Ninth Edition

TECHNIQUES AND GUIDELINES FOR SOCIAL WORK PRACTICE

Bradford W. Sheafor
Professor, Colorado State University

Charles R. Horejsi
Professor Emeritus, University of Montana

Allyn & Bacon
Boston   Columbus   Indianapolis   New York   San Francisco   Upper Saddle River
Amsterdam   Cape Town   Dubai   London   Madrid   Milan   Munich   Paris   Montreal   Toronto
Delhi   Mexico City   São Paulo   Sydney   Hong Kong   Seoul   Singapore   Taipei   Tokyo

Executive Editor: Ashley Dodge
Editorial Product Manager: Carly Czech
Senior Marketing Manager: Wendy Albert
Marketing Assistant: Shauna Fishweicher
Production Manager: Pat Brown
Art Director: Jayne Conte
Editorial Production and Composition Service: Kalpana Venkatramani/PreMediaGlobal
Cover Designer: Suzanne Behnke
Printer/Binder: Bind-Rite Graphics

Library of Congress Cataloging-in-Publication Data

Sheafor, Bradford W.
Techniques and guidelines for social work practice / Bradford W. Sheafor,
    Charles R. Horejsi.—9th ed.
        p. cm.
    Includes index.
    ISBN-13: 978-0-205-83875-2
    ISBN-10: 0-205-83875-8
    1. Social service—United States.   I. Horejsi, Charles R.   II. Title.
    HV91.S48 2012
    361.3'2—dc22   2010049761

10 9 8 7 6 5 4 3 2 1   [BRR]   14 13 12 11 10

Allyn & Bacon
is an imprint of

www.pearsonhighered.com

Student Edition:
ISBN-10: 0-205-83875-8
ISBN-13: 978-0-205-83875-2

Instructor Edition:
ISBN-10: 0-205-83554-6
ISBN-13: 978-0-205-83554-6

à la Carte Edition:
ISBN-10: 0-205-02273-1
ISBN-13: 978-0-205-02273-1

Dedication

To the next generation of social workers,
who have chosen to devote their time and talents to the service of others and the
struggle for social justice,

and

To our families,
Nadine, Laura, Brandon, Perry, Christopher,
Gloria, Angela, Martin, and Katherine,
for their love and support

CONTENTS

PREFACE

Many people are influenced, directly and indirectly, by the decisions and actions of social workers. Working in courts, clinics, hospitals, schools, businesses, private practice, and a myriad of private and public social agencies, social workers deliver a wide variety of services directly to clients while they also work toward positive community and social changes. Improving the quality of life for an individual, a family, or the people of a community will ultimately have an impact on society as a whole and elevate the health, happiness, safety, and productivity of all its members.

This book is about what social workers actually do when helping their clients solve problems and/or enhance their functioning. Although many books describe the general principles and theories used by social workers, *Techniques and Guidelines for Social Work Practice* focuses on a more specific and concrete level. It describes many of the basic and specific techniques and guidelines that social workers use in everyday practice.

Most social workers have been exposed to a variety of practice theories and conceptual frameworks reported in the literature and taught in programs of social work education. Although that knowledge base is essential, practice is much more than a set of ideas. In reality, practice is a set of actions and behaviors by the social worker. Clients are not directly affected by the worker's theory; rather, they are influenced by what the worker actually does—by the specific actions taken by the social worker. We do not intend to suggest that attention to the techniques can or should replace attention to theoretical frameworks. Rather, techniques and specific guidelines complete the package of knowledge and skills needed by the social worker.

PLAN AND STRUCTURE

Understanding the design of a book helps the reader make use of its contents. This book has five major parts.

Part I, "Social Work and the Social Worker," reviews the background knowledge and characteristics we believe a social worker must possess:

- A clear conception of the domain of social work and the competencies the social worker is expected to bring to the change process (Chapter 1)
- An understanding of the challenges a social worker faces in merging his or her personal life with professional roles and responsibilities (Chapter 2)
- The native talents or artistic abilities necessary for perceptively creating and entering into the interpersonal relations that are at the heart of practice as well as a commitment to draw upon and apply the science of social work—that is, the profession's knowledge base and its ethical principles (Chapter 3)

Part II, "The Building Blocks of Social Work Practice," stresses the need for the social worker to become familiar with the central features of effective helping. To serve clients ranging from individuals to communities, a social worker must have these qualities:

- An understanding of the varied roles performed by social workers in delivering human services and the specific functions associated with these roles (Chapter 4)
- The ability to apply the fundamental practice principles of social work (Chapter 5)
- A basic knowledge of the various perspectives, theories, and models that have proven useful in practice (Chapter 6)
- Skill in selecting the best evidence available to inform the process of guiding clients through the planned change process and in helping them make sound decisions about how to improve their lives (Chapter 7)

From this point to the end of the book, we present specific techniques and guidelines. Each presentation or item has a Number and Name (e.g., 10.4: Making a Referral). In this example, 10.4 signifies the fourth item in Chapter 10. This system of numbering is used to refer the reader to related information in other parts of the book. These numbers are also the keys to using the "Cross-Reference Guide," found inside the front cover, which is intended to help the reader easily locate techniques that may be useful when working with specific client groups.

Next, several paragraphs describe the technique or guideline and its application. At the end of this discussion, we present a Selected Bibliography, which usually lists two to four books or articles that we consider particularly useful for obtaining additional information.

In Part III of the book, "Techniques Common to All Social Work Practice," we have included techniques that strengthen the social worker's performance regardless of agency setting and independent of whether the client is an individual, family, group, organization, or community. Underlying our selection was the belief that the social worker must have these basic skills:

- The interpersonal competence to carry out effective communication and to engage in a set of basic helping activities (Chapter 8)
- The organizational ability to address the details of service delivery and to effectively manage his or her own workload (Chapter 9)

Part IV, "Techniques and Guidelines for Phases of the Planned Change Process," lists techniques and guidelines for both direct and indirect practice in chapters organized around the five phases of the planned change process. Although various authors use differing descriptions of this process, we have elected to use the following:

- Intake and engagement (Chapter 10)
- Data collection and assessment (Chapter 11)
- Planning and contracting (Chapter 12)
- Intervention and monitoring (Chapter 13)
- Evaluation and termination (Chapter 14)

We describe what should be accomplished in these phases in the introduction to each chapter. Then, these general concepts are elaborated to more clearly describe the direct practice applications (Section A) and the indirect practice applications (Section B) of those chapters. A worker can readily examine several suggested techniques or guidelines by identifying the phase of the change process, determining if the activity is a direct or indirect intervention, and then locating the appropriate chapter and section.

Part V, "Specialized Techniques and Guidelines for Social Work Practice," includes some items that cut across the five phases of the planned change process and thus did not fit into the classification system used in Part IV. To address these issues, we created chapters containing the items related to serving vulnerable client populations (Chapter 15) and the items related to maintaining a social work position and enhancing one's professional performance (Chapter 16).

DEFINITION OF TERMS

Writing about social work practice inherently presents some language problems. One has to read only a few social work texts or articles to become at least a little confused with the terminology describing practice. Perhaps that is to be expected in a profession that focuses on complex and dynamic human and social interactions. This book cannot overcome these long-standing problems of terminology, yet the ideas presented here will be more readily understood if we make the meanings of three terms more explicit.

The reader should be alert to the term *client*. Common usage implies an individual who is the consumer of services. However, as used in this book, the term has a broader connotation. The *client* of the social worker may be an individual, a family or another form of household, or even a small group, committee, organization, neighborhood, community, or larger social system. Throughout the book, the term *client* is occasionally expanded to mention clientele, clients, client groups, or client systems, reminding the reader that the traditional narrow definition of client is not intended.

A *technique* is viewed as a circumscribed, goal-oriented behavior performed in a practice situation by the social worker. It is a planned action deliberately taken by the practitioner. The application of a simple technique (e.g., making the first telephone contact) may take only a few seconds, whereas more complex techniques (e.g., assessing a client's social functioning) may require an hour or more.

Guidelines, by comparison, are a set of directions intended to influence the social worker's behavior and decisions. Guidelines are essentially lists of do's and don'ts. They might be used when working with a specific type of client (e.g., a child or a client with mental illness) or when carrying out workload management tasks (e.g., recording or writing reports).

NEW TO THIS EDITION

Techniques and Guidelines for Social Work Practice has been carefully updated to provide students with easy access to the most current information on fundamental techniques required for social work practice from the generalist perspective. New features of the ninth edition of *Techniques and Guidelines* include:

- The important social work role of researcher/evaluator and the associated functions is made more explicit in Chapter 4.
- A new item in Chapter 8 addresses the difficult task of enhancing client motivation to actively address their situations.
- In Chapter 10 a new item addresses power differentials between workers and clients.
- New items on helping clients address harmful habits and financial problems appear in Chapter 13, as well as an item on organizing neighborhoods and communities.
- Two new items in Chapter 15 address clients impacted by the criminal justice system and clients affected by war.
- A new item is added to Chapter 16 to aid students in preparing for state or national competency examinations.
- Throughout the book we have streamlined materials by combining related items and placing some items on Brad Sheafor's website (http://www.ssw.cahs.colostate.edu/faculty_staff/sheafor) to help keep the size of the print editions of the book manageable.
- Finally, additional appendix materials will help students find quick reference to many of the acronyms used in social work and to locate useful websites related to this profession.

SUPPLEMENTS FOR INSTRUCTORS

To assist instructors using this book in their classes, we have created an Instructor's Manual and Test Bank. In addition to teaching suggestions, this supplement contains sample test questions (Chapters 1 through 7) and suggested exercises for applying these materials. This manual can be obtained from your campus Allyn & Bacon representative or by writing to Allyn & Bacon (75 Arlington Street, Suite 300, Boston, MA 02116).

ACKNOWLEDGMENTS

We would like to recognize a number of people who have contributed to the techniques and guidelines presented in this book, including current and former students and professional colleagues who have graciously given their time and expertise to offer constructive criticisms on selected sections. A special thank-you is extended to each of the following individuals:

- Angeline Barretta-Herman, Ph.D. (staff meetings)
- Barbara Benjamin, M.S.W.; Bob Jackson, Ph.D.; Maxine Jacobson, Ph.D.; and Lowell Jenkins, M.S.W. (practice frameworks)
- Mary Birch, M.S.W. (small groups)
- Vicky Buchan, Ph.D. (understanding quantitative data)
- Kim Bundy-Fazioli, Ph.D. (worker/client power differentials)
- Timothy Conley, Ph.D.; Ted Lewis, B.S.W.; and Detective Mark Long (chemical dependency)
- Donna DeAngelis, M.S.W. (competency exams)
- Robert Deaton, Ed.D. (suicide)
- Jim Demuth, M.A.; Sr. Dot Feehan, M.A.; Janet Wallersheim, Ph.D. (spirituality and religion)
- Kathleen Gallacher, M.A.; and Kristin Dahl Horejsi, M.S. (child development)
- Cindy Garthwait, M.S.W. (motivational interviewing, the older client, spirituality and religion)
- Cynthia J. Geissinger, M.S.W. (bisexual and transgender)
- Jeffrey Gliner, Ph.D. (effect size)
- Helen Holmquist-Johnson, M.S.W. (eating disorders)
- Ken Hoole, M.S.W.; Suzanne Grubaugh, B.S.W.; and Deanna Morrow, Ph.D. (gay and lesbian issues)
- Mike Jakupcak, Ed.D.; and George Camp, Ph.D. (intellectual disability)
- Mike Johnson, M.A.; Danielle Wozniak, Ph.D.; Joan Bartkowski, M,Ed.; and Sue Kenney, M.S.W. (poverty)
- John Means, Ph.D. (psychological testing)
- Dan Morgan, M.S.W.; Cindy Bartling, M.S.W.; and Charlie Wellenstein, M.S.W. (children and adolescents)
- Kevin Oltjenbruns, Ph.D. (grief and loss)
- Peter Pecora, Ph.D. (evaluation)
- Steven Price, Ph.D.; and Bob Seiz, Ph.D. (clients affected by war)
- Maria Puig, Ph.D. (immigrants and refugees)
- Jeannette Sale, B.S.W.; Kelly Slattery-Robinson, B.S.W.; and Frank Clark, Ph.D. (battered women)
- David Schantz, Ph.D. (leadership)
- Mona Schatz, D.S.W. (social work roles and functions)
- Barbara W. Shank, Ph.D. (sexual misconduct)
- Tom Shilke, M.A.; Kaycee Shilke, B.A., and Malcolm Scott, Ph.D. (criminal justice)
- Michael Silverglat, M.D.; James Moody, Pharm.D.; and Mel Mason, M.S.W. (psychotropic medication and mental illness)
- John Spores, Ph.D.; Iris Heavy Runner, M.S.W.; Rodney Brod, Ph.D.; Victor Baez, Ph.D.; and Janet Finn, Ph.D. (cultural competence)
- Ryan Tolleson-Knee, M.S.W.; and Shaen McElravy, M.S.W. (merging person and profession)
- Elizabeth Tracy, Ph.D.; and James Whittaker, Ph.D. (social support assessment)
- Carmen Underwood, B.S.W. (family group conferencing)
- Deborah Valentine, Ph.D. (mentoring, narrative therapy, and mediation)
- Sue Wilkins, B.S.W.; and Charlotte Booth, M.S.W. (involuntary and manipulative clients)

We would also like to acknowledge the following individuals, who reviewed this edition and offered suggestions for improving this publication: Janice Adams, Indiana Wesleyan University; Carolyn Bradley, Monmouth University; and Cathleen Faruque, Winona State University.

Social Work and the Social Worker

Social work is an indispensable profession in our complex and ever-changing society. But it is an often misunderstood profession, as well, in part because it cannot be easily described or explained. It is a profession characterized by diversity. Social workers engage in a broad range of activities within many types of settings and with many different people. Some work intensely with individuals and families, while others work with small groups, organizations, or whole communities. Some deal primarily with children, while others deal with older persons. Some are counselors and psychotherapists, while others are supervisors, administrators, program planners, or fund-raisers. Some focus on family violence and others on how to provide housing or medical care to the poor. This variety is what makes social work so challenging and stimulating. But it is because of this diversity of both clients and activities that it is so difficult to answer the simple question: What is social work?

The task of concisely defining social work in a manner that encompasses all of the activities in which social workers engage has challenged the profession throughout its history. At a very fundamental level, social work is a profession devoted to helping people function at their maximum levels within their social environments and, when necessary, to changing their environments to make that possible. This theme of person-in-environment is clarified and illustrated throughout this book.

The authors' perspective of social work is captured in the following three-part definition of a social worker. A social worker

1. has recognized professional education (i.e., knowledge, ethics, and competencies) and the requisite skills needed to provide services sanctioned by society,
2. that engage vulnerable populations (e.g., children, older people, the poor, minorities, persons with disabling conditions) and others in efforts to bring about needed change in themselves, the people around them, or related social institutions,
3. so that these individuals and groups are able to meet their social needs, prevent or eliminate difficulties, make maximum use of their abilities and strengths, lead satisfying lives, and contribute fully to society.

In order to be a responsible professional, the social worker must understand and function within the profession's accepted areas of expertise. The primary resource the social worker brings to the helping process is his or her own capacity to develop positive helping relationships and assist clients to take actions that will improve the quality of their lives. Throughout its history, social work has been portrayed as both an art (one's personal characteristics) and a science (a base of knowledge required to be an effective professional). Part I, then, addresses the most fundamental elements of social work practice—the blending of the person and the profession—in order to most effectively assist individuals, families or other households, small groups, organizations, and communities as they work to prevent or resolve the complex social problems that arise in their daily lives.

The Domain of the Social Work Profession

When a person sets out to help others, especially those most vulnerable to social problems, he or she assumes a serious responsibility. The responsible professional must practice within his or her **professional domain** (i.e., the profession's area of expertise, or its "professional turf") if clients are to receive the services that the profession is sanctioned to provide. Indeed, professional helpers can harm clients if their activities extend beyond their professional boundaries because these boundaries establish the content of the profession's formal education and identify the services its members are best prepared to deliver.

This book is concerned with the profession of social work and how social workers assist people in addressing a variety of different issues that confront them. Social work is, indeed, a curious name for a profession. In times that emphasize image over substance, it is clearly a title that lacks pizzazz. In fact, the use of the word work makes it sound burdensome and boring. It is a title that many social workers have wished they could change, possibly without understanding where it came from in the first place.

The title is attributed to Jeffrey Brackett (1860–1949) who served for nearly 30 years on the Massachusetts Board of Charities and later became the first director of what is now the Simmons College School of Social Work. In the early 1900s, Brackett argued that the word *social* should be part of this developing profession's title because it depicts the focus on people's interactions with important forces that shape their lives, such as family members, friends, or a myriad of other factors, including their relevant cultural or ethnic group, school, job, neighborhood, community, and so on. He added the word *work* to differentiate professional practice from what he considered the often misguided and self-serving philanthropic activity of wealthy volunteers. He believed including the word *work* in the profession's title emphasized that its activities were to be orderly, responsible, and disciplined—not something to be engaged in by someone unprepared for these tasks.

Social work is an accurate title for a profession that applies helping techniques in a disciplined manner to address social problems. During the years since Brackett convinced early helping services providers to accept this title, the domain of social work has expanded and its approach has been reshaped by the increasing knowledge generated by the social and behavioral sciences. Yet the title continues to describe this profession's central focus today.

THE SOCIAL WORK DOMAIN

It is important for the social worker to carefully examine the domain of social work (i.e., to understand its purpose, focus, scope, and sanction). This is especially important for students because educational programs divide the study of social work into units, or courses, and this can lead to familiarity with the parts without necessarily understanding the whole.

One reason for understanding of the social work domain is to help guard against **professional drift**: the neglect of the profession's traditional purpose and functions in favor of activities associated with another professional discipline. This happens most often in clinical settings when social workers align themselves too closely with models and theories used in medicine, psychology, and other disciplines, which tend to minimize social policy and social justice issues. These practitioners may come to view themselves as psychotherapists first and social workers second—or perhaps not as social workers at all. Professional drift is also seen among administrators and managers who were trained as social workers but are identified primarily with their specific organizations rather than the social work profession. When professional drift occurs, it is a disservice to one's clients, employing social agency, and community for it diminishes the commitment, perspective, and competencies unique to social work.

A precise and generally agreed-upon understanding of the boundaries that mark the several helping professions does not exist. Different disciplines (e.g., social work, clinical psychology, school counseling, and marriage and family therapy) have claimed their domains without collaboration or mutual agreement about where one profession ends and another begins or where they appropriately overlap. This problem is further complicated by the fact that each state that chooses to license the practice of these professions is free to establish its own descriptions of professional boundaries. It is important, therefore, to approach learning about social work's domain with the recognition that boundaries between professions are sometimes blurred.

Social Work's Purpose

An understanding of the social work profession begins with a deep appreciation of humans as social beings. People are, indeed, social creatures. They depend on other people to help address many of their own needs. An individual's growth and development requires the guidance, nurturing, and protection provided by others. And that person's concept of self—and even his or her very survival, both physically and psychologically—is tied to the decisions and actions of other people. It is this interconnectedness and interdependence of people and the power of social relationships that underpins a profession devoted to helping people improve the quality and effectiveness of those interactions and relationships—in other words, to enhance their social functioning.

SOCIAL FUNCTIONING   The concept of social functioning is a key to understanding the unique focus of social work and distinguishing social work from the other helping professions. *Positive social functioning* is a person's ability to accomplish those tasks and activities necessary to meet his or her basic needs and perform his or her major social roles in the society. Basic needs include such fundamental concerns as having food, shelter, and medical care, as well as being able to protect oneself from harm, finding acceptance and social support, having meaning and purpose in life, and so on. Major social roles include, for example, those of being a family member, a parent, a spouse, a student, a patient, an employee, a neighbor, and a citizen. A person's social roles change through his or her life, and expectations associated with these roles differ somewhat depending on the person's gender, ethnicity, culture, religion, occupation, and community. (See Item 11.8 for more description of social role performance.) In sum, the concept of social functioning focuses on the match or fit between an individual's capacities and actions and the demands, expectations, resources, and opportunities within his or her social and economic environment.

Although the social work profession is concerned with the social functioning of all people, it has traditionally prioritized the needs of the most vulnerable members of society and those who experience social injustice, discrimination, and oppression. The most vulnerable in a society are often young children, the frail elderly, persons living in poverty, persons with severe physical or mental disabilities, persons who are gay or lesbian, or persons of minority ethnic/racial backgrounds.

To carry out their commitment to improving people's social functioning, social workers are involved in the activities of social care, social treatment, and social enhancement. **Social care** refers to those actions and efforts designed to provide people in need with access to the basics of life (e.g., food, shelter, protection from harm) and opportunities to meet their psychosocial needs (e.g., belonging, acceptance, and comfort in times of distress). In social care, the focus is on providing needed resources and/or on helping the client be as comfortable as possible in a difficult situation that either cannot be changed or modified in the immediate future. Examples of social care would be efforts to address the needs and concerns of young children who must live in foster care, adults who have a serious and persistent mental illness, and persons who are dying.

Social treatment involves actions designed to modify or correct an individual's or a family's dysfunctional, problematic, or distressing patterns of thought, feeling, and behavior. In social treatment, the focus is primarily on facilitating individual or family change through education, counseling, or various forms of therapy. In many cases (e.g., work with children in foster care), the social worker may provide both social care and social treatment to the same client.

A third form of intervention seeks to enhance, expand, or further develop the abilities and performance of persons who are already functioning well. **Social enhancement** services emphasize growth and development of clients in a particular area of functioning without a "problem" having necessarily been identified. Some examples of enhancement-oriented services are youth and senior citizen recreation programs, well-baby clinics, marriage enrichment sessions, and job training programs.

IMPROVED SOCIAL CONDITIONS   Social work's second area of emphasis is on shaping and creating environments that will be supportive and empowering. Underpinning this goal is one of the most fundamental social work values: a strong belief in the importance of achieving and maintaining social justice. **Social justice** refers to fairness and moral rightness in how social institutions such as governments, corporations, and powerful groups recognize and support the basic human rights of all people. A closely related belief of social workers is that the society should strive for *economic justice* (sometimes called *distributive justice*), which refers to fairness in the apportioning and distribution of economic resources, opportunities, and burdens (e.g., taxes). In other words, the economic resources of a society should be distributed (and redistributed) through structures of taxation and other economic mechanisms so that all people have opportunities for economic advancement and can meet their basic needs.

Very often, political controversy has its origin in differing conceptions of what is truly fair and just and in differing beliefs on whether and how society should assume responsibility for addressing human needs and problems. Most social workers would argue that social and economic policies must recognize that all people have basic human rights—that is, claims on humanity at large, not because of individual achievement or by actions of government but simply by virtue of one's existence and one's inherent worth and dignity. Among those *basic human rights* are the following:

- The right to have the food, shelter, basic medical care, and essential social services necessary to maintain one's life
- The right to be protected from abuse, exploitation, and oppression
- The right to work and earn a sufficient wage to secure basic resources and live with dignity
- The right to marry, to have a family, and to be with one's family
- The right to a basic education
- The right to own property
- The right to be protected from avoidable harm and injury in the workplace
- The right to worship as one chooses—or not at all, if one chooses
- The right to privacy
- The right to associate with those one chooses
- The right to accurate information about one's community and government
- The right to participate in and influence the decisions of one's government

Social workers would also agree that along with rights come responsibilities. Rights and responsibilities cannot exist without the other. Situations of injustice develop when people are concerned only about their own rights and no longer possess a sense of responsibility for others and society in general. To protect each right, there must be associated acts of responsibility. For example, in relation to the first three rights identified earlier:

- If a human has the right to be alive, then others have the responsibility to make sure that he or she has food, shelter, and essential medical care.
- If people have the right to be protected from abuse, exploitation, and oppression, then others have the responsibility to create social programs and take actions that will provide this protection when required.
- If a person has the right to work and earn a living, then others have the responsibility to make sure that employment opportunities exist and that those who work are paid a living wage.

Social workers sometimes perform services to help achieve people's rights; at other times, they serve as a voice for those whose rights are ignored or abused by calling on others to recognize the basic rights of all people and to act responsibly, with fairness and justice. When a social worker is providing services to individuals, families, or groups, these changes would be considered *environmental modifications*. An example would be efforts by a school social worker to prepare students for the return of a former classmate who was badly scarred in an automobile accident. Another example would be providing special training to a foster mother so that she can respond thoughtfully and constructively to a young foster child who exhibits inappropriate behaviors.

Even when working with an organization or a community, a social worker may seek to modify its wider environment. That may entail efforts to influence local decision-makers, businesses, political leaders, and governmental agencies so that they will be more supportive of the organization's mission or more responsive to a community's needs and problems. Such macro-level interventions may involve the worker in social research, social planning, and political action intended to develop and improve laws, social policies, institutions, and social systems so that they will promote social and economic justice, expand opportunities for people, and improve the everyday circumstances in which people live. Specific examples would be expanding the availability of safe and affordable housing, creating incentives for businesses to hire people with disabilities, amending laws so that they better prevent discrimination, and helping neighborhood and community organizations become politically active in addressing the issues they face.

Efforts to modify environments are sometimes labeled programs of prevention. **Prevention** consists of those actions taken to eliminate social, economic, psychological, and other conditions known to cause or contribute to the formation of human problems. To be effective in prevention, social workers must be able to identify the specific factors and situations that contribute to the development of social problems and then select actions and activities that will reduce or eliminate their impact (see Item 12.13). Borrowing from the public health model, three levels of prevention can be identified:

Level 1: Primary prevention.   Actions intended to deter the problem from developing

Level 2: Secondary prevention.   Actions intended to detect a problem at its early stages and address it while it is still relatively easy to change

Level 3: Tertiary prevention.   Actions intended to address an already serious problem in ways that keep it from growing even worse, causing additional damage, or spreading to others

Social Work's Focus

Social work is certainly not the only profession concerned with how individuals and families function, nor is it the only profession interested in social conditions and social problems. However, it is social work's simultaneous focus on and attention to both the person and the person's environment that makes social work unique among the various helping professions.

One's environment may be either a support or a barrier to his or her effective social functioning. Because both the person and the environment are constantly changing, adaptations and adjustments must be ongoing. Social workers, therefore, must be especially vigilant regarding those aspects of a person's environment that are shaped by the social policies and programs that make up the social welfare system.

The social work profession's unique focus on the **person-in-environment** requires that the social worker attend to several interrelated dimensions of the person: biological, intellectual, emotional, social, familial, spiritual, economic, communal, and so on. This concern for the **whole person** contributes to the breadth of concern by the social work profession—for example, the individual's capacity to meet basic physical needs (food, housing, health care, etc.), the person's levels of knowledge and skills needed to cope with life's demands and to earn a living, the person's thoughts about others and his or her own life, the individual's goals and aspirations, and the like. It is important to note the person-in-environment construct uses the word *person*, not *personality*. Personality is but one component of the whole person. A focus only on personality would be incongruous with the domain of social work and slant it toward psychology.

The term **environment** refers to one's surroundings—that multitude of physical and social structures, forces, and processes that affect humans and all other life forms. Of particular interest to social workers are those systems, structures, and conditions that most frequently and most directly affect a person's day-to-day social functioning (i.e., the person's *immediate environment*). One's immediate environment includes the person's family, close friends, neighborhood, workplace, and the services and programs he or she uses.

Social workers devote a major part of their attention to clients' efforts to improve interactions with their immediate environment. Social workers focus to a lesser extent on the broader environment, possibly because the impact of problems in the more *distant environment* is less evident and more difficult to change. In order to grow, develop, and survive, humans need clean air, drinkable water, shelter, and good soil to produce food. And because biological well-being is a prerequisite to positive social functioning, social workers must also be concerned with problems such as prevention of disease and pollution. In addition, they seek to change damaging societal values, correct human rights violations, and address unjust political and economic structures that may affect their clients. Concern over factors in both the immediate and distant environments is central to fulfilling social work's mission.

Because social relationships are of central concern to their profession, social workers must understand the power of a social environment—both its potentially helpful and harmful influences. Humans are social creatures and have a strong need to be accepted by others. Observing what others in our social environment are doing can be a powerful force for change—either positively or negatively. Social workers understand that if a person's environment changes and becomes more favorable for the client, that individual will be more likely to make positive changes in what he or she thinks and how he or she behaves.

Social Work's Scope

A profession's **scope** can be thought of as the range of activities and involvements appropriate to its mission. One way of describing social work's scope involves classifying the intervention by the size of the client system. Practice at the **micro level** focuses on the individual and his or her most intimate interactions, such as exchanges between husband and wife, parent and child, close friends, and family members. The terms *interpersonal helping*, *direct practice*, and *clinical practice* are often used interchangeably with micro-level practice.

At the other extreme, **macro-level** practice may involve work with an organization, a community, a state, or even a society as a whole. Obviously, macro-level practice also deals with interpersonal relations, but these are the interactions between people who represent organizations or who are members of a work group such as an agency committee or interagency task force. When engaged in macro-level practice, the social worker is frequently involved in activities such as administration, fund-raising, testifying on proposed legislation, policy analysis, class advocacy, and social resource development.

Between the micro and macro levels is **mezzo-level** (midlevel) practice. Practice at this level is concerned with interpersonal relations that are somewhat less intimate than those associated with family life but more personally meaningful than those that occur among organizational and institutional representatives. Included would be relationships among individuals in a self-help or therapy group, among peers at school or work, and among neighbors.

Some practice approaches address more than one intervention level. For example, social treatment, as defined by Kemp, Whittaker, and Tracy (1997), includes the micro and mezzo levels, and the generalist perspective (Schatz, Jenkins, and Sheafor, 1990) requires the social worker to be capable of practice at the micro, mezzo, and macro levels.

Social Work's Sanction

The concept of **sanction** refers to the authorization, approval, or permission needed to perform certain professional tasks or activities. Sanction has the effect of defining the profession's domain. Four major sources provide sanction for social work activities. One source is government agencies—federal, state, and city—that authorize the actions of social workers through several means: legislation that creates social programs, the allocation of funds for social work activities, the licensing of organizations (e.g., licensed child-placing agencies) that employ social workers, and the licensing and regulation of individual social work practitioners.

A second source of sanction includes the many private human services organizations (both non-profit and profit-making agencies) that endorse social work by recruiting and hiring social workers to provide services or by purchasing services from those who are in private practice or employed by other agencies. Indirectly, then, the community sanctions and pays social workers to provide specific services. In return for this sanction to practice, social workers are obliged to provide high-quality services and to take reasonable steps to make sure that social work practitioners are competent and ethical.

Third, the profession, acting through the National Association of Social Workers (NASW), sets standards for appropriate and ethical practice. By requiring adherence to its *Code of Ethics*, offering certification (see http://www.socialworkers.org/credentials/default.asp), and providing education to its membership through publications and conferences, the NASW serves as a vehicle for protecting the public trust.

Finally, the true test of public sanction for practice is the willingness of clients to seek out and use services offered by social workers. In order to win the trust of clients, social workers must demonstrate on a daily basis that they are capable of providing effective services and are committed to conducting their practice in a responsible and an ethical manner.

AN OVERVIEW OF SOCIAL WORK PRACTICE

Figure 1.1 presents a model of the key factors that influence social work practice. It shows the client (or client system) and the social worker joined in an effort to bring about a desired change in the client's functioning or situation, while both are being influenced by the social agency (e.g., its policies and programs) and by the wider social environment. This **planned change process** involves several phases during which the client and social worker move from their decision to initiate a course of action, through assessment and action phases and on to an evaluation of its success and a decision to terminate the helping activity (see Chapter 7). Although the social worker is expected to guide this process, the client must ultimately decide to commit to the change process and utilize the helping resources identified by or provided by the worker.

The Client side of Figure 1.1 indicates that the problem or situation the client seeks to change is, most likely, the product of a combination of personal and environmental factors. Each client has a unique set of *personal characteristics* (e.g., life experiences, goals, beliefs, perceptions, strengths, limitations, needs) that may have contributed in some way to the situation or problem being addressed and that might also be a resource that helps to bring about the desired change.

Clients do not exist in isolation. Their *immediate environment* might include friends, family, school personnel, employers, natural helpers, neighborhood or community groups, or even

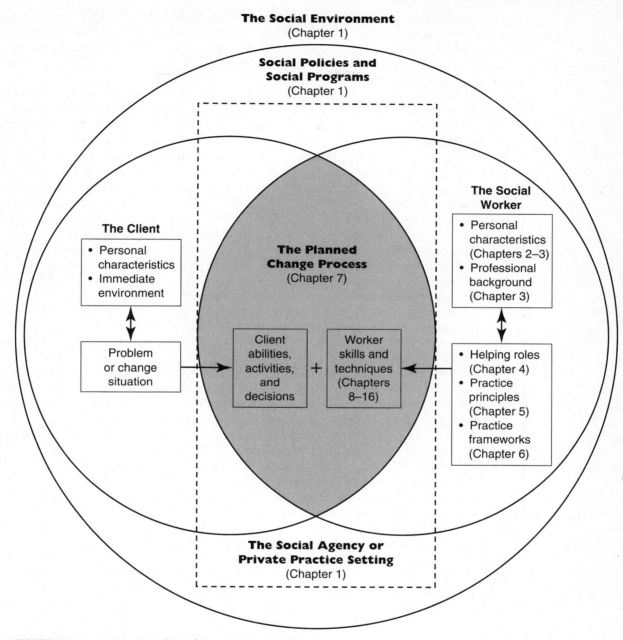

FIGURE 1.1   An Integrative View of Social Work Practice

other professional helpers, to mention just a few. These individuals and environmental influences are also possible resources in the helping process. And in some cases they have contributed to the client's problem and will need to become a target for change.

The Social Worker side of Figure 1.1 suggests that the worker brings unique personal characteristics and a professional background to the change process. These are experienced by the client through what the social worker actually does (i.e., the worker's activities and application of skills and techniques). What the worker does is a function of the specific professional role he or she has assumed and the conceptual framework he or she has selected to guide practice. The social worker's *personal characteristics* encompass such factors as life experience, talents, training, and commitment to serving others. (Chapter 2 offers an in-depth discussion of these characteristics.) The social worker's unique perspectives on the human condition, as well as his or her particular values, are inevitably introduced into the change process. Those perspectives will have been shaped by his or her unique life experiences and his or her socioeconomic background, gender, age, sexual orientation, and the like. All of these characteristics affect the social worker–client relationship.

At the same time, the practitioner brings the special contribution of a *professional background* to social work, which differentiates the social worker from the client's friends, family, natural helpers, and the professionals representing other disciplines who may also be working with the client or who attempted to help in the past. What is this professional background? First and foremost, the social worker brings the belief system, values, ethical principles, and focus on social functioning that are common to the domain of social work. Through education and experience, the social worker develops practice wisdom and an ability to use his or her personal characteristics, special talents, and unique style to help clients. In addition, the social worker brings a knowledge base, much of it derived from the social and behavioral sciences. Chapter 3 presents an overview of the necessary artistic abilities, knowledge base, and value positions relevant to practice.

As social workers carry out their responsibilities, they perform various *helping roles*. As Chapter 4 describes more fully, social workers must be prepared to perform a wide variety of roles and functions, ranging from linking clients to appropriate resources, to assessing case situations and providing direct services, to planning and conducting social action.

The social work profession has informally tested the applicability of its approach to providing human services, largely through trial and error. Some of these tried-and-true guidelines for practice have been reduced to *practice principles* that serve as the most fundamental directives to practice (see Chapter 5).

An important element of professional background is that portion of the social worker's knowledge base consisting of various *practice frameworks* that guide one's work (e.g., practice perspectives, theories, and models) and provide direction to the change process. The ways in which these frameworks might be selected and utilized are discussed in Chapter 6.

Finally, the social worker's *skills* and mastery of *techniques* are his or her most evident and tangible contribution to the change process (Chapters 8–16). The skills or techniques selected by the social worker will depend, of course, on the nature of the client's problem or concern, the expectations of the practice setting, and the worker's own competence in using them.

Returning again to Figure 1.1, it is important to recognize that social work practice takes place within a **social environment** (sometimes called a *distant environment*) and, more specifically, usually within the context of a social agency. Typically, the agency has been shaped by local, state, and/or national social policies and its programs are a reflection of society's values and beliefs. Commitment to the social welfare of its members varies among societies; within the United States, it even varies among regions, states, and communities. We know that having sound social programs supports quality living for all people—the more secure as well as the most vulnerable members of that society. Yet every social worker knows that our social policies and programs leave much to be desired. Moreover, U.S. society has demonstrated an ambivalent and transient commitment to people whose needs are not adequately met. Therefore, social workers, who serve as agents of society must frequently work with fewer than the desired tools for assisting their clients.

Through its legislative and other decision-making bodies, society creates **social programs** intended to help certain people. These programs take three forms:

- *Social provisions* involve giving tangible goods (e.g., money, food, clothing, and housing) to persons in need.
- *Social services* include intangible services (e.g., counseling, therapy, and learning experiences) intended to help people resolve and/or prevent problems.
- *Social action* programs are concerned with changing aspects of the social environment to make it more responsive to people's needs and wants.

The particular philosophy on which social programs are built has a significant bearing on how they operate, how effective they are, and how they affect both the client and the social worker.

The dominant social welfare philosophy in the United States contends that social programs should be a *safety net* that is available only to people who can demonstrate "real need." In other words, social programs should exist only to help people solve already serious problems and be available only to those who are deemed needy. A second philosophy, the *social utilities* conception, considers social programs to be first-line functions of society (similar to education and law enforcement). This approach places greater emphasis on prevention and avoids forcing the client to identify a problem or admit to some personal failure in order to benefit from human services.

The benefits and services associated with a particular social program are typically offered through a **social agency**. Thus, for the most part, social work is an agency-based profession and most social workers are agency employees. A social agency might be a public welfare department, mental health center, school, hospital, neighborhood center, or any of a number of differing organizational structures. It may be a public agency supported by tax funds and governed by elected officials or a private agency operating under the auspices of a volunteer board and supported primarily by fees and voluntary donations. The basic functions of the agency are to administer social programs and to monitor the quality of the helping process.

To perform these functions, the agency must secure money, staff, and other resources; determine which people are eligible for its services; and maintain an administrative structure that will meet targeted social needs in an efficient and effective manner. The most important ingredient of a social agency is its people. Receptionists, custodians, administrators, and service providers all must work together to deliver successful programs. Often, several helping professions are employed in the same agency. In such interdisciplinary programs, each profession brings its own perspective on helping—as well as the special competencies appropriate to the domain of that profession.

Increasingly, social workers are providing services through **private practice**. In this setting, social workers and other professionals maintain an independent practice, as is typical in medicine and law, and contract directly with their clients to provide services.

Conclusion

Social work is one of several human services professions that have been sanctioned by society to help improve the quality of life for its people. Other such helping professions include clinical psychology, drug and alcohol counseling, marriage and family counseling, school psychology, medicine, rehabilitation counseling, nursing, and so on. The uniqueness of social work among these professions is its focus on the social functioning of people and helping people interact more effectively with their environments—both their immediate and distant environments. Social workers perform this role by assisting people to address issues in their social functioning and working to prevent social problems from emerging or, if they already exist, from getting worse.

Increasingly, conflict and competition arise among the various human services professions over issues of the domain (or turf) of each. These conflicts tend to center around competition for jobs, salary, status, and control, as well as disagreements over which profession is most qualified to perform certain tasks. To minimize the effect of these problems on clients, it is important for the members of these professions to engage in **interprofessional collaboration** as they provide their services. However, each discipline must avoid letting its practice activities drift into the areas of expertise of the other professions.

Social workers have historically claimed they represent the profession best prepared to help people resolve problems in social functioning and to guide social change efforts to prevent problems from occurring or becoming worse. It is important that social workers maintain their focus on these central features of their domain.

Selected Bibliography

Kemp, Susan P., James Whittaker, and Elizabeth Tracy. *Person-Environment Practice: The Social Ecology of Interpersonal Helping*. New York: Aldine de Gruyter, 1997.

National Association of Social Workers. *Code of Ethics*. Washington, DC: NASW, 1999.

Schatz, Mona S., Lowell E. Jenkins, and Bradford W. Sheafor. "Milford Redefined: A Model of Initial and Advanced Generalist Social Work." *Journal of Social Work Education* 26 (Fall 1990): 217–231.

Merging Person with Profession

A social worker's professional role and responsibilities are always, to some degree, intertwined with his or her personal life. A social worker will try to keep professional concerns separate from his or her personal and family life but the very nature of social work makes this rather difficult.

The social work profession views the client as functioning within a particular situational and environmental context. Social workers must function within both personal and professional contexts. They have many roles and responsibilities in addition to those associated with their jobs. For example, a social worker is part of a family or household, often a spouse or partner, often a parent, part of friendship and social networks, and a resident in a particular neighborhood and community. Moreover, he or she may be a member of an ethnic group, affiliated with a religious denomination or faith community, a member of a special-interest group or political party, and a member of service organization. Given this multitude of connections and contexts, a social worker is challenged to cope with the tensions and conflicts that can easily arise between personal matters and professional obligations.

The social work profession strives to view the client, when an individual, as a whole person, with many dimensions such as the physical, emotional, psychological, social, spiritual, and the intellectual. This, of course, also describes the social worker for he or she responds as a whole person to the demands of job and profession. Thus, the social worker's beliefs, values, physical and emotional well-being, and all other dimensions will both influence and be influenced by what the social worker encounters in his or her professional practice.

Although this book focuses primarily on the activities that occur during the hours that the social worker devotes to his or her professional activities and job, this chapter examines how the realities of practice may impinge on the worker's private life. The observations presented here are intended to assist workers strike a healthy balance between their personal needs and responsibilities and the demands and responsibilities of social work practice.

SELECTING SOCIAL WORK AS A CAREER

Our lives are shaped by the choices we make. Because choosing social work as a career has some unique implications for self and family, those attracted to this profession must consider (and periodically reconsider) if social work should be their life's work. There must be a good fit between the person and his or her occupation. A mismatch can cause stress and threaten one's health and well-being. A person who feels trapped in the profession cannot bring the desired energy and commitment to the helping process, and consequently, clients will be poorly served.

Social Work as a Life Companion

An individual considering a social work career must be satisfied with his or her answers to the following questions:

- Is being a social worker a meaningful and worthwhile way for me to live my life?
- Will the practice of social work be an appropriate use of my special gifts, abilities, and skills?
- Is there a good fit between my personal beliefs and the values, ethical standards, and goals of the profession?
- What impact will my career in social work have on my family?
- What impact will this career have on my physical and mental health and the overall quality of my life?

Each person needs to identify his or her core beliefs and values and decide what is truly important. The work and rewards that accrue from being a social worker should be consistent with those priorities.

Earning a Living as a Social Worker

People do not choose the social work profession because of what they will earn, but they cannot devote their time to the practice of social work unless they can earn a living. Social work has never been a high-paying profession and in contrast to some occupations, the earning power of social workers does not rise rapidly or continually as they gain skill and experience. Social workers earn a modest income and have limited opportunity to climb the economic ladder. However, the satisfaction of doing something truly worthwhile and making a difference in the lives of people is often viewed by social workers as an offsetting form of compensation.

Most entry-level jobs are ones involving the provision of services directly to clients. After several years in direct services, many social workers seek higher-paying jobs in supervision and administration as a way of increasing their income and status. This may be a wise move for those attracted to management tasks such as budgeting, policy development, public relations, personnel selection, and staff training. It may be an unwise decision for those whose job satisfaction comes primarily from direct contact with clients.

Those entering social work should expect to change jobs from 5 to 10 times during their working years. Sometimes a job change is prompted by an agency's staff reductions, but most often it is a matter of personal choice. Among the reasons why social workers change jobs are the following:

- Desire for higher salary, better benefits, or job security
- Desire to learn a new field of practice and work with clients having a different set of problems or concerns
- Desire for more discretion and control over practice decisions and methods
- Desire to work in a setting that is more accepting of new ideas and new approaches to practice
- Desire for a less stressful or a safer work environment
- Opportunity to receive better supervision and more training
- Desire to remove self from conflicts with a supervisor or agency administrator
- Need to adjust work schedule to changes in personal or family life (e.g., marriage, divorce, birth of child, illness, etc.)

Those preparing to enter social work are advised to identify their personal and career goals and formulate a plan for reaching those goals. Examples of goals include becoming skilled in work with certain client populations, having the opportunity to design an innovative program, becoming an administrator of a certain type of agency, conducting research on a particular topic, and so on. In these times of rapid change, it can be difficult to develop such a plan and even more difficult to follow it. However, career planning provides a framework for making decisions about what experiences and training to pursue as preparation.

The School-to-Job Transition

Social work is a rewarding career but it is full of challenges. For many social workers these challenges will become apparent as they transition from the role of student into that of being a paid professional within an agency setting. Many new social workers will experience a reality shock. For example, in describing her new job, a very capable recent graduate told one of the authors: "I simply had no idea that my clients would be so troubled, my job so difficult and that my agency setting would be so complex."

Those beginning their first social work job soon realize that there is seldom enough time to do all that needs to be done. Many discover that in far too many social agencies, core social work values and principles have taken a backseat to the forces of political pressure, administrative expediency, budget limitations, the fear of lawsuits, and the day-by-day struggle to cope with an overwhelming workload. Many are disillusioned when they find that some colleagues have lost their enthusiasm and are too fatigued and demoralized to be effective. If the work place environment is rushed, overwhelmed, and stressful, it can be a challenge to maintain one's professional ideals and standards.

Every new social worker is somewhat frustrated by the slowness of change, whether that change is by individual clients, organizations, or communities. They also discover that identifying what needs to change or should be changed is relatively easy compared to actually achieving the change. Programs of social work education teach about the process of change and the techniques for facilitating change, but they cannot teach the personal qualities of patience, perseverance, tenacity, and tolerance so necessary to turning good ideas into reality.

New social work graduates who were high academic achievers may face a special challenge as they move into agency-based practice. Simply put, they are accustomed to doing grade-A, academic work and they expect to always do high-quality work on the job. They discover, however, that there is not enough time for perfection and probably only enough for C-level or average work.

Some of the agencies and organizations that employ social workers provide a superb working environment for their employees but far too many work settings are noisy, crowded, and even dangerous. Dissatisfaction with such conditions has led many experienced social workers to enter private practice in search of a more agreeable work environment and more control over what they do and how they do it. Although this is an understandable response to frustration, it has the effect of drawing talented social workers away from the profession's traditional commitment to serving the poor and the oppressed. Throughout their careers, social workers must struggle to reconcile their desire for adequate income and a decent work environment with their concern for the poor and a commitment to social and economic justice.

Many new social workers are surprised and disenchanted to discover that office or organizational politics plays a sizeable role in the decisions and functioning of their agency settings. Within every group and organization—whether a business, a social agency, a religious body, or a professional association—people use their power and authority to move the organization in directions they consider to be desirable. Thus, all organizations are inherently political. Social workers must, however, guard against becoming so absorbed in the politics of the workplace that they lose sight of their agency's real purpose and the people it is to serve.

ESTABLISHING ONESELF AS A SOCIAL WORKER

It is not enough for the new social worker to carry his or her credentials and skills into a job and simply assume that everything will fall in place for a satisfying and effective practice. The social worker must first demonstrate to clients, colleagues, and other agencies in the community that he or she is competent and trustworthy.

Acquiring a Reputation

Every social worker will acquire a reputation within his or her agency, within the local human services network, and among the clients he or she serves. That reputation has a significant impact on his or her work with clients, professional communications, interagency cooperation, and whether he or she is considered for promotion or offered other social work jobs. Social workers should regularly review how their statements, actions, and associations are forming their reputations. Socrates observed that, "the way to gain a good reputation is to endeavor to be what you desire to appear."

One needs to only sit in on a few support group meetings or spend an hour in an agency waiting room to realize that many clients talk freely about the social workers, doctors, teachers, and other professionals. They tell friends, neighbors, and other clients about how they have been treated and who does a good job and whom to avoid. Clients are especially sensitive to whether social workers really listen to what they are saying, are available when needed, and are fair in the decisions they make.

Within an agency, each social worker acquires a reputation as an employee. Over time, other agency employees form an opinion about the worker's competence, whether he or she is honest and dependable, and if he or she is a good team member. That reputation will affect the willingness of the other employees to offer their support, assistance, and cooperation.

Reputation is a determining factor in whether a private practice or a fee-for-service program will succeed. If they have a choice, people will avoid using agencies and professionals who have poor reputations. In addition, those who are in a position to refer clients to a social worker will select a practitioner who has a reputation for being competent, ethical, and effective.

A good reputation can take years to develop but can be quickly destroyed by others. For this reason, many cultures consider slander and the spreading of gossip that can ruin a person's reputation to be among the most reprehensible of moral transgressions.

Conflict over Agency Policy

Every social worker comes to his or her practice setting with a set of personal beliefs, values, standards, and expectations. It is inevitable that he or she will, from time to time, disagree with his or her agency's policy decisions and methods of operation. How is a worker to respond to such situations? The worker's decision on what to do must be based on a thoughtful examination of the issue or conflict. One might begin this examination by seeking answers to the following questions:

- Which of my beliefs, values, or standards is threatened or violated by my agency's position or policy? Is my concern or conflict a matter of principle or possibly arising from my own bias or perhaps from differences in personal, professional, or administrative style?
- Why has my agency taken this position? What are the arguments for and against this position? What political, economic, and social forces gave rise to this position? Is it an attempt to allocate scarce resources in a fair and responsible manner?
- What impact does this position or policy have on those to be served by my agency? How will it affect those who are most at risk and most in need of agency services?
- What impact does this position or policy have on the community? Does it enhance and strengthen the functioning of individuals, families, and the community? Does it recognize the obligation of communities and society to promote the common good, expand social and economic opportunities, and provide assistance to those unable to meet their basic needs?
- Does the position or policy recognize the dignity and worth of every person and that every person has a right to self-determination, as long as his or her actions do not harm others?
- Does the position recognize that every competent person is responsible for his or her own actions and must accept the consequences for violating legitimate laws?

Once the social worker understands why the agency has taken the action or position in question and is clear about why he or she disagrees, the worker must decide on a course of action. If the worker concludes that this is indeed a serious matter and demands a response, he or she should seek further advice and direction from trusted peers and/or the agency supervisor. If the offensive policy or procedure cannot be reversed, the worker faces a critical decision as to his or her future with the agency. In extreme cases and when there is no acceptable alternative, the worker will need to seek employment in a different agency.

One of the most painful situations social workers can experience is to find themselves employed by an organization that does not respect its clients, value professional competence, or expect ethical conduct. Such situations can arise when an organization's administration and policy board is more concerned about politics, cost cutting, or profit than providing needed services.

All organizations develop a culture consisting of its values, expectations, and group norms. Once formed, an organization's culture tends to perpetuate itself while exerting a pervasive effect on employees and their job performance. Employees are rewarded when they accept this culture and ostracized when they do not. A social worker employed by an organization with a destructive culture will need to work to change that culture or else look for another job.

If the worker is expected by his or her agency to perform a task or take an action that would violate his or her professional or personal moral standards, the worker should voice these concerns, document them in a letter to the appropriate administrator, and formally request to be excused from having to participate in the questionable activity.

When issues are complex, knowing what is right is never easy and doing what is right is always difficult.

Promoting Social Justice

Most individuals attracted to social work are somewhat idealistic. They want to make the world a better place. As discussed in Chapter 1, the social work profession and social workers strive to create a more just and humane society. Social workers believe that every individual has certain rights, such as those identified in the Declaration of Independence, the Bill of Rights, and the Universal Declaration of Human Rights issued by the United Nations. In short, they seek **social justice**, a time when everyone in the society shares the same rights, opportunities, and protections.

All considerations of social justice rest on the core belief that every human being is intrinsically valuable. This worth is not something that must be earned or proved, nor is it a function of one's skin color, nationality, gender, income, social status, health, education, political affiliation, occupation, or other external characteristics or life circumstances. Simply by virtue of being human, every person has a right to be treated with fairness and respect, protected from abuse and exploitation, and granted opportunities to have a family, secure an education and meaningful work, and have access to basic health care and social services. The Universal Declaration of Human Rights (United Nations, 1948, p. 1) observes that the "recognition of the inherent dignity and of the equal and inalienable rights of all members of the human family is the foundation of freedom, justice and peace in the world."

A multitude of interrelated economic, political, historical, and social forces can give rise to unjust and dehumanizing conditions. Because a social injustice is so often woven into a society's dominant belief systems and into its social and economic structures, an injustice such as exploitation, oppression, and discrimination may go unnoticed by all but those who are directly harmed. Social workers must always be open to the possibility that they or their agencies may unintentionally and unknowingly contribute to a social injustice.

All too often, we do not feel personally responsible for the existence of social injustice. When an injustice is brought to our attention, we are likely to conclude that it is the fault of society and beyond our control. When we examine a situation of injustice, we may feel helpless and conclude that we are too small a force to make any real difference. Social injustice is indeed a community or societal problem, but the responsibility to oppose injustice rests with the individual. Dr. Martin Luther King, Jr., reminded us that "whoever accepts evil without protesting against it, is really cooperating with it."

Achieving social justice is a complex undertaking, and even among people of goodwill and compassion, there will be different perspectives on what is truly fair and what actions and changes will move us toward a more just and humane society. Social workers must work for social and economic justice and for needed change in ways that recognize these legitimate differences of opinion while maintaining respect for those with whom they disagree.

In order to correct an injustice, people must become politically involved, speak out, and propose practical and feasible solutions. However, those who seek social reform must also understand that they will pay a price for challenging powerful individuals and groups that stand to lose money, power, or position if the status quo is altered. Those who speak out for justice may be ridiculed, lose their jobs, or, in extreme cases, subjected to physical threats and injury.

Political Involvement

Efforts to advance social and economic justice require participation in the political process. **Politics** is the art of gaining, exercising, and retaining power. Some social workers are attracted to politics; others find it distasteful. The degree to which one becomes involved in political activity will reflect such factors as level of interest, available time, and temperament. Being an informed and conscientious voter is of course essential, but more is required of social workers if they are to remain true to the "soul" of their profession. A social worker's participation in the political process will usually involve one or more of the following activities:

- Assessing the impact of an existing or proposed law, social policy, or program on people, especially the most vulnerable member of society
- Participating in the development and formulation of beneficial and effective social policies
- Educating the public about the social dimensions and ramifications of existing and proposed laws and public policies
- Entering into the public debate and advocating for needed changes
- Working for the election of those who will advance social and economic justice

As social workers become involved in the political process, they must make hard decisions about where they stand on complex issues. This can be difficult because there are usually some valid arguments both for and against any proposed policy. Most social workers tend to be on the liberal side of the conservative-to-liberal continuum. However, it is a mistake for social workers to assume that they must choose between being either a liberal or a conservative. Rather, they will need to be something of both. Everyone who is intellectually and spiritually alive will be liberal in the sense of being open to the truth, regardless of its source; desirous of needed change; and accepting governmental action if it is just and will, in fact, improve the lives of people. Similarly, every thoughtful and responsible person is conservative in the sense of wanting to preserve those values, social arrangements, and approaches that have been fair and beneficial to people. The newest idea is not necessarily the best one and not infrequently there is a negative side to government intervention. Thus, depending on the issue, a social worker might line up on either the liberal or conservative side of a debate. The merits and wisdom of a proposal, and not political ideology or political party, should dictate one's stance on an issue.

The political health of a nation, state, or city depends on informed citizens debating the issues and finding ways of achieving social and economic justice and advancing the common good. Such a debate requires not only mutual trust and goodwill among all involved but also a respect for diversity, a common language and terminology and agreement on a core of beliefs about people, society, and government. Debate, discussion, and decision-making can be constructive only within a context of such fundamental agreement. People destroy the possibility of finding common ground and a workable compromise if they replace dialogue with monologue, reason with slogans, and civility with coercion.

Political involvement can be tiring and frustrating. Some social workers begin to lose heart when confronted with setbacks. In order to continue working for justice and desirable social change, year after year, social workers must strive to develop the personal qualities of patience, perseverance, and tolerance. They need to present their positions without being shrill and offensive. They need to be engaged without being used and manipulated. They must hold to their core beliefs and principles without becoming narrow and partisan. And they need to focus on what brings people together rather than on what divides them.

Many social workers are in a position to directly observe the impact of social policies and programs on the lives of people. These observations are seldom available to the politicians who consider legislation and the administrators who implement policy and design programs. Thus, the social worker has both the opportunity and the obligation to document and communicate the effects of legislation and administrative decisions, as well as to offer ideas on how policies and programs can be made more humane, effective, and efficient. Social workers with special abilities to speak and write can make valuable contributions to the education of legislators and the citizenry.

THE INTERPLAY OF ONE'S PERSONAL AND PROFESSIONAL LIVES

Social workers meet many people who have overcome great obstacles and who care deeply about their families and communities. Getting to know these individuals can be an inspiring and uplifting experience. At the same time, social work practice is often stressful and requires a heavy commitment of time and energy. Those demands affect the social worker and his or her family.

Being Changed by Your Clients

In every type of practice, social workers will meet clients and other people who are truly remarkable because of their courage, wisdom, compassion, and generosity. Many will have faced great challenges and hardship. Social workers have the wonderful opportunity of learning from these individuals. Workers open themselves to this learning experience when they set aside their desire to learn *about* their clients and, instead, seek to learn *from* them. Many professional relationships with clients are an exchange of intangible gifts and both the social worker and client stand to be changed by what they give to and receive from each other.

One cannot begin to really know a client without coming to understand how the client thinks and feels about life. In many cases, the client's perspectives, beliefs, and values will be significantly different from those of the social worker. This may challenge the worker to rethink his or her own life experiences and reevaluate priorities. Whenever we begin to understand things in a new way or look at the familiar from a different angle, we begin to change.

A social worker may be nudged toward further self-examination by a client's criticism. A client might, for example, accuse a social worker of being rushed, insensitive, or unfair. The worker must remain open to the possibility that a client's uncomplimentary evaluation is accurate and, if that is the case, strive to modify the attitudes and behaviors that have offended clients.

The clients that cause a social worker to feel great anguish are a particularly painful source of worker self-examination. Not infrequently, the worker's skills and the available resources are insufficient or ineffective in helping a troubled client modify destructive behavior. In such situations, the worker will feel powerless and helpless as these clients make choices that disrupt family relationships, damage their health, or get them into trouble with the law. These frustrating and humbling experiences teach the social worker that he or she is but one small influence in a client's life.

Personal Responses to Clients in Need

Many of the clients served by social workers live in poverty and experience much distress because they cannot pay for even the basics such as food and shelter. By comparison, the social worker, with only a modest income, seems quite well off. This situation confronts the worker with a troubling question about his or her individual responsibility. Once a social worker has done all he or she can do as a professional and as an agency's representative, what, if anything, remains as a purely personal responsibility? Should a social worker use his or her own money to address a client's emergency?

Some would quickly answer no and argue that meeting peoples' basic needs is a community and governmental responsibility. For a social worker to do so, even occasionally, would be an unfair and unreasonable drain on the worker's personal finances and, moreover, it might make it too easy for the community or government to avoid or ignore their responsibilities. On the other hand, some professionals might answer that even when our social welfare systems fail to meet basic needs, the social worker still has a moral and ethical responsibility to respond in certain cases. It can be argued that a social worker, because of his or her knowledge, has a unique obligation beyond that of the ordinary citizen.

Ultimately, one's answer to this complex question is a matter of conscience and a judgment call as to what action would be helpful to the client and reasonable for the social worker. The social worker might consider the following questions in formulating his or her response:

- What situations, if any, require some extraordinary and essentially personal or private response by the professional (i.e., above and beyond what the agency provides)? What if the situation involves a person who is especially vulnerable?
- Given that social workers may encounter desperate and emergency situations on a daily basis, is it realistic to even consider using one's personal financial resources to address these situations? If a personal response is not reasonable, is some type of political or community action required of the worker?
- If a social worker decides to make a personal contribution to deal with some client emergency (e.g., to buy food, pay for a night's lodging, pay cab fare) how is this to be done? Can it be done in a way that keeps the donor's identity confidential so the client is not placed in a position of feeling beholden to the worker? What personal, ethical, and legal pitfalls might result from making a money contribution directly to a client?
- Should agencies have a policy on whether, when, and how a personal contribution can occur? Would it be appropriate for the workers of an agency to create and donate to a special, non-agency emergency fund?

The Social Worker's Family

It is difficult to keep work-related concerns from affecting one's personal life and family relationships. It is also difficult to keep one's personal and family responsibilities and concerns from affecting professional performance. Nevertheless, social workers must strive to maintain a healthy separation.

The social worker must protect his or her family from being adversely affected by work-related responsibilities. Those who provide direct services to seriously troubled and highly dysfunctional clients will observe behaviors and situations that are extreme, depraved, and cruel. Long-term exposure to such behavior and circumstances can distort one's sense of normality and moral compass. In an adult correctional setting, for example, the daily exposure to intimidation, violence, and manipulation can dull one's sensitivity and stretch one's tolerance for and acceptance of abuse and inhumane treatment. Skewed views on what is usual and normal behavior, if brought home to one's family or into one's friendships, can strain those relationships.

Social workers, like everyone, experience personal and family problems. Sometimes the problems are serious and a source of anxiety or depression. When worry associated with personal concerns is added to the stress of practice, the social worker may become overwhelmed. During these times, the social worker needs the support of colleagues and must be open to guidance provided by those able to see more objectively what is happening.

A FITNESS PROGRAM FOR THE SOCIAL WORKER

To be of maximum assistance to clients, a social worker must maintain a proper boundary in professional relationships. The worker's own need for meaningful relationships and friendships must be met outside his or her relationships with clients. In addition, effective practice requires that the worker be intellectually alert and physically, emotionally, and spiritually healthy.

Friendships and Community

Good friends provide us with support and encouragement and help us to examine our assumptions, test reality, and maintain perspective. Good friends also provide constructive criticism when we behave inappropriately.

Because people tend to choose friends who are similar to themselves in age, interests, and socioeconomic status, many friendships develop within the workplace. While this is a natural occurrence, it has a downside. It can, for example, limit one's exposure to differing perspectives and points of view. If a social worker's friends are mostly other social workers, he or she may come to believe that only another social worker can understand his or her concerns, interests, and frustrations. In some cases, a narrow circle of friends gives rise to an "us against them" mentality. The social worker should cultivate friendships with people from outside the work setting and outside the profession in order to attain varied perspectives on life, the community, and society.

All people need to feel that they belong to something greater than themselves. Unfortunately, a sense of community is often missing in our fast-moving, urban society. Some people feel unconnected and lonely because they are self-absorbed and more interested in receiving than in giving. A genuine sense of belonging and community cannot be artificially manufactured or forced into existence. Rather, it is something that grows slowly as individuals share what they have—time, energy, creativity, or money—with others in order to reach a common goal. Long-term associations, personal sacrifices, trust, mutual respect, and loyalty are the building blocks of community; there are no shortcuts.

Social workers often find a spirit of community and camaraderie through their participation in professional associations such as the National Association of Social Workers. Professional organizations are indeed important because they advance the profession. However, social workers should not limit their involvements to professional groups and organizations. They should also participate in neighborhood and local community events, projects, and activities.

Self-Worth and Self-Image

Social work is not an esteemed profession. To a large extent, this is because its identity and purpose is not clear to the public and because social work is inherently controversial. Social workers call attention to problems and social conditions that many would prefer to ignore and deny. Because so many of the people served by social workers and social agencies are devalued and disliked (e.g., the poor, parents who abuse their children, the mentally ill, individuals addicted to drugs, the homeless, etc.), social workers are by association, also devalued. All too often, images of social work and social workers are linked to unpopular governmental welfare programs that many people perceive as a waste of taxpayer money.

Given the type of concerns they address, it is not surprising that social agencies and social workers become targets for criticism by politicians and others who do not want to be reminded of unmet human need, injustice, and the inadequacy of existing programs. Not infrequently, social workers are blamed for systemic and societal problems that are beyond the control of any one person, profession, or agency. Even when social workers understand that such criticism is unreasonable or misdirected, it is still painful and frustrating. Social workers, like all people, want to be understood, valued, and respected.

In order to counteract feelings of being devalued and misunderstood, social workers must possess a strong sense of personal worth and confidence. This comes from belief in the importance of their work and the value of the services they provide. If the social worker doubts his or her own worth or the importance of the profession, he or she is easily demoralized. No one should feel apologetic for being a social worker; the profession's mission and values are truly noble and reflect the very best of the human spirit.

Physical and Emotional Well-Being

There must be a suitable match between a person's physical and emotional stamina and the demands of his or her job. Thus, when selecting a particular type or field of practice, a social worker needs to consider his or her temperament, physical limitations, and health problems. In addition, the worker must consider the normal developmental changes that will occur during the years of work. As people grow older, their level of energy decreases and they often experience some degree of loss in vision and hearing. These ordinary changes can affect the performance of specific social work tasks. Family and group therapy, for example, require excellent hearing. Also, one's age can make it either easier or more difficult to build relationships with clients who are in certain age categories.

For the most part, social work is a sedentary occupation. Physical inactivity can place the worker at greater risk of heart disease and other health problems. In order to counter this risk, it is important for workers to adhere to a program of regular exercise.

The expression of empathy and compassion by the social worker for the client is necessary to support and encourage the client during the change process. However, those efforts to "be with" and to "feel with" the client are sometimes exhausting and even painful to the worker. The social worker must strive to strike a healthy and realistic balance between empathy for the client and maintaining the emotional distance, objectivity, and personal boundaries appropriate to a professional relationship.

Social workers must be able to cope with and respond appropriately to the intense feelings and emotions (e.g., sadness, anger, fear) they encounter when working with clients who are in gut wrenching situations such as the father who has abused his child or the family that has lost a member to suicide. The frequent and long-term exposure to the distress of others can contribute to *compassion fatigue* and a numbing or hardening of the worker's own feelings (see Item 16.4).

Many clients are so overwhelmed by their problems that they develop *learned helplessness*—a pervasive feeling of hopelessness and a belief that no matter what they do, their pain will continue. Social workers who meet these clients on a daily basis are vulnerable to developing this same sense of helplessness. The gallows humor observed in some agencies suggests that the workers are struggling to maintain perspective in the face of human conditions that defy acceptance when, at the same time, they have neither the time nor the resources to respond in a humane manner.

Social workers who have not satisfactorily resolved issues in their own family relationships or who carry emotional baggage related to traumatic life experiences may sometimes distort and mishandle a professional relationship when clients are struggling with issues similar to their own. In extreme cases, vulnerable workers have been so knocked off balance emotionally that they could no longer function as professionals. It is critically important that social workers acknowledge their emotional weak spots and, if needed, obtain professional help. If that is not possible or successful, they should arrange for work assignments that avoid handling the types of cases and situations that might threaten their emotional well-being (see Item 16.3).

Life-Long Learning

The risk of mental stagnation exists in every profession. Learning and intellectual growth, both personal and professional, must continue throughout one's life. People put themselves in touch with new ideas and clarify their thinking by reading, listening to presentations by experts, and participating in thoughtful discussions with family, friends, and colleagues. It is helpful to occasionally place oneself in situations that generate pressure to study and think. Examples include teaching a class, making a presentation, or writing an article (see Item 16.10). Ideally, every new social worker will find a mentor who can provide encouragement and direction as the worker seeks to learn a new job or develop his or her knowledge and skills (see Item 16.9).

Learning, especially learning in adulthood, requires some special effort and the willingness to let go of comfortable and familiar ideas. In order to learn, people must first feel unsure about what they "know" and be ready to consider new and sometimes disturbing ideas. Learning begins with a question and an inner dissatisfaction with one's level of understanding or skill. It continues as the individual searches for answers, either alone or with others.

It is hard to imagine a type of work that can evoke as many truly significant and challenging questions as does the practice of social work. The situations social workers encounter each day touch the very heart of questions about social justice; human rights and responsibilities; ethical behavior; the causes of individual, family, and organizational problems; and the nature of personal and social change. However, social work is not an academic discipline, nor a pure science wherein the search for knowledge is driven by the excitement of ideas and the joy of discovery. Those who want most of all to deal with theoretical matters and knowledge building are usually not content in the role of a social work practitioner. Social workers spend much of their time trying to patch together practical solutions to very serious but quite ordinary and common human problems, dilemmas, and crises.

Religion and Spirituality

What motivates some people to pursue a career in social work? Undoubtedly, there are a variety of answers but many social workers would say that it had something to do with their spiritually and religious beliefs and values.

Both spirituality and religion grapple with the primal questions of life such as: Does my life have some ultimate purpose and meaning? How should I live my life? How am I to decide what is right and wrong? Why is there so much evil and suffering in the world? Why is there so much good and love in the world? How do I relate to God? Is there a God? What is God?

These are not questions that the scientific method can answer. Rather, they are matters of spirituality, faith, and choice. The major religions of the world offer some answers and perspectives that have been meaningful to countless people over thousands of years, but, ultimately, each individual must choose his or her own spiritual path.

Although religion and spirituality are intertwined, it is helpful to make a somewhat arbitrary distinction. A **religion** is a set of beliefs, stories, traditions, and practices that nurture and support particular approaches to spiritual growth. A religion provides a language and a conceptual framework for describing and understanding the spiritual life. A religion is passed from one generation to another through various forms of leadership and institutional structures. The elements of a religion typically include public prayer and worship by the community of believers, various rituals that mark transitions in the life cycle or the spiritual journey, a moral code, and reverence for certain sacred writings and sacred places.

As compared to a religion, which is public and institutional in nature, **spirituality** is more a quality of the inner self or soul—that deepest recess of our being, where we confront our "true self" and judge ourselves in light of what we believe to be right and wrong. An individual's spirituality is his or her unique way of interpreting and assigning meaning to life. Our spirituality is revealed in how we respond to other people, what we do with our money, how we react to our success and setbacks, and the meaning we give to the very ordinary aspects and events of living. Observers conclude that a deeply spiritual person is real or genuine, self-aware, non-defensive, unpretentious, and accepting of all people. They do not waste time or energy trying to be successful, unique, liked, or respected. They simply accept themselves for who they are, including their strengths and their limitations.

Both religion and spirituality involve a sense of the sacred and the recognition that some creative power, life force, great mystery, or divine presence transcends the visible and material world and, at the same time, is somehow present within all that exists and all that we experience. Both emphasize the importance of human qualities such as compassion, forgiveness, hope, gratitude, justice, reconciliation, humility, self-awareness, and service. Both involve ideals and visions of the way things should be or could be.

Every day, social workers meet people who have been hurt by injustice, dishonesty, discrimination, and violence. Every day social workers encounter people who have unmet needs for food, shelter, and health care. How do social workers make sense of such a harsh reality? How do social workers keep up their spirits when in such a discouraging situation? In order to keep from being consumed by outrage and frustration and in order to maintain their motivation, the social worker must strive to develop a hopeful spirituality—one that views all people, including those who cause harm to others, as having inherent worth and dignity and capable of positive change. The social workers need a spirituality that helps them celebrate the goodness of people.

As people struggle to make sense of their life experiences, especially those that bring great joy or cause great distress, they often gain new insights and their beliefs and perspectives slowly change. Thus, spirituality is dynamic and an ongoing journey. The deeply religious and spiritual people who describe their spiritual struggles emphasize the importance of occasional solitude for reflecting on life experiences, striving to achieve self-knowledge and self-discipline, providing service to others, developing a sense of humility, and having patience with themselves and compassion for others. They also identify common barriers to spiritual growth such as a desire for control, power, prestige, and possessions, and the fear of change.

One's spirituality needs to be durable in the sense that it provides meaning and direction during both good times and bad, throughout the life cycle, and especially as the person faces great hardship, suffering, and death. As Moore (1992) suggests, the development and nurturing of such spirituality is difficult without the assistance of a group or community that provides guidance, encouragement, and challenge.

> Religions around the world demonstrate that spiritual life requires constant attention . . . For good reason we go to church, temple, or mosque regularly and at appointed times: it's easy for consciousness to become lodged in the material world and forget the spiritual. Sacred technology [e.g., prayer, meditation, solitude, ritual, study, fasting, etc.] is largely aimed at helping us remain conscious of spiritual ideals and values. (p. 204)

As people grow spiritually, they see more clearly that they are themselves capable of great love and generosity as well as hate and selfishness. An important task in one's spiritual journey is to come to terms with one's own potential to be cruel, dishonest, and destructive as well as one's capacity for self-deception (see Item 15.17).

Artistic Expression

Another piece of the social worker's fitness program should be to develop and/or maintain his or her capacities for artistic expression. There is evidence that effective social workers are often creative people. It is not uncommon to meet social workers who are talented in various forms of artistic expressions such as music, painting, acting, creative writing, sewing, photography, dance, woodworking, and so on.

It is important for social workers to cultivate and share their artistic talents. Such activities can be a diversion from the stress of practice and a gift that enhances the quality of life of other people.

HAVING FUN IN SOCIAL WORK

Human beings need to play and have fun. Adults often satisfy this need by introducing various forms of humor (e.g., jokes, kidding, playful pranks, and silly antics) into their work environment. How is a social worker to reconcile his or her need for fun with the serious business of social work? In many ways, the practice of social work is a rather grim and emotionally heavy endeavor. Clients are often in truly desperate and tragic situations, and the helping resources at a social worker's disposal are woefully inadequate. Although human distress is not a laughing matter, humor can be a counterbalance to the frustrations experienced in practice.

Despite the risks associated with inappropriate expressions of humor, without an active sense of humor, social work practice can be unbearable and social workers can be very boring. Social workers must take their work seriously, yet acknowledge and appreciate those things that are genuinely funny about themselves, their jobs, and the situations they encounter. They must allow themselves to laugh at the absurdities of life and to temporarily to slip out from under societal demands for conformity and the many restrictions they place on themselves.

The use of humor with clients is always somewhat risky, but given proper precautions, it has a place in helping relationships. Often, it is the clients who teach the workers the importance of finding the humor in the clients' situations. Many who live with harsh realities come to appreciate the importance of humor as a way of achieving a degree of detachment from their painful situations. Humor is an essential coping mechanism that should be affirmed and supported. It is always wrong to laugh at clients, but it may be appropriate and even helpful to laugh with them as they describe the humorous aspects of their experiences.

Conclusion

When an individual chooses social work as a career, he or she is faced with all of the challenges involved in blending or merging a unique human being with a set of professional responsibilities. The social worker, as a whole person, has many dimensions, including the physical, emotional, intellectual, social, and spiritual. These dimensions both affect and are affected by social work practice and the workplace environment. The social worker's family is affected by the modest earning capacity associated with the profession and by how the social worker handles the everyday demands and stresses common to social work practice.

A social worker will attempt to keep his or her personal and family life separate from his or her professional responsibilities but this is inherently difficult. Each social worker must strive to achieve a healthy balance between his or her personal and professional lives.

Selected Bibliography

Gibelman, Margaret. *What Social Workers Do*, 2nd ed. Washington, DC: NASW Press, 2005.

Ginsberg, Leon. *Thinking About a Social Work Career*, 3rd ed. Boston: Allyn & Bacon, 2008.

Moore, Thomas. *Care of the Soul*. New York: Harper Collins, 1992.

Payne, Malcolm. *What is Professional Social Work*. Chicago: Lyceum, 2006.

Reichert, Elisabeth. *Social Work and Human Rights*. New York: Columbia University Press, 2003.

Ritter, Jessica, Halaevalu Vakalahi, & Mary Klernan-Stern. *101 Careers in Social Work*. New York: Springer, 2008.

Rosenberg, Jessica. *Working in Social Work: Real World Guide to Practice Settings*. New York: Routledge, 2009.

United Nations General Assembly. *Universal Declaration of Human Rights*. New York: United Nations, December 1948.

Merging the Person's Art with the Profession's Science

The social worker must combine his or her personal qualities, creative abilities, and social concerns with the profession's knowledge in order to help clients enhance their social functioning or prevent social problems from developing. Each social worker has unique qualities that provide an artistic component to his or her practice. Professional education cannot teach these artistic features, although it can help the learner to identify such strengths and develop the ability to focus and apply them in work with clients. Professional education can also assist the learner in developing a beginning understanding of the knowledge (or science) that is necessary for effective practice. This merging and blending of one's art and the profession's science is initiated in social work education programs, but it is a lifelong activity, as social work knowledge is constantly expanding and the worker is being continually changed by life experiences.

THE SOCIAL WORKER AS ARTIST

Art is "skill arising from the exercise of intuitive faculties" (*American Heritage Dictionary of the English Language*, 2000, s.v. "art"). One need not look far to observe successful helpers who rely almost entirely on their artistic or intuitive abilities. Natural helpers, volunteers, and untrained human services providers demonstrate daily that even without formal education, they can be helpful in many situations. Similarly, it is not uncommon to see well-educated and knowledgeable people fail in their efforts to serve clients because they lack the necessary intuitive skills.

What factors comprise the art of social work? There are numerous components: the compassion and courage to confront human suffering; the capacity to build a meaningful and productive helping relationship; the creativity to overcome barriers to change; the ability to infuse the change process with hopefulness and energy; the exercise of sound judgment; the appropriate personal values; and the formation of an effective professional style.

Compassion and Courage

A prerequisite to effective social work practice is the social worker's compassion. The word **compassion** means to suffer with others; it refers to a willingness to join with and enter into the pain of those who are distressed or troubled. Although most people see themselves as compassionate, it is important to recognize that a high level of compassion is not typical of most people. In fact, it is quite natural to want to avoid involvement in the pain of others. A social worker who lacks compassion is likely to distance himself or herself from client concerns.

Social work also demands courage, not in the sense of being bold or daring but rather in being able to confront on a daily basis human suffering and turmoil and, not infrequently, negative and destructive human behaviors. Day after day, case by case, the social worker must be able to respond constructively to people who are directly affected by illness, disability, violence, neglect, sexual abuse, addiction, criminal exploitation, poverty, bizarre and chaotic family life, separation from a loved one, loneliness, abandonment, and other types of human suffering. Moreover, the social worker must be able to respond constructively to people who have directly or indirectly inflicted suffering on others. They must be able to deal with sometimes appalling human problems without becoming distracted or immobilized by their own emotional reactions. Over time, an individual can develop this fortitude or courage, but it is not something that can be learned from books or in a classroom. People who have this courage are able to value and treat with dignity even those who have hurt others.

Professional Relationship

A bond of trust must exist before people are willing to risk that difficult human experience—change. Thus, the most fundamental tool of the trade is the use of a **professional relationship** (see Item 8.1) to help people become open to the possibility of change and engage in the change process. A positive relationship is a precondition for effective work with individuals, families, or groups of clients, and also in work with the people who make up organizations and communities.

How important is this relationship to the helping process? Lambert (1992) has reviewed the research on factors that contribute to successful helping and concluded there are four:

1. *Client factors* (e.g., quality of the client's participation in treatment, satisfaction with what the worker is doing, the client's personal strengths and resources)
2. *Relationship factors* (e.g., the trust and connection between client and helper)
3. *Expectancy factors* (e.g., the client's positive expectations from the helping process)
4. *Model/technique factors* (e.g., the specific practice approach used by the worker)

Lambert's research indicates that client factors account for 40 percent of successful outcomes, relationship factors for 30 percent, expectancy factors for 15 percent, and helping approach factors the remaining 15 percent. In other research, Hubble, Duncan, and Miller (1999) did not find significant differences in the success rates among the many intervention models now available to therapists. They conclude that the elements of a particular model are less important than the worker's confidence that following a certain approach will achieve the desired change and thus encourage the client's trust in the process. Of the variables the worker can affect, relationship is the most important.

What are the essential qualities of successful helping? Within many Native American tribes there is a saying: "If you want to understand another person, you must first walk a mile in his [or her] moccasins." In other words, one must get inside that person's thoughts, beliefs, and life experiences. But before that is possible, one must first set aside his or her own values, attitudes, and judgments. This ability to take on another's perspective is known as having **empathy**.

Although no one can ever fully appreciate the viewpoint of another person, the social worker needs to get as close as possible to that level of understanding. Empathy is needed, for example, to understand the fear and anger of a battered wife and her possible love and concern for the man who hurt her; to be sensitive to the anger and guilt of an abusive parent; to appreciate the difficulty of a teenager risking criticism by peers for speaking up in a group; or even to hear out the frustrations of an overworked staff member.

Warmth is another quality of relationship that communicates respect, acceptance, and interest in the well-being of others. However, warmth is much more than just saying "I care," although at times, that is important. Warmth is transmitted in many forms of communication, from a reassuring smile to an offer of concrete and tangible assistance. Warmth is a highly individual quality that is expressed differently by each person, but inherent in all expressions of warmth is acceptance and a nonjudgmental attitude.

Linked to warmth and empathy is the quality of **genuineness**. Trite as it may sound, the social worker must behave like a "real" person and must truly like people and care about their well-being. The social worker may know the correct words to say or the proper action to recommend, but the client will assign them little value if the worker appears phony.

Creativity

Creative thinking is characterized by the integration of diverse facts and information leading to the formation of original ideas. Creativity is important in social work because each client's situation is unique and constantly changing. So-called textbook answers to human problems cannot accommodate this uniqueness.

A social worker with **imagination** can identify a variety of ways to approach and solve a problem, whereas the unimaginative one sees only one or two options—or perhaps none at all. For example, an area in which the social worker must be imaginative is in interpreting and implementing agency policies. Policies are created to serve the typical client, yet people are characterized by infinite variety. Although the social worker cannot ethically (or legally) ignore or subvert agency policy, he or she must find ways to adapt or bend a policy to meet unique client needs. The social worker who is bound by a literal interpretation of "The Manual" is simply not able to make the system work for many clients.

Flexibility is also a dimension of creativity. Helping others change requires an ability to continually modify and adapt prior plans and decisions. The social worker making a foster home placement, for example, must have the flexibility to adapt his or her thinking to the often differing perspectives of biological parents, foster parents, the child, the court, the agency, and even the neighborhood. To align oneself rigidly with any of the affected parties limits the social worker's ability to help resolve problems and conflicts. At times, one needs to be supportive; at other times, it is necessary to challenge the client; and at still other times, the social worker must be hard nosed, directive, or exercise legitimate legal or professional authority. The effective social worker must be able to shift from one approach to another and correctly decide when a shift is appropriate.

In addition, the creative social worker must possess the trait of **persistence**—the capacity to continue on a course of action, despite difficulties and setbacks. Self-discipline and goal directness are needed to translate creative ideas into action. The term *flexible persistence* emphasizes the need for both flexibility and persistence in the problem-solving process.

Hopefulness and Energy

The willingness and motivation of a client to work for change, when the prospect of change is anxiety producing or painful, is often a reflection of the social worker's ability to communicate the perspective that together the worker and client can improve the client's situation. Two characteristics of the social worker that are central to increasing client motivation are hopefulness and energy.

Hopefulness refers to a firm belief and a trust in the basic goodness of people, in their capacity to change in positive ways, and in their willingness to work cooperatively with others for the common good. Clients have typically been unsuccessful when attempting other avenues to address their issues or they would not be seeking professional help. Consequently, they often approach professional services with a carryover of skepticism. Given the serious and intractable nature of many of the situations encountered in practice, the social worker, too, is vulnerable to feelings of discouragement. The worker's hopefulness makes it possible to approach each practice situation with a genuine sense that this time the helping effort can make a difference.

Energy is the capacity to move things along, get results, and bounce back from mistakes and failures. The social worker's energy is needed to activate the client and counteract the client's hesitation. One's willingness to commit time and effort to the change process can encourage clients to also invest themselves in that activity. The worker should be careful, however, to avoid communicating a false or counterfeit optimism.

Judgment

The responsibilities that are inherent in any professional activity, the complex nature of the helping process, and the uniqueness of every client's situation requires social workers to make difficult and important judgments. **Judgment** is the ability to discern relationships, make distinctions, choose between alternatives, and arrive at a decision on how to proceed. Judgment is at the very core of such professional activities as assessing client situations, formulating intervention plans, choosing techniques or procedures to utilize, and deciding when to terminate services. Ultimately, professional judgment depends on clear and critical thinking by the social worker.

Needless to say, some of us are better than others when it comes to forming judgments and making decisions. Some of us make poor judgments because it is easier to feel than to think; given that, we may be inclined to make decisions on the basis of emotion rather than careful and logical thinking. The qualifier *mature* is often used to describe the type of judgments expected of a social worker. Sometimes, we assume that chronologically mature people are better at making sound judgments. Certainly, life experience presents opportunities to gain insight, and if one learns from those experiences, then age and wisdom are surely associated. Similarly, providing human services over many years affords opportunities to test and refine one's ability to make wise practice decisions. However, the repetition of an experience by itself does not assure that the social worker will gain insight. To grow in practice wisdom, the social worker must be analytical, reflective, and open to learning from successes as well as failures.

Personal Values

The reasons one might enter social work are varied, but the motive is almost always a concern for others and a desire to make the world a better place. However, it is important to remember that when a person becomes an instrument for change, there is in that person's mind some notion about what constitutes a desirable and good life for people. In other words, social workers, like all people, possess personal values. A **value** is a consistent preference that affects one's decisions and actions and is based on that person's deepest beliefs and commitments. Values are our fundamental beliefs about how things should be and what is right and worthwhile.

The dilemma arises when there is a difference of opinion over what is "right." The social worker's view of the "right" outcome or the best course of action may be different from the client's, and both may differ from those who fund and sanction the agency that employs the social worker. Is it "right," for example, to encourage a single mother to find employment if having a job necessitates placing her young children in day care? Is it "right" to refer a woman to an abortion clinic? Is it "right" to withhold further financial assistance from a client who has violated an agency rule by not reporting income from a temporary job? Is it "right" to force homeless people to reside in shelters against their will? Whose "right" is right? Whose values are to be followed?

Given that one person's values cannot serve as absolute guides for all others to follow, is it appropriate to expect the client to conform to what the social worker or his or her agency considers desirable or the right thing to do? Logic would answer no, but many clients feel subtle pressure to go along with what they think the agency or social worker expects. If a social worker accepts the principle of maximizing clients' self-determination, he or she must allow clients to make the decisions and to move toward outcomes they believe are most desirable. And apart from those values codified in law and universally recognized moral principles, the social worker should hold his or her personal beliefs and values in abeyance in favor of client self-determination.

This is not to suggest that the social worker is always to remain neutral with regard to client behaviors or decisions that are socially irresponsible, self-destructive, or harmful to others. A social worker is of little help to a client if he or she sidesteps or avoids discussing moral and ethical issues directly related to a client's concerns. Laws, basic moral principles, and even the rules of civility do matter. They are an essential part of our social fabric, and they are an important aspect of the client's social functioning. However, when such issues are discussed, it must be done in ways that are respectful of the client's perspective.

Prerequisite to maintaining a nonjudgmental attitude is knowledge of one's own belief system. As new value conflicts arise, it is important for the social worker to consider what he or she believes about the situation and why. It is useful to discuss values and various moral dilemmas with family, friends, and colleagues to obtain alternate views that might contribute to refinements in one's thinking.

It is desirable for the social worker's personal values to be compatible with the values of the social work profession. If these two value systems are in conflict, one of the following two things is likely to happen: (1) the worker will go through the motions of being a professional social worker but because his or her heart is not in it, the lack of genuineness will be apparent to both clients and colleagues or (2) the worker will reject the profession's values and principles as a guiding force and respond to clients entirely on the basis of personal beliefs and values. In both instances, the client and the employing agency will lose the benefit of the social work perspective.

What values characterize professional social work? The *National Association of Social Workers Code of Ethics* (NASW, 1999) is predicated on six core values that drive this profession:

1. ***Service.***   The primary purpose of social work is to help clients deal with issues of social functioning. The obligation to serve clients takes precedence over the workers' self-interests.

2. ***Social justice.***   As social workers engage in efforts to change unjust societal conditions, they are particularly sensitive to the most vulnerable members of the population (i.e., those individuals and groups who have experienced poverty, discrimination, and other forms of injustice). In doing this, social workers are committed to promoting public understanding of the effects of such oppression and encouraging an appreciation of the richness to be gained from human diversity.

3. ***Dignity and worth of the person (and the society).***   Social workers are committed to considering each client as a person of value, and therefore treating the client with respect—even when his or her behavior may have been harmful to self or others. At the same time, social workers are committed to improving societal conditions and resolving conflicts between clients and the broader society.

4. ***Importance of human relationships.***   Social workers understand that relationships are central to human development as well as to a successful helping process, whether serving individuals, families, groups, organizations, or communities. Further, clients are hesitant to risk change unless they are true partners in the helping process, feel supported by a meaningful relationship with the social worker, and maintain as much control as possible over the decisions about how to achieve change.

5. ***Integrity.***   A helping relationship cannot be sustained unless clients can trust social workers to be honest and to respect the clients' rights to privacy. Moreover, workers are obligated to assure that any human services agency with which they are affiliated treats clients and client information in an appropriate and professional manner.

6. ***Competence.***   Social workers are committed to bringing the best knowledge and skill possible to the helping process. They are obligated to practice within their areas of expertise (i.e., the social work domain), to search for the best knowledge and skills related to the practice situation (i.e., evidence-based practice), and to contribute to the profession's knowledge base.

None of these values is unique to social work, but the effect of the combined set of values differentiates social work from other professions.

Professional Style

In the final analysis, it is the social worker who is the instrument of change and, as such, each social worker has a unique style of practice. According to Siporin (1993, p. 257), "The social worker's personality, craftsmanship, and artistry in the application of knowledge and skill are articulated through professional and personal styles." One's style can open up and facilitate the helping process or close it down.

Style is expressed in how social workers relate to clients—their energy, creativity, wisdom, and judgment, as well as their passion and commitment to addressing social issues. In addition, their uniqueness is expressed in their clothing, hairstyle, posture, speech, and in a hundred other choices and behaviors that send out messages about who they are and what they believe about themselves and others.

One's professional style must be appropriate to the situation, the clients served, and the agency setting. For example, a worker might dress casually when working with children and families but should dress more formally when making a court appearance on the clients' behalf.

"Know thyself" is an important admonition for the social worker, but putting that advice to practice is never easy. It is helpful for the social worker to step back periodically and examine how others perceive his or her style. Clues from clients, family, friends, colleagues, and supervisors are helpful in making these assessments.

A social worker's practice style emerges as he or she balances individuality with the behaviors required for practice. Inherent in professional socialization is pressure to conform. The need to balance expectations of profession, agency, and clients with one's individuality is an issue for every social worker. The social worker must ask: How far am I willing to compromise my individuality and personal preferences in order to serve my clients and meet agency expectations? So long as clients are properly served and not alienated or harmed, one has considerable latitude. In fact, the profession is enriched by the varied styles of its members.

THE SOCIAL WORKER AS SCIENTIST

Social workers must use both heart and head when interacting with clients and providing services. With artistic abilities as a foundation, the social worker builds professional capacity by drawing from the available knowledge about his or her clients and the most effective methods of helping. One form of knowledge, *practice wisdom*, is derived from the worker's personal observations and the collective experiences for several generations of social workers who informally share their understanding with colleagues. It is expected that professionals will also use tested knowledge (i.e., science). **Science** is "the objective identification, description, experimental investigation of theoretical explanations and phenomena" (*American Heritage Dictionary of the English Language*, 2000, s.v. "science"). Like other professions, social work strives to increase the amount of scientific knowledge available to its practitioners.

The scientific method is the most accepted approach in Western societies for studying phenomena and building knowledge. In its most rigorous applications, the **scientific method** involves carefully defining and isolating the problem under study, precisely defining all concepts and terminology used, formulating hypotheses to be tested, following appropriate sampling procedures and an established protocol for gathering data, using control and experimental groups for comparison, applying valid and reliable tools of measurement, and, finally, submitting the research findings to scrutiny by professional peers so they can replicate the study and either confirm or repudiate the findings. Although the use of the scientific method is not the only source of knowledge, it is one that helps to minimize errors of judgment caused by bias and subjectivity.

The application of the scientific method is difficult within social work because many of the problems that concern social workers cannot be easily quantified, client confidentiality prohibits some studies, and identical client situations seldom exist for rigorous comparison and testing. Also, for ethical reasons, social workers and agencies cannot assign vulnerable, at-risk clients (e.g., an abused child) to a no-treatment or control group. Single-subject designs may be used or the relative effectiveness of two or more interventions may be studied, but seldom can the effectiveness of an intervention be directly compared to doing nothing at all.

For ethical reasons, social work may never be a completely scientific discipline, nor should it. Practice wisdom, values, and beliefs will inevitably shape the social worker's practice. Nevertheless, the worker must strive to be scientific in his or her thinking. Social work is not a science to the same degree as, for example, physics, botany, or chemistry. However, social work can be said to be scientific in the following ways:

- It gathers, organizes, and analyzes data that describe the social functioning of people.
- It uses its observations, experiences, and formal studies to create new techniques, formulate new practice guidelines, and develop new programs and policies.
- It uses data as the basis for formulating propositions and conceptual frameworks that guide social work interventions.
- It objectively examines its interventions and their impact on the social functioning of people.
- It exchanges and critically evaluates the ideas, studies, and practices described by others in the profession.

To the extent that social work is scientific, it should be viewed as an **applied science**, rather than a pure science. And like many other professionals, the social worker is more a technologist than a scientist. For example, as a technologist, the physician draws upon and applies the findings derived from the biological sciences; likewise, the mechanical engineer applies knowledge derived from the science of physics. The social worker, too, is a technologist who draws upon and applies the knowledge derived from the social and behavioral sciences. Whereas the primary goal of the scientist is to understand, the primary goal of the technologist is to bring about certain types of change.

To assist clients with problems of social functioning, social workers need knowledge of the social phenomena (e.g., individual, family, group, organization, or community) with which they will be working. Because social workers are also concerned with the social environment of people, they must be knowledgeable about the social conditions in communities, agencies, and the human services delivery system. Finally, because they are representing one of several helping professions, social workers need to have knowledge of the social work profession and possess the requisite knowledge about effective intervention approaches used in social work practice.

Knowledge of Social Phenomena

Given their focus on the social functioning, social workers are especially concerned with interactions between and among people and interactions between people and the systems that deliver social programs. Thus, they must understand social phenomena and the various levels of person-in-environment interaction. As described in Chapter 1, social work requires an exceptionally broad knowledge base.

In addition to understanding the interrelatedness of the various system levels and the kind of situations being addressed in the social worker's practice, the worker must understand the individual person, for which knowledge of physical and psychological development (including both normal and abnormal functioning) is essential. The social worker must also understand families and other households. The family has long been a dominant point of intervention for social workers, and knowledge of family dynamics is critically important. With the increase of nontraditional family structures, understanding alternate living and intimacy patterns has become especially important. Further, a considerable amount of practice takes place with small groups, including support groups, therapeutic groups, and committees. Thus, the social worker needs to understand small-group behaviors and processes.

Most social work practice takes place under the auspices of a formal organization, such as a social agency, school, hospital, or correctional facility. The social worker must understand how clients and other members of the community view these organizations and how people are affected by the behavior of organizations. To work effectively within an agency or program, a social worker must understand organizational development, structure, methods of operation, and communication patterns. Indeed, the social worker is required to possess substantial knowledge regarding the people and organizations with which he or she works.

The social worker must also understand cultural and religious differences and personal and social issues related to ethnic identity, cross-cultural interaction, and the impact of racism and discrimination. Since people are influenced by the neighborhoods and communities in which they live, the social worker must be familiar with, for example, theories of decision making, intergroup conflict, and community change, in addition to community beliefs and attitudes related to ethnicity, race relations, gender roles, aging, sexual orientation, and disabling conditions.

Knowledge of Social Conditions and Social Problems

Social workers must not only understand the problems commonly brought to the attention of social agencies but also must recognize how human problems (e.g., adolescent crime, school-age childrearing, school dropout, poverty, unemployment, drug abuse, and family violence) cluster together and overlap. The interrelatedness of human problems is an inescapable fact.

As background for dealing with social problems, the social worker should be familiar with factors that contribute to the overall quality of life on this planet. Some of these are clean air and water, a safe and sufficient supply of food and energy, opportunities for employment, worldwide political and economic conditions that support personal freedom and social justice, the use of technology to improve human welfare, success in controlling communicable illnesses and promoting wellness, and a world free of racial hatred and war. In short, the well-informed social worker possesses a world view.

Social work practice and related social programs and services are particularly influenced by conditions at the national or regional level. When practicing in the United States, for example, the social worker must understand the beliefs, values, and organization of U.S. society and its governmental, political, and economic systems.

Although some social conditions and problems are national and international in scope, others are a function of regional and state characteristics. For instance, regional drought conditions or low prices for farm products directly affect people in the agricultural states of the Midwest or Rocky Mountains differently than people in urban centers.

Finally, some social conditions affect local communities but not whole states or regional areas. The well-publicized crime rate in Washington, DC, and the high incidence of juvenile gang activity in Los Angeles have dramatically affected those cities, whereas towns a few miles away are relatively free of those problems. Rural areas may also experience locality-relevant social and economic problems caused by, for example, a decline in the timber harvested in Montana and Oregon or the closing of a small town's single industry in Alabama.

When social conditions are perceived as either harmful to people or a threat to the community or the society, social policies may be formulated and social programs created to help those in need. Essentially, a **social policy** is a set of principles, usually expressed in law and governmental regulations, that guide the assignment of specific benefits and opportunities or the regulation of behavior. We have policy clusters related to areas such as health care, mental illness, crime, child welfare, education, disabilities, old age, poverty, unemployment, and so forth. Social workers must be familiar with the policies that most strongly influence the programs through which they work and understand how these policies affect the clients served by those programs.

Social programs consist of three major elements: organizational structure, benefits or services, and providers. Social programs must be delivered through some form of organization or agency. No matter what service or benefit is provided, there must be an organizational and administrative structure that determines who is eligible, how it will be provided, who will provide it, and what costs are acceptable. Thus, social workers must be knowledgeable about the fiscal, administrative, and organizational aspects of service delivery.

The benefits and services provided by a social program can take the form of social provisions, social services, and/or social action. The social worker must understand the programs offered by his or her own agency and be familiar with those provided by the agencies to which clients might be referred.

Finally, social programs require providers, people who are in direct contact with the client, or the consumers of the services and benefits. Providers may be volunteers, but most often they are paid professionals. Social work is only one of the professions that deliver services and benefits. Teachers, psychologists, physicians, nurses, occupational therapists, and others provide a wide array of human services. Each has its own focus but there are areas of overlap. Understanding the competencies of each profession, as well as the dynamics of teamwork and interprofessional cooperation, is important to developing the social worker's knowledge base.

Knowledge of the Social Work Profession

The social worker must understand the functions that a profession performs in society and the benefits, as well as the responsibilities, that accrue from this status. When society grants professions the authority to provide the specific services that fall within their domain, in essence, a monopoly is given to that profession to determine the qualifications of its members (e.g., educational and experiential prerequisites for membership). In return, the profession is charged with monitoring and policing its members to protect the public against abuses of that monopoly.

Social workers have been ambivalent about professionalizing their discipline. They have devoted considerable effort to identifying their knowledge base, creating professional organizations, staking out their domain, specifying criteria for identifying qualified social workers, and taking other steps to become a valued profession. At the same time, they have been uncomfortable about the inherent elitism that characterizes any profession and have struggled with the conflict between assuring quality services to clients and keeping access to the profession open to as many people as possible.

The balance between maintaining openness and having clear standards for recognition as a professional social worker changes through time. At this time in history, the entry point is through completion of a baccalaureate or master's degree from a social work education program that is accredited by the Council on Social Work Education. To move to more advanced or more specialized levels of recognition, one must gain experience, and through demonstration of appropriate levels of knowledge and competence, he or she can receive one or more specialized certifications through the National Association of Social Workers. Additionally, all states have some form of licensing or certification for at least some social work practice activities.

Closely linked with professional recognition is the social worker's compliance with the profession's ethical principles. Workers must be both competent and ethical in their practice if the profession is to maintain the public trust. Thus, it is essential that the social worker possess a thorough understanding of the ethical principles that guide practice. Ethics are concerned with what is morally right or, in a profession, what is the correct course of professional action. Perhaps no single document is more important to the practice of a social worker than the *National Association of Social Workers Code of Ethics* (1999). When a social worker joins the NASW, he or she pledges to practice within the profession's ethical code. The NASW uses the Code as a standard for determining if charges of unethical practice have a basis. If accusations are made that an individual worker has violated the Code, the local NASW chapter and NASW's National Committee on Inquiry may review the complaint and possibly apply negative sanctions to that social worker.

Knowledge of Social Work Practice

In a profession such as social work, it is not possible to separate theory from practice or concept from action. In fact, practice is the process of using knowledge and applying theory in order to bring about specific change. A practice uninformed by theory tends to become repetitive and sterile, whereas theory uninformed by the realities of practice tends to be merely interesting and often irrelevant.

The many theories, models, and perspectives discussed in the social work literature can all be considered conceptual frameworks. A **conceptual framework** is composed of a coherent set of concepts, beliefs, values, propositions, assumptions, hypotheses, and principles. Such a framework can be thought of as an outline of ideas that help one to understand people, how people function, and how people change. These frameworks are important because they have utility. Consider the following:

- They provide a structure for analyzing complex and often highly emotional human problems and situations.
- They organize information, beliefs, and assumptions into a meaningful whole.
- They provide a rationale for action and decision making.
- They promote a systematic, orderly, and predictable approach to work with people.
- They facilitate communication among professionals.

Social workers use a variety of theories, models, and perspectives. Although these terms have somewhat different meanings, they are often lumped together and simply termed theory. However, it is helpful to make some distinctions when describing these conceptual frameworks (see Figure 3.1). Howe (1987, 166) explains that there are theories of social work and theories for social work. The **theories of social work** focus on the profession and explain its purpose, domain, and character within a society. They describe what the profession is all about and why it functions as it does. By contrast, the **theories for social work** focus on clients and helping activities. They explain human behavior, the social environment, how change occurs, and how change can be facilitated by the social worker in order to benefit clients.

In their work, social workers make use of orienting theories and practice frameworks. Mailick (1990) indicates that **orienting theories** describe and explain behavior and how and why certain problems develop. They provide important background knowledge and are

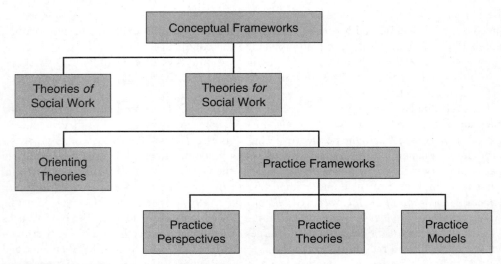

FIGURE 3.1 Types of Conceptual Frameworks

usually borrowed from other disciplines such as biology, psychology, sociology, economics, cultural anthropology, and the like. Examples include the various theories related to human development, personality, family systems, socialization, organizational functioning, and political power, as well as theories related to specific types of problems such as poverty, family violence, mental illness, teen pregnancy, crime, and racial discrimination. Orienting theories, by themselves, provide little guidance on how to bring about change. For such guidance one must look to **practice frameworks**. There are three types: practice perspectives, practice theories, and practice models.

A **practice perspective** is a particular way of viewing and thinking about practice. It is a conceptual lens through which one views social functioning and it offers very broad guidance on what may be important considerations in a practice situation. Like a camera lens, a perspective serves to focus on or magnify a particular feature. The ecosystems perspective is commonly used in assessing relationships between people and their environment. The generalist perspective focuses a worker's attention on the importance of performing multiple practice roles and the possibility of various levels of intervention. Others, such as the feminist and the ethnic-sensitive perspectives, remind the worker of special challenges faced by certain groups in society.

A second type of framework, a **practice theory**, offers both an explanation of certain behaviors or situations and guidance on how they can be changed. A practice theory serves as a road map for bringing about a certain type of change. Most practice theories are rooted in one or more orienting theories. An example is psychosocial therapy, which is based primarily on psychodynamic theory and ego psychology. Another is behavioral therapy, which derived from the psychology of learning.

A distinction is made here between a practice theory and a practice model. A **practice model** is a set of concepts and principles used to guide intervention activities. However, in contrast to a practice theory, a model is not tied to a particular explanation of behavior. For example, crisis intervention is viewed as a practice model rather than a practice theory because it does not rest on a single explanation of crisis situations. For the same reason, task-centered practice is termed a model. Most often, a model develops out of experience and experimentation rather than from a theory of human behavior.

The term **model** is also used when referring to a conceptual framework that is borrowed from one field and applied in another. For example, when someone refers to an approach to change based on the medical model, he or she is describing practice activity that mirrors that used in medicine—one that places emphasis on the practitioner as an expert and an authority figure, the careful gathering and categorization of data (study), the application of a classification system to properly label the problem (diagnosis), and an intervention (treatment) dictated by the diagnosis. Similarly, social workers may refer to the legal model as a way of describing an approach to social action and client advocacy—one that involves competition and conflict among adversaries. Other innovations in practice are spread from agency to agency by borrowing the essence of a successful program. Thus, we hear such terms as the self-help model, the grass-roots model, the 12-step model, the case-management model, and so on.

It is rare for a social worker to use a single orienting theory or a single practice framework. Rather, most social workers utilize a variety of orienting theories and a set of compatible and complementary perspectives, theories, and models. Such a combination can be termed one's **theoretical frame of reference** or theoretical orientation to practice.

This book presumes that social workers use many of the same techniques and guidelines, regardless of practice perspective, theory, or model. A **technique** is a set of actions directed at accomplishing a particular outcome. Although a worker's frame of reference might lead him or her to select particular techniques, they are, for the most part, independent of specific theories. **Guidelines**, however, are typically a mix of prescriptions (do this) and proscriptions (avoid this).

Conclusion

In order to perform effectively, the social worker uses a combination of art and science. It is recognized that a worker brings certain intangibles to the practice situation that affect both the process and the outcome—the art encompassed in building relationships, creative thinking, compassion and courage, hopefulness and energy, using sound judgment, and committing to appropriate values. At the same time, the social worker must combine his or her artistic abilities with the profession's knowledge and scientific base. Without art, the knowledge base is of little value. But without the knowledge, the art is of limited effectiveness.

The social worker merges his or her art and the profession's science into a practice framework. Chapter 6 provides descriptions of over two dozen selected practice perspectives, theories, and models that commonly are included in practice frameworks. The intent is not to provide a comprehensive description of any of these frameworks nor is it to provide a complete listing of all those available to the social worker. Rather, the chapter is intended to supply enough information to suggest how practice frameworks differ and what might be required for constructing one's own theoretical orientation to practice.

Selected Bibliography

American Heritage Dictionary of the English Language, 4th ed. Boston: Houghton Mifflin, 2000.

Howe, David. *An Introduction to Social Work Theory*. Hants, England: Wildwood House, 1987.

Hubble, Mark A., Barry L. Duncan, and Scott D. Miller. *The Heart and Soul of Change: What Works in Therapy*. Washington, DC: American Psychological Association, 1999.

Lambert, Michael J. "Implications of Outcome Research for Psychotherapy Integration." In *Handbook of Psychotherapy Integration*, edited by John C. Norcross and Marvin R. Goldstein. New York: Basic Books, 1992.

Mailick, Mildred. "Social Work Practice with Adolescents: Theoretical Saturation." In *Serious Play: Creativity and Innovation in Social Work*, edited by Harold Weissman. Silver Spring, MD: NASW, 1990.

National Association of Social Workers. *NASW Code of Ethics*. Washington, DC: NASW, 1999.

Siporin, Max. "The Social Worker's Style." *Clinical Social Work Journal* 21 (Fall 1993): 257–270.

The Building Blocks of Social Work Practice

Once the social worker is personally prepared to engage in practice, several other factors will shape the nature of that practice. An understanding of these four building blocks is prerequisite to the selection and application of the techniques and guidelines described in the remainder of this book.

First, the social worker will be expected to perform a variety of roles and functions in an agency, as well as with specific clients or groups of clients. One can readily discern that social work differs from other helping professions simply by examining these roles. Although other disciplines perform some of these roles and the associated functions, the collection of roles (e.g., broker, advocate, case manager, social change agent) reflects social work's breadth and its emphasis on helping people interact more effectively with their environments.

Second, over time a number of principles have evolved that should guide each social worker's approach to practice activities. These principles provide the "bottom line" for offering appropriate and effective service to clients. To many social workers, the phrases used to communicate these principles have become clichés: "Begin where the client is," "Help the client help himself (or herself)," "Guide the process, not the client." The casual use of these phrases too often masks the wisdom of these principles.

Third, in helping clients formulate plans for addressing the issue(s) for which they seek help from the social worker, the worker draws on various conceptual frameworks that provide an overall strategy for the change process. There are literally hundreds of these conceptual frameworks, which we term perspectives, theories, and models. Each social worker must select or assemble a set of conceptual frameworks that can address his or her clients' concerns that are compatible with agency context.

Finally, two key elements in successful practice are the social worker's critical thinking and ability to (1) guide clients through the phases of the change process and (2) assist clients in making decisions that will result in enhancement of their social functioning or the improvement of a social condition.

By examining these building blocks for social work practice as presented in Chapters 4 through 7, the foundation is established for the rest of the book.

The Roles and Functions Performed by Social Workers

Every person in an occupation (e.g., engineer, teacher, farmer) is expected to perform a set of activities. For example, a physician is expected to conduct tests to diagnose a patient's condition, prescribe treatment, and monitor the results. Similarly, when in the role of social worker, an individual is expected to carefully analyze the practice situation, apply the most effective intervention techniques, and assess the success or failure of the effort. Although there is individuality in how a person performs an occupational role, there are also professional boundaries and standards that determine what a social worker can and cannot do.

Associated with each role are several job functions that can best be described as the activities one performs within a specific role. This chapter describes 11 roles and nearly 40 associated functions expected of social workers. In the course of a day, most social workers engage in several practice roles. Someone in specialized practice will assume a more limited number of these roles and functions, whereas the generalist worker will engage in a broader array of activities.

IDENTIFYING PROFESSIONAL ROLES

The roles and job functions expected of the members of a given profession are defined by social norms and historical traditions, by the legal codes and administrative regulations that sanction the activity, and by agency policies and procedures. In any practice role, the performance of several distinct functions may be required. Similarly, a specific job function may be applied in the performance of more than one role. For example, a social worker might engage in an assessment of a client's situation in the role of a broker of human services, a counselor or clinician, and a case manager. In the following pages, however, each function is described only once.

The Social Worker as Broker

Social work's particular emphasis among the helping professions is to assist people in relating to their social environment. That places the social worker in the position of being the professional person most likely to facilitate linkage between client and community resources (i.e., to bring together a person needing a service and a provider of that service). To carry out the broker role, the social worker identifies clients' needs, assesses their motivation and capacity to use various resources, and helps them gain access to those resources.

As a broker of human services, the social worker must be knowledgeable about the various services and programs available, maintain an up-to-date assessment of each one's strengths and limitations, and understand the procedures for accessing those resources. These resources may include social provisions (e.g., money, food, clothing, and housing) and/or social services (e.g., counseling, therapy, group interaction experiences, and rehabilitative services).

FUNCTIONS

Client Situation Assessment.   The first step in brokering is to thoroughly understand and accurately assess the needs and abilities of the client or clients. An effective broker should be skilled at assessing such factors as the client's vulnerability, culture, verbal ability, emotional stability, intelligence, and commitment to change.

Resource Assessment.   The social worker must also assess the various resources available to meet client needs. For his or her own agency, as well as for other community agencies, the social worker must be familiar with what is offered, the quality of services offered, the eligibility requirements, and the costs of those services. Additionally, the social worker must know the best way for clients to gain access to those resources.

Referral.   The process of connecting clients to resources requires that the social worker make a judgment regarding the motivation and ability of the client to follow through and the likelihood that the resource will accept the client for service. Depending on these judgments, the social worker will be more or less active in the referral process. A proper referral also entails follow-up activity wherein the worker checks to assure the client–resource connection is working to meet the client's needs. If there has been a breakdown, further action may be warranted.

Service System Linkage.   Brokering requires that the social worker facilitate continuing interaction between various segments of the service delivery system. To strengthen the linkage among agencies, programs, and professionals, the social worker may engage in networking to strengthen communication channels, negotiate resource sharing, and/or participate in interagency planning, information exchange, and coordination activities.

Information Giving.   Brokering often requires the transmittal of information to clients, community groups, and legislators or other community decision makers. As a repository of knowledge about the service delivery system, the social worker helps others by sharing this knowledge. Also, the social worker may make the general public aware of gaps between client needs and available services.

The Social Worker as Advocate

Advocacy is fundamental to social work's mission and is clearly embodied in the *Code of Ethics* (National Association of Social Workers, 1999). For example, Section 3.07 of the Code calls for social workers to advocate "within and outside their agencies for adequate resources to meet clients' needs" and to assure that the resource allocation procedures are open and fair for all clients. Section 6.04 indicates that social workers engaged in macro-level practice are expected to "advocate for changes in policy and legislation to improve social conditions in order to meet human needs and promote social justice."

Advocacy is "the act of directly representing, defending, intervening, supporting, or recommending a course of action on behalf of one or more individuals, groups, or communities with the goal of securing or retaining social justice" (Mickelson, 1995, p. 95). Social workers must balance their methods of advocacy with the principles of maximizing client self-determination and client participation in the change process. To the extent possible, advocacy should take the form of assisting clients to be their own advocates.

Advocacy within one's own agency or with the community service system is a necessary function performed by social workers. What is needed, however, is not always popular. The social worker must choose his or her battles with great care and should be prepared for negative and even hostile responses to advocacy activities.

FUNCTIONS

Client or Case Advocacy.   A common goal in this type of advocacy is to assure that the services or resources to which an individual client is entitled are, in fact, received. Critical steps include gathering information and determining if the client is entitled to the desired service. If so, negotiation, mediation, and, if necessary, more strident and confrontational tactics are used to secure the service. The client is helped to make use of available appeal procedures and, in some instances, to initiate legal action against an agency or service provider.

Class Advocacy.   The social worker must often serve as an advocate for groups of clients or a segment of the population that have a common problem or concern. Typically, class advocacy entails action intended to remove obstacles or barriers that restrict a group of people from realizing their civil rights or receiving benefits or services due to them. It usually requires efforts aimed at changing agency regulations, social policies, or laws. Consequently, class advocacy requires activity within the political and legislative arena and building coalitions with organizations that are concerned about the same issue.

The Social Worker as Teacher

Much of social work practice involves teaching clients or client groups to deal with troublesome life situations or to anticipate and prevent a problem or crises. This is empowering to clients. The **teaching role**, as it plays out is social work, involves teaching them how to adapt to conditions that negatively affect them or providing understandable information, advice, and describing possible alternatives and their consequences to help clients make informed decisions about issues in their lives.

A fundamental purpose of social work practice is to help clients change dysfunctional behavior and learn effective patterns of social interaction. This may require teaching clients to adhere to the various rules or laws and norms of society, develop social skills, learn role functioning, or gain insights into their own behavior. The teaching may occur informally during one-on-one interviews or in more structured educational activities such as presentations and workshops.

The teaching role also has a macro-level application. Social workers should be prepared to engage in activities that educate the public about the availability and quality of needed human services and the adequacy of social policies and programs for meeting client needs.

FUNCTIONS

Teach Social and Daily Living Skills.   Teaching clients skills in conflict resolution, money management, use of public transportation, adjusting to new living arrangements, personal care and hygiene, and effective communication are examples of activities regularly engaged in by some social workers.

Facilitate Behavior Change.   The social worker may use instructional approaches such as role modeling, values clarification, and behavior modification in teaching clients more effective interpersonal behaviors. When dealing with larger social systems, the social worker may, for example, educate a board of directors about an emerging social issue or teach a client advocacy group how to redesign a change strategy that is failing.

Primary Prevention.   Throughout its history, the social work profession has been mostly concerned with addressing and modifying serious human problems and conditions. In recent years, social workers have given greater attention to primary prevention (i.e., preventing the development of problems). Many such prevention efforts place the social worker in the role of a teacher or even a public educator. Examples include such activities as providing premarital counseling, teaching parenting skills, offering information on family planning, and informing the public of ways to address a social problem or issue.

The Social Worker as Counselor/Clinician

Perhaps the most visible and frequently performed role in social work is that of counselor or clinician. The **counselor/clinician role** involves the application of evidence-based assessments and interventions to assist individuals, families, or small groups to address the social and emotional issues in their lives.

In order to perform this role, the social worker needs a knowledge of human behavior and an understanding of how the social environment impacts on people, an ability to assess client needs and functioning and to make judgments about what interventions can help clients deal with these stresses, skill in applying intervention techniques, and the ability to guide clients through the change process.

FUNCTIONS

Psychosocial Assessment and Diagnosis.   The client's situation must be thoroughly understood and his or her motivation, capacities, and opportunities for change assessed. This involves selecting conceptual frameworks to organize the information in ways that promote an understanding of both the client and the social environment. The labeling and categorizing inherent in diagnosis is necessary in some settings for purposes of interprofessional communication, research, program planning, and obtaining payment for services provided.

Ongoing Stabilizing Care.   The counselor/clinician role does not always involve efforts to change the client or social situation. Sometimes it consists of providing support or care on an extended basis. For example, counseling people who are severely disabled or terminally ill—or working with their families—may involve efforts to increase their choices and help them to more comfortably deal with difficult but unchangeable situations or conditions.

Social Treatment.   This function involves such activities as helping clients understand the relationships among relevant persons and social groups, supporting client efforts to modify social relationships, engaging clients in the problem-solving or interpersonal change efforts, and mediating differences or conflicts between individuals and/or between individuals and social institutions. Direct strategies might include face-to-face meetings with the client, whereas indirect strategies often involve helping the client negotiate the human services system by using such tools as advocacy and referral.

The Social Worker as Case Manager

The social worker's role as case manager is of critical importance for clients who must utilize services provided by several agencies. As a case manager, the job of the social worker typically begins with identifying the type of help needed and moves on to exploring ways to overcome barriers to successful living, advocating for clients as they attempt to connect with potential helpers, and, on occasion, providing some of the services directly to the client. Finally, the worker monitors the success of the services plan and helps solve problems that may emerge. Effective case management requires a social worker to be goal oriented, proactive, and assertive.

FUNCTIONS

Client Identification and Orientation.   This involves directly identifying and selecting those individuals for whom service outcomes, quality of life, or the cost of care and service could be positively affected by monitoring and guiding the change process.

Client Assessment.   This function involves gathering information and formulating an assessment of the client's needs, life situation, and resources. It may also involve reaching out to potential clients who have not requested services.

Service/Treatment Planning.   In concert with the clients and other relevant actors, the social worker identifies the various services that can be accessed to meet client needs. Bertsche and Horejsi (1980, p. 96) describe these tasks as the work necessary to "assemble and guide group discussions and decision-making sessions among relevant professionals and program representatives, the client and his or her family, and significant others to formulate goals and design an integrated intervention plan."

Linkage and Service Coordination.   As in the broker role, the case manager must connect clients with appropriate resources. The case manager role differs, however, in that the social worker remains an active participant in the delivery of services to the individual or family and places emphasis on coordinating the clients' use of resources by becoming a focal point for interagency communication.

Client Support.   During the time the services are being provided by the various resources, the case manager assists the client and his or her family as they confront the inevitable problems in obtaining the desired services. This activity includes resolving personality conflicts, counseling, providing information, giving emotional support, and, when appropriate, advocating on behalf of clients to assure that they receive the services to which they are entitled.

Follow-Up and Monitoring Service Delivery.   The case manager makes regular and frequent follow-up contacts with both the client and the service provider to ensure that the needed services are actually received and properly utilized by the client. If not, action is taken to correct the situation or modify the service plan. Typically, it is the case manager who completes the necessary paperwork to document client progress, service delivery, and adherence to the plan.

The Social Worker as Workload Manager

Social workers must simultaneously provide the services needed by clients and adhere to the requirements of the employing social agency. In other words, they must balance their obligations to both clients and agency. Although the emphasis on accountability to funding sources has increased in recent years, social workers have always needed to maximize the services provided within an environment of scarcity.

FUNCTIONS

Work Planning.   Social workers must be able to assess their workloads, set priorities according to importance and urgency, and make plans that will accomplish work in the most efficient and effective way possible. They must be effective in managing heavy workloads.

Time Management.   If the social worker is to give each client proper attention, priorities for the use of one's time must be set and the available time carefully allocated. Time management requires that the worker learn to use the agency's computer systems and other time-saving office equipment.

Quality Assurance Monitoring.   The social worker should regularly evaluate the effectiveness of his or her own service provision and also be involved in the assessment of services provided by colleagues. These activities might include reviewing agency records, conducting job performance evaluations, and holding performance review conferences with colleagues.

Information Processing.   Social workers must collect data to document need and justify service provision, complete reports, maintain case records, and substantiate various expenditures. Further, information about agency regulations and procedures must be understood by all, which requires that workers be skilled at preparing and interpreting memoranda, participating in staff meetings, and engaging in other activities that facilitate communication.

The Social Worker as Supervisor/Staff Developer

Social workers often serve in middle-management positions. In that capacity, they devote a part of their energies to maintaining and improving staff performance. That might involve working with secretaries, receptionists, and volunteers, but most often the supervisor role centers on maximizing the effectiveness of professional helpers.

Staff development requires many of the skills used in the teacher role. In this case, however, the knowledge is transmitted to peers rather than clients or the general public. Staff development is predicated on an accurate assessment of the training needs, with the training taking the form of individualized instruction such as job coaching, consultation, and/or conducting or participating in training sessions and workshops.

FUNCTIONS

Employee Orientation and Training.   Orientation to the agency and training for specific job assignments are necessary for all new employees and volunteers. The tasks required to perform this function include specifying job expectations, orienting workers to organizational policies and procedures, and teaching helping skills and techniques used in the agency.

Personnel Management.   Personnel management activities may range from the selection of new employees to the termination of someone's employment. These middle-management activities affect the professional growth of other social workers. For example, the selection of case assignments not only involves judgments about workers' capacities but also provides opportunities for workers to have new and challenging professional experiences.

Supervision.   This function involves overseeing and directing the activities of staff members to enhance the quality of services they provide and make sure that agency rules and regulations are followed. It includes such tasks as making and monitoring work assignments, developing performance standards, and negotiating staffing changes to better address the needs of clients.

Consultation.   As compared to supervision, which is a part of the agency's administrative hierarchy, consultation is given on a peer level—from one professional to another. The consultee is free to use or not use the advice offered by the consultant. Typically, consultation focuses on how best to handle a particularly challenging practice situation.

The Social Worker as Administrator

In an administrative role, the social worker assumes responsibility for implementing the agency's policies and managing its programs. When performing this role, the social worker might be an agency's chief administrative officer or executive director. Or he or she might be in a middle-management position, in which the administrative responsibility spans only the social workers in an agency or perhaps one program area (e.g., the child welfare division). The tasks one would be expected to perform might include leading program planning initiatives, implementing programs that have been adopted, and evaluating the effectiveness of the programs. At the same time, social worker administrators often continue to carry a small caseload or otherwise engage in the primary work of the agency in order to have firsthand knowledge of the day-to-day issues in operation of the agency.

In the role of administrator, the social worker is responsible for implementing policies, programs, and laws made by others. Agency boards or elected officials typically define agency purposes, establish administrative guidelines, and allocate the funds required to operate the agency. Normally, either the governing board of a volunteer agency or, in a public agency, an elected official or officials appoints the executive director to administer the organization. The social worker in an administrative position in the agency may perform all or some of the following functions.

FUNCTIONS

Management.   The management function calls for the administrator to maintain operational oversight of a program, service unit, and/or the entire organization. It includes such responsibilities as facilitating the work of the agency board, recruiting and selecting staff, directing and coordinating staff activities, developing and setting priorities, analyzing the organizational structure, promoting professional standards within the organization, adjudicating employee conflicts, and allocating the financial resources. In addition, management involves budgeting, documenting the use of resources, and arranging for the acquisition and maintenance of buildings and equipment.

Internal and External Coordination.   A primary task of the administrator is to coordinate the work of the agency. Internally, this involves developing plans for implementing the agency's programs in an efficient and effective manner, which may involve negotiating among several units or programs or working with staff to assure that new programs are integrated into the agency's functioning. The administrator also serves as the primary representative of the agency to external constituencies. These external tasks include serving as a buffer to protect staff from external pressures, negotiating disputes with consumers, and interpreting programs to the community in order to enhance viability. Thus, the administrator is a key figure in the agency's public relations and communication with consumers, other social agencies, and the general public.

Policy and Program Development.   The effective administrator is proactive. Although considerable time and energy must be devoted to maintaining established programs, an administrator should regularly assess the need for new or different services by conducting needs assessments, being knowledgeable about social trends, generating alternative policy goals for the governing body to consider, and translating new program or policy goals into services.

The Social Worker as Social Change Agent

Social work's dual focus on both the person and environment requires that the social worker facilitate needed change in neighborhoods, communities, or larger social systems. The role of social change agent in the social worker's repertoire of practice roles distinguishes social work from the many other helping professions.

When working directly with clients, social workers are in an excellent position to recognize conditions that contribute to people's distress and the need for human services. The social worker must take responsibility for assuring that resources are available to meet those needs and/or for stimulating action to create resources or change conditions that contribute to social problems. Social change does not occur rapidly or easily, and the authority to make the political decisions to achieve change is rarely held by social workers. Rather, change requires skill in stimulating action by influential groups and decision-making bodies that have the power to address the problems.

FUNCTIONS

Social Problem or Policy Analysis.   A first requirement for social change is to understand the nature of the problem. Trends must be analyzed, data collected and synthesized, and findings reported in ways that are understandable to decision makers. Without this background work, change efforts have little chance of success. The tasks involved in such analysis include identifying criteria for the analysis, ascertaining the impact of the policy on clients and social problems, and analyzing community values and beliefs that may affect the issue (see Item 11.21).

Mobilization of Community Concern.   Translating one's understanding of problems into social change efforts requires mobilizing and energizing concerned individuals, groups, and organizations. This might involve encouraging clients, human services organizations, and/or other citizen groups to address and speak out on the problem. Mobilization for action might involve assembling interested parties and presenting an analysis of the situation, helping expand their understanding of the issues and identify goals they could achieve, aiding in the selection of change strategies, identifying the decision makers who can effect the desired change, and planning and/or carrying out the activities necessary to induce change.

Social Resource Development.   The social change agent might also work toward the development of needed programs and services. Resource development involves creating new resources where they do not exist, extending or improving existing resources, planning and allocating available resources in order to avoid unnecessary duplication of human services, and increasing the effectiveness and efficiency of services offered by a unit, an agency, or a group of agencies. This may involve lobbying and providing expert testimony to legislative committees or more informal communication with decision makers.

The Social Worker as Researcher/Evaluator

If it is to remain a viable contributor to the society, it is not sufficient for a profession to simply continue doing what it has always done. In today's rapidly changing world, social workers must regularly evaluate the knowledge, values, and skills that guide their practice; make use of new knowledge that is developing in related disciplines; and position themselves in the forefront of strengthening knowledge that specifically supports social work practice. To do that, the social worker must perform the role of a researcher and evaluator.

FUNCTIONS

Research Consumption.   New knowledge is built on existing knowledge. Thus before a social worker can engage in knowledge-guided practice or add new information to the profession's knowledge base, he or she must be skilled at consuming the knowledge that is already available. Some of that knowledge is in the form of theories of human behavior or the functioning of the social environment drawn from social work and related disciplines, while increasingly social workers rely on knowledge that has been empirically tested through scientific research. Evidence-based practice calls for the social worker to maximize the use of tested knowledge. The social worker, then, must be competent to evaluate the merits of existing knowledge, both theoretical and empirical. This requires sufficient background knowledge to critically examine the many human behavior and practice theories, plus the general knowledge of sound research design and the appropriate application of qualitative and quantitative research data.

Practice Evaluation.   Social workers are increasingly expected to engage in evaluation of their work—their direct practice activities with their clients (i.e., individuals, families, or groups) and the programs they deliver—to determine the relative success or failure of their efforts. Direct practice evaluation requires measuring client change on a case-by-case basis. This requires skill in selecting and using individualized and standardized tools to empirically measure change, as well as the ability to select appropriate formats for organizing the data (e.g., goal attainment scaling, single-subject designs). Program evaluation, too, is often a function performed by the social worker. He or she must monitor and evaluate the agency's programs and collect data that will help document the adequacy of the services and/or suggest actions that might be taken to improve them.

Research Production.   It is not enough for social work to depend on related disciplines such as sociology and psychology to conduct the research that social workers might use, especially research related to the effectiveness of social work interventions. Thus, it is incumbent on the profession to produce social workers who can conduct research that advances the practice of social work. This research might range from a practitioner making a qualitative analysis of recordings from interviews with clients to a highly specialized social worker conducting a complex quantitative study funded by a major government agency requiring sophisticated data collection and analysis techniques.

The Social Worker as Professional

Basically, a professional is a person whose actions are thoughtful, purposeful, competent, responsible, and ethical. It is incumbent on the social worker to practice in a manner that reflects the highest professional standards. The social worker must constantly seek to develop his or her knowledge and skills, to examine and increase the quality of his or her practice, and to perform in a highly ethical manner.

As one who benefits from professional status, the social worker should actively engage in the enhancement and strengthening of the profession. Active participation in professional associations at the local, state, and national levels is an essential component of the professional role.

FUNCTIONS

Self-Assessment. The autonomy required for professional decision making carries with it the responsibility for ongoing self-assessment. Social workers in every type of human services organization (including private practice) and those performing every social work role are expected to devote substantial effort to self-assessment and engage in their own professional development based on that assessment.

Personal/Professional Development. The corollary to self-assessment is further developing one's abilities and addressing any performance problems that have been identified. Social workers are expected to regularly read articles in professional and scientific journals related to their job responsibilities; seek critique of their practice from colleagues; and periodically attend workshops, seminars, and other programs intended to improve their job knowledge and skills for practice.

Enhancement of the Social Work Profession. Social workers should contribute to the growth and development of the profession and the expansion of its knowledge base. Maintaining membership in the National Association of Social Workers, for example, and contributing time and energy to the efforts of NASW to strengthen the quality of professional practice and support legislative initiatives are obligations of each social worker. In addition, social workers should share the knowledge gained from their practice or research with their colleagues through presentations at conferences and make contributions to the professional literature.

Conclusion

The range of practice roles performed by the social worker is large and varied. The effective social worker must master at least the basic job functions associated with most of these roles. The specialist practitioner might develop more in-depth competence in fewer roles, but the generalist social worker, in particular, must continually seek to expand his or her competence in each.

Selected Bibliography

Bertsche, Anne Vandeberg, and Charles R. Horejsi. "Coordination of Client Services." *Social Work* 25 (March 1980): 94–98.

Mickelson, James. "Advocacy." In *Encyclopedia of Social Work*, Vol. 1, 19th ed., edited by Richard L. Edwards, 95–100. Washington, DC: NASW Press, 1995.

National Association of Social Workers. *NASW Code of Ethics*. Washington, DC: NASW, 1999.

Guiding Principles for Social Workers

Within each profession there exists a number of fundamental principles that guide practice decisions and actions. These principles apply in all practice situations regardless of client characteristics, practice setting, or roles assumed by the professional. In addition, they are independent of any specific theories, models, and techniques selected in a practice situation. **Principles** are basic rules or guides to one's practice behavior, but they are not to be applied without careful analysis.

Social work's practice principles are grounded in the profession's philosophy, values, ethical prescriptions, and practice wisdom. Most are not supported by empirical verification nor are they compiled in a single document. Social work's practice principles are largely unwritten and are passed on informally from seasoned workers to those who are entering the profession. They are often expressed as clichés such as "start where the client is" or "accept the client as he or she is." Many of the principles seem so obvious to the experienced worker that they often are not consciously taught in professional education programs or during supervision. However, they are central to effective social work practice and should be fully understood.

This chapter presents a synopsis of 24 fundamental principles that should guide social work practice. The first six focus on the social worker. The others are concerned with the social worker in interaction with a client or client group—whether it is an individual, family, small group, organization, neighborhood, community, or even larger social structure.

PRINCIPLES THAT FOCUS ON THE SOCIAL WORKER

The Social Worker Should Practice Social Work

This fundamental principle seems so obvious that it appears trite. We expect the teacher to teach, the physician to practice medicine, and the social worker to practice within the boundaries of the social work profession. Yet it is not uncommon to find professionals extending their activities into the domain of another profession. This principle admonishes the social worker to do what he or she is sanctioned and prepared to do.

Social work is sanctioned to focus on social functioning and help improve the interaction between people and their environment—that is the social work domain. The requisite educational preparation equips the social worker with the knowledge, values, and skills to work at the interface of person and environment, and that, more than anything else, is the unique contribution of social work among the helping professions.

Due to areas of overlap, the "turf" problems among the disciplines are difficult enough when each practices within professional boundaries. Such problems are magnified when a member of one discipline strays into another discipline's area of operation. Ethical practice requires that the social worker function within his or her professional expertise. Although individual social workers may have special talents that exceed the profession's domain, the social worker who drifts from the profession's area of focus deprives clients of a critically important perspective on human problems and associated change activities.

The Social Worker Should Engage in Conscious Use of Self

The social worker's primary practice tool is the self (i.e., his or her capacity to communicate and interact with others in ways that facilitate change). The skilled worker is purposeful in making use of his or her unique style of relating to others and building positive helping relationships with clients.

In professional relationships, workers reveal—verbally or nonverbally, directly or indirectly—their values, lifestyles, attitudes, biases, and prejudices. Workers must be consciously aware of how their own beliefs, perceptions, and behaviors may have an impact on their professional relationships, as these personal attributes will surely affect the ability to be helpful to clients. Part of the "art" that the social worker brings to the helping process (see Chapter 3) is his or her enthusiasm for helping people improve the quality of their lives. This personal commitment to serving others facilitates communicating energy and hope to the client.

The social worker must be comfortable with his or her unique personality and be at peace with whatever problems he or she has experienced in life. For most people, acquiring such self-knowledge and self-acceptance is a lifelong journey that requires a willingness to take risks, for taking a close look at who we are can be disquieting. (See Item 16.3 for more information on developing self-awareness.) But the worker must discover and build on his or her special strengths and minimize the impact of deficiencies, identify the types of clients and situations that respond positively to his or her practice style, and develop a pattern of regular, objective, and non-defensive examination of how one's professional self is functioning.

The Social Worker Should Maintain Professional Objectivity

By the time most clients come into contact with a professional helper, they have attempted to resolve their troublesome situation themselves—by either struggling alone or seeking assistance from family, friends, or other helpers. Often, these efforts are thwarted by high levels of emotion and the conflicting advice they receive. This may only add to the person's frustration and preclude clear understanding and response to the situation.

The professional adds a new dimension to the helping process by operating with a degree of personal distance and neutrality. Maintaining this neutrality without appearing unconcerned or uncaring is a delicate balancing act. The worker who becomes too involved and identifies himself or herself too much with the client's concerns can lose objectivity. At the other extreme, the worker who is emotionally detached fails to energize clients or, even worse, discourages clients from investing the energy necessary to achieve change. The social worker can best maintain this balance through a controlled emotional involvement.

Further, this professional objectivity is important to the social worker's own mental health. A degree of emotional detachment is needed, allowing the worker to set aside the troubles of clients and society and separate the professional and personal aspects of one's life. Professional objectivity is perhaps the best antidote to worker burnout.

The Social Worker Should Embrace Human Diversity

The practice of social work involves activity with and in behalf of people from virtually all walks of life, most racial and ethnic backgrounds, a variety of cultures and religions, a range of physical and intellectual abilities, both genders, as well as various sexual orientations and ages. This diversity is expressed in the beliefs, behaviors, and values of clients.

The worker must understand and respect such differences and recognize that what may appear to be unusual behavior from one perspective may be quite appropriate given a different set of values and life experiences. To the social worker, diversity brings richness to the quality of life and failure to accept and appreciate difference creates barriers to helping.

Respect for diversity requires sensitivity to the fact that various population groups have had differing experiences in U.S. society. In addition, individuals within a particular group or class may have had quite different experiences from other persons in that group. The social worker, then, must also appreciate the variations within any group and avoid making assumptions about any one person's cultural identity, beliefs, or values on the basis of that person's external characteristics or membership in a particular population or demographic group. Practitioners who respect diversity are careful to guard against making decisions based on overgeneralizations and stereotypes.

The Social Worker Should Challenge Social Injustices

Central to social work is the recognition that many human problems are caused by discrimination, oppression, or more subtle social factors that limit people's opportunities or create difficulties for them. The failure of employers to accommodate the needs of persons with disabilities and the tradition of higher pay for men over women doing comparable work are just two well-known examples of social injustices. If not addressed, these social injustices will continue to burden the individuals affected and the society as a whole. Eliminating these injustices will improve the quality of life for all and, for the most vulnerable members of society, will prevent many social problems from occurring in the first place.

Challenging social injustices is a long-term proposition. The social worker cannot expect social issues that developed over time to dramatically be resolved with only short-term effort. However, unless social workers and other concerned citizens effectively identify, document, analyze, strategize, and carry out social change efforts, social injustices will surely continue.

The Social Worker Should Seek to Enhance Professional Competence

Social work is a contemporary discipline. Its focus is on the here-and-now concerns of ever-changing people living in a dynamic environment. Helping people interact more effectively with their environments requires that the social worker be in tune with the world as it is experienced by others. One cannot be empathic and creative in working with a wide range of clients while holding a narrow and uninformed view of life. The social worker must continuously seek growth and development—both personally and professionally.

The person who becomes immersed in social work to the exclusion of other activities and experiences actually limits the ability to be helpful by restricting his or her knowledge and awareness of broader issues that affect human functioning. To appreciate the infinite variety of the human condition one must understand life from various orientations. Gathering ideas from history, science, the arts, and travel and interacting with a wide range of people are vital to the continuing development of the social worker.

However, the social worker must also be current with the latest professional information. The rapid change in the relevant knowledge requires constant updating of the social worker's knowledge base. New concepts, theories, and intervention techniques regularly appear in the literature and are presented at workshops and conferences. It is incumbent on the social worker to regularly participate in such activities in order to continue to grow as a competent social worker.

PRINCIPLES THAT GUIDE PRACTICE ACTIVITIES

In addition to the principles related to the social worker, a number of other principles are concerned with the social worker's intervention with individual clients and client groups.

The Social Worker Should Do No Harm

Social work practice is about the facilitation of desired change. However, there is always an element of risk in any effort to bring about change, no matter how well intended or desirable the goal. Because planned change is a very human process, the responsible professional must anticipate that mistakes will be made. The social worker must anticipate such possibilities and have plans for dealing with the things that can go wrong in an intervention. In the effort to enhance the social functioning of people, the social worker must strive to at least minimize any harm.

Professional actions and the programs social workers implement should in no way discourage or undermine responsible client behaviors nor erect barriers to appropriate social functioning. Furthermore, social workers engaged in efforts to change an unjust condition or unfair social policy must avoid creating other injustice to people affected by the change.

The Social Worker Should Engage in Evidence-Based Practice

At the very core of society's trust in professions is the expectation that the professional will bring to the change effort the latest knowledge and the most effective tools. Consciously using the best available evidence regarding the client condition and successful interventions in one's practice requires considerable discipline. With the pressure of heavy caseloads and busy schedules, there is a tendency to fall into a pattern of reacting to client situations without carefully considering what is known about people who experience similar conditions and what research has shown about the effectiveness of different intervention approaches related to this condition. Unless one's work is knowledge driven, it will fail to meet the expectation for professional practice.

A social worker cannot possibly stay abreast of all the knowledge that relates to the many dimensions of social work practice. However, the worker is obligated to be familiar with the most current evidence that directly relates to his or her practice activities and to be able to retrieve needed knowledge from the social work literature, from the vast resources on the web, from presentations at professional conferences, and from colleagues. After all, it is the clients who are most at risk if practice assessments and intervention decisions are based on faulty information. Each social worker should be prepared to engage in critical review of social work's theoretical knowledge and "best practices" research before adopting an approach to his or her practice activities.

The Social Worker Should Engage in Value-Guided and Ethical Practice

It is critical that the social worker make a conscious effort to identify and address relevant value and ethical issues in social work practice. Value choices and value conflicts are at the center of many practice situations. The social worker must recognize that one's values are powerful forces in human behavior and that helping clients clarify and understand value issues in their lives can be a critical step in bringing about change. However, in many cases, if clients are to change themselves or their situations, they must take some action to adjust or adapt their values to be more congruent with those of others in their lives—or learn to help others adjust or adapt their values to be more congruent with those of the client. When working directly with clients, then, the social worker must be sensitive to the value issues that inevitably arise.

Organizations and communities also operate from values about who should be served, who should pay for the services, and how the services should be delivered. When engaged in practice activities that relate to the agencies that employ them, the social conditions that exist in the community, or the social programs that are created at the city, state, or federal level, the social worker should attempt to understand the values that have influenced that situation. Societal problems are often a result of value differences, and an important step in finding solutions to those problems is to address the value issues.

Social workers must also be sensitive to their own values and beliefs and be prepared to suspend or set aside their own preferences and perspectives to avoid inappropriately imposing their beliefs on their clients. Social work practice, however, is not value free. At times, the social worker must take actions to protect the health and safety of others or achieve a broader social benefit than the interests of a single client. Making those practice decisions ethically requires careful consideration. The National Association of Social Workers (1996) *Code of Ethics* provides a useful guide for making ethical choices in one's practice.

The Social Worker Should Be Concerned with the Whole Person

Most professions focus on a single dimension of the person. Physicians are primarily interested in physical well-being, teachers focus on intellectual development, and psychologists are concerned with emotional and cognitive processes. Social work, however, is unique among the professions because of its concern for the whole person—biological, psychological, social, and spiritual. For the social worker, practice activities rarely relate to a single dimension of human life and living.

Concern for the whole person requires attention to the client's past, present, and future. It requires the social worker to look beyond the client's immediate or presenting problem and be alert to the possible existence of other issues, ranging from a lack of food and shelter to a lack of meaning and purpose in life. The social worker must focus attention on both the client's problems and strengths. He or she must attend to the client's presenting problem or concern and to possible underlying causative factors (i.e., the symptoms as well as their causes). In keeping with the person-in-environment construct, the social worker must be concerned with the well-being of the client and also the many other people who may be affected by the client's behavior and by the worker's intervention. Finally, the social worker must be concerned with both the short-term and long-term implications of the change process for both the client and others.

The Social Worker Should Serve the Most Vulnerable Members of Society

From its inception, the profession of social work has concerned itself with those people most likely to experience difficulties in social functioning. This includes persons who are poor, mentally or physically disabled, from a minority race or culture, and who otherwise may be devalued and face discrimination, ostracism, and neglect by the dominant society. Needless to say, not every person who is part of a vulnerable population actually experiences problems and requires the assistance of a social worker. But as a group, these individuals are at risk and frequently encountered by workers when delivering various social programs.

Not infrequently, ill-conceived social policies and laws treat devalued groups unfairly and place them at a social and economic disadvantage. Social workers have often been champions of efforts to remedy these conditions, even though advocacy for (and with) these groups may be politically unpopular. Such advocacy, if successful, forces members of the dominant society to face the existence of social and economic injustice and the need for change in the social order. In fact, those who have power and privilege often benefit from the status quo and resist change. They may therefore dislike what social workers are trying to do and seek to discredit the profession. To be a social worker, one must be willing to accept the criticism that follows from service to devalued groups and engage in the advocacy needed to accomplish social change.

The Social Worker Should Treat the Client with Dignity

Philosophically, the social worker must accept the proposition that each person or group deserves to be treated with dignity, respect, and understanding. The phrase "Accept the client as he or she is" reminds and encourages the social worker to approach clients as people with dignity who deserve respect, regardless of behavior, appearances, and circumstances. Acceptance occurs when the worker views the client as he or she is, with all of the endearing and maddening characteristics that every human possesses. That means recognizing that clients sometimes make wise decisions and at other times make irrational choices that harm themselves and others. Nevertheless, the social worker is obligated to treat each client as a person who is valued and deserves to maintain his or her dignity throughout the helping experience.

Communicating acceptance and respect requires that the social worker avoid making moral judgments concerning clients. The worker's nonjudgmental attitude helps clients overcome the common fear of being criticized and frees up the helping relationship for positive, rather than defensive, action. The need to treat each and every client with respect and acceptance does not imply approval of all behavior by a client. One can accept and treat the client with dignity without approving of, for example, illegal, harmful, or socially destructive behavior. The key to adhering to this principle is to remember that the purpose of social work is to help people make changes, and it has been amply demonstrated that acceptance of and respect for the person are prerequisite for change, while condemnation and judgmentalism erect barriers to such change.

The Social Worker Should Individualize the Client

To individualize the client is to be cognizant of and sensitive to the uniqueness of the client and the uniqueness of his or her situation, concerns, history, and possibilities. The social worker must adapt his or her approach to this uniqueness and to the client's capacities, limitations, and readiness to participate in a particular intervention or change effort. What works well with one client may not work at all with another.

Closely related to the principle of individualization is the precept "Start where the client is." In other words, the social worker must strive to identify and tune in to the client's current thoughts, feelings, and perceptions. The worker should always begin the professional relationship, an intervention, and each contact with the client by focusing first on the concerns, issues, and circumstances that are most relevant to and most pressing for the client. The client's highest priority or greatest concern may, of course, change from day to day or week to week. A skillful social worker will be alert to such shifts and adapt his or her approach accordingly.

The Social Worker Should Consider Clients Experts on Their Own Lives

Who knows more about a client than the client himself or herself? Too often, social workers and other helping professionals become enamored with their theoretical knowledge of human functioning and forget to consult with their clients to learn the actual circumstances of their lives. There are many things social workers will never know about their clients—and, in fact, many things that are not the business of the workers to know. Where possible, clients should be viewed as the primary experts on their lives. Weick, Rapp, Sullivan, and Kisthardt (1989, p. 353) observe that social workers should recognize that clients have "an inner wisdom about what they need and that ultimately, people make choices based on their own best sense of what will meet that need [and that] it is impossible for even the best trained professional to judge how another person should best live his or her life."

What, then, is the social worker's role in assessing a client's situation? The expertise a social worker brings is to help the client recall factors that have affected his or her life, to provide alternative interpretations of the meanings of those factors, to provide possible explanations by connecting multiple factors, to link this information to knowledge that aids in understanding, and to help the client decide how to act on the basis of this knowledge. The client will be empowered to realize that the worker recognizes him or her as the expert on his or her own life.

The Social Worker Should Lend Vision to the Client

A central feature of professional helping is to bring vision: new ideas, new perspectives, and more effective change strategies to a problem situation. If an individual or group is to invest in the difficult process of changing, they must be convinced that the outcome will be worth the effort. The social worker must introduce and nurture a sense of hopefulness that change is indeed possible and that there are new and better ways for the client to deal with the situation. The client will become more hopeful and more open to change if the worker displays a genuine belief and faith in the client's potential for change, in his or her power to overcome obstacles, and in the capacity to build working alliances with others who can become resources to the client.

While offering new perspectives, encouragement and support, and techniques for change, the social worker must also be realistic and honest about limits and possibilities. Clients are not helped by raising false hopes or by projecting unrealistic outcomes for the helping process. A tempered infusion of energy and vision allows the client or client group to make real progress toward achievable outcomes.

The Social Worker Should Build on Client Strengths

All too often, social workers and other human services professionals become preoccupied with client problems and invest considerable effort in identifying the specific limitations or deficiencies of a client or client group. Such an essentially negative way of thinking about clients and their situations is reinforced by the diagnostic labels now required for statistical purposes within many human service agencies or by insurance companies that pay for social work services.

For the social worker, it is the clients' abilities and potentials that are most important in helping to bring about change. Since a change in social functioning is largely under the control of the client, it is important to help clients recognize and utilize their strengths. The emphasis on building on clients' strengths helps change the tone of the helping relationship from one of gloom over problems to one of optimism.

The Social Worker Should Maximize Client Participation

"Help your clients to help themselves" is a principle based on the belief that if meaningful and lasting change is to occur for an individual, group, community, or other client system, the people who will need to change must be active participants in the change process. It is the responsibility of the social worker in guiding the process to be sure that, as far as possible, all relevant persons participate in identifying the problem, formulating a plan of action, and implementing that plan.

In order to maximize client participation, the social worker should "Do *with* the client and not *to* or *for* the client." For example, it does little good for the social worker to construct a sophisticated diagnosis of a client's situation if that client does not understand or accept those conclusions. Meaningful change will occur only when those who must change clearly understand the need for change and are willing and able to take action.

Similarly, an intervention plan is most likely to be followed when it is developed with active client participation. As compared to an attorney, who single-handedly presents a case for the client, or a physician, who injects the patient with a chemical that can cure an illness with minimal patient involvement, a social worker must view himself or herself as primarily a collaborator, facilitator, and catalyst. Although situations do arise in which a social worker must act in behalf of clients, the social worker should always seek to maximize client involvement.

The Social Worker Should Maximize Client Self-Determination

The instruction to "Guide the process—not the client" captures another important principle. This principle maintains that those who must ultimately live with the outcomes of decisions should have the freedom to make those decisions. The job of the social worker is to help clients explore alternatives and the implications of various options but not to prescribe their final choices.

The principle of self-determination must be qualified in its application. It assumes that the client is capable and legally competent to make decisions in relation to self and others. Sometimes that is not a valid assumption. Some clients may not understand the consequences of an action or may lack the mental capacity to make sound judgments and might therefore make choices that are clearly harmful to themselves or others. At times, the social worker must take on a decision-making role for these clients (e.g., children, the person who is mentally ill). This may involve persuading them to take a particular action, using the authority or power that the social worker's position might command, securing a court order declaring mental incompetence, or, in the most extreme situations, calling for police assistance in order to prevent a tragedy.

The social worker should reluctantly assume the responsibility for making decisions on behalf of clients, but then only after careful review of the situation, after consultation with others, and always with the intent of returning that responsibility to the client as soon as possible. In the final analysis, the social worker should attempt to maximize the client's ability to determine his or her own destiny.

The Social Worker Should Help the Client Learn Self-Directed Problem-Solving Skills

Most social workers are familiar with the idea of helping people help themselves. Perhaps this should be extended to "helping people help themselves now and also in the future." Too often, the changes in social functioning made by a client with the assistance of a professional helper come unraveled unless the client is prepared to sustain that change over time. Ideally, a social work intervention helps prepare clients to cope successfully with future difficulties and to engage in self-directed problem solving when faced with another problem.

Hopefully, what the client learns during his or her interaction with the social worker can be applied to other concerns that emerge in day-to-day living. The admonition "Don't do for clients what they can do for themselves" relates to this principle of helping clients learn the skills needed to be independent and self-reliant.

An important aspect of preparing clients for the future is to teach them how to identify and make use of resources that might be found in their immediate environment. Such resources may include family members, friends, self-help groups, service clubs, and church, mosque, or synagogue groups.

The Social Worker Should Maximize Client Empowerment

Because social workers are committed to serving society's most vulnerable citizens, they regularly work with people who have been victims of various forms of discrimination and oppression. One especially helpful contribution social workers can make to their clients' social functioning is to help them gain increased power over their lives. While some of the principles described here have the effect of giving clients more control over some dimensions of their lives (e.g., maximizing participation, maximizing self-determination, or helping to develop problem-solving skills), a principle that should guide all of a social worker's practice activity is the goal of empowerment.

Helping people, both individually and collectively, secure the power needed to gain control over how they live their lives has been part of social work's philosophy from its founding. The term *empowerment* reflects efforts to help people gain control over their life circumstances, to obtain needed information and resources, and to develop skills needed to make the decisions and take the actions necessary to attain a higher level of self-reliance and modify one's social and political environment. In order to empower others, social workers place a special emphasis on the activities of encouraging, teaching, and facilitation, as well as collaboration and shared decision making within the professional relationship.

The Social Worker Should Protect Client Confidentiality

Individuals and families seeking help from a social worker often reveal very private aspects of their lives. In groups, clients may discuss secrets and self-perceptions that could be embarrassing or damaging if made public. The community worker, too, encounters instances when information about individuals, agencies, and organizations must be protected. All social workers must therefore be capable of handling private and sensitive information in a confidential manner.

There are two basic forms of confidentiality: absolute and relative. *Absolute confidentiality* refers to a situation when information imparted by the client can never go beyond the social worker. That degree of confidentiality is rare in social work practice. It is only under the protection of some professional licensing statutes that a client can claim a legal right to privileged communication. Most social work practice involves *relative confidentiality*, meaning that the most the social worker can promise is to treat information responsibly, as prescribed in the profession's code of ethics; adhere to existing laws; and to follow agency policy concerning the handling of client information.

The degree of confidentiality that can be provided will depend on the type of information communicated, the nature of the agency where the practice occurs, the state and federal laws and regulations that govern its operation, and the existence of other legal requirements such as the mandated reporting of child abuse. In correctional programs (e.g., prison, parole, probation), the client can expect little confidentiality. On the other hand, a client who receives social services within a hospital setting will have a much higher level of protection. But even here, a client's records might be reviewed by nonhospital personnel such as insurance companies, Medicaid or Medicare authorities, worker's compensation officials, hospital accreditation teams, and others who have the authority to review patient records for purposes of quality control. The clients should be advised early in the helping process of the limits of confidentiality the social worker can guarantee.

The social worker must be prudent regarding what information is placed in agency files, and care must be taken in preparing clerical staff to respect the confidential nature of any materials they may type, file, or inadvertently overhear. To protect confidential information, social workers must carefully plan the location of interviews and cautiously select the information to be discussed during professional consultations and in case conferences. Further, clearly separating one's personal life and work life is important in protecting against breaches of confidentiality that might occur when discussing work experiences with family and friends.

The Social Worker Should Adhere to the Philosophy of Normalization

Many social work clients have evident mental and physical disabilities and often experience discrimination and social isolation. The philosophy of normalization is a powerful force in efforts to integrate persons who appear "different" into the life of the community and ensure that their lives resemble that of the so-called normal person as much as possible.

Normalization connotes helping people, especially those experiencing disabling conditions, to live their lives within an environment and in a manner considered typical and culturally normative for persons without disabilities. This approach has the effect of minimizing social stigma and increasing social acceptance of persons who are in some way different from most others. For example, a person with mental retardation should, to the greatest extent possible, live in a typical or ordinary home, attend a conventional school, and perform work that is useful and valued. His or her recreation, religious participation, clothing, transportation, and daily routines should be as conventional and mainstream as possible.

The Social Worker Should Continuously Evaluate the Progress of the Change Process

The practice of social work is far from an exact science. It involves working with ever-changing people and ever-changing situations. The objectives of helping activities, therefore, must be clearly delineated and regularly reviewed to be certain that they remain relevant to the client's needs. It is not enough to set the course of an intervention strategy and assume that the desired outcome will be achieved. Rather, a continuous monitoring and evaluation of the change process is necessary. To achieve this, both the worker and the client or client group must regularly collect and record data that are indicators of change and these data must be reviewed and carefully analyzed. If the desired change is not occurring, the worker is obligated to try another approach or redesign the intervention plan.

The Social Worker Should Be Accountable to Clients, Agency, Community, and the Social Work Profession

One factor that complicates practice is that the social worker must answer to a number of parties. Practitioners in some disciplines might feel that they are accountable only to the client, but the social worker—working at the interface of person and environment—faces multiple sources of accountability.

Social workers are obligated to give their best service to all clients at all times and therefore must be accountable to those individuals, families, and groups they directly serve. In addition, since most social workers are employed by a social agency or as part of a private practice group, they must be accountable to their employing organizations by carrying out their work as effectively and efficiently as possible. Furthermore, the existence of a professional monopoly demands that the members of a profession also be accountable to the community.

The social work profession, as reflected in the National Association of Social Workers (1999) *Code of Ethics*, expects accountability to clients, colleagues, employers, the profession, and society. At times, practice situations place the individual worker in a position that makes it impossible for him or her to be fully and equally accountable to all audiences. In those situations, the social worker should attempt to maximize the accountability to each—but accountability to one's clients should be given priority.

Conclusion

The new social worker is often inundated with information that reveals, in bits and pieces, the knowledge and values that guide social work practice. Some of this information is formally taught in professional education programs, whereas other information, such as the principles described in this chapter, is typically transmitted in a more subtle and informal manner.

Practice principles reflect that combination of values and knowledge that should underlay all practice activities.

If all else fails, the worker cannot go too far wrong if he or she is operating within these principles. They might be viewed as a fail-safe mechanism in social work practice. With these principles firmly in mind, the social worker is prepared to engage the client in a change process and to identify and select appropriate techniques for addressing the client's problems, needs, or concerns.

Selected Bibliography

National Association of Social Workers. *Code of Ethics*. Washington, DC: NASW, 1999.

Weick, Ann, Charles Rapp, W. Patrick Sullivan, and Walter Kisthardt. "A Strengths Perspective for Social Work Practice." *Social Work* 35 (July 1989): 350–354.

Practice Frameworks for Social Work

It has been said that there is nothing so practical as a good theory. Some social workers may question that notion when faced with the rather daunting task of trying to understand and sort through the multitude of theoretical orientations described in social work textbooks and journals and at conferences and workshops.

At the end of Chapter 3, under the heading Knowledge of Social Work Practice, the topic of practice frameworks was introduced and three types of frameworks—perspective, theory, and model—were briefly described. The reader may want to review those pages before proceeding. Basically, a **practice framework** consists of a coherent set of beliefs and assumptions about how and when human behavior and social systems can be changed. Some focus mostly on individual change, whereas others focus on changing the functioning of families, small groups, organizations, or communities. This chapter suggests criteria for selection of a practice framework, provides brief descriptions of ones commonly used in social work, and offers information on when a particular framework is most appropriately applied. Also, suggested readings about each framework are provided. Additional references are offered in the Selected Bibliography at the end of this chapter.

REQUIREMENTS OF A PRACTICE FRAMEWORK

A framework used in social work practice should meet the following criteria:

- It is consistent with the purpose, values, and ethics of the profession.
- Its key concepts, principles, and terminology are clearly described and defined.
- It provides guidance and direction to the change process.
- It rests on an empirical foundation (i.e., based on facts and observations).
- It helps the worker analyze and understand complex situations.

Because social workers practice in a wide variety of settings and encounter clients with many different types of problems and concerns, it is not possible to identify a single framework that is superior to all others. However, a practice framework is most likely to yield the desired outcomes for the client if it encourages the social worker to do the following:

- Build a collaborative worker–client relationship based on trust and the worker's respect, empathy, caring, and compassion for the client.
- Assess and address the client's concern within an environmental context (e.g., view children's problems within context of family and family problems within a community context).
- Allow and encourage the client to make decisions related to the intervention's goals and the methods to be used to reach those goals.

- Recognize and build on client strengths and avoid focusing exclusively on limitations, deviance, and psychopathology.
- Be proactive and reach out to the client with offers of services that he or she considers relevant.
- Offer services and use approaches that are congruent with the client's values, culture, and religion.
- Offer services for which the costs to the client in time and money are reasonable, given the probable benefits or outcome.
- Achieve some immediate success, even if a small one, so as to demonstrate the usefulness of intervention and maintain client's motivation.
- Encourage the client to utilize mutual support and self-help groups.
- Facilitate the client's acquisition of knowledge and skills that will decrease his or her need for professional assistance and formal resources in the future.

GUIDELINES FOR SELECTING A PRACTICE FRAMEWORK

The choice of a particular practice framework can either enlarge or constrict the social worker's vision and options. Students and new workers especially must guard against becoming overly committed to a single practice framework. During their formal education, social workers may become immersed in or captivated by a particular modality and remain overly invested in or overly confident in that approach throughout their careers. Such a "Have theory—will travel" mentality can constrict one's professional growth and ultimately it is a disservice to one's clients.

Social workers must also avoid falling into the habit of using practice frameworks in an uncritical manner. The concepts, beliefs, and assumptions from which frameworks are constructed must be continually reexamined and tested against changing times and new research findings.

When selecting a framework, one must grapple with the question: With what types of clients, with what kinds of problems, in what practice settings, and under what circumstances will a particular practice framework provide relevant and useful guidance? The utility of a given framework depends on the nature of the problems or issues receiving the worker's attention, the characteristics of the clients or consumers, the phase in the helping process, and the setting or organizational context of practice. For example, a framework that is helpful in guiding work with voluntary clients may be of limited value in work with mandated, court-ordered clients. A framework that is useful with teenagers may not be useful with older adults, and one that is useful with persons of one ethnic group may prove ineffective when used with a different cultural background.

Social workers must beware of adopting frameworks that are either so narrow or so abstract that they no longer describe life's complex realities as experienced by the clients. An additional caution is important: Within the human services, the term *theory* is loosely used. For example, some people apply the term to ideas that have no empirical basis or are so vague that they cannot be tested. For others, the ideas called a "theory" are little more than a description of someone's personal style.

In working with a specific client or client group, social workers may use several practice frameworks together or sequentially. They may shift from one to another as they move through the phases of the helping process (see Chapter 7). For example, the ecosystems perspective is most helpful in the beginning phases (e.g., problem definition and assessment), but less so during the later phases of planning, implementing, or evaluating an intervention. On the other hand, a framework such as behavior modification provides detailed guidance on implementing behavior change, but its application presupposes that changing a specific behavior will be the focus of the intervention. Questions that a social worker might consider when selecting a practice framework include the following:

1. What client system does the framework address? Does the framework focus on the individual? Couple? Family unit? Peer group? Organization? Community?
2. What type of client change is expected? For example: Changes in attitude? In behavior? Acquisition of new knowledge or skill? Access to a needed resource?

3. Does the framework explain or describe how and why change occurs?

4. When applying the framework, what is the role of the social worker? For example: Advisor? Teacher? Counselor? Broker of services? Case manager? Administrator? Planner? Researcher? Advocate?

5. What are the implicit or explicit assumptions concerning the preferred or expected relationship between the professional and the client? Consider these possibilities: The professional is the expert who knows what the client needs and what should be done, whereas the client is to follow the professional's directions. The professional is to control and distribute services, whereas the client is to utilize the services provided in a cooperative and appreciative manner. The professional presumes that clients will often know what type of intervention or service will prove beneficial and will, therefore, solicit suggestions from the client.

6. What is the primary medium of communication? Does the framework rely on verbal exchanges? Expression through art or games? Writing? Reading? Precise and deliberate communication or spontaneous exchanges?

7. Does the framework specify when its use is appropriate as well as when its use would be inappropriate or possibly harmful?

8. Does the framework recognize the importance of the client's cultural or ethnic background and religious values and beliefs? Can it be adapted to clients of various backgrounds?

9. Does the framework presume a particular setting, such as an office? Agency-based practice? Private practice? In the client's home?

10. Is the framework applicable when the client is uncooperative, involuntary, or court ordered?

11. Does the framework describe how it is similar to and different from other commonly used frameworks?

12. Does the framework utilize a special set of helping techniques or skills or are they ones that are used also with other frameworks?

13. Does the framework exclude certain clients or situations, either explicitly or implicitly? For example: An individual unable to pay a fee? An individual who cannot meet in the professional's office during regular office hours? An individual with a significant physical or mental disability? An individual whose primary concerns are a lack of food, shelter, health care, protection from harm, and so on? An individual who cannot read?

14. Does the framework emphasize keeping the client within his or her family and usual social network? Or does it emphasize removing the client from the influence of family, friends, or peer group?

The social worker's choice of a practice framework is never a completely objective process. A worker brings subjective factors to the selection process, such as the feeling or intuition that a particular approach fits best with his or her personality and practice style or that it simply works better than other approaches. However, subjective factors alone are not sufficient. By passing the various practice approaches through a screen of questions, such as those just described, a greater degree of rationality can be applied to the worker's selection of a practice framework.

SELECTED PRACTICE FRAMEWORKS

Typically, a social worker draws upon several practice frameworks that offer guidance and direction in work with the types of clients served. This repertoire of perspectives, theories, and models can be termed a **practice frame of reference**. When first developing one's frame of reference, the worker may adopt and utilize only a limited number of frameworks. Gradually, the number can be expanded to fit the needs of one's agency and clients and one's interests and abilities.

To aid in the selection process, a sampling of commonly used frameworks is described next. Each of these brief descriptions highlights a few key concepts and assumptions that set the framework apart from others. The descriptions also reveal how practitioners might view client concerns differently and how and why workers might differ in their beliefs about the change process. These descriptions begin with five perspectives: generalist, ecosystems, strengths, ethnic-sensitive, and feminist. A sampling of practice theories and models is also provided, beginning with those that are more individually oriented and progressively moving to families, small groups, organizations, and concluding with the identification of a few frameworks used in work with communities. The reader is reminded that most social workers will draw ideas and techniques from several frameworks and are therefore somewhat *eclectic.*

Selected Practice Perspectives

As identified in Chapter 3, a practice perspective is like a lens that directs the worker to focus most attention on certain especially relevant factors and considerations when approaching a practice situation. One or more of the following (or other) perspectives might be part of the worker's frame of reference.

GENERALIST PERSPECTIVE   The generalist perspective directs the social worker to approach every client and every situation with openness to using various models, theories, and techniques and a willingness to consider more than one level of intervention, from micro to macro. Such an orientation is especially relevant during the beginning phases of the helping process when the client's problem or concern is being identified and clarified and when decisions are being made concerning what approaches might be effective.

Social work practice has been described as inherently generalist. The word *generalist* refers to a person with broad general knowledge and possessing skills in several disciplines, fields, or areas. Thus, the terms **generalist practice** and *generalist social work* refer to a practitioner who has a broad range of knowledge and skills, who draws on several perspectives, theories, and models, and who can move with minimal difficulty from one field of practice to another. The opposite of generalist practice is one characterized by specialization, either by type of problem addressed, method used, or level of intervention.

The generalist social worker is prepared to engage and work with a variety of client systems—for example, an individual; a whole family; a group formed for a purpose such as therapy or social support; a committee or task group; a formal organization, such as an agency or a network of agencies; and legislators and policymakers. In addition, the generalist is prepared to assume a variety of social work roles—for example, advocate, case manager, counselor or therapist, group facilitator, broker of service, fund-raiser, program planner, policy analyst, and researcher. The generalist expects to mold and fit his or her approach to the client's unique situation and to characteristics of the local community, rather than expecting the client to conform to the professional's or agency's preferred way of dealing with clients. Four elements most clearly characterize the generalist perspective:

1. *A multidimensional orientation that emphasizes the interrelatedness of human problems, life situations, and social conditions.* At the heart of this perspective is an appreciation for the interplay and interdependency of people and the various social systems that constitute the environment or context in which they live. The level of an intervention (e.g., micro, mezzo, macro), the practice framework, and specific techniques and procedures are not to be selected until after a careful consideration of the various and multiple ways that a client's concern and situation might be defined, conceptualized, and approached.
2. *An approach to assessment and intervention that draws ideas from many different practice frameworks and considers all possible actions that might be relevant and helpful to the client.* The generalist perspective requires that the social worker be eclectic (i.e., draw ideas and techniques from many sources) and versatile enough to at least initiate practice activities in a variety of situations. That is not to say that the generalist is expected to be an expert in the application of all theories and models. Rather, the generalist is knowledgeable enough to know when he or she can responsibly serve the client and when to refer elsewhere for more specialized interventions.

3. *Selection of intervention strategies and worker roles are made primarily on the basis of the client's problem, goals, situation, and the size of the systems that are targeted for change.* The generalist perspective calls for the social worker to adapt his or her practice activities to the client situation. Sometimes that may require working directly with the client, with key persons in the client's immediate environment, and at other times working to change agency and community factors that affect the clients or the services.

4. *A knowledge, value, and skill base that is transferable between and among diverse contexts, locations, and problems.* The more specialized frameworks may, implicitly or explicitly, prescribe or limit the settings where a worker is prepared to practice or the type of client, problem, or concern the worker is prepared to address. However, the generalist perspective can be applied in any human services organization or geographic context and used with a wide variety of clients and concerns. That transferability has job mobility value to the worker, but is a trade-off for the more in-depth knowledge and skills that are required in specialized settings.

The flexibility offered by the generalist perspective is particularly useful when the social worker's job description demands the performance of multiple roles (see Chapter 4). However, it must be recognized that some agencies have missions, job descriptions, and policies that limit the scope of a worker's activities or point them in certain directions (e.g., emphasis on individual change, group services, community development). In such settings the perspective would have less relevance.

Suggested Readings

Johnson, Louise, and Stephen Yanca. *Social Work Practice: A Generalist Approach*, 10th ed. Boston: Allyn & Bacon, 2010.

Kirst-Ashman, Karen, and Grafton Hull. *Understanding Generalist Practice*, 5th ed. Belmont, CA: Brooks/Cole, 2009.

Poulin, John. *Strength-Based Generalist Practice*, 2nd ed. Belmont, CA: Brooks/Cole, 2005.

Timberlake, Elizabeth, Michaela Zajicek-Farber, and Christine Anlauf Sabitino. *Generalist Social Work Practice*. Boston: Allyn & Bacon, 2009.

ECOSYSTEMS PERSPECTIVE   The ecosystem perspective draws selected concepts from ecology, a branch of biology, and uses them as analogies and metaphors to describe client situations and how clients might adapt to an ever-changing environment. It is attractive to social workers because it provides a way of describing the interdependencies and transactions between and among people and social systems. Since all parts of a system and all aspects of a client's environment are connected to and dependent on all other parts, a change in any one part will affect all other parts. Thus, for example, a social worker's assessment must anticipate how an intervention might affect others within the client's family or social network. If a client is concerned about a marital problem, social workers will usually want to work with both the husband and wife, since a change by one will affect the other. This perspective also reminds the social worker that the process of planned change is both facilitated by and limited by a myriad of forces and factors within the client's environment. This perspective is especially useful during the phases of assessment and planning.

It is important to understand that when social workers borrow concepts from a science such as ecology the fit will not be perfect. For example, the unit of study in ecology is the *ecosystem*, which consists of many interacting species and their exchanges with their physical and chemical environment (i.e., a category of organisms). Ecology is focused primarily on the adaptations and functioning of a species and not on the individuals of that species. By contrast, social work places a very high value on the individual and considers environmental factors as they impinge on the individual.

The term *carrying capacity* is defined as the maximum number of individuals of a species that can live within an ecosystem. If the carrying capacity is exceeded, disease and starvation will decrease that population. Either a rapid growth or a rapid decline in population numbers can upset the delicate balances necessary to the health of an ecosystem. Given the values and ethics of the social work profession, we cannot stand by and watch the raw forces of nature control human populations. However, these ecological ideas do have relevance to social workers and public health personnel when they anticipate the effects of problems such as the mass movement of refugees and the formation of crowded slums in economically depressed areas.

The ecological concept of *niche* refers to that combination of conditions and circumstances (e.g., temperature, soil chemistry, food supply) needed by a particular species. When niche is used as a metaphor in social work practice, we recognize that clients or client systems can function better in some situations and environments than in others. Many social work interventions are designed to help a client find a social niche in which they can make the most of their particular abilities.

Ecosystems are never static, and each species within an ecosystem is constantly adapting to an ever-changing environment. If the environment changes rapidly or if the species cannot adapt, the species may be overpowered or replaced by a more adaptable species. One form of adaptation is *specialization*. A species that is specialized in terms of what it needs to survive is at an advantage because its specialization has the effect of reducing competition. However, a highly specialized species is vulnerable in a rapidly changing environment. As a general rule, specialization increases survivability in a stable environment but decreases survivability in a changing environment. Such ideas might, for example, guide the thinking of those who design job-training programs. Is it better to train individuals for a highly specialized job or provide them with a broader and more general type of training? Having specialized skills will make them more competitive in a stable job market but more vulnerable to lay off if the job market is in flux or if new technologies can make a particular set of skills obsolete.

The interactions between the different species of an ecosystem can take several forms. In one type of interaction, termed *predation*, one species (the predator) feeds on or utilizes another species (the prey). *Symbiosis* refers to a type of interaction wherein either one or both species benefit. There are three major types of symbiosis: In *mutualism*, both species benefit from the interaction (e.g., bees and flowers); in *commensalism*, one species benefits while the other is neither helped nor harmed; and in *parasitism*, the parasite benefits while its host is harmed.

Because the resources needed by a species (e.g., food, water, space) are limited and needed by many other species, a species must compete in order to survive. The ones that are most adaptive will have an advantage in this *competition*. When the resources needed by a particular species are scarce, the individuals of that species must, in addition, compete with each other. In that situation, the strongest individuals will survive.

Competition is built into our economic system, job markets, and schools. Competition can be positive in that it may push people to work harder, stay focused, and realize their innate abilities. However, unbridled competition can be a destructive force that gives rise to social and economic oppression and exploitation and to personal feelings of inadequacy and despair. Personal and social factors such as illness, disability, advanced age, immaturity, and lower levels of intelligence can limit a person's capacity to successfully compete. If all of the individuals in a society are to be valued and treated with dignity (a core social work goal and value), then various forms of cooperation and mutualism are needed to counterbalance the negative effects of raw competition. When viewed through the lens of the ecosystems perspective, the social work profession strives to enhance the adaptive capacities of people, remove environmental obstacles that limit effective social functioning, and expand the availability of resources that meet the basic needs for those who cannot secure them through usual competitive means.

It should be apparent that there is not always a good fit between concepts borrowed from another field, like ecology, and the values and purposes of the social work profession. Nevertheless, these ideas stretch our thinking and encourage us to view human behavior and problems and consider planned change in ways that are new and fresh. Above all else, ecology teaches us that people are shaped and influenced by their environment and, in turn, the environment is shaped and changed by humans. That reality is all too apparent as we face such problems as global warming, over population, and environmental degradation.

Suggested Readings

Dale, Orren, Rebecca Smith, Julia Norlin, and Wayne Chess. *Human Behavior and the Social Environment: A Systems Model*, 5th ed. Boston: Allyn & Bacon, 2009.

Germain, Carel, and Alex Gitterman. *The Life Model of Social Work Practice*, 3rd ed. New York: Columbia University Press, 2008.

Kemp, Susan, James Whittaker, and Elizabeth Tracy. *Person-Environment Practice*. New York: Aldine de Gruyter, 1997.

Meyer, Carol, and Mark Mattaini. "The Ecosystems Perspective: Implications for Practice." In *The Foundations of Social Work Practice*, 3rd ed., edited by Mark Mattaini, Christine Lowery, and Carol Meyer, 3–19. Washington, DC: NASW, 2002.

STRENGTHS PERSPECTIVE   The strengths perspective encourages the social worker to identify and build upon client strengths. A **client's strength** can be defined as any client attribute, capacity, or experience that contributes to positive and satisfying life and effective social functioning. Client strengths can take many forms, such as an ability or skill, the desire to learn and change, personal integrity, fortitude, and a commitment to help others. This perspective presumes that all clients have strengths, even when the client's behavior is seriously dysfunctional. Strengths are presumed to exist in all environments no matter how harsh they might appear. For example, within every neighborhood and community there will be individuals and groups that care deeply and contribute their time and resources to be of help to others. Creative and persistent efforts by the social worker can identify and mobilize those resources.

The strengths perspective offers an important counter balance to the emphasis on identifying problems and pathology that characterizes so many human service programs and is implicit in some other practice frameworks. Many of models and theories used by helping professionals focus mostly on what is going wrong in a client's life. Those problem-oriented or deficit-oriented approaches often overlook the positive and functional aspects of a client's behavior and situation.

When a social worker helps a client to identify and build on his or her strengths, it has the effect of increasing client motivation, elevating the client's sense of hope and self-confidence, and reducing resistance to needed change. While it is true that traumatic life experiences or an illness or disability can impose limitations on a person's functioning, even these experiences and conditions can become a source of personal strength and opportunity. No one can know for certain the upper limits of a person's ability to overcome life's difficulties.

The strengths perspective presumes that clients will usually know what types of interventions will be effective and helpful in addressing their concerns. Thus, the professional helping relationship is intentionally collaborative in nature and the practitioner's role is primarily that of a consultant. The client is viewed as an expert on his or her life situation and circumstances and the social worker will ask for and use the client's ideas on how best to proceed. The strengths perspective is relevant in work with all clients and during all phases of the helping process. It has much in common with the Solution-Focused Model described later. (See Item 11.5 for information on client strengths.)

Suggested Readings

Glicken, Morley. *Using the Strengths Perspective in Social Work Practice*. Boston: Allyn & Bacon, 2004.

Rapp, Charles, and Richard Guscha. *The Strengths Model*, 2nd ed. New York: Oxford University Press, 2006.

Saleebey, Dennis. *The Strengths Perspective in Social Work Practice*, 5th ed. Boston: Allyn & Bacon, 2009.

ETHNIC-SENSITIVE PERSPECTIVE   Given that people are shaped by their backgrounds and life experiences, factors such as a client's ethnicity, culture, religion, and socio-economic class will influence a client's thoughts and behavior. These factors will also affect what an individual defines as a problem, whether he or she will seek assistance from a professional or human services agency, how he or she expects to be treated by service providers, and what types of services he or she considers relevant and helpful. The ethnic-sensitive perspective draws the social worker's attention to these important factors and influences. This conceptual lens is especially important when the client is a member of an ethnic or minority group and whenever the client's presenting problem or concern is related to discrimination or oppression. It is applicable during all phases of the helping process.

It is important for every social worker to become a culturally competent practitioner, one who has the ability to work with a client in ways that are congruent with the client's beliefs, values, traditions, and expectations. In order to develop this ability, the social worker, must, first and foremost, develop self-awareness and become cognizant of how his or her own beliefs, values, and expectations have been shaped and molded by his or her personal experiences of culture, ethnicity, religion, and social class. In addition, the social worker must learn about a client's background and be able to use that knowledge in practice. (For related information on this perspective and cultural competence, see Items 8.10, 15.17, 15.20, and 16.3.)

Suggested Readings

Appleby, George, Edgar Colon, and Julia Hamilton. *Diversity, Oppression, and Social Function*. Boston: Allyn & Bacon, 2007.

Diller, Jerry. *Cultural Diversity: A Primer for the Human Services*, 3rd ed. Belmont, CA: Brooks/Cole, 2007.

Lum, Doman. *Culturally Competent Practice*, 3rd ed. Belmont, CA: Brooks/Cole, 2007.

Sisneros, Jose, Mildred Joyner, and Cathryne Schmitz. *Critical Multicultural Social Work*. Chicago: Lyceum, 2008.

FEMINIST PERSPECTIVE   The feminist perspective heightens the practitioner's awareness of how societal beliefs and attitudes related to sex, gender, and sex roles may shape how a client views and explains a problem or situation and the ways that a professional or agency responds to people's concerns and requests for services. This perspective is especially important when one recognizes that male-dominated institutions and decision-making groups have designed most of the laws, policies, and programs that impact women. This perspective is needed whenever a client's problems or concerns are linked to sexism and sex role stereotyping. It is applicable throughout the helping process and especially during the phases of problem definition and assessment.

The terms *sex* and *gender* are often used interchangeably but they have somewhat different meanings. The concept of *sex* refers to the classification of people as either male or female, based on anatomy and a particular assemblage of the X and Y chromosomes. By contrast, the concept of *gender* refers to socially constructed differences as reflected in the meanings people assign to biological differences and associate with ideas of femininity and masculinity. For example, in many societies femininity is associated with the qualities of compassion, cooperation, loyalty, intuition, caring, sharing, openness, and attention to human relationships. Masculinity, on the other hand, is often associated with rationality, competition, authority, leadership, courage, decisiveness, fortitude, honor, and attention to things and objects. Needless to say, many of the perceived differences between the sexes have their origin in historical forces and cultural and societal dynamics, rather than in biological differences.

The feminist perspective challenges those belief systems and social structures that give rise to the oppression and exploitation of women. Two examples are sexism and patriarchy. As a set of beliefs and attitudes, *sexism* presumes that one sex (usually the female) is inferior to and should be subordinate to the other, thus resulting in an unfair ordering of roles and responsibilities and to social and economic inequalities. *Patriarchy* refers to a hierarchical system of societal organization in which men control the family, political, and economic structures. It, like sexism, rests on the belief that the male is inherently superior and naturally suited for leadership and decision making.

Central to the feminist perspective is the belief that the professional helping process cannot be limited to clinical or direct service activities; it must also emphasize political action and advocacy. Here are some other characteristics:

- The helping process emphasizes empowerment and building on client strengths. It has a strong educational component, including teaching the client about sexism, sex-role stereotyping, discrimination, and the historical factors that have shaped societal attitudes toward women and also how women view themselves.
- Client concerns and personal problems are assessed within a sociopolitical context with attention to sex-related power differentials within male-female relationships, marriage, family, and employment.
- The helping relationship is egalitarian; the professional seeks to be a partner or colleague to the client, not an expert or authority figure. The client is expected to be an active participant in the helping process. The professional willingly shares relevant personal experiences.
- There is an emphasis on creating and utilizing women's social networks and support groups.

The feminist perspective is especially important in work with women, but its emphasis on empowerment, social justice, and political action should be a part of social work practice in all settings and also in work with male clients.

Suggested Readings

Bricker-Jenkins, Mary, and F. Ellen Netting. "Feminist Issues and Practices in Social Work." In *Social Workers' Desk Reference*, 2nd ed., edited by Albert Roberts. New York: Oxford University Press, 2008.

Kopala, Mary, and Merle Keitel, eds. *Handbook of Counseling Women*. Thousand Oaks, CA: Sage, 2003.

Saulnier, Christine. *Feminist Theories and Social Work*. Binghamton, NY: Haworth, 1996.

Selected Practice Theories and Models

A practice perspective does not stand alone; it is always used in conjunction with various practice theories and models. For example, a social worker operating from the generalist perspective may elect to use behavioral techniques, small group theories, and/or theories of organizational change, depending on the practice situation. More specialized practitioners may draw on a smaller number of theories or models, but apply them with more depth of knowledge and skill. In the remainder of this chapter we offer brief descriptions of practice theories and models commonly used by social workers.

BEHAVIORAL THEORY   The behavioral approach to social work practice is based on knowledge drawn from the laboratory study of the learning process. It presumes that most of our behavior and even certain types of emotional reactions are learned according to known principles and that both functional (healthy) and dysfunctional behaviors (psychopathology) are learned in essentially the same ways. People will repeat behaviors that are rewarded and gradually abandon behaviors that are not rewarded or are punished. In other words, how a person behaves is determined by the consequences that a particular behavior elicits within his or her social environment.

The application of this approach begins with a specification of the behavior to be changed (i.e., a target behavior). Behavioral change refers to an increase or decrease in frequency, duration, or intensity of the target behavior. Either the client or practitioner must have control over whether or how the target behavior is reinforced (rewarded). Detailed and precise data collection is necessary in order to determine what factors encourage or suppress a target behavior and to know if a specific intervention is being effective. The decisions that guide the change process are made on the basis of data and not on beliefs about what should work.

The behavioral approach is frequently used in residential treatment and correctional settings, where it is possible to closely observe the behavior of clients and exercise control over the rewards they receive. In some applications, the client is taught how to modify his or her own behavior through the self-administration of reinforcers.

This approach can be used to improve the functioning of individuals, couples, families, and organizations. It is applicable in work with the non-voluntary or mandated client if the professional has the authority to allocate or withhold reinforcements. It is usually not an appropriate approach when the client's concerns or problems are value conflicts, decision making, and distorted thinking. (See Item 13.3 for additional information on the behavioral approach.)

Suggested Readings

Bronson, Denise. "A Behavioral Approach to Social Work Treatment." In *Social Workers' Desk Reference*, 2nd ed., edited by Albert Roberts. New York: Oxford University Press, 2008.

Sundel, Martin, and Sandra Sundel. *Behavior Change in the Human Services*, 5th ed. Thousand Oaks, CA: Sage, 2005.

Thyer, Bruce, and John Wodarski. *Handbook of Empirical Social Work Practice*. New York: Wiley, 1998.

COGNITIVE BEHAVIORAL THEORY   This framework integrates selected concepts from learning theory with ones drawn from the study of cognitive processes (i.e., how people interpret and assign meaning to their experiences and the interplay of thoughts, emotions, and behavior). Many personal problems and troublesome moods and feelings are caused by the person's faulty, irrational, and rigid thinking about the way things are and should be. In a sense, we humans live at the mercy of our thoughts and beliefs; we react to and become what and how we think about our experiences. In large measure, the degree to which we are satisfied, happy, and content in life is a function of how well what is happening in our life fits with or matches what we believe should or ought to be happening. A person's expectations and habits or patterns of thought (termed *schemas*) are largely formed during childhood. Basically, a *schema* is an enduring conviction about one's self, others, and what one can and expect in life.

As a general rule, people strive to behave in ways that are consistent with their beliefs, values, and moral standards. When a person perceives a discrepancy or disconnect between his or her beliefs about what is right and appropriate and how he or she is actually behaving, the person experiences *cognitive dissonance* (i.e., some degree of inner discomfort, regret, or guilt). The person will then try to bring his or her behavior more in line with his or her beliefs and standards. However, sometimes people respond to such dissonance by adopting new beliefs that will better fit their behavior. To take an extreme example, consider a soldier placed in a situation where he must kill others. But killing is repugnant because he has always believed that it was wrong to kill another human being. To resolve this inner conflict, this dissonance, the soldier may adopt beliefs that justify or rationalize the killing, such as: "If I don't kill the enemy, he will kill me," "The enemy is less than human and not like me," "The enemy lives in such a terrible society, he is better off dead." In this example, behavior (killing) gives rise to a change in beliefs about killing.

An intervention based on cognitive-behavioral principles will teach the client to recognize the content and impact of their cognitions (thoughts) and schemas, to evaluate the validity of his or her beliefs and assumptions, and to view events and situations with greater objectivity. As clients change how they interpret and understand their situation, they start to think, feel, and behave differently. Within this framework there are subdivisions, such as rational emotive therapy and cognitive therapy. Practitioners and theoreticians tend to differ on whether to emphasize the cognitive side or the behavioral side of the cognitive-behavioral construct and the degree to which they work to modify fundamental cognitive process such as perception, memory, information processing, judgment, and decision making.

The cognitive-behavioral approach is helpful in addressing problems of depression, low self-esteem, and various self-defeating patterns. The client must possess the requisite intellectual capacity and a willingness to invest the time needed to monitor and analyze his or her patterns of thought and behavior. An interesting and promising elaboration of this approach is termed *dialectical behavioral therapy* that was originally designed to treat persons with borderline personality disorder. It combines common cognitive behavioral techniques with the techniques of meditation and mindfulness (derived largely from Buddhist meditation) to help the client learn to tolerate discomfort and exercise control over their emotional reactions (see Items 8.6, 13.6, 13.7, and 13.10).

Suggested Readings

Corcoran, Jacqueline. *Cognitive Behavioral Methods: A Workbook for Social Workers*. Boston: Allyn & Bacon, 2006.

Eamon, Mary. *Empowering Vulnerable Populations: Cognitive-Behavioral Interventions*. Chicago: Lyceum, 2008.

Ledley, Deborah, Brian Marx, and Richard Heimberg. *Making Cognitive-Behavioral Therapy Work*. New York: Guilford, 2005.

Ronen, Tammie, and Arthur Freeman, eds. *Cognitive Behavior Therapy in Clinical Social Work Practice*. New York: Springer, 2006.

EXCHANGE THEORY   The basic principles of *exchange theory* are drawn from the fields of behavioral psychology and economics (see the previous section on behavioral theory.) This approach emphasizes the fact that self-interest is a powerful factor in human motivation and will frequently explain and predict the behaviors and decisions of individuals, families, groups, and organizations. Most people, most of the time, place their own wants and desires above those of other people. People behave in ways that move them closer to whatever they perceive to be valuable and beneficial. Moreover, people strive to protect or preserve that which they value. In short, people seek to maximize benefits and minimize costs. Knowing how to appeal to a client's self-interest is an essential skill in work with all clients and especially with non-voluntary and uncooperative clients.

Clients' values and belief systems are the key predictors of what they will define to be a benefit, advantage, or reward and what they will judge to be a cost, disadvantage, or punishment. Different individuals and groups will have different ideas about what is desirable. For example, some people may want money, possessions, power, status, and privilege, whereas others may believe that personal freedom, honor, social approval, friendship, a sense of belonging, or the feeling of a "job well done" are of the greatest value. For still others, adhering to a moral code, performing religious practices, and holding onto tradition may be more important than anything else. Similarly, costs are defined differently by different people. Examples of costs are the loss of money or time, the loss of status or respect, dishonor, humiliation, or knowing one has done wrong. Understanding how clients define costs and benefits is central to understanding their motivation, predicting how they will behave in certain situations, and formulating an effective intervention.

Among the core principles of exchange theory are the following:

- When a client must choose from among various alternatives, the client will engage in the behaviors that will secure the greatest benefits and incur the least costs, as the client defines benefits and costs.
- When a client concludes that all possible alternatives will result in about the same level of reward or benefit, the client will usually select the alternative that has the fewest perceived costs (i.e., disadvantages) and risks.
- When a client believes that all possible alternatives will have immediate outcomes that are about equal, he or she will usually select a course of action that may result in some long-term benefit.

- When a client believes that all possible alternatives will have long-term outcomes that are about equal, he or she will usually select a course of action that might provide an immediate benefit.
- When a client's values have been shaped by a Western industrialized society, the client will usually choose a course of action that promises the greatest financial gain or the least financial cost.

In the context of micro-level social work practice, exchange theory suggests that a client will make use of a service (e.g., counseling, treatment group) only if and only as long as he or she believes the benefits (e.g., feeling better, avoiding negative consequences) outweigh the costs. In this situation, costs might include fees, time, loss of privacy, and stress.

Exchange theory helps to predict inter-group and inter-organizational behavior. As a general rule, the desire to obtain rewards and avoid costs will determine whether people cooperate and collaborate with others or adopt a strategy of competition and conflict. For example, organization A will cooperate with organization B if doing so helps it get what it wants. But, organization A will compete with organization C if it believes it can gain more through competition than through cooperation. If, for example, social agencies are expected to cooperate and work together, there must be clear advantages for them to do so. If there is no incentive to cooperate and collaborate, the agencies will compete for limited resources, such as funding, press coverage, status, staff, and the like.

Closely related to exchange theory is the conceptual framework known as *rational choice theory*. This theory is drawn from the study of economics and rests on the assumption that people are always rational and logical and will, when given a choice, select those alternatives or behaviors that maximize their benefits and minimize their costs. Thus, by creating a system of incentives and penalties, it is possible to guide people toward desired social goals and away from behaviors that are deemed undesirable. This theory has been the rationale for many proposed social policy changes in the areas of health care and social welfare. A major weakness is this approach and other economic models is that they overlook the fact that people are not always rational and make many decisions on the basis of emotion, peer pressure, tradition, and other psychological and social factors.

Suggested Readings

Blau, Peter. *Exchange and Power in Social Life*. New York: Wiley and Sons, 1964.

Nye, F. I., ed. *The Relationships: Rewards and Costs*. Beverly Hills, CA: Sage, 1982.

Robbins, Susan, Pranab Chatterjee, and Edward Canda. *Contemporary Human Behavior Theory*, 2nd ed. Boston: Allyn & Bacon, 2006.

PSYCHODYNAMIC THEORY   This direct practice framework focuses mostly on the client's deeply personal and often hidden thoughts, feelings, and inner conflicts. It gives much attention to the power of intense emotions and feelings (e.g., fear, hatred, anger, guilt, lust) and the psychological turmoil they can cause. It presumes that many of our choices and behaviors are determined by forces that are largely unconscious or beyond our awareness.

The psychosocial development of an individual is viewed as a progressive movement through a sequence of phases, beginning in early infancy. Accomplishing the developmental tasks of a particular phase sets the stage for the next phase. Negative childhood experiences can disrupt the normal phases of development and result in various psychological problems. The concepts of *object relations* (people relations) describe how current patterns of thought, feelings, and behavior often reflect, at an unconscious level, one's childhood experiences with parent figures.

The dynamics or the workings of the mind are conceptualized as the interplay between the ego, id, and superego. The term **ego** refers to the reality-oriented, problem-solving, and decision-making component of the personality that mediates the tension and conflicts between one's primitive drives and impulses (the id) and one's values, norms, and moral standards that have been absorbed from family and society (the superego). Largely unconscious *defense mechanisms* (e.g., repression, projection, rationalization) operate to minimize or mask the anxiety associated with these inner conflicts (see Item 11.7).

Change results from the client's cathartic expressions of conflict and feelings; from gaining insight (understanding) into how life experience gave rise to troublesome thoughts and behaviors; and from facing up to and working through one's inner turmoil. The change process usually requires an in-depth professional relationship wherein the client feels safe to explore and express very private thoughts and feelings. It is presumed that the client will often act and feel toward the practitioner as he or she did toward other significant persons such as parents or ones who inflicted psychological trauma, a phenomenon termed *transference*. In some instances, the client is asked to examine this transference in order to gain self-understanding. The term *ego supportive treatment* refers to an intervention intended to maintain or enhance a client's capacity to resolve inner conflict, solve a problem, or make a needed adjustment.

Social workers have adapted various therapeutic methods rooted in psychodynamics to the realities of an agency-based practice and to the social work profession's emphasis on viewing the client within an environmental context. As a general rule, however, a practice that is based on psychodynamic concepts will give relatively more attention to the client's psychology (inner thoughts and feelings) than to social, situational, and environmental factors. A client is expected to be motivated, verbal, and willing to participate in numerous therapy sessions. This approach is seldom appropriate if the client has limited intellectual ability, is chemically dependent, or is overwhelmed by adverse social and economic conditions (e.g., poverty, inadequate housing). Recent contributions to this approach incorporate concepts drawn from the cognitive-behavioral approach and various theories of family treatment.

Suggested Readings

Borden, William. *Contemporary Psychodynamic Theory and Practice*. Chicago: Lyceum, 2009.

Brandell, Jerrold. *Psychodynamic Social Work*. New York: Columbia University, 2004.

Goldstein, Eda. *Object Relations Theory and Self Psychology in Social Work Practice*. New York: Free Press, 2001.

Leiper, Rob, and Michael Maltby. *The Psychodynamic Approach to Therapeutic Change*. Thousand Oaks, CA: Sage, 2004.

Person-Centered Theory

The person-centered approach, borrowed from counseling psychology, seeks to help clients free themselves from feelings and attitudes that block their innate potential for personal growth and self-actualization. With roots in humanistic and existential philosophy, it is constructed around a very positive and optimistic viewpoint—people are basically good, wanting to do what is right, and striving to discover and develop their full potential. This approach presumes that change will occur when the practitioner offers the client a relationship that is validating, accepting, and non-judgmental. Within such a relationship, clients will lower their defenses, examine their attitudes and behavior, and begin to perceive themselves and their situation in a more realistic and positive manner.

For the most part, the helping process and the professional relationship is non-directive, meaning that the practitioner accepts the client's choice of issues to be discussed and does not guide the discussion toward any particular topic. The worker refrains from giving advice, labeling, and diagnosing. The practitioner's role is to help clients help themselves. The professional places much emphasis on conveying the qualities of acceptance, empathy, warmth, and genuineness and using the techniques of active listening (see Item 8.4).

The application of the person-centered approach presumes that the client will be voluntary, highly motivated, articulate, and interested in self-examination. It is most often used in individual counseling and in personal growth and human potential groups. It is usually not appropriate for clients who are manipulative, have an addiction, are highly dysfunctional, or are burdened by adverse social and economic conditions.

Suggested Readings

Purton, Campbell. *Person-Centered Therapy*. New York: Palgrave, 2004.

Rowe, William, and Alicia Stinson. "Client-Centered Theory and Therapy." In *Social Workers' Desk Reference*, 2nd ed. New York: Oxford University Press, 2008.

Tudor, Keith. *Person-Centered Therapies*. Thousand Oaks, CA: Sage, 2008.

INTERACTIONAL MODEL   As the name suggests, this approach primarily focuses on a client's interactions with others and with various social systems. This is one of the few practice frameworks that developed within the social work profession, rather than being borrowed from another profession. It grew out of experiences with typical social work clients in a variety of social agencies, and it is applicable in work with individuals, families, groups, and organizations.

People naturally seek connectedness, even though disputes, conflict, and ambivalence are a part of their interactions and relationships. In this model of helping, the social worker becomes an active "third force" who functions as a mediator between and among the individuals, groups, and systems impacting on the client. The practitioner seeks to resolve conflicts and facilitates the formation of more effective and satisfying exchanges.

This approach gives primary attention to the client's here-and-now experiences and realities. It presumes that many clients will be struggling with problems such as poverty, inadequate housing, or the lack of health care. Neither the client's relationships nor the client's concerns or problems can be understood apart for their social and environmental contexts. It is presumed that many clients will be reluctant or resistant to entering into a professional relationship.

This model has four major components: (1) the client, (2) the social systems and people with whom the client interacts, (3) the interactions that are particularly troublesome to the client, and (4) the element of time and the four phases in the helping process. The phases are the preliminary or preparatory phase, the beginning contracting phase, the middle or work phase, and the ending or transition phase. The model describes specific skills or techniques that are especially applicable during each of these phases. (For more description of these phases and techniques, see Item 8.4.)

Suggested Readings

Shulman, Lawrence. *The Skills of Helping Individuals, Families, Groups, and Communities*, 6th ed. Belmont, CA: Brooks/Cole, 2009.

———. *Interactional Supervision*. Washington, DC: NASW, 1993.

———. *Interactional Social Work Practice*. Itasca, IL: F. E. Peacock, 1991.

STRUCTURAL MODEL   The structural approach to direct practice rests on the belief that most of the client problems addressed by social workers are a manifestation of inadequate social arrangements and insufficient resources, rather than, for example, a manifestation of individual pathologies or deficiencies. A client who is experiencing a problem is not necessarily its cause and therefore, the individual is not always the appropriate target or focus for a change effort or intervention.

The social work profession strives to maintain a focus on the person-in-environment. However, it is inherently difficult to give equal attention to both the individual and his or her environment. The structural approach addresses this tension by directing practitioners to consider, first, changing the client's environment. Whereas other approaches to counseling and therapy focus mostly on helping individuals make changes in their own behavior and attitudes and adjust to their situation, the structural model aims to modify the client's environment so it can better meet the needs of the individual. Improving social conditions and structures (i.e., social change) is the responsibility of all social work practitioners and not an exclusive concern of those practicing in the areas of community organization, social policy development, and social planning.

The model identifies four key social work roles (conferee, broker, mediator, and advocate) and assumes the worker will move from one role to another depending on the needs of the client. This model is built around several fundamental principles: Be accountable and responsible to the client; take actions that identify and engage others who have concerns or problems similar to those of the client; maximize the supports that exist in the client's environment; proceed on the basis of "least contest" (e.g., take on the role of broker before mediator and mediator before advocate); help the client understand social forces impacting on his or her situation, and teach behaviors and skills that will help the client take control of his or her life.

Suggested Readings

Middleman, Ruth, and Gail Goldberg Wood. *Skills for Direct Practice*. New York: Columbia University Press, 1990.

Mullaly, Robert. *Structural Social Work: Ideology, Theory and Practice*, 2nd ed. New York: Oxford University Press, 1997.

Wood, Gale Goldberg, and Carol T. Tully. *The Structural Approach to Direct Practice in Social Work*, 2nd ed. New York: Columbia University Press, 2006.

CRISIS INTERVENTION MODEL   The crisis intervention model is used to help individuals who are experiencing an acute, psychological crisis. A crisis is defined as a time-limited period of psychological disequilibrium, usually set in motions by a personal loss or traumatic event. During a crisis the individual's usual methods of coping prove ineffective. Typically, this period of turmoil, anxiety, and disorganization lasts a matter of weeks, after which the person will gradually regain his or her ability to cope. If the individual does not reestablish a pattern of adequate functioning, he or she is at risk of developing more serious and long-term problems. Thus, crisis intervention is an effort to cushion the immediate impact of the disruptive event by providing "emotional first aid" and prevent mental health problems.

When using this approach, the professional is quite directive and will usually offer advice and guidance. Key elements of the model include: (1) quick access to the client and rapid response by the helper; (2) frequent contact during the crisis period (e.g., five or six counseling sessions over a four-week period); (3) focused attention on the precipitating event and its subjective meaning to client; (4) emphasis on helping the client make decisions and take action; and (5) contact with the client's social network. Those using the model may draw on a variety of theories, techniques, and intervention procedures. (For more information on crisis intervention, see Item 13.14.)

Suggested Readings

James, Richard. *Crisis Intervention Strategies*, 6th ed. Belmont, CA: Brooks/Cole, 2008.

Kanel, Kristi. *A Guide to Crisis Intervention*, 3rd ed. Belmont, CA: Brooks/Cole, 2007.

Roberts, Albert. *Crisis Intervention Handbook*, 3rd ed. New York: Oxford University Press, 2005.

TASK-CENTERED MODEL   After discussing their problem or situation, clients often know what they need to do but are unable to move ahead and take the action necessary to change their situation. The task-centered approach is designed to help clients (individuals, couples, families, and groups) to specify and perform these important tasks and activities. It developed out of work with typical social work clients who were experiencing a wide variety of problems and challenges. This approach is especially useful with clients who are attempting to manage problems caused by a lack of resources and works well with non-voluntary clients.

A specific action or step toward change is termed a *task*. The tasks to be worked on can take many forms: making a decision within a certain time frame, securing a needed resource, learning a skill, communicating with another person, and so forth. Large tasks are broken down into several smaller ones so they are more manageable and so the client will experience progress and maintain motivation. Priority setting is used to limit the number of tasks to only two or three per week. The use of an unambiguous and understandable plan of action and time lines or time limits enhance client motivation and help the client stay focused on what needs to be done. The model is largely empirical, stressing the close monitoring and measurement of task completion.

The model's emphasis on taking action and the completion of tasks should not be interpreted as a lack of concern about clients' feelings or inner conflicts. However, this approach rests on the belief that people are more likely to change as a result of action than from simply discussing their thoughts and feelings. Task-centered practitioners draw on a variety of theories and techniques to help clients accomplish agreed-upon tasks (For more information on this approach, see Items 12.1, 12.2, and 14.4.)

Suggested Readings

Epstein, Laura, and Lester Brown. *Brief Treatment and a New Look at the Task-Centered Approach*, 4th ed. Boston: Allyn & Bacon, 2002.

Fortune, Anne. "Task-Centered Practice." In *Social Workers' Desk Reference*, 2nd ed. New York: Oxford University Press, 2008.

Reid, William. *The Task Planner*. New York: Columbia University Press, 2000.

Tolson, Eleanor, William Reid, and Charles Garvin. *Generalist Practice: A Task-Centered Approach*, 2nd ed. New York: Columbia University Press, 2003.

PSYCHOEDUCATION MODEL   When faced with a specific problem or condition, such as a mental illness, both the client and members of the client's family need information in order to understand what is happening and what they can do about it. When people have accurate information they are better able to make informed decisions, focus their efforts, and utilize services. The psychoeducation model is designed to improve the functioning of individuals and families by educating them about the psychosocial problems they are experiencing and about possible interventions. This model originated within the field of psychiatric treatment, but is now used in a wide variety of practice settings.

Psychoeducation is seldom a stand-alone intervention, but it is used to complement or supplement other interventions or therapies. As an illustration of psychoeducation, consider the case of John, a man recently diagnosed with schizophrenia. Both John and his family need information about this disorder, its etiology, progression, prognosis, and the treatment options so that they can secure treatment and better cope with the bewildering symptoms associated with this illness. Another example of psychoeducation exists in most alcoholism treatment programs when the family of an alcoholic is invited to educational sessions that explain the nature of addiction, the effects of alcohol on mind and body, the 12-step program, signs of relapse, the phenomena of co-dependency, and the like.

A wide variety of problems or situations might become the focus of psychoeducation sessions; for example, living with bipolar disorder, going through a divorce, parenting a teenager, dealing with the death of a loved one, managing a child with attention deficit disorder, and so on. A program of psychoeducation lessens anxiety and worry, corrects possible misunderstandings, and teaches relevant problem-solving skills and coping strategies. A social worker using psychoeducation must be clear on the goals for the educational session(s), what a client expects and needs to learn, and how content can be presented so that the client can most easily grasp and make use of the information. (See the section titled, "The Social Worker as Teacher" in Chapter 4 and Item 13.32.)

Suggested Readings

Brown, Nina. *Psychoeducational Groups: Process and Practice*, 2nd ed. New York: Brunner-Routledge, 2003.

DeLucia-Waak, Janice. *Leading Psychoeducational Groups for Children and Adolescents*. Thousand Oaks, CA: Sage, 2006.

Lefley, Harriet. *Family Psychoeducation for Serious Mental Illness*. New York: Oxford University Press, 2009.

ADDICTION MODEL This model recognizes the special challenges of helping a client control an addiction or a similar compulsive pattern. It rests on a number of beliefs and assumptions about how addictions develop and their effect on a person's life. When we think of an addiction we usually think of a dependency on alcohol and drugs. However, other problems such as certain eating disorders, gambling, and compulsive sexual activity are appropriately viewed as having the qualities of an addiction. Even the extreme pursuit of money and physical exercise can take on the characteristics of an addiction. Given the nature of an addiction, the addiction model pre-supposes that most clients will be resistant and non-voluntary and will typically deny that they have a problem. The model is applicable in work with individuals and with groups.

In the very beginning stage of the addiction process, the individual uses the substance or activity mostly as a means of meeting an emotional need or coping with some other personal problem. When the substance makes the person feel better, its use is reinforced and, subsequently, it is used again and again. Over time, the substance or activity consumes more and more of the individual's attention and resources and displaces other relationships and activities. As the addiction spins out of control, the individual develops a system of denial, rationalizations, and behaviors that will ensure access to the substance or activity.

The process of treatment and recovery from an addiction typically moves through six stages:

1. The person with an addiction lets go of denial and defensiveness and acknowledges that he or she has a serious problem.
2. The person develops a sense of hope based on awareness that people with similar problems have made a successful recovery.
3. The person comes to understand how the addiction developed and why it has gotten worse over time.
4. The person acquires the resolve, strength, and social support necessary to change the patterns of thought, behavior, and lifestyle that reinforce the addiction.
5. The person takes action to battle and abandon the addiction.
6. The person continually monitors his or her life so as to stay free of the addictive substance or activity.

Both one-on-one counseling and small-group experiences (e.g., 12-step programs) help the person move through these stages and achieve sobriety and a healthy lifestyle. Even after the individual is able to function without the addictive substance or activity, he or she must constantly work to avoid being drawn back into the addiction. (For further information on chemical dependency and addiction, see Item 15.11.)

Suggested Readings

Barsky, Allan. *Alcohol, Other Drugs, and Addictions*. Belmont, CA: Brooks/Cole, 2006.
Doweiko, Harold. *Concepts of Chemical Dependency*, 7th ed. Belmont, CA: Brooks/Cole, 2009.
McNeece, C. Aaron, and Diana DiNitto. *Chemical Dependency*, 3rd ed. Boston: Allyn & Bacon, 2005.

SELF-HELP MODEL Alcoholics Anonymous, Parents Without Partners, and Overeaters Anonymous are but a few of the many self-help groups that exist in most communities. Most self-help groups rest on five assumptions and beliefs:

• People have a need to tell their story and to be heard by others. They are most receptive to suggestions from those who have similar concerns and life experiences.
• People are helped as they help others. We can learn from others and have much to teach others.
• People are attracted to and feel most comfortable in small groups that are welcoming, informal, and noncompetitive.

- People are attracted to simple rules and principles that offer practical guidance on how to cope with day-to-day problems (e.g., "live one day at a time," "walk your talk").
- Helping and caring for others is a natural human activity and not a commodity to be bought and sold.

In order for self-help approach to be effective, a participant must be willing and able to listen attentively to others, tell his or her own story, and share personal information. Self-help groups work best with voluntary participants but some will welcome non-voluntary and even court-ordered participants. These groups usually depend on leaders who are indigenous to the group. Some rotate the leadership role from one member to another. A few look to leadership by professionals or members who have received special training on how to facilitate meetings.

Sometimes self-help takes the form of neighborhood groups and associations that help each other with, for example, home maintenance chores, child care, sharing transportation or tools, food coops, bartering, providing emergency financial assistance, or offering micro-loans to persons trying to start a small business.

Suggested Readings

Gitterman, Alex, and Lawrence Shulman. *Mutual Aid Groups, Vulnerable and Resilient Populations, and the Life Cycle*, 3rd ed. New York: Columbia University Press, 2005.
Kurtz, Linda. *Self-Help and Support Groups*. Thousand Oaks, CA: Sage, 1997.
Powell, Thomas. *Understanding the Self-Help Organization*. Thousand Oaks, CA: Sage, 1994.

SOLUTION-FOCUSED MODEL   A variety of influences, most of them economic, are forcing social workers and agencies to do more with less, to emphasize efficiency, and to limit the number of times they meet with a client. This reality has given birth to models of brief and time-limited counseling and therapy. The solution-focused approach is one of the better-developed models. It is built on several assumptions and principles:

- Real change and the resolution of problems can occur in a relatively short period of time. Because of the ripple effect, even small positive changes will, over time, have a positive impact on all other parts of the client system.
- Clients do not resist proposed changes that make sense and provide relief from distress.
- It is not necessary to understand the cause of a problem in order to resolve it.
- There are many possible ways of viewing a situation and many right ways of dealing with a troublesome concern.
- Clients are the true experts on their situations and are in the best position to know what will and will not solve their problems.
- Clients (individuals and families) will have ideas, strengths, and resources that can be identified and mobilized by the social worker to help resolve client problems.

This approach to working with individuals, couples, and families does not seek to analyze and understand the client's problem. Rather, the social worker strives to help the client clarify what he or she really wants to change and to then identify what he or she is already doing to effect those changes. In other words, it facilitates change by assisting the client to amplify those behaviors and actions that are already helping to address the presenting problem. Emphasis is placed on helping the client envision ways to expand on those the actions that are making a positive difference, no matter how small the immediate impact. The social worker uses various questioning techniques to help the client recognize that he or she already has some control over the troublesome situation and already has some good ideas on how to resolve it (see Item 11.4).

Because this approach accepts the client's definition of the problem and vies on how to change it, it is inherently more culturally sensitive than approaches that place the social worker in the position of identifying, diagnosing, and treating the client's problem. It can be adapted for use with court-ordered non-voluntary clients and those with substance abuse problems.

Suggested Readings

DeJong, Peter, and Insoo Kim Berg. *Interviewing for Solutions*, 3rd ed. Pacific Grove, CA: Brooks/Cole, 2008.

O'Connell, Bill. *Solution-Focused Therapy*, 2nd ed. Thousand Oaks, CA: Sage, 2005.

Nelson, Thorana, and Frank Thomas, eds. *Handbook of Solution-Focused Brief Therapy*. New York: Haworth Press, 2007.

Sharry, John. *Solution Focused Group Work*. Thousand Oaks, CA: Sage, 2007.

NARRATIVE MODEL   The narrative model or narrative therapy is built around the observation that individuals and families construct stories or narratives about themselves in order to describe and explain who they are and why life is the way it is. In short, we construct stories to help us make sense of what we experience. Moreover, people react to and are shaped by the assumptions and beliefs they have built into their own stories. For example, the words we choose to describe our life and situation influences whether we value and respect ourselves, whether we are hopeful or discouraged, whether we feel adequate or inadequate, and what we expect of ourselves and of others. Because individuals can assign various interpretations to their life experiences, they do, in a certain sense, construct their own "reality."

The stories or narratives that people construct are strongly influenced by societal, community, and even neighborhood values and beliefs. They also incorporate themes and plots drawn from movies, magazines, and pop cultures. For example, and unfortunately, many people derive their expectations and evaluations of their own marriage, parenting, children, and job from the images and stories they see on television.

The narrative therapy approach helps clients to examine their stories and understand how some story content can generate unhappiness and dysfunction. A professional using this approach places great emphasis on careful listening and on striving to understand the client's perceptions about his or her life and situation. Clients are helped to unravel the assumptions, experiences, and interpretations on which they have based their personal stories and then to construct alternative interpretations and new and more positive stories that explain and guide their lives.

A key technique in narrative therapy is termed "externalizing the problem." This is an effort to separate the person from the problem or their story about the problem. A problem may be discussed as an "opponent" and "oppressor." The client and therapist work together to "combat" the problem. The problem, not the person with the problem, is the target of change. (Items 11.4, 11.9, and 13.7 provide some insight into how a social worker might help clients examine their stories.)

Concepts and techniques of narrative therapy are used in work with individuals, families, and small groups. In some ways it is similar to strengths perspective and the solution-focused model. However, narrative therapy is different in that it draws heavily on presumptions common to postmodern philosophy and to related ideas of constructivism and social construction. This set of beliefs questions the existence of objective reality and doubts the usefulness of the scientific method. Thus, in contrast to most of the other practice frameworks, the narrative model does not incorporate concepts of data collection, assessment, a specification of desired outcomes, treatment plans, or evaluation. Neither does it strive to be methodical.

Suggested Readings

Brown, Catrina, and Tod Agusta-Scott. *Narrative Therapy*. Thousand Oaks, CA: Sage, 2006.

Kelly, Patricia. "Narrative Therapy." In *Social Workers' Desk Reference*, 2nd ed. New York: Oxford University Press, 2008.

White, Michael. *Maps of Narrative Practice*. New York: Norton 2007.

FAMILY THERAPIES   The use of a family therapy approach is appropriate when the purpose of the intervention is on changing the interactions among family members and on changing the way the family functions as a system. Such an approach is feasible if it is possible to assemble all or most family members for a series of sessions and the members have at least a minimal level of interest in strengthening their family. Most family members should be voluntary participants, although it is expected that some members will have been pressured to attend by the more powerful family members.

While there are numerous theories and models to guide work with families, they have much in common such as, the family system is the unit of attention, all or most family members are engaged in the change process, the focus is mostly on changing relationships rather than on solving a specific problem, attention is on current behavior (here and now), the practitioner is especially sensitive to the context and subtleties of family communication, and active techniques are employed (e.g., family sculpture, role-play, homework). The differences between the various approaches are mostly a matter of emphasizing certain concepts and procedures over others. A family therapist is usually quite eclectic and draws ideas and techniques from many sources. In order to illustrate how one approach might differ from another, a few of the key assumptions associated with commonly used approaches are presented here.

The **communications approach** presumes that family problems and conflicts are caused mostly by faulty communication. Change occurs when family members learn to really listen to each other and speak honestly. The practitioner models clear and forthright communication and uses various experiential exercises to help family members express themselves and practice skills of effective communication.

As suggested by its name, the **structural approach** focuses primarily on a family's structures and organization. Special attention is given to the delineation and interaction of the spousal, parental, and sibling subsystems. Unhealthy alliances and splits among these subsystems and either overly rigid or overly flexible boundaries are a seen as a major source of family dysfunction. Change occurs when the roles and responsibilities of the family's members and the subsystems are clarified and agreed to by all.

The **family systems approach** focuses on the struggle of family members to simultaneously be a part of a family and be an individual apart from that system. Problems arise when an individual either suppresses the self and is enmeshed with his or her family or, at the other extreme, rejects his or her connection to family. This approach recognizes that families tend to repeat the patterns of prior generations (i.e., the intergenerational transmission of dysfunction) and is especially sensitive to issues that arise during the various stages in the family life cycle.

An approach known as **strategic family therapy** gives special attention to the distribution and use of power within the family and to family rules (i.e., the often unstated family beliefs about how family members should think and behave). The word *strategic* connotes an active and directive role by the therapist in strategically selecting interventions that move the family toward a pattern of behavior deemed desirable and healthy by the therapist.

The **social learning approach** draws concepts and techniques from behavior therapy and behavior modification. It presumes that family conflicts and problems arise because the members have not learned basic skills such as communication and conflict resolution, and/or that appropriate and functional behavior is not reinforced within the family system. Thus, the practitioner places a heavy emphasis on teaching. *Functional family therapy* resembles the social learning approach but also examines the social context of family problems and the subtle psychological purposes that can be supported by problem behaviors. Problem behaviors are viewed as unsuccessful efforts by family members to cope with issues of dependence versus independence, freedom versus control, and intimacy versus distance.

The **narrative approach** to working with families focuses on the personal and family stories and anecdotes that family members use as frames of reference when they explain and interpret their own lives, situations, and problems. People also use the stories embedded in a community and culture (e.g., fables, novels, biographies, movies) to make sense of their experiences of family. Special questioning techniques are used to help family members examine the way they think about themselves and to help them construct alternative stories and interpretations that lead to improved patterns of interaction. (See section on narrative model in this chapter.)

As is true of psychotherapy in general, most approaches to family therapy developed out of work with middle- and upper-class families. Thus, they may not work as well with families that are economically poor or members of an oppressed minority group. Social workers are challenged to select approaches that can be adapted to agency-based practice and their profession's emphasis on social functioning and the person-in-environmental construct. To help them make that selection, Kilpatrick and Holland (2009) offer a practical **integrative model** that ties the use of various family therapies or family interventions to four levels of family need and functioning. For example, the approaches recommended for a family struggling to meet basic needs (food, safety, equality, etc.) would be different from the approaches recommended for the family having problems around issues of unclear boundaries or a lack of intimacy. (For additional information on families, see Items 11.3, 11.10, and 12.7.)

Selected Readings

Becvar, Dorothy, and Raphael Becvar. *Family Therapy*, 7th ed. Boston: Allyn & Bacon, 2009.

Bitter, James. *Theory and Practice of Family Therapy and Counseling*. Belmont, CA: Brooks/Cole, 2009.

Collins, Donald, Cathleen Jordan, and Heather Coleman. *An Introduction to Family Social Work*, 2nd ed. Belmont, CA: Brooks/Cole, 2007.

Kilpatrick, Allie, and Thomas Holland. *Working with Families: An Integrative Model by Level of Functioning*, 5th ed. Boston: Allyn & Bacon, 2009.

Nichols, Michael. *Essentials of Family Therapy*, 4th ed. Boston: Allyn & Bacon, 2009.

SMALL GROUP THEORIES   Work with groups occurs in a variety of social work settings for a multitude of purposes. For example, small groups are created and designed for the purposes of teaching and training, therapy, mutual support, social action, and recreation. There are a number of approaches or models in group work but their differences are related mostly to the purpose of the group (e.g., a task group versus a treatment group); the role assumed by the professional (e.g., group leader, therapist, teacher, mediator, or facilitator); and whether the professional is focused mostly on the behavior of the individuals within the group or mostly on the functioning of the group as a whole or a social system. Numerous orienting theories provide social workers with background knowledge on small groups such as leadership, goals, structure and norms, group cohesion, conflict, stages of group development, and communication. For purposes of illustration, we will identify some applications of group work, some ways in which the group approaches may differ, and a few of the frameworks that influence practice.

When groups are used for the purpose of **teaching and training**, they are goal oriented and the social worker assumes the roles of leader and teacher. Depending on the topic being addressed (e.g., parent training, learning job skills, learning about a medical condition) and the number of times the group will meet, there may or may not be an emphasis on promoting member interaction, building trust, and developing a sense of belonging to the group.

Task-oriented groups are formed for the purpose of carrying out a specified set of activities or achieving a certain goal. Examples include committees and agency boards. These goal-oriented or goal-driven groups tend to be quite structured. The group's leadership and officers are elected by the membership. Typically, a written agenda and *Robert's Rules of Order* guide the discussion and decision-making process.

The **group treatment approach** views the group as a therapeutic environment and a tool to change the behavior or attitude of members. The focus is mostly on the members as individuals and on the problems they are having outside the group. A member's behavior within the group will often mimic his or her functioning in other environments such as family and school. In a treatment group, the social worker assumes the role of a therapist, expert, and group leader. In some groups, such as those used in the treatment of sex offenders and persons addicted to alcohol or drugs, there is heavy use of challenge and confrontation and members are required to complete assigned homework and adhere strictly to established rules. In such groups, self-determination is not a priority.

The **developmental approach** is used to promote normal growth and development, and the learning of ordinary skills for living, rather than for the purpose of correcting dysfunctional behavior or coping with serious problems. Many of the groups that are part of the YMCA/YWCA programs, summer camps, after-school programs, and senior citizen programs are of this type. In these developmental groups, the worker typically assumes the role of leader, planner, and arranger of group activities and makes heavy use of programming (see Item 13.21).

The **interactional model** of group work, places the social worker in the role of a mediator between members of the group and between the group and its environment, including the agency that has sanctioned the group's formation. The worker gives attention to both the functioning of individual members and to the functioning of the group as a whole. This approach assigns a high value on client self-determination. (See description of the interactional model in this chapter.)

A number of theoretical influences from outside the social work profession have had an impact on how social workers approach their practice involving groups and, of course, also practice with individuals and families. These include Gestalt therapy, transactional analysis, encounter groups, psychodrama, behavior modification, and positive peer culture. (For additional information on group work, see Items 11.11, 12.8, 13.20, and 13.25.)

Selected Readings

Fatout, Marian, and Steven Rose. *Task Groups in Social Services*. Thousand Oaks, CA: Sage, 1995.

Garvin, Charles, Maeda Galinsky, and Lorraine Gutierrez. *Handbook of Social Work with Groups*. New York: Guilford, 2004.

Gitterman, Alex, and Robert Salmon, eds. *Encyclopedia of Social Work with Groups*. New York: Routledge, 2009.

Greif, Geoffrey, and Paul Ephross, eds. *Group Work with Populations at Risk*, 2nd ed. New York: Oxford University Press, 2004.

Macgowan, Mark. *Guide to Evidence-Based Group Work*. New York: Oxford University Press, 2008.

Toseland, Ronald, and Robert Rivas. *An Introduction to Group Work Practice,* 6th ed. Boston: Allyn & Bacon, 2009.

ORGANIZATIONAL CHANGE MODELS   Various models of organizational development and change can be used to modify the functioning of a human services organization in order to increase its ability to address the needs and concerns of its clients and staff. A change effort may be the result of a carefully articulated process to analyze agency functioning and establish a plan for incrementally making needed changes (i.e., strategic planning), or it may stem from concerns by staff members and/or clients that some problem in agency functioning must be immediately repaired. In either case, the change effort will typically involve the agency's top administrative staff, the board of directors of a private agency, or elected officials and legislative committees of a public agency.

The complexity of organizational change becomes evident when one recognizes that organizations are made up of numerous individuals, each with a unique personality and each with specific roles and tasks to perform; a set of formal and informal structures, procedures, and norms; and established power and authority relationships. Moreover, an organization is a legal entity whose purpose and functioning is tied to a charter and bylaws (private agency) or to certain legislation and statutes (public agency), as well as available resources and budgets that further shape their functioning. Organizations must constantly adapt to an ever-changing social, political, and economic environments.

Every social worker employed by an organization, regardless of position, must give some attention to how well it is functioning. A social agency must be efficient in using its resources, yet, provide appropriate services to meet the needs of its clients. As one moves from line worker to supervisor or middle manager, or to agency administrator, the responsibility to engage in organizational maintenance and change activities increases. These activities typically include informing upper-level administrators of staff concerns and client needs, proposing specific changes in agency policies and procedures, arranging for input from consultants, participating on committees to study specific aspects of the organization's performance, conducting program evaluations, and so on.

The selection of an approach to planned organizational change will depend on the organization's culture regarding its nature and functioning. An organization's culture might reflect one of three conceptual models. The **rational model** assumes that those who are part of the organization are in agreement about its goals and committed to those goals. Thus, an organization is primarily a way of structuring the work that needs to occur in order to reach a goal. Given that view, proposed changes (e.g., restructuring, personal assignments, adoption of new technologies, reallocation of resources) will be accepted if it becomes apparent that they would improve the organization's capacity to achieve its goals. Change following the rational model results from such activities as self-study, obtaining the advice of consultants, examining the complaints or suggestions made by clients or consumers, in-service training on new technologies, and so forth.

The **natural-system model** views an organization as a system made up of a multitude of individuals, roles, subsystems, and formal and informal processes striving to function and survive in a wider social environment. It recognizes that the personnel of an organization can be easily distracted from the organization's official mission by such things as job stress, unclear work assignments, and disagreements over duties and responsibilities. This model views an organization as needing to balance its goal achievement with maintenance functions. Change efforts emphasize the clarification of goals and objectives, improving communication, recognizing and addressing the social and emotional needs of personnel, morale building, and the like.

The **power-politics model** assumes that an organization is essentially a political arena in which various individuals, departments, and other units compete for power, resources, and personal advantage. Consequently, the achievement of the organization's official or stated goals may take a backseat to other agendas. To change such an organization, one needs access to persons in positions of influence over the organization and must be able to persuade them that a specific change is in their self-interest. External forces such as media exposure, investigations by citizen groups, legislative oversight, and lawsuits might be necessary for modifying these organizations.

Depending on the organizational model that best reflects the agency, a social worker might adopt one or more of the following approaches for generating change in a human services organization. The **policy approach** achieves change by developing and adopting new policies that will guide the organization and its operation. Those working for change direct their efforts toward the groups and individuals who are authorized to make policy and allocate resources at either the local, state, or national level. They provide these decision makers with data and new insights concerning a specific condition, problem, need, or issue, and advocate for a specific policy change.

A **program approach** seeks to change the organization by designing and introducing new or additional programs and services to better express and implement existing policy. Change efforts are directed primarily at people in administrative and managerial positions (i.e., those with authority to modify specific programs and alter the procedures and technology used in the work of the organization).

The **project approach** introduces change at the interface between line staff and the clients or consumers of the organization's services. Small-scale projects are used to try out or demonstrate new ways of working with agency clients. Policies and programs remain the same but staff skills and performance are enhanced, often through in-service training and increasing sensitivity to clients' needs.

An approach termed **client-centered management** focuses mostly on the relationship between organizational procedures and client outcomes. It is predicated on the belief that an excessive emphasis on powerful decision makers, funding bodies, interagency communication, and personnel issues diverts the attention of administrators from their primary purpose—assuring that the social agency provides high-quality services that truly respond to client needs. This approach strives to secure client input into agency decision making and planning (see Item 14.10).

The **teamwork approach** is primarily concerned with the manner in which workers interact to implement agency programs. It is based on two premises. First, it recognizes that the typical bureaucratic organization places excessive control in the hands of administrators, which, in turn, reduces innovation and consensus among workers about how best to provide services. Second, it recognizes that given the explosion of knowledge and technology, specialization is increasingly required in almost every occupation, but with specialization comes the need for better coordination. The providers of human services must be able to coordinate practice activities since services to clients are often provided simultaneously by several disciplines and several different agencies. Unfortunately, the department structure used in many agencies may erect barriers to coordination because the lines of communication and decision making are organized by profession, role, and job title, rather than by the need for an integrated approach to service delivery.

The teamwork approach has proven especially useful as a means of retaining the specialized knowledge and competencies of the several helping professions, and at the same time coordinating their practice activities. To make multidisciplinary teams viable working units, they are given the authority to plan and implement programs and to make decisions about the personnel and resources necessary to carry out their assignments. In this process, the teams become powerful forces for innovation and policy and program change.

Suggested Readings

Austin, Michael J., Ralph P. Brody, and Thomas Packard. *Managing the Challenges in Human Services Organizations: A Casebook.* Thousand Oaks, CA: Sage Publications, 2009.

O'Connor, Mary Katherine, and F. Ellen Netting. *Organization Practice: A Guide to Understanding Human Services*, 2nd ed. Hoboken, NJ: Wiley, 2009.

Patti, Rino J. (ed.). *The Handbook of Human Services Management.* Thousand Oaks, CA: Sage Publications, 2009.

COMMUNITY CHANGE MODELS   Social workers are frequently involved in efforts to improve the functioning of a community and increase its capacity to address the concerns of its members. Whenever such a change is being considered, it is important to recognize that the word *community* can be defined in several ways. For example, a community might be defined as the people who live in a particular geographical area (e.g., neighborhood, town, or city) or the word *community* might be applied to the people who share a common interest, focus, or concern (e.g., people who are working to protect the environment or those who share a particular religious orientation). The selection of a particular approach to community change must be based on an assessment of the problem or concern targeted for change and, to a large extent, on political factors. If the social worker has the authority, responsibility, and/or support of others to work toward a specific community change, his or her efforts will most likely succeed. Yet even under the best circumstances, community change is a slow and time-consuming process.

Social work embraces three models of community practice, and each rests on a different set of assumptions concerning how community is defined, the change process to be followed, and the role of the professional.

The **locality development model** (or community development) presupposes that the community consists of people who share a sense of belonging to their local area and can reach a consensus on how to address community problems. It emphasizes broad citizen participation, sharing of ideas, democratic decision making, cooperative problem solving, and self-help. In the process of working on problems, people learn the practical and leadership skills needed to tackle other concerns of the community. In performing most community-level social work practice, the professional performs such functions as enabling, facilitating, coordinating, and teaching.

The model of change known as **social planning** zeroes in on specific social problems (i.e., crime, inadequate housing, lack of health care) and seeks to improve the responses of the human services delivery systems to these problems. It recognizes the complex legal, economic, and political factors that must be addressed in solving a community problem. Although involvement by ordinary citizens is welcome, the key to community problem solving and change is involvement by influential persons, government officials, and organizations that have authority, power, and influence. This approach also recognizes the vertical dimension in community dynamics and therefore the need to involve people and organizations from outside the immediate locality such as state and federal government agencies, and on some matters corporations that do business in the community. The social worker using this approach gives much attention to fact gathering, data analysis, policy analysis, sharing technical information, and program planning.

The third model, **social action**, is usually associated with efforts to correct a social injustice or achieve a needed change for a devalued or disadvantaged group (e.g., those living in poverty, those who experience discrimination). It views a community as consisting of diverse groups and special interests that are competing for power and limited resources. Thus, in order to bring about a change in human services programs, there must be a shift in the decisions of those who exercise power and influence—or new decision makers must be given authority to take action. Since it is assumed that those in control will not easily relinquish their power, change requires confrontation with those who have power. The functions of the professional within this model include those of organizing, advocating, and negotiating.

Suggested Readings

Eichler, Mike. *Consensus Organizing: Building Communities of Mutual Self Interest*. Thousand Oaks, CA: Sage, 2007.

Netting, F. Ellen, Pether Kettner, and Steve McMurty. *Social Work Practice with Communities and Organizations*, 4th ed. Boston: Allyn & Bacon, 2008.

Kirst-Ashman, Karen, and Grafton Hull. *Generalist Practice with Organizations and Communities*, 3rd ed. Belmont, CA: Brooks/Cole, 2006.

Rubin, Herbert, and Irene Rubin. *Community Organizing and Development*, 4th ed. Boston: Allyn & Bacon, 2008.

Weil, Marie. *The Handbook of Community Practice*. Thousand Oaks, CA: Sage, 2005.

Conclusion

As suggested by this survey of conceptual frameworks, the intervention approaches used by social workers have similarities but may differ in what they emphasize. Some differ in terms of basic assumptions about how and why change occurs (see Chapter 7 for additional ideas about the nature of change) and others differ in the characteristics of the clients they are intended to serve. A lifelong activity of the social worker is to carefully select a configuration of perspectives, theories, and models that matches his or her practice style and best meets the needs of his or her clients.

The reader is reminded that no one approach is always or inherently superior to others and that a social worker needs to have a basic understanding of several. One's practice framework might include multiple perspectives and an ever-growing repertoire of practice theories and models. Since all frameworks are concerned with helping people change, the worker must always be cognizant of the whole person—humans are thinking, feeling, and behaving biological beings whose survival, growth, and development depend on constant interaction with others and their environment.

Selected Bibliography

Allen-Meares, Paula, and Charles Garvin. *Handbook of Social Work Direct Practice*. Thousand Oaks, CA: Sage, 2000.

Brandell, Jerrold, ed. *Theory and Practice in Clinical Social Work*. New York: Free Press, 1997.

Coady, Nick, and Peter Lehmann. *Theoretical Perspectives for Direct Social Work Practice*, 2nd ed. New York: Springer, 2007.

Cooper, Marlene, and Joan Lesser. *Clinical Social Work Practice*. Boston: Allyn & Bacon, 2008.

Corsini, Raymond, and Danny Wedding. *Current Psychotherapies*, 9th ed. Belmont, CA: Brooks/Cole, 2011.

Dorfman, Rachelle, ed. *Paradigms of Clinical Social Work*, vol. 1. New York: Brunner/Mazel, 1994.

———, ed. *Paradigms of Clinical Social Work*, vol. 2. New York: Brunner/Mazel, 1998.

Encyclopedia of Social Work, 20th ed. (in four volumes). edited by Terry Mizahi and Larry Davis. New York: Oxford University Press, 2008.

Forte, James. *Human Behavior and the Social Environment*. Belmont, CA: Brooks/Cole, 2007.

Gilliland, Burl, and Richard James. *Theories and Strategies in Counseling and Psychotherapy*, 5th ed. Boston: Allyn & Bacon, 2003.

Gray, Mel, and Stephen Webb. *Social Work Theories and Methods*. Thousand Oaks, CA: Sage, 2008.

Payne, Malcolm. *Modern Social Work Theory*, 3rd ed. Chicago: Lyceum Books, 2005.

Prochaska, James, and John Norcross. *Systems of Psychotherapy*, 6th ed. Belmont, CA: Brooks/Cole, 2007.

Roberts, Albert, ed. *Social Workers' Desk Reference*, 2nd ed. New York: Oxford University Press, 2008.

Rothman, Jack. "Approaches to Community Intervention." In *Strategies of Community Intervention*, 6th ed., edited by Jack Rothman, John Erlich, and John Tropman, 27–64. Itasca, IL: F. E. Peacock, 2001.

Schatz, Mona S., Lowell E. Jenkins, and Bradford W. Sheafor. "Milford Redefined: A Model of Initial and Advanced Generalist Social Work." *Journal of Social Work Education* 26 (Fall 1990): 217–231.

Sommers-Flanagan, John, and Rita Sommers-Flanagan. *Counseling and Psychotherapy Theories in Context and Practice*. Hoboken, NJ: Wiley, 2004.

Sowers, Karen, and Catherine Dulmus, editors in chief. *Comprehensive Handbook of Social Work and Social Welfare*. Hoboken, NJ: Wiley, 2008.

Walsh, Joseph. *Theories of Direct Practice*. Belmont, CA: Brooks/Cole, 2006.

Using Evidence to Guide the Change Process

The admonition that the social worker should "Guide the process, not the client" is fundamental to effective professional practice, yet perhaps oversimplifies the complexity of guiding client change. One must first fully understand the client situation, help identify the change needed, engage the client in efforts to bring about that change, and, finally, evaluate the success of the change effort. To perform these tasks, the social worker must select the best knowledge and intervention strategies, engage in critical thinking about the application of the knowledge to the practice situation, and guide the client through the often difficult process of changing.

EVIDENCE-BASED PRACTICE

Increasingly, social work and other helping professions are emphasizing **evidence-based practice**, a term suggesting that the practitioner is to draw upon the strongest documented information to guide practice-related judgments and decisions. This way of thinking about practice seeks to identify and utilize those interventions that are most likely to be effective and to abandon those shown to be ineffective. This orientation strengthens the scientific basis of practice and is consistent with the National Association of Social Workers (1999) *Code of Ethics*, which states: "Social workers should base practice on recognized knowledge, including empirically based knowledge, relevant to social work and social work ethics" (Section 4.01c, p. 22). This approach calls on social workers to critically examine and evaluate their own practice, keep current on the professional literature, and remain open to the implications of new research, especially research findings on the effectiveness of various interventions.

In the past, many social workers assumed that their good intentions, compassion, common sense, and adherence to core social work values were sufficient to bring about desired changes. We now recognize that something more is required. Research tells us that some approaches and interventions are more effective than others; some approaches are ineffective; and some are even harmful. Clients deserve social workers who will think critically about their practice-related beliefs and assumptions and will search out and apply interventions that have been evaluated and found effective.

Given their heavy caseloads and time demands, social workers can easily find excuses for not spending precious time searching professional journals, textbooks, and the Internet for information to guide their practice. All too often, those excuses provide only a short respite from the time crunch and, in the long run, often create added time pressures because the most effective assessments and interventions were not applied to the client's situation and, as a result, the client's concerns or problems continue to occupy the worker's time.

Because many client situations are unique and highly complex, not all social work practice can or should be based only on evidence. Indeed, many decisions and actions must be based largely on professional values, ethics, legal statutes, agency policy, and court orders. Moreover, practice-related decisions must always consider such factors as the client's personal preferences and values and any special circumstances. But, to the extent possible, social workers must strive to base their practice on the best evidence available. The three components of evidence-based practice are evidence-based assessment, evidence-based intervention, and evidence-based evaluation.

When making an *evidence-based assessment* the social worker seeks out and makes use of theory and research data that will expand his or her understanding of the practice situation. Two sets of data are utilized; one focuses on the client's specific condition or problem while the other focuses on the client group or population being served.

In social work education, the courses that fall under the heading of "human behavior and the social environment" provide knowledge about the behavior and functioning of individuals, families, groups, and communities. Although this information is typically extensive, it usually does not provide enough depth to adequately guide interventions related to a client's particular condition or problem. Thus, the worker must search the literature for more specific information to better understand, for example, the implications for a family if a child is diagnosed with Down syndrome, or if an older parent is exhibiting signs of dementia, or perhaps if a couple is experiencing sexual dysfunction.

Another aspect of evidence-based assessment seeks to learn more about the client group or client population being served. For example, if the worker's client is an adolescent, what does the worker need to know about adolescence as a stage in human development? When working with a client who is a member of a vulnerable population group, the worker may want a better understanding of what it is like to experience discrimination. Or the worker may need to find information about a religion that is central to a specific client's life.

Fortunately, much information on various human problems, illness, disabling conditions, social problems, and various population groups is now available online, and various search engines (see Inside Back Cover) provide links and easy access to relevant websites. Additional sources are, of course, social work journals, textbooks, and documents published by organizations that focus on particular conditions, social problems, and issues.

Evidence-based practice also involves drawing on the most substantial information available about the many approaches for helping clients make needed changes, that is, *evidence-based intervention*. But how does one decide which approach is most appropriate? To answer that question, the professions are beginning to engage in "best practices" research, in which intervention approaches are carefully scrutinized in relation to success rates when applied to specific client conditions or specific client populations. Best practices research typically begins with a keyword search around the intervention being assessed and involves identifying published articles. These articles are then screened to a small number, analyzing only those that empirically evaluate the effectiveness of the intervention. The articles or research reports making the final cut are then subjected to a rigorous protocol by which a panel of experts rates each study on the quality of evidence for factors such as the alignment of the intervention to commonly held ideas regarding this intervention, the replicability of the intervention approach, the adequacy of the outcome measures used, if the intervention tested statistically across important populations that might be served, and the adequacy of controls placed on the manner in which the intervention approach was applied to the clients in the study. Where the studies that stand up to this rigorous assessment agree, best practices are identified. The National Association of Social Workers maintains a source for identifying current best practices relative to social work (http://www.socialworkers.org/research/naswResearch/0108EvidenceBased/default.asp).

The third component of evidence-based practice is *evidence-based evaluation*. In part, this is a response to those who demand that social workers document the quality of their work. For example, a managed care organization may refuse to pay for client services unless the social worker offers evidence that a particular intervention is both appropriate and effective when working with a specific client. Increasingly, social workers must clearly describe the changes or outcomes that they anticipate from the application of a specific intervention and empirically measure these changes, a topic addressed in Chapter 14.

CRITICAL THINKING WHEN MAKING PRACTICE DECISIONS

The social worker's skills in critical thinking are also essential for successful practice outcomes. Kersting defines **critical thinking** as "a process used by social workers to determine which if any sets of beliefs about a given issue warrant our using these beliefs in practice . . . (when we) do not find absolute answers." The skills of critical thinking include the following:

- Clarifying and defining key terms and concepts and using them in a consistent manner
- Determining the credibility of an information source
- Differentiating relevant from irrelevant information
- Distinguishing between verifiable and unverifiable claims and statements
- Checking the accuracy of a statement or claim
- Recognizing proper and improper use of statistics
- Separating thoughts and logic from emotions and feelings
- Identifying biased, ambiguous, irrelevant, and deceptive arguments
- Recognizing logical fallacies and inconsistencies in an argument or line of reasoning
- Reaching conclusions about the overall strength of an argument or conclusion

Critical thinking is especially important in social work because all people develop systems of beliefs or bundles of ideas that they draw upon to interpret new experiences. While such frames of reference or conceptual maps are necessary to human thought and reasoning, they are also a potential source of errors, bias, and distortion. A critical thinker, however, recognizes that all ideas (e.g., concepts, theories, definitions) are essentially inventions constructed to describe and explain our understandings and judgments at a particular point in time. Critical thinking requires recognition that these inventions may not represent "truth" about the topic, are invariably incomplete, and are likely to shift as we have new experiences or acquire more information.

Critical thinking requires an ability to distinguish between a fact, an assumption, an opinion, and a value. A *fact* is a statement of what is or of what happened that can be independently verified by empirical means. A fact is more or less solid, depending on how easily it can be confirmed. An *assumption* is an idea that is taken for granted or presumed for the sake of making an argument but is recognized as possibly untrue or inaccurate. An *opinion* puts forward one particular interpretation or viewpoint when it is understood that other credible interpretations are also possible. An opinion based on critical thinking has some factual basis, is rooted in extensive experience, and is derived from careful judgment. A value is a strongly held belief concerning what is truly worthwhile, right or wrong, and the way things are supposed to be.

In our efforts to think clearly, it is useful to distinguish between information, knowledge, and wisdom. The term *information* refers to a more or less random collection of concepts, facts, and opinions. *Knowledge* refers to an orderly and coherent arrangement of relevant and trustworthy information related to a specific topic. The term *wisdom* refers to a higher level of knowledge that has a truly lasting quality. Typically, wisdom is a distillation of key ideas and principles drawn from a broad base of knowledge, a careful and in-depth examination, and many years of practical experience. These distinctions help us realize that a person can possess much information but lack real knowledge. Also, a person can be very knowledgeable on a topic but still lack wisdom.

The critical thinker is aware of his or her susceptibility to self-deception. All too often, we believe what we want to believe and what is convenient and comfortable for us to believe. We tend to ignore facts and ideas that do not fit with our expectations. We often hold tightly to whatever we believe even in the face of evidence to the contrary. Another aspect of self-deception is our tendency to find what we are looking for. When we want support for our ideas, positions, and personal agenda, we usually find it. Moreover, we tend to look harder for evidence that supports our view than for evidence that refutes it.

An important dynamic giving rise to uncritical thinking is our desire to be right and to convince others we are right. That is why we so often become defensive when our beliefs are questioned. The more fragile our self-esteem, the more likely we are to be threatened by new ideas; the more likely we are also to uncritically accept ideas proposed by others.

To think critically about a claim or assertion, consider the following:

Purpose

- Who is making this claim? How reliable and trustworthy are these individuals or sources?
- Why do those making the claim or assertion want me to believe it?
- What motives or circumstances might cause them to make erroneous claims?
- Do they have something to gain from my acceptance of this claim or assertion?
- Am I attracted to this argument or claim because I want to believe it or perhaps because it meets some emotional need?

Evidence

- Are the terms used to present the claim clearly defined and explained?
- Is the claim or assertion rooted in facts? Opinion? Values? Ideology?
- Does the claim or assertion recognize the complexity of the matter being considered, or is it based on an oversimplification or superficial understanding of the topic?
- Are the facts and figures used to support the argument correct and complete? Have relevant facts been omitted or distorted?

Interpretation

- Could the facts and figures be interpreted in other ways or assigned different meanings?
- Have irrelevant and extraneous facts been added to the argument in order to create confusion or divert the focus from the central question?
- Has the claim or assertion been framed or stated in a way that allows it to be subjected to independent verification, objective observation, and scientific study?
- Has the claim been subjected to careful studies? Were the studies as free as possible from bias? Have the studies been replicated?

Critical thinking and a search of the literature for best practices are especially important when an unconventional intervention (such as rebirthing or conscious energy breathing, aromatherapy, crystal therapy) has been requested or suggested for use in a particular case situation. A social worker must first decide if this is a valid approach and make an informed judgment about its effectiveness and the risk of this approach for the client—and the social worker. A social worker is more vulnerable to a malpractice suit if he or she is unable to demonstrate that an intervention or treatment is the one most effective and appropriate to the client's problem or situation (see Item 16.6). Reamer (2005) suggests that a social worker should follow the procedural standard of care guidelines to help consider the ethical and legal implications of selecting such intervention approaches. He notes that this includes "eight key elements: 1) consulting colleagues; 2) obtaining proper informed consent; 3) obtaining proper supervision; 4) reviewing relevant ethical standards; 5) reviewing relevant regulations, laws, and policies; 6) reviewing relevant literature; 7) obtaining legal consultation when necessary; and 8) documenting and evaluating decision-making steps" (p. 194).

GUIDING THE PLANNED CHANGE PROCESS

Change is inevitable. Humans and all of the social systems created by humans are constantly adjusting and adapting within their ever-changing environments. Many of the changes experienced by individuals and families are set in motion by the natural consequences of biological maturation and aging, and also by personal choices such as selecting a certain occupation, taking a specific job, choosing a particular person as a spouse or partner, raising children, or getting a divorce. Still other changes are imposed on people by illness, accidents, natural disasters, and even world events such as wars and shifts in the economy. These events and experiences change the way people think, feel, and behave, and they may constrict or expand their choices and opportunities.

Although many of the changes experienced by individuals, families, groups, and organizations are unplanned, unintended, and unwelcome, others are deliberately chosen and achieved through individual and group effort. These can be termed *planned changes*. Within social work, professional efforts to help clients bring about a planned change are called *interventions*. Interventions are designed to alter some specified condition, pattern of behavior, or set of circumstances in an effort to improve a client's social functioning or well-being.

An intervention or a **planned change** is a process: a planned series or sequence of actions directed toward the achievement of a specific end. However, the use of the word *process* should not be interpreted to mean that the change effort, once begun and underway, will naturally unfold and proceed on a predictable path toward its goal. Quite the opposite is usually true. Given the complexity of change, change efforts can easily lose momentum, and movement toward a goal can easily be derailed.

In some ways, a planned change is similar to a scientific experiment: Based on knowledge and a working hypothesis, the social worker takes certain steps and then monitors the effects to determine what, if any, change has occurred. However, an intervention will usually have both expected and unanticipated outcomes.

Change—even if wanted and planned—is often difficult to achieve and requires time and effort. Consequently, some degree of reluctance and conflict, accompanied by emotion, can be expected during periods of change. The social worker who is helping others make a change must be ready to address these conflicts and be comfortable with the client's expressions of fear, frustration, and anxiety.

Resistance to change is a characteristic of humans and their social systems. People tend toward preserving the status quo. They resist change, particularly if it is rapid or especially upsetting to familiar patterns. The social worker must anticipate and be prepared to deal with resistance, even in a case where the client has demonstrated a strong desire to change.

Closely related to resistance is *ambivalence*, which is a condition of both wanting and not wanting a particular change. For example, an abused wife may want to leave her abusing husband in order to escape the abuse but at the same time not want to risk the loss of the financial security she has while married. Such a client is pulled in opposite directions and may become immobilized and unable to make decisions or take action to change the situation.

Helping clients sort through their perceptions of the risks and rewards associated with change is another important social work activity. If the potential rewards outweigh the risks, most clients will attempt the change. However, if the change involves high risk or promises few or uncertain rewards, clients may be reluctant to work toward change.

Success in making changes is largely a function of the client's motivation to change, capacity for change, and opportunity to change. *Motivation*, which can be viewed as a state of readiness to take action, represents the balance of the pull of hope and the push of discomfort. Clients will work toward a desired change if they believe this change is truly possible (i.e., the pull of hope) and if they are dissatisfied or distressed with their current situation (i.e., the push of discomfort). A client can be highly motivated toward one action while having little or no motivation toward another. Moreover, a person's level of motivation varies over time and from one social context to another. Thus, a meaningful and useful description of a client's motivation must be tied to some specified goal or action rather than being viewed as a personal trait or characteristic.

One's *capacity* for change can be thought of as the various abilities and resources that clients or other people in the clients' environment bring to the change process. These capacities include time, energy, knowledge, experience, self-discipline, optimism, self-confidence, communication skills, problem-solving skills, money, political power, and so on. Different types of change require different capacities. For example, the capacities needed by someone to perform successfully as a participant in a therapy group may be significantly different from those needed to communicate effectively with his or her teenaged son and different still from those needed to adjust to the limitations of a chronic illness.

Further, change requires *opportunities*—that is, various conditions and circumstances within the client's immediate environment that invite and support positive change. For example, consider the situation of a young man on probation who wants to find a job and stay out of trouble. His environment consists of his family, peer group, neighborhood, law-enforcement agencies, and so on, that will influence his ability to bring about the desired change. His opportunity for change may also be affected by community attitudes, the availability of jobs, discrimination, and other social forces.

When a social worker becomes involved in the change process as a facilitator of planned change, he or she adds professional resources and knowledge to the client's motivation, capacities, and opportunities. The role of the social worker in helping people to make changes can be conceptualized as taking action and applying knowledge and skills designed to increase motivation, expand capacity, and create or uncover opportunities for change.

THE CONTEXT OF PLANNED CHANGE

Whether the social worker's client is an individual, a family, a group, an organization, or a community, the client's concern or problem always exists within a wider context. A multitude of social, economic, cultural, legal, and political factors affect client functioning. However, many of these factors are beyond the influence of both the client and worker. Reality demands that the client and social worker narrow their focus and zero in on those aspects of the situation that can be influenced and changed.

For the purpose of further explaining the process of planned change, the term **client situation** is used here to describe that segment of the client's total existence, experience, and circumstances that are the focus of the planned change effort. *Decision making* is the activity of consciously choosing among available options. The social worker must be able to make difficult decisions—and help clients make difficult decisions—and do so with an awareness of the evidence being used to inform those decisions.

The *observed situation* (or objective situation) is the client's situation as observed by people in the client's environment and perhaps described by professionals using commonly understood terminology, categories, and classifications. By contrast, the *perceived situation* (or the subjective situation) is the situation as it is felt by and uniquely interpreted and subjectively constructed by the client. It consists of the client's hopes and fears, desires and aspirations, and it usually reflects the client's history and life experiences. The situation as perceived by the client may be significantly different from the client's observed situation as understood and interpreted by the social worker and others in the client's environment.

The importance of the client's perceived situation to the change process is recognized in the social work axiom, "Start where the client is." It is necessary for the worker to understand the client's concern and situation from the client's subjective point of view. It is this element of subjectiveness that makes it so difficult to predict how clients will respond to a given intervention.

An awareness of the contextual and situational aspects of social functioning and planned change yields several fundamental guidelines for social work practice:

- The social worker must give primary attention to the client's problem or concern as it is defined, perceived, and experienced by the client.
- The worker must focus primarily on those aspects of the situation and the client's environment that most immediately and directly affect the client.
- The intervention must address those aspects of the situation over which the client and/or the worker have some control and influence.

- The social worker must recognize the multitude of forces pushing and pulling on the client but understand that the actual impact of those forces is at least partially dependent on the client's subjective interpretation.
- The worker must be prepared to intervene at one or more levels (e.g., individual, family, organization, community), depending on the nature of the client's concern, the client's interpretation of the situation, what the client wants to do about it, and what the client can reasonably expect to be able to do about it.
- The worker must be prepared to use a variety of techniques, approaches, and services since whatever is done must make sense to the client, given his or her perceptions and interpretations of reality.

Within all client situations, there are factors and forces pushing and pulling the client toward healthy, positive, and constructive functioning. These are often called strengths (see Item 11.5). At a fundamental level, most social work approaches to planned change are efforts to encourage, guide, and build on the positive forces already at work in the client's life and, at the same time, to remove or overcome barriers that block change.

IDENTIFYING ACTORS IN PLANNED CHANGE

Efforts by a social worker or agency program to facilitate change typically involve numerous individuals, groups, and organizations. In complex situations, and especially in mezzo- and macro-level practice, dozens or even hundreds may be involved. To be effective, the social worker must be clear about the purpose and goal of each intervention and clear as to what is expected of each of the many actors in the change process. Drawing from a conceptualization proposed by Pincus and Minahan (1973, p. 63), we suggest the following terminology to help make needed distinctions among the various actors:

- *Change agent system.* The social worker and the worker's agency
- *Client system.* The person, group, or organization that has requested the social worker's or agency's services and expects to benefit from what the worker does
- *Target system.* The person, group, or organization that needs to change and is targeted for change in order for the client system to benefit and overcome its problem. (In many situations, the client system and the target system are one and the same.)
- *Action system.* All of the people, groups, and organizations that the change agent system (e.g., the social worker) works with or through in order to influence the target system and help the client system to achieve the desired outcome

An episode of practice typically begins with the client system and the change agent system coming together and contracting to address a particular client concern. They identify the person(s), group(s), or organization(s) that need to change and then reach out to and involve others to help facilitate the change. For example, a single mother (the client system) may approach and contract with a human services agency to receive counseling from an agency social worker (the change agent) on how to help her 10-year-old son who is withdrawn and socially isolated because he is ridiculed or teased by schoolmates. If both the mother and child need to change, both would be target systems. If the social worker draws the child's teacher, the school principal, and the school psychologist into the helping process, these become part of the action system. If the intervention also attempts to change the behavior of the other children at school, they are also part of the target system.

PHASES OF THE PLANNED CHANGE PROCESS

An intervention or planned change activity typically moves through several sequential phases, with each phase building on previous ones. The uniqueness of each phase is that the social worker is focusing on a specific action, information, decision, or outcome. If the social worker is to guide the change process, he or she must become an expert regarding the tasks that must be accomplished at each phase.

Descriptions of these phases have been a part of the social work literature throughout the history of the profession. In her classic book, *Social Diagnosis*, Mary Richmond (1917) described several steps necessary in helping people. Forty years later, Helen Perlman (1957) echoed the same theme when describing helping as a problem-solving process that involved three major phases: (1) beginning with *study* that would ascertain and clarify the facts of the problem, followed by (2) *diagnosis*, where the facts would be analyzed, and concluding with (3) *treatment* that involves making choices and taking actions to resolve the problem. In subsequent years, various authors divided these phases into more discrete units, described them in more detail, and demonstrated their application in a range of helping approaches and in work with client systems of various sizes. Elements of the planned change process typically include:

- Identify, define, and describe the client's concern, troublesome situation, or problem.
- Collect data needed to better understand the client's concern or situation and its context.
- Assess and analyze the concern and situation and decide what needs to change, what can be changed, and how it might be changed.
- Identify and agree upon the goals and objectives (outcomes) to be achieved by the process of planned change.
- Formulate a relevant and realistic plan for reaching the goals and objectives.
- Take action based on the plan (i.e., carry out the intervention).
- Monitor progress of the intervention and determine if it is achieving the desired outcomes and if not, modify the plan and try again.
- Once goals and objectives have been reached, terminate the intervention and evaluate the change process to inform future practice activities.

The logical progression of these phases makes the process appear to be a linear, step-by-step set of activities. In reality, change rarely proceeds in an orderly fashion; rather, it is more of a spiral, with frequent returns to prior phases for clarification or a reworking of various tasks and activities (see Figure 7.1). During each phase, the worker also anticipates future phases, tasks, and activities and lays the groundwork for their completion.

Intake and Engagement	Data Collection and Assessment	Planning and Contracting	Intervention and Monitoring	Final Evaluation and Termination
Begin the relationship; identify and define the client's concern or problem; determine eligibility for service.	Gather information and "study" the problem or situation; decide what needs to change, what can be changed, and how it can be changed.	Formulate objectives; evaluate possible strategies; agree on an intervention plan; determine who will do what and by when.	Carry out the plan; monitor progress; revise the plan if it is not achieving the desired results.	Evaluate overall progress; bring the relationship to an end; give feedback to the agency about how services and programs might be improved.

FIGURE 7.1   Phases of the Planned Change Process

At any given time, it is helpful to be clear about where the client is in the process of planned change, because the worker draws on somewhat different techniques to accomplish the tasks of each phase. What is helpful in one phase might be ineffective or even counterproductive in another. For example, it would be an error for a worker to discuss with an abusive mother her possible participation in an anger management group (i.e., planning and contracting) when she has not yet concluded that there is something inappropriate and harmful about how she disciplines her child (i.e., data collection and assessment).

Conclusion

The belief that planned change can resolve problems or create better lives for people is embedded in Western culture and especially in U.S. society. Faith in the ability to change human interactions and social conditions is at the very heart of social work practice and is a prerequisite characteristic of effective social workers.

When engaged in guiding a planned change process, the social worker makes several important contributions. The social worker understands the whole process necessary for change and guides the client(s) through the several phases, being sure that the key decisions or actions to be accomplished at each phase are indeed completed. The social worker also contributes critical insights that the client would not normally be expected to possess. This includes seeking out and engaging in evidence-based assessment—in terms of drawing on the best evidence found in the literature regarding people with the client's characteristics, evidence regarding the issues to be addressed in the practice situation, and the relationship between the two factors. In addition, the social worker

should have researched the "best practices" to use in that client's situation (evidence-based intervention) and should be competent in using that approach or skilled in referring the client to someone who is. Finally, throughout the process the social worker must engage in critical thinking that can lead to sound decision making to improve the chances of a successful practice outcome.

The five phases of the planned change process described in Figure 7.1 are an important part of the structure of this book. Because the phases reflect activities that should be accomplished as the practice episode unfolds, it is possible to identify various practice techniques and guidelines that are most likely to be helpful in each phase. In Chapters 10 through 14 more than 100 techniques and guidelines are presented. A description of the work to be done in each phase is provided in each chapter's introduction and the various items are divided into those most likely to be used in providing services directly to clients, and those that support the indirect practice activities in which social workers are typically engaged.

Selected Bibliography

Briggs, Harold E., and Tina L. Rzepnicki, eds. *Using Evidence in Social Work Practice*. Chicago: Lyceum, 2004.

Cournoyer, Barry R. *The Evidence-Based Social Work Skills Book*. Boston: Allyn & Bacon, 2004.

Fischer, Joel. *Toward Evidence-Based Practice: Variations on a Theme*. Chicago: Lyceum, 2008.

Kersting, Robert C. "Critical Thinking and Evidence-Based Practice in Social Work." Paper presented at 25th Annual BPD Conference, March, 2008. rkersting@wsc.ma.edu.

National Association of Social Workers. *Code of Ethics*. Washington, DC: NASW, 1999. (http:\\www.naswdc.org/pubs/code/default.asp).

Perlman, Helen. *Social Casework: A Problem Solving Process*. Chicago: University of Chicago Press, 1957.

Pincus, Allen, and Anne Minahan. *Social Work Practice: Model and Method*. Itasca, IL: F.E. Peacock, 1973.

Reamer, Frederic G. "Nontraditional and Unorthodox Interventions in Social Work: Ethical and Legal Implications." *Families in Society: The Journal of Contemporary Social Services* 87 (2006): 191–197.

Richmond, Mary. *Social Diagnosis*. New York: Russell Sage Foundation, 1917.

Techniques Common to all Social Work Practice

The two chapters in Part III focus on techniques and guidelines that are fundamental to social work practice, regardless of agency setting or type of client served. This content lays a foundation for understanding and applying the more specialized techniques and guidelines that appear in Parts IV and V.

In every setting, the social worker must be a skillful communicator and able to develop relationships. Thus, several items focus on the skills and tools of effective communication and relationship building. Although many of the examples are drawn from direct service, most are also applicable in administrative, community organization, and social planning activities.

Few beginning-level workers are prepared to cope with the time pressures and paperwork they encounter. Items in Part III also offer information on time management, managing a workload, maintaining client records, and writing reports. Given an expansion of computer applications in social work, a worker must acquire at least the basics of information technology and know how to access online resources.

Because social work can be a stressful occupation, workers must be able to apply principles of stress management in order to handle job-related pressures. Throughout his or her career, the social worker must strive to continually learn and grow as a professional. The worker's ability to master these tasks often determines whether he or she will be successful and thrive in social work.

Basic Communication and Helping Skills

This chapter presents what might be called "the basics" of social work communication and relationship building. It focuses on generic communication and basic helping skills—those used with all clients, whether an individual, a family, a small group, an organization, or a community.

The purpose of a social worker's interaction with a client will determine what type of relationship he or she attempts to create and, of course, his or her messages to the client. A worker providing direct services (e.g., counseling) to individuals and families will strive to develop a professional relationship characterized by those qualities known to positively affect the outcome of the helping process, such as acceptance, empathy, personal warmth, and genuineness. By contrast, the indirect-services worker who is, for example, interacting with the members of an agency board or a committee, will build relationships that are more formal and place an emphasis on communication characterized by precision, clarity, and goal directness.

Essentially, **communication** is a process in which one individual conveys information—either intentionally or unintentionally—to another. Communication is a form of behavior, but not all behavior is communication; it depends on whether a person perceives a message in the words or behavior of another. Communication occurs when one person attaches meaning to the verbal or nonverbal behavior of another. Communication is primarily a receiver phenomenon; regardless of what the sender may say in words or intend to communicate, it is the person on the receiving end who assigns meaning to another's words and gestures.

It is important to recognize the complexity and limitations inherent in our efforts to communicate. Because each individual is a unique personality and has had a unique set of life experiences, he or she has various perceptual filters and patterns of thought that affect how messages are sent and received. Thus, one individual may notice things that others overlook, and messages that are important to one person may seem inconsequential to another.

Communication involves the use of words. A word is but a symbol. Thus, a word may have somewhat different meanings to different people, depending on their belief system, life experiences, capacity of abstract thinking, and familiarity with the language being used. The words of a language have literal, or denotative, meanings (i.e., dictionary definitions) and they may also have an implied or connotative meaning. Moreover, the meaning of a word, phrase, or nonverbal gesture may depend on who is using it and the social or situational context.

Communication depends on the functioning of the physical senses (e.g., vision, hearing) and the cognitive activities of the brain, which include **attention** (focusing on certain stimuli while disregarding others); **perception** (using pattern recognition and sensory memory to interpret stimuli picked up by our senses); **memory** (retaining information over time); **language** (interpreting, expressing, and remembering verbal and written words and symbols); **conceptualization** (organizing information and ideas into categories); **reasoning** (drawing conclusions from information); and **decision making** (choices based on an anticipation of future events). These cognitive processes are interrelated and overlapping. If the senses are impaired (e.g., a hearing loss) or if the brain has been damaged, the ability to communicate will be limited to some degree.

One of the most important factors affecting people's communication is their **self-concept**, or how they define and view themselves in relation to others (see Item 11.9). One's self-concept acts like a screen through which he or she sees, hears, and interprets the messages from others. For example, an individual who feels incompetent or inferior may be guarded and find it difficult to speak honestly and listen attentively to others. The defensive and insecure individual may find it difficult to accept direction, instruction, or constructive criticism.

The capacity to send and receive messages accurately can also be limited by one's emotional state and expectations. In general, we tend to hear what we want to hear and what we expect to hear. We may also distort messages sent by others in order to meet our emotional needs or avoid discomfort. Individuals with certain personality disorders characteristically distort messages in a self-serving fashion.

The lack of clear communication is a common cause of problems within families and organizations. In general, communication problems develop in these situations:

- When we speak for others rather than allowing them to speak for themselves
- When we discourage or suppress communication by ordering, threatening, preaching, patronizing, judging, or blaming
- When we allow our prejudices and presumptions to color our interpretations of what others are saying
- When we do not take the time or make the effort to really listen
- When we do not speak honestly and truthfully because we want to avoid conflict or fear disapproval from others
- When we assume that others already know or should know what we think

8.1   CREATING AN EFFECTIVE HELPING RELATIONSHIP

The nature of a professional relationship is shaped by the reason why the social worker and client are meeting, the clients presenting concern or request, an agency's program and procedures, and the practice framework utilized by the social worker. A positive relationship between the social worker and client is necessary but by itself is not sufficient to facilitate change. The application of change-producing techniques is also necessary. Without a positive relationship, change is not likely to occur. With a positive relationship, the various helping techniques and skills are more likely to have their intended effect. It is important to note that a positive and effective helping relationship is not free of interpersonal tension. Because change is difficult, a relationship intended to promote change will be somewhat stressful and taxing for both the client and the social worker.

Some type of relationship will develop whenever a social worker and client interact. It may be either positive or negative, depending mostly on the client's interpretation of the worker's words and actions. A social worker cannot make a positive relationship happen. At best, the worker can strive to be the type of professional that most clients find helpful. Research has identified a number of qualities that characterize a helpful and therapeutic relationship. At the very heart of these relationships is **human caring**. A social worker must genuinely care about his or her clients. Clients expect a social worker to be knowledgeable, but they will not pay much attention to what the worker knows until they are convinced that he or she really cares. **Trust** is always basic to the relationship. When clients trust a social worker they have faith and confidence in the worker's integrity, ability, and character. Trust develops when the client experiences the social worker as truthful, dependable, and competent.

The quality of **empathy** is the social worker's ability to perceive the client's inner experiences of thought and feeling. It is often described as the capacity to step into the client's shoes.

Empathy is conveyed by giving the client undivided attention and by applying the techniques of active listening to demonstrate that the worker understands the client's feelings and perceptions (see Item 8.4).

Unconditional positive regard exists when the social worker views a client as having inherent worth and treats him or her with respect, regardless of what the client may have done in the past or how he or she behaves during an interview. The word *unconditional* is meant to convey the notion that clients are to be treated with fairness and thoughtfulness simply because they are human beings, not because they have somehow earned the right to such treatment.

The display of unconditional positive regard is closely related to the admonition that a social worker should maintain a *nonjudgmental attitude* in his or her work with clients. We are judgmental when we make harsh and negative moral judgments and express them in ways that disparage clients, whether verbally or nonverbally. Whenever clients feel they are being judged or criticized, they become defensive and may withdraw from the relationship. Thus, in order to be helpful and to facilitate positive change by the client, the social worker must be able to suspend making moral judgments within the professional relationship. Needless to say, there are times when this is difficult to do. A social worker is most likely to become judgmental when the client has violated the worker's own cherished values and moral principles such as having abused a child or committed a murder or rape.

To say that the social worker should strive to be nonjudgmental is not to suggest that he or she cannot or should not make professional and objective judgments concerning the client's attitude, behavior, or functioning. Neither does it mean that the worker must condone harmful and inappropriate behavior. A client's inappropriate and destructive behavior will need to be discussed and confronted if it is related to the client's presenting concerns and/or the reason he or she is involved with the worker's agency. However, the unacceptable behavior must be discussed in an objective manner, not in a way that will denigrate or deprecate the client.

The relationship characteristic of **personal warmth** exists when the social worker responds to clients in ways that help them to feel safe and accepted. Without the quality of warmth, the worker's words will sound hollow and insincere and have no therapeutic impact. Warmth and acceptance are conveyed mostly through nonverbal communication, such as a smile, a soft and soothing voice, a relaxed but interested posture, and appropriate eye contact.

The quality of **genuineness** refers to a professional who is real and speaks from the heart. Social workers who are genuine and authentic are unpretentious and spontaneous. What they say matches what they do. They lack any hint of phoniness. However, genuineness is not the same as being totally honest about all things, for the worker must be sensitive to the needs and emotional state of the client. When a worker has negative feelings toward a client, he or she exercises self-discipline so that these thoughts and feelings do not damage the professional relationship.

Those who are new to social work sometimes worry that they cannot simultaneously assume a professional role and at the same time, be real and genuine in their relationships with clients. That concern reflects a misunderstanding of professionalism. Being a professional has nothing to do with playing the role or trying to imitate some image of a professional person. A true professional is caring, knowledgeable, self-disciplined, responsible, ethical, and, most of all, effective. There is no conflict between those qualities and being genuine.

In addition to caring, trustworthiness, empathy, positive regard, personal warmth, and genuineness, certain other conditions have been identified as important to a helping relationship: **concreteness** (being able to communicate one's thoughts and ideas in ways that are understandable and clear to the client), **competence** (proficiency in carrying out professional tasks and activities), and **objectivity** (being unbiased and able to appreciate differing points of view).

In some situations the building of a professional relationship can be enhanced through the use of **structuring**, a term that refers to various arrangements (e.g., worker–client matching) and symbols (e.g., worker dress and office environment) intended to make the professional more attractive to and trusted by the client. The use of structuring is based on the premise that clients are most likely to be influenced by someone they respect and with whom they feel comfortable. This will often be someone who the client perceives as similar to themselves in terms of fundamental beliefs and life experiences. Thus, a social worker might find it useful to mention similarities they share. For example, the worker might point out that he or she and the client both have children of about the same age or that they share the experience of having grown up on a farm.

Whether the similarities and differences between the client and the worker have a significant impact on the helping relationship is mostly a function of the client's expectations and perceptions. Davis and Proctor (1989, p. ix) suggest that a client who is different from the social worker in terms of race, gender, or socioeconomic status is likely to have three concerns:

- Is this social worker a person of goodwill? Does he or she have my best interests at heart? Does he or she dislike people like me?
- Does this worker have the expertise and skills necessary to resolve my problems?
- Can this worker understand my social reality, background, and life experiences?

How the client answers these questions will determine if the worker is viewed as trustworthy and credible and whether the guidance offered by the worker are accepted as worthwhile.

Expertness, or the appearance of expertness, can have a positive impact on the initial phases of the helping process. Such things as certificates and diplomas on the wall, a well-furnished office, and professional attire can help to provide a positive first impression. To the extent possible, offices and meeting rooms should be inviting, private, and comfortable. The social worker's waiting room and office can have an impact on clients, either positive or negative. If a client must talk with the social worker in a space that lacks privacy and comfort, respect for the worker is diminished. While the social worker must be alert to the importance of such factors, he or she should remember that clients, like all people, make deliberate decisions about whose influence they accept and whose they reject.

Selected Bibliography

Brammer, Lawrence, and Ginger MacDonald. *The Helping Relationship*, 8th ed. Boston: Allyn & Bacon, 2003.

Davis, Larry, and Enola Proctor. *Race, Gender and Class: Guidelines for Practice with Individuals, Families and Groups*. Englewood Cliffs, NJ: Prentice Hall, 1989.

8.2   VERBAL COMMUNICATION SKILLS

Social workers make frequent use of two broad categories of verbal skills: (1) those intended to facilitate interpersonal helping and (2) those intended to facilitate the exchanges of information within an agency, between agencies, and among professionals. Those used in direct-practice activities (e.g., face-to-face work with individual clients, families, therapeutic groups) are described in Item 8.4. The verbal skills in the second category are presented here.

Communication involves both a message sender and a message receiver. The sender has a responsibility to convey his or her message in a way that is easily received and understood. The receiver has a responsibility to make sure that he or she has accurately received the sender's intended message and has not, in some way, distorted or misinterpreted that message. Thus, when **sending a message**, follow these rules:

- Use clear, simple language. Speak distinctly and not too fast.
- Pay attention to your body language; make sure it is congruent with your message. Maintain appropriate eye contact and utilize gestures.
- Do not overwhelm or overload the receiver with information. Break up a lengthy or complex message into several parts so that it can be more easily understood.
- Ask for comments, questions, or feedback so that you will know whether your intended message is received and understood.

When in the position of listening to or **receiving a message**, remember these rules:

- Stop talking. You cannot listen when you are talking.
- Put the message sender at ease and remove distractions.
- Be patient with the message sender and do not interrupt.
- Ask questions if it will help you understand or help the sender to clarify his or her message.

The skill of **planning a message** refers to anticipating an upcoming episode of communication and structuring your message around the answers to questions or concerns, such as the following:

- How much time is available for this exchange?
- When and where am I most likely to have the full attention of the person who is to receive my message?
- What are the essential points of my message?
- What aspects of my message are most likely to be misunderstood?
- How can I organize and present my message so it will be understood and accepted by the receiver?
- Do I have the necessary credibility, position, and status to deliver this message or should someone else present this message?

Because it is the middle portion of a message that is most likely to be distorted by the receiver, the most important points should be placed at the beginning and the end of your message.

The skill of **identifying self** is a concise description of who you are and how your role and responsibilities relate to the conversation. For example:

> You may remember me from a previous meeting, but let me begin by introducing myself. My name is Mary Jones. I am a social worker with the Evergreen Family Services Center. A client of mine has asked me to speak with you to find out if . . .

The skill of **explaining the purpose of the communication** refers to the sender's statements that explain the reason or purpose of the communication. This helps the receiver place the message in a proper context. For example, a child welfare worker speaking to a prosecuting attorney might say:

> As you know, my agency has 10-year-old Billy Johnson in one of our foster homes. I need to speak with you in order to get a clear idea about when you plan to have Jimmy testify in court. This is important to me because I have to inform his school of a planned absence and also work out Billy's transportation to the courthouse.

Sometimes, it is important to respond to a receiver's nonverbal communication if it suggests some confusion over the sent message. The skill of **following up on nonverbal communication** refers to such efforts. For example:

> John, I noticed that you looked a bit puzzled when I was explaining the new agency procedure. If you have a question, please ask me at this time.

Such follow-up efforts are especially important when the receiver's nonverbal behavior or communication suggests that he or she disagrees with the message. Here is an example:

> When I was explaining the proposed policy change, I could not help but notice that several of you were looking rather distressed. As your supervisor, I want to know how you feel about the proposal. Bob, Anna, and Judy—please share your thoughts on the proposed policy change.

Sending a message of complaint or constructive criticism is always a challenge because it can so easily put the receiver on the defensive and block further communication. The technique called the **I-statement** or *I-message* refers to a particular way of structuring and wording a message so as to minimize that possibility. To understand the I-message, it is important to recognize that during times of conflict, confrontation, and hurt feelings we so often use "You-statements"; for example: "You need to study more," "You make me angry," and "You are being selfish and rude." Such you-messages cause the person on the receiving end to feel put down and wanting to strike back.

An I-statement consists of three parts: (1) a brief, clear description of the troublesome behavior, (2) the resulting feeling experienced because of that behavior, and (3) a description of the tangible impact this behavior has had on the message sender. For example:

> When you did not show up for our scheduled appointment (troublesome behavior), I felt upset and angry (feeling) because I don't like having to wait around and because I could have spent that time with another client (tangible impact).

The structure of an I-statement allows the sender, the person bothered by the behavior of another, to say, in effect: "This is my concern, this is how your behavior affects me, and this is how I am feeling." Implicitly it says: "I will trust you to decide what change is needed." It gets a point across without sounding accusatory.

The skill of **checking for message reception** refers to the use of questions and probes to determine whether your message has been accurately received. For example:

> I am aware that what I have just described is complex and potentially confusing. I want to make sure you understand. Would you please repeat to me what you heard me say?

When on the receiving end of a message, it is desirable to use the skill of **checking one's receipt of a message**. This involves using probes and questions to verify that you have, in fact, accurately received and understood the message. For example:

> Before we end this conversation, I want to make sure that I understand what you have told me. Let me take a minute and repeat what I heard you say. If it sounds like I have misunderstood something, please correct me.

It is surprisingly difficult to ask questions. All too often, we attach unnecessary words or extraneous concerns to our basic question, and this can confuse the point of our query. In order to receive a clear answer, your question must be clear. This calls for the skill termed **asking a focused question**. Consider first this example of a very awkward question directed to an agency administrator:

> I am confused about these new agency policies, especially the ones about foster care and, in some ways, about a lot of the policies. This policy manual is organized in an unusual way. What is really expected of us? I mean, what are we supposed to do with new cases and how do we handle the court-ordered evaluations?

It would be difficult for the administrator to give a clear answer because several questions have been asked and all of them are rather vague. The question would be much more focused if phrased like this:

> I have a question about the policy described on page 86 of our agency manual. My question is, do I need my supervisor's written approval before I request a psychological evaluation on a foster child?

The skill of **answering a question** refers to the ability to formulate statements that respond directly to the question asked and answer the question in a clear and complete manner. This seems simple; however, people often fail to carefully listen to a question. In the following example, a supervisor makes this error but then makes a correct response:

> WORKER: I need some direction on where to send this report. Do I send it to the County Attorney or directly to Judge Smith?
>
> SUPERVISOR: Just remember that Judge Smith is a stickler for details and he wants the report to be concise.
>
> WORKER: Well, yes, I know that but what I need to know is where to send the report.
>
> SUPERVISOR: Oh, I'm sorry. I didn't answer your question. Send it directly to Judge Smith.

Many communication problems arise because people attach different meanings to words or phrases. The skill of **checking for word meaning** refers to inquiries intended to make sure that all parties to a message exchange agree on the meaning of key words. Consider the following example:

> CHAIR OF PLANNING GROUP: I think we need to shift about 20 percent of our budget into child abuse prevention programs.
>
> COMMITTEE MEMBER (checking for meaning of words):   Well, I may or may not agree, depending on what you mean by prevention. Are you thinking of primary or a secondary level of prevention?

Selected Bibliography

Allen, Gina, and Duncan Lanford. *Effective Interviewing in Social Work and Social Care.* New York: Palgrave, 2006.

Burley-Allen, Madelyn. *Listening: The Forgotten Skill.* New York: John Wiley and Sons, 1995.

Sidell, Nancy, and Denice Smiley. *Professional Communication Skills in Social Work.* Boston: Allyn & Bacon, 2008.

8.3   NONVERBAL COMMUNICATION SKILLS

Experts tell us that about 65 percent of the communication occurring during a face-to-face exchange is nonverbal. In other words, the messages are conveyed mostly by means of gestures, facial expressions, eye movements, and tone of voice. Much of this nonverbal activity is habitual and beyond our awareness. Consequently, we sometimes say one thing with our words and without knowing it communicate something quite different in our nonverbal behavior.

Eye contact is a powerful means of communication. Our eyes reveal much about our emotional state and our reactions to other people. In most Western cultures (e.g., North America, Europe), making eye contact indicates openness and a willingness to engage in communication, whereas avoiding eye contact is viewed as being closed to communication and sometimes suggesting a dishonest intention. In other cultures, such as those of many Native Americans and people from Asia and the Middle East, making direct eye contact is considered to be intimidating, disrespectful, and/or even sexually aggressive. Moreover, in these and other cultures, a private conversation between unmarried men and women may be judged as inappropriate.

Gestures of greeting are important to relationship building. In North America a firm handshake is the expected gesture among both males and females. However, for many people from Asia and the Middle East, a strong and firm handshake suggests aggression. An embrace or hug is a common greeting among males in Russia, the Middle East, and Latin America. Bowing is the appropriate gesture among the people of Japan, Thailand, and India; the lowest ranking person bows first, and the depth of the bow reflects the status of the person for whom the bow is offered.

Personal space is another important nonverbal element in interpersonal communication. In general, being close to someone communicates trust and interest, but being too close is threatening. People from North America typically prefer to be about an arm's length from one another, whereas those from Asian cultures usually prefer a greater distance. People from the Middle East and Latin America are often toe-to-toe during their conversations. The worker can avoid invading a client's personal space by reading the client's body language and adjusting accordingly.

Body positioning conveys various attitudes and intentions. It is usually best to face the client at a 90-degree angle, since this suggests both safety and openness. Facing the client directly may communicate aggressiveness. Leaning slightly toward the client communicates attention and interest. A desk separating the client and social worker restricts closeness, encourages formality, and suggests the worker is in a superior position.

Facial expressions—such as smiling, frowning, nodding and shaking the head, lip quivering, and blushing—register our thoughts and emotions. The face is the most expressive part of our body and makes us most vividly present to others. Facial expressions may reveal a worker's disapproval of a client, even when the worker is trying to be nonjudgmental.

Touch is a powerful communication. For example, by touching another's hand, arm, or shoulder or by offering a gentle hug, we can convey reassurance, sympathy, or understanding. However, a social worker must be cautious about touching a client, especially if the client is of the opposite sex or from an unfamiliar cultural background. A social worker's innocent and well-meaning touch can be misinterpreted as a sexual advance or as intimidation by someone who has been physically or sexually abused or by someone with an intense need for attention and affection.

Arm and hand movements frequently communicate strong emotions. Crossed legs, arms folded across the chest, and a rigid posture suggest a defensiveness and resistance, whereas arms and hands in an outreached position or at the body's side suggest openness to others. Clenched fists indicate anger or anxiety. Fidgety movements, finger tapping, and leg bouncing suggest impatience, nervousness, or preoccupation.

Tone of voice will often reveal the emotion we are feeling. A loud and forceful tone suggests anger, aggressiveness, and control. A meek and scarcely audible voice suggests fear and submissiveness. A monotonous or flat voice suggests a lack of interest.

Dress and appearance are also important forms of nonverbal communication. Our choices of clothing and accessories (e.g., jewelry) and our hairstyle send a message about who we are or who we want to be and may display our membership in a particular social group or subculture. A social worker must give careful thought to his or her appearance and avoid choices that might distract clients or make them feel uncomfortable. Clothing that is highly unusual or sexually suggestive should always be avoided.

Selected Bibliography

Kavanagh, James. *Worldwide Gestures*. Blaine, WA: Waterford Press, 2000.

Knapp, Mark, and Judith Hall. *Nonverbal Communication in Human Interaction*, 7th ed. Florence, KY: Wadsworth-Cengage Learning, 2010.

Remland, Martin. *Nonverbal Communication in Everyday Life,* 3rd ed. Boston: Allyn & Bacon, 2009.

8.4   HELPING SKILLS

As used here, the term **helping skill** refers to a message that the practitioner deliberately sends to the client because the worker believes it will have a beneficial effect. The moment-to-moment decisions concerning what message to send is guided by the purpose of the interview and by what the social worker knows about the client and his or her situation. All helping skills have nonverbal components (see Item 8.3).

Below we offer brief descriptions of commonly used helping skills. In several instances, terminology is borrowed from Shulman (1981, 2009). The examples used to illustrate a particular skill are drawn from one-on-one interviews, but these skills can also be applied in work with families and therapeutic groups. Many of the more specialized techniques presented in the remainder of this book are elaborations and special adaptations of the skills described here.

GETTING READY

Prior to the meeting the client face to face, the worker should imagine and consider what the client might be thinking and feeling as he or she enters the agency expecting to discuss some personal and possibly a very painful matter. By trying to anticipate how the client might feel, the worker begins to develop empathy for the client and prepares to address the client's initial reactions and feelings (e.g., anger, fear, confusion) and plan ways to ease the client into the helping relationship. Shulman (2009) has termed this the *tuning-in phase* of the helping process (see Items 10.1, 10.2, and 13.1).

GETTING STARTED

During the intake and engagement phase of the change process and also at the beginning of each session with a client, the social worker must clarify the purpose of the meeting and the worker's role. The helping skill of **explaining purpose** refers to a simple, non-jargonized statement by the worker that describes the general purpose of the meeting. It serves to define expectations and reduce client confusion and anxiety. For example:

> WORKER: I am pleased that you were able to meet with me today. As you know, your wife first came to this agency about three weeks ago. She expressed concern about your marriage. I would like to hear your thoughts and find out if you also believe there are problems in the marriage.

When the client initiates the first contact, the worker should encourage the client to begin by describing his or her reason for requesting the interview. If the client has a hard time doing this, the worker might ask some general questions about the circumstances that led up to the request for the interview and what the client hopes will come from the meeting.

When the social worker has initiated the first contact, he or she should begin by explaining its purpose in a manner that is clear, direct, and to the point. Consider these two examples of explaining purpose:

> GOOD EXPLANATION: I need to talk with you about your son, Max. He has missed 14 of the last 20 school days. I am concerned and I would like to get your thoughts on this problem.

> POOR EXPLANATION: Hi there. I know your son Max. I was in the neighborhood so I decided to stop by to chat. How are things going?

The skill of **encouraging the client's feedback on the purpose of the communication** (Shulman, 1981) refers to statements that encourage the client to respond to the worker's explanation. This gives the client an opportunity to ask questions or perhaps voice disagreement. Here are two examples:

> WORKER: What are your reactions to what I have said about the purpose of this meeting? Do you perhaps see things differently?

> WORKER: It's quite possible you and I have different thoughts about why we are talking today. I want to know if you were expecting something else.

The skill of **describing the worker's role and method** refers to statements intended to give the client a beginning idea of how the worker might be able to help and the methods to be used. For example:

> WORKER: As you get ready to leave this hospital, it is important to anticipate the problems you may face when you get home. That is why I want to meet with you two or three times before you leave. I will ask for your thoughts about what your adjustment will be like and I will share my ideas, as well. Between the two of us, I hope we can come up with a plan that will minimize the difficulties that you encounter when you return home.

Each session with a client has three time phases: (1) getting started, (2) the central work of the session, and (3) drawing the session to a close. At the beginning of each session, the social worker should provide an opportunity for what Shulman (1981) has termed **sessional contracting**. Even when there has been a prior agreement on how the session's time will be used, it is important to check once again for consensus. Quite possibly, some change in the client's situation has altered the client's priorities. The skill of **reaching for between-session data** (Shulman, 1981) may be used to initiate the sessional contracting. This form of checking-in involves asking the client to bring the worker up to date and to identify the key topics to be discussed. This effort is an attempt to adhere to the principle of *starting where the client is*. For example:

> WORKER: You will recall that during last week's session we agreed to spend today's session talking about your reluctance to visit your children who are in foster care. Do you still think that is how we should spend our time today, or do you now have a more pressing concern?

ASKING QUESTIONS

A social worker uses various types of questions to obtain needed information and assist the client in expressing his or her thoughts and feelings. A question such as "What are the names of your children?" is termed a *closed-ended question* since it limits how the client can respond. By contrast, a question such as "Tell me about your children" is called an *open-ended question* because it gives the client an opportunity to say whatever he or she thinks is important. However, open-ended questions can vary in the amount of freedom they allow. These three questions are all open ended, but some are more open than others:

> "Tell me about your job."

> "What do you like and what do you dislike about your job?"

> "What tasks and responsibilities are parts of your job?"

During counseling sessions, the worker will use mostly open-ended questions. Closed-ended questions are useful when the worker needs specific information or when the client is so confused or overwhelmed that some structure is needed to maintain a focus and direction.

The skill of **narrowing the focus** (or *funneling*) refers to a series of questions intended to assist the client in describing his or her concerns or situation with more specificity. For example:

> CLIENT: Things are a real mess at home.

> WORKER: What do you mean by "a mess"? What happened?

> CLIENT: Well, we were eating when Dad came home from work. He was drunk again and ended up hitting Mom.

> WORKER: What did you do when all this was happening?

> CLIENT: First, I ran out of the house. Then I came back and yelled at my dad to stop or I would call the cops.

> WORKER: What were you thinking and feeling at the time you threatened to call the police?

A worker should never ask questions out of mere curiosity or to fill a silence. Other common errors in questioning include the overuse of closed-ended questions, stacking questions, asking leading questions, and asking too many "why" questions. **Stacking questions** refers to the undesirable practice of asking several questions at once. Consider this example of stacking:

> WORKER: So, you are interested in adoption. How long have you been thinking about adoption? Have you known others who have adopted? Are you thinking about an infant? Have you thought much about an older child or one who has a disability?

Stacked questions are confusing to clients. It is best to ask questions one at a time.

Leading questions are those that push or pull the client toward giving a certain response—for example, "Didn't you think that action was wrong?" or "I assume that you explained to your boss why you missed work?" or "Isn't it true that you were hoping for a fight?" A leading question may prompt the client to lie rather than openly disagree with the worker. Leading questions often offend or insult the client.

Another common error is to ask **why questions**—for example, "Why do you get so angry when Maria spills food?" Essentially, "why" questions ask the client to justify his or her behavior and this tends to produce defensiveness. Moreover, most people do not know or cannot articulate the "whys" of their behavior, so, when asked "why" they simply guess or give socially acceptable answers. Instead of asking why, use questions that focus on the what, where, when, and how of the client's behavior and situation.

ACTIVE LISTENING

Listening—really listening—is exceedingly difficult. Everyone wants to believe that he or she is a good listener, but few of us are. We humans are by nature rather self-centered; we like to be the center of attention and the object of interest. That is why listening to others is so difficult. In order to listen, we must set aside our self-centeredness and make another person the center of our attention.

In active listening, the worker attends to both the client's verbal and nonverbal messages and reflects back to the client what has been heard so that the client will know that his or her message has been received and understood. The skills of active listening are those of using encouragers, clarification, paraphrase, reflection, summarization, and exploring silences.

An **encourager** (also called a *prompt*) refers to a word, short phrase, or nonverbal gesture that encourages the client to continue talking or expand on what he or she has said. Examples of verbal encouragers are "Uh-huh," "Tell me more," "Please go on," and the repetition of a key word just uttered by the client. Nonverbal encouragers include nods of the head and hand gestures that signal an invitation to continue and say more.

The technique or skill of **clarification** refers to asking a question intended to encourage a client to become more explicit or to verify the worker's understanding of what the client has said. Such questions might begin with "Are you saying that . . . " or "Do you mean that . . . " and continue with a rephrasing of the client's words. For example:

CLIENT: My life is a disaster. I thought I could get things squared away, but it doesn't look like that will be possible.

WORKER: I am not sure I am following you. Are you saying that things are changing more slowly than you expected or that your situation is now worse than before?

When confused by what a client is saying, it is best to acknowledge the confusion and seek clarification. For example:

WORKER: You are talking very fast. I cannot keep up and I am getting confused. Please start over, one point at a time. Also, try to slow down so I will not miss anything.

A skilled social worker focuses on both the client's words and on the affect or the emotion associated with the words. To do this, the worker will make frequent use of the paraphrase and reflection. The skill known as **paraphrasing** is a rephrasing of the literal meaning of the client's statement, whereas the skill termed **reflection of feeling** is an expression of the feeling or emotional component of the message. Examples of paraphrase and reflection are as follows:

CLIENT: That guy down at the employment office is a real jerk. How does he get away with treating people like that? I feel three inches tall when I go down there.

WORKER: I hear you saying that when you go to that office you are treated badly.
(a paraphrase)

Or

WORKER: It sounds like you are angry and feel humiliated at the employment office.
(a reflection of feeling)

The skill of **summarization** refers to pulling together both the content and affective components of several client messages. For example, a worker might use summarization to draw together the key elements of what was discussed during the previous five minutes. Here is an example of summarization:

WORKER: From what you have been saying, I am hearing a number of things. You are desperate for a job and feel a mix of anger and discouragement because you haven't found one. You have been going to the employment office but that adds to your feelings of shame and frustration. On top of that, you are beginning to feel regret for having dropped out of high school. Is that an accurate summary of what you have been telling me?

Active listening requires careful attention to times when the client is silent. Silence is a behavior that has meaning. Sometimes it is important to uncover that meaning. The skill of **exploring the client's silence** refers to efforts to gently probe the silence. For example:

CLIENT: (thoughtful silence)

WORKER: You appear to be puzzling over something. Can you tell me what you are thinking about?

An error commonly made by beginning social workers is to respond to silence with a change of topics. This happens because the worker feels uncomfortable when the client is quiet. A brief silence is best responded to with patience and polite quietness. If the silence is a long one, the worker should explore the silence.

DISPLAYING EMPATHY, GENUINENESS, AND WARMTH

Item 8.1 of this chapter described the importance of empathy, genuineness, and personal warmth in a helping relationship. A number of skills or techniques are used to display these qualities to the client. The skill of **displaying understanding** refers to verbal and nonverbal communication intended to demonstrate that the social worker comprehends and can identify with the client's thoughts and feelings. For example:

CLIENT: Having to place Susan in foster care is one of the most difficult decisions I have ever made.

WORKER: It must be hard and painful to make a decision that will be upsetting to Susan. It seems like this decision is tearing you apart inside.

It is especially important to acknowledge and display an understanding of a client's negative feelings such as anger and resentment. For example:

CLIENT: I am sick of this place. I don't need to be in this treatment program. I feel like punching the next person who asks me about my drinking.

WORKER: Well, I am a part of this treatment program and you know that I will ask about your drinking. I guess that means you want to hit me. I am not sure how to respond to your threat. What are you expecting me to do?

The skill of **putting the client's feelings into words** refers to the articulation of what the client appears to be feeling but has stopped just short of expressing it in words. For example:

WORKER: How did the visit with your mother go?

CLIENT: OK, I guess, but I don't know if I can take this much longer.

Worker: Watching your mother die is causing you unbearable distress. It sounds like you hope death will come soon, but I am wondering if such a thought makes you feel guilty. Is that the way you are feeling?

This helping skill gives the client a supportive invitation to express what he or she is reluctant to say aloud. Here is another example:

WORKER: Do you have any other questions about adoption or our agency's adoption program?

CLIENT: No, I don't think so. You explained it pretty well. I guess it's a lot different from what I expected.

WORKER: You sound disappointed. Can you tell me how you are feeling about what I have told you?

It is important to recognize that encouraging a client to express feelings is appropriate only when those feelings are related to the overall goals of the professional relationship and intervention.

The helping skill of **self-disclosure** refers to a worker's statements that reveal some of his or her own thoughts, feelings, or life experiences. When properly used, self-disclosure can make it easier for the client to talk about a sensitive topic and feel more comfortable with the worker. Consider these two examples of worker self-disclosure:

WORKER: I can understand how frustrated you feel about your teenaged son. I went through a similar experience when my son was an adolescent. There were times when it seemed like he was from another planet. His self-centeredness and preoccupation with what I felt were superficial fads just drove me nuts! But eventually things change. Now, 15 years later, my son is married, has two kids, he is a good father, and he has a very responsible job. I once heard grandchildren described as "God's reward for not killing your children."

WORKER: I am sorry about how I reacted to you on the phone. I guess you have noticed that I get kind of weepy when we talk about your mother's death. That touches me deeply. I am struggling with grief since my mother died a year ago.

As a general rule, the use of self-disclosure should be avoided in the early stages of relationship building and used sparingly at other times. The personal information revealed by the worker should always have a clear connection to the client's concern. It is inappropriate for the worker to talk about personal experiences that are unrelated to the client's concerns or the purpose of the interview.

Another complicated issue for social workers is deciding how to go about **answering personal questions**. Clients might ask workers a whole range of personal questions, such as: Do you have children? Did you ever go through a divorce? What is your religion? Have you ever used drugs? Have you ever been fired from a job? Whether and how the worker answers such questions will depend on his or her best guess as to why the client wants to know and how an answer will affect the professional relationship. There are many reasons clients might ask social workers personal questions. For example, the client may want to know if the worker is capable of understanding the client's situation. The client may be checking out whether the worker is going to be judgmental. Not infrequently, the client asks personal questions simply because he or she is curious. And in some cases, the client is trying to manipulate the worker (see Item 10.8).

Typically, we feel most comfortable with people whom we perceive are similar to us in terms of values, beliefs, and life experiences. This holds true for the client–worker relationship, as well. Thus, when asked a personal question, the worker may want to offer a simple, straightforward answer, if doing so will establish some common ground for mutual understanding. On the other hand, the worker should side step the question if the answer will underscore or highlight their differences in values, beliefs, and so on. Also, the worker should side step any question that seems to be a client's attempt to manipulate the worker or divert the discussion away from the purpose of the meeting.

SUSTAINING CLIENT MOTIVATION

In order for people to make a change, they must be motivated to change. They must feel hopeful about the possibility of change and in addition, feel some discomfort or dissatisfaction with their current situation. Several skills can be used to increase or sustain a client's motivation for change.

Displaying a belief in the potential of work (Shulman, 1981) refers to statements intended to convey the worker's belief that professional intervention can be helpful. For example:

WORKER: The problems you have described are serious. I can understand why you feel overwhelmed. But if we work together and start chipping away at the problems, one at a time, I believe you will be able to successfully deal with these problems. It won't be easy, but I believe you will make some progress over the next few weeks.

The skill of **recognizing client strengths** refers to expressions of confidence in the client's capacity to accomplish some specific task or to cope with a difficult situation (see Item 11.5). For example:

WORKER: I know it is going to be painful for you to visit your kids in their foster home, but your visits are important to the children. You possess the special quality of being honest and upfront with your children. For those reasons, I think you will be able to explain to them why you must now get inpatient treatment and why you cannot take care of them at this time.

The skill of **pointing out negative consequences** refers to statements that remind the client that change is needed in order to avoid undesirable consequences. For example:

WORKER: When you talk about wanting to drop out of the sex offender treatment program, I must warn you of the consequences. If you do not work on your problems and demonstrate a capacity to control your attraction to children, the judge may revoke your probation and you will go to prison.

MAINTAINING PROGRESS TOWARD CHANGE

Effective helping involves encouraging and assisting the client to make decisions, take action, and move ahead. From time to time, the worker must make realistic, gentle, and supportive demands that the client face his or her problems and take the steps necessary to make a needed change. Tackling a personal problem usually involves examining one's assumptions and behavior. This can be difficult, painful, and even embarrassing. Real change requires having to try out new behaviors and perform unfamiliar tasks. A degree of fear, ambivalence, and resistance is a normal part of the change process. In fact, a lack of some ambivalence and resistance by the client may indicate that what may appear like an effort to change is, in reality, only an illusion. Shulman (1981) explains that:

The worker must make a consistent **demand for work**. The demand may be expressed in many ways, but it is generally experienced by the client as the worker saying: "I mean business." It is a critical skill because it conveys to the client the worker's . . . willingness to deal with even the toughest problems and feelings faced by the client. It is precisely this additional pull that clients need at that moment to mobilize their strength and to take their next steps. . . . The demand for work needs to be linked closely to the empathic skills. . . . A worker who is demanding, but not empathic, will be seen by the client as rejecting. On the other hand, the worker who is empathic, but makes no demands, will appear to the client as easy to put off. It is a critical synthesis of these two behaviors that will lead to effective work. (p. 20)

The word *encouragement* literally means to give courage or to help another overcome fear. Thus, the skill of **providing encouragement** will often take the form of statements that express confidence in the client's ability to overcome an obstacle or deal with a difficult situation. The worker's words must be genuine and individualized to the client's situation. For example:

> WORKER: I know that the reoccurrence of your cancer is devastating news and that you want to spare your children the pain of knowing the truth. However, they are waiting to hear what you have learned from the doctor. This is one of those times when it is especially difficult to be a mother. This is a time when you must be very strong for your children. It will be hard to tell them but it needs to be done.

Statements of **reassurance** are used when the client is experiencing doubt and uncertainty about his or her decisions and actions when they are, in fact, reasonable and realistic. Such worker statements must be based in reality. Trite and thoughtless comments such as "I am sure everything will be OK," or "You can do anything you set your mind to" are inappropriate and insulting to the client. By tying words of reassurance to the facts of the client's situation, the worker can provide reassurance and support without sounding phony or naïve. For example:

> WORKER: Even though you are now feeling scared and unprepared, I think you will be able to handle this new job assignment. I say that because over the past two months you have successfully taken on three new and difficult job-related responsibilities. That prior success is a clear demonstration that you possess the skills needed for the new assignment.

The skill of **partialization** refers to the activity of breaking down a large problem or action into several smaller and more manageable components, steps, or phases so that the client can more effectively focus his or her attention and energy. For example:

> CLIENT: I cannot believe this is happening. Jimmy fell and cut his head and I took him to the hospital. That crazy doctor notified child protective services and accused me of abusing Jimmy. Then my oldest son got into a fight with the landlord, and now the landlord has asked me to find another apartment. I cannot afford a lawyer, my child support check is late, and, on top of everything else, my car won't start. Things are so screwed up I cannot even think straight. The whole world has fallen in on me.

> WORKER: I think we better talk about your concerns one at a time. Otherwise, we will feel overwhelmed and get confused. Let's first focus on the child abuse report. Later, we will return to the other problems. First, tell me more about Jimmy's injury and the abuse report. For now, let's talk only about that problem, OK?

The skill of **staying on track** involves worker statements intended to keep the client focused on a particular concern or objective. This skill is especially important when a client tends to ramble, go off on tangents, or wants to avoid facing a pertinent issue. For example:

> WORKER: Because your boss has now threatened to fire you, I think we better focus on that concern.

> CLIENT: Yeah. I guess so. I really wish I could get a transfer. But the company has such old-fashioned policies on things like that. I'm surprised they make any money at all. With the economy the way it is, you would think they would modify the whole operation. They are not prepared for global competition. I recently read an article on new styles of management and. . . .

> WORKER: We need to come back to the conflict between you and your supervisor. You have lost other jobs because of conflict and disagreements. I know you need this job, so I think we need to figure out a way of dealing with the problem you are having with your supervisor.

The skill of **building a communication link** refers to efforts by the worker to establish a connection or link between the client and those individuals with whom he or she needs to communicate. For example:

WORKER: This is the third time you have told me that you haven't been able to tell your doctor about your concerns. Would you give me permission to call her office and explain that you have a worry and that you need to talk to her about it? I think that might cause her to spend more time with you when she visits you in the hospital tomorrow. Is that OK with you?

Sometimes, a client will display the outward appearance of having agreed to a certain action but inwardly lack a real commitment to the plan. It is also fairly common for a client to decide on an action without fully considering the challenges he or she will encounter. The skill of **checking for acquiescence** is used to flush out a client's hesitation, ambivalence, or disagreement. For example:

WORKER: I certainly agree that you should talk to your math teacher about your failing grade. That needs to be done and I am pleased to hear that you intend to do it. But I also know that you have felt intimidated by that teacher. In what way will talking to him be a difficult or stressful thing to do?

Because facing up to a personal problem and trying to make a change is inherently difficult, a client's strong feelings (e.g., frustration, anger, discouragement) and emotionally charged exchanges between the client and worker are to be expected during the helping process. If over a period of several sessions, the client displays little or no emotion and little frustration with self and the slowness of change, it is likely that the client is not really engaged or invested in the change process. The skill of **challenging the client's avoidance of change** is an effort to point out the client's resistance to taking on the hard work of personal change. The next example illustrates the use of this challenge during a couple's marriage counseling session:

WORKER: Something concerns me. When you two came to this agency a few weeks ago, you requested help with your marriage. We have met three times. However, both of you have spent most of our time talking about your jobs and your desire for a new house. You seem to be avoiding any real discussion of your marriage and how you get along. Unless we focus on your marriage we are not going to make progress. What is your response to what I am saying?

A client's progress is sometimes blocked because he or she does not want to grapple with especially painful feelings. The skill of **identifying emotional blocks** refers to messages aimed at increasing the client's awareness of how these feelings are getting in the way of progress. For example:

WORKER: I have noticed something and we need to talk about it. We started meeting together because you wanted help in learning how to handle your children's behavior. Yet, each time I ask about your daughter Gloria, you become tense and fidgety and start talking about the other children. What is it about your relationship with Gloria that makes you so uncomfortable?

In some cases, the change process is blocked when a client has unusual difficulty talking about a pertinent but embarrassing or perhaps disgraceful situation such as irresponsible sexual behavior, damaging spending habits, or crimes. The skill of **supporting the client in taboo areas** (Shulman, 1981) refers to worker communication intended to support or assist the client in discussing a sensitive or awkward topic. For example:

CLIENT: I always feel nervous when I get to the topic of sex. It's hard for me to talk about it because of the way I was raised.

WORKER: You are not alone. Many of us were raised the same way. But it is clear that you and your husband need to discuss your sexual relationship. That area in your marriage is causing you some serious problems. It's difficult to discuss and sort of embarrassing for you, but let's keep at it.

Some clients have had difficulties with authority figures (e.g., parents, employers, police) and view the social worker as one more authority wanting to boss them around and exert control (see Item 10.7). The skill of **addressing the authority issue** refers to a worker's message that invites the client to express concerns or complaints about the worker's real or perceived authority and power in the helping process. Consider this illustration:

CLIENT: I think things are now a lot better at home. I don't think we need to set up another meeting.

WORKER: I hope things are better, but I think something else is going on here. I have the impression that you think my job is like that of a parole officer and that I am trying to catch you doing something wrong. How about that? Are you possibly afraid of me because I could make trouble for you?

BRINGING THINGS TO A CLOSE

Not infrequently, clients will wait until the last few minutes of a session before bringing up an important issue. There are several possible motives behind this *doorknob communication*, such as fear of the topic, wanting to inform the worker of a concern but not wanting to discuss it, and so on. The skills of **setting time limits** and **giving a 10-minute warning** are ways of encouraging the client to bring up and to remain focused on high-priority concerns. Here are a couple of examples:

WORKER: Before we begin, I want to remind you that we can talk until 4:00 P.M. I say that because I want to make sure that we use our time to discuss issues that are of greatest importance to you.

WORKER: I just noticed that we have about 15 minutes left until we need to end this session. Have we gotten to all the topics you wanted to discuss or is there something else that you wanted to talk about today?

The skill of **looking ahead to the end** is designed to remind the client of a planned ending for the intervention so that the best possible use can be made of the remaining sessions. For example:

WORKER: When we began meeting a month ago, we agreed to meet for eight times. We have three sessions left. Let's discuss what remains to be done so we will use those three sessions to focus on your high-priority concerns.

The client–social worker relationship may end because their work together is finished, because the social worker must transfer the client to another professional, because insurance benefits have elapsed, or for other reasons. If the relationship has been a meaningful one, the ending may be difficult. Because many clients have experienced losses during their lives, the ending may be painful because it reactivates feelings attached to prior losses. These feelings must be addressed directly by the worker. Shulman (1981) explains that

> . . . because of the general reluctance to face endings, both on the part of the worker and the client, endings often are handled too quickly, without an opportunity for the client and worker to deal with the complex feelings involved. . . . Since the client needs time to deal with the ending . . . it is important for the worker to point out the ending well in advance . . . . It is only when workers can come to grips with their own feelings that they can begin to help the client in this important phase. (pp. 26–27)

The social worker can help the client deal with the separation by voicing feelings about termination. This skill is named **sharing ending feelings** (Shulman, 1981). For example:

WORKER: I have been thinking about our relationship. Since you came to this hospital in September, we have gotten to know each other very well. I am glad you are finally able to go home, but I want you to know that I will miss our discussions and miss your positive, upbeat attitude.

It is important to encourage the client to express his or her feelings about termination. These may be positive or negative or a mix of both. The skill of **reaching for ending feelings** (Shulman, 1981) refers to worker communication that helps the client articulate these feelings. For example:

WORKER: I know you are pleased about getting off probation. You are no longer required to see me. But I also sense that you have some mixed feelings about our meetings coming to an end. Am I correct about that?

A review of what the client and worker have done to address the client's concerns is another important element in termination. This skill is referred to as **reviewing progress**. Here is an example:

WORKER: Altogether, we have been meeting for about four months. A lot has happened since you were reported for child abuse. You have made some positive changes in how you deal with your son, Michael. As you think back over the past four months, what specific changes do you see in your behavior and attitude?

(See Item 14.7 for more information on termination.)

Selected Bibliography

Farber, Barry A. *Self-Disclosure in Psychotherapy*. New York: Guilford Press, 2006.
Hill, Clara. *Helping Skills*, 2nd ed. Washington, DC: American Psychological Association, 2004.
Murphy, Bianca, and Carolyn Dillon. *Interviewing in Action*, 3rd ed. Belmont, CA: Brooks/Cole, 2007.
Shulman, Lawrence. *Identifying, Measuring and Teaching Helping Skills*. Alexandria, VA: CSWE, 1981.
———. *The Skills of Helping: Individuals, Families, Groups, and Communities*, 6th ed. Belmont, CA: Brooks/Cole, 2009.
Sommers-Flanagan, John, and Rita Sommers-Flanagan. *Clinical Interviewing*, 4th ed. Hoboken, NJ: Wiley, 2009.

8.5   ENHANCING CLIENT MOTIVATION

If a person is to make changes in his or her functioning and situation, the desire or motivation to change is an indispensable ingredient. But what can be done when the client lacks motivation and is denying a serious personal problem such as an addiction, a mental illness, or abusive behavior? In such situations, **motivational interviewing** may offer a strategy and helpful guidelines. This approach is built on the premise that one's level of motivation is ever changing. Motivation is not a personality trait: rather it comes and goes and its strength varies in response to one's perceptions, thoughts, mood, and situation. Since motivation develops within the person, external pressures do not, by themselves, increase motivation. In fact, threats or jarring confrontations often generate additional defensiveness and resistance.

Clients are more committed to a goal or a plan (e.g., treatment, sobriety) when the goal is of their own choosing, rather than imposed by others. Thus, motivational interviewing avoids argumentation and debate and simply creates a safe and supportive environment in which the client can lower his or her defenses and examine his or her thoughts, feelings, and desires. When using this approach, the practitioner is especially sensitive to how the client is responding to the idea of having a problem or needing to change and adapts his or her messages to these responses and to the client's ever-changing level of motivation.

The skills and techniques of active listening (see Item 8.4) are used to engage the client in a discussion of his or her situation in ways that will highlight the discrepancy between the client's behavior (e.g., drug use) and his or her values and goals such as, for example, his or her desire for improved self-esteem, health, success on the job, and being a good parent. Gradually, he or she will come to the conclusion that his or her current behavior (e.g., the drinking) is indeed a barrier to achieving what is important and conclude that change is in his or her self-interest. The social worker uses affirmations (recognizing client strengths) to build the client's confidence that change is possible and will also offer information and suggestions but always in ways that respect the client's right to decide whether and how to address the problem.

The following guidelines will prove useful when a social worker encounters a client who denies the existence of a serious problem or is resistant to the idea of addressing the matter.

1. Any attempt by a social worker to increase a client's motivation must be based on an understanding of when and why people seek change and the factors or situations that may trigger a client's decision to work toward a needed change. Examine your own assumptions about personal change. Recall the challenges and frustrations that you have experienced when trying to rid yourself of some annoying habit.

We humans are surprisingly adaptable. After living with a problem or troublesome situation for many years, we may, simply accept it, organize our lives around its existence, and quit trying to change it. Once we get use to having a problem, we may have a hard time even imagining a life apart from the problem. Our adaptations to the problem become intertwined with the other aspects of our lives, such as the choice of friends, job and career, household budgets, leisure time activities, and dozens of other choices and daily routines. Strange as it seems, we can reach a point where we are afraid to eliminate a long-standing problem because its absence would disrupt so many of our other habitual and familiar patterns of thought and behavior.

2. People naturally resist changes to their usual patterns, lifestyle, and ways of making sense of life. It is normal for people to be ambivalent about change. We are especially annoyed when others tell us that we have a problem and need to change. Realize that the resistant client has reasons for not wanting to change; examples include: the sheer difficulty of change, a history of prior unsuccessful efforts to change resulting in a pessimism about the possibility of change, a fear that a change will bring with it more disadvantages than benefits, the existence of other concerns requiring attention, a disagreement on what constitutes a problem and who might need to change, and so on.

Demonstrate empathy for and an understanding of your client's reasoning about why change is unnecessary, even when you see things differently. Avoid making any statements that may sound argumentative, fault-finding, or critical such as: "How can you really believe that you do not have a problem?" or "Can't you see that your life would be better if you would change?" If your client is becoming more defensive or resistant, it is probably because you are saying things in a way that is judgmental, confrontational, or insensitive to the client's situation.

3. Since the timing of what is said to the client is of critical importance, a social worker is continually assessing and monitoring the client's readiness to change. To facilitate that assessment, DiClemente and Valasquez (2002) describe the five levels or stages in a cycle of change. These are pre-contemplation, contemplation, preparation, action, and maintenance.

Individuals are said to be in the *pre-contemplation stage* when they have no intention of changing, either because they are unaware of their problem or because they completely reject the concerns expressed by others. During the next stage, *contemplation,* individuals are aware that a problem exists and they are at least thinking about and considering the need to do something about it. When in the third stage, *preparation,* individuals have decided that they want to change and are beginning to formulate a plan for making the desired change. During the *action stage* individuals are taking steps to bring about the desired change. And finally, during the *maintenance stage* the individuals are striving to maintain the changes they have made and are working to prevent backsliding or a relapse. A person who is in the process of making changes will cycle through these various stages numerous times. Change does not proceed in a step-by-step or linear fashion. Meaningful change always entails some steps forward and some backward. Setbacks, stumbles, and relapses are a normal and expected part of the overall change process.

It is critically important to offer messages and ideas especially relevant and suited to a particular stage or level. Thus, the social worker is always listening and watching for indications of where the client is at in this cycle of change. What the workers says to the client must be tailored to that particular stage and the client's readiness for change. If the client resists the worker's message that indicates the worker is getting ahead of the client.

The three guidelines presented below focus on the first three stages: pre-contemplation, contemplation, and preparation. Many techniques and guidelines appropriate for use during the fourth stage (action) and the fifth stage (maintenance) appear in Chapters 12 and 13 of this book.

4. When interacting with a client who is in the stage of *pre-contemplation,* the social worker seeks to plant some seeds that may germinate later. Explore, listen with empathy, and seek to truly understand the client's perceptions, rationale, and explanations of why he or she does not have a problem (i.e., a problem or concern reported by or complained about by others). Encourage the client to identify his or her goals and values and then in a gentle and non-threatening manner explore how the client's current choices, behavior, or patterns do and do not help the client reach those goals and conform to his or her stated values and ideals. For example, if a man says something like "I want to be a better father to my children than my own father was to me," the worker might then explore and discuss whether the time he spends at the bar or with his drinking buddies helps him to be a better father or keeps him from being the father he wants to be. Call to the client's attention the obvious discrepancies between what they want for themselves and loved ones and what they are actually doing. It may take weeks, months, or even years for the client to struggle with and mull over the reality of his or her situation and finally reach a point or decision and a readiness to work on the problem.

5. When the client is in the stage of *contemplation* it is important to realize that just because the client is now acknowledging a problem that does not necessarily mean that he or she is ready and willing to actually work toward a change. Many people can accurately describe their problems and wish aloud that things were different, but they never get around to changing anything. Before they make the hard choice to take action, they must believe and feel that change is really possible and that they are capable of doing what will be required. During this contemplation stage, the worker's task is to engage the client in an analysis of the risks and rewards and the advantages and disadvantages of addressing the problem.

Because the client is ambivalent, maybe fearful of change, and has doubts about whether change is possible, the worker's messages should be ones that tip the balance in favor of deciding to change. Thus, encourage the client to elaborate on any of his or her statements that sound as if the client is thinking about the disadvantages of his or her current situation (the status quo) and or thinking about the possible advantages or benefits of a changed situation. Do this no matter how tentative the client might be. Also, encourage the client to expand on any of his or her statements related to the potential for change and wishing to try something different. Call to the client's attention his or her prior successes with change and facing difficult life challenges.

Provide information on the realities and stresses to be faced during a change effort so that the client will understand what is required and possibility of success.

6. During the stage of *preparation* the client is ready to change and has made at least a tentative commitment to change, but is still wrestling with ideas about how to go about making a change. The client is unsure of what steps or actions might actually work. For the social worker, the task is to help the client maintain this momentum toward change and to select specific steps or actions that will be appropriate, realistic, and effective. Some clients will start to have second thoughts about trying to change as they see more clearly what it will actually require.

When working with clients who are in the preparation stage, the social worker will be asking questions and encouraging discussion that helps the client examine the various ways that change might be achieved and anticipate possible barriers and pitfalls. For example, the worker might ask: When will you start? What is the first step? The second? Why is that particular action needed and important? What will your first week of change be like? Who else needs to be involved in making and carrying out this plan of action? Who will encourage you and who might sabotage your plan? How will you know if your plan is working? If it does not work, do you have a backup plan?

A client's plan for change is more likely to succeed if it identifies and lists the many small but necessary steps needed to bring about the change and includes a method for the ongoing monitoring of progress. (Also see Items 10.7. 11.5, and 13.9.)

Selected Bibliography

Arkowitz, Hal, Henry Westra, William Miller, and Stephen Rollnick, eds. *Motivational Interviewing in the Treatment of Psychological Problems*. New York: Guilford Press, 2008.

DiClemente, Carlo, and Mary Valasquez. "Motivational Interviewing and the Stages of Change", in Miller, William, and Stephen Rollnick, eds. *Motivational Interviewing*, 2nd ed. New York: Guilford Press, 2002.

Miller, William, and Stephen Rollnick, eds. *Motivational Interviewing*, 2nd ed. New York: Guilford Press, 2002.

Rollnick, Stephen, William Miller, and Christopher Butler. *Motivational Interviewing in Health Care*. New York: Guilford Press, 2008.

Smith, Jane, and Robert Meyers. *Motivating Substance Abusers to Enter Treatment*. New York: Guilford, 2008.

8.6   UNDERSTANDING EMOTIONS AND FEELINGS

Many of the clients served by social workers are confused, frightened, or overwhelmed by their emotions, and many have not learned to express their feelings in a healthy manner. A social worker must be able to discuss the nature of emotions in ways that clients can understand and gain greater control over troublesome feelings and emotions.

Although the words *emotion* and *feeling* are often used interchangeably, it is useful to view an emotion as a particular physiological and psychological response or reaction and a feeling as one's subjective awareness of that response. **Emotions** are complex, physical, biochemical, and psychological reactions to conscious and unconscious interpretations of an event or an experience. Neuroscience is just beginning to understand how emotions arise within us and how normal emotions can go awry, as when, for example, fear grows into a phobia or sadness turns into a disabling depression.

The word *emotion* means "to move." Our emotions move us or motivate us to take action. They are a form of primitive survival wisdom that is programmed into our very being. Emotions warn us of danger and pull us toward actions that will meet our basic needs. For example, the emotion of fear moves us to withdraw from a dangerous situation, whereas anger moves us to attack those who threaten harm. The emotion of sadness attracts the attention and caring of people. The emotion of remorse or guilt moves us to correct misbehavior, rebuild damaged relationships, and make amends for the harm we have caused. The emotion of anticipation moves us to persist in our efforts to reach a goal.

Emotion is a type of communication that signals our state of mind and intentions to others. The facial expressions that reflect emotions such as joy, sadness, fear, and anger are recognizable around the world, regardless of culture.

Emotions vary in intensity. For example, joy can range from serenity to ecstasy, fear can range from apprehension to terror, and anger from mild annoyance to rage. While all emotions involve some level of physiological change, the bodily reactions that accompany the primitive fight-flight emotions such as fear, anger, panic, and terror are the strongest of all. Emotional reactions can overpower one's capacity to think clearly and make rational decisions. The power of emotion to influence behavior is most evident in the reactions of children and adolescents. As an individual matures, he or she grows in the ability to maintain self-control.

It is important to understand that emotions are a response to our subjective interpretation of what we have encountered. The usual sequence is as follows: (1) an event or situation occurs; (2) we notice, interpret, and think about that event; (3) depending on our interpretation, we have a particular emotional response; and (4) this emotion may elicit a certain behavior.

Out interpretations may or may not be accurate. Also, because of past conditioning (learning), we may interpret certain experiences in a habitual (unconscious) manner that involves little or no analysis. The conditioning associated with a prior painful life experiences may cause us to misread a situation and thereby elicit emotions and behaviors that others judge to be inappropriate or irrational. An example is a woman who is afraid of all men because she was sexually abused by one man. Some emotional reactions are immediate and do not involve conscious thought. For example, no analysis is necessary to interpret an attacking dog as a danger and quickly move to escape.

We respond emotionally not only to our interpretations of an event but also to our own feelings and behavior. For example, as we experience an emotion, we may think about whether it is right or wrong to be feeling as we do, and these thoughts may elicit still other emotions. In other words, we often pass judgment on our own emotional reactions and these judgments or thoughts cause still other emotions to arise within us.

Because of the interplay between thought and emotion, we can to some degree alter and control our emotions and feelings by striving to modify the ways we think about and interpret events and experiences. Several steps are involved:

1. *Noticing our feelings.*   Certain bodily sensations inform us that an emotional response is occurring. However, many of us tend to ignore or deny these sensations. Consequently, we may need help in learning to recognize the bodily reactions associated with emotion. One approach is to stop periodically throughout the day and reflect on our body's sensations and ask, for example, "What part of my body is experiencing emotion?" "Does some part of my body feel tense or strange?" "Is my body trying to get my attention?" "What thoughts and interpretations are giving rise to these emotions?"

2. *Naming our feelings.*   Assigning a name to our emotions and feelings helps us to accept them as real and provides a beginning sense of control. But attaching a label to something as nebulous as a feeling is not easy. Many people lack a vocabulary for feelings. A list of feeling words may be of assistance in this naming process (see Item 13.16).

3. *Owning our feelings.*   Before we can gain control over an emotion or feeling we need to acknowledge its existence and claim it as our own. That can be a challenge if we are in the habit of denying our feelings. Owning a feeling can be made easier if its name is spoken aloud, possibly to another person (e.g., "I am afraid" or "I am feeling sad"). Many people are surprised to discover that this simple acknowledgement and verbalization helps them cope with troublesome feelings.

4. *Looking under and behind our emotions.*   Our emotions are a window through which we can glimpse our underlying and often unconscious interpretations. For example, when feeling anxious or fearful, we might ask ourselves, "Why does this situation seem so frightening or threatening?" "Is it really threatening or am I interpreting it this way out because of a prior painful experience?" "Are there alternative ways of interpreting this experience?" By looking at things from a different angle, we can often lessen the impact of negative emotions and feelings.

5. *Examining our habits of thought.*   Our ways of interpreting and thinking about our experiences are often learned during childhood. Thus, in order to understand and modify troublesome thoughts and feelings, it may be necessary to reevaluate what we learned and experienced during our childhood. We must decide if what we habitually tell ourselves about ourselves and our situation (i.e., our self talk) is valid in our current situation (see Item 13.7).

6. *Choosing a course of action.*   Even when we cannot change our emotional reaction to a particular situation or event, it is still possible to make choices about how to act and behave. We can make better choices if we ask ourselves the following questions: "When I feel this way, what choices do I have?" "Is my first or instinctive response (e.g., attacking if I am angry) an appropriate one under the circumstances?" "What destructive behaviors must I avoid?" "What responses hurt me or others?" "Which response would be most beneficial to me and others?"

Selected Bibliography

Greenberger, Dennis, and Christine Padesky. *Mind Over Mood.* New York: Guilford, 1995.

Lewis, Michael, Jeanette Haviland, and Lisa Barrett, eds. *Handbook of Emotions*, 3rd ed. New York: Guilford, 2008.

Plutchik, Robert. *Emotions in the Practice of Psychotherapy.* Washington, DC: American Psychological Association, 2000.

8.7   RESPONDING TO DEFENSIVE COMMUNICATION

A social worker, especially one who is working with mandated clients, will encounter individuals who are angry, afraid, defensive, and guarded in their communication. The client may use a number of defensive maneuvers to keep the social worker at a distance. These include, for example, *denial* (e.g., I do not have a drinking problem!), *blaming others* (e.g., I wouldn't have to hit her if she didn't make me so mad), *avoidance* (e.g., I forgot about our appointment), and *pleading helplessness* (e.g., It's no use trying; nothing can ever change). Some clients may curse or ridicule the worker. Some use their physical environment (e.g., drawn shades, vicious dogs) and style of dress as means of intimidation and a way of keeping people at a distance.

It is likely that the individual who is defensive and resistant within a professional relationship was defensive and perhaps resentful and defiant long before he or she met the social worker. However, in some cases a worker's behavior or style can make the situation even worse. For example, the worker is likely to increase a client's defensiveness and anger if he or she keeps the client waiting, is brusque and insensitive, is judgmental or authoritarian, uses bureaucratic jargon and often quotes agency rules, and calls the client by his or her first name without permission.

By following these guidelines, the social worker can help to reduce a client's defensiveness:

1. View defensiveness as an attempt to protect oneself from some real or imagined danger. Within a context of social service delivery, the threats perceived by clients might be embarrassment, loss of privacy, loss of control over one's life, or the failure to receive a desired service or benefit. You may lessen the client's fear by acknowledging the awkwardness of the situation (e.g., "I know that it can be embarrassing to ask for financial assistance"). To the extent possible, give your client opportunities to make choices and thereby maintain some control over what is happening. When appropriate, use words and phrases such as "we," "together," and "it will be your decision" for such words imply choice and cooperation. Because people become defensive when they experience a loss of individuality, do not label or categorize your client by saying something insensitive like, "All Medicaid recipients have to fill out this form."

2. Understand that the client's defensiveness may have served a useful purpose in the past. If the guardedness, defensiveness, and resistance are a long time pattern rather than situational behavior, consider how it may have protected the client from pain associated with some prior experience (e.g., rejection by a parent, breakup of one's family, or separation from loved ones) or from a frightening and traumatic event (e.g., family violence). Your own gut reactions may provide clues as to the psychological function of the client's defensiveness. For example, if you feel a strong desire to simply walk away from the client, the client's defensiveness may serve as a protection against interference by outsiders. If the client's apparent helplessness makes you want to rescue the client, this behavior may help the client avoid responsibility.

3. Look for ways to reinforce any indications of openness exhibited by the client. Use the technique of **mirroring**, which can be described as responding to his or her positive messages in a manner that matches the client's nonverbal behavior. For example, if the client lets down his or her guard, ever so slightly, follow up with a tone of voice, cadence, posture, and gestures that are similar to or mirror those displayed by the client. On the other hand, if your client's conversation speeds up because of anxiety or anger, respond with a slower pace and nurturing message for this will often calm the client. If your client assumes a defensive tone and closed posture, respond with a comforting tone of voice, gestures of openness, and an unguarded posture.

4. Use words and phrases that match your client's primary or dominant mode of receiving information. The three basic modes are visual, auditory, and tactile. A client reveals his or her dominant mode in the frequent use of certain predicates in phrases such as "I see what you mean" (visual), "I hear what you are saying" (auditory), or "That goal is beyond my reach" (tactile). If you can identify your client's dominant mode, try to match your phrases to his or her mode—for example, "Do you have a clear picture of what I am suggesting?" (visual), "Does this plan sound OK to you?" (auditory), or "I think the plan you have suggested is one we can both grab hold of" (tactile).

5. Display empathy and understanding by using the technique of **joining the resistance.** It involves aligning yourself with the client's feelings—for example, "After such a long wait, you deserve to be angry. I would be angry also." Such an alignment or joining tends to remove the client's need to keep up his or her defenses and it gives the client permission to vent feelings.

6. If your client uses obscene or abusive language, remain calm and do not respond with anger. Perhaps say something like, "I know you are upset but it is important that we have a respectful conversation." If the client persists in making verbal attacks, consider using the technique termed **fogging**. This name comes from the notion that rocks thrown into a fog bank have no effect. If the person under a verbal attack can become like the fog, the verbal "rocks" have no impact and, hopefully, the attacker will soon abandon efforts to inflict discomfort. This technique works because the person under attack does not retaliate in kind and calmly acknowledges that the angry person may indeed have a point and is possibly justified in his or her criticism. For example:

ANGRY CLIENT: All you ever do is talk!

WORKER: You're right. I do talk a lot.

ANGRY CLIENT: If you would pay attention to what I have been saying, you wouldn't have to ask these dumb questions!

WORKER: That may be true. I should be very attentive to what you say.

ANGRY CLIENT: You are just like all the other lazy government employees and state social workers! You are always telling people what to do and butting into things that are none of your damn business.

WORKER: I am a state employee. It does make sense that state employees would do their job in similar ways.

7. In situations where it is critically important to engage the defensive and resistive client (e.g., in cases of child abuse), you may need to adopt an assertive and direct approach. For example, if your client refuses to talk, you might say something like, "I can see that you do not want to talk to me about how your child was injured, but I must stay here with you until we have discussed this serious matter." If your client behaves in a threatening manner, you will need to say something like, "I have no intention of harming you. I will not argue with you and I cannot continue the interview under these threatening conditions. If you are too angry to talk now, I will come return this afternoon with a police officer. Would you rather talk now or later?" If your client attempts to avoid the central issue by talking about tangential concerns, you will need to take control by saying something like, "I can understand that you have other concerns and other problems, but for right now we must discuss how Joey got those bruises." In some cases, clients defend themselves by trying to make the worker feel guilty and intrusive. When that happens, you might say, "I know you are upset and I don't like to see people cry, but your child has been injured. Take a few minutes to compose yourself. Then we must discuss what happened to Joey" (see Items 10.7, 10.8, and 10.9).

Selected Bibliography

Cormier, Sherry, Paula Nurius, and Cynthia Osborn. *Interviewing and Change Strategies for Helpers*, 6th ed. Belmont, CA: Brooks/Cole, 2009.

Kottler, Jeffrey. *Nuts and Bolts of Helping*. Boston: Allyn & Bacon, 2000.

Rooney, Ronald. *Strategies for Work with Involuntary Clients*, 2nd ed. New York: Columbia University Press, 2009.

8.8	ELEMENTS OF PROFESSIONAL BEHAVIOR

It has been said that "A professional is someone who knows what to do and can be counted on to do it, even when he or she does not feel like doing it." That is an insightful description. It suggests that a professional knows what should be done, can be trusted to do it, and does not let matters of personal convenience or personal bias interfere with his or her performance.

It is important for social workers to continually examine their performance and make sure their behavior is of a professional nature. Figure 8.1 offers a comparison of professional and nonprofessional behavior.

Professional Behavior	*Nonprofessional Behavior*
A deep and abiding committed to the profession's goals, values, and ethics	Views social work as simply a job that can be easily abandoned if something better comes along
Bases practice on a body of knowledge learned through formal education and ongoing training	Bases practice mostly on personal opinions agency rules, or a political ideology
Makes decision on basis of fact, critical thinking, and scientific research	Makes decisions on basis of feelings, attitudes, or whims
Practice is guided by the profession's *Code of Ethics*	Practice is guided by personal preferences and inclinations
Professional relationships with clients are individualized, purposeful, and goal directed; does not expect to meet own needs within professional relationships	Relationships with clients are routine, perfunctory, and without direction; looks to meet own needs within relationships with clients
Client's well-being is of primary importance;	Own wants and convenience are of highest priority
Adheres to principles of professional practice, regardless of other pressures	Political and organizational pressures easily sway or influence decisions and actions
Continually upgrades knowledge and skills so as to better serve clients	Learns only the minimum required to keep job
Expects and invites peer review and critical evaluations of his or her performance	Avoids having others examine or observe his or her performance
Strives to develop new knowledge and share it within the profession	Does not invest self in search of new knowledge
Assumes responsibility for quality of services provided and for improving own agency's policies, programs, and services	Only concerned with doing a job as assigned by others and does not see self as responsible for improving agency policy and programs
Exercises self-discipline and self-awareness; keeps own emotions in check	Expresses emotions and personal views in thoughtless and hurtful manner
Documents professional decisions and actions, completely and accurately	Avoids recordkeeping, records are incomplete and cursory

FIGURE 8.1 Comparison of Professional and Nonprofessional Behavior

Selected Bibliography

Lauffer, Armand. *Working in Social Work.* Newbury Park, CA: Sage, 1987.
Payne, Malcolm. *What Is Professional Social Work*? 2nd ed. Chicago: Lyceum, 2007.
Sheafor, Bradford W., Armando T. Morales, and Malcolm E. Scott. *Social Work: A Profession of Many Faces,* 12th ed. Boston: Allyn & Bacon, 2010.

8.9   MAKING ETHICAL DECISIONS

Everyday, social workers encounter complex ethical issues. Sometimes the task is to help clients sort out their own ethical concerns, and at other times it involves the social worker determining if an action he or she is about to take is ethically appropriate. Occasionally all possible practice options will cause harm to someone, creating an ethical dilemma for the social worker.

Essentially, an **ethical dilemma** is a situation in which the worker has two or more ethical obligations but cannot follow or adhere to one without violating another. For example, ethical dilemmas faced by social workers increasingly involve decisions on how best to allocate scarce resources in times of budget cutbacks or to limit services when an insurance company will not pay for the cost of services required by a client. Or, in some cases, the decision to provide services to one client may result in limiting or withholding the services needed by others.

A first step toward resolving ethical dilemmas is to answer several questions that supply important background information and clarify the matter:

- Who is your primary client (i.e., usually the person, group, or organization that requested the social worker's services and expects to benefit from them)?
- What aspects of the agency's or your practice activities give rise to the dilemma (e.g., legal mandates, job requirements, agency policy, questions of efficient use of resources, possible harm caused by an intervention)?
- Who can or should resolve this dilemma? Is it rightfully a decision to be made by the client? Other family members? You? The agency administrator? A combination of people?
- For each decision possible, what are the short-term and long-term consequences for the client, family, agency, community, and so on?
- Who stands to gain and who (if anyone) stands to lose from each possible choice or action? Are the affected people of equal or unequal power (e.g., child vs. adult)? Are some who might be affected particularly vulnerable and thus require special consideration?
- When harm to someone cannot be avoided, what decision will cause the least harm with fewest long-term consequences? Who of those who might be harmed are least able to recover from the harm?
- Will a particular resolution to this dilemma set an undesirable precedent for future decision making concerning other clients?

Once those questions have been answered, the worker must answer three additional questions:

- What ethical principles and obligations apply in this situation?
- Which, if any, ethical principles are in conflict in this situation and therefore create an ethical dilemma?
- In this situation, do certain ethical obligations take priority over others?

To answer these questions, the social worker should first be very familiar with the National Association of Social Worker's (1999) **Code of Ethics**, which describes basic ethical standards and principles and provides general guidelines for professional conduct. The *NASW Code of Ethics* is organized into six sets of ethical principles:

1. *Ethical responsibilities to clients.* This section addresses such factors as the social worker's primary responsibility to the client, including maximizing client self-determination; securing informed consent; demonstrating cultural competence and competence in any intervention approach used; avoiding conflict of interest; protecting client privacy; and prohibitions regarding sexual involvement, physical contact, sexual harassment, and other boundary matters; as well as appropriate termination of services.

2. *Ethical responsibilities to colleagues.* Section 2 is concerned with treating colleagues with respect; maintaining professional confidentiality; engaging in collaboration and teamwork; proper handling of disputes; making referrals; and reporting colleagues who may be impaired, incompetent, or unethical in their practice.

3. *Ethical responsibilities in practice settings.* The items addressed in this section include competence in providing supervision, consultation, education, and training; the evaluation of the performance of other workers; responsible recording and billing; assuring an appropriate work environment; and so on.

4. *Ethical responsibilities as a professional.* Section 4 addresses items related to accepting assignments only when one is competent to perform the work; addressing any form of discrimination; avoiding private conduct that compromises one's professional responsibilities; engaging in dishonesty, fraud, and deception; addressing personal issues if impaired; and making it clear when acting as a private citizen and making statements that are not part of professional activities.

5. *Ethical responsibilities to the social work profession.*   Section 5 concerns issues related to promoting high standards for social work, contributing to the growth and development of the profession, as well as evaluating quality of the programs one offers and assessing his or her own practice as a quality control device.

6. *Ethical responsibilities to the broader society.*   This section reflects that social workers are charged with promoting the general welfare of the society; the realization of social justice; participating in public debates to shape social policies and institutions; providing services in emergencies; and actively engaging in social and political action to strengthen quality of life for all persons.

A copy of the *Code* should be on the desk of every social worker and can be downloaded from the NASW website at http://www.naswdc.org. It is an important screen that may be used to analyze a practice situation to determine if a specific alternative or action is ethically responsible and to help identify ethical conflicts that may arise in a practice situation. Addressing similar ethical issues, the Canadian Code of Ethics (http://www.casw-acts.ca) is organized into 10 areas: (1) primary professional obligation, (2) integrity and objectivity, (3) competence, (4) limits on professional relationships, (5) confidential information, (6) outside interests, (7) limits on private practice, (8) responsibilities to the workplace, (9) responsibilities to the profession, and (10) responsibilities for social change.

A limitation of a professional *Code of Ethics* as a tool for resolving ethical issues is that its standards are listed one after another giving the impression that all are of equal importance. However, when dealing with an individual case and its special circumstances, some standards should be given priority over others. For example, if a social worker learns that a client intends to harm himself, the standard assuring confidentiality should be temporarily set aside in order to protect his life, a higher good. Sorting out such issues, especially if more than one ethical issue is involved, is difficult.

A second useful screen when addressing ethical issues is provided by Dolgoff, Loewenberg, and Harrington (2009) who provide a useful prioritization of seven fundamental principles. They list these principles in the following order: (1) the protection of life; (2) increasing equality among relevant persons affected by the situation; (3) maximizing clients' autonomy and freedom (including self-determination); (4) following the "least harm" principle; (5) promoting the quality of life; (6) protecting privacy and confidentiality; and (7) practicing with truthfulness and full disclosure of all important information. Thus in evaluating an ethical dilemma in a practice situation, a social worker might seriously consider encouraging clients to determine what actions they will take (Principle #3) over protecting confidentiality (Principle #6). Any individual social worker might identify additional principles or order the priorities differently, yet the ranking by Dolgoff, et al. provides a useful starting point.

It is important to understand that ethical and legal codes are not synonymous. There may be times in social work practice when legal requirements conflict with ethical principles. In fact, social workers can place themselves in legal jeopardy when they do what is ethically correct, if a state and federal law mandates a different course of action (see Item 16.6).

It is also important to distinguish between personal morality and the ethics of a profession. The term *morality* (or personal ethics) usually refers to an individual's standards of conduct and beliefs as to what is right and wrong. In the case of legal–ethical conflicts, there may be times when the social worker's personal standards are in conflict with either the *Code of Ethics* or legal codes. These are indeed thorny situations that require very careful discernment and probably consultation with trusted peers or experts.

Finally, in addition to serving as a guide for practice decisions, social workers should recognize that their profession's ethical code also serves as a guide for judging if actions they have performed are unethical.[*] Just as various laws become the standards against which person's

---

[*]NASW maintains a hotline a few hours each week (800–638–8799) where members can receive consultation regarding ethical issues in social work practice.

actions are judged in a trial, so the profession's ethical standards serve as guidelines by which one's actions are judged if charged with unethical social work practice.

Selected Bibliography

Dolgoff, Ralph, Frank M. Loewenberg, and Donna Harrington. *Ethical Decisions for Social Work Practice*, 8th ed. Belmont, CA: Brooks/Cole, 2009.

National Association of Social Workers. *Code of Ethics*. Washington, DC: NASW, 1999.

Reamer, Frederic. *Ethical Standards in Social Work*, 2nd ed. Washington, DC: NASW Press, 2006.

_____. *The Social Work Ethics Casebook: Cases and Commentary*. Washington, DC: NASW Press, 2009.

Sommers-Flanagan, Rita, and John Sommers-Flanagan. *Becoming an Ethical Helping Professional*. Hoboken, NJ: Wiley, 2007.

Strom-Gottfried, Kim. *Straight Talk About Professional Ethics*. Chicago: Lyceum, 2007.

8.10 APPLYING CULTURAL COMPETENCE TO HELPING

Social workers must understand how one's culture may influence a client's behavior, values, expectations, communication, and decisions. Culture, ethnicity, and religion influence, for example, how parents raise their children, how men and women define their roles in a marriage, and how people evaluate or judge their own behavior and that of others. It is also important for social workers to be aware of how their own cultural perspectives, values, and belief systems may sometimes get in the way of providing appropriate services to a client.

Section 1.05 of The National Association of Social Workers' (1999) *Code of Ethics* states that social workers should:

a. . . . understand culture and its function in human behavior and society, recognizing the strengths that exist in all cultures.

b. . . . have a knowledge base of their client's cultures and be able to demonstrate competence in the provision of services that are sensitive to clients' cultures and to differences among people and cultural groups.

c. . . . obtain education about and seek to understand the nature of social diversity and oppression with respect to race, ethnicity, national origin, color, sex, sexual orientation, age, marital status, political belief, religion, and mental or physical disability.

The National Association of Social Workers' social policy statement (NASW, 2000, p. 61) calls on all social workers and human services systems to acquire **cultural competence**, which consists of a set of congruent behaviors, attitudes, and policies that enable professionals and agencies to work effectively in cross-cultural situations. The NASW Cultural Competence Standards (2001) further identify several elements that contribute to an agency's or a professional's ability to become more culturally competent. Among these are: (1) to value and respect human diversity, (2) diligent self-assessment in regard to one's own or one's agency cultural perspectives, values, and beliefs, (3) awareness of the special dynamics that are in play whenever people of different cultures interact, and (4) develop programs and services that reflect an appreciation and understanding of the diversity. These elements should be built into a human services organization and reflected in the attitudes and performance of those employed by the agency.

What is a culture? From the perspective of anthropology, a **culture** can be defined as a set of shared ideals, values, and standards that make the actions of individuals intelligible and understandable to the other members of their society. Culture shapes the way people make sense out of their experiences, cope with life's problems, and negotiate power relationships, both within their own group and with outsiders. Culture is a lens through which people view life. One's culture is, to a large degree, the source for what one expects of self and others and one's ideas about the way things should be. A culture does not create reality but it does influence what people believe to be reality. A person's culture is often so internalized and so habitual that he or she does not even recognize its existence and its power in shaping thoughts and behavior. All people, social workers included, tend to be somewhat **ethnocentric**—that is, they assume that their own way of life is a reasonable and an appropriate standard for judging others.

When people encounter a culture that is different from their own, some will find it confusing, unreasonable, and even silly. Others will be fascinated and find everything about this new culture to be interesting and an improvement over their own culture. Reality usually lies somewhere in between these two extremes. No culture is perfect. All have strengths and weaknesses. All have features that are admirable, sensible, and prudent. And, all cultures contain elements that are problematic.

Cultures are dynamic. Some shifts and changes are gradual whereas others are rapid and disruptive. Cultures are altered by economics, technology, science, politics, and by large-scale societal events such as a war or an economic depression. The younger generation may welcome and embrace changes to their culture, whereas the older generation often feels threatened and will resist change.

The patterns inherent in a culture are passed from generation to generation or gained from a common experience. Thus a common culture may exist among members of a population group, or might develop among individuals who have in common a significant life experience, such as being together in military combat, experiencing a particular disease or disability, or being the subject of various forms of discrimination or oppression.

The word *culture* is often used rather broadly, as for example in the terms *teen culture* or *drug culture*. These are not true cultures, as defined above, because the beliefs, values, and patterns associated with a particular generation of teens or drug users are not usually passed on to the next generation. The transmittal of a culture to the next generation requires the influence and reinforcement of multiple societal institutions and social forces such as family, schools, language, laws, religion, and public policies.

An **ethnic group** is a segment of the larger population that identifies itself and is regarded by others as a distinct group because of its language, religion, ancestry, physical appearance, or some combination of these characteristics. If people believe that they are somehow different and belong to a distinct group, that belief will affect their interactions—including how they interact with social workers.

Whereas culture and ethnicity have to do with differences concerning values, beliefs, and traditions, the idea of **race** is a categorization of people on the basis of physical characteristics, such as skin color, hair texture, and body structure. **Racism** exists when the members of one group (usually one that is politically and economically powerful) views those of another race as inherently inferior. Racism gives rise to discrimination and oppression, as when, for example, opportunities, protections, liberties, and resources are denied on the basis of race. Although the United States has made progress in dealing with the problem of racism, it still falls short of Martin Luther King Jr.'s dream of a society in which people "would not be judged by the color of their skin, but by the content of their character."

There are few issues that engage us so viscerally as that of racism. The emotions of anger, defensiveness, guilt, denial, sadness, shame, and despair are not uncommon among those who feel that they are the victims or racism, among those who perceive the existence of prejudice and racism in their own attitudes and beliefs, and also among those who are accused—accurately or inaccurately—of being prejudiced or racist. Those of the dominant group may be morally troubled as they come to realize that many of their privileges and benefits exist because other groups have been economically oppressed and exploited.

It is helpful to distinguish between prejudice and discrimination. Whereas *prejudice* is an attitude, *discrimination* is an action or behavior that harms the members of a particular group. Prejudice (i.e., to pre-judge) refers to attitudes or beliefs that devalue or disparage others simply because they are of a certain race, ethnic group, religion, age, or gender. Prejudice does not always result in acts of discrimination. And discrimination can exist apart from a prejudice as, for example, when an employee thoughtlessly follows an organizational policy that is unfair and discriminatory to a particular group.

Acts of *individual discrimination* may be as blatant, such as deliberately causing physical injury to a member of a particular group (hate crimes) or refusing to hire a qualified individual because of his or her skin color. More subtle and difficult to detect is *institutional discrimination*. It exists when prejudice and racism are woven into laws, social structures, organizational policies, and the ordinary patterns of community life. The term *internalized racism* refers to the effects that racism has on the psychology of some of its victims, those who absorb or incorporate the messages of racism and come to view themselves as inherently inferior.

Discrimination, in its many forms, may limit people's access to jobs, housing, health care, education, job training, credit, and business contracts. Directly and indirectly, it is a cause of poverty and many forms of injustice. For example, a person with few employment opportunities may be too afraid to question unfair wages or to protest abuse in the workplace if doing so could jeopardize his or her job.

A particular ethnic or racial or group may or may not be a minority group. A **minority group** is one whose members have significantly less political and economic power and control over their own lives as compared to a dominant group in society. Minority status has to do with power, not the numerical size of the group. Within every society, and usually within any racial, cultural, ethnic, or religious grouping, there will be *socio-economic classes* or status rankings based usually on income, education, and occupation.

GUIDELINES FOR CULTURALLY SENSITIVE SOCIAL WORK PRACTICE

Self-awareness is critical for social workers. Strive to understand how your own culture, ethnicity, religion, and socio-economic background have shaped your views. Frequently ask yourself, "What is my attitude toward people of different cultural backgrounds?" "How do I feel about people who have a different skin color, are elderly, or speak a different language?" "How do I feel about people who have religious beliefs different from my own?" Be alert to the possibility that you may make judgments based on bias and prejudices. Below are some indicators that a professional is possibly prejudiced:

- The professional gives stereotyped explanations for the actions of people belonging to a particular group.
- The same practice strategies, methods, and techniques are used for all clients who are members of a particular ethnic or racial group.
- The factors of culture, race, and ethnicity are minimized or dismissed as irrelevant, or at the other extreme, used to explain nearly all behavior and social problems.

Agencies must also constantly examine their policies and procedures to make sure they are not, in some way, discriminating against certain groups of people. An agency can be helped to develop culturally sensitive and appropriate ways of addressing issues of cultural difference by, for example, including representatives from diverse groups on its governing or advisory boards, soliciting reviews of agency performance by persons from the various segments of the community it serves, and conducting program evaluations.

Here are some guidelines the social worker might consider:

1. Strive to learn about the cultural backgrounds of the clients you serve while recognizing that we can seldom acquire much more than a superficial knowledge of another culture, especially when language differences are involved. Even so, the social worker can achieve at least a beginning level of understanding by interacting frequently with people from that ethnic and cultural group, consulting with the leaders of the group, attending cultural festivals and religious events, reading ethnic newspapers and literature, and so on.

2. Never assume that a client's cultural background or race will predict his or her values, beliefs, or behavior. Rather, always individualize the client. Every attempt to describe a group of people—whether the white middle class, people who are blind, African Americans, Republicans or Democrats, rich or poor, is a generalization and thus, always runs the risk of over-generalization, stereotyping, and even using caricatures. Within every cultural or ethnic group there are various subgroups and certainly a wide range of differences among individuals.

3. All people struggle to balance and reconcile two sets of beliefs, values, and social expectations. One set consists of the somewhat impersonal influences of the dominant culture that are embedded within a society's economic, commercial, political, legal, and educational systems. The second set is very personal and exists within one's family and social network. When these two sets of beliefs, values, and expectations are quite different for an individual, he or she may be confused or uncertain about his or her place in society and about what to expect of self and others. Such a tension is most likely to occur among those who are members of an ethnic, cultural, or religious minority and for new immigrants (see Item 15.20).

4. Show an interest in your client's name, place of birth, and home community, for these topics are usually good icebreakers and lead naturally to a discussion of the client's cultural and ethnic background. Early in the professional relationship, acknowledge the existence of obvious differences of culture or race as a way of giving the client permission to talk about these matters and perhaps express concerns about not being understood. Encourage the client to identify important cultural values, beliefs, or customs that may need to be considered or accommodated in the professional relationship and service delivery.

A major obstacle in working cross-culturally is that the professional helper and the client may have quite different notions of what constitutes genuine help and how a person can be helpful. Moreover, a particular model or approach to professional helping or therapy may strike a client from certain cultures as strange or even offensive. For example, a short-term or task-oriented approach may seem abrasive to a client who believes that extended periods of time spent just getting to know each other is the appropriate way to enter into a new relationship. To some clients, techniques like reaching for feelings or putting the client's feelings into words may appear intrusive. An individual from an Asian culture may consider it shameful to discuss a personal problem with someone from outside the family. Many Hispanics will expect a helper to offer advice and tangible forms of assistance and may feel confused by a professional using non-directive counseling and the techniques of active listening. Cognitive behavioral or rational emotive techniques, which tend to challenge or question a client's beliefs and assumptions may offend a client whose culture places a high value on displaying respect and deference. Discussing a personal problem with a professional who is from the dominant group may be particularly difficult for a person who is from a minority and oppressed group, since it presumes a degree of trust that does not exist and may cause the client to feel especially vulnerable.

Overlooking client strengths, misreading nonverbal communication, and misunderstanding family dynamics are among the most common errors made in cross-cultural helping. Behaviors motivated by religion, family obligation, and sex roles are frequently misunderstood or misinterpreted by professional helpers. The worker should be cautious about using techniques such as reaching for feelings, confrontation, and supporting the client in taboo areas.

5. Because members of many ethnic minority groups have experienced discrimination, it is to be expected that they will be somewhat distrustful of professionals and the agencies that represent and reflect the beliefs and values of the dominant groups in society. They will enter a helping relationship with caution as they size up the social worker. They may evaluate the worker's trustworthiness by asking, directly or indirectly, about his or her life experiences, family, children, and opinions. The worker needs to respond to these probes with honest, non-evasive answers. Since visiting people in their own home is usually an indication of caring and respect, the home visit may help the worker build trust.

6. Be aware that an extended family structure is common to many cultures and ethnic groups. In these families, the members feel a strong obligation to assist and support other family members. The misbehavior of a family member brings shame to the whole family and an honor bestowed on one member is recognition of the whole family. Typically, the elders are held in high esteem, command deference and respect, and exert much influence on the decisions and actions of other family members. For example, in many Hispanic families the husband and father will have considerable authority and his wife and even his adult children may feel obligated to obtain his approval before making an important decision, even one involving medical treatment. Within the large extended families common to the American Indian tribal cultures, family members will often delay making a decision until they have obtained an elder's advice on the matter. Thus, it is always a good idea to ask the client if he or she wants to invite others to the interview or somehow involve them in decision making. Not infrequently, clients will simply bring these respected advisors to important meetings.

7. Closely related to the necessity of cultural competence is the need to adapt social work practice to the client's religious beliefs and spirituality. Very often, a client's ethnicity, culture, and religion are interwoven. A professional who ignores a client's spirituality, religious beliefs, and moral code may fail to accurately assess the client's situation and overlook resources that could prove helpful to the client (see Item 15.17).

8. Clients who may experience difficulty with the society's common language (e.g., English) should be asked if an interpreter would be helpful. If you will be working with many people who speak another language, strive to learn as much of that language as possible. Make an effort to speak some of the client's language, even if you can master only a few phrases. Doing so will be viewed as a courtesy and as respect for the client's native language and culture.

9. Societal or systemic problems (poverty, unemployment, poor housing, lack of access to health care, etc.) bring ethnic minorities to agencies more often than do psychological problems. Thus, the provision of concrete services and the practitioner roles of broker and advocate are of special importance.

Selected Bibliography

Harper-Dorton, Karen, and Jim Lantz. *Cross-Cultural Practice*, 2nd ed. Chicago: Lyceum, 2007.

Lum, Doman. *Culturally Competent Practice*, 3rd ed. Belmont, CA: Brooks/Cole, 2007.

National Association of Social Workers. *Code of Ethics.* Washington, DC: NASW Press, 1999.

—————. Cultural Competence in the Social Work Profession. In *Social Work Speaks: NASW Policy Statements.* Washington, DC: NASW Press, 2009.

—————. *NASW Standards for Cultural Competence in Social Work Practice.* Washington, DC: NASW Press, 2001.

Rothman, Juliet. *Cultural Competence in Process and Practice.* Boston: Allyn & Bacon, 2008.

Sisneros, Jose, Catherine Stakeman, Mildred Joyner, and Cathryne Schmitz. *Critical Multicultural Social Work.* Chicago: Lyceum, 2008.

Sue, Derald, and David Sue. *Counseling the Culturally Diverse,* 5th ed. Hoboken, NJ: Wiley, 2008

Basic Skills for Agency Practice

Regardless of their practice settings, most social workers struggle with two sets of tasks: managing their time and managing the required documentation and other paperwork. This chapter offers guidance on how social workers might increase their efficiency by incorporating into their daily routines the skills of time management, effective phone use, and information technology. Also included are guidelines on report and letter writing and maintaining client records. A social worker must strive to be efficient, but measures taken in the name of efficiency must not compromise an effective helping process or shortchange client services.

Recordkeeping is an essential component of service provision. Professional records must be complete, concise, useable, legible, and accurate. Ideally, an agency's recordkeeping system will create documentation useful for the following purposes: (1) provide an accurate account of services provided; (2) provide data that can be used to identify needed changes in policy, service delivery, and staff deployment; (3) provide data for retrospective and prospective research; (4) provide data that are useful in the planning of staff training and professional education; (5) provide documentation of adherence to relevant legal and policy requirements; and (6) provide information that is understandable to and will withstand scrutiny by external reviewers (e.g., accreditation bodies, ombudsmen, lawyers, insurance companies, quality control personnel).

In our litigious society, social workers are sometimes named in lawsuits alleging professional negligence or misconduct. Accurate and complete documentation and recordkeeping is critical to defending oneself against such an allegation. In the absence of proper documentation, there may be no evidence that a social worker's decision or action was appropriate and responsible.

9.1   WRITTEN REPORTS AND CORRESPONDENCE

Professional reports and letters must be carefully written. Ones that are unclear or inaccurate can create misunderstanding and sometimes costly or embarrassing errors. A number of guidelines should be kept in mind.

1. Before you begin to write, carefully consider who will be reading the report or letter. Decide what information the readers need and expect. Also, consider whether the document might be sent to still others such as other agencies, newspapers, or clients. Keep these potential readers in mind as you write and imagine how they are likely to interpret or perhaps misinterpret your words.

2. Reports that are to be submitted to a court, doctors, psychologists, lawyers, schools, human services agencies, businesses, and committees need to be formal and tightly organized. Give close attention to agency protocol and prescribed format, accurate use of terminology, and proper names and titles. A less formal style is usually appropriate for internal communications (i.e., within one's organization) and in these reports and memos the use of first names, abbreviations, and jargon is usually acceptable. Copies of well-written reports—ones judged by others in the agency to be good examples—can be used as a model to guide your report writing.

3. Before writing the first draft or a formal report, organize the content to be presented. Outline the main topics, the various subtopics, and the key points under each. If you present your ideas in an orderly manner and use headings to set sections apart, the reader will be better able to follow your reasoning and understand your message. Two or three drafts or revisions of a formal report may be needed before the final version is produced. Ask peers to review your draft and offer constructive criticism.

4. A formal letter will have at least the following parts: letterhead, date, inside address, reference line or subject line, salutation, body, complimentary close, typed signature, and written signature. When appropriate, there should also be an enclosure notation (enc.) and a copy notation (cc or pc) that names others receiving a copy of the letter.

Use proper titles, such as Mr., Mrs., Ms., Miss, Dr., Rev., and so on. First names should be used only when addressing children or adults with whom you have a close personal relationship.

As a general rule, all letters to other agencies, professionals, and clients should be typed on letterhead stationery. However, in special instances, a personalized note to a client can be handwritten.

Be cautious about including any information that might violate a client's right to confidentiality if read by persons other than the intended recipient. Also, be alert to the fact that an agency's name on an envelope may reveal the client's involvement with the agency.

A copy of all letters sent should be retained in agency files or the case record because they document a professional action and the service provided. Use certified or registered mail when necessary to document that a specific letter was delivered.

5. Select your words carefully, using only those your reader will understand. Wordiness lessens the force of expression and may distract the reader from the point you want to make, so use only the number of words necessary. The use of shorthand phrases and symbols that appear in email and telephone text messages are not appropriate in professional reports and letters. Keep your sentences relatively short, usually 15 to 20 words or less. Most often, the straightforward subject-verb-object sentence is the best structure because it can be read quickly and is seldom misunderstood. Always use complete sentences, proper grammar, and correct spelling. Use the spell check, grammar check, dictionary, and thesaurus available in your computer's word-processing program.

6. Avoid cramming many ideas into a single paragraph. Typically, a page of text should have several paragraph breaks. Ideally, each paragraph should focus on a single idea. In its first sentence state the central point of the paragraph. Then, if necessary for purposes of clarification, restate the central point in different words. Additional sentences are to present the evidence, examples, background information, and the logic supporting the central point or idea. Finally, draw the paragraph to a close, summarizing the key point in a single sentence. By reading only the first and last sentence of a paragraph, the reader should be able to grasp the core of what you are trying to communicate.

7. Avoid so-called weasel words such as *feel* and *seems*. Instead of saying "I feel placement is necessary," be direct and state, "I believe placement is necessary" or "I recommend placement for this child." Weak and evasive language gives the impression that the writer is uncertain or unwilling to take responsibility for what is being said.

Selected Bibliography

Davis, Kenneth. *Business Writing and Communication*. New York: McGraw Hill, 2005.

Glicken, Morley. *A Guide to Writing for Human Services Professional*. Lanham, MD: Rowman and Littlefield, 2008.

Healy, Karen, and Joan Mulholland. *Writing Skills for Social Workers*. Newbury Park, CA: Sage, 2007.

9.2 EFFECTIVE TELEPHONE COMMUNICATION

The telephone is used frequently in social work practice. However, a phone is not always the most effective and accurate method of communication because the messages must be delivered entirely by voice and without body language. The telephone can be used when a quick response is needed, when the matter under discussion is easily understood and when it is not critical to establish a permanent record of the transaction. The use of a letter, memo, or email may be preferred when the message is complex and involves many details. Following these guidelines will help improve telephone use:

1. Before placing a phone call, consider its purpose and jot down the major points you wish to address. Plan to take notes during the phone conversation. Such notes can be placed in the agency file or case record to document the phone call.

2. Begin all phone communications by identifying yourself and your organization. Take time to enunciate clearly. Give complete attention to the person with whom you are speaking; do not "multitask" while on the phone. If the person on the other end is talking at length, interject a brief comment at intervals: "Yes, I see" or "I understand." This lets him or her know that you are listening. If your caller gets sidetracked, steer him or her back to the point of the call. Before saying "good-bye" it may be appropriate to summarize the information you intended to convey and the information you received.

3. Social workers must be careful about where they use cell phones. Cell phone use, especially in public places, can jeopardize client confidentiality. Also, it is difficult for a social worker to give undivided attention to a cell phone conversation while also driving or walking down a busy street. Common courtesy requires that cell phones be turned off during client interviews and agency meetings.

4. If you must leave a message for a person you did not reach by phone, keep that message short (e.g., your name, phone number, and reason for calling). Repeat the phone number two times, and speak slowly while doing so. Suggest a time for the person to return your call. However, you will save time by calling back rather than waiting for your call to be returned.

5. Master the skills of using your agency's phone system such as transferring calls, using voice mail, and so on. When transferring calls to other lines, let callers know what you are doing: Tell them the name and title of the person to whom they will be speaking and why you are transferring their call. If you must leave the phone for a minute, say something like: "Please hold on while I get that file." Unless you are sure you will be away for only a few moments, tell your caller that you will call back.

6. The automated answering and voice mail systems used in many agencies can be confusing to callers. For example, a client may be upset after having to listen to a recorded voice, select from a menu of options, and perform numerous dialing maneuvers. Instruct your clients and other frequent callers how to use the system.

Selected Bibliography

Tarbell, Shirley. *Office Basics Made Simple*. New York: Learning Express, 1997.

9.3 USING INFORMATION TECHNOLOGY

Computers are an essential part of social work practice, agency operation, and administration. At a minimum, social workers should be skilled at word processing, the use of a spreadsheet program, inputting client data, accessing online information, and communicating via email. A desktop or laptop computer equipped with a basic software package and a high-speed Internet connection is usually sufficient for performing these activities—although for some specialized applications more sophisticated technology is required.

Here are some applications and information technologies used in social work settings:

1. *Online resources.* The information technology used most often by social workers is **electronic mail** or **email**. It is an excellent communication tool for transmitting information, scheduling meetings, obtaining consultation, and providing support for both professionals and clients. At an advanced level, email can be used for client counseling and advice giving. Email improves efficiency as messages can easily be sent and stored, meetings can be efficiently announced and scheduled, clients can be contacted, and reports can be transmitted and received. Participating in email-based professional discussion groups can also add to social workers' practice knowledge and provide stimulation, especially for workers who live in remote areas. Clients, too, can use email and electronic discussion groups to connect with people experiencing similar social issues as a form of self-help or mutual-aid group experience.

Another widely used online resource is the **World Wide Web** (WWW), which links Internet information through webpages. Once the basic web access fee has been paid, an unlimited amount of information is available to the user at no cost. Many government agencies, human services organizations, universities, and individuals create and maintain webpages. These pages often provide built-in links to related pages, making it relatively easy for a social worker to access multiple sources of information on a specific topic. Many articles and some books are available on the web and can be downloaded free or at a nominal cost. With the growing emphasis on evidence-based social work practice, it is essential to be able to search for evidence of best practices or the latest information on specific client conditions.

Web-based online advocacy represents a growing use of this technology. Groups who are concerned about local, state, national, and even international matters of social policy are able to rapidly exchange social and political information and reach large numbers of people to encourage them to take action regarding these issues. The inside back cover of this book contains a listing of some useful web resources for social workers.

2. *Word processing.* Another almost universal use of computer technology by social workers is word processing. Much of the necessary correspondence; preparation of case summaries; completion of agency information sheets; preparing memoranda, agendas, reports, and journal articles; as well as other routine agency paperwork now typically bypasses clerical staff and is done entirely by social workers. A specialized form of word-processing software, known as **desktop publishing**, is used in many agencies to prepare newsletters, bulletins, flyers, and public relations information (see Item 13.34). Finally, **presentation software** packages assist in creating text and graphics for making presentations at professional meetings (see Item 16.10) and for interpreting agency services to other agencies, civic clubs, United Way allocation committees, potential clients, and so on.

3. *Spreadsheets.* When the information to be recorded is numerical, **spreadsheet software** is extremely useful. Spreadsheets are used in maintaining data about services provided and clients seen, in accounting and bookkeeping tasks, and in collecting program evaluation and research data. The primary advantage of using a spreadsheet is being able to use formulas so that data summaries can be quickly compiled. In addition, columns can be accurately summed, basic statistical formulas can be applied to data, and professional looking graphs and charts developed. One particularly useful application of spreadsheet software is in making projections; namely, "what if" questions can be tested by changing one value and then observing how doing so will modify other values. This application is useful, for example, in estimating the need for financial resources when preparing a grant application (see Item 13.36), in identifying the potential savings from purchasing more efficient office equipment, or in changing the fees charged for services.

4. *Database programs.* As the electronic equivalents of filing cabinets and file folders, **database programs** provide an efficient way of maintaining and accessing important information. Regarding a specific client, social workers might include in a database such items as demographic characteristics, a social history, intake information, treatment plans, and progress notes. These data can be readily retrieved to track the progress of the client or merged with data from other clients to prepare a report. Database programs also can be used to schedule appointments, manage "to do" lists, and otherwise reduce paperwork.

5. *Research-related software.* Social workers are obligated to assess their practice effectiveness. That might be done by tracking the progress of individual clients (see Items 14.3 through 14.6) or by engaging in program evaluation (see Item 14.9). In addition, social workers are expected to add to the knowledge base of the social work profession as they become interested in answering questions and testing hypotheses that arise in their practice. Software is available to facilitate such research by selecting a sample size, constructing data-entry forms, calculating the margin of error for a given return rate, suggesting and performing statistical tests, analyzing qualitative data, and presenting the results in graphic format.

6. *Distance learning.* Social work practice constantly changes, which means social workers at all levels must learn new theories and techniques. Whenever a worker moves from one practice setting or field to another (e.g., from mental health to corrections), a period of intensive retooling is usually required. In addition, some state licensing boards require licensed social workers to update their credentials periodically by participating in workshops, classes, and other instructional activities. These educational needs can often be met through participation in distance learning programs or online workshops. Some are offered in an online format, which will allow the worker to participate in courses from his or her home or office.

7. *Job searches, graduate school applications, and competency exams.* Finding and qualifying for social work positions increasingly requires the social worker to be comfortable in using computer technology. Human services agencies regularly post job openings on their websites and the application process typically involves completing an online application form (see Item 16.1). Similarly, master's and doctoral level graduate education programs often expect that most of the application process will be conducted electronically. Skill in basic use of word processing technology for completing forms and writing short essays as part of the application process for jobs and advanced education are required.

The use of paper and pencil competency tests is still required by a few human services agencies, but most large agencies and the national social work licensing exams are now conducted using computerized programs (see Item 16.2). Because these tests are usually time-limited, social workers are likely to be able to devote more attention to the content of the exams when they are comfortable with the mechanics of the computer technology.

As social work practice makes increasing use of information technology, practitioners at all levels must participate in shaping the technology to fit the practice, rather than permitting the technology to shape and drive practice. Social workers should also understand both the benefits and the dangers associated with this technology. For instance, they should be aware of inherent ethical issues, such as the risk of transmitting confidential information electronically, as well as the potential to further distance disenfranchised populations from mainstream society by expecting that people have ready access to this technology. (This is sometimes referred to as the *digital divide*.)

In the end, however, social workers must recognize that electronic technology only provides tools to assist practice. It is the workers themselves who must decide how to use this technology in an appropriate and responsible manner.

Selected Bibliography

Dunlop, Judith, and Michael J. Holosko, eds. *Information Technology and Evidence-Based Social Work Practice.* New York: Haworth Press, 2006.

Hick, Steven F., and John G. McNutt, eds. *Advocacy, Activism, and the Internet: Community Organization and Social Policy.* Chicago: Lyceum Books, 2002.

Martin, Jennifer, and Linette Hawkins, eds. *Information Communication Technologies for Human Services Education and Delivery: Concepts and Cases.* Hershey, PA: Information Science Reference, 2010.

9.4   CLIENT RECORDS AND DOCUMENTATION

What and how much information should be included in the client's record? How should this information be arranged and organized? Every social worker and agency must come up with workable answers to those questions. The answers will depend on factors such as the agency's mission, the type of service provided, relevant state and federal laws and regulations, and who will have access to the records.

A client record describes the client and his or her situation or problem and the social work intervention. It shows the rationale underlying the intervention, provides a coherent picture of the specific services provided, documents the client's involvement in pivotal decisions, and documents compliance with key agency policies. All client records contain *identifying data* such as names, addresses, and phone numbers. Records must be accurate, up to date, unbiased, clearly written, and well organized. Maintaining client confidentiality is an overriding concern in all recordkeeping and documentation (see Item 10.5).

Depending on agency policy, a client record may be handwritten, dictated, or typed directly into a computerized record. Increasingly, agencies use software programs that aid in the preparation and the management of client records and make the retrieval of information easier (see Item 9.3).

Given that a court can subpoena client records for use as evidence in lawsuits and because a social worker providing court testimony may be asked to read aloud from a client record, a worker must be very thoughtful about what information is placed in a record and how it is stated (see Item 16.7). Conjecture, rumors about the client, and information irrelevant to the services provided should never appear in a client record.

The use of *progress notes* or *case notes* is a common method of recording in direct service agencies. This approach describes the worker's contacts with the client, chronologically arranged. After each contact with the client or with persons collateral to client service, the worker writes a few sentences or paragraphs (progress notes), which succinctly captures the essence of what happened during the session and, typically, states what the worker plans to do in future sessions.

In order to prepare progress notes for easier reading and retrieval, the information is often placed within an organizing structure. Examples include the DAP (Data, Assessment, Plan); TIPP (Themes/Topics, Interventions, Progress, Plans); PIG (Problem, Intervention, Goal); and the SOAP or SOAPIER formats. The acronym SOAPIER refers to the following headings or categories of information:

S *Subjective data* reports worker's impressions of client's mood and feelings and how the client is interpreting his or her situation. This data is derived mostly from a client's self-report. By definition, subjective information does not lend itself to independent or external validation.

O *Objective data* is that which has been obtained by way of a professional's direct observation, clinical examinations, testing, systematic data collection, and the like. This category of information can be independently verified.

A *Assessment/Analysis* refers to the professional's working hypothesis or tentative conclusions derived from reviewing the subjective and objective information. This action connects the current session to the overall goals of work with client.

P The *Plan* focuses on the future and spells out how the professional and/or client intend to address the client's concern or problem.

I *Interventions* describes the steps or actions actually taken to address the clients problem or concerns.

E *Evaluation* presents data that describes the results, outcome, or effectiveness of the interventions.

R *Revision* describes how the intervention plan is being revised or needs to be modified in light of evaluation data.

Figure 9.1 is an illustrative SOAPIER entry related to problems faced by a client, Mrs. Brown.

At monthly or quarterly intervals, the information contained in progress notes or case notes may be consolidated into a *narrative summary* and used to update or modify a client's service contract or treatment plan (see Item 12.5).

Subjective: Jane Brown says she is feeling in a "panic" and is "frightened" of losing her children to foster care because she cannot make ends meet. She is "scared and embarrassed" by her financial situation. Since she grew up on welfare, she says she will "never to go on the dole." She expressed a desire to eventually get her GED and maybe some technical training.

Objective: Ms. Brown, age 24, earns about $1,800 per month for her work at a dry cleaning establishment. She rents a one-bedroom apartment from her uncle for $750 per month. She was divorced three years ago but receives no child support. She dropped out of a GED preparation program because its class schedule conflicted with her work.

She appears anxious and jumps from topic to topic. Agency records indicate that she was neglected as a child and spent four years in foster care. Her two children are ages 4 and 7. The 7 year old attends Paxton School. A friend watches the children when Ms. Brown is at work but this friend is not reliable because she drinks.

Assessment: Client does not have sufficient money. She needs to find a different child care arrangement. Ms. Brown is overwhelmed by family and job responsibilities. Her worry, disorganization, and inability to think clearly are due, in part to a fear that she will lose her children to foster care. That fear is, in turn, related to her own experiences of having been in foster care. She believes that accepting any form of welfare will label her as a "bad parent" and for that reason is resistant to the idea of attempting to secure financial assistance.

Plan: Schedule two sessions with Ms. Brown. Help her explore the possibility of securing job training, looking for a higher paying job, and finding a dependable and safe childcare arrangement. Explore options on how she might restart her work toward a GED. Gather information about why she receives no child support from the children's father. Encourage and assist her to apply for SNAP (food stamps). Assure her that such an application is a way for her to be a "good mother" under these difficult circumstances.

Intervention: Active listening. Problem solve her scheduling conflicts. Provide examples and stories of other mothers in her situation that have had to ask for outside assistance. Accompany her to information gathering meetings with representatives from GED program and a job-training program.

Evaluation: After the first two sessions, Ms. Brown says she is less worried. She feels reassured that she will not lose her children if she is being a responsible mother, even if she needs to utilize food stamps or some other welfare assistance. Because her ex-husband is in jail there is no chance that she will be receiving child support. She is making progress on working out a childcare arrangement with a responsible older neighbor who lives on her block. This neighbor will watch the children in exchange for help with shopping, some weekly house cleaning, and doing some home maintenance tasks.

Revision: Schedule two more sessions to teach Ms. Brown about managing self-talk as a way of helping her gain control over her tendency to dwell on negative thoughts and worry excessively. Help her develop a family budget. Follow up on her desire to enroll in GED program that begins in February. Inform Ms. Brown about the MOMS support group and encourage her to attend.

FIGURE 9.1   Sample SOAPIER Entry

Many agencies utilize various *forms and outlines* to collect, organize, and record client information. These are prepared by professionals familiar with the work of the agency and with the type of client concerns usually addressed. The headings written into the forms and outlines remind the social worker of the types of data to be recorded and also facilitate the retrieval of information. Examples of headings that appear on such forms are: client's presenting concern or problem, client's family and social supports, client's health, client's employment and occupation, client's cultural background, activities, and changes since last contact with client, and so on.

A consideration in all approaches to preparing client records is developing a mode of documentation that can monitor and measure client progress in order to determine if a given intervention is working. The starting point for all such measurement is clarity regarding the intervention goals and objectives (see Items 12.1 and 12.4). Chapter 14 describes scales and techniques used to measure client change. The documentation of client change is critically important when a client is using a public or private insurance to pay for the service. Numerous books offer guidance on the preparation of a client record that will meet requirements imposed by managed care. Such books list hundreds of prewritten progress notes that are keyed to various client problems and to the *Diagnostic and Statistical Manual (DSM-IV)* categories (see Item 11.16).

Selected Bibliography

Jongsma, Arthur. *The Adult Psychotherapy Progress Notes Planner.* Hoboken, NJ: Wiley, 2003.
Jongsma, Arthur, L. Mark Peterson, William McInnis, and David Berghuis. *The Child Psychotherapy Progress Notes Planner*, 3rd ed. Hoboken, NJ: Wiley, 2007.
Kagle, Jill, and Sandra Kopels. *Social Work Records*, 3rd ed. Long Grove, IL: Waveland Press, 2008.
Wiger, Donald. *Clinical Documentation Sourcebook*, 4th ed. Hoboken, NJ: Wiley, 2009.
Wiger, Donald. *The Psychotherapy Documentation Primer*, 2nd ed. Hoboken, NJ: Wiley, 2005.

9.5 MANAGING TIME AND WORKLOAD

Nearly every social worker is faced with having too much work and too little time. Thus, the worker must use time management skills, strive to control his or her workload, and increase efficiency on the job. Consider these guidelines:

1. Understand your agency's mission and your job description. Unless you are clear on exactly what needs to be done, you cannot figure out ways to do it effectively and efficiently. If your assignments and responsibilities are not clear, discuss them with your supervisor or administrative superiors. Find out what tasks and assignments are of highest priority.

2. Plan your work. At the end of each day, as well as at the end of each week, write down what you must work on or accomplish the next day and the next week. Start each day with a "to do" checklist. Estimate how much time is needed for each item on the list and plan to allocate the time needed. Anticipate deadlines and begin work on those tasks that must be completed within a certain time frame. It is usually best to tackle lengthy tasks before those that can be completed in a short time. Work on the most difficult tasks when your energy level is highest (e.g., first thing in the morning). Reserve some time at the end of each day for clearing your desk and taking care of any last-minute activities.

3. Adopt a system for setting priorities. One such system is the ABC priority system. On your list of work tasks, write A's next to those that are most important and have highest priority. Write C's next to tasks that are of least importance and B's next to tasks in the middle range. Next, prioritize the A tasks in order of importance, labeling them A–1, A–2, A–3, and so on. The B tasks can be labeled in the same way: B–1, B–2, and so on. At the beginning of the working day, start work on task A–1 and stay with it until it is completed. Then move to A–2 and on down the list.

A less complex approach is to classify all tasks into three categories: (1) tasks that must be completed today, (2) tasks that should be started today, and (3) tasks that can wait a few days.

Realize that priorities may change over the course of a day or week. Thus, it is necessary to continually review and revise your "to do" list.

4. Make decisions in a timely manner. Some workers are afraid of making mistakes and delay or avoid making decisions. Some avoid making a decision because they cannot arrive at a perfect solution. There are few, if any, perfect solutions in the real world of social work practice. One must strive for excellence, but striving for perfection will result only in frustration. If you make a mistake, learn from it, do not waste time brooding over it. A "good" mistake is one from which you learn and do not repeat. A "bad" mistake is one you will repeat.

5. Organize your desk and eliminate clutter in your workspace. Keep the materials you are working on in front of you, but clear your desk of other things. This will help keep your attention on the task at hand. Focus on one thing at a time until you either complete the task or reach a preset time limit for that activity. Avoid jumping from task to task.

Keep your agency's policy and procedures manual up to date and handy. Much time can be lost searching for misplaced information or following an outdated procedure.

An important rule in managing paperwork and paper flow is to handle each paper only once. If you pick up a letter or report, take the action required or discard it if no action is necessary. Do not set it aside; do not let papers pile up on your desk.

6. Develop *a tickler file* to keep track of deadlines for submitting monthly reports and other tasks that must be completed according to a schedule. A tickler file can take several forms: notations on a calendar, a desktop file, a computerized calendar, or electronic date book. Also, develop a workable system for rapid retrieval of frequently used information such as the names, addresses, phone numbers, and email addresses of professionals and agencies that you regularly contact. That system might be a Rolodex or a personal digital assistant.

7. Minimize the time spent in meetings. Unnecessary and poorly planned meetings waste much valuable time. Do not schedule a meeting if an alternative is possible, such as a telephone conference call or email exchanges. If you must have a meeting, make sure all those attending know its purpose and agenda so that they can properly prepare. Start on time and end on time. Stick to the agenda and stay on task. Consider attending the meeting for only the time necessary to make your contribution. (See Items 13.23 and 13.25 for additional guidelines on meetings.)

8. When possible, structure your day by using scheduled appointments for interviews, collateral contacts (contacts with other service providers), and the like. However, plan also for the unexpected and allow time in your schedule for emergencies. Remember Murphy's Laws: "Nothing is as simple as it seems," "Everything will take longer than you think," and "If anything can go wrong, it will." When possible, reduce travel time by scheduling all meetings in a given locality for the same day.

9. Reduce interruptions to a minimum. Drop-in clients are usually less of a problem than staff members who like to chat. When you are interrupted, maintain control of the situation by giving the interruption full attention, and if appropriate, setting a time limit on the interruption. Being able to say no to the question "Do you have a minute?" is an important time-management skill. Closing your office door or standing up to converse with someone who stopped by can help limit unnecessary interruptions.

10. If the lack of a skill is slowing you down or causing time-consuming mistakes, obtain the additional training you need. Ask experienced colleagues to help you devise more efficient approaches to your work. For example, secure their suggestions on how to reduce time spent on writing agency records and reports (see Item 9.1). Become proficient in the use of office machines and communications systems (e.g., email, fax, word processor).

11. To the extent feasible, exercise control over your workload. If you do not you will be spread too thin and your effectiveness will diminish. When asked to take on additional work, consider the following:

- Decide if the proposed assignment or request for your time is reasonable, given your job description and current workload. Ask yourself: Is this a matter of high priority?

Am I responsible for this matter or is someone else? If I take on the extra work, will I soon feel put upon and angry?

- When unsure if the request is reasonable, obtain more information. If still in doubt, ask for some time to think about the request and set a deadline for making the decision (e.g., "I'll let you know in a half hour").
- If you must refuse, give a simple and straightforward explanation without making excuses. If you have a good reason for refusing, there is no need to apologize.

The above discussion of refusing additional work assignments presumes a situation in which there is opportunity to negotiate. In many practice settings that possibility does not exist. An agency supervisor or an administrator has the authority to make work assignments, even when he or she knows you are already overloaded.

In some work situations you can reduce an excessive workload by assigning or delegating certain tasks to other agency staff such as a secretary, case aide, or paraprofessional. However, do not ask others to perform tasks that are beyond their ability or job description.

Selected Bibliography

Morgenstern, Julie. *Time Management from the Inside Out*, 2nd ed. New York: Henry Holt and Co., 2004.

Zeigler, Kenneth. *Getting Organized at Work*. New York: McGraw Hill, 2008.

Zeller, Dirk. *Successful Time Management for Dummies*. Hoboken, NJ: Wiley, 2009.

Techniques and Guidelines for Phases of the Planned Change Process

Social work supervisors have often heard practicum students and new social workers say something like "I understand the basic theory of working with people, but what should I do when I see Mrs. Jones and her daughter this afternoon?" Obviously, these novice workers have discovered that there is a difference between the knowing and the doing in social work practice. They sense a need for direction and guidance that is more specific than that provided by theories and models.

Part IV of this book addresses this need. As was explained in the Preface, the authors chose to prepare a book focusing mostly on techniques and guidelines. This decision reflects their belief that many textbooks do an excellent job of presenting the theoretical frameworks of practice, yet few provide the concrete guidance so often requested by students and new workers.

The five chapters of Part IV correspond to the five phases of the planned change process, as described in Chapter 7. The reader will notice that each of these chapters has a Section A and a Section B. Techniques and guidelines related to direct social work practice are provided in Section A, whereas techniques and guidelines relevant to indirect practice are provided in Section B. The term **direct practice** refers to those activities that involve frequent face-to-face interaction with an individual or family who has requested a service or is experiencing some difficulty. Direct social work practice might include, for example, individual and family counseling, case management, referral work, group treatment, guiding a support group, advocating for the services needed by a specific individual, and so on. By contrast, the term **indirect practice** refers to activities that do not usually involve extensive contact with the clients or consumers of services but which indirectly benefit those who need various types of services or forms of assistance. Examples of indirect practice include administration, staff supervision, program planning, program evaluation, fund-raising, public education, work with community groups and coalitions of agencies concerned about a particular social problem or condition, advocacy on behalf of a persons in need, and efforts to enact legislation and establish social and economic policies that would enhance peoples' lives.

Intake and Engagement

This chapter presents guidelines and techniques for use during the beginning, or start-up phase, of the change process. Although the activities differ somewhat when providing direct services (Section A), as compared to indirect services (Section B), the intent is essentially the same. During this phase, the social worker typically undertakes three sets of activities: preparation, initial engagement, and intake. First, he or she *prepares* for the first contact by reviewing whatever information is available on the client (e.g., agency records), selecting a meeting time and place that will be convenient and comfortable for the client, determining who should be involved in the initial meeting, and remaining alert to other factors that might affect the client's perspective on and investment in the helping process.

Second, the worker will begin the process of *initial engagement* by establishing rapport and helping clients articulate and clarify the nature of their concerns or requests. Typically, clients have tried unsuccessfully to deal with their concerns through friends or other helpers before deciding to seek assistance from a social worker. Given this fact the client, whether an individual or organization, is likely to approach the social worker and the change process with some degree of hesitation, skepticism, and ambivalence. It is important, therefore, to quickly help the client become truly invested in this process by starting to build trust and actively engaging the client in working toward meaningful change.

Third, the worker must determine if he or she can appropriately address the client's need or request. In short, some form or *intake* or screening decision is necessary. In most communities, the human services delivery system is complex and people in search of help or assistance may approach an agency or a professional that will not be able to address the client's specific concern. Or, at the indirect service level, the initial group created to address an agency or community issue may not, on more thorough examination of the matter, be the best structure or the right set of actors to proceed with the change process. The intake decision to be made by the social worker, then, is whether it is appropriate to continue with the client or to refer the client to another organization or professional better suited to address the client's situation.

SECTION A

TECHNIQUES AND GUIDELINES FOR DIRECT PRACTICE

Many clients are anxious and ambivalent during the start-up phase of a helping relationship. They may wonder, for example: Will I be treated with respect? Will this person be able to help? Will he or she really understand my concerns? Will this worker listen to what I have to say? Can my concern or situation be resolved in a reasonable amount of time at a reasonable cost to me?

Preparatory Activities.   Since the first contact is critical because it sets the tone for a helping relationship, the worker should carefully plan for this meeting. However, adequate preparation may not be possible if the initial meeting takes place under crisis conditions. One useful pre-intake activity is to reflect on the fact that the typical client has had some prior experience with other helping professionals and may be skeptical or distrustful of entering still another professional relationship. If the client is involuntary and has been *mandated* (i.e., court ordered) or somehow pressured to see the worker, he or she may be angry or resentful.

Some clients cannot conveniently leave their place of work to see a social worker during usual business hours, and thus weekend or evening appointments may be necessary. Depending on the client's situation, the meeting might take place in the worker's office, in the client's home, or perhaps, in a hospital, jail, group home, or neighborhood center. To the extent possible, the social worker should secure a meeting space that offers comfort, privacy, and accommodations for special needs (e.g., room for a wheelchair). The worker, too, should be concerned with such matters as being on time, having in hand any needed agency intake forms or documents, and if the client had prior involvements with the agency, being familiar with the nature of those contacts.

The social worker should also be sensitive to how the agency environment or milieu might affect the helping relationship. For instance: Is the receptionist courteous and helpful when the client telephones or stops by the agency to initiate contact? Is there a comfortable waiting area for clients? Is childcare available, if needed? Is the worker's office or group meeting room appropriately furnished to create an environment favorable to communication and interaction?

Engagement Activities.   The following activities can help clients take the risk to invest themselves in a helping relationship:

- Greet and speak with the client in a way that is non-threatening and puts him or her at ease.
- Demonstrate genuine interest in the client and his or her request, problem, or situation.
- Explain any legal or ethical rules or obligations related to confidentiality and the handling of information divulged by the client.
- Help the client articulate his or her requests, concerns, and expectations of the agency and worker.
- Identify any fears or misunderstandings the client may have about the social worker, the agency, or its services.
- Explain pertinent eligibility requirements that may affect service provision.
- Address the client's possible ambivalence about receiving services.

During this phase, the worker should be alert to a client's possible fear of the unknown and to people's inherent resistance to change. Making even a small change can create discomfort or fear for clients, especially if they tend to be inflexible and rigid. When clients are anxious or unsure of what is happening or what is expected, they are likely to become somewhat more defensive and hold tightly to their usual patterns of thought and behavior.

Intake Activities.   One decision the social worker must make during the intake and engagement phase is concerned with the continuation of service. The worker must rapidly determine if there is a fit between the client's need or request and the agency's eligibility criteria and requirements. If so, the next decision is whether the worker should provide continuing services (i.e., guide the remainder of the helping process) or transfer the matter to another worker within the agency. That decision will depend on the division of labor in the agency and the competence of the worker to address the client's specific issues. If it is determined that the worker should continue to provide services to the client, some actions that should be taken include the following:

- Assess the urgency of the client's needs or presenting problem and attend to the emergency, if one exists.
- Explain the responsibilities that both the client and worker will assume during the helping process.

- Explain to the client that he or she will need to provide information (in some cases, very personal information) needed to assess the problem or situation.
- Secure the client's signed release of confidential information (if one is needed).
- Reach tentative agreement on the minimum and, if possible, maximum number of meetings that probably will be necessary.
- Explain any fees to be charged. If the provision of services must be authorized by an insurance company, initiate the request for approval.
- Reach agreement on the time, place, and frequency of future meetings.

If the client's request or needs do not match this agency's programs, a referral to an appropriate source of help must be made. Social workers are expected to know about available human services resources (see Item 10.4).

10.1 MAKING THE FIRST TELEPHONE CONTACT

When clients approach an agency for the first time, many will be nervous, confused, and uncertain about what to expect. Responding to this client is a special challenge when the first conversation is by telephone. The worker must use this time on the telephone to lessen the client's fears, obtain a general understanding of the client's concern or request, and, if appropriate, arrange for the first face-to-face interview. Several guidelines should be kept in mind:

1. During a telephone conversation, you cannot read the client's nonverbal behavior. Thus, miscommunication is more likely because you will not always know how the client is reacting to what you are saying. Minimize this possibility of a miscommunication by trying to keep your messages simple, short, and factual. An explanation of details related to your agency's services should be saved for a face-to-face meeting.

2. If speaking with a voluntary client, briefly explore his or her presenting concern or request so that you can evaluate the appropriateness of this referral to your agency. However, avoid gathering detailed intake information by phone; that is best done during a face-to-face interview.

If speaking to a mandated or involuntary client, it is best to confine the phone conversation for simply arranging the first face-to-face interview. The mandated client often has negative feelings about having to meet with a social worker. Such feelings are much easier to read and address during a face-to-face interview (see Item 10.7).

3. When arranging the first office visit, make sure the client knows your name and the location of your office. Some clients may need guidance on how to use public transportation to reach the agency. In some cases, a follow-up letter should be sent to the client, repeating the time and place of the appointment.

4. Be aware of the client's relationships and roles (e.g., child, spouse, parent), and how other family or household members might be impacted by the caller's decision to seek professional assistance. Ask the caller if his or her significant others know of this request for assistance. If the call is being kept secret from others, ask why secrecy is important. Determine if making the call places the caller in danger, as might be the situation in cases of domestic abuse (see Item 15.6).

5. The first telephone contact can be an opportune time to ask the caller if others in his or her family or household should perhaps also attend the first face-to-face meeting. Except in situations in which secrecy is necessary to protect the caller, encourage the caller to consider involving significant others (e.g., spouse, child) in at least the assessment phase of the helping process. Explain, for example, that the assessment of a problem will be more accurate and the intervention more effective if everyone affected can share his or her perception of what is happening and voice ideas on what actions or services might prove helpful. If the caller is open to involving significant others and they are willing to participate, hold out for such a meeting. If the caller does not want others involved, then respect his or her wishes and set up a meeting with the caller alone. Later in the helping process, you might again try to involve the client's significant others, if their participation will make the helping process more effective.

Selected Bibliography

Martin, David, and Allan Moore, eds. *First Steps in the Art of Intervention*. Belmont, CA: Brooks/Cole, 1995.

Ragg, D. Mark. *Building Effective Helping Skills*. Boston: Allyn & Bacon, 2001.

10.2 CONDUCTING THE FIRST FACE-TO-FACE MEETING

It is quite common for the social worker to feel a bit nervous when meeting a client for the first time. It is safe to assume that the client has similar feelings. It is during this first meeting that the worker and client size up each other and form initial impressions. These first impressions can have a powerful effect on what follows. Several guidelines can help the social worker get the interaction off to a good start:

1. Before meeting a client for the first time, try to anticipate what he or she might be thinking and feeling about this meeting. Prepare yourself to respond to the client's possible feelings of fear, confusion, ambivalence, and anger. Realize that the client may perceive you as an unwanted intrusion, an unwelcome stranger, and an authority figure. Be prepared to offer a simple but accurate description of your role, responsibility, and approach to helping and providing services.

2. Create a physical arrangement conducive to good communication. For a two-person meeting, the chairs should face each other. The chairs for a family interview should be arranged in a circle. Make sure the room is comfortable and offers privacy.

3. If the client requested the meeting, begin with some introductory remarks and possibly some small talk, but soon move the focus to the concern that brought the client to the agency. If you initiated the interview, begin by explaining who you are, who you represent, and why you need to speak to the person.

4. Explain the rules of confidentiality that apply and inform the client if what he or she says cannot be held in complete confidence. For example, you might say, "Before we begin, I want to make certain you understand that I will be preparing a report for the court that is based on our meetings. So, what you tell me may end up in my report to the judge. Do you understand that?"

5. Begin with whatever topic the client considers important and wants to talk about (i.e., begin where the client is at). Realize, however, that many clients will at first test the worker's trustworthiness and competence before deciding whether to reveal their real concerns or the whole story. If you have only limited time to spend with a client, explain this at the beginning of the interview so that the topics of highest priority to the client will receive attention.

6. Do not rush the client. Rather, convey the message, "I will give you the time necessary to develop your thoughts and decide what you want to say." Do not jump to conclusions about the nature or cause of the client's presenting concern or problem. Do not display surprise or disbelief in response to what the client tells you.

7. When you do not know the answer to a service-related question asked by the client, explain this in a non-apologetic manner and offer to find the answer. Be careful not to make promises that you may not be able to keep.

8. Some note taking during the intake phase is usually necessary and appropriate. Writing down pertinent client information can demonstrate your desire to understand and remember what the client is saying. Note taking can be distracting, however. If the client is bothered by note taking, show him or her your notes and explain why they are needed. If the client still objects, cease taking notes. If you are completing an agency form, give the client a copy to follow along as you speak.

9. If you and the client agree to a second meeting, be sure the client has your business card and that it lists your name and phone number. Also, be sure that you obtain the client's full name, address, and phone number.

The social worker will encounter a number of clients who have significant *physical or sensory disabilities*. The place and usual patterns of first meetings may need to be altered in order to accommodate their special needs. A few guidelines should be kept in mind:

1. When interviewing a person who is lying in a hospital bed or using a wheelchair, sit or position yourself at eye level with the client. Do not force the client to strain his or her neck or body in order to look at you. Do not stand over him or her for that might place the client in a psychologically inferior position.

2. If the client moves about in a wheelchair or with the aid of a walker or crutches, do not offer assistance unless it is clearly needed. Respect the client's desire to remain in control and decline your offer of assistance. Be patient if it takes the client longer to complete tasks and movements. Avoid fixation on the client's medical equipment or prosthesis.

3. When you meet with a person who is blind and in an unfamiliar physical environment, you may need to provide information he or she needs to move about. For example, you can alert him or her to obstacles or dangers such as overhead obstructions, sharp turns, and stairs. When walking with a person who is blind, simply stay at his or her side and let the person maneuver. Never grab or move the individual, for this is both insulting and frightening. If the client wants your assistance, he or she will ask or reach out; respond by offering your elbow to hold and then walk about a half-step ahead. If the client has a guide dog, be aware that these dogs are trained to walk down the center of a sidewalk or hallway. Do not touch or speak to a guide dog or a service dog unless you have the owner's permission.

4. Individuals with a hearing loss will have difficulty accurately interpreting the human voice, especially when there is background noise and/or several people are talking at once. They may confuse words that sound similar. A type of hearing loss caused by long-term exposure to loud sounds is fairly common among older people, especially men. Because it involves diminished capacity to hear high-frequency sounds, individuals with this type of hearing loss may understand a male voice more easily than a female voice. Even persons wearing hearing aids will have some trouble hearing in a noisy environment.

If your client is struggling to hear, ask what you can do to minimize the client's difficulty. You may need to move to a quieter environment, speak louder, or more slowly. Check often to see if the client is able to follow the conversation. Do not mistake nodding and smiling as a sign of comprehension, for that may be simply the client's response to being embarrassed.

If your client uses speech reading (lip reading), be sure to position yourself so he or she can see your face. Do not position yourself in front of a window or bright light. Do not look away or down at papers while speaking. A heavily mustached mouth may impede speech reading, as well. Do not exaggerate your words, since this will make speech reading more difficult. Realize that even adept lip-readers seldom comprehend more than two-thirds of what it said orally. They must guess at the rest.

A person who is functionally deaf is usually prepared to communicate in writing, by sign language, or through adaptive technology. If the individual will be using sign language, find out what system he or she uses and arrange for the services of an interpreter. Some who are deaf use hearing dogs trained to detect certain sounds such as traffic signals and alarms.

5. Most governmental offices, hospitals, and other essential services are equipped with devices that can be used by persons who have difficulty communicating because of blindness, hearing loss, or speech impairments. A social worker likely to encounter clients with these limitations should become familiar with amplifiers, signaling devices, puff-blow devices, electronic artificial larynx devices, telebraille, telecommunications device for the deaf (TDD), teletypewriter (TTY), and other assistive technology.

Selected Bibliography

Allen, Gina, and Duncan Lanford. *Effective Interviewing in Social Work and Social Care.* New York: Palgrave, 2006.

Morrison, James *The First Interview*, 3rd ed. New York: Guilford, 2008.

Murphy, Bianca, and Carolyn Dillon. *Interviewing in Action*, 3rd ed. Belmont, CA: Brooks/Cole, 2008.

10.3 CLARIFYING THE CLIENT'S PROBLEM, CONCERN, OR REQUEST

An important activity performed by the social worker during the phase known as intake and engagement is to obtain from the client a description of the problem or concern that brought him or her into contact with the social worker or agency. Careful interviewing and questioning is necessary in order to obtain a description that is clear, accurate, and useful. The ways in which clients describe their concerns depends, in part, on whether or not the client is voluntarily seeking assistance. Mandated or non-voluntary clients will often minimize the seriousness of their problem, describe it in only a vague and general manner, and withhold significant information. On the other hand, some voluntary clients overstate the seriousness of their problem and the urgency of their request for service.

Here are examples of questions or statements that a social worker might use to encourage adult clients to more clearly describe their problems or concerns:

- Did someone suggest that you come here and talk to me (or come to this agency)? Who was that? Why did he or she think it was important for you to come here?
- Describe the most recent example of the problem or situation that is adversely affecting your life.
- Describe the time when this problem was the most serious it has ever been.
- If today's meeting with me accomplishes what you hope it will, what will then be different in your life? How will your situation have changed?
- Do you, your family, and your friends agree or disagree on the nature and cause of this problem?
- What have you attempted to do about this problem? How well did that work?
- Do you know of other people who have a similar problem or concern? What did they do about this problem?
- Who else have you talked to about this concern? What did they have to say about it? What suggestions did they offer?
- How have you managed to cope with this problem up to now? What have you done to keep it from getting even worse or even more serious?
- If you could do it, what is the one thing that you would do immediately to make things better for yourself?
- If someone close to you—such as your spouse, child, or parent—were to describe and explain your problem or concern, what would they say about it?
- If someone videotaped your problem and then I watched that tape, what would I especially notice, hear, or see? What would stand out in that video?
- On a scale of 1 to 10—with 1 meaning "of little concern" and 10 meaning "of great concern"—how would you rate the seriousness of your problem today? How would you have rated it two weeks ago? What has changed in the last two weeks? On this scale of 1 to 10, how would your spouse (or child, parent, probation officer) rate this problem?

- Is there a time of day or a particular time of the week when this problem is the most troublesome to you?
- In what places or in what situations is this problem most evident or most serious? Less evident and least serious?
- Think of times when you have experienced this problem. Now, tell me what has usually happened just before the problem occurs or turns worse? What usually happens after you have experienced an episode of this problem?
- If your best friend came to you with this same problem or request and asked for your advice, what would you tell him or her?
- If, all of a sudden, this problem or concern disappeared, what would you then do different-ly? How would each day or week of your life be different if you didn't have this problem? What would you do instead of trying to cope with this problem?
- What is your theory about your problem or concern? Why has it developed or appeared at this point in your life? How do you explain it? Do you think your problem could have been prevented?

Selected Bibliography

Hill, Clara. *Helping Skills*, 2nd ed. Washington, DC: American Psychological Association, 2004.
Kottler, Jeffrey. *Nuts and Bolts of Helping*. Boston: Allyn & Bacon, 2000.

10.4   MAKING A REFERRAL

An important social work activity is to link people to the resources, services, and opportunities they need, want, and can use. Many professionals view referral as a relatively simple task. However, studies indicate that attempted referrals are often unsuccessful. This high rate of failure, possibly 50 percent, indicates that the activity of referral is complex and challenging. By follow-ing these guidelines, the worker can increase the rate of success in the referral process:

1. A **referral** is a carefully planned intervention, based on an assessment, and intended to help a client address a specific problem, concern, or request. Thus, a clarification of the client's situation or problem and some level of data gathering and assessment are prerequisite to making a successful referral. That assessment must determine what the client wants and needs and the type of service he or she is willing to utilize. Any attempt to refer a client for help with a concern or issue that the client does not consider important and a priority is likely to end in failure.

View a referral as the first step in a new helping process. It sets the stage for what will follow. If done well, the referral process can be an empowering and therapeutic experience for the client. The client's active involvement in the referral process can help them to learn commu-nication and problem-solving skills such as problem definition, gathering information, and deci-sion making.

2. Referral is necessary when you or your agency cannot provide the service needed and wanted by a client. Referral to another professional is appropriate when you do not have the knowl-edge or skills needed to work with a particular client or when you have reason to believe your own values, attitudes, religious beliefs, or lack of language skills would be a significant barrier in devel-oping an effective helping relationship. Attempting to shed responsibility for having to deal with a difficult and frustrating client is never an acceptable reason for referral. "Passing the buck" or "dumping" a troublesome client on another agency or professional is unprofessional and unethical.

3. Before deciding that referral is necessary, make sure you have considered all possible sources of assistance available within your own agency. Because any attempted referral carries a risk of failure, the social worker should first utilize all the relevant resources of an agency to which the client is already linked. Also, be sure to consider the client's friends, relatives, neighbors, and other informal resources as possible sources of assistance.

Be realistic about what other agencies and professionals have to offer your client. Recognize that just because a service or a program exists, that does not mean that it will be available to your client. And, just because a service is available, that does not mean that your client is ready and willing to use it.

4. Before considering a referral, make sure you know of all the agencies and professionals already involved with the client. Some client concerns are best handled through interagency case coordination and improved case management, rather than by a referral that expands the number of agencies and professionals involved. The professionals and agencies already working with a client should be consulted before attempting to refer the client to yet another program. The client's permission will usually be needed before this discussion can take place. Whenever necessary, obtain releases of information signed by the client prior to engaging in the referral process.

5. In order to make an effective referral, you must know about existing community resources. Thus, a social worker must invest the time and energy necessary to learn about resources and keep up with the constant change that occurs within the community resource system. Most communities have a clearinghouse and/or computerized database designed to help the user identify existing health and social service agencies, programs, and providers.

Just knowing that a resource exists is seldom sufficient. It is also important for the worker to know someone employed at the agency or program who can be used as a contact point. Use agency visits as well as NASW and other professional meetings as opportunities to meet people working in the agencies to which you might be referring clients.

6. A client's prior experiences with helping professionals and programs will affect a client's willingness to consider a referral. If they were negative, the client may hesitate to seek assistance from another resource, even if it offers an important service. A discussion of those experiences and how the client approached and interacted with these resources may yield clues as to what needs to be done to facilitate a successful referral.

The success of a referral will often depend on whether others in the client's social network support the plan. Thus, it is often a good idea to ask the client if family members or friends agree or disagree with the referral being discussed. Also, ask the client if he or she wants certain trusted friends or family members to participate in discussing a possible referral. Whenever appropriate and desired by the client, the client's family and significant others should be involved in making these decisions. Their participation will, of course, increase the number of opinions and may slow down the process. However, in the long run, involving those persons who exert an influence on the client will increase the chances that the referral will be successful. In addition, it will reduce the chances that they might later sabotage the client's utilization of the service or program to which the client was referred.

7. When the client is in need of a service for which there is a fee, you must address the issues of cost and the client's ability to pay. Some clients will need guidance and assistance in order to obtain information from insurance companies, managed care organizations, or public programs and then determine whether they have a way of paying for a service. In this era of managed care, you must consider the questions of whether the client's private health insurance or public medical program (e.g., Medicaid) will cover certain medical procedures or specific types of services and whether a particular professional is on the list of providers acceptable to the managed care company. Helping a client secure the proper preauthorization from the managed care company may be an important step in making a successful referral to a health care provider.

8. Agency decisions concerning eligibility for services, benefits, and entitlement are often tied to questions about whether the applicant fits into a legally defined category and meets eligibility or intake criteria. Thus, referral work requires skill in gathering information and documentation related to, for example, citizenship, marriage, parent–child relationships, prior employment, income, household composition, medical conditions, and so forth. It is important for the worker to know how to verify information and obtain key documents such as citizenship papers, birth certificates, marriage certificates, divorce decrees, death certificates, tribal enrollment numbers, and military service papers.

9. All agencies and private practitioners have their own methods of operation, policies, and eligibility criteria. Do not expect them to suspend these procedures as a favor to you or your client. Be careful not to tell a client that he or she is eligible for a particular service, unless you have the authority to make such eligibility decisions. Do speak for or second-guess another professional or agency.

10. If possible, give the client several options from which to choose the agency or professional he or she wishes to utilize. If the client asks for your advice or recommendation, you have an obligation to give your honest assessment.

When assisting a client in the selection of service provider, especially if the service is counseling or psychotherapy, ask yourself this question: Would I refer my own mother or my own child to this professional? Refer clients only to those professionals whom you know to be competent and ethical.

Ordinarily, when telling a client about services available through another professional or agency, you should explain both the advantages and limitations of those services. However, with clients who are confused, fearful, or highly dysfunctional, it is best to avoid focusing on the limitations because doing so may create an added barrier to the client's use of an important and needed service.

11. Whenever possible, clients should make their own arrangements for securing the services they want. In some cases, however, the client who is frightened, immature, or overwhelmed will need considerable help and guidance in setting up an appointment, securing transportation, arranging child care, and the like. Do whatever is needed to establish the linkage. If the client is very confused or fearful about going to an agency, you will need to accompany the client or perhaps you can arrange for a family member or volunteer to provide this assistance.

Give special attention to the practical problems that may become barriers to a successful referral (e.g., client's lack of transportation or phone, inability to read, lack of child care during appointments, fearfulness associated with travel in a high-crime area, inability to take time away from job).

12. Going to a new or unfamiliar agency will be stressful for many individuals. They may encounter a rude or harried receptionist, an overwhelmed intake worker, complex application forms, confusing eligibility requirements, and waiting lists. Some clients will need a great deal of emotional support during the referral process, and some will need to be coached on how to approach an agency and apply for services. Without this extra help, they may abandon their effort to obtain the services they need.

13. In some cases, the referral of a client to another agency or professional means that the client must end a satisfying, familiar relationship and face the task of building new relationships with unfamiliar persons. Although the client may see the logic of the referral and the need to use another resource, he or she may be fearful, ambivalent, or even resentful about having to do so. Explore and address those feelings of separation so that they do not block the referral.

14. Take steps to make sure your client successfully connects with the resource (professional, agency, or program) to which you are referring him or her. These **connecting techniques** have proven effective:

- Write out for the client the name, address, and phone number of the resource, and, if necessary, provide him or her with detailed instructions on how to get there (e.g., draw a map or plot the bus route).
- Provide the client with the name of the person he or she is to contact.
- Compose a brief letter addressed to the resource that the client will hand deliver to the resource. This statement should briefly describe the client's concern or request, and the client should be involved in composing this message.

- Contact the resource by phone when the client is with you. Then after speaking to the resource and explaining the intended referral, hand the phone to the client so that he or she will experience some conversation with the resource.

Sometimes an individual's initial contact at the agency will be with an employee who does not listen carefully and launches into a detailed explanation of the service, program, eligibility, and so on. Some instruction and guidance may be necessary to prepare the client to ask the right questions and to be assertive during the phone conversation or meeting.

15. Even after the client has had the first interview with the resource, take steps to cement or solidify this connection. Various **cementing techniques** increase the chance that the client will continue using this resource. For example:

- Ask the client to call you after he or she has had the first contact and discuss what happened. Find out what he or she is thinking and feeling about making use of this resource.
- With the client's agreement, contact him or her after the first scheduled meeting with the resource to see if things went as expected.
- Plan a series of interviews with the client while he or she is using the new resource in order to provide encouragement and detect possible problems that the client may be encountering with the new resource.

16. Evaluate your referral work. Determine whether the client actually received what he or she wanted from the professional or agency, if the client is making progress, and if your approach to making referrals needs to be modified.

Selected Bibliography

Abramson, Julie. "Six Steps to Effective Referrals." In *Agency-Based Social Work,* edited by Harold Weissman, Irwin Epstein, and Andrea Savage, 65–71. Philadelphia: Temple University Press, 1983.

Crimando, William, and T. F. Riggar. *Community Resources: A Guide for Human Service Workers*, 2nd ed. Long Grove, IL: Waveland Press, 2005.

Levinson, Risha, ed. *New Routes to Human Services: Information and Referral.* New York: Springer, 2002.

Reamer, Frederic. *Pocket Guide to Essential Human Services*. Washington DC: NASW, 2005.

10.5   OBTAINING, PROTECTING, AND RELEASING CLIENT INFORMATION

During the engagement and intake phase, the social worker will begin to gather client information and construct a client record. Once obtained, this information must be handled in ways that protect the client's privacy. In recent years, the laws and regulations concerning the creation, storage, and exchange of client information have grown more complex and restrictive. Moreover, different federal and state laws apply in different practice settings (e.g., hospitals, schools, substance abuse programs, child protection agencies, correctional programs).

In general, the newer laws provide the consumers of health and social services with greater privacy and make providers more accountable for the records they keep. They give clients and patients greater access to their own records and more control over who can read the record. For example, the Health Insurance Portability and Accountability Act (HIPAA)[*] is a federal law that

---

[*]The purpose of HIPAA is broader than addressed here. That is, the legislation is intended "to improve portability and continuity of health insurance coverage in the group and individual markets, to combat waste, fraud and abuse in health insurance and health care delivery, to promote the use of medical savings accounts, to improve access to long-term care services coverage, to simplify the administration of health insurance, and for other purposes" (Preamble to Public Law No. 104–191, 110 Stat.1936). For human services providers, the requirement for accountability relative to clients' private information is what makes being familiar with this legislation especially important.

applies to providers of health and mental health services, including clinical social workers and social workers employed in medical settings, if they or their organization engages in the electronic exchange of information with health insurance providers, clearinghouses, or other health or mental health care providers. Among the many HIPAA rules and regulations, the following are critical for social workers:

- At the beginning of the professional relationship, the client or patient must be notified of his or her privacy rights and informed how the provider of services intends to use and possibly share his or her health information.
- The client or patient has a right to see, copy, and supplement (i.e., correct) his or her records. However, the provider may deny a patient access to records in certain circumstances, such as when there is reason to believe that disclosure will cause harm to the patient or some other person or result in the disclosure of other protected information.
- The provider of services is required to have in place certain technical and administrative procedures designed to safeguard client information, especially information that is stored in a computer or transferred electronically.
- Providers are barred from disclosing health information to a client's employer.
- Under ordinary circumstances, the provider can release a client's health information only with the client's permission. However, a provider may share client information with others on a need-to-know basis if his or her purpose is to secure a professional consultation; to arrange care, treatment, and other services for the client or patient; to secure payment; and/or to conduct an audit, quality of care assessment, or the like.
- Providers of mental health services can refuse to disclose psychotherapy notes to the client's health insurance company without the client's authorization.
- Health insurance companies and health plans may not condition enrollment or the delivery of benefits on obtaining the client's authorization to release information.
- A hospital patient has a right to opt out of having his or her name and health status made available to interested and concerned persons.
- When records and notes are to be discarded, they must be shredded. They should not be placed whole in a waste container.

In all practice settings, social workers must follow the ordinary procedures intended to safeguard client information. For example:

- All client information and files should be stored in locked files. Only those professionals or agency employees with a legitimate need to know can have access to these materials.
- Computer screens, appointment books, and files containing client information must be kept out of the sight of all other clients, persons in waiting rooms, janitors, and other agency personnel.
- Professionals should discuss matters related to clients only when behind closed doors. Phone conversations with clients or about clients should not occur in areas where they might be overheard.
- When a client's file is being used, it should be placed face down on the desk so as not to display the client's name or any other client information.
- The possibility of violating a client's privacy must by evaluated before sending a client a letter (e.g., an appointment reminder), since even the return address on an envelope and letterhead stationary connects the client to a certain type of professional or organization.

Fundamentally, the client record maintained by a social agency or a private practitioner belongs to the client. This means that the client decides whether and to whom this information will be released. (Parents and legal guardians control the release of information concerning minor-age children.) If a social worker wants information contained in a record maintained by another agency or professional, the worker must first obtain the client's written permission. Similarly, a worker must never release client information to someone outside his or her own agency without first obtaining the client's written permission to do so. There are, however, some exceptions to this general principle. For example, a client's records may be released in response to a court order, and in most states, a protective services investigator (e.g., someone investigating child or elder abuse or neglect) may by law access a client records without the client's permission.

The written permission granted by the client is often called a *consent to release confidential information* or simply, a *consent form.* Typically, agencies have a standard form for this purpose. Legally and ethically, the client's permission must constitute informed consent. In other words, before signing a release, the client should do the following:

- Know what information is being requested, by whom, and for what purpose.
- Have an opportunity to read the material being requested, or if necessary, have it read and explained in words he or she can understand.
- Have an opportunity to correct any errors in the record before it is released.
- Be informed of the possible negative consequences if the information is released and possible consequences if the information is not released.
- Understand that a signed consent form can be revoked at a later date.

In most situations, the consent will automatically expire six months after being signed by the client.

The rules surrounding the release of client information can make it difficult for professionals and agencies to share information needed for an accurate diagnosis or assessment and can create an added barrier to effective case management and the coordination of services provided to the client by several different agencies. In addition, laws giving clients easy access to their records have had an effect on what is actually written into the record. Professionals may be reluctant to include information that could be upsetting to the client or his or her family if they were to read the record. A school social worker, for example, may be reluctant to record the content of a discussion with a student about the parent–child relationship if the worker knows that the parent can review the school record.

When a social worker is documenting service to a client (i.e., writing an entry into the client record), the worker should always assume that the client—or the client's parent or guardian if the client is a minor or legally incompetent—has a right to read this record. Moreover, the social worker should assume that the client may copy the record, question what is written, and ask that the record be changed to correct any errors.

Deciding what is and is not part of an official agency record is more difficult than it might seem. For example, is a report prepared by a private psychologist part of the agency record just because it has been placed in the client's file? Or, what about a report that the social worker obtained from a school? The social worker must understand agency policy and procedure concerning such questions before responding to a written request to release a client record.

In the absence of legal guidance to the contrary, the social worker should presume that records and reports prepared by and/or obtained from a third party (e.g., a doctor, another agency) are not a part of the worker's own agency's record. In other words, an agency's client record consists only of those materials that were prepared by or written by the agency's personnel. Thus, the worker should not release letters or reports that were prepared by persons outside his or her agency, even if they are contained in or stored in the agency file.

Some professional licensing laws provide for what is termed *privileged communication,* a protection that usually applies to doctor–patient, attorney–client, husband–wife, and priest–penitent relationships. However, a state's law might extend the privilege to the social worker–client relationship. This privilege belongs to the client or patient, not to the professional. It is claimed or asserted by the client when he or she learns that personal information covered by the privilege has been subpoenaed and could be disclosed in a legal proceeding. The client asks the judge to recognize the privilege and prevent the disclosure. The judge must then decide if there is a compelling need to reveal the information.

Whenever a social worker is uncertain about his or her legal or ethical responsibility regarding the handling of client information, the worker should consult an attorney and the agency administrator and also review the general legal information offered online by the NASW (www.socialworkers.org/ldf).

Selected Bibliography

Dickson, Donald. *Confidentiality and Privacy in Social Work*. New York: Free Press, 1998.
National Association of Social Workers. "HIPAA Highlights for Social Workers." 2004. Available online:
    www.naswdc.org/hipaa/default.asp.
Saltzman, Andrea, and David Furman. *Law in Social Work Practice*, 2nd ed. Chicago: Nelson-Hall, 1999.
Zur, Ofer. *The HIPPA Compliance Kit*, 3rd ed. New York: Norton, 2005.

10.6   CONDUCTING AN IN-HOME INTERVIEW

The term **in-home interview** (or home visit) refers to a meeting between the social worker and client in the client's home. In the early days of social work, home visiting was the modus operandi of the worker but it was gradually abandoned by many social workers because it did not seem professional and did not fit the popular office-based models of therapy. Of course, the home visit has always been used by social workers employed by child protection and public health agencies and by those engaged in out-reach and the provision of home-based services, and those providing assistance to the frail elderly. Despite its usefulness and necessity in many cases, the in-home interview is a source of anxiety for many social workers. Following these guidelines can help the worker make proper use of this valuable diagnostic and treatment tool:

1. Understand the rationale for meeting with clients in their natural environment. Meeting in an agency building or in a professional's office is often necessary and appropriate, but such a setting can be awkward and stressful for many clients. When in a convenient and familiar setting, such as their own home, clients are more likely to be open, relaxed, and authentic.

The home visit or in-home interview is especially valuable in helping the worker obtain an accurate picture of the client's family and neighborhood contexts and for gaining an appreciation of how various forces within the client's environment either support or impinge on his or her social functioning. Ebeling and Hill (1983) explain that a person's home is his or her sacred space and a reflection of the individual's personality and lifestyle:

> Within the walls of a home, people experience the intimate moments of their lives. They sleep, wake up, bathe, eat, drink, make love, and raise children. They fight, scream, and rejoice; they cry, laugh, and sing. They may experience the warmth of positive object relationships, the anguish of negative ones, or isolation and loneliness. . . . Their outer space reflects their inner space. The way the homes are decorated and furnished can reveal either the chosen lifestyle of the occupants or their economic position. It can also indicate depression, despair, and disorganization. (p. 64)

2. Do not confuse the in-home interview with a purely social or friendly visit. This technique, like all others, is to be used in a purposeful manner. When the social worker requests an in-home interview, the client should be given a clear explanation as to how and why it can make the service more effective.

An in-home interview should be scheduled. Unannounced and unscheduled visits should be avoided but this may not be possible if a client does not have a phone or is unable to read a letter.

If you must stop by a client's home unannounced, explain immediately your previous efforts to reach him or her and use the conversation to set up a scheduled visit. (Often, the client will immediately invite you in.)

3. When you enter the client's home extend the same respect and courtesy you expect when someone visits your home. Ask where you are to be seated. Accept an appropriate offer of food or drink. Convey a genuine interest in family pictures and household furnishings that are an expression of the client's identity, interests, and culture. Ebeling and Hill (1983, p. 66) remind us that the social worker must never show shock or disapproval upon entering the client's home: "No matter what the condition of the building, . . . regardless of the number of dogs, the darkness of the halls, or the odors of the stairways; no matter how barren or cluttered or 'hospital' clean; even no matter what signs of impulsivity, violence, or sexual acting out are encountered."

4. Obtaining privacy is sometimes a problem during a home visit. Children may run in and out, neighbors may stop by, the telephone may ring, and the TV may be blaring. This will be distracting to you but probably not to your client. On the positive side, it provides a glimpse into the client's daily routine and environment. Significant distractions are best dealt with directly by expressing a need for privacy and for attention to the meeting's purpose. When friends or neighbors are in the home, the client should be asked if it is permissible to discuss private matters in their presence. Some clients may invite trusted and supportive friends to sit in on the interview, and this choice should be respected.

5. If the client lives in a dangerous neighborhood, it is important to schedule the home visit for a time of day when the risks are minimal. Ask the client for suggestions on how best to minimize the risks. If the client or others in the household are possibly dangerous and/or if you are concerned that you might be falsely accused of inappropriate behavior, you should bring along a colleague for added protection and to serve as an observer or witness (see Item 10.9).

Selected Bibliography

Allen, Susan, and Elizabeth Tracy. *Delivering Home-Based Services: A Social Work Perspective.* New York: Columbia University Press, 2009.

Ebeling, Nancy, and Deborah Hill, eds. *Child Abuse and Neglect.* Boston: John Wright, PSG, 1983.

Newton, Nancy, and Kadi Sprengle. *Psychosocial Interventions in the Home.* New York: Springer, 2000.

Wasik, Barbara, and Donna Bryant. *Home Visiting: Procedures for Helping Families,* 2nd ed. Newbury, CA: Sage, 2000.

10.7   ENGAGING THE MANDATED CLIENT

As used here, **mandated client** (or *involuntary client*) refers to an individual who is required or mandated to utilize professional counseling or some other service by a legal authority, such as a judge, probation officer, or child protection agency. Not infrequently, such a client is often resentful, angry, and sometimes belligerent. Consider these guidelines when working with a mandated client:

1. Prepare yourself for meeting this client by recalling how it feels when you are forced to do something you do not want to do or are forced to do something that seems unfair and unnecessary. Assume that the client will have negative feelings and that you will encounter hostility, anger, shame, fear, and embarrassment, and a number of defensive reactions. Do not ignore or sidestep the client's feelings; rather acknowledge them and respond with sensitivity and empathy. Maintain your self-discipline and do not respond to the client's hostility with anger or threats for this will generate even more hostility and resistance. Use the skills of active listening to help the client articulate his or her perspectives and to tell his or her side of the story (see Items 8.1, 8.4, and 8.6).

2. When you first meet with your client, reveal the factual information you have about why he or she has been mandated to utilize certain services. If the client denies the accuracy of this information, explain that you will check the records and reports and speak with authorities in order to clarify and verify the information and resolve any disagreements or misunderstandings. Seek clarification from the referring source (e.g., probation officer) if there is a significant discrepancy between the client's perspective and the information you received from the person who referred this client.

3. Provide a clear and honest explanation of both your role and responsibility, as well as what you or your agency expect of the client. Also, explain the rules of confidentiality that apply. For example, if you are required to prepare a report to the court, the client has a right to know that what he or she reveals may end up in this report and be discussed by the judge and attorneys in open court.

Inform the client of any adverse consequences that may occur if he or she does not cooperate. However, respect the client's right to choose the consequences rather than your services. Remind the client who decides not to cooperate that he or she is, in effect, giving up the control he or she has to influence the outcome.

4. In some cases it may be helpful to discuss the client's previous experiences—especially the negative experiences—with professionals or the social services system, along with any preconceived notions he or she has about social workers, counselors, or other professional helpers. Also, be aware of the client's cultural background or experience with discrimination and how this might add to his or her feeling of being overpowered by or alienated from social institutions.

5. Within the limits and legal constraints placed on the client, give him or her as much choice as possible. Allowing the client to make some decisions and choices and have some control over even minor details will usually lower his or her resistance—for example: "We have to meet each Wednesday for the next six weeks. We can meet either at 2:00 p.m. or 4:00 p.m. What is your choice?"

6. Do not ask questions that could be interpreted as trickery or an attempt to catch him or her telling a lie. Make it clear to the client that you do not want him or her to lie or fabricate, using an explanation something like this:

> I am aware that you are angry about having to talk to me. I can understand that. I can also understand that there may be times during our session when you will be tempted to lie to me. More than anything else, I do not want you to lie. If you lie, you may then feel guilty or also worry about me catching you in that lie. That would not be good for you. Rather than lie, I want you simply to tell me that you do not want to answer my question. Is that something you can agree to?

7. If usual efforts to engage the client and establish a beginning level of cooperation have not worked and the client remains resistant, consider using the "Let's make a deal" tactic. In this approach, the worker agrees to do something that will lessen the client's discomfort or help the client get something he or she wants (something legal and legitimate) in exchange for the client's cooperation or the client's completion of certain specified tasks. An example of this approach would be a worker who says something like the following:

> Well John, it is apparent that you do not want to come here for counseling. But you and I both know that your probation officer, Mr. Roberts, is insisting that you get help with what he calls your anger problem. If you don't do what your PO wants, then he may make your life even more difficult. How about us making a deal? If you see me for five one hour sessions, answer my questions, and talk honestly about your relationships with your wife and children, I will, in return, write a letter to Mr. Roberts and say that you have made a good faith effort to use our counseling sessions to examine what others say is your anger problem.

8. Unmotivated clients do not exist. All clients are motivated and all have wants, needs, and preferences. When a professional labels a client as "unmotivated," he or she is simply acknowledging that what the client wants is different from what the practitioner wants for the client. Successfully engaging the mandated client requires that the worker tap into the client's own needs and wants and establish intervention goals that are at least partially consistent with the client's preferences and inclinations. Thus, strive to identify something that both you and the client agree is a legitimate goal or a desirable course of action. Once there is an agreed-upon goal, you can more easily engage the client in problem solving. For example, you might say, "Well, we both want you to get off probation so you won't have to see me each week. We can agree on that. What ideas or suggestions do you have on how we can work together to achieve that goal?"

9. With most clients, some degree of self-disclosure by the worker has the effect of decreasing the client defensiveness and resistance. However, when working with persons who are skilled manipulators or sociopaths, you should avoid sharing personal information. The use of worker self-disclosure with these individuals will usually have serious and unwanted consequences because of their uncanny ability to spot, exploit, and twist a helper's personal weakness and mistakes (see Item 10.8).

Selected Bibliography

Harris, George. *Overcoming Resistance: Success in Counseling Men*. Laurel, MD: American Correctional Association, 1995.

Ivanoff, Andre, Betty Blythe, and Tony Tripodi. *Involuntary Clients in Social Work Practice*. New York: Aldine de Gruyter, 1994.

Rooney, Ronald. *Strategies for Work with Involuntary Clients*, 2nd ed. New York: Columbia University Press, 2009.

Trotter, Chris. *Working with Involuntary Clients*, 2nd ed. Thousand Oaks, CA: Sage, 2006.

Welo, Beverly, ed. *Tough Customers: Counseling Unwilling Clients*. Laurel, MD: American Correctional Association, 2001.

10.8   RESPONDING TO THE MANIPULATIVE CLIENT

Most people, at least occasionally, attempt to manipulate others as a way of getting what they want. Some individuals, however, rely on manipulation and "conning" as a primary means of interacting with others and coping with life. Such individuals can be difficult clients because they are skilled in the art of using other people. Social workers who are unable to detect a manipulation may quickly find themselves in legal, ethical, and moral difficulties.

Some of the most practiced manipulators are labeled as sociopaths or psychopaths or as having an antisocial personality disorder. Many have a history of criminal activity. A hallmark of psychopaths is their lack of conscience. They seem to lack the capacity for empathy and for experiencing genuine remorse or guilt. Additional common characteristics include a glib and superficial manner of relating, egocentric and grandiose thinking, shallow emotions, impulsiveness and poor self-control, strong need for excitement and risk taking, and antisocial behavior. For them, truth is whatever fits their purpose at the moment. Many of these individuals grew up in environments where manipulation was the key to physical and psychological survival; thus, it is useful to view their manipulation as the continuation of patterns that proved effective in the past.

Here are a few guidelines for dealing with a manipulative client:

1. The manipulative client, like all clients, is deserving of respect. With this client, however, you need to be very cautious. Yochelson and Samenow (1985) remind us that the habitual manipulator is always behaving in ways that help him or her gain control of others:

> He tries to determine what others want to hear and feeds it to them. He finds and uses opportunities for digression and diversion. He discloses as it suits his purposes.

He slants his version of events to make himself a victim and blames others for his plight in life. He tries whatever he thinks will impress the [professional helper], enlist his sympathy and compassion, or convince him of a particular point of view. Failing this, he uses a variety of tactics to put [the helper] on the defensive. These may be couched in highly intellectual terms as the criminal argues the meaning of a word, disputes a philosophic issue, and generalizes a point to absurdity. However, there are also open power plays as he intimidates, threatens, ridicules and erupts with angry reactions.

The [helper will not be] . . . successful if he allows a criminal to set the conditions of a meeting. . . . The [helper] must stand firm. . . . [A professional] who is indecisive or lacks confidence does not instill confidence or respect in a criminal. Nor can [a professional] who is permissive later establish himself as a firm authority. Many criminals have had experience with permissive [helpers] and have exploited them. A person who is shy, timid, or reserved may do well in many endeavors, but he will fail to effect change in criminals. (p. 541)

2. When working with an individual who is manipulative your must be explicit in outlining your role, what you can and cannot do as a professional person, and your expectations of the client. You must demonstrate firmness. You must remain in control. Be reasonable and fair but unwavering in your expectations. Hold the client accountable and do not rescue him or her from the natural consequences of their dishonesty. Before deciding to change their behavior, a habitual manipulator will usually need to experience the punishing consequences of their actions.

Do not go along with or overlook the client's attempts to minimize or side step personal responsibility. Many will make frequent use of the word *but* as a way of avoiding responsibility or downplaying the seriousness of a behavior (e.g., "Well yes, I did steal some money *but* only 30 dollars" or "I hit him with a baseball bat *but* not very hard").

Never break or even bend agency rules as a favor to this client because even a minor concession leads quickly to additional requests or a blackmail situation (e.g., "Look, if you won't do this for me, I'll tell your supervisor that you violated program rules when you allowed me to smoke in the hallway").

3. Suspect manipulation whenever your client takes an inordinate interest in your personal life or your feelings about your job. Be especially cautious when your client says things such as "You are the only person who really understands me," "No one else has ever been as helpful as you," "You are the most caring person I have ever met," "I need to tell you something but you must promise not to tell this to anyone else," "If you could do this one thing for me, I can get my life straightened out," and "I have a wonderful opportunity to pull my life together—I just need a small loan."

4. If you suspect that you are being drawn into manipulation, consult with another professional. If you are part of a team, raise your concerns with team members; you may discover that the client is saying very different things to other team members. An elevated level of communication and coordination is necessary to keep team members from being drawn into a manipulation where one is played against another.

5. Unfortunately, there is no completely reliable way of detecting a lie, especially when the person who is lying has little conscience and is practiced in the art of deception. Nevertheless, a few observations and special techniques may help you detect a lie:

- Engage the person in several minutes of friendly small talk before addressing a topic about which he or she might lie. A deception is suggested by an obvious change in the client's voice, facial expressions, or other body language when you begin to focus on the sensitive area.
- Most people feel somewhat uncomfortable when they lie. Consequently, when lying, their voices often become higher in pitch, they are more likely to stumble over words, and they are more prone to frequent blinking and fidgeting.

- Even a clever, confident, and experienced liar cannot completely control his or her facial expressions. Thus, the individual may exhibit a momentary look of panic if he or she begins to fear that he or she has made a mistake and the lie has been detected.
- When lying, people tend to use fewer descriptive phrases and fewer hand motions than when not engaged in a deception.
- The experienced liar has prepared and practiced responses to commonly asked questions, but his or her response often sounds emotionally flat. Asking an unusual or unexpected question may catch him or her off guard and uncover a deception.
- When asked a question, someone telling the truth will respond quickly because he or she has only one thing to say—the truth. By contrast, someone who wants to deceive will hesitate before answering because he or she must first weigh the pros and cons of various answers.
- A person who is lying tends to decrease the level of intimacy. Thus, he or she will look away, avoid touching, and move back slightly from the person to whom he or she is lying. The person who is lying will use words that are less intimate. For example, he or she will avoid the pronouns *I*, *me*, *my*, and *we* and instead use more distant, objective words such as *them*, *that*, or *it*.
- People who are telling the truth will not hesitate to give detailed and specific answers to questions. Those who are lying will usually answer with generalities because they fear being tripped up by details and specifics. However, some who are very skilled at lying will attempt to bolster their credibility by overwhelming the questioner with details. If these skillful liars are told that their answers can and will be checked for accuracy, they usually back away from specifics.
- Individuals who are right-handed typically move their eyes up and to the left when trying to accurately remember an image or set of details. When trying to fabricate a visual image or put together a deceptive story, their eyes usually move up and to the right. The right and left movements are reversed for a left-handed person.

Selected Bibliography

Allen, Bud, and Diana Bosta. *Games Criminals Play*. Sacramento: Rae John, 1981.

Lieberman, David. *You Can Read Anyone: Never Be Fooled, Lied To, or Taken Advantage of Again*. New York: MJF Books, 2009. St. Martin's Press, 1998.

Simon, George. *In Sheep's Clothing: Understanding and Dealing with Manipulative People*. Little Rock, AK: A.J. Christopher, 1996.

Yochelson, Samuel, and Stanton Samenow. *The Criminal Personality*, vol. 2. Northvale, NJ: Jason Aronson, 1985.

10.9   INCREASING PERSONAL SAFETY IN DANGEROUS SITUATIONS

At times social work practice places the worker in dangerous situations. The workers most at risk are those who work directly with clients who are angry, highly stressed, and prone to violence. Such clients are most likely to be found in criminal justice settings, child protection, hospitals for the criminally insane, and addiction treatment programs. Some social workers may encounter bio-hazardous materials in health care facilities and possibly during visits to clients' homes, especially if the client's home has been involved in the use or manufacture of illegal drugs. To minimize the risk of being injured, the social worker should adhere to the following guidelines:

1. Never enter a dangerous situation without first consulting with others about your intentions. Consider the situation to be high risk whenever you are to meet with an individual who has a history of violence and whenever you are to meet an unfamiliar client in a nonpublic or isolated location. If you must enter a very dangerous situation, request police protection. Social workers may unexpectedly find themselves in danger if they inadvertently encounter an illegal activity such as drug dealing.

2. A history of violent behavior is the most reliable predictor of future violence. Statistically speaking, an individual most likely to commit violent acts has one or more the following characteristics and life experiences:

- Has a history of committing violent acts
- Is violent when under the influence of alcohol or drugs
- Is or was the target of family violence during childhood
- Is or was the target of violence in his or her community
- Has been publicly humiliated
- Is part of a violent peer group or gang
- Is experiencing a high level of stress
- Is a male teen or a young adult
- Has experienced a traumatic brain injury

3. An agency's recordkeeping system should use some method of flagging the case record of a dangerous client so that the social worker meeting with this client can take appropriate precautions. In especially dangerous practice settings, a professional's desk or office should be equipped with an emergency call button. At minimum, agencies should have an internal telephone code so that the staff will recognize a disguised call for help. For example, in a telephone message such as "Hello, Bob. This is Jim. Would you send a copy of our red resource book to my office?" might be code for "I am in danger; send security to my office."

4. The office or meeting room where the social worker will encounter a potentially dangerous client should be set up so that the worker has quick assess to the door or another escape route. Also, the room should be cleared of items that could be grabbed and used as weapons (e.g., letter openers, staplers, umbrellas, paperweights).

5. When making a home visit, keep your office informed of your itinerary and check in by phone according to a prearranged schedule. Before entering a client's home or building, take a few seconds to look around and think seriously about your safety. Are you alone? Where are the escape routes? Do you hear a violent argument in process? Do the people inside sound out of control? If I go in will I be able to get out?

6. Never move through a doorway and into a room as a response to an invitation to "come in" unless you can see the person who is speaking and he or she has seen you. Being mistaken for someone else can be dangerous. When entering a room containing a hostile person, move in slowly. Remain on the periphery until you assess the situation and advance slowly. Do not quickly move into the person's space because intrusive movements may trigger violent behavior.

7. Be alert to anything about the situation that feels or looks unusual or out of place. We all possess an unconscious danger detector. Thus, trust your gut feelings. If you feel afraid, assume that you are in danger, even if you cannot pinpoint why you are feeling this way.

8. Most people who are very angry will vent (e.g., scream, curse) for two or three minutes and then begin to gradually calm down. However, some individuals are further stimulated and agitated by what they say and think. If an angry individual is not starting to calm down after a few minutes of angry venting, assume that the situation has become more dangerous.

9. Do not touch an angry person; do nothing that could be interpreted as a threat, challenge, or a dare. Encourage the client to sit down, as this will usually have a calming effect. If safe to do so, sit rather than stand, because sitting is a less aggressive stance. However, avoid sitting in an overstuffed chair because it can be difficult to rapidly get up and out of a well-cushioned chair. Also, it is best to avoid sitting on a cushioned chair or sofa because it might contain a needle left over after a drug injection. Rather, pick a hard and movable chair that could also serve a protective shield if you are attacked.

10. Be alert to signs of imminent attack, such as flaring nostrils, rapid breathing, dilated pupils, pulsing veins, grinding teeth, pointing fingers, clenched fists, crouching, and choppy and bobbing (boxer-like) movements of the body. Do not turn your back to an angry or distraught person or let that person or others in the room walk behind you. If the danger level of the situation escalates, leave.

11. When in the home of a potentially violent person, be alert to the facts that guns are usually kept in the bedroom and that the kitchen contains numerous potential weapons. If the person has threatened you and then moves quickly to one of these rooms, leave immediately.

Do not attempt to disarm a person who has a weapon. Leave that to the police! If your client has a weapon, calmly explain that you intend no harm and then slowly back away or otherwise extricate yourself from the situation.

12. An attack on others is often a reaction to being afraid; thus, do what you can to lessen the person's need to be afraid of you. Remain composed and speak in a gentle and soothing manner. Do not argue or threaten. Demonstrate empathy for the person's feelings of frustration and anger. Use active listening skills to secure an understanding of his or her perceptions and feelings. If an inappropriate statement on your part has caused the client to become angry, admit your error and apologize.

13. Aggressiveness and attacks often arise out of a feeling of being trapped or controlled by others. To the extent possible, increase the client's sense of being in control by offering options and choices and using a cooperative tone and language such as: "Of course, it is up to you to decide what is best" and "Think about what we have discussed and decide on a course of action."

14. Maintain a neat, well-groomed appearance and an attitude of confidence so as to project the impression that you take your job seriously and can take care of yourself. An angry person is more likely to attack someone who appears weak, afraid, and insecure. Select clothing and shoes that permit running and a rapid escape from danger. Do not wear earrings that can be easily grabbed to inflict pain and control.

15. If you work with dangerous clients, your phone number, home address, and personal email address should be protected from public disclosure. In rare instances, a social worker's family (e.g., spouse, children) may become the target of a client's anger and violence. A worker's family should be prepared for that possibility.

16. If you work in a dangerous neighborhood, secure guidance from experienced peers, local merchants, and the police on how to protect yourself. If you are likely to encounter dangerous clients, ask your agency for in-service training on nonviolent self-defense. You must be able to protect yourself from harm without inflicting physical injury on your clients. If you secure training in self-defense be sure to select an instructor who has had personal experience with violent persons. Even excellent training does not adequately prepare you for the real thing. Never overestimate your ability to handle a threatening situation or underestimate the paralyzing effect of fear.

17. If you work in a hospital or another health care setting, be alert to biological hazards and obtain instruction on how to protect yourself and vulnerable patients against exposure to an infection. That includes knowing how to handle items stained with body fluids, such as bandages, tissues, clothing, and bed sheets. In some instances, the social worker will need to wear a protective mask and gloves when interviewing a hospitalized client.

18. Social workers and other human services personnel who make home visits should be alert to the possibility of inadvertently encountering a clandestine laboratory where illegal drugs are being manufactured. For example, methamphetamine, or "meth," can be cooked using easily obtained chemicals and ordinary kitchen equipment. These labs are extremely dangerous because the chemicals used in making drugs are highly corrosive and flammable. Someone who is manufacturing drugs may take impulsive and drastic action to prevent the lab from being reported to law enforcement. In some cases, clandestine laboratories are booby-trapped with explosives.

Selected Bibliography

Cambell, Jacquelyn. *Assessing Dangerousness*. New York: Springer, 2006.

Jones, David, ed. *Working with Dangerous People*. San Francisco: Radcliff Medical Press, 2004.

Newhill, Christina. *Client Violence in Social Work Practice*. New York: Guilford, 2004.

Weinger, Susan. *Security Risk: Preventing Client Violence against Social Workers*. Washington, DC: NASW, 2001.

10.10 ADDRESSING POWER DIFFERENTIALS WITH CLIENTS

The very nature of a professional relationship places the social worker in a position of power in relation to the client. Sometimes that power differential has little influence on the helping process as, for example, when the client is completely voluntary and the social worker is in a private practice setting where agency authority is not part of the practice context. However, in many practice settings, the social worker and his or her agency or organization has some inherent power or authority. This is most apparent in correctional or child protection settings and when the client is involuntary or mandated to obtain services (see Item 10.7). In these practice situations the social worker has considerable power and must always use it in a thoughtful and cautious manner.

Current thinking regarding the sociology of professions describes the professional–client relationship as one in which the professional is an expert on the issues his or her client is experiencing, competent to guide the change process, and able to select and use appropriate evidence-based interventions. Although some practice perspectives view the professional and client roles as more equal (e.g., the feminist perspective), most intervention models view the professional as having some control or authority over how the change process plays out.

Power can be defined in several different ways. Power to control the actions of others can be held by individuals, groups, or institutional structures such as human services agencies. In the context of professional client relationships, **power** is defined as "the ability or official capacity to exercise control; authority" (American Heritage Dictionary of the English Language, 2000, s.v. "power"). Similar to the teacher having the authority to assign grades in a college class, the social worker can use the power in the position in a number of ways. The power can be applied, for example, in ways ranging from motivating clients to address an issue, to reward clients for their progress, or to punish clients for past deeds.

Bundy-Fazioli, Briar-Lawson, and Hardiman (2008) conceptualize a useful continuum of power for social work practice. At one end of this continuum are *hierarchical/imbalanced* power relationships, those that are *negotiated/reciprocal* fall in the middle, and the *shared/balanced* power relationships are at the other end. The traditional conception of professionals based on the medical model views the professional/client relationship at the hierarchical/imbalanced end of this continuum. Given that perspective, the physician or other professional studies the problem, makes a diagnosis, and treats the condition with relatively little involvement or guidance by the patient or client. Increasingly, all of the helping professions have moved toward greater client engagement and input throughout the helping process. At present, professional–client relationships are more likely to be negotiated and reciprocal. Various legal mandates, agency restrictions, and concerns over legal liability constrain most social workers and other professionals from creating or achieving a truly shared/balanced professional relationship.

Several of the social work practice principles identified in Chapter 5 reflect the movement of social work to a mid-ground of meaningful client involvement in decision making. For example:

- The social worker should consider clients experts on their own lives.
- The social worker should maximize client participation.
- The social worker should maximize client self-determination.
- The social worker should help the client learn self-directed problem-solving skills.
- The social worker should maximize client empowerment.

The concept of client empowerment expands the scope of the professional–client relationship to also address the societal causes of the client's powerlessness (see Item 13.18).

The following guidelines related to worker–client power dynamics should be considered by the social worker:

- Be clear about the degree of power/authority the worker legitimately possesses.
- Help the client understand the limits placed on the worker due to the nature of the issues addressed in the case situation, the requirements of the agency or, in some cases, the referring agency, and demands of the legal system.
- Determine the degree to which the client is capable of assuming or sharing responsible decision-making authority.
- Establish a plan with the client to negotiate shared decision-making power in the relationship where appropriate.

Selected Bibliography

Alexander, C., and Grant, C. "Caring, Mutuality, and Reciprocity in Social Worker-Client Relationships: Rethinking Principles of Practice." *Journal of Social Work* 9(1): 5–22, 2009.

Bundy-Fazioli, Kimberly, Katharine Briar-Lawson, and Eric R. Hardiman. "A Qualitative Examination of Power between Child Welfare Workers and Parents. *British Journal of Social Work* 38, 1–18, 2008.

SECTION B

TECHNIQUES AND GUIDELINES FOR INDIRECT PRACTICE

At the indirect service level, the planned change process usually involves the social worker in activities aimed at making existing programs work better or creating new programs to meet client needs or to prevent problems from developing. For example, the social worker might give formal or behind-the-scenes leadership to a change effort, or he or she may advocate with agency administrators, legislators, or others to effect change. Usually, indirect service work is done with a committee or some other group that comes together in an effort to provide services more effectively and efficiently or develop strategies to accomplish needed change in a policy, program, or budget.

As in most change efforts, it is important for the participants to be invested in the process, committing their time, talent, and (sometimes) financial or other resources. Participants need to be involved early in the process and have opportunities to influence its direction as the change effort evolves.

Preparatory Activities.   Social workers attempting to facilitate organizational or community change must know their "turf." Even new social workers must be able to assess the agency where they are employed (see Item 10.11) and the dynamics of their community (see Item 10.13). Attaining that knowledge is prerequisite to any effort to facilitate change in an agency or community.

Typically, the work of the social worker involves bringing together groups of people from within an agency or from a community to address new problems or ones that have not been successfully resolved in the past. Gaining knowledge of past efforts, barriers that existed, and the people or organizations who were involved is a necessary part of one's homework. When providing indirect services, it is rare that the worker faces an emergency or crisis situation that does not allow time for gathering this background information.

When leading a group for the purpose of addressing an issue, the worker should carefully select, invite, and recruit participants; identify a meeting time that accommodates as many potential participants as possible; select a convenient meeting place and arrange the meeting room to facilitate interaction; and have a prepared agenda that includes ample opportunity for participants to discuss the issue at hand (see Item 13.28).

Engagement Activities. A social worker rarely will have the power or authority to individually resolve problematic issues in an agency or community. Rather, the worker must secure support and resources from others in order to address issues. It is important, then, that the first meeting of a group or committee is structured to involve the participants in identifying concerns and issues from their own perspectives and encourage the expression of differing viewpoints. Also, participants should leave the meeting having some responsibility for an action to be reported at the next meeting as a means of maintaining their involvement.

Intake Activities. The first meeting of a group or committee must, among other things, reach a decision regarding the desirability of this group continuing to address the matter, deferring to another group that may already be addressing this topic, joining a parallel effort to deal with the matter, or dissolving. The social worker's role, as convener of the group, is to help the group decide which of these options should be followed.

10.11 LEARNING ABOUT YOUR AGENCY

Social workers are usually employed by either a private or a public agency. **Public agencies** (whether at the city, county, state, or federal level) are established by legislation written by elected officials and are largely funded by tax dollars. By contrast, most private agencies are **nonprofit organizations** funded primarily by voluntary contributions and possibly by fees, grants, or contracts or they may be **for-profit corporations** designed to yield income for investors and stockholders. Some private agencies enter into the purchase of service contracts with public agencies and are paid to deliver specified services; thus, such private agencies are funded, in part, by tax dollars. The term **membership agency** refers to a private agency that derives a significant portion of its funds from membership fees (e.g., YMCA or YWCA). The term **sectarian agency** describes a private agency that is under the auspices of a specific religious body (e.g., Jewish Community Services, Catholic Social Services).

In order to deliver social services and programs effectively, the social worker must understand the agency's mission, structure, funding, policies, and procedures. The following activities will help the worker learn about his or her agency:

1. Ask your supervisor and experienced agency staff for guidance on how best to become familiar with the agency's purpose, policies, and operation. Study the agency's organization chart and determine how you and your department or unit fit into the agency structure.

2. If your agency is a public agency, read the law(s) that established the agency and those describing the specific programs that the agency is to administer (e.g., state child protection laws) and examine relevant state and federal administrative rules and regulations. If your agency is a private agency, read the bylaws that describe the agency's purpose and the functions of the board of directors and its officers and committees. The bylaws will also describe the responsibilities assigned to the executive director, who is typically responsible for the organization's day-to-day operation.

3. Examine your agency's manual of policies and procedures. Pay special attention to any ethical guidelines that prescribe employee behavior. For example, many agencies will have guidelines for such potential issues as the following:

- Use of time at work for personal matters
- Use of agency property (e.g., telephones, fax, automobiles, copy machines, computer, office space) for personal activities
- Receipt of gifts from clients, other employees, or use of the agency's name or the worker's affiliation with the agency in outside activities

- Provision of agency services to friends and family
- Situations wherein personal or financial interests might conflict, or appear to conflict, with official duties
- Publication and dissemination of research reports or other information prepared or developed during agency employment
- Sale of materials prepared on agency time or with agency resources
- Matters related to the confidentiality of client information
- Persons who are in a position to receive referrals of fee-paying clients from agency employees

4. Read documents that describe your agency's history, mission, and philosophy. Find out how the agency has changed during the past 5–10 years and what community or political forces are having a significant impact on the agency. Seek information about the agency's goals and objectives for the current year and its strategic plan for the next three to five years.

5. Examine the agency's personnel policies, the tools or forms that will be used in the evaluation of your job performance. Read the union contract, if one exists.

6. If your agency must conform to standards issued by a national accrediting organization (e.g., Child Welfare League of America, Council on Accreditation of Rehabilitation Facilities), review those portions of the accreditation standards that apply to your areas of service.

7. Examine your agency's budget. Pay special attention to the sources of income, because the agency must be responsive and accountable to these sources if it is to continue to attract needed funding. Also review any "purchase of service" arrangements, interagency agreements, or protocol statements that tie the services and operation of your agency to other agencies or funding sources. If you are working on a project funded by a grant or a contract, read the relevant documents so that you know what the funding source is expecting of the project.

8. Examine annual reports and statistical data compiled by your agency, and determine which of its programs and services are most used and least used by clients and consumers. Also, examine data that describe the people served by your agency in terms of age, gender, socioeconomic status, race, ethnicity, religion, and so on.

9. Determine what procedures are used to evaluate agency performance and the quality of services provided. Also determine how the agency's clients and consumers are involved in the evaluation and planning of services and programs.

10. Identify the agencies and organizations with which your agency frequently interacts. Determine which community or state agencies have an impact on your agency and how the services and programs provided by your agency are to be coordinated with other agencies in the community.

11. Determine what specific roles, tasks, and activities are assigned to the agency's social work staff (see Chapter 4) and those assigned to persons of other disciplines and professions. Also find out what practice frameworks guide service delivery (see Chapter 6).

12. Talk to community leaders and professionals outside your agency to ascertain how your agency and its programs are perceived by others. Determine the public image attached to your agency and how it acquired that reputation.

Selected Bibliography

Hassenfeld, Yeheskel. *Human Services as Complex Organizations,* 2nd ed. Newbury Park, CA: Sage Publications, 2010.

O'Connor, Mary Katherine, and F. Ellen Netting. *Organizational Practice: A Social Worker's Guide to Understanding Human Services,* 2nd ed. Hoboken, NJ: John Wiley & Sons, 2009.

10.12 RECRUITING, SELECTING, AND TRAINING STAFF AND VOLUNTEERS

Although tangible resources (e.g., social provisions, office equipment, and supplies) are important to the operation of human services agencies, the heart and soul of helping rests with the people who deliver those services. Perhaps no indirect service task is more important than getting the right personnel in place to provide needed services.

Selecting and training professional staff for an agency is expected of persons in management roles. Although the agency managers may have the final decision regarding who will be chosen, an important prior step is to screen applicants and recommend the strongest candidates. Virtually every social worker, whether or not in management, will at some time be part of a search committee. And once a new employee has been selected, the agency social workers may also have a role in helping the hiree develop or sharpen his or her competencies to better fit the needs of the agency.

Securing a group of competent and committed volunteers is also essential to the operation of most social agencies. The U.S. Bureau of Labor Statistics (2009) reports that 26.4 percent of the U.S. population volunteer to serve in their communities each year. However, if this level of volunteer effort is to continue, it is essential that there is a good match between the volunteer and the service needed, that the work is carefully planned and rewarding, and that volunteers are properly recognized for their contributions. Many human services agencies have a staff member (often a social worker) assigned to the tasks of recruiting, screening, selecting, orienting, training, supervising, and evaluating volunteers.

Before staff and volunteers can be used effectively, it is vital to identify the service tasks that would be appropriately performed by volunteers and those that require professional expertise. Assigning appropriate tasks for the person's level of competence is prerequisite to achieving worker or volunteer job satisfaction.

SECURING A COMPETENT PROFESSIONAL STAFF

For professional staff (i.e., persons with specific professional preparation who are to be employed and compensated for their work), a successful job search should carefully match the abilities of each applicant with the requirements of a given job. Therefore, being clear about the requirements of the job is prerequisite to a good search. A beginning point for the specification of competencies usually is found in a job description. Most agencies will have such descriptions, but it is helpful to review the list of tasks and then identify the competencies (i.e., knowledge and skills) required to perform each task.

The position should be advertised widely to attract a diverse and qualified pool of applicants. The advertisement should appear on the agency's website and in local newspapers. It should identify the minimum requirements (e.g., experience in working with older adults, a bachelor's or master's in social work degree, grant-writing skill), the closing date for applications, a description of how to apply, and the expected starting date for the position. If a position requires a professional social worker, advertising in the newsletter of the NASW chapter, sending flyers to other human services agencies, or contacting schools of social work may further stimulate applications from qualified persons.

Typically, the staff-screening process has two phases: a credential review based on information submitted by the applicant and a personal interview with a small number of applicants who appear from their credentials to be the most prepared to assume the responsibilities of the position. The goal of the credential review is to obtain sufficient information for the search committee to rate the applicants on the characteristics established in the job description. In most cases, the candidate will have been asked not only to submit a professional résumé but also to provide a narrative statement regarding his or her interest in and preparation for the position.

With this information, the committee will review the applications completed, compare their independent assessments of the candidates and discuss differences in perception, eliminate unacceptable candidates from consideration, and create a priority list of applicants to invite for interviews.

When interviewing a person for a staff position, the process usually involves members of the organization beyond the committee membership. This interview process should be viewed as providing opportunities to identify the best candidate(s) for recommendation to the person with final hiring authority, to provide a chance for the applicant to learn about the agency and job and judge if he or she is a good fit, to allow the candidate to ask questions about the job and agency, and to provide an opportunity to persuade the applicant to accept the position if it should be offered. The search committee will often prepare a list of questions to be asked of all candidates and/or develop a short case example to be discussed so that comparisons among finalists can be made. Questions such as these might be asked:

- What is it about the population group served by this agency makes you interested in our position?
- What special skills do you bring to working with these clients?
- Why are you considering leaving your current position, and what about this job seems more attractive to you?
- From a career development perspective, how would taking this job fit into your future plans?
- What can we tell you about this agency (or community) that would assist you in considering this position?
- What support, training, supervision, or professional development opportunities would you see as necessary or valuable in getting started on this job?

All agency personnel engaged in conducting interviews should be warned against asking inappropriate personal questions about a candidate's marital status, plans for having children, child care arrangements, sexual orientation, and so on. It should be assumed that professionals make appropriate provisions for their personal lives. If such questions are asked, the candidate should assure the committee that he or she would be responsible for making sure that personal matters do not negatively affect professional performance.

Before a search committee offers its recommendations, the committee must collect feedback from all persons who were involved in the interview process (a form might be developed to get consistent feedback on key factors), contact the finalists' references (often by telephone) to gain a more detailed and candid appraisal of each candidate than might be included in a reference letter, analyze all the information gathered, and rank the candidates or designate those who would be acceptable or unacceptable in the committee's judgment. The committee should compile the documentation underpinning its recommendations, and the agency should maintain that information for three years in case an unsuccessful applicant should challenge the fairness of the selection process. The final decision maker will then have the responsibility to offer the job, negotiate the conditions, and plan for the entry of the new employee into the agency.

All new staff members will require orientation to the agency. Some of the orientation should relate to the basics of how the agency functions, whom to ask when needing various types of information, where to find supplies, procedures to maintain confidentiality, and so on. Also, new staff members usually require some training to adapt their general skills to the unique needs of the agency. This might involve in-service training or the investment of agency funds for participation in professional workshops or conferences. Bringing new personnel into an agency should not be considered complete until he or she is given appropriate training.

At least at first, the work of the new hire will be closely monitored. The person who provides this administrative supervision (see Item 16.8) is critical to helping the new staff member get off to a good start. The monitoring function offers both the clients and the agency a level of protection by closely observing the service activities being performed and, if necessary, using administrative authority to protect clients from errors or incompetence until the new person becomes more experienced. It is also useful for another person in the agency to support the new worker as a mentor (i.e., a trusted counselor or guide) to help the new worker develop into a competent staff member (see Item 16.9). While a supervisor must be responsible for monitoring the new employee's work and protecting agency interests, a mentor should focus on the new worker's professional development.

DEVELOPING A CADRE OF VOLUNTEERS

The first step in conducting any successful search for volunteers is to determine as precisely as possible the competencies that are needed. For a volunteer (i.e., a person who provides services without compensation), this requires clear specification of who the clientele will be, what services he or she will be expected to provide, and how much time will be required to perform the duties. Nothing is more frustrating for a volunteer than being recruited to an agency and then not having his or her time and talents used efficiently.

A second step in securing volunteers is to advertise the agency's need for such help. In general, widely circulated announcements in local newspapers and on the agency website should be the minimum effort at advertising. These formal announcements should describe the major tasks to be performed, the time demands, and specific skills required. It is important for these ads to target specific organizations or groups of people in order to reach those most likely to be interested in the position. Word-of-mouth recruiting by experienced volunteers is one of the best ways to secure new volunteers.

Once the applications have been received from a potential volunteer, the screening process begins. The initial screening is usually restricted to reviewing information provided on an application form. In general, this information is intended to determine, at a minimum, if anything in the person's background might place the agency's clients at risk and if the person would bring some unique skills or strengths to the agency.

Following the paper screening, the face-to-face interviewing process will begin. When interviewing persons for volunteer positions, the goal should be to assess each person's motivation, commitment, and capacity for addressing the identified agency or client needs. Questions such as these should be asked:

- Why are you interested in being a volunteer in this agency?
- What type of activity is of greatest interest to you? Are there tasks or activities you might be asked to perform that are of little or no interest to you?
- Are you hoping to have direct contact or involvement with clients? If yes, with what type of clients and what types of interaction?
- What do you expect to gain personally from this volunteer experience?
- Have you been a volunteer for other agencies? If so, what was satisfying about that experience? Not satisfying?
- For how long do you expect to serve as a volunteer? How much time can you contribute each week or month?
- What special skills and experience would you bring to the agency? Do you have any limitations that would affect your work at the agency?
- What type of training and supervision do you expect from the agency?
- What is your view of the importance of the confidentiality of client information?

The final selection of volunteers usually rests with a volunteer coordinator or other staff member assigned to that function. Once capable volunteers have been identified, the coordinator will be responsible for matching each volunteer's talents with the agency's needs and initiating the volunteer into the agency. Each volunteer should be given a thorough orientation to the agency and will usually need training to perform the assigned tasks. This training might be conducted on an individual basis, or it might be conducted in a group session for new volunteers. The important point is that the orientation and training should be specific to the tasks to be performed.

Formalizing an ongoing support system for new volunteers is also important. A staff member should have the responsibility for assisting new volunteers in understanding the tasks they are to perform and identifying the best means of carrying out this work.

Selected Bibliography

Doelling, Carol Nesslein. *Social Work Career Development: A Handbook for Job Hunting and Career Planning*, 2nd ed. Washington, DC: NASW Press, 2005.

Sherr, Michael E. *Social Work with Volunteers*. Chicago: Lyceum, 2008.

U.S. Bureau of Labor Statistics. Volunteering in the United States, 2008. *Economic News Release*. Available online: www.bls.gov/news.release/volun.nr0.htm.

10.13　LEARNING ABOUT YOUR COMMUNITY

The term **community** describes people who feel a bond with each other because they share an identity, a sense of belonging, and usually a common locality. For example, the people may share a common interest (e.g., the social work community, the African American community) or identify themselves with a geographical area such as a particular neighborhood, town, or city. *Geographic communities*, which provide the context in which most social work practice is conducted, typically perform one or more of the following functions:

- *Provision of goods and essential services.*　Water, electricity, gas, food, housing, garbage disposal, medical care, education, transportation, recreation, social services, information, and the like.
- *Business activity and employment.*　Commerce and jobs exist from which people earn the money needed to purchase goods and services.
- *Public safety.*　Protection from criminal behavior and hazards such as fire, floods, and toxic chemicals.
- *Socialization.*　Opportunities to communicate and interact with others and to develop a sense of identity and belonging beyond those provided by the family system.
- *Mutual support.*　Tangible assistance and social supports beyond those provided by one's family.
- *Social control.*　Establishment and enforcement of laws and rules needed to guide and control large numbers of people (e.g., laws, police, courts, traffic control, pollution control).
- *Political organization and participation.*　Governance and decision making related to local matters and public services (e.g., streets, sewer, schools, public welfare, public health, economic development, zoning of housing and businesses).

All of these community functions affect the form and availability of social programs and thus directly help shape social work practice.

For the social worker who is new to a geographic area, conducting an informal study of the community where he or she is employed is an important part of moving into a new job. Such an assessment has three purposes:

1. *To understand the context of one's practice.*　The social worker must become knowledgeable about the community's history and demographics, economic base, political structures, and the prevailing values, norms, and myths that affect decision making and intergroup behavior.
2. *To evaluate the existing human services system.*　The social worker needs to know what services are available and to understand community attitudes toward people who have psychosocial problems and utilize the human services. Communities differ in their willingness to respond to human needs and in regard to how well local professionals and agencies work together.

3. *To acquire understanding of the community decision-making structure.* At some point, the social worker's desire for more adequate human services should lead to efforts to bring about changes in the community's response to a particular problem or need. To succeed in those efforts, he or she must understand the power structure operating in the community, the beliefs and values of the leaders and key actors who decide what programs and services will be provided and funded, and the formal and informal processes used to reach those decisions.

Information that describes a community and its functioning can be gleaned from documents such as census data, economic forecasts, public health reports, prior studies of a community problem, reports related to community planning projects, directories of health and human services agencies, and the like. Helpful documents may be available from the local library, Chamber of Commerce, United Way, and government offices. Supplemental data might be obtained by reading historical accounts of how the community grew and developed and how it has responded to recent problems, by interviewing long-time residents, and by closely following current issues and controversies reported in the local news. It is important to record the names of the organizations and individuals who are important decision makers, especially those associated with human services concerns.

Although the social worker's area of practice will determine the nature and depth of information sought in relation to particular aspects of the community and its service systems, certain general information is essential. The following points will help the social worker develop a profile of the community in which he or she is working:

1. ***Demographics***
   - Total population
   - Age distribution, levels of education, occupations
   - Minority and ethnic groups; languages spoken by various groups

2. ***Geography and environmental influences on community:***
   - Effect of climate, mountains, valleys, rivers, lakes, and so forth on local transportation patterns, economic development, and population distribution
   - Effect of transportation routes and other corridors and barriers on neighborhood patterns, social interaction, agency location, and service delivery

3. ***Beliefs and attitudes:***
   - Dominant values, religious beliefs, and attitudes of the population and its various subgroups
   - Types of human services agencies and programs that are valued and respected and that attract community support, favorable publicity, and funding

4. ***Local politics:***
   - Form of local government
   - Relative power and influence of political parties and various interest groups
   - Current political debates, issues, and controversies at the local level

5. ***Local economy and businesses:***
   - Types of jobs and work available in area (i.e., wages; part time or full time; seasonal or year-round; hours and times of work)
   - Percentage of labor force unemployed

6. ***Income distribution:***
   - Median income for women; for men; for minority groups
   - Number of persons/families below official poverty line

7. ***Housing:***
   - Most common types of housing (e.g., single-family dwellings, apartments, public housing)
   - Cost and availability of housing
   - Percentage of units overcrowded or substandard

8. *Educational facilities and programs:*
   - Locations and types of schools (i.e., public, private, neighborhood, magnet)
   - School programs for children with special needs
   - Dropout rate for all students; for members of various socioeconomic and minority groups

9. *Health and welfare systems:*
   - Names and locations of providers of health care (e.g., emergency services, acute care, home health programs, long-term care, public and private hospitals, public health programs, private clinics)
   - Names and locations of agencies providing social and human services (e.g., housing, substance abuse treatment, child welfare, protection from child abuse and domestic abuse, financial assistance)
   - Self-help groups and informal helping networks

10. *Sources of information and public opinion:*
   - Influential TV and radio stations and newspapers to which the people look for information and perspectives on current events
   - Key leaders and spokespersons for various segments of the community, including racial or ethnic and religious groups

11. *Summary assessment of community issues:*
   - Assessment of major social problems within the community (e.g., inadequate housing, inadequate public transportation, insufficient law enforcement, lack of jobs, youth gangs, poverty, teen pregnancy, domestic abuse)
   - Major gaps among existing social, health care, and educational services
   - Efforts underway to address these issues; leaders in these efforts

Selected Bibliography

Hardina, Donna. *Analytical Skills for Community Organization Practice.* New York: Columbia University Press, 2002.

Kirst-Ashman, Karen K., and Grafton H. Hull, Jr. *Generalist Practice with Organizations and Communities,* 4th ed. Belmont, CA: Brooks/Cole, 2009.

Weil, Marie, ed. *Handbook of Community Practice.* Thousand Oaks, CA: Sage, 2005.

Data Collection and Assessment

The social worker's focus during the second phase of the planned change process is on collecting information needed to comprehend the client's concern and current situation and determine how it might be addressed. The social worker brings to this activity an expertise not usually possessed by the general public, including skill in determining what data are needed, where they can be obtained, and how they should be interpreted.

Data collection is the activity of securing information directly from the client, from other involved people, and, in some cases, from documents such as medical records, school reports, probation records, community surveys, and so on. The worker is especially interested in gathering facts but in addition the worker will be alert to subjective perceptions and opinions regarding the situation held by the client, family members, key people in the client's environment, and perhaps from the referring agency (e.g., a court, school).

When does data collection end? To some degree, new data are always being collected. Certainly, it is essential that a social worker obtain sufficient information to have a clear picture of what is occurring in the client's life before formulating an intervention plan. However, it is equally important to avoid delaying or stalling the change process by gathering unnecessary or excessive data.

Assessment is the thinking process by which a worker reasons from the information or data to arrive at working hypothesis and tentative conclusions. During assessment, the available information is organized and analyzed to make sense of the client's situation and to lay the foundation for a plan of action. An assessment should be *multidimensional*—that is, based on numerous data sources that reflect varying points of view. If the worker, the client, and others involved in the client's situation reach highly divergent conclusions, it will be necessary to collect additional data and do a more in-depth analysis in order to reach a consensus or at least, reduce the range of opinions.

Social workers must guard against unconsciously or inadvertently making the client's situation or the data collected fit a particular theoretical orientation, model, or a preconceived diagnostic category. One protection against the worker's own biases having undue influence on the assessment is to have the client actively involved in identifying the relevant sources of information and in sorting through the information when arriving at an assessment. Further, when a conclusion is reached, the worker should view it as tentative and open to revision as additional information is obtained during other phases of the change process.

SECTION A

TECHNIQUES AND GUIDELINES FOR DIRECT PRACTICE

In direct practice with individuals, families, and small groups, the social worker's data gathering and assessment will be shaped and guided by the *person-in-environment* framework. In other words, attention is given to the client as a unique and whole person as well as the demands and constraints placed on the client by the context or environment in which he or she must function. Ultimately, it is finding, facilitating, or negotiating a workable match between the person and his or her environment that is the focus of a social work intervention (see Chapter 13).

Data-Collection Activities.   A social work assessment should give some attention to all dimensions of the *whole person* and to any factors that impinge on his or her social functioning. For example:

- *Volitional:*   the personal choices and decisions, both large and small, that shape one's life; the impact of these decisions and choices on oneself and others
- *Intellectual:*   the ideas, knowledge, and beliefs used to understand oneself, others, and the world; the ability to interpret and give conceptual order to one's experiences; the cognitive processes needed to understand, form judgments, and make decisions
- *Spiritual and religious:*   one's deepest core beliefs concerning the meaning and purpose of life; one's relationship with his or her God, the meaning assigned to pain and suffering; one's religious identity, traditions, and practices
- *Moral and ethical:*   one's standards of right and wrong; the criteria one uses to make moral decisions; one's conscience
- *Emotional:*   one's feelings and moods, such as joy, love, sadness, anger, fear, shame; the inclination to be drawn toward or move away from certain situations and persons
- *Physical:*   one's level of energy; capacity for movement; health and nutritional status (e.g., illness, disabilities, pain, care and treatment needed)
- *Sexuality:*   one's sexual identity and orientation; libido; the place of sexual attraction in relationships; the meaning assigned to being male or female; one's sex-role expectations; the capacity for and desire for reproduction
- *Familial:*   relationships with one's parents, siblings, spouse, partner, children, and relatives; one's sense of loyalty to and responsibility for family members; one's family history and traditions
- *Social:*   interactions with friends and peers; one's social support network; one's interests and leisure time/recreational activities
- *Community:*   one's sense of belonging to a group beyond family and friends; one's sense of loyalty to and responsibility for others in the neighborhood and local area; one's place or status in the community; one's use of various formal and informal resources to meet personal and family needs
- *Cultural:*   ones beliefs, values, traditions, and customs as related to one's ethnicity, cultural background, and language
- *Work and occupation:*   the nature of one's work; job skills, one's source of income; relationship with one's work organization or occupation; the place and meaning of work in one's life
- *Economic:*   one's material resources; one's capacity to secure and manage the money needed to purchase goods and services
- *Legal:*   one's rights, responsibilities, protections, and entitlements as defined in law

There are several modes or methods of data collection. Since each has limitations, the social worker should use more than one whenever possible for this will increase the accuracy of the inferences drawn from these data. Data-collection modes a social worker might use include the following:

- Direct verbal questioning, such as the face-to-face interview (see Chapter 8)
- Direct written questioning, including the use of questionnaires and problem checklists (see Item 11.12)
- Indirect or projective verbal questioning, such as the story completion or the use of vignettes (see Item 11.12)
- Indirect or projective written questioning, such as sentence completion
- Observation within the client's natural environment, such as home visits (see Item 10.6), visits to a classroom, and so forth
- Observations of the client in a simulated situation that is analogous to real life, including such techniques as role-playing a job interview
- Client self-monitoring and self-observation with the aid of a recording tool, such as a log, checklist, or journaling
- The use of existing documents, such as agency records, school records, physician reports, newspapers, and so forth

Assessment Activities. As described above, assessment is the activity of drawing meaning, inferences, and tentative conclusions from the data. During assessment (but hopefully earlier), there must be clarity as to who is the client and who is to be the target of an intervention. In other words, who is asking for and expects to benefit from the social worker's services (*the client system*) and who is expected to change (*the target system*). They are not always the same. For example, when a mother requests counseling for a rebellious daughter who is forced to attend the counseling sessions, who is the client? We would probably conclude that the mother is the client and the daughter is the target of intervention.

Special effort should be devoted to assessing client strengths. All too often, both client and worker become preoccupied with the presenting problem and all that is going wrong. This can give rise to an incomplete or distorted intervention plan. Including an analysis of client strengths builds hopefulness and usually uncovers resources for dealing with the client's problems and concerns.

Value preferences will of course affect assessments. Both the client and social worker will hold beliefs about the way things could be or ought to be and such views affect the way a problem is defined and the outcomes sought. To the extent possible, these values and beliefs should be made explicit and discussed during the assessment process.

An *assessment tool* combines data collection with some form of a scoring procedure that will facilitate or guide the interpretation. Typically, these tools provide a way to compare the client's responses to a set of questions, for example, with the answers of a larger collective to whom the instrument has been administered (i.e., a standardized assessment tool; see Item 14.2). Hundreds of such instruments have been published and are available to the social worker. However, sometimes, it is useful for the worker to develop a tool that is tailor-made for use in a particular practice setting or with clients facing a particular type of challenge (see Item 14.1). Tools and techniques for organizing data for the ongoing evaluation of a client's progress and change are reported in Chapter 14.

It is in direct social work practice that social workers encounter the concept of diagnosis, which is related to the processes of data gathering and assessment, yet essentially different. In *diagnosis*, the client's problem, condition, or situation is classified and assigned to a particular category within a given taxonomy, such as the Person-in-Environment (PIE) system or the *Diagnostic and Statistical Manual of Mental Disorders (DSM)* (see Item 11.16). The act of diagnosis applies a standardized terminology to the client's condition or situation in order to facilitate communication among professionals and to aid in the gathering of data needed for research and program administration. Labeling and categorization may or may not make a useful contribution to the worker's intervention planning, however. In many instances, clients assigned the same *DSM* diagnostic label require somewhat different approaches to treatment and intervention.

11.1 ASSESSING A CLIENT'S SOCIAL FUNCTIONING

As explained in Chapter 1, the fundamental purpose of the social work profession is to enhance client's social functioning and capacity to live a satisfying life and also to prevent and correct problems in social functioning. It is this focus on a client's social functioning that distinguishes a social worker's assessment from an assessment conducted by, for example, a psychologist, nurse, or counselor. The concept of **social functioning**, when applied to an individual, can be thought of as the person's motivation, capacity, and opportunity to meet his or her basic needs and perform his or her major social roles, such as those of parent, spouse, partner, family member, employee, student, citizen, and so on. The word **social** refers to the interactions between and among people and between people and the significant systems of their social environment (e.g., family, school, job, hospital). Social workers are particularly concerned about the match (or lack thereof) between a client's needs and the resources available to meet those needs.

The statements listed below are intended to remind the social worker of various dimensions or aspects of a client's social functioning. Depending on the client's presenting concerns or problem, some areas of social functioning would be examined in more depth than others. Because these statements are written in a positive manner, they constitute a list of possible client strengths (see Item 11.5). If an individual's current functioning or situation departs significantly from the description provided, he or she is probably facing some special challenge or problem. This list can also serve as a starting point when writing the goals and objectives to be included in a service agreement or treatment plan (see Items 12.4 and 12.5).

INDEPENDENT LIVING AND SELF-CARE (ADULTS)

- Manages basic self-care tasks such as eating, food preparation, dressing, bathing, and toileting.
- Grasps new information, makes logical decisions, and implements plan necessary to performing ordinary roles and responsibilities.
- Possesses physical mobility and energy level necessary to care for self and perform ordinary roles and responsibilities.
- Recognizes dangerous situations (e.g., medical emergencies, criminal activity, gas leak) and knows how to call for help.
- Initiates interactions with others and can secure their cooperation and assistance in order to care for self.
- Speaks, reads, and writes the language(s) needed for such activities as shopping, working, attending school, obtaining medical care, and calling for assistance.
- Has access to needed transportation.

HOUSING AND HOME SAFETY

- Has housing that is safe and provides adequate space and privacy and protection from weather, intruders, and so forth.
- Has access to clean drinking water, a method of safe food storage, and sanitary toilet.
- Keeps food preparation area clean.
- Can safely use the various tools, soaps, and household chemicals needed to keep the home safe from disease-causing microbes, roaches, and rodents.

NUTRITION AND HEALTH CARE

- Prepares nutritious meals within the food budget.
- Engages in health-building behaviors (e.g., adequate sleep, proper diet, exercise) and avoids excessive alcohol, street drugs, and the misuse of medicines.

- Has access to health care and ability to pay for services.
- Avoids high risk or daredevil activities that could result in injury.

FAMILY LIFE

- Relationship with spouse or partner is mutually satisfying and meets need for intimacy and companionship; sexual activity is non-exploitative and satisfying to self and partner.
- Family members care for each other and are a source of support, assistance, and encouragement for each other.
- Parents or caretakers provide children with nurturance, guidance, protection, encouragement, and limits.
- Parents or caretakers put needs of children before their own wants and are willing to make sacrifices for the welfare of family and children.
- Children consider the parents' guidance, limits, and discipline to be fair and reasonable.
- Adults encourage family members to participate in activities that further their development and build healthy relationships with people outside the family.

FRIENDSHIPS AND SOCIAL SUPPORTS

- Builds and maintains wholesome relationships with relatives, friends, and neighbors.
- Has access to a social support network that can provide encouragement, information, and some forms of tangible assistance.
- Selects companions who provide acceptance and encouragement and avoids individuals who are manipulative or exploiting.

SPIRITUALITY

- Possesses values, beliefs, and perspectives that provide meaning, purpose, and direction in life.
- Possesses and uses a framework of moral and ethical principles for making decisions and choices.
- Is free to be part of a faith community or religion that provides acceptance, encouragement, support, and guidance.
- Is able to attend religious services of his or her choice.

INTERACTION WITH COMMUNITY

- Lives in a community that provides adequate public safety and protection (e.g., police, fire, emergency medical response).
- Feels accepted by and has a sense of belonging to a supportive and helpful neighborhood and community.
- Able to maintain meaningful ethnic, cultural, and language connections and associations.
- Participates in social, recreational, and political activities of the neighborhood and community.
- Contributes to activities that benefit and improve the community and the lives of its people.
- Not adversely affected by discrimination or oppression.

PERSONAL APPEARANCE AND HYGIENE

- Maintains the level of personal hygiene needed to prevent illness and infections and secure social acceptance.
- Able to obtain and afford items and services needed to maintain appropriate appearance (e.g., hair care, deodorant, shampoo, washing machine).

- Selects clothing, accessories, and body decorations that are appropriate to the occasion and enhance appearance and social acceptance.

EDUCATION AND TRAINING

- Is free of cognitive or sensory difficulties that impede learning or is able to effectively compensate for these limitations.
- Explores new areas of learning in order to challenge self and discover new interests and abilities.
- Is aware of and has access to types of education and training needed to maintain and develop important job skills.
- Assesses own learning needs and seeks out instruction needed to perform social roles and fulfill responsibilities at work, home, and school.
- Has realistic understanding of own capacity to complete various programs of education and training.

EMPLOYMENT AND JOB PERFORMANCE

- Has a satisfying job that is appropriate to his or her level of skill and experience and provides an adequate amount of income.
- Working conditions are safe and supportive. If the client is a parent, he or she has access to suitable and affordable day care.
- Is a responsible employee, is able to perform assigned work, and understands employment-related policies and procedures.
- Prepares for those job changes and promotions that can increase opportunity, income, benefits, and job satisfaction.
- Client knows about various types of jobs, how to apply and interview for a job, and can determine if a particular job matches his or her skills and income needs.

INCOME AND MONEY MANAGEMENT

- Has an income sufficient to meet the basic needs of self and family.
- Uses budgeting to plan and monitor financial situation.
- Understands the difference between necessities and wants and has self-discipline to avoid unwise expenditures and debt. Recognizes that the purpose of advertising is to encourage spending.
- Understands basic money concepts such as interest, debt, charge accounts, loans, and late payment penalties.
- Understands work-related concepts such as payroll deductions, income taxes, FICA, and health insurance.

CITIZENSHIP AND LAW

- Understands right and wrong and abides by laws and basic moral principles that recognize the rights of others and the common good.
- Understands basic legal rights and responsibilities and the functions of police, lawyers, and courts.
- Is aware of laws related to marriage, parent–child relationships, contracts, insurance, leases, loans, taxes, driving an automobile, use of alcohol and drugs, firearms, and so on.
- Expresses views on public policy and legislation through such activities as voting and participation in advocacy organizations.
- Avoids situations, associations, and activities that could draw him or her into dangerous or illegal conduct.

USE OF COMMUNITY RESOURCES

- Knows how to access community resources such as those providing medical care, mental health services, legal counsel, consumer counseling, employment services, recreation, library services, and so on.
- Knows of organizations/resources that provide services pertinent to his or her concerns, needs, and circumstances.
- Knows how to use telephone book, directories of community services, and perhaps the Internet, in order to obtain needed resources.

RECREATIONAL AND LEISURE ACTIVITY

- Participates in recreation or leisure activities that provide a respite from ordinary roles and responsibilities.
- Participates in activities that expand opportunity for physical exercise, new learning, creativity, and new friendships.
- Selects recreation and leisure activities that are safe and wholesome and does not expose self to social influences that could prove harmful (e.g., excessive drinking).

COPING WITH ORDINARY PROBLEMS OF LIVING

- Has self-confidence and positive self-worth. Client does not overlook own abilities and strengths and does not deny or ignore real limitations.
- Uses knowledge drawn from past experiences to decide how best to cope with current difficulties and to anticipate challenges.
- Assumes responsibility for own behavior and choices and performs roles and responsibilities, even when they are sometimes a source of frustration. Perseveres in order to complete important tasks.
- Recovers from anxiety, depression, and emotional turmoil brought on by an upsetting event or life disruption such as a death in the family, loss of job, or breakup of a relationship.
- Rebuilds alternate intimate relationships following a loss such as one caused by a divorce, separation, or death.
- Is comfortable with his or her own identity, ethnicity, gender, sexual orientation, economic situation, and life circumstances.
- Sets reasonable limits on demands by others for his or her time and energy.

COPING WITH MENTAL HEALTH PROBLEM OR ADDICTION

- Recognizes the nature of his or her problems and their consequences. Does not deny the existence of significant problems.
- Makes use of effective therapies, medications, and support groups.
- Prior problem behaviors and addictions are controlled and monitored in order to prevent relapse.
- Interacts with a wide variety of people; relationships and activities are not limited to ones involving people having similar problems.

ADJUSTMENTS TO PHYSICAL DISABILITY

- Makes use of rehabilitation programs, medications, and assistive technology (e.g., communication devices, artificial limbs, wheelchair) to minimize the impact of the disability.
- Is able to discuss the disability and need for assistance without embarrassment or apology. Lets others know what he or she can and cannot do.

- Recognizes disability-related risks and vulnerabilities and plans how to reduce risks and handle possible emergencies or accidents.
- Expressions of frustration over his or her disability are reasonable and appropriate and do not drive away family members, friends, and other helpers.

SCHOOL PERFORMANCE OF A CHILD OR ADOLESCENT

- Performs in school at a level consistent with ability, as indicated by observed reasoning and problem-solving activities, and by standardized tests.
- Communicates with teachers and school personnel and enjoys these exchanges.
- Is able to attend school without concern for personal safety.
- Participates in both planned school-related social activities (e.g., sports, dances, and clubs) and in spontaneous activities involving other students and peer group.
- The youth (in keeping with age level) is interested in learning about various career choices and educational opportunities.

RELATIONSHIP OF A YOUTH TO PARENTS, SIBLINGS, AND FAMILY

- Usually does what parent expects and performs age-appropriate chores and assigned duties (e.g., taking care of clothing, cleaning room, supervision of younger siblings).
- Frequently joins in the family's recreational, social, or spiritual activities, such as family gatherings, outings, and so on.
- Interacts with extended family members such as grandparents, aunts, uncles, and cousins.

CHILD OR ADOLESCENT SEXUALITY

- Has basic knowledge of sex and expresses comfort with own sexuality (consistent with age).
- Speaks with parents or responsible adults about feelings, thoughts, and questions related to sexual matters.
- Is respectful of others in dating situation. Sexual activity is kept within the limits of the partner's and own sense of morality. Sexual activity is not compulsive. Does not coerce or force others to participate.

ORDINARY PROBLEMS OF CHILDHOOD AND ADOLESCENCE

- Handles feelings and emotions without letting them seriously disrupt relationships at home and school.
- The youth (if necessary to adjust to new parent figures) accepts the support and guidance offered by new parent figures, such as stepparents, guardians, or foster parents.
- Acknowledges and faces up to own problems. Can recognize a problem that is blocking positive interactions and does not underestimate nor exaggerate its effect.
- Takes steps to avoid a recurrence of prior problem behavior.

Selected Bibliography

Daniel Memorial Institute. *Independent Living Skills Assessment.* Jacksonville, FL: Daniel Memorial Institute, 1995.

MacNair, Ray. *Assessment of Social Functioning: A Client Instrument for Practitioners.* Vol. 6, Human Service Series. Athens: Institute of Community and Area Development, University of Georgia, 1981.

11.2   THE SOCIAL ASSESSMENT REPORT

A **social assessment report** (often called a *social history*) is a particular type of professional report prepared frequently by social workers in direct practice. It presents background information and describes the client's current situation and psychosocial functioning. Because past behavior is the best predictor of future behavior, the social worker will gather and report information on how the client behaved and reacted to various situations and challenges in the past. Those using the report can then make informed predictions about how the client will respond in the future.

A well-written social history or social assessment report is especially useful to professionals responsible for making decisions regarding the type of program or service that would be appropriate for a particular client and also to professionals and staff responsible for facilitating a client's adjustment to a new environment such as, for example, a foster home, treatment program, or nursing home. The report's content will vary somewhat depending on the audience for whom it is prepared (e.g., other social workers, doctors, judges, psychologists, school personnel, interdisciplinary teams). A social assessment report has these qualities:

1. *Concise and Relevant.*   Keep the intended reader in mind as you prepare this report. Provide what they need to know. The report should be as brief as possible. Avoid using jargon and diagnostic labels; rather include descriptions of the client's actual behavior and performance.

2. *Objective.*   Be as factual as possible. Do not present an opinion as if it were a fact. Label your interpretations or hypothesis as such; the best way to do this is to place your conclusions and inferences under a separate heading called "Worker's Impressions and Assessment."

If possible and appropriate, invite the client to review a draft of the report and offer additions and corrections. Because the report will become part of the client record, you should assume that the client may want to read it and has a right to do so (see Item 10.5). Avoid using words or phrases that could appear judgmental. When it is necessary to include observations that might offend the client, do so, if possible, by using the client's own words. Note these examples:

INAPPROPRIATE: It is apparent that Jane is a hostile and uncaring individual who is too self-centered and immature to cope with the demands of her elderly father.

ACCEPTABLE: While I was talking with Jane, her father requested a glass of water. She responded in a loud voice and said, "Go to hell, you old fool. I hope you dry up and blow away."

3. *Attention to client strengths.*   Successful interventions are built on client strengths. Thus, the report should focus on client strengths and abilities. Avoid giving undo attention to a client's limitations, deficiencies, and psychopathology (see Item 11.5).

4. *Organization.*   Use headings to sort the information into easy-to-find, topical categories. Here are some topical headings commonly used in social assessment reports:

- Identifying information (name, date of birth, address, phone, etc.)
- Reason for social workers or agency involvement with client
- Statement of client's concern, problem, or need
- Family background (data on family of origin, parents, siblings)
- Current family/household composition
- Client's significant others (e.g., spouse, children, friends)
- Ethnicity, religion, and spirituality
- Physical functioning, health concerns, nutrition, home safety, illness, disabilities, medications
- Intellectual functioning, education, school performance
- Psychological and emotional patterns
- Strengths, ways of coping, and problem-solving capacities
- Employment, income, work experience, and skills

- Housing, neighborhood, and transportation
- Recent use of community and professional services
- Social worker's impressions and assessment
- Descriptions of proposed intervention and service plan

The sample social assessment report presented in Figure 11.1 illustrates the use of topical headings.

Greystone Family Service Agency

Identifying Information

Client Name: Shirley McCarthy	Case Record #: 3456
D.O.B: July 4, 1991 Age: 20	Date of Referral: Oct. 8, 2011
Soc. Security #: 505–67–8910	Social Worker: Jane Green, BSW
Address: 2109 B Street	Report Prepared: Oct. 13, 2011
Greystone, MT 09876	
Phone: 555–0123	

Reason for Report

This report was prepared for use during consultation with Dr. Jones, the agency's psychiatric consultant, and for purposes of peer supervision. (The client is aware that a report is being prepared for this purpose.)

Reason for Social Work Involvement

Shirley was referred to this agency by Dr. Smith, an emergency room physician at City Hospital. Shirley was treated there for having taken an unknown quantity of aspirin in an apparent suicide attempt. She is reacting with anxiety and depression to her unwanted pregnancy. The father is a former boyfriend with whom she has broken off. She does not want him nor her parents to learn that she is pregnant.

She does not want an abortion and does not want to care for a child. She has thought about adoption but knows little about what would be involved. She agreed to come to this agency in order to figure out how she might deal with her dilemma.

Source of Data

This report is based on two one-hour interviews with the client (Oct. 9 and 11) and a phone conversation with Dr. Smith.

Family Background and Situation

Shirley is the youngest of three children. Her brother, John, age 30, is a chemical engineer in Austin, Texas. Her sister, Martha, age 27, is a pharmacist in Seattle. Shirley does not feel close to either sibling and neither knows of her pregnancy.

Her parents have been married for 33 years. They live in Spokane, Washington. Her father, Thomas, is an engineer for a farm equipment company. Her mother, Mary, is a registered nurse.

Shirley describes her parents as hard-working, honest people who have a strong sense of right and wrong and a commitment to family. The family is middle class and of Irish

FIGURE 11.1 Sample Social Assessment Report

heritage. The McCarthy's are life-long Catholics. The three children attended Catholic grade and high schools. Shirley says that if her parents knew of the pregnancy "it would just kill them." Her wish to keep her parents from learning of the pregnancy seems motivated by a desire to protect them from distress.

Physical Functioning and Health

Shirley is 5'7" tall and weighs 115 pounds. She is about three months pregnant. Dr. Smith reports that she is underweight but otherwise healthy. He has concern about her willingness to obtain proper prenatal care; he had referred Shirley to Dr. Johnson (an OB/GYN physician), but she did not keep that appointment.

Shirley says that she is in good health, eats well, exercises minimally, and reports no medical problems. She is not taking any medication.

Intellectual Functioning

Shirley completed two years at the University of Washington and then transferred to the University of Montana where she is currently a junior in computer science. She has an overall GPA of A–. Despite her good grades, Shirley describes herself as a "mediocre student."

She is attracted to subjects where there is a clear right and wrong answer. She does not like courses such as philosophy, which seems "wishy-washy" to her. Although she values the logical and precise thinking that is part of computer science, she explains that she tends to make personal decisions impulsively and "jumps into things without considering the consequences."

Emotional Functioning

Shirley describes herself as "moody." Even before the pregnancy, she had bouts of depression when she would sit alone in her room for hours at a time. She never sought treatment for the depression. In describing herself, Shirley uses the words "childish" and "immature"; she has always felt younger than others her age.

She often feels anger and sadness, but tries to keep her feelings from showing. In this sense, she is like her father, who always keeps things to himself until he finally "blows up."

In spite of her accomplishments, Shirley seems to have poor self-esteem and focuses more on her limitations than her strengths.

Interpersonal and Social Relationships

Shirley has no "close friends." She says it is difficult for her to interact with others and she wishes she had better social skills. She has held various part-time jobs during high school and college, but socialized only minimally with co-workers. In college, Shirley had trouble getting along with her roommates in the dorm, so she moved to an apartment so that she could be alone.

When she drinks alcohol, she feels more outgoing and friendly. However, this fact scares her because several uncles are alcoholic. For the past year, she worked hard at not drinking at all. She was not drinking when she took the aspirin.

Her former boyfriend, Bob (father of her baby), was the first person she ever dated for more than a few months. The relationship ended one month ago. Bob is also a student.

Religion and Spirituality

Shirley was raised as a Catholic and retains many of the beliefs and values she learned as a child. She describes herself as a spiritual person and one who prays quite often. She has clear ideas of right and wrong but also feels she is in a stage of life when she is trying to

FIGURE 11.1 Continued

decide what she really believes and is in the process of constructing a system of values, morals, and ethical principles.

Strengths and Problem-Solving Capacity

Although Shirley tends to minimize her strengths, she exhibits intelligence, an ability to work hard, a desire to make friends, a loyalty to her family while also wanting to make her own decisions, and a moderate motivation to deal with her situation constructively. She displays a good vocabulary and expresses herself in a clear manner.

She tends to avoid making hard decisions and lets things pile up until she is forced by circumstances to follow the only option still open to her. She usually knows what she "should do" but does not act; she attributes this to a fear of making mistakes. When faced with interpersonal conflict, she is inclined to withdraw.

Economics/Housing/Transportation

Shirley's parents are assisting her with the costs of her education. She also works about 30 hours per week at the Baylor Department Store, earning minimum wage. With this money, she pays rent and keeps her eight-year-old car running.

Aside from her college student health insurance, she has no medical coverage. She does not know if that policy covers pregnancy. Shirley lives alone in a two-room apartment which she says is located in a "rough area" of town. She is afraid to be out alone after dark.

Use of Community Resources

This is the first time Shirley has had contact with a social agency. During our sessions, she asked many questions about the agency and expressed some confusion about why she had been referred here by Dr. Smith. She acknowledged that feelings of embarrassment and shame make it difficult for her to talk to about her concerns.

Impressions and Assessment

This 20-year-old is experiencing inner conflict and depression because of an unwanted pregnancy. This gave rise to a suicide attempt. In keeping with her tendency to avoid conflict, she has not told others of the pregnancy, yet the father (Bob) will need to be involved if she chooses the legal procedure of relinquishment, and her parents' involvement may be needed for financial support. Prenatal care is needed, but it too has been avoided. Abortion is not an acceptable solution to Shirley, and she is ambivalent about adoption and how to manage her life while pregnant.

Goals for Work with Client

In order to help Shirley make the necessary decisions to deal with this pregnancy, I hope to engage her in pregnancy options counseling. Issues to be addressed include making a further assessment of her depression and suicide attempt, obtaining and paying for medical care, and deciding on whether to inform Bob and her own parents. She will need emotional support, some structure, and a gentle demand for work so she can overcome her avoidance, make decisions, and take necessary action.

Note: The names in this report are fictitious.

FIGURE 11.1   Continued

Selected Bibliography

Andrews, Arlene. *Social History Assessment*. Thousand Oaks, CA: Sage, 2007.
Kagle, Jill, and Sandra Kopels. *Social Work Records*, 3rd ed. Long Grove, IL: Waveland Press, 2008.
Zuckerman, Edward. *The Clinician's Thesaurus: The Guide for Wording Psychological Reports,* 6th ed. New York: Guilford, 2005.

11.3 MAPPING CLIENT CONDITIONS

Social workers make use of several forms of diagramming client conditions that present client information in a graphic or visual format. Descriptions and explanations that might require several pages of narrative can often be reduced to a single page using these diagrams. Three of the most popular diagrams are the **genogram** (a diagram similar to a family tree that depicts family structures and relationships), a specialized version of the genogram that focuses on exploring the cultural background of clients (i.e., the **cultural genogram**), and the **ecomap** (which depicts and individual or a family within a social context).

The symbols used for both genograms and ecomaps are similar and client information such as the following can be easily be diagramed:

- Age, sex, marital status, and household composition
- Family structure and relationships (e.g., biological children, stepchildren, parents)
- Job situation, employment, and responsibilities
- Social activities, interests, hobbies, recreation
- Formal associations (e.g., church involvement, membership in service club)
- Sources of support and stress in social interactions (between people and between people and community systems)
- Utilization of professional and community resources
- Informal resources, social supports, and natural helpers (e.g., extended family, relatives, friends, neighbors)

Although the user of these diagrams can create his or her own symbols and abbreviations, certain symbols are commonly used, as shown in Figure 11.2. In addition to the symbols, various words and notations—such as "m" for "married," and "div" for "divorced"—may also be used in the family diagram and ecomap.

GENOGRAMS

Figure 11.3 is an example of a genogram that describes a reconstituted family. That family appears within the dotted circle (boundary). It indicates that a man (age 45), his wife (age 33), and three children (ages 3, 1, and 10) live in the household. The 10-year-old is from his mother's former marriage; the boy's biological father died in 2007. The 45-year-old husband was divorced from his former wife (age 42) in 2005. Also, we see that he has two daughters (ages 20 and 18) by this former wife and is now a grandfather, since his 20-year-old daughter has a 1-year-old daughter. The former wife is now married to a man who is age 44. Inserting the actual names and other notations adds even more clarity. Information on the purchase of software that facilitates making genograms, as well as examples of genograms, may be found at www.genogramanalytics.com.

CULTURAL GENOGRAMS

The purpose of preparing a cultural genogram is to help clients better understand their identities by describing cultural groups that helped shape their identity and life experiences. It helps to clarify cultural influences on their family system. The diagram can assist in surfacing cultural conflicts within a family and also an individual's culturally based emotions, assumptions, and stereotypes.

In addition to the mapping provided by a conventional genogram (described above), the cultural genogram incorporates the use of shading or coloring of the person symbols to represent differing racial, ethnic, nationality, and language backgrounds and influences. Completing a cultural genogram with a client can help to flesh-out a family's experience with discrimination,

FIGURE 11.2 Symbols for Ecomaps and Genograms

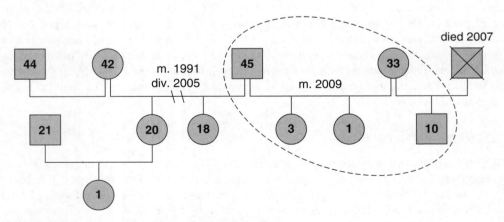

FIGURE 11.3 Genogram of a Reconstituted Family

a history of intergroup conflict, differences in religious/spiritual perceptions, the value placed on various occupational roles, pride/shame issues, and so on. This form of genogram can also depict generation-to-generation cultural shifts and the merging of different cultures in the offspring in multicultural families.

As a result of working with a social worker in developing a cultural genogram, the client should have been helped to address such questions as:

- What parts of your cultural background and identity do you embrace or reject?
- What beliefs, biases, and prejudices have been transmitted to you from your family and cultural background?
- How do the examination of your cultural background and the blending of your culture with other cultures in your relationships affect how you will think and feel when experiencing cultural conflict?

ECOMAPS

Typically, an ecomap uses circles to represent the significant people, organizations, or other factors that interact with and impact on a client. In addition, various symbols, directional arrows, and short phrases are used to identify and describe the nature of these interactions. Figure 11.4 is an ecomap of Dick and Barb and their two children, John and June.

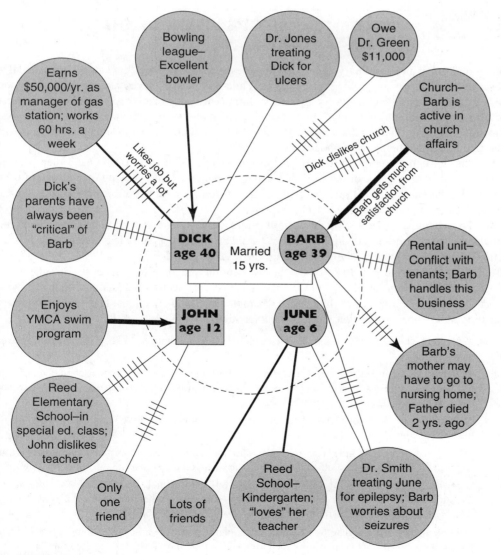

FIGURE 11.4   Ecomap

Ideally, the development of a genogram or ecomap is a joint effort between the social worker and client during a face-to-face interview. The worker's use of these diagrams can help strengthen a professional relationship and demonstrate a desire to better understand the client. The process of drawing these diagrams and clarifying and discussing the relationships and factors depicted can help both the social worker and client understand the client's situation more clearly. In many situations, it is best for the social worker to simply guide the client in using the mapping tools to construct his or her own ecomap.

Selected Bibliography

DeMaria, Rita, Gerald Weeks, and Larry Hof. *Focused Genograms: Intergenerational Assessment of Individuals, Couples, and Families.* Philadelphia: Brunner/Mazel, 1999.
Hardy, Kenneth V., and Tracey A Laszoffy. "The Cultural Genogram: Key to Training Culturally Competent Family Therapists."*Journal of Marital and Family Therapy* 21, no.3 (July 1995): 227–237.
McGoldrick, Monica, Randy Gerson, and Sueli Petry. *Genograms*, 3rd ed. New York: W. W. Norton, 2008.

11.4 EXPANDING A CLIENT'S VISION OF CHANGES THAT ARE POSSIBLE

Many traditional and customary approaches to assessment require the client to provide a detailed description of his or her problem or concern. While this may be necessary for some purposes, such as making a clinical diagnosis, these descriptions are not necessarily helpful to the process of planning or facilitating change. In fact, giving undo attention to the client's problems, dysfunction, pathology, and all that may be going wrong in a client's life and situation can cause the client to feel rather helpless and hopeless.

An alternative approach, one based on the principles of solution-focused therapy (see Chapter 6), is to ask a type of question that will draw the client into viewing their situation from new and different angles. Three especially useful techniques are termed *exploring exceptions*, *scaling questions*, and *using the miracle question*.

The technique of **exploring exceptions** refers to questions intended to help the client realize that there are times or situations when the problem is less apparent, less frequent, or less intense. Even when the client feels that the problem exists "all the time" and "everywhere," it is usually possible to find exceptions. Once these exceptions are identified and described, the social worker can then encourage the client to consider why these exceptions occur and figure out what might be done to recreate or prolong these desirable times and situations. Here are examples of questioning intended to uncover and explore exceptions:

"This is obviously a very serious problem. How have you managed to keep it from getting even worse?"

"You have said that you are in trouble with your parents most of the time. Tell me about a time in the last couple of weeks when you and your parents were getting along at least somewhat better than usual. What did you do to make that happen?"

"You are failing all of your school courses except for History. What have you done in order to pass the History course?"

"Have things been even a little better since you called me to arrange this appointment [the answer is usually yes]? If things are now a little bit better, tell me what you did to make things better for yourself?"

"Are those times when things are going a little bit better usually in the morning? Afternoon? Evening? Are you alone or is someone with you? If someone is with you, what are they saying and doing to help make things go more smoothly?"

"During the next week and before we meet again, please notice the times when things are going better and write down what is happening each time your problem becomes less troublesome."

The technique of **scaling questions** is designed to help the client realize that the seriousness and the impact of a problem varies over time and also that bringing about change is a matter of taking many small steps. The technique consists of asking a core scaling question and several follow-up questions, as in this example:

SOCIAL WORKER: On a scale of 1 to 10—with 1 being the worst your problem has ever been and 10 meaning that the problem had been solved and is no longer of concern to you—how would you rate your situation today?

CLIENT: Oh, probably about a 4 today, but it was a 2 last week.

SOCIAL WORKER: Great! I am glad to hear that things are going better. Given that improvement, I have two questions for you. First, how did you manage to change your situation from a 2 to a 4? And second, what do you think you can do in the next week to move the rating from a 4 to about a 4.5 or a 5?

Here is an application of the scaling question intended to assess the client's motivation:

SOCIAL WORKER: We have talked about some things that you might be able to do in order to address your dilemma. On a scale of 1 to 10—with 1 meaning that you are not willing to do anything to solve the problem and 10 meaning that you are willing to try just about anything to find a solution—how hard are you willing to work on this problem?

CLIENT: Probably about a 9.

SOCIAL WORKER: Wow! That is wonderful! Tell me, why do you feel so strongly motivated today?

A third solution-focused technique, the **miracle question**, encourages the client to visualize what his or her life would be like without the current problem and to identify more clearly the changes he or she needs to make. The miracle question is asked deliberately and rather dramatically. De Shazer (1988, p. 5) suggests wording something like this:

"Now, I want to ask you a rather strange question. Suppose that while you are sleeping tonight, a miracle happens: The problem that brought you here for professional help has been solved! However, because you were sleeping, you do not know that this miracle has occurred. So, after you wake up tomorrow morning, how will you know? What will be different? What will tell you that something miraculous has happened and that the problem that brought you into counseling has disappeared?"

The social worker will then ask various follow-up questions to help the client further describe the hoped-for changes. The following examples are from work with a married woman:

"What might your husband notice about you that would give him the idea that your problem has miraculously disappeared?"

"When he notices that positive change in you, what might he do differently in response to how you have changed?"

"When he behaves differently toward you, what will you do in response to how he is now behaving toward you?"

"When you are free of this problem, how will your relationships at home and at work be different than they are now?"

As clients begin to visualize and think seriously about their everyday lives without or in the absence of their problems, they typically come up with practical ideas about what they can do to better cope with their problems.

Selected Bibliography

DeJong, Peter, and Insoo Kim Berg. *Interviewing for Solutions*, 3rd ed. Belmont, CA: Brooks/Cole, 2008.
de Shazer, Steven. *Clues: Investigating Solutions in Brief Therapy*. New York: W. W. Norton, 1988.
O'Hanlon, Bill, and Michele Weiner-Davis. *In Search of Solutions*. New York: Norton, 2003.
O'Hanlon, Bill, and Sandy Beadle. *A Guide to Possibility Land*. New York: Norton, 1999.

11.5 IDENTIFYING CLIENT STRENGTHS

An assessment of a client's functioning should identify a client's strengths. A **client strength** can be defined as something positive and important that the client is doing, can do, or wants to do. That "something important" may be a behavior, a situation, or even an attitude. This is not to suggest a Pollyannaish approach that ignores or overlooks real problems, but it does ask the social worker to search for strengths even in the most dysfunctional and chaotic of cases. The reason for this emphasis is simple: To be successful, an intervention must be built on and around client strengths. If the worker focuses only on a client's problems and on what is going wrong in the client's life, the client will become even more discouraged and the worker will start to doubt his or her ability to be of help.

For many in the helping professions, focusing on client strengths requires a paradigm shift—a new way of thinking. It is important to recognize the forces that have encouraged excessive attention on client problems and limitations. Consider the following:

- *Agency policy and funding.* Most human services agencies are created for the purpose of addressing or correcting some personal or family problem, pathology, deficiency, or dysfunction. Consequently, those employed by the agency may presume that they should focus primarily on a client's problems.
- *Diagnostic labels.* Commonly used reference books (e.g., *DSM*) focus on pathology. The frequent use of this terminology creates a negative mindset that looks for and finds only client problems and pathology.
- *Lack of skill.* Identifying a client's problems is an elementary skill. Most people can do it with little or no training. On the other hand, identifying strengths is an advanced or higher level skill.
- *Personality and temperament.* Many people tend to see the glass as "half empty" rather than "half full." They just naturally focus on what is missing and on what is wrong. Some socio-biologists believe that the human tendency to notice quickly what is wrong, different, and out of place has a survival value for animals and the human species. Consequently, evolution has "wired" our senses and perceptual processes so that we will quickly notice things that are somehow out of the ordinary because it helps us to detect and avoid dangers in our environment.

The social worker can identify strengths by carefully observing individual and family behavior. Here are some examples of *individual strengths*:

- Assuming responsibility for one's actions
- Loyalty and a sense of duty to family and friends
- Showing affection, compassion, and concern for others; demonstrating willingness to forgive others
- Assisting and encouraging others and protecting them from harm
- Seeking employment, holding a job, being a responsible employee, meeting one's financial obligations
- Exercising self-control and making thoughtful decisions and plans; choosing not to engage in irresponsible or self-defeating behavior (e.g., an angry youth wanted to beat up another teen but chooses to walk away)

- Taking reasonable risks in order to make needed changes
- Being trustworthy, fair, and honest in dealing with others
- Experiencing appropriate sorrow and guilt; making amends or restitution for having harmed others
- Seeking to understand and accept differences among people
- Willingness to keep trying despite hardship and setbacks
- Participating in organizations that improve one's neighborhood and community
- Expressing one's point of view and standing up for one's own rights and the rights of others
- Making constructive use of abilities and aptitudes

Important *family strengths* include the following:

- Members trust, respect, and enjoy each other
- Family has traditions, rituals, and stories that provide a sense of history, belonging, and identity
- Family has clear and reasonable rules that govern behavior and interaction
- Family members share and make personal sacrifices in order to help each other; members stick together and support each other
- Members listen to and respect each other's opinions, even when they disagree
- Each member's ideas, preferences, and needs are considered before making decisions that would affect the whole family
- Conflicts are acknowledged, negotiated, and resolved

Strengths can be uncovered by asking questions such as: What would you not change about yourself, your situation, and your life? What advantages or benefit do others see in your approach to life? Despite your current problems, what parts of your life are going fairly well? Tell me about times when you successfully handled a serious problem? Where did you find the courage to keep going in this challenging and stressful situation? What do other people like about you?

Building on client strengths may require looking at a client's problems from a very different angle. For example, consider the man who has been labeled as uncooperative and unmotivated. If one views his behavior from a different angle, this behavior may reveal a strength, namely his ability to assert himself and the courage to resist doing what does not make sense to him. In other words, when viewed from another perspective, he is being logical and assertive. When problems are reframed in this way, one usually also discovers more effective ways of helping or at least communicating with the client (see Item 13.10).

Another way of orienting your approach to one that recognizes and builds on client strengths is to assume that within all people, there are innate tendencies toward psychological health and prosocial behavior. Just as there are natural healing processes constantly repairing our body, there are natural forces that, over time, tend to heal and repair psychological damage, ruptured relationships, and the many other hurts that are a part of life and living. If such a belief is a reasonable one, it lends hope to the social worker's efforts and underscores the importance of creating conditions and environments that allow the client's natural healing processes to work.

The more adept a social worker becomes at identifying client strengths, the easier it becomes to build a helping relationship, formulate an individualized intervention plan, and select services that will be used by and useful to the client. These guidelines will help the worker maintain a focus on client strengths:

1. Assume that the client is honest and trustworthy, unless it is proven otherwise. Assume that most people, most of the time, are doing the best they can, given their situation and circumstances. At the same time, assume that everyone is capable of making positive change if provided with support, encouragement, guidance, and resources.

2. Assume that the client is an expert on his or her own behavior, life, and situation, and probably knows best what will and will not work in a treatment plan or change effort. To the extent possible utilize the client's understanding of his or her troublesome situation and his or her suggestions on what can be done to change it. View the assessment and the service planning processes as a collaborative activity.

3. Anticipate that somewhere within the client's family, social network, and community there is an oasis of potential helping resources. Every family, neighborhood, and community contains people who are willing and capable of offering assistance to others.

4. Avoid discussions of blame and what the client or others could have or should have done previously. Attempts to find and assign blame usually lead nowhere. Also, avoid pointless discussions of what has caused the problem. Typically, problems of social functioning arise from a combination of many personal and situational factors. Trying to figure out the exact cause is seldom helpful. Even when a cause can be identified, that may say little about what can be done to address a problem or concern.

5. Call to the client's attention all indicators, displays, or demonstrations of his or her strengths such as a skill, competence, motivation, or attitude.

Selected Bibliography

Clifton, Donald, and Edward Anderson. *Strength Quest: Discover and Develop Your Strengths*. Washington, DC: Gallop Organization, 2004.

Corcoran, Jacqueline. *Building Strengths and Skills*. New York: Oxford University Press, 2004.

Glicken, Morley. *Using the Strengths Perspective in Social Work Practice*. Boston: Allyn & Bacon, 2004.

Saleebey, Dennis, ed. *The Strengths Perspective in Social Work Practice*, 4th ed. Boston: Allyn & Bacon, 2009.

11.6   ASSESSING A CLIENT'S SOCIAL SUPPORT

The term **social support** refers to assistance and caring provided by others and perceived by the person on the receiving end as desirable and beneficial. Family, friends, or neighbors most often provide social support. It can take several forms, such as *tangible* or *concrete assistance* (e.g., a ride to a doctor appointment, a small cash loan, help with grocery shopping, child care); *guidance and teaching* (e.g., providing information, helping a friend make a difficult decision, teaching a needed skill); *care and comfort* (e.g., listening with empathy, reassurance) and *companionship* (e.g., friendship, social activity). The availability of social support can be a significant factor in one's physical and mental health and in recovery from an illness or injury. In some situations, social support is provided by agency employees or volunteers.

In order to help a client make appropriate use of his or her social supports, the social worker will need to engage the client in an effort to identify current or potential sources of support. A series of questions might guide this assessment process:

- What people are important to you? As you answer that question, think of and list the people who are in your household or family, your friends and neighbors, people at work or school, and the people who are members of the organizations or religious groups to which you belong.
- Of those you have listed, which ones are especially supportive and helpful and a positive influence on your life? And of these individuals, which ones do you see, talk to, write to, or email on a regular basis?
- Are there individuals to whom you often turn to for advice or help in making decisions?
- Are there individuals that you would feel comfortable asking for a ride to work, a ride to the grocery store, or for a small loan?
- Who among those in your network of relatives and friends knows you and understands you quite well?

- Do you have individuals in your life whom you really trust and could turn to for help or advice concerning a personal problem?
- Who is the one person you can always count on for help, no matter what the problem or situation?

Once a client has identified individuals who are potential social supports, the worker engages the client in a discussion of whether and how the client might reach out to them and enlist their assistance. Whether these individuals are likely resources will depend on the nature of the client's needs and the client's willingness to ask for and use these sources of supports. In some situations, a client may experience emotional support just knowing that there are people or agencies that they could call upon, even if they never utilize these potential resources.

It should be noted that social support is one component of a person's larger **social network** (all the individuals and groups with whom one interacts on a regular basis). The size or extent of a person's social network is not necessarily correlated with the availability of social supports. Some people belong to a large family and have many friends but few social supports. By definition, social support is a positive influence whereas some aspects or a client's social network may, in fact, be harmful, as, for example, in the negative influence exerted by an anti-social peer group or gang.

Selected Bibliography

Kemp, Susan, James Whittaker, and Elizabeth Tracy. *Person-Environment Practice*. New York: Aldine de Gruyter, 1997.

Tracy, Elizabeth. "Identifying Social Support Resources of At-Risk Families." *Social Work* 35, no. 3 (May 1990): 252–258.

Uchino, Bert. *Social Support and Physical Heath*. New Haven, CN: Yale University Press, 2004.

11.7   ASSESSING A CLIENT'S COPING STRATEGIES AND EGO DEFENSES

During the assessment phase, it is often necessary to identify a client's usual ego defenses and methods of coping in order to anticipate how the client will react to an effort to bring about needed change. Some professionals use the terms *coping strategy* and *defense mechanism* interchangeably, but there is a distinction based on the degree to which the response is under conscious and voluntary control and whether self-deception and reality distortion are involved. Thus, we define a **coping strategy** as a deliberate and conscious effort to solve a problem or handle personal distress. By contrast, an **ego defense** is a habitual or unconscious and problem-avoiding maneuver.

Coping strategies have two functions: to solve a problem (*task-focused coping*) and to reduce emotional discomfort (*emotion-focused coping*). These two functions may be in play concurrently. In some very difficult situations, an individual will need to first manage his or her emotional reactions before being able to engage in problem solving.

Individuals vary widely in their emotion-focused coping strategies. For example, given a situation that causes much anxiety, some individuals might elect to go off by themselves, others might visit friends, some pray and meditate, and still others might engage in a physical workout. Other coping strategies—some functional and some not—include ignoring the problem, sleeping more, eating more, and immersion in work. Since an individual will tend to use certain strategies habitually, the social worker can form a fairly accurate picture of which ones a client uses by asking how he or she has responded to or dealt with prior stressful situations.

Regardless of their culture, people react to shocking events and intense distress by using certain **emotion-focused coping strategies**:

- *Crying.* This is a common means of alleviating tension and responding to loss. It is a necessary part of successful grief work.

- *Talking it out.* People who have undergone traumatic experiences often need to repeatedly describe and talk about the experience. Over time, this natural desensitization process lessens the intensity of the emotional pain associated with the traumatic experience.
- *Laughing it off.* Joking and viewing a painful experience with a sense of humor may release tension and put the matter in perspective. In healthy grieving, for example, there is often a good mix of crying and laughter among those adjusting to the death of a loved one.
- *Seeking social support.* It is natural for both children and adults to seek reassurance and comfort from others as a means of regaining a sense of security and emotional equilibrium.
- *Dreaming and nightmares.* These do not fit the authors' definition of a coping strategy (i.e., conscious and voluntary) but they are a common reaction to traumatic experience. And, like the desensitization process involved in talking it out, recurring dreams have the benefit of drawing the individual into consciously grappling with the experience.

When working with a client who has not experienced a traumatic event and has moved beyond the emotion-focused responses described above, the social worker should help him or her adopt **task-focused strategies**. These are deliberate actions that will likely bring about changes in one's functioning, one's environment, or both. The task-focused strategies listed below are of a rather general nature, but they illustrate what the social worker should be looking for in data collection and assessment. A client with good task-oriented coping strategies will have the motivation, the capacity, and the opportunity to do these things:

- Express thoughts and feelings in a clear, positive, and, when necessary, assertive manner.
- Ask questions and gather new information, even when the information challenges one's current beliefs.
- Recognize that one has choices and can, with effort, modify one's behavior and situation.
- Cut one's losses and withdraw from relationships or situations that are unhealthy, stressful, and unchangeable.
- Examine the spiritual and religious dimension of life and draw on one's beliefs for insight, strength, and direction.
- Identify early indicators of a developing problem so that corrective action can be taken before the problem becomes serious.
- Take steps to solve one's problems, even when such actions are a source of fear and anxiety.
- Release pent-up emotion in ways that do not harm self or others.
- Delay immediate gratification in order to stick with a plan that will attain a desired, but more distant goal.
- Use visualizations of future actions or events to mentally rehearse how to handle anticipated difficulties.
- Seek out and use additional skills training and needed professional services.

If the assessment reveals that a client lacks necessary coping strategies, the intervention plan should focus on helping the client learn specific skills. For example, an abusing parent may need to learn parenting skills, an individual in need of a job will need to focus on job-finding skills, a married couple in conflict may need communication skills, and a youth leaving the foster-care system will need to acquire independent living skills.

A **defense mechanism** is usually defined as a mostly unconscious mental process that protects the individual against anxiety, psychological threat, and emotional pain. Everyone uses these mechanisms to some degree when coping with the ordinary problems and stresses of living. However, the excessive or rigid use of defense mechanisms is problematic because they often get in the way of realistic problem solving. Extreme defensiveness and distortions of reality are characteristics of a mental disorder.

An individual who uses the ego defense of **denial** screens out unpleasant realities by refusing to acknowledge them. The ego defense of **rationalization** involves offering arguments that justify one's inappropriate behavior. Denial and rationalization are predominant defenses used by people who are addicted to drugs or alcohol. An example of rationalization would be the mother who justifies the physical abuse of her child by arguing that inflicting pain is the only thing that works to control her child's misbehavior. Although it is a distortion of the truth, a rationalization is not the same as a lie because the defensive pattern is so habitual that the person is not consciously and deliberately trying to fabricate a falsehood. Behaviors that suggest rationalization by a client include: (a) groping for reasons to justify a behavior or belief, (b) inability to recognize inconsistencies in one's "story," and (c) unwillingness to consider alternative explanations and becoming angry when one's reasoning is questioned.

The defense mechanism of **projection** is in play when one attributes to others one's own unacceptable thoughts or behavior. For example, an individual who has molested a young child may convince himself that he was seduced by the child and is therefore the victim rather than the offender.

The defense of **intellectualization** involves the use of abstractions and theoretical considerations as a means of separating oneself emotionally from a troubling situation. For example, the individual who was turned down for a sought-after job may cope with feelings of rejection and disappointment by explaining the inability to get the job as caused by free-trade economics and changing global markets.

Emotional insulation is a maneuver aimed at withholding one's attachment to or investment in a desired but unlikely outcome. It creates a shield that protects the individual from a recurrence of emotional pain. For example, a child who is moved frequently from foster home to foster home may withhold all attachment to the foster parents as a defense against experiencing yet another painful separation and loss. Unfortunately, such a child often carries this pattern into adulthood and is then unable to form an emotional bond to a marriage partner or to his or her own children. This defense is closely related to the concept of *learned helplessness*—after a long period of frustration, some individuals may simply give up and quit trying to escape their misery. These are the "broken" individuals who become passive recipients of whatever life brings them. Emotional insulation is commonly observed in persons who have grown up in extreme deprivation.

The person using **fantasy** as a defense spends much time daydreaming and dwells on imaginary situations, either as a way of meeting emotional needs or as shields against anxiety and feelings of inadequacy. Problems develop when the person chooses an imaginary existence over reality. The inability to distinguish between fantasy and reality is a symptom of serious mental illness.

The defense of **repression** unconsciously excludes an extremely threatening experience from one's awareness. For example, a child may repress the experiences of having been sexually abused and not remember this until many years later.

Regression is a retreat from one's present level of maturity and its responsibilities to one that has fewer demands. For example, when a new child is born to a family, the 5-year-old may begin behaving like an infant (e.g., wetting pants, sucking thumb) as a way of getting more attention and coping with fears of being overlooked by his or her parents. Some degree of regression is fairly common among persons who are seriously ill and experiencing much pain and distress.

When using **reaction formation** a person adopts behaviors that are the opposite of his or her desires, ones that are abhorrent and unacceptable. An example is an individual who comes to realize that he is sexually attracted to children and, in response, works tirelessly to create programs designed to prevent child sexual abuse.

Displacement refers to transferring troublesome emotions (often hostility) and acting-out behaviors (e.g., violence) from the person who arouses the emotion to another less threatening and less powerful person or thing. The classic example is the man who kicks his dog because he is angry with his boss.

Acting out is an attempt to cope with frustration or inner turmoil by taking action, often impulsively, or by striking out physically. For example, a frustrated adolescent boy who is unable to verbally express his feelings may seek a release from tension by attacking the person he views as the source of his problems. Another example would be the battered wife who is feeling the tensions build and knows she will soon be beaten by her abusive husband, so she proceeds to provoke him so she can "get it over with." Soldiers in combat who can no longer tolerate the stress and fear of waiting to be attacked have been known to leave the safety of their foxhole and blindly charge the enemy.

Several guidelines will assist the social worker in assessing and responding to a client's defense mechanisms:

1. When using defense mechanism terminology, certain precautions are necessary. The patterns that we call ego defenses are only hypothetical constructs inferred from the way people behave. At best, they are a shorthand language for describing people's behavior and inner struggles. Simply labeling a client's behavior as projection or rationalization, for example, in no way changes or even explains the behavior. You must look behind the surface behavior and identify the unmet needs and pain that cause the client to rely on the defense mechanism.

2. Because defenses are mostly learned and habitual, an individual tends to repeat those defenses he or she has used in the past. For example, if an individual has a history of frequently using denial and rationalization, you can expect him or her to use those same defenses when again faced with anxiety or conflict.

3. People hold tightly to their defensive patterns. The more anxiety they experience, the more rigidly they use the defense. It is usually only within a relationship characterized by empathy, warmth, and genuineness that a person can feel safe enough to let down his or her defenses and examine the underlying pain.

Selected Bibliography

Blackman, Jerome. *101 Defenses: How the Mind Shields Itself*. New York: Routledge, 2003.
Conte, Hope, and Robert Plutchik. *Ego Defenses: Theory and Measurement*. New York: Wiley and Sons, 1995.
Cramer, Phebe. *Protecting the Self: Defense Mechanisms in Action*. New York: Guilford, 2006.

11.8 ASSESSING A CLIENT'S ROLE PERFORMANCE

As explained in Item 11.1, the social work profession is especially focused on a people's social functioning. To examine social functioning, one must understand the concept and dynamics of social role. The notion of **social role** derives from the observation that certain behaviors, attitudes, and norms are expected of a person when he or she has been assigned a certain status or occupies a certain position in society. For example, once a person becomes a parent (a social role), he or she is expected to provide his or her young children with food, shelter, protection, guidance, and so on. Within a school setting, the teacher (a social role) is expected to deliver instruction, and the student (another social role) is expected to study, learn, and adhere to school rules. The term *role*, borrowed from theater, implies that a script (role descriptions), an actor, and an audience (society) are components of our social functioning. Because the concepts and terminology of role theory bridge psychological and social perspectives on human behavior, they help social workers to assess and describe a client's functioning. The purpose of many social agencies and programs is to enhance or improve people's performance of their social roles such as parent, spouse, employee, student, and citizen.

The concept of **role expectation** suggests that for a given role, there is a cluster of behaviors that are deemed appropriate and acceptable by a reference group or by society as a whole. In other words, the reference group (e.g., peer group, a community, religion, organization) expects the individual to behave in a certain way and will either approve or disapprove of the person, depending on whether he or she conforms to those expectations. Role expectations define the limits of acceptable and tolerated behavior.

The term **role conception** refers to an individual's beliefs and assumptions about how he or she is supposed to behave when in a particular role. An individual's role conception may or may not conform to the role expectations, as defined by a community or the wider society.

An individual's actual behavior while performing a role is termed his or her **role performance** (or *role enactment*). In some instances, an individual's role performance may be consistent with his or her role conception but not conform to other peoples' role expectations. For example, a father may be living up to his own beliefs about parenthood, but his behavior may be judged to be child neglect by the community or the court system. In order to successfully perform a given role, an individual must possess certain knowledge, values, attitudes, and skills. These prerequisite abilities are often termed **role demands** (or *role requirements*).

A number of terms are used to describe problems in role performance. **Interrole conflict** refers to an incompatibility or clash between two or more roles. For example, a woman may experience a conflict between her role as the parent to a young child and her role as a corporate executive who is expected to travel out town and work long hours. **Intrarole conflict** exists when a person is caught up in a situation where two or more sets of expectations are assigned to a single role. For example, a high school boy may not be able to reconcile the role of student as defined by his teacher with how being a student is defined by his friends who prefer parties to homework. The problem of **role incapacity** exists when, for some reason, an individual lacks the capacity to perform a certain role; possible reasons include physical or mental illness, lack of the prerequisite skills, drug addiction, mental retardation, and so on. **Role rejection** occurs when an individual refuses to perform a role; an extreme example is when a parent abandons his or her child.

A problem of **role ambiguity** (or *role confusion*) exists when there are few clear expectations associated with a role—a condition most likely to occur in times of rapid societal change. Consequently, the individual is unsure of what is expected and is unable to evaluate his or her own performance. **Self-role incongruence** exists when there is little overlap or a poor match between the requirements of a role (i.e., role demands) and the individual's personality or self-concept. For example, an individual may occupy the role of trial lawyer but not feel comfortable in that role because he or she is by temperament rather submissive and passive. Another example is when an individual finds that his or her values, ethics, or lifestyle are at odds with the expectations of a role.

The problem of **role overload** exists when a person occupies more roles than he or she can perform adequately. In reality, most people are unable to or do not choose to meet all of the expectations associated with their roles. Thus, most people live with some degree of **role strain**, a situation that necessitates making compromises and trade-offs, setting priorities, and using various coping strategies to reconcile their role conceptions with their limited time and energy.

A number of questions can help the social worker analyze problems of role performance and make decisions concerning the type of intervention needed. The questions that follow are based, in part, on ones proposed by Mager and Pipe (1997) for the analysis of job-related performance problems:

1. *What is the nature and degree of discrepancy between the client's actual role performance and the role expectation?*

- How does the client's behavior differ from that considered appropriate or normal for this particular role?
- What observations, events, or experiences have caused you, the client, or others to conclude that a discrepancy exists?
- Why are you and/or the client dissatisfied with or concerned about the client's role performance? Why is this role important? What will happen if there is no change in the client's role performance?

2. *Is the discrepancy caused by a lack of knowledge, skill, or motivation?*

- Does the client possess the knowledge or skill needed to perform this role?
- Could the client satisfactorily perform this role if he or she had to or really wanted to?

3. *If the discrepancy is caused by a lack of knowledge and skill, how might this limitation be addressed?*

- Was there a time when the client could perform this role? If so, what has caused the client to lose this capacity or motivation?

- Is the client able to learn the prerequisite knowledge and skills?
- What teaching methods or techniques will help the client acquire the knowledge and skills needed to perform this role?

4. *If the discrepancy is caused by a rejection or a lack of interest in the role, how can the problem be addressed?*

- Does this role really matter to the client?
- What roles or activities does the client consider more important?
- Does the client see any benefits in performing this role?
- Is the client rewarded or reinforced for performing this role? If not, how can incentives be increased?
- Is the client being punished by others or by social systems for performing this role? Can this punishment be avoided?

Selected Bibliography

Davis, Liane. "Role Theory." In *Social Work Treatment*, 4th ed., edited by Francis Turner, 581–600. New York: Free Press, 1996.

Mager, Robert, and Peter Pipe. *Analyzing Performance Problems*, 3rd ed. Atlanta: Center for Effective Performance, 1997.

11.9   ASSESSING A CLIENT'S SELF-CONCEPT

The term **self** refers to that private and inner world of assumptions, perceptions, and thoughts about the "I" or the "me." The self is the center of consciousness, thought, and action. One's sense of self answers the questions: Who am I? What am I really like, regardless of what others may think of me? The term **self-concept** refers to a set of beliefs and images that a person has about himself or herself. Those beliefs may or may not be shared by others. Moreover, our self-concept will vary somewhat in response to differing situations, circumstances, and how we are performing certain tasks. Although the foundation of our self-concept is formed during childhood, experiences throughout life can lead us to reevaluate and possibly modify what we think of ourselves. Self-concept is of critical importance to our social functioning because how we respond to others and to life events and how we perform our social roles is influenced by how we think and feel about ourselves.

Several other concepts help to describe aspects of the self. **Self-identity** is how we define and describe ourselves to ourselves and differentiate ourselves from other people. What we think about ourselves may, of course, be different from the image we try to present or project to other people. Thus, we have a private self and a public self.

Self-worth (or *self-esteem*) refers to our evaluation of our own worth or value as a human being. Self-worth is a highly subjective evaluation. The term **ideal-self** (or *self-expectation*) refers to our deeply personal thoughts about who we could be, should be, or want to be. **Body image** refers to our perceptions and evaluations of our own body and physical appearance. The term **self-acceptance** can be thought of as the degree to which we are satisfied and at peace with what we see as our qualities and attributes, strengths, and limitations. **Self-efficacy** has to do with the beliefs we have about our effectiveness and competence as a human being.

Whether a particular facet of a client's self-concept needs to be discussed during the assessment process depends on the client's presenting concern and the reasons the client and professional are meeting. Some clients are reluctant to share such personal information, whereas others are eager to tell their stories and share innermost thoughts about themselves. To draw out this type of information, the social worker can ask questions that are organized around five common themes in life: love, loss, fear, having been hurt, and having hurt others. Many clients will respond non-defensively to questions like these:

1. *Who and what do you really love?*   Who and what are of greatest importance to you? For whom do you make personal sacrifices? For whom and for what purposes do you give of your time and money? Are you, perhaps, unable to care for or love someone as you want?

2. *Who and what have you lost?*   Have you lost parents, children, siblings, and close friends to separation, estrangement, disability, or death? Have you lost purpose and meaning in life or your hopes and dreams? Have you lost some physical or mental abilities as a result of illness or injury? Have you lost your sense of security and safety as a result of abuse, exploitation, violence, or war? Have you lost contact with your homeland or native language? Have you lost touch with meaningful religious and cultural activity? Have you lost a home or possessions to a flood, fire, or natural disaster?

3. *Who and what do you fear?*   Do you live with a fear of hunger, violence, illness, pain, disability, or death? Do you fear that no one really cares for you? Do you fear that you are incapable of loving others? Do you fear the loss of respect and status? Do you fear the loss of important relationships, a job, money, or a home?

4. *How have you been hurt in life?*   How have you been hurt by family and friends (physically, emotionally, financially, etc.)? How do you explain these painful experiences? Have these past hurts given rise to fears of being hurt again or a desire for revenge? How have these painful experiences affected the way you feel about yourself and others?

5. *Whom have you hurt?*   How and when have you hurt others, either deliberately or inadvertently? How do you explain these experiences? Have those experiences altered the way you feel about yourself? What have you done to make amends or restitution for the pain and injury you have caused?

Next are some other lines of questioning that might be used, in one form or another, to explore a client's sense of self:

1. *Family membership.*   Who is your family (tribe or clan)? For whom do you feel responsible and obligated to care for, help, or look after? With whom do you live? How often do you talk with family members? To which family members do you feel especially close or perhaps distant and estranged? Are you comfortable in your family?

2. *Identity.*   How do you define yourself in terms of the labels and categories commonly used to describe people? For example: Gender? Sexual orientation? Marital status? Occupation? Nationality? Ethnicity? Religion? Socioeconomic class? Political orientation?

3. *Body image.*   Are you satisfied with your body? What do you notice most about your body? What do others see when they look at your body?

4. *Self-acceptance.*   In what ways are you unique? Are you comfortable with your truthful answer to the question: Who am I? Do you enjoy being alone with yourself? When by yourself, are you comfortable with your thoughts and feelings? Are you usually at ease or usually tense when with people who know you extremely well? What if anything, would you change about yourself?

5. *Self-worth.*   What criteria or standards do you use when you judge the worth or value of another person? How do you measure up on those same criteria? What are your major strengths, talents, and abilities? What, if anything, causes you to think that you are less valuable than others?

6. *Ideal-self.*   To what degree are you doing or accomplishing what you expect of yourself? How do you define success? In what areas of life are you successful? In what areas are you falling short of your expectations? What do you want to accomplish or achieve in your lifetime? What special contributions do you want to make to others, your family, or your community? How do you want to be remembered after you die?

7. *Self-efficacy.*   Do you feel that you are in control of your life? Which has more influence or sway in your life: the decisions that you make or the decisions that other people make? Do you usually respond to change with anticipation and enthusiasm or with apprehension and fear? Are you hopeful or pessimistic about your future?

8. *Spirituality.*   Do you have a set of deeply held beliefs that provide meaning, purpose, and direction in life? How do you make sense out of the pain and suffering that you and others experience in life? Do you have certain spiritual or religious beliefs, or particular moral standards that I should know about in order to better understand your concerns?

9. *Past self and future self.*   Do you think you are now similar to or different from the person you were five years ago? Ten years ago? Do you have regrets or guilt feelings about the past? Do you expect that you and your life situation will be different in five years? If you expect it to change, will this be a desirable or an undesirable change?

10. *Sense of place.*   In what physical environment are you most comfortable, content, and happy? Are you satisfied living in your neighborhood or community? Is there another place where you want to live? Where? Why?

Selected Bibliography

Bracken, Bruce, ed. *Handbook of Self-Concept.* Hoboken, NJ: John Wiley and Sons, 1996.
Elson, Miriam. *Self Psychology in Clinical Social Work.* New York: Norton, 1988.
Mallory, Hershel. *Concept of the Self: Implications of Social Work.* Rochester: NY: MOBIZ Publishers, 2003.

11.10   ASSESSING FAMILY FUNCTIONING

Given the dramatic societal changes of recent decades, it is increasingly difficult to define the term *family*. The U.S. Census Bureau defines a *family* as "two or more persons related by birth, marriage or adoption who reside in the same household," and it defines a *household* as "all the persons, related or not, occupying a housing unit." For purposes of planning human services programs and maintaining a family-centered approach in the delivery of social and health services, the authors prefer a definition based on family functions. Thus, a **family** will be defined as a group of persons related by biological ties, a legal relationship, or expectations of long-term loyalty and commitment, often comprising at least two generations, and usually inhabiting one household. Moreover, some of the adults of this group must have the intention and the capacity to carry out all or most of the activities or functions common to a family, such as to:

- *Provide for the rearing and socialization of children*   (e.g., prepare children for adulthood; prepare children to function within a particular culture and society; teach and model basic values and morals such as honesty, responsibility, cooperation, compassion, and sharing).
- *Provide its members with intimacy and a sense of belonging*   (e.g., acceptance and love).
- *Provide a private and emotionally secure environment for sexual expression by consenting adults.*
- *Provide its members with a place of privacy and respite*   (e.g., respite from other roles and responsibilities such as those related to occupation, work, and community).
- *Provide its members with a legal and social identity*   (e.g., an identity and location for the purposes of legal transactions).
- *Serve as an economic unit*   (i.e., manage money, purchase goods and services, budget and plan for future, and care for possessions).
- *Protect and care for vulnerable family members*   (e.g., young children, frail elderly, sick or disabled).
- *Advocate for family members in need of community resources*   (e.g., the parent who seeks out medical care for sick child, the parent who makes sure his child gets a proper education).

In addition to nuclear and extended family structures, other variations are common. These include *single-parent families* (i.e., one biological parent or adoptive parent or foster parent, plus children), *blended families* or stepparent families (i.e., two married adults plus each one's children from a prior relationship and possibly children born to them as a couple), and *functional families* (i.e., two or more unmarried and unrelated adults plus their children). A growing number of families are headed by *second-time-around parents*, referring to grandparents who have assumed responsibility for rearing their grandchildren, often because the biological parents have been incarcerated or impaired by an addiction or illness.

The family is a complex and dynamic social system and it is a challenging task to identify and assess a family's patterns of interaction and communication. The social worker should keep these dimensions of family functioning as he or she gathers assessment data:

1. *How is family membership defined?* Who are members of the *biological family* (e.g., bio-parents, biological offspring)? Members of the *legal family*, as defined by the laws of marriage, divorce, and adoption and by court orders affecting child custody? What is the composition of the *functional family* (i.e., those who make up the household and assume responsibility for child care, cooking, and other tasks of daily living)? Who belongs to the *perceived family,* those considered to be family, regardless of biological and legal ties? And finally, who belongs to the *family of long-term commitments*, as defined by an expectation of lifelong loyalty, duty, and responsibility.

2. *What facts and realities describe the family?* What are the names and ages of the members? What language is spoken within the family? Level of education? Are family members employed and in what occupations? Level and adequacy of income? Does the family have a particular ethnic or religious identity? Does the family observe certain holidays, holydays, or food rituals? What circumstances surrounded the marriage or the formation of the family and the birth of the children? Is there a history of divorce, abandonment, or violence? Do any family members have a serious physical or mental illness, disability, or addiction?

A social worker's effort to gather information will often be more productive if the client brings family photographs or albums and perhaps scrapbooks to an interview devoted to data gathering and assessment. Browsing through these collections will make it easier for the client to describe family members, explain interactions, and recall important events.

3. *Is the family's functioning supported by its community?* In what neighborhood and community does this family live? Is this a safe place? An attractive place? Is decent and affordable housing available? Are jobs available? Do the local schools provide the programs needed by the children? Do stores carry needed products for a reasonable cost? Are public utilities and services adequate (e.g., police protection, sanitation, transportation, library)?

4. *What boundaries and subsystems describe the family?* Over time, the interactions within a family become patterned and organized. In short, a social system is created. Once these patterns are established, there is a tendency for the members and the family as a whole to maintain the status quo, even when a particular pattern becomes a problem.

As a system, a family has a *boundary* that delineates the family from its environment. The nature of that boundary will determine whether the family is open or closed to outside influences. The boundary must be sufficiently permeable or open so the family can incorporate information needed to adapt to an ever-changing social environment. However, if the boundary is too porous or weak, the family will be indiscriminately pushed and pulled by outside influences and the family will lose its structure, organization, or "systemness." On the other extreme, if a family's boundary is too rigid and impervious to outside influence, the family will become isolated, estranged, and separated from other people and its community. An extreme example would be parents who prohibit their children from having any exposure to, or contact with neighbors, schools, newspapers, and TV. In that case the children might be protected from potentially harmful outside influences but they are not being prepared to function in their society.

Within a family consisting of both adults and children, there are typically four *subsystems*: the *spouse subsystem* (i.e., two adults, usually involved in a sexual relationship); the *parental subsystem* (i.e., the family members—usually adults—responsible for childrearing); one or more *parent–child subsystems* (i.e., special relationships between a particular parent and a particular child); and the *sibling subsystem* (relationship patterns among the siblings). In a healthy family, the boundaries that define these subsystems are clear and in keeping with societal norms. By contrast, for example, in an incest family, the child is drawn into the spouse subsystem and sexual involvement with a parent. In a similar vein, the child with an alcoholic parent may enter the parental subsystem, reverse roles, and end up taking care of and protecting his or her parent.

5. *What rules and roles govern family interaction?*   *Family rules* are the explicit and implicit principles that govern member behavior and maintain the family's structure and organization. The existence of such rules is evident in something so simple as the seating arrangement during meals or in who is responsible for putting gas in the car. An explicit family rule might be: "You must clean the bath tub when finished." Although most family rules are practical, innocuous, and sometimes even silly (e.g., "Don't take a trip in the car without first changing your underwear."), others can be dysfunctional. Rules that suppress emotion, cover up irresponsible behavior, encourage dishonesty, or generate feelings of shame are especially harmful. Examples include: "When Dad is drinking, never mention his brother Ed," "Pretend you don't see Mom and Dad fighting," or "Only an evil child would ever feel anger toward a parent." The children of parents who are alcoholic often grow up with the family rules of *don't talk* (about the drinking or other real issues), *don't feel* (suppress all feelings), and *don't trust* (always be on guard and keep people at a distance). A social worker conducting a family assessment needs to identify troublesome family rules and what happens when rules are broken.

Families also develop a certain role structure. Role expectations guide many of the common tasks of living, such as who cares for the children, who drives the car, and who manages the money. The role structure is often shaped by the family's culture and religion.

During childhood, individuals often take on a certain role within their family. Pet expressions for such roles include "mama's boy," "peacemaker," "family worrier," "disciplinarian," "lone wolf," "message carrier," "family banker," and "black sheep." Family therapy literature often makes reference to the roles of "scapegoat," "hero," "mascot," "lost child," and "rescuer."

The boundaries, subsystems, rules, and roles within a family can only be inferred after careful observation. Some family members may be able to describe some rules and roles, but most of these patterns are so ingrained that they feel natural and are never questioned. When adults form a new family they may repeat or reproduce the patterns they learned within their family of origin. Thus, both family strengths and family problems can be transmitted from one generation to another.

6. *How do family members balance separateness and togetherness?*   Humans have a need for closeness but at the same time have some fear of intimacy. We may avoid getting too close to others because we fear becoming vulnerable and worry that others will take advantage of an exposed weakness. Even within a family, members experience a tension between the need to belong to the family group and the need to be a unique and independent individual. They want to belong and be connected but not consumed or controlled by family loyalty. Within a well-functioning family, members are able to reveal many inner thoughts and feelings but also maintain a comfortable and workable level of privacy and independence.

When personal boundaries are weak and unclear, family members may become intrusive or overly involved in the lives of other members. Such family relationships are termed *enmeshed* or *fused*. The opposite is when there is very little meaningful communication or interaction among family members. Such a family is termed *disengaged* or *disconnected*. In an extreme form, it is little more than a group of people who happen to live under the same roof.

To understand a troubled family, the social worker must see beyond and behind the most obvious problems and wonder why members interact in ways that create so much distress and misery. When observing the behavior of a family member consider: How does this behavior draw members closer together and provide a sense of belonging? How does this behavior provide a protective distance from others?

7. *How well does each member fit within the family system?*   Although there is value in viewing the family from a systems perspective, it is important to remember that a family is made up of individuals, each with a unique genetic makeup, personality, and life experience. Each family member will have a unique set of thoughts and feeling, hopes and dreams, sense of identity, spirituality, emotional needs, strengths, and limitations. It is useful to consider whether there is a good match, or a possible mismatch, between the individual and his or her family's norms, rules, and expectations.

8. *How do family members handle differences?*   A common source of conflict is the inability to accept others as being different from one's self and/or the inability to accept one's self as being different from others. The members of a family can vary widely in terms of personality, temperament, interests, and values. For example, some may be outgoing while others reserved and introverted. Some may be flexible and open to change whereas others prefer stability and predictability. Some may be organized, methodical, and neat while other members are disorganized and messy. Some may be calm and others excitable. There are four basic ways of handling such differences. Three are rather dysfunctional: *Eliminating others* (i.e., suppressing the individuality of others by finding fault, threatening, blaming, attacking); *eliminating self* (i.e., suppressing one's own individuality by always agreeing, submitting to others, and hiding one's true feelings); and *avoiding issues* (i.e., denying the existence of a conflict or avoiding topics that would reveal differences). The most healthy and functional method of handling conflict and differences is through *open and honest communication* (i.e., acknowledging that a difference exists, discussing it a respectful manner, and negotiating a solution).

Like all social systems, a family will tend to resist change, especially rapid change. Family members use various maneuvers to maintain the status quo or hold onto their usual and habitual patterns. In some extreme cases and when other adaptations have not worked, a family may attempt to preserve itself from a real or perceived threat by *scapegoating* or sacrificing a member for the good of the whole family. A request by parents to have their disruptive teenager placed in foster care might be such a maneuver. A related phenomenon, termed *re-peopling,* refers to the family's efforts to regain stability by adding a member. The decision by a couple with marriage problems to have a child could be a re-peopling maneuver.

9. *What communication patterns exist within the family?*   A pattern of communication develops whenever two or more people interact on a regular basis. Certain unwritten rules and expectations emerge and subtly guide their interaction. To decipher this pattern, the worker might observe the following: Who speaks to whom? Who speaks first? Who responds? Who listens and pays close attention to whom? Who speaks most? Who speaks least? Who speaks last? Who sits next to whom? Are messages directed to one person but meant for someone else? Do the words say one thing but also imply something else? Are communications characterized by clarity, respect, and openness or instead by evasiveness, double messages, blaming, threats, hurtful jokes, or interruptions?

10. *How does the family make decisions?*   All families develop patterns or styles of decision making. In some families, all members participate in decision making. On the other extreme are families in which one member makes all major decisions. A social worker can learn about a family's way of making decisions by meeting with the whole family and asking them to perform a task such as planning a vacation or a family outing and observing the decision-making process.

11. *What is the mood of the family?*   Much like an individual, a family is often characterized by a prevailing mood. For example, is the family warm and caring? Cool and distant? Optimistic? Pessimistic? Playful? Excitable? Depressed? Outgoing? Spontaneous? Controlled? Content? Angry?

12. *What are the moral, ethical, and spiritual aspects of the family's functioning?* Matters of loyalty, fairness, obligation, sacrifice, accountability, and entitlement within a family relate rather directly to its moral and ethical standards. Many family conflicts revolve around moral issues and the conduct expected of family members.

Some aspects of family behavior can only be understood by first knowing about a family's sense of the sacred—that which is in the sphere of the mysterious, the awesome, the uncontrollable, and the supremely important. This will be closely related to their spirituality and religious beliefs and to meanings assigned to life, conflict, suffering, and death.

13. *To what tasks and activities do the adults and older children devote their time?* Family functioning is tied to the question of what the members do with their time and what portion of each day is spent with other family members? Consider, for example, how many hours each day are devoted to job and work? Travel to and from work? Family meals? Child care? Cooking? Cleaning and laundry? Study and homework? Shopping? Care of a sick or disabled member? Clubs and organizations? Religious activities? Recreation? Reading? TV? Telephone? Computer? Sleep?

14. *Who supports and who opposes change?*   In most families, some members will tend to invite and welcome change while other are inclined to oppose it. In order to assess this area, the social worker might ask the family members to speculate on the effects of a hypothetical change. For example, the worker might ask: "How would a move to another city affect your family and each of its members? Who would be most upset? Who would like a change? What would each family member do in order to adjust?"

Selected Bibliography

Collins, Donald, Cathleen Jordan, and Heather Coleman. *An Introduction to Family Social Work*, 2nd ed. Belmont, CA: Brooks/Cole, 2007.
Manuchin, Salvador, Michael Nichols, and Wai Yung Lee. *Assessing Families and Couples: From Symptom to System*. Boston: Allyn & Bacon, 2007.
Thomlison, Barbara. *Family Assessment Handbook*, 2nd ed. Belmont, CA: Brooks/Cole, 2007.
Walsh, Froma, ed. *Normal Family Processes*, 3rd ed. New York: Guilford, 2003.

11.11   ASSESSING SMALL-GROUP FUNCTIONING

Social workers work with and within many small groups, including, for example, committees, interagency planning groups, therapeutic groups, and self-help groups. In general, a *well-functioning group* is one in which the members are clear about the group's purpose and are all working together to achieve that purpose. Such a group energizes its members, brings out their creativity, and, of course, achieves its purpose. A *dysfunctional group*, on the other hand, seldom achieves its goals and frustrates its members.

Whenever a social worker is involved in the formation of a new group, he or she should encourage discussions and deliberations that clarify the group's purpose and anticipate the tasks to be performed. The worker should encourage those involved in forming the group to consider how the group should be structured, its ideal size, and the type of leadership and membership necessary to be effective. The worker should assist those who are planning the group to anticipate problems and snags and take steps to minimize these problems. Common group-related problems are poor attendance, lack of leadership, inability to make decisions and resolve conflicts, disruptive or ineffective members, and a lack of resources needed by the group.

When working with or within a group, the social worker should constantly observe and assess its functioning in order to decide what he or she can do to increase the group's effectiveness and efficiency. To do this, the worker must be attentive to both content and process. Basically, *content* refers to the observable actions and activities, whereas *process* refers to the less visible how and why behind what the group does or perhaps, avoids doing. It is group content that is described by the formal minutes of a committee meeting. Content is shaped by the group's stated purpose, formal structure, and official agenda. Process is revealed by the emotional mood of meetings, how members interact, who influences whom, how decisions are made, and the degree to which members are invested in the group.

The following sections identify several aspects of small group functioning and provide questions to consider when examining a group's functioning and deciding what might be done to improve its effectiveness.

Purpose. Agreement and clarity on the group's purpose is fundamental to effective functioning. Unless members are working toward the same outcome or goal, the group is likely to drift or get bogged down in conflict. To assess a group's clarity of purpose, the answers to the following questions should be informative: What is the group's stated or official purpose? Who selected the group's purpose? Are all group members in agreement on the purpose? If the members disagree, what is the source of this disagreement?

When a group lacks agreement on its purpose and goals, the social worker should bring this to the group's attention and encourage a discussion about the group's purpose and goals. Conflict may arise as members voice their differing expectations of the group.

Organizational and Community Contexts. A small group exists within an organizational or community context that impacts its functioning. These external influences are often the source of hidden agendas and conflict within a group, especially disagreements over the group's purpose and composition. For example, an agency administrator or a powerful person in the community may exert pressure on the group's leader or on a member to make a certain decision or move in a particular direction.

Answers to the following questions will help reveal external influences: What organization sponsors, hosts, or funds this group or wanted it formed? What does this organization expect of the group? In what way is the group impacted by, for example, political pressures, policy and program requirements, and current community controversies? When it is apparent that external influences are having an adverse or inappropriate effect on the group, it is usually best for the group to acknowledge this reality and discuss how it should be handled.

Leadership. Effective leadership is a key to guiding a small group toward its goals. If the designated or official leader lacks leadership skills, the group will flounder and the inevitable conflicts will likely smolder and eventually undermine group functioning. The answers to several questions can help to assess the leadership dimension within a group: How was the leader selected? Does the leader provide the vision and direction needed to help the group achieve its goals? Does the leader clarify and test out ideas, build consensus, promote needed compromises, and resolve conflicts within the group? Does the leader display the behavior and commitment that he or she expects from the group's members? Does the leader have credibility and command the respect of members? Do members look to someone other than the official leader for leadership? Do some members undermine or sabotage the leader?

When the work of a group is being impeded by the lack of effective leadership, a change is usually necessary. Problems of poor leadership can be at least minimized by holding regularly scheduled elections of the leader of perhaps an agreed-upon rotation of the leadership role. In some cases, an open and critical evaluation of the group's functioning and performance may prompt a change in leadership (see Item 16.12).

Composition and Member Participation. In order for a small group to achieve its purpose, its members must have the motivation, commitment, skills, and authority to achieve that purpose. Having a few highly motivated and skilled members can be pivotal to a group's success. On the other hand, a few negative, unmotivated, or disruptive members can severely limit the group's effectiveness.

To assess a group's composition and the level of participation, seek answers to the following questions: Given its purpose, is the group about the right size? Is it composed of the individuals necessary to achieve its purpose? What values, attitudes, beliefs, skills, needs, and problems does each member bring to the group? Has the membership or level of participation changed significantly since the group was first formed and if so, why? What draws the members to this group and what keeps others from joining? Which members are most active? Least active? Do some dominate the group? Are some ignored or isolated? Are quiet or hesitant members encouraged to participate? Do members feel free to express disagreement, address conflicts, and take risks? Is open and honest communication expected or perhaps, discouraged? Does each member attend the group's meetings because he or she wants to or because attendance is required?

If a group's effectiveness is hampered because some members do not have the motivation or ability to perform essential tasks, there needs to be a change in the group's size or composition. If an individual's poor attendance is a problem this should be discussed privately with the member and if he or she cannot meet the minimum expectation on attendance, the member should be replaced. If a member is disruptive, the leader or a few influential members should speak privately with this individual and request a change of behavior. In some cases, it may be necessary to find a way of excluding a continually disruptive member. Whenever the social worker is group member, he or she should model behaviors and attitudes that are important to effective group functioning.

Structure, Norms, and Rules.   Over time, a small group will develop a formal and an informal structure, as well as some norms or rules that shape its activity and how members behave. Various structures will be more or less effective, depending on the group's size, purpose, and history. The norms and rules are typically a mix of explicit and implicit guidelines.

The answers to several questions can help to assess the appropriateness of the group's structure, norms, and rules: Are the frequency and length of meetings suitable to the group's purpose? Are the time and place of the meetings convenient to the members? Do the group's norms and rules encourage all members to participate and stay focused on the group's purpose and activities? What formal or informal rules govern behavior in the group (e.g., seating arrangement, agendas, *Roberts Rules of Order*)? Is the discussion of certain topics or certain viewpoints encouraged or discouraged? Does an informal structure or status hierarchy determine who speaks and who makes decisions?

If a group is not achieving its goals because it lacks the structure and rules needed to keep it on course, the group should be encouraged to examine this matter and possibly modify or create an agreed upon set of procedures.

Decision Making.   An effective group makes wise and timely decisions. Good decisions depend on a membership that is sufficiently diverse so as to provide a variety of opinions and perspectives but not so diverse and divided that it frequently gets bogged down in a stalemate or impasse. A group's decision-making process can be examined by seeking answers to the following questions: Do all members contribute to the group's decisions? Are the decisions deliberate and thoughtful or perhaps rushed, partisan, or ideological? Are poor decisions the result of a subgroup or clique pushing its own agenda? Does the group use a formal procedure to arrive at its decisions (e.g., *Robert's Rules of Order*)? If so, do all members understand this procedure?

Physical Environment and Resources.   A group's effectiveness will often depend on having access to essential resources such as a suitable meeting space and money for supplies and photocopying. This concern can be assessed by these questions: Is the meeting space comfortable and arranged to facilitate participation? Do all members have copies of the agenda, minutes of previous meetings, copies of reports under discussion, training handouts, and so forth? If some members have a very limited income, is it possible to cover their expenses for travel, child care, and so forth.

Selected Bibliography

Corey, Marianne, and Gerald Corey. *Group Process and Practice*, 7th ed. Belmont, CA: Brooks/Cole, 2006.

Northhouse, Peter. *Leadership: Theory and Practice*, 4th ed. Thousand Oaks, CA: Sage, 2006.

Toseland, Ronald, and Robert Rivas. *An Introduction to Group Work Practice*, 6th ed. Boston: Allyn & Bacon, 2009.

11.12 USING QUESTIONNAIRES, CHECKLISTS, AND VIGNETTES

When meeting with a social worker, some clients find it difficult to describe their problems or concerns, either because they feel confused or embarrassed or because they have trouble verbalizing their thoughts and feelings. In such a situation, certain types of data-gathering tools can be useful. Such tools (e.g., questionnaires, checklists) are also used when an agency needs to collect a set of data from all clients and do so in an efficient manner.

The data-collection tool known as a ***problem checklist*** is designed to help the client identify his or her concerns. It is essentially a list of the problems and concerns commonly reported by the clients served by a particular agency. A client having difficulty articulating his or her concerns is presented with the problem checklist and asked to identify those statements that come close to describing his or her own concerns.

Consider, for example, the case of a 15-year-old who has just given birth to a baby in a hospital and will be dismissed in one day. In such a situation, the hospital social worker would like to meet with this young mother, do a quick assessment, and refer her to relevant community resources. The worker's goal is further complicated because there is so little time to build a relationship. Figure 11.5 is a checklist that could be used with this new mother. In addition to helping her state her concerns, it focuses the communication so that she and the worker can make the best possible use of their very limited time together.

Not infrequently, clients are unaware of the services that can be offered by the social worker. If a worker and a client examine a problem checklist together, the client begins to understand how the worker or agency might be of assistance. In this sense, the checklist can serve as an educational tool. If a client is easily distracted, the checklist can help to structure an interview and in some situations a client could be asked to study the problem checklist as homework prior to the next session (see Item 13.15).

A simple ***questionnaire*** is another useful tool for gathering information from a client. Figure 11.6 is a questionnaire developed by a social worker who provides marriage counseling. Its purpose is to help the clients identify those aspects of their marriage relationship that are satisfactory and those that are troublesome. Because the questionnaire is simple and brief, clients can complete it in only a few minutes. By substituting a different set of items or questions, the basic format illustrated in this example can be modified for use with clients with other types of problems.

In some practice situations, the worker needs a type of information that cannot be elicited by direct verbal or written questions. For example, social workers often need to gather information about a client's values and attitudes but recognize that a direct question is not likely to yield accurate information. Consider, for example, a child welfare worker faced with the task of deciding whether an individual should be licensed as a foster parent. Among other things, the worker needs to learn about the person's beliefs and attitudes about discipline. Of course, the worker could ask direct questions such as: Do you believe in spanking a child who misbehaves? But such a question is likely to elicit the answer that the individual thinks the worker wants to hear and not reveal much about underlying attitudes that are so central to parenting.

An alternative approach is for the worker to write a set of vignettes and use them as springboards for discussion and exploration. Basically, a ***vignette*** is a brief story to which the client is

Concerns of Young Mothers: A Checklist

The birth of a baby is a time of happiness and joy. But along with the good feelings are concerns about the changes in lifestyle and responsibility that lie ahead. A new mother often feels uncertain and a bit scared about the responsibility of caring for a baby. If we know about your concerns, we may be able to help you find ways to address them.

Directions: Below is a list of worries and concerns that have been expressed by other new mothers who have had babies in this hospital. Please read through this list and place a check (✓) by all statements that are similar to the concerns you now have. Your responses will be held in strict confidence.

1. _____ Have worries about paying hospital and doctor bills.
2. _____ Have worries about my baby's health and physical condition.
3. _____ Have worries about my own health and physical condition.
4. _____ Uncertain about how to feed and care for an infant.
5. _____ Uncertain where to turn when I have questions about child care.
6. _____ Afraid I may become pregnant before I am ready to have another child.
7. _____ Worried about not having enough money to care for my baby.
8. _____ Concerned about whether I can finish school.
9. _____ Worried about getting or keeping a job when I have a baby to care for.
10. _____ Concerned when I feel resentment or anger toward my baby.
11. _____ Worried about the effects of drugs or alcohol on me and my baby.
12. _____ Worried that my friends will not accept me and my baby.
13. _____ Worried about my relationship with my baby's father.
14. _____ Concerned that I do not feel love toward my baby.
15. _____ Feeling sad and depressed about my situation.
16. _____ Worried that I will be a burden to my own parents.
17. _____ Worried about living alone with my baby.
18. _____ Concerned that my own parents and family will not accept me and my baby.
19. _____ Afraid I am going to lose my independence and freedom.
20. _____ Please describe or list any other concerns not covered by the checklist:

_____

Now, look over all of those items you have checked and draw a circle around the one or two that seem most important. Please feel free to discuss these concerns with a hospital social worker.

_____

FIGURE 11.5 Sample Problem Checklist

asked to respond. Thus, this technique is an indirect or a projective method of questioning. Figure 11.7 presents two vignettes written for use in the foster home-study process. Needless to say, the social worker using this tool must create vignettes that will engage the client and elicit the type of information needed in the assessment process.

In general, social workers underutilize data-gathering tools such as those described above. However, they are useful in many practice situations and not difficult to create. Here are some guidelines that will help in the preparation of these tools:

1. As you consider the construction of a data-gathering tool, be clear about its intended purpose, the type of information you seek, and the clients and situation for whom it is being prepared. Rather than developing one all-purpose tool, it is better to design several, each with a specific purpose or client group in mind.

Questionnaire on the Husband-Wife Relationship

Explanation: Below are questions about how satisfied you are with what goes on between you and your spouse. Your answers will help us understand and clarify your concerns. To the right of each statement, place a check (✓) to indicate if you are mostly satisfied, or mostly dissatisfied, or perhaps unsure and confused about this aspect of your marriage relationship. If a statement does not apply to your situation, write NA next to the statement.

	Mostly Satisfied	Mostly Dissatisfied	Unsure or Confused
The way we make decisions			
The way we divide up responsibility for child care			
The way we handle and budget money			
The way we divide up housework			
The way we talk to the children			
The amount of money we earn			
The way we resolve conflict			
The way we discipline our children			
The way we get along with in-laws			
The way we use our free time			
The way we talk to each other			
The way we care for our home			
The amount of time we have together			
The way we help and encourage each other			
The amount of privacy we have			
The way alcohol or drugs affect our relationship			
The way we handle birth control			
The sexual part of our relationship			
The way we plan for our future			
The way we get along with the neighbors			
The way we deal with moral or religious concerns			
The way we handle anger and frustration			

Please list here any other concerns you may have about your relationship:

_____

_____

What do you consider to be the major strengths in your marriage?

_____

_____

What do you consider to be the one or two major problems in your marriage?

_____

_____

FIGURE 11.6   Sample Questionnaire

2. The wording used should be clear and concise and free of jargon, bias, and offensive language. The words should be ones that client will easily understand. A brief questionnaire is more likely to be accurately completed than a long one. In general, the higher the client's level of education and motivation, the more likely he or she is to deal successfully with a paper-and-pencil, data-gathering tool. Remember, many people lack the basic skills of reading and writing.

The Peterson Family: A Situation to Discuss

The Petersons have been foster parents to 15-year-old Sharon for about six years. Religion is very important to Mr. and Mrs. Peterson. They attend church services and participate in several church-related activities on a regular basis. Until about two months ago, Sharon also attended the Petersons' church even though she had been raised in another religious denomination. Sharon now refuses to attend church and tells her foster parents that religion is a bunch of superstition and foolishness. The Petersons are worried and upset by Sharon's attitude because religion is so central to their life and family.

1. What could have caused this situation?
2. How should the Petersons respond to Sharon?

The Allen Family: A Situation to Discuss

Mr. and Mrs. Allen have three children. In order to celebrate Mrs. Allen's birthday, the whole family goes to a restaurant. During the meal, 6-year-old Jimmy throws a tantrum—he cries and throws food at his parents. Others in the restaurant stare at the Allens and obviously disapprove of what they are seeing.

1. What is your evaluation of Jimmy's behavior?
2. How should the parents respond to Jimmy?

FIGURE 11.7 Sample Vignettes

3. The writing of items to be included in a data-gathering tool requires knowledge of possible and probable responses by clients. For example, if a question requires the client to select an answer from a list of possible answers, the questionnaire designer must know beforehand the answers most likely to be given by clients. When it is difficult to anticipate the range of probable client answers, it will be necessary to ask an open-ended question to which the client writes out his or her answer. Because such written answers are often difficult for a worker to read and understand, open-ended written questions should be used sparely. A questionnaire containing numerous open-ended questions offers few advantages over the ordinary verbal questioning during a face-to-face interview.

4. Each question or statement should focus on a single idea and should in no way lead or point the client toward a particular answer. When possible, the wording of each question in a series of questions should follow a similar format and structure because this helps the client move easily from question to question and minimizes the chances that he or she will misread or misinterpret a question.

5. A sequence of questions should follow a logical and unfolding order and should usually begin with the general questions and end with the more specific ones. Questions that will be easiest for the client to answer should usually appear at the beginning of a series, whereas the most personal or probing questions should appear toward the end.

6. A pretest should be used to determine if clients will understand the wording and questions, whether clients can complete the questionnaire in a reasonable time, and whether the data collected in this way are indeed useful to practitioners.

Selected Bibliography

Abell, Neil. *Developing and Validating Rapid Assessment Instruments*. New York: Oxford University Press, 2009.

Horejsi, Charles. *Assessment and Case Planning in Child Protection and Foster Care Services*. Englewood, CO: American Humane Association, 1996.

Millon, Theodore, and Caryl Bloom. *The Millon Inventories: A Practitioner's Guide to Personalized Clinical Assessment*, 2nd ed. New York: Guilford, 2008.

11.13 IDENTIFYING DEVELOPMENTAL DELAYS IN YOUNG CHILDREN

Social workers who have frequent contact with families are often in a strategic position to observe preschool-age children and conduct a cursory assessment of a child's physical and mental development. Children who are malnourished or chronically ill, many who are abused and neglected, and, of course, those who have mental retardation or sensory or neurological problems will fall behind developmental norms. However, there can be considerable variation in the growth and development of normal children. Moreover, for a given age, it is not unusual to find some unevenness across the various domains of development as, for example, the child who is quick to walk but slow to talk.

Figure 11.8 lists a number of markers that can be used to judge a child's developmental progress. If it appears that a child cannot perform the motor, mental, language, and social skills and tasks expected at a given age, the child should be referred to a specialist for an in-depth evaluation. An early diagnosis and intervention can limit the negative impact of a developmental problem.

Here are some early warning signs of *sensory problems* and developmental delays in a young child:

INDICATORS OF HEARING PROBLEMS

- Exhibits delays in speech and language development
- Does not turn toward source of strange sounds or voices by six months of age
- Has frequent earaches or runny ears
- Talks in a very loud or very soft voice
- Does not respond when you call from another room
- Turns the same ear toward a sound he or she wants to hear

INDICATORS OF DELAYS IN SPEECH DEVELOPMENT

- Does not say "Mama" and "Dada" by age 1
- Does not say the names of a few toys and people by age 2
- Cannot repeat common rhymes or jingles by age 3
- Does not talk in sentences by age 4
- Cannot be understood by people outside the family by age 5

INDICATORS OF DELAYS IN MOTOR DEVELOPMENT

- Unable to sit up without support by age 1
- Cannot walk without help by age 2
- Does not walk up and down steps by age 3
- Unable to balance on one foot for a short time by age 4
- Cannot throw a ball overhand and catch a large ball bounced to him or her by age 5

INDICATORS OF VISION PROBLEMS

- Holds head in strained or awkward position when looking at a person or object
- Is often unable to locate and pick up small objects within reach
- Has one or both eyes crossed

At about 1 month, child will:
- Turn eyes and head toward sound
- Cease crying if picked up and talked to
- Lift head when lying on stomach
- Follow a moving light with eyes
- Stretch limbs and fan out toes and fingers
- Display pupil response when a flashlight is moved in front of eyes

At about 3 months, child will:
- Make cooing sounds
- Respond to loud sounds
- Turn head toward bright colors and lights
- Move eyes and head in same direction together
- Recognize bottle or breast
- Make fists with both hands
- Grasp rattles or hair
- Wiggle and kick with legs and arms
- Lift head and chest while on stomach
- Smile in response to others

At about 6 months, child will:
- Babble
- Recognize familiar faces
- Turn toward source of normal sound
- Follow moving object with eyes when head is held stationary
- Play with toes
- Roll from stomach to back
- Reach for objects and pick them up
- Transfer objects from one hand to other
- Help hold bottle during feeding
- Bang spoon on table repeatedly
- Look for fallen object

At about 12 months, child will:
- Have a 5- to 6-word vocabulary
- Sit without support
- Pull self to standing position
- Crawl on hands and knees
- Drink from cup
- Wave bye-bye
- Enjoy peek-a-boo and patty cake
- Hold out arms and legs while being dressed
- Put objects into container
- Stack two blocks

At about 18 months, child will:
- Use 8 to 10 words that are understood
- Feed self with fingers
- Walk without help
- Pull, push, and dump things
- Pull off shoes, socks, and mittens

- Step off low object and keep balance
- Follow simple directions ("Bring the ball")
- Like to look at pictures
- Make marks on paper with crayons

By age 2 years, child can:
- Use 2- to 3-word sentences
- Say names of favorite toys
- Recognize familiar pictures
- Carry an object while walking
- Feed self with spoon
- Play alone and independently
- Turn 2 or 3 pages at a time
- Imitate parents
- Point to own hair, eyes, ears, and nose upon request
- Build a tower of four blocks
- Show affection toward others

By age 3 years, child can:
- Use 3- to 5-word sentences and repeat common rhymes
- Walk up stairs or steps alternating feet
- Jump, run, climb
- Ride a tricycle
- Put on shoes
- Open door
- Turn one page at a time
- Play with other children for a few minutes
- Name at least one color correctly
- Use toilet with occasional accidents

By age 4 years, child can:
- Ask "what," "where," "who" questions
- Give reasonable answers to simple questions
- Give first and last names
- Show many different emotions
- Say "no" or "I won't" with intensity
- Balance on one foot for 4 to 8 seconds
- Jump from a step and maintain balance
- Dress and undress with little help
- Cut straight with scissors
- Wash hands alone
- Play simple group games

By age 5 years, child can:
- Speak clearly
- Print a few letters
- Count 5 to 10 objects
- Skip, using feet alternately
- Catch a large ball
- Bathe and dress self
- Draw a body with at least five parts
- Copy familiar shapes (e.g., square, circle, triangle)

FIGURE 11.8   Child Developmental Markers

INDICATORS OF DELAYS IN SOCIAL AND MENTAL DEVELOPMENT

- Does not react when name is called by age 1
- Does not play games such as peek-a-boo, patty cake, and waving bye-bye by age 1
- Unable to identify hair, eyes, ears, nose, and mouth by pointing to them by age 2
- Does not imitate parents doing household chores by age 2 to 3

- Does not understand simple stories told or read by age 3
- Does not enjoy playing alone with toys, pots and pans, sand, and so on by age 3
- Does not play group games such as hide-and-seek, tag-ball, and so on with other children by age 4
- Does not give reasonable answers to such questions as "What do you do when you are sleepy?" or "What do you do when you are hungry?" by age 4
- Does not seem to understand the meanings of the words *today*, *tomorrow*, and *yesterday* by age 5
- Does not share and take turns by age 5

A governmental website designed especially for parents concerned about their child's development is: http://www.cdc.gov/ncbddd/autism/ActEarly/default.htm

Selected Bibliography

Allen, K. Eileen, and Lynn Marotz. *Developmental Profiles: Pre-birth Through Twelve*, 5th ed. Clifton Park, NY: Thomson/Delmar, 2007.
Berk, Laura. *Child Development*, 8th ed. Boston: Allyn & Bacon, 2009.
Leach, Penelope. *Your Baby and Child: Birth to Age Five*, 3rd ed. New York: Alfred A. Knopf, 1997.

11.14   ASSESSING A CHILD'S NEED FOR PROTECTION

State laws require social workers to report cases of suspected abuse or neglect. (Many states also mandate the reporting of elder abuse.) Below is a list of physical and behavioral signs that suggest the possible existence of physical abuse, neglect, and sexual abuse.

INDICATORS OF PHYSICAL ABUSE

- Unexplained bruises or welts, especially if on both sides of child's face or body, or on back, buttocks, or torso
- Bruises in different stages of healing (suggesting repeated injury)
- Multiple bruises clustered in one area and/or bruises with shape or pattern of an instrument (e.g., loop marks, lineal or parallel marks, punch marks)
- Bruises that regularly appear after a weekend or a visit
- Bruises on shoulders or neck with a shape of hand or fingers (i.e., grab marks)
- Unexplained burns, such as those caused by cigarettes, and especially if on palms, feet, back, or buttocks
- Hot water immersion or dunking burn on hands or feet (e.g., sock like, glove like) or doughnut shaped burn on buttocks
- Burns patterned like an electric stove burner, hot plate, curling iron, etc.
- Rope burns or tie marks on wrists or ankles
- Unexplained mouth injuries such as frenulum tears or broken teeth (caused by rough feeding)
- Human, adult-size bite marks on child's body
- Unexplained broken bones, head injuries such as skull fractures, or a subdural hematoma
- Retina detachment or whiplash injuries to neck caused by violent shaking (i.e., shaken baby syndrome)
- Internal injuries caused by a punch to the body
- Poisoning caused by ingestion of street drugs, alcohol, prescription medicines, or household chemicals
- Attempts by child to hide injuries with clothing or embarrassment or shame over injury including reluctance to talk about injury (non-abused children quickly and proudly display accidental injuries)

- Hyper-vigilant, fearful, and guarded when around adults; avoids physical contact with people including his parents (i.e., seems fearful of human touch)
- Overly adaptive behavior in an attempt to meet parents' needs (i.e., by taking care of and comforting parent the child seeks to keep things calm and prevent abusive episodes)
- Becomes uneasy when another child cries or acts up (i.e., has learned to associate crying with parent getting upset and inflicting abuse)
- Serious behavioral problems at young age (e.g., runs away, self-mutilation, suicide attempts, violence, withdrawn)

INDICATORS OF NEGLECT

- Begging, stealing, or hoarding food; underweight; failure to thrive; bald patches on scalp caused by being left in crib for long periods
- Poor school attendance (sometimes the neglectful parent is so lonely he or she keeps the child home for company; sometimes the child remains home to care for younger siblings)
- Untreated medical and dental problems, even though parent has resources to get medical services
- Primitive and unsocialized eating and toilet behaviors
- Unusual fatigue and listlessness; falling asleep at unusual times
- Stays at school, in public places, or at another home for extended periods
- Poor hygiene, filthy clothing, clothing inappropriate for weather
- Child not supervised or protected from dangerous activity

INDICATORS OF SEXUAL ABUSE

- Bruises, scaring, or tissue tears around vagina and anus; bruised or swollen penis (caused by rough fondling and masturbation)
- Blood on child's underwear
- Redness or rash in genital area of child not wearing diaper (caused by frequent fondling)
- Redness or abrasions between upper legs (caused by adult penis placed between child's legs)
- Recurrent bladder infections (i.e., bacteria from rectum introduced into vagina when there is both anal and vaginal penetration)
- Pregnancy or a sexually transmitted disease in younger child
- Semen in vagina, rectum, or mouth (may be detected by medical exam within three days of intercourse)
- Inappropriate masturbation by child that has a driven or compulsive quality
- Unusual sexual play with or exploration of pets or dolls
- Aggressive and forced sexual activity with other children, usually of a younger age
- Inappropriate and suggestive sexual behavior toward adults
- Unusual level of knowledge about sexual activity (e.g., can describe sexual movement, smells, taste, feelings)
- Preoccupation with sexual matters or on the other extreme, unusually fearful of anything sexual
- Unusual fear of showers, bathrooms, bedrooms
- Unwilling to change clothes for gym or to expose body (caused by extreme shame of body)
- Frequent and patterned absences from school that are justified by one adult, the offender
- Unusual or bizarre sexual themes in artwork or drawings
- Wearing many layers of clothing (seeking protection of body)
- Frequent use of dissociation as coping mechanism
- Unusually close relationship with an adult that has secretive or sexual overtones
- Extreme protectiveness of child by an adult who keeps child from talking to or getting close to responsible adults

While certain signs and symptoms can establish that a child has been abused or neglected, these signs do not determine with certainty who is responsible for the maltreatment.

Many parents believe in and utilize corporal punishment as discipline. Thus, the social worker must be able to differentiate abuse from ordinary spanking. That decision will, of course, be tied to the definition of physical abuse found in a state's legal code. In addition, we offer three criteria for making that distinction:

1. In corporal punishment, the child experiences some pain and discomfort. In abuse, there is actual injury to body tissue.
2. In using corporal punishment, the parent maintains self-control and is aware of where and how hard the child is being spanked. In an abusive situation, the parent typically loses control and strikes the child with excessive force or in places that are easily injured.
3. Parents who use corporal punishment may, in rare instances, hit too hard but they quickly realize what has happened and are able to make changes in how they discipline the child so this does not happen again. In situations of abuse, there are repeated episodes of excessive punishment and injury.

While cases of physical abuse and sexual abuse are most likely to attract media attention, child neglect is the more frequent form of child maltreatment. In the United States about one-half of all child maltreatment–related fatalities are caused by neglect. A high percentage of the neglect cases occur in families where the parents are addicted to drugs or alcohol.

Most children who are sexually abused do not tell anyone because they are either afraid or feel great shame. Most cases of child sexual abuse involve fondling and masturbation, but not penetration. When penetration occurs it might be of the child's mouth, vagina, or rectum. Even if there has been penetration of the vagina or rectum there will be no physical evidence in most cases. It is also important to understand that the majority of sexually abused children will not exhibit unusual sexual behavior. However, sexually abused children are more likely than nonabused children to display adult-like sexual behavior.

The social worker must report suspected cases of child sexual abuse. However, he or she must also be alert to the fact that false or mistaken accusations do occur. Both children and adults are suggestible and may misinterpret facts, and occasionally will level false accusations as a means of hurting someone. Although false accusations by a child are relatively rare, the rate increases if the child's accusation is being encouraged or urged by a parent. That rate becomes even higher in cases involving child custody fights between parents.

Once a case of abuse or neglect has been identified, the question of risk must be addressed. In other words, is the child now at risk of serious harm and in need of immediate protection? Presented here are factors that should be considered when conducting this *assessment of risk.*

CHILD-RELATED RISK FACTORS

- Child is vulnerable and unable to protect self because of young age, illness, disability, need for medication, etc.
- Child was previously subjected to abuse or neglect
- Injuries to child are at vulnerable body locations (e.g., head, face, genitals) or required medical attention or hospitalization
- Alleged perpetrator now has access to child
- Child's relationship to others in the household is tenuous or troubled, thus decreasing chances that others would intervene to protect the child

PARENT/CAREGIVER-RELATED RISK FACTORS

- Existing physical or mental illness, mental retardation, or substance abuse limits caregiver's ability to protect child

- History of domestic violence (e.g., spouse abuse) or other violent criminal activity by parent or caretaker
- Parent has history of having abused or neglected other children
- Lack of basic parenting skills or knowledge
- High levels of anger, hostility, or rejection toward child
- Child's behavioral problems or special needs (e.g., a disability) place stressful demands on parent or caretaker
- Existence of other serious family problems that place added stress on parent (e.g., marital conflict, financial, health, chaotic lifestyle)
- Unrealistic and unreasonable expectations of child
- Denial of problem, evasiveness, or refusal to cooperate with child protection workers or other helpers
- Prior efforts to work with family were rejected or ineffective

ENVIRONMENTAL RISK FACTORS

- Condition of home is a clear danger to child (e.g., exposed electrical wiring, unprotected household chemicals, lack of sanitation)
- Family is socially or physically isolated, no access to assistance in times of emergency

An *out-of-home placement* may be necessary if a child is in danger and there is no less drastic means of protecting the child. Such placements can be traumatic to the child and, of course, upsetting to the parents. If a child must be placed into foster care, it is to be done for one reason only: to protect the child from a specific harm. It is unethical to place a child in order to coerce the parent into taking some action. A child should be placed in the least restrictive alternative. To the extent possible, the parent(s) should participate in preparing the child for the separation and placement. During a placement it is important to encourage visits to the child by the parent. It is also important to respect and maintain the child's religious traditions and cultural heritage. Special requirements to maintain the cultural connection of a Native American child are outlined in the Indian Child Welfare Act, a federal law.

Selected Bibliography

Brittain, Charmaine, and Deborah Hunt. *Helping in Child Protection*, 2nd ed. New York: Oxford University Press, 2005.

Giardino, Angelo, and Eileen Giardino. *Recognition of Child Abuse for the Mandated Reporter*, 3rd ed. Elk Grove Village, IL: American Academy of Pediatrics, 2002.

Myers, John, and Jordan Greenbaum, eds. *The APSAC Handbook on Child Maltreatment*, 3rd ed. Thousand Oaks, CA: Sage, 2010.

Tower, Cynthia. *Understanding Child Abuse and Neglect*, 8th ed. Boston: Allyn & Bacon, 2010.

11.15   ASSESSING A CLIENT'S MENTAL STATUS

When a social worker encounters a client who exhibits highly usual behavior or seems to lack a capacity for rational thought and is, therefore, possibly in danger, the social worker needs to do at least a cursory mental status exam to detect symptoms of a mental illness, neurological disorder, or dementia. A mental status exam consists of careful observation and asking several simple questions that gauge the client's orientation to time and place, short- and long-term memory, accuracy of perceptions, judgment, and appropriateness of affect. To the extent possible, the questions should be worked into the ordinary flow of conversation. Engaging the client in a description of his or her typical day—from awakening to bedtime—can provide a context for asking these questions. If the questions are asked, one after another, the client may be offended or embarrassed. Following are 11 categories of information that should be considered in assessing mental status:

1. *General appearance and attitude*   considers whether the client's appearance is appropriate to his or her age and social and economic status. The client's dress, hygiene, speech, facial expressions, and motor activity provide information about self-perception and awareness of others. Marked inappropriateness in appearance may be associated with psychological disturbance, particularly if the client's appearance has changed over a short period of time.

2. *Appropriateness of behavior*   considers whether the client's behavior during an interview and as reported by others is understandable and expected, given the current situation and social norms. Irrational and bizarre behavior, compulsions (repeated acts that the client feels compelled to do) and phobias (avoidance of places, persons, or objects because of unfounded fears), are symptoms of a mental disorder.

3. *Orientation to time and place*   refers to whether the client is aware of who he or she is, where he or she is, and what time it is (year, month, date, and day). Disorientation and confusion is a symptom of a possible brain disorder.

4. *Memory*   deficits may be associated with psychiatric, neurological, and other medical problems. Four types of memory may be assessed:

- *Immediate recall*   refers to the ability to recall things within seconds of their presentation.
- *Short-term memory*   is generally defined as covering events transpiring within the last 25 minutes.
- *Recent memory*   refers to the client's recollection of current events and situations occurring within the few weeks preceding the interview.
- *Remote memory*   refers to the recollection of events occurring months or years ago and of a significant life happening, such as marriage, first job, high school graduation, and so on.

Immediate and short-term memory can be assessed by asking a question such as, "What did you have to eat at your last meal?" Or one might ask the client to remember a word, number, or object then after the lapse of either a few seconds or a few minutes ask the client to recall it. Recent memory is tested by asking questions like: When was the last time it rained? Where do you live? What is the name of the building we are in? Remote memory can be tested by asking questions such as: Where were you born? Where did you go to grade school? Who was president of the United States when you got married?

5. *Sensorium*   refers to an individual's ability to utilize data from his or her sense organs (hearing, vision, touch, smelling, and taste) and more generally, to overall attentiveness and alertness to the surroundings. If a client cannot comprehend visual symbols (and has no visual impairment), ordinary conversation (and has no hearing impairment), or does not respond to other ordinary sensory stimuli, he or she may have a neurological disorder.

6. *Intellectual functioning*   is screened by evaluating the client's abilities to read, write, and follow simple instructions, do simple arithmetic, think abstractly (e.g., How are an apple and orange alike?), and by testing the client's awareness of common knowledge consistent with his or her level of education. Poor comprehension and deficits in abstract thinking are symptoms of several different psychological disorders. Gauging educational attainment is important because low levels of intellectual performance may be attributable to a lack of education. Poor intellectual performance among educated persons, however, may be indicative of organic disorders. The symptom of gradual intellectual deterioration is most often associated with brain disorders.

7. *Mood and affect*   refer to the client's prevailing emotional state and the range of emotions displayed during the interview. A problem is suggested if the client's emotions (e.g., sadness, elation, anger, anxiety, apathy) seem unreasonable or unconnected to the situation or the topic being discussed. For example, rapid shifts in mood or smiling and laughter when talking about a sad or tragic situation may suggest a psychiatric disturbance. The symptom of labile emotions (i.e., unstable or erratic) is often associated with brain disorders and is fairly common among people who have had a stroke (see Item 15.9).

8. *Perceptual distortions* may occur among some psychologically impaired individuals. Two of the most significant perceptual problems are illusions and hallucinations. *Illusions* are misinterpretations of actual stimuli. *Hallucinations* are perceptual experiences in the absence of external stimuli (e.g., hearing voices) (see Item 15.12).

9. *Thought content* refers to the logic and consistency of an individual's attitudes, ideas, and beliefs. Symptoms include delusional thinking (false beliefs that cannot be altered by logical arguments) and obsessions (fixed or repetitive ideas that the client cannot get out of his or her mind).

10. *Insight* can be evaluated by asking questions that determine whether the client is aware that he or she is exhibiting unusual behavior or has symptoms that are of concern to family members, the social worker, or a physician, and whether the client can describe reasons why he or she might be having this problem. Ironically, the more severe the mental disorder, the more likely it is that the individual will not recognize that his or her thoughts and behavior are unusual and symptomatic.

11. *Judgment* refers to the individual's ability to think rationally in regard to an obvious problem. It also refers to a client's mental capability to make ordinary decisions, particularly ones about self-care.

Selected Bibliography

Applegate, Jeffery, and Janet Shapiro. *Neurobiology for Clinical Social Work*. New York: Norton, 2005.

Sadock, Benjamin, and Virginia Sadock. *Kaplan and Sadock Synopsis of Psychiatry*, 10th ed. Philadelphia: Walter Kluwer/Lippincott, 2007.

Sommers-Flanagan, John, and Rita Sommers-Flanagan. *Clinical Interviewing*, 4th ed. Hoboken, NJ: Wiley, 2009.

11.16 USING THE *DIAGNOSTIC AND STATISTICAL MANUAL OF MENTAL DISORDERS* (DSM) AND THE PERSON-IN-ENVIRONMENT (PIE) ASSESSMENT TOOLS

Social workers should be familiar with two classification systems, the *Diagnostic and Statistical Manual of Mental Disorders (DSM)* and the *Person-in-Environment* (PIE). These taxonomies facilitate communication between mental health professionals and among practitioners, administrators, and researchers.

In the widely used *DSM* nearly 300 mental disorders are classified within 17 broad categories such as substance-related disorders, schizophrenia, mood disorders, sexual and gender identity disorders, sleep disorders, and personality disorders. Each disorder is described in terms of its symptoms, diagnostic criteria, age of onset, prevalence, level of impairment, and so on. A clinician using the *DSM* evaluates the client within five separate clusters or categories of information, each of which is called an axis:

Axis 1: Disorders with usually obvious symptoms and often the primary focus of clinical attention (e.g., anxiety disorders, schizophrenia, substance abuse, eating disorders)

Axis 2: Long-standing problems that might be overlooked when a client has an Axis 1 disorder (e.g., mental retardation, personality disorders)

Axis 3: Medical conditions or diseases that may be relevant to the understanding, treatment, and management of a person's mental disorder (e.g., high blood pressure, pregnancy, brain injury, diabetes)

Axis 4:   Psychosocial and environmental problems or situations that may have a bearing on the understanding, treatment, and management of a mental disorder (e.g., lack of family support, lack of housing, unemployment, poverty, life cycle transitions)

Axis 5:   A rating of the client's overall psychological, social, and occupational functioning using the *Global Assessment of Functioning* (GAF) Scale

Knowledge of the *DSM* is important because many social workers and agencies look to third-party payments from Medicaid, Medicare, and private health insurance companies as sources of fees for the psychotherapy they provide to clients. Prior to submitting a claim for payment of fees, the client must be assigned to a *DSM* category.

The *DSM* is a classification of mental disorders. It is not a classification of people. Thus a term such as *schizophrenic* should be avoided in favor of an expression such as "an individual with schizophrenia." The American Psychiatric Association (2000) warns the users of the *DSM-IV-TR* of the inherent difficulties of assessing the behavior of a person who is from an ethnic or cultural group different from that of the clinician: "A clinician who is unfamiliar with the nuances of an individual's cultural frame of reference may incorrectly judge as psychopathology those normal variations in behavior, belief, or experiences that are particular to the individual's culture" (p. xxxiv).

The **Person-In-Environment System (PIE)** is designed for use by social workers and is built around two core social work concepts: social functioning and viewing the person within an environmental context. The PIE system is intended as a supplement to the *DSM*, not a substitute. It classifies client problems or concerns into four classes or *factors*. The terminology used to describe social functioning problems (Factor I) and environmental problems (Factor II) is unique to social work practice. Factor III (mental health problems) utilizes the terminology and taxonomy found in the *DSM*. PIE Factor IV (physical health problems) records a client's diseases and health problems that have been diagnosed by a physician or reported by the client or others. An abbreviated outline of the Factor I and Factor II categories and subcategories is presented here.

PIE FACTOR I: SOCIAL FUNCTIONING PROBLEMS

1. Social role in which problem is defined (four categories and numerous subcategories):

- Familial roles (parent, spouse, child, sibling, other family member, and significant other)
- Other interpersonal roles (lover, friend, neighbor, member, and other)
- Occupational roles (worker-paid, worker-home, worker-volunteer, student, and other)
- Special life situation roles (consumer, inpatient/client, outpatient/client, probationer/parolee, prisoner, immigrant-legal, immigrant-undocumented, immigrant-refugee, and other)

2. Type of problem in social role (nine types: power, ambivalence, responsibility, dependency, loss, isolation, victimization, mixed, other)

3. Severity of problem (rated on a 6-point scale)

4. Duration of problem (six categories)

5. Ability of client to cope with problem (six levels)

PIE FACTOR II: ENVIRONMENTAL PROBLEMS

1. Social system where each problem is identified (six major systems and numerous subcategories):

- Economic/basic needs system problems
- Education and training system problems
- Judicial and legal system problems
- Health, safety, and social services problems

- Voluntary association system problems
- Affectional support system problems

2. Specific type of problem within each social system (71 subcategories; number varies for each of six social systems. Examples of social system problem subcategories: lack of regular food supply, absence of shelter, lack of culturally relevant education, discrimination, lack of police services, unsafe conditions in home, regulatory barriers to social services, absence of affectional support system, lack of community acceptance of religious values)

3. Severity of problem (rated on a 6-point scale)

4. Duration of problem (six categories)

Selected Bibliography

American Psychiatric Association. *Diagnostic and Statistical Manual of Mental Disorders,* 4th ed., text rev. Washington, DC: APA, 2000.

Karls, James, and Maura O'Keefe, eds. *Person-in-Environment System Manual*, 2nd ed. Washington, DC: NASW Press, 2007.

_____, Compu PIE [computer software]. Washington, DC: NASW Press, 2000.

Corcoran, Jacqueline and Joseph Walsh. *Clinical Assessment and Diagnosis in Social Work Practice,* 2nd ed. New York: Oxford University Press, 2010.

11.17 REFERRAL FOR PSYCHOLOGICAL TESTING

In some situations, the social worker will want to refer a child or adult to a psychologist for testing. Testing can provide useful information about a client's intellectual capacity, level of anxiety or depression, coping behavior, self-concept, patterns of motivation, and general personality integration. In some cases, a psychiatrist will need to be involved if it appears as if a client might have a psychiatric, neurological, or drug-induced disorder. Below are guidelines that should be considered when considering or planning a referral.

1. List the questions you want a psychological evaluation to answer. The testing or assessment procedures selected by a psychologist (and sometimes by a psychiatrist) will depend on the type of information sought, client characteristics, and suspected problems. Thus, describe for the psychologist the type of information that would be most helpful in your work with this client and the specific case management decisions you face.

Provide the psychologist with data concerning the client's age, education, occupation, employment, ethnicity, any unusual fears of testing, and any disabilities, such as hearing or visual problems, mobility problems, reading problems, or difficulty with the English language. If possible, provide the results and reports of any previous testing, including the dates of testing and the names of the tests used.

2. After consulting with the psychologist who will do the testing, prepare the client by giving him or her basic information on what to expect, where the testing will be done, and about how long the testing will take.

3. Have realistic expectations of psychological testing. In many cases, the test results will simply confirm the impressions already formed by people who have closely observed or worked with the client. Important case management decisions should not be based exclusively on test results. Ask the psychologist to explain the strengths and limitations of the testing procedures and to discuss how the test results might shape the client's treatment or service plan.

Selected Bibliography

Aiken, Lewis, and Gary Groth-Marnat. *Psychological Testing,* 12th ed. Boston: Allyn & Bacon, 2006.

Neukrug, Edward. *Essentials of Testing and Assessment: A Practical Guide for Counselors, Social Workers, and Psychologists.* Belmont, CA: Brooks/Cole, 2006.

Van Ornum, Bill, Linda Dunlap, and Milton Shore. *Psychological Testing Across the Lifespan.* Boston: Allyn & Bacon, 2008.

SECTION B

TECHNIQUES AND GUIDELINES FOR INDIRECT PRACTICE

Large system change is difficult and time consuming. Rarely can a single person, or even a few people, decide on changes to be made and easily implement the actions to bring about that change. It takes careful planning, education, negotiation, and patience to achieve meaningful changes in agency policies and programs or the legislative changes that affect the larger community.

Data-Collection Activities.   The first step in preparing for agency or community change is to collect sufficient information to be well informed. For example, change requires working through, or sometimes around, the agency's or community's decision-making structure. To do this, the worker needs to learn about the feasibility of various options, the costs (in dollars and the expenditure of human resources) of changing the current situation, the positive and/or negative implications for other associated individuals or systems, and the most effective ways to bring about change.

Like direct practice data collection, indirect practice requires that the worker be skilled at interviewing people to obtain information regarding their experiences and attitudes about the situation being considered for change. However, these impressions typically are obtained from a number of people who have knowledge of or may be affected by the situation. The worker must also be able to accumulate data regarding differing perceptions and accurately summarize the information obtained.

Often this data collection occurs in a staff meeting, in a board meeting, or from members of a committee appointed to consider the situation. On other occasions, *focus groups* are created where intensive verbal interaction is stimulated in order to air various opinions on a topic. Another format for data collection involves creating a questionnaire that invites written responses to a series of questions that can be tabulated and summarized to yield a description of the thoughts and opinions of the respondents. Finally, data collection may mean securing relevant reports and documents and then writing a report that organizes these data so that they might be readily analyzed.

Assessment Activities.   Once data are collected and summarized, the social worker must have some tools to help interpret the meaning of the data and to arrive at conclusions. When working at the organizational level, a social worker is typically concerned with issues such as understanding alternative ways to structure the work to be done in a human services agency (see Item 11.18) or ways to organize data that leads to an assessment of needs that clients typically experience (see Item 11.19).

At the community level, a social worker needs to be able to assess the factors that impinge on decision makers in that particular community (see Item 11.20). Also, before moving to action, the social worker must accurately assess the social policies that are in place and understand the ramifications of various changes that may be proposed. Having at least a general sense of the elements of a sound policy analysis is important for any social worker (see Item 11.21).

11.18   ASSESSING AGENCY STRUCTURE

The organizational structure of an agency has a significant impact on the ability of the social worker to provide effective services. In any type of organization, the structure can be expected to vary according to the complexity of the tasks being performed, the amount of authority reserved for central decision making, and the degree to which policies, rules, and procedures are formalized. For example, many successful industrial organizations are based on the bureaucratic model. That model is most viable when the work requires the performance of relatively simple tasks (e.g., putting together parts on an assembly line) that are coordinated through very specific rules of operation. The bureaucratic organizational model, however, is less viable in human services agencies where the work is complex and must be adapted to the unique needs of clients. This work requires individualized judgments by professionals that cannot be readily subjected to centralized control and formalized rules and procedures.

The structures of human services organizations range from highly bureaucratized operations to those that permit considerable worker autonomy. For example, public agencies tend to be bureaucratized, allowing the policymakers and program administrators to maintain a high degree of control over agency functioning. Private nonprofit agencies, by contrast, are usually smaller, offer fewer programs, and tend toward decentralized authority and a minimum of rules and regulations, thus allowing staff members more control over their practice activities and substantial flexibility in how they perform their jobs.

For social workers in all types of human services organizations, it is useful to recognize that various degrees of bureaucratization can exist and that adaptations can be made that create a balance between management and workers in order to facilitate the provision of high-quality services. At times, workers must advocate for structural changes when they find that the agency's structure interferes with service to clients. To inform these advocacy efforts, it is useful to examine several examples of structural formats commonly found in human services agencies.

At one end of the continuum of organizational structure is the **bureaucracy**. In its pure form, a bureaucracy has an elaborate *division of labor* in which work activities are clearly defined and assigned to specialized workers; a *hierarchy* of several of layers of managers, supervisors, and front-line workers is developed; a formalized set of very specific *rules and regulations* is rigidly applied; and the work is carried out in a spirit of *impersonality* that is not adjusted to accommodate individual uniqueness. Bureaucracies are characterized by fairness and equal treatment, but they suffer from lack of flexibility and the ability to individualize. They are stable and consistent yet slow to change.

At the other end of the continuum of organizational structure is the **adhocracy** (i.e., the organization that forms internal structures on an issue-by-issue basis with various collectives of staff members addressing each issue). The ad hoc groups have considerable authority and operate with few agency-wide rules and regulations. This type of organization has a "flat" administrative structure, in which all staff positions are somewhat equal. Ad hoc agencies are weak on both structure and stability, but are able to respond to new issues and undergo change rapidly. They are particularly effective when the nature of the work is dynamic or fluid.

In reality, most human services agencies fall somewhere between a fully developed bureaucracy and a completely ad hoc structure. In smaller agencies, it is possible to have a relatively flat structure with an executive director heading the organization (e.g., representing the staff with the board and the board with the staff) and at least the professional staff members having somewhat equal status. As agencies become larger and more complex and when the span of control or number of staff members for the director to supervise becomes too great for one person to manage, the work must be divided into segments. In this situation, a functional structure is likely to serve the agency well. In the **functional model**, a second-level administrative layer reports to the director and also leads a program unit or supervises a group of workers. A family services agency, for example, might have a counseling unit, a day treatment unit, a social action unit, and an administrative support unit—each with its own unit manager. The executive director would facilitate coordination of these units and oversee the work of the unit managers.

At times, an agency may temporarily supplement one of these structures with a **project-team model**. This model provides for groups of staff to be organized around specific tasks for limited periods of time. In addition to being assigned to a specific unit or supervisor for their primary job, workers may be temporarily assigned on a full- or part-time basis to a team that cuts across units to address a specific problem. An example would be staff members from a family agency's clinical and day treatment units temporarily joining with staff members from the social action unit to plan and carry out a strategy of public education and to reduce the incidence of spouse abuse.

Selected Bibliography

Jones, Gareth R. *Organizational Theory, Design, and Change*, 6th ed. Upper Saddle River, NJ: Pearson/Prentice Hall, 2010.

Patti, J. Rino, ed. *The Handbook of Human Services Management: Purposes, Practice, and Prospects in the 21st Century*, 2nd ed. Thousand Oaks, CA: Sage, 2009.

Schmid, Hillel, ed. *Organizational and Structural Dilemmas in Nonprofit Human Service Organizations*. Binghamton, NY: Haworth, 2004.

11.19   ASSESSING HUMAN SERVICES NEEDS

The perspective of the agency board and staff is a valuable source of information for determining agency goals and services, it is also important that decisions be based on a formal evaluation of the need for these services.

Agencies should periodically conduct needs assessments. **Needs assessment** refers to the process of identifying the incidence, prevalence, and nature of certain conditions within a community or target group. The ultimate purpose is to assess the adequacy of existing services and resources in addressing those conditions. The extent to which those conditions are not adequately addressed denotes a need for different services or resources.

Before conducting a needs assessment, two decisions must be made by those conducting the analysis and those who will use the findings (e.g., agency board, city council, United Way). First, there should be agreement about what constitutes a need. Second, there must be a willingness to take action if an unmet need is identified. It is not a good use of time or resources to conduct a needs assessment when it is known in advance that any needs identified by the study process cannot or will not be addressed with corrective action.

GUIDELINES FOR CONDUCTING A NEEDS ASSESSMENT

These guidelines should be kept in mind when conducting a needs assessment:

1. It is essential to have a clear understanding of the policy issues and administrative concerns that prompted the decision to conduct a needs assessment. In other words, what problems do the decision makers hope to address through the use of a needs assessment? Some possible reasons why situations of unmet need might exist include the following:

- Insufficient services are available in the community.
- Existing services are not accessible because of transportation problems, eligibility criteria, and the like.

- Persons in need are not aware that services exist.
- Existing services are not integrated or coordinated to provide a continuity of service to individuals and families with multiple problems and needs.
- Existing programs do not have adequate resources to provide quality service.
- Existing services are unacceptable to residents of a particular community. For example, they may be perceived as degrading, threatening, or in conflict with existing ethnic, religious, or cultural norms and values.

2. The goals and objectives of the needs assessment must be clear before it is possible to select appropriate methods of data collection and analysis. All too often, those planning a needs assessment jump ahead to the question of what to ask the people being interviewed before they are clear on exactly what kind of data will be useful in the planning of new services or the modification of existing services.

3. It is helpful to know how other communities or agencies have approached the task, but it is usually a mistake to just borrow someone else's objectives and methodology. Those who are in a position to use the data should decide what approach would be useful and work best in their community. Such decisions should not be made by outside consultants or by persons or agencies that have a vested interest in seeing the assessment yield certain results.

4. A needs assessment should not only identify unmet service needs; in addition, it should shed light on the quantity, quality, and direction of existing services. For example:

Quantity.   Does the level of service meet the need? This involves some assessment of the number of persons in need of service compared with the capacity of providers to serve those persons.

Quality.   Are the services effective? Do they accomplish what they are intended to do? Do they work?

Direction: Are the approaches used in service delivery appropriate or possibly out of touch with the real needs of clients? Does the philosophy or beliefs that gave rise to existing programs coincide with ones espoused by experts in the field?

Selected Bibliography

Brun, Carl F. *A Practical Guide to Social Service Evaluation.* Chicago: Lyceum, 2005.

Royse, David, Michele Staton-Tindall, Karen Badger, and J. Matthew Webster. *Needs Assessment.* New York: Oxford University Press, 2009.

11.20   COMMUNITY DECISION-MAKING ANALYSIS

If social workers seek to influence decisions that affect the quality of human services in a community, they must develop a strategy for convincing the people in authority that a particular course of action is the best choice among the possible options. Ideally, decisions should be made on the merit of the proposal; in reality, however, decision makers usually respond to external pressures and various personal considerations.

Research on community decision making and community power structures does not yield a consistent picture of the forces that lead to these decisions. However, several generalizations can be made regarding variables that partially explain why some communities tend to center the decision making in a small, elite group of people while others are more pluralistic and involve a broader spectrum of the community:

1. *Size.*   Large cities tend to be pluralistic. They are likely to become more diverse and competitive as they grow, resulting in a greater range of people and interest groups involved in making decisions.

2. *Population diversity.*   Communities that have more varied and complex class and ethnic structures develop more special interest groups and many different community organizations that compete for power and resources. Consequently, there are more challenges to any dominant elite group and a tendency to increase pluralism in decision making.

3. *Economic diversity.*   More diversified communities in terms of varied sources of employment, high levels of industrialization, and the presence of absentee-owned industry (as opposed to local people owning the major industries) all tend to make communities more pluralistic in how decisions are made.

4. *Structure of local government.*   Cities with council-manager format and nonpartisan-at-large elections tend to be more elitist than partisan governments with representatives elected by districts. Further, the greater the competition or balance among political groups, the more likely the community will have a pluralistic decision-making structure.

Most communities in the United States have a pluralistic type of decision-making structure, although some small rural communities maintain elite power structures. Influencing decisions requires a careful assessment of the people who are authorized to make the decisions. For example, the critical decision maker regarding an issue of interest to social workers may be an agency board member, an elected official, or the manager or management team for a social program. In most cases, relatively few people are involved in making a decision, and they will tend to be focused on particular issues where they have self-interest (e.g., realtors and bankers focused on housing and economic issues, physicians and other health care professionals focused on health care).

One task for the social worker is to assess the various factors that may affect a decision maker's choice. As identified in Figure 11.9, personal characteristics of the person or persons attempting to influence the decision maker, as well as the institutional power the influencer represents, will potentially affect the decision. Also, personal considerations such as the repercussions of the decision on one's finances, self-esteem, judgment about the merits of the proposed change, and

FIGURE 11.9 Factors Influencing Community Decision Makers

so on, will affect the choice. An assessment of the sources for influencing the decision makers for both the proponents and opponents of the change, as well as the personal issues that might affect the decision, should serve as the basis for mapping a strategy for change.

Selected Bibliography

Chaskin, Robert J. *Building Community Capacity.* New York: Aldine de Gruyter, 2001.
Pilotta, Joseph J. *Communication and Social Action Research.* Cresskill, NJ: Hampton Press, 2001.
Scott, John. *Network Analysis: A Handbook*, 2nd ed. Thousand Oaks, CA: Sage, 2000.

11.21   ANALYZING SOCIAL POLICY IMPLICATIONS

When a social worker engages in activity to change an existing social policy, or to introduce a new one, it is important that he or she conduct a careful analysis of that policy. The depth of that analysis will depend on the social worker's role in making the analysis and the scope of the change to be accomplished.

It is helpful to recognize that every realistic social policy is a compromise and the worker must be prepared to compromise. At a minimum, the social worker should be prepared to analyze the major elements of a policy proposal to assure that compromise does not negate the central goal of the change.

Chambers and Wedel (2009) provide a relatively simple and straightforward guide for analyzing policy proposals. The questions in each of the following categories suggest the kinds of information the worker might seek in order to gain sufficient understanding to engage in a successful policy change process:

1. *Social problem analysis.*   The first step in the analysis of a social policy or program is to have a clear understanding of what created the situation requiring such a policy. To make this assessment, it is useful to undertake the following activities:

   - Identify the problem or troublesome situation that gave rise to the social policy. How is this problem described or defined? Are there other more appropriate or accurate definitions? How many people experience this problem? What subpopulations are most likely to experience this problem?
   - Determine the causes and consequences of the problem. What forces or factors have caused the problem? Are there multiple causes? Are there multiple consequences from a single cause?
   - Identify the ideological beliefs embedded in the description of the problem. The definition of a problem is influenced by beliefs about what "ought to be," or the values one holds. Is there a difference of opinion about the seriousness of the problem? Do different groups hold varying views about the nature and cause of the problem?
   - Identify the gainers and losers in relation to the problem. Who benefits from the existence of the problem? What do they gain and how much? Who loses? What do they lose and how much? How serious are the negative consequences on the lives of the losers?

2. *Social policy and program analysis.*   Once the problem is understood, the second step is to assess the social policy and/or program being considered as a means of addressing the problem or offering relief to the victims of the problem. The following are useful for this analysis:

   - Search out the relevant program and policy history. Is this a new problem? Have conditions, values, or perceptions changed over time? What is different about the proposed program or policy from past efforts to deal with the problem?
   - Identify the key characteristics of the proposed policy or program. What are the goals and objectives of the proposal? Who would be eligible to benefit from the plan? What

benefits or services would be delivered if this proposal gains approval? What administrative structure would be required and how would it work? How would the program be financed and how much money would be required?

3. *Draw conclusions.* After the preceding information has been collected, it is necessary to judge the merits of the policy or program under analysis. Ultimately, it is the weight of the evidence matched with one's beliefs about what the quality of life should be for members of the society that results in a recommendation favoring or opposing the proposal—or suggesting compromise.

Answers to the following questions might be considered in arriving at conclusions about this program or policy proposal: Does the remedy proposed adequately deal with the causes as well as the consequences of the problem? Will it yield an outcome different from ones attempted in the past? Would the costs associated with the proposed remedy justify the possible outcomes? Are there better remedies that might be proposed?

When addressing a social policy, it is particularly important to be conscientious about using accurate data. If challenged by those with competing interests, credibility can be lost by not having sufficient and accurate data to support conclusions and underpin recommendations for change.

With a solid analysis of the policy or program proposal, the social worker is prepared to influence the decisions that would impact the problem under consideration. At times, the social worker will work through committees or other groups to affect these decisions; on other occasions, it is appropriate to contact a policymaker directly and express a position on the proposal.

Selected Bibliography

Chambers, Donald E., and Kenneth Wedel. *Social Policy and Social Programs: A Method for the Practical Social Policy Analyst,* 5th ed. Boston: Allyn & Bacon, 2009.

Jimenez, Jullian. *Social Policy and Social Change: Toward the Creation of Social and Economic Justice.* Thousand Oaks, CA: Sage, 2010.

Midgley, James, and Michelle Livermore. *Handbook of Social Policy,* 2nd ed. Thousand Oaks, CA: Sage, 2009.

CHAPTER 12

Planning and Contracting

Upon completing an assessment of the client's concern and situation, the social worker and the client enter the third phase of the change process, planning and contracting. **Planning** is the bridge between assessment and intervention. In some cases of direct practice, the decision on what needs to be done to address the client's concern is fairly obvious, but in other cases the appropriate action is less apparent and requires careful discernment. In an effort to change complex systems such as organizations and communities, the length of the planning phase will often exceed the time required for the intervention itself.

Effective planning places a special demand on the creativity of the social worker and the willingness of the client to consider alternative courses of action. Each possible option must be evaluated in an effort to predict its probable impact and effectiveness, identify possible unintended consequences, determine the resources required, and estimate the time needed to implement the plan. In addition, the worker must select the most appropriate practice frameworks—perspectives, theories, and models that can guide the process (see Chapter 6). Recognizing that some methods of securing change may be effective but unethical, the *Code of Ethics* should be considered at this point, as it is an important screen or filter when selecting intervention strategies (see Item 8.9). Clients, and sometimes inexperienced workers, may be tempted to rush or shortcut this planning activity. However, action, without a clear plan, is a recipe for confusion and failure.

Once a tentative plan has been developed, it is important for the worker and client to explicitly agree to this plan. In other words, they enter into an agreement or a **contract**. The content of a contract is essentially the same whether working at the individual, family, group, organization, or community level. At a minimum, this agreement should delineate the following:

- Problems or concerns to be addressed
- Goals and objectives of the intervention
- Activities the client will undertake
- Activities to be performed by the social worker
- Expected duration of the intervention (in weeks or months)
- Probable place and number of sessions or meetings
- Identification of additional persons, agencies, or organizations expected to participate and their role in the change process

Recognizing that even the most carefully developed plan may need to be modified as the intervention evolves and circumstances change, the social worker and client must be open to such revisions.

SECTION A

TECHNIQUES AND GUIDELINES FOR DIRECT PRACTICE

When working with individuals, families, and groups during the planning and contracting phase, the social worker must strive to maximize client participation and client self-determination. After all, it is the client who must live with the results of the intervention. The client has certain rights that need to be respected when selecting or planning an intervention:

- Make decisions and have input concerning the intervention's goals and objectives and the approach to be used.
- Know the likelihood of success and know about any risks or adverse effects associated with the proposed intervention.
- Know about how long it will take to achieve the agreed-upon objectives.
- Know how much time and money (if any) will be required of the client.
- Know how progress and success of the intervention will be evaluated.
- Know of any consequences for terminating the intervention against the advice of the social worker or agency.
- Know what rules of confidentiality apply and who else (e.g., court, probation officer, school officials, parent) may have access to information about the client's participation and the outcome of the intervention.
- Know about appeals or grievance procedures that can be used to challenge a decision made by the social worker or agency.

Planning Activities.   Some of the most critical decisions a social worker must make occur as part of planning. In some cases, a decision can have lifelong consequences for a client—for example, whether to plan the separation of an abused child from his or her parents, whether to recommend probation or incarceration for a youth, and so on.

One possible mistake is to move too quickly toward selecting an intervention without considering various options and the likelihood of their success. That error may occur because the worker hurries the decision, considers only a narrow range of strategies for change, or interprets agency policy and procedure in an excessively rigid manner, thus stifling creativity and resourcefulness. A related error is to make decisions on the basis of untested assumptions without first weighing information that might contradict the client's or the worker's presumptions about the nature of, cause of, and solution to the client's concern or problem. Finally, an uncritical application of a particular practice theory or model can lead to bad decisions. A social worker overly committed to a particular framework may disregard information that does not fit his or her preferred approach or theory.

Contracting Activities.   Having a plan is critical. Having agreement on that plan is just as important. The greater the specificity about who will do what, when, where, and how, the more likely it is that everyone involved will understand the intervention plan and the more likely it will be fully implemented. A social worker who has navigated the steps of the change process many times may be tempted to assume that the client, too, knows what lies ahead and already agrees to a particular course of action. That can be a serious mistake. The discipline of carefully developing and discussing a contract is often reassuring to clients, while also encouraging the social worker to rethink steps that may have become routine.

Of the three forms of contracts—implied, oral, and written—*implied contracts* offer the least clarity and are most vulnerable to misunderstanding. *Oral contracts* add an element of clarity, but the details of oral communication can be quickly forgotten. Although more time consuming to develop, *written contracts* (see Item 12.5) are the most beneficial for both the client and worker. A document can be reviewed between sessions to remind the participants of their responsibilities and it provides a solid foundation for evaluation and accountability.

12.1   SELECTING TARGET PROBLEMS AND GOALS

During the planning and contracting phase, the social worker and the client must agree on the goal(s) toward which they are working. A **goal** is a desired outcome or the end sought. If the client's need and the action required are readily apparent, the worker and client can quickly agree on their goals. However, in many cases, the social worker and client will see things differently and must struggle to reach an agreement on the nature of the problem and on what can and should be done about it. In direct service helping, the goals of an intervention can take many forms. For example:

- Learn a skill or acquire needed knowledge (e.g., learn how to interview for a job, manage time, make decisions, resolve interpersonal conflict, manage stress).
- Make an important decision (e.g., decide on a college major, whether to get a divorce, whether to relinquish custody of a child, whether to seek help for an emotional problem).
- Assess and examine a troubling problem or concern.
- Make a plan (e.g., formulate a plan on how best to address the concern or problem).
- Change a behavior (e.g., learn a desirable behavior, decrease or eliminate a troublesome behavior or habit).
- Alter attitudes about self or about some other person(s).
- Gather information about availability of certain types of services or programs.
- Become linked to or enrolled in a program or service provided by some agency or professional.
- Rebuild a damaged relationship (e.g., reach out to an estranged parent or child, improve husband–wife relationship).
- Change the way life circumstances or a life event is perceived or interpreted (e.g., learn to assign new meaning to events and circumstances, view things from a different angle).
- Achieve a better adjustment to an unchangeable condition or situation (e.g., strive to adapt to a chronic illness, permanent disability, or the death of a loved one).
- Advocacy to address an injustice.

If the client has numerous problems and concerns, the worker and client must devote considerable time to priority setting in order to decide the primary focus of the intervention and the order in which the problems will be tackled. The value-based principle of *client self-determination* dictates that, to the extent possible, the client has the right to make these decisions. There are also some very practical reasons for expecting the client, rather than the social worker, to select the target problems and goals of the intervention. Namely, it is seldom possible to encourage or motivate a client to do something that he or she does not consider important. Unless the problem to be worked on is a priority to the client and the goal and proposed intervention make sense to the client, the client will not invest himself or herself in the process of change. Even in work with a mandated client, it is important to give the client as much choice as possible (see Item 10.7).

Both research and practice wisdom suggest that, in order to be effective, the helping process must concentrate available time and energy on just one, two, or perhaps three problems at a time. If too many problems are tackled at once, and if priorities are not established, the helping effort flounders and usually ends in frustration for both client and worker. The following steps will help the client and worker select targets for change and set priorities:

1. The client identifies and lists what he or she sees as the problems or concerns needing attention (i.e., what the client wants to change).

2. The social worker offers his or her recommendations, if any, and explains why they also need to be considered. The worker makes sure that any mandated problems or goals are included (a mandated problem or goal is one imposed on the client by some legitimate authority such as a court, probation officer, or child protection agency).

3. The problems and concerns are reviewed and sorted into logical groupings so that their interrelatedness is identified. The client examines the list and selects the two or three problems or concerns of highest priority. Then the worker selects the two or three items he or she considers to be of highest priority.

4. Together, the client and worker discuss the concerns identified in step 3 and examine them against the following criteria:

- Which ones weigh most heavily on the client's situation (e.g., which ones cause the most worry and anxiety)?
- Which ones, if not addressed and corrected, will have the most negative and far-reaching consequences for the client?
- Which ones, if corrected, would have the most positive effects on the client?
- Which ones can be addressed and corrected with only a moderate investment of time, energy, and other resources?
- Which ones are relatively unchangeable or would require an extraordinary investment of time, energy, or resources?

5. After considering these criteria, the three problems of highest priority are selected. As mentioned earlier, it is usually counterproductive to address more than three concerns at one time. Task-centered practitioners have termed this principle the *rule of three*.

6. It is important for the social worker to remember that the client's problems and concerns will almost always affect or involve significant others (e.g., spouse, children, parents, friends, employer). Unless these individuals, who are either part of the problem or part of the solution, are considered in the intervention planning, they may knowingly or unknowingly become an obstacle to the change process. In some cases, they may actively sabotage the client's attempt to make desired changes.

Selected Bibliography

Fortune, Anne. "Task-Centered Practice" in *Social Workers' Desk Reference*, 2nd ed., edited by Albert Roberts. New York: Oxford University Press, 2008.

12.2	THE PROBLEM SEARCH

The technique termed **problem search** is essentially a mini-contract or an agreement between the client and the social worker to devote some time to discuss the client's situation in order to determine if the client has a problem and, if so, whether it should be addressed by some type of professional intervention. Most often a problem search is used when (1) the client has been referred by an authoritative agency (court) or by family but does not acknowledge the existence of a problem as defined by others, or (2) the client has requested a specific service, but in the worker's opinion, it is desirable to help the client to modify that request or redefine the presenting problem. In this later situation, the social worker is concerned that the client's definition of his or her problem or need is not accurate or realistic, or that the service requested will not resolve the problem. An example might be the father who requests foster care placement for his children because he and his wife are having marital problems.

The problem search asks the client to participate in one or two sessions in order to explore his or her situation. The client is asked to withhold judgment about the need for professional intervention and the worker's usefulness until after these meetings. When using this technique, the social worker moves through these four steps:

1. Explain why you are suggesting this exploration. For example: "I realize that you see no problems that deserve my attention, but what you said about getting fired from a couple of jobs leads me to believe that even though you try to get along at work, you and your supervisors often clash. May I suggest that we meet two times and talk more about your job experiences? If, after the second session, we cannot figure out what might be done to improve your situation, we will stop meeting."

2. Solicit the client's thoughts and feedback on the proposal. For example: "What do you think about my suggestion that we meet two times to discuss the stress you experience on the job?" (If client responds with a no, you might say, for example: "Well, I can understand your reluctance and I will respect your decision, but let me give you one other reason why I think it is a good idea. . . .")

3. Set up a plan for a future meeting. For example: "I am glad that you agreed to meet with me. As I said, we will meet just two times. If it proves useful, that will be great. But, if after the second session, it doesn't seem useful, then we will not continue. How about meeting next Wednesday at 4 P.M.?"

4. Identify two or three topics to be discussed. For example: "When we meet next week, let's start with a discussion of the jobs you have liked and why. Second, I would like to discuss the type of supervision you expect on the job. Does that sound reasonable?"

Selected Bibliography

Epstein, Laura, and Lester Brown. *Brief Treatment and a New Look at the Task-Centered Approach*, 4th ed. Boston: Allyn & Bacon, 2002.

Marsh, Peter, and Mark Doel. *The Task-Centered Book*. New York: Routledge, 2005.

12.3 THE CLIENT NEEDS LIST

A **client needs list** is a tool used to guide the case-management activities related to a certain category of clients. Most often it is used with clients who are highly dependent on the services provided by health care and social agencies (e.g., the frail elderly, children in foster care, people with a serious disability). This tool is especially useful when the case-planning activity is being performed by a multi-agency or multidisciplinary team because it helps to clarify responsibilities, facilitates interagency coordination, and reduces misunderstandings within the team. A needs list reminds all involved of the concerns that should be addressed in a client's service plan. Those involved in formulating this plan review the list and decide how each of the client's needs and concerns can be addressed and which service provider will take on that responsibility.

Figure 12.1 is an example of a needs list used in work with adults who have a developmental disability but are capable of living in a semi-independent living arrangement. Also, see Item 11.1 for ideas on specific areas of client functioning that might be included in a needs list.

Selected Bibliography

Frankel, Arthur, and Sheldon Gelman. *Case Management: An Introduction to Concepts and Skills*, 2nd ed. Chicago: Lyceum Books, 2004.

Rothman, Jack, and Jon Simon Sager. *Case Management: Integrating Individual and Community Practice*, 2nd ed. Boston: Allyn & Bacon, 1998.

Summers, Nancy. *Fundamentals of Case Management Practice*, 3rd ed. Belmont, CA: Brooks/Cole, 2009.

Needs List for Independent Living

1. Housing suitable for client's level of mobility and physical limitations (consider stairs, wheelchair accessibility, etc.)
2. Safe heating and electrical system and usable toilet facilities
3. Home furnishing (chairs, tables, TV, radio, etc.)
4. Bed, blankets, sheets, etc.
5. Clothing for all seasons of the year
6. Food, food storage, stove
7. Telephone or other means of requesting assistance
8. Items needed for food preparation (e.g., utensils, pots, pans)
9. Items needed to maintain personal hygiene (razor, soap, sanitary napkins, etc.)
10. Financial resources/money management system
11. Transportation
12. Medical and dental care
13. Medication and monitoring of dosage, if needed
14. Social contacts and recreational activities
15. Concern and interest shown by family, friends, and neighbors
16. Protection from harm or exploitation
17. Appropriate level of supervision
18. Training (job-related, community, survival skills, etc.)
19. Employment or work-related activity
20. Adaptive aids (e.g., eyeglasses, hearing aids, leg braces, etc.)
21. Therapy and other special treatments (e.g., physical therapy, speech therapy, etc.)
22. Maintenance of cultural and ethnic heritage
23. Participation in spiritual or religious activities
24. Legal advice

FIGURE 12.1   Sample Client Needs List

12.4   FORMULATING INTERVENTION OBJECTIVES

Unless there are agreed-upon goals and objectives for an intervention, the helping process will falter and it will be impossible to measure an intervention's effectiveness. Although the term's goals and objectives are often used interchangeably, they do not mean the same thing. A goal is a broad and rather global statement (e.g., "to better cope with the demands of my child who has a disability"). Not infrequently, a goal is simply a restatement of a problem in a way that suggests a solution. For example, if the stress felt by a parent erupts in abuse of the children, a logical goal would be to reduce stress.

As compared to a goal, an **objective** is more specific and written in a manner that allows for measurement and evaluation. An objective describes who will do what, by when, and under what conditions. Consider these examples:

STATEMENTS PREPARED BY A HOSPITAL SOCIAL WORKER

Goal: Improve responsiveness of social work staff to new referrals.

Objective: To conduct at least 80 percent of initial patient or family member interviews within four hours of receiving a referral from a doctor or nurse.

STATEMENTS PREPARED BY THE ADMINISTRATOR OF A BIG BROTHERS PROGRAM

Goal: Obtain more Big Brothers or mentors for our children.

Objective: To recruit, select, train, and match 35 new Big Brothers before August 1.

STATEMENTS PREPARED BY A CHILD WELFARE WORKER

Goal: To promote better parent-child relationships.

Objective: To encourage and facilitate parental visitation so that by January 15 at least 70 percent of parents in my caseload visit their children in foster care at least once a month.

When examining the above sample objectives, notice that an objective makes use of verbs that describe actions to be taken. Examples of verbs that commonly appear in objectives are: attend, visit, learn, practice, discuss, plan, obtain, demonstrate, select, arrange, conduct, decide, and so on.

A properly developed objective meets the following criteria:

1. It usually starts with the word *to*, followed by an action verb.
2. It specifies a single outcome to be achieved.
3. It specifies a target date for its accomplishment.
4. It is as quantitative and measurable as possible.
5. It is understandable to the client and others who are participating in the intervention.
6. It is attainable, but still represents a significant challenge and a meaningful change.

When an objective is especially complex and cannot be written in a single sentence, it will be necessary to attach further statements of condition and criteria as a means of clarification. *Conditions* describe the situation or context in which the desired behavior or action is to take place; *criteria* are the rules or the definitions that will be used to decide whether the desired behavior or action has occurred at an acceptable level.

When developing an objective, it is important not to confuse an *input* with an *outcome*. This common error results in statements like "Mr. Jones is to obtain counseling," which describes an input (counseling) but says nothing about the intended outcome. In this example, counseling is presented as an end, but in reality, it is only the input or a means to an end. What is the intended outcome of the counseling? What is the counseling to accomplish? A better statement would be "Mr. Jones will obtain counseling focused on his physical abuse of his son, Johnny, and designed to help him learn to use time-out and positive reinforcement as alternatives to harsh spanking and screaming as discipline." Given that statement, it would be possible to measure whether or not Mr. Jones did in fact learn how to use time-out and positive reinforcement.

It is important to write an objective in behavioral language using words that describe observable actions in terms of their frequency, duration, and intensity. Also, positive language should be used whenever possible. The words should describe what the client will do, not what the client will not do (e.g., "learn and adhere to specified table manners" versus "stop being so messy when eating").

A *timeframe* is an essential part of an objective. In interpersonal helping, for example, an objective usually should not take more than a few weeks or a couple of months to accomplish. Thus, a large or ambitious objective that could take many months to accomplish should be broken down into several sub-objectives, stages, or phases. This is important because the client needs to see evidence of progress. If the client can perceive he or she is making concrete gains (i.e., reaching an objective), even if the steps are small, he or she will be motivated to continue.

The concept of a task, as used by social workers favoring the task-centered approach, is both similar to and different from the concept of an objective. Basically, a *task* is some specified and observable action or step that can be evaluated in terms of whether it was achieved or completed. A task can be viewed as one of the many steps that must be completed in order to reach an objective. Whereas an objective is something that might be achieved in a couple of months (e.g., "Learn new methods of discipline with the help of a parent training program"), a task can be completed in a matter of days or a couple of weeks (e.g., "Call a friend to arrange

FIGURE 12.2 Relationship of Goals, Objectives, and Tasks

transportation to the parent training program"). Thus, when working toward a single goal, the client may need to achieve several objectives, and in order to reach an objective, the client may need to complete numerous tasks. The relationship between goals, objectives, and tasks is depicted in Figure 12.2.

An objective is intended to give direction to the helping process and facilitate the evaluation of the intervention's effectiveness. However, the utilization of written objectives should never stifle the humanness and individualization that are essential ingredients in the helping process. A willingness to revise objectives in response to changing circumstances is critical to effective helping.

Selected Bibliography

Gronlund, Norman. *How to Write and Use Instructional Objectives*, 6th ed. Upper Saddle River, NJ: Merrill, 2000.

Mager, Robert. *Goal Analysis*, 3rd ed. Atlanta: Center for Effective Performance, 1997.

———. *Preparing Instructional Objectives*, 3rd ed. Atlanta: Center for Effective Performance, 1997.

12.5   WRITTEN SERVICE CONTRACTS

Arriving at an agreement on the service to be provided by the social worker and to be used by the client is fundamental to social work practice. In most cases and in most agencies and programs, a verbal agreement is sufficient. However, many social workers use written service contracts (or service agreements). This is especially true in public agencies and in the fields of child welfare, mental health, developmental disabilities, and probation and parole.

A **written service contract** is a document that specifies the desired outcome of the service(s) to be provided, the key actions that will be taken to achieve this outcome, the major roles and responsibilities of those involved in this effort, and the relevant timelines. Typically, the document is signed by the client and service provider(s). These agreements reduce possible misunderstandings and thereby also reduce the possibility of a malpractice suit. Except in those cases in which the contract is written into a court order, a service contract is not considered to be legally binding. However, it is intended to describe and demonstrate commitment to a mutually agreed-upon course of action. The core elements of a service contract are depicted in Figure 12.3.

While the authors prefer the term service contract, other practitioners and agencies use the terms service agreement, case plan, treatment plan, intervention plan, or individual family support plan when referring to this type of document. Often these terms are used interchangeably.

Service contracts should not be confused with behavioral contracts (see Item 13.5). The two have similarities but also important differences. A behavioral contract is much more specific and covers a shorter period of time—often a matter of days or a week or two. The period covered by a service contract may be several months, although it is ordinarily renegotiated and updated every three or six months.

This agreement is between _____(client's name)_____ and _____(social worker's name)_____, who is employed by the Mountain State Department of Family Services.

The purpose or goal of this agreement is to _____

_____

_____

In order to achieve this purpose or reach this goal, the following objectives must be met:

1. _____ (by date) _____

2. _____ (by date) _____

3. _____ (by date) _____

In order to reach these objectives, ____(client's name)____ is to perform or engage in the following tasks or activities before the dates shown:

1. _____ (by date) _____

2. _____ (by date) _____

3. _____ (by date) _____

In order to reach these objectives, ___(social worker's name)___ is to perform or engage in the following tasks or activities before the dates shown:

1. _____ (by date) _____

2. _____ (by date) _____

3. _____ (by date) _____

Progress toward the objectives will be reviewed and evaluated by means of the following procedures or methods:

_____

_____

The consequences, if any, of not reaching the objectives are the following:

_____

_____

The following steps or actions are required to renegotiate terms of this agreement:

_____

_____

Signed _____ Date _____

Signed _____ Date _____

FIGURE 12.3 Sample Form for Client–Social Worker Contract

A service contract should answer the following questions:

- What is the desired outcome of service to the client?
- What is to be done by the client? By when?
- What is to be done by the client's significant others (family, friends, neighbors, etc.)? By when?
- What is to be done by the social worker and other agency staff? By when?
- What services are to be obtained from other agencies or providers? How and when?

- What events will trigger a reassessment of the client's situation and/or a revision of the service contract?
- What fees, if any, will be charged for these services?
- What are the consequences, if any, for not adhering to the plan?

Follow these guidelines for using written service contracts:

1. Understand your agency's policy regarding written service contracts and any legal requirements or legal interpretations relevant to their use with the clients you serve. Understand the advantages and disadvantages of using written service contracts. The major advantages are that they clarify purpose, set priorities, delineate roles and responsibilities, increase ownership of the plan, provide a means of measuring progress, and reduce the potential for client-worker misunderstanding. Needless to say, contracts work best with voluntary and motivated clients. They do, however, have a special advantage when working with a reluctant or involuntary client because they facilitate clear and above-board communication and will often lessen the client's hostility and fear of being manipulated or set up by some hidden agenda.

An obvious disadvantage of written service contracts is that considerable time may be needed to prepare a clear and easily understood contract. Also, there is the danger that an unassertive client or one who feels powerless may agree to a contract provision out of fear of being penalized if he or she does not agree with what the service provider has suggested.

2. Develop the contract only after a thorough social assessment during which you and the client study and agree on the problems to be tackled. From the client's perspective, the goals and objectives listed in the contract must be realistic and worth achieving. And, since the purpose of the contract is to facilitate change, it must focus on behaviors or situations that can, in fact, be changed.

When selecting and formulating objectives, logical sequences must be built into the plan. Some problems must be tackled one step at a time and in a certain order. New behaviors may need to be learned in a particular sequence. For example, the client who wants a job must first learn how to complete a job application.

3. By definition, a service contract specifies what the client will do and what the worker/agency will do. A contract must never be one-sided and list only that which is expected of the client. The provisions of a contract must be consistent with the client's capacities, the worker's skill, and the agency's mission.

4. The contract should be written in simple, clear language so that the client will know exactly what it means. It will be necessary to prepare the contract in the client's first language (e.g., Spanish) if he or she has a poor understanding of English. In cases where the client cannot read, the worker should consider preparing an audio recording of the agreement, in addition to preparing a written statement.

5. A contract should be developed in a way that makes success probable without sacrificing relevance. It must not focus on trivial outcomes, so as to easily attain success while avoiding objectives that are more important but more challenging. If the worker believes that the client will be unable to meet the terms of a particular contract, that alone is an indication that its objectives are too ambitious, or the timeframe is too short.

6. Provisions of the contract should be modified as necessary to stay in step with changing realities of the situation. This flexibility is important in maintaining the trust of the client.

Selected Bibliography

Rothman, Juliet. *Contracting in Clinical Social Work*. Chicago: Nelson-Hall, 1998.
Wodarski, John, Lisa Rapp-Paglicci, Catherine Dulmus, and Arthur Jongsma. *The Social Work and Human Services Treatment Planner*. New York: John Wiley and Sons, 2001.

12.6   MAKING USE OF INFORMAL RESOURCES

When appropriate and acceptable to the client, an intervention plan should consider drawing upon the informal resources available within the client's support network, such as family, friends, neighbors, and faith groups. These individuals and groups may be able to provide the client with needed information, encouragement, emotional support, material assistance (e.g., housing, money), physical care (e.g., caretaking during an illness), and sometimes the mediation of interpersonal conflicts. While some clients desire to keep others from learning about their troubles, others like the idea of enlisting the help of informal resources. Informal resources may be attractive to a client because help is available 24 hours a day at no cost; one does not have to be categorized, diagnosed, or otherwise meet agency-eligibility requirements in order to secure assistance; and this informal helping involves a relationship among equals or peers—rather than the expert–client relationship that is so often a part of the professional helping process.

A *self-help group* is usually considered to be an informal resource, even though some may be affiliated with a state or national level organization and some may utilize professionals as advisors. Another important informal resource is the *natural helper*, an individual who has often resided in the community for a long time and is known for his or her ability to help others. An example would be the "neighborhood Mom" to whom children gravitate for nurturing and advice. Other natural helpers include respected elders, religious leaders, and healers. Another informal resource—one often overlooked by professionals—is other agency clients. Clients can be of help to each other; however, in some cases, they can also exacerbate each other's problems.

Although informal resources are the oldest and most common form of helping activity, some professionals are reluctant to encourage their clients to use them. Possible reasons include the following:

- The professionals assume that formal resources are inherently more effective than nonprofessionals, regardless of the client's problem or situation.
- They have little awareness of the informal helping networks and informal resources available to their clients.
- They assume that the client has already thought about using informal resources and for some reason has rejected the idea.
- They doubt the capacity of informal resources to protect a client's right to confidentiality.

When considering the appropriateness of looking to informal resources as a source of additional help to a client, the social worker should keep the following guidelines in mind:

1. The fundamental goal of social work practice is to help clients improve their social functioning. The resources used—whether formal, informal, or a mix of both—are simply the means to that end. Both formal and informal resources are important, and both may be needed. A professional should not feel threatened by a client's use of or preference for informal resources. While invaluable in many situations, informal resources are neither a panacea nor an inexpensive alternative to professional services and the formal resources needed by a client.

2. The client's social support network should always be viewed as a potential reservoir of helping resources. If a source is identified, the advantages and disadvantages of attempting to use it should be discussed with the client. However, in the final analysis, it is the client who decides whether to contact others and involve them in the helping process. Some clients may need guidance on how to reach out to an informal resource and also handle the expectation of reciprocity (see Item 11.6).

3. The ethical and legal codes concerning client confidentiality need not be a barrier to the use of informal resources. In almost all situations it will be the client who first approaches the informal resources. Thus, the client is in control of what he or she chooses to reveal. In cases where the social worker needs to talk with an informal resource, the worker must, of course, first secure the client's permission.

4. Some clients are reluctant to approach or join a self-help group or support group because they do not want to admit that they have a problem. They may find a group more attractive if they come to view their own participation as a means of helping others. Thus, a worker attempting to connect a client with such a group might emphasize that because of the client's life experiences, he or she will be able to offer valuable guidance to the group's members.

5. A worker should not attempt to "professionalize," train, or direct the actions of an informal helping resource. Generally, these people are most effective when they follow their judgments and respond spontaneously.

Selected Bibliography

Gitterman, Alex, and Lawrence Shulman, eds. *Mutual Aid Groups, Vulnerable Populations and the Life Cycle*, 3rd ed. New York: Columbia University Press, 2005.

Kurtz, Linda. *Self-Help and Support Groups*. Thousand Oaks, CA: Sage, 1997.

Norcross, John, John Santrock, Linda Campbell, Thomas Smith, Robert Sommer, and Edward Zuckerman. *Authoritative Guide to Self-Help Resources in Mental Health*, rev. ed. New York: Guilford, 2003.

Steinberg, Dominique. *The Mutual Aid Approach to Working with Groups*. New York: Haworth, 2004.

12.7   FAMILY GROUP CONFERENCING

The technique termed **family group conferencing** (also known as *family group decision making* and *family unity meetings*) was developed during the 1980s by child welfare personnel in New Zealand. It was designed to engage the large extended families and kinship groups (common to indigenous peoples) in decision making and planning for a child who has been abused or neglected by a parent. A family group conference (FGC) brings together in a face-to-face discussion the parent and other individuals who are concerned about both the parent and the child. The facilitator asks the group to come up with a plan for keeping the child safe. In many cases, planning for the child involves making a plan that will help the parent change his or her behavior or situation.

In addition to the parent and his or her family and relatives, those attending the FGC might include some of the parent's close friends, the parent's clergy person, the child's school personnel or day-care providers, attorneys, foster parents, social and mental health service providers, and others who are somehow involved with and concerned about the child and the child's parent. However, the professionals or service providers who attend an FGC are there to only provide information and do not propose solutions or make decisions.

A typical FGC session lasts from 2 to 3 hours, but some go on for an entire day. Young children aren't allowed but an adolescent might be invited to participate. The FGC technique is based on these assumptions, values, and beliefs:

- The individuals who are most deeply concerned about and committed to the long-term well being of the child are, most likely, his or her blood relatives and close friends of the family.
- Family members know one another's histories and their strengths, limitations, and problems.
- A plan that is developed by family, relatives, and trusted family friends is more likely to be accepted and implemented than is a plan developed by a social worker, a social agency, or a court.

The FGC approach is attractive to many social workers because it is inherently culturally sensitive, it is family-centered, and it builds on family strengths. An FGC demonstrates to the abusive or neglectful parent that many people care and want to help. As the parent comes to this realization, his or her denial and resistance will often fall away. Many who are experienced in the use of the FGC express amazement at the creativity and resourcefulness displayed by the people attending a family group conference, as they strive to come up with feasible solutions to the problems. Not infrequently, individuals from the parent's family or kinship group will step forward and offer invaluable resources to address the parent's problems. A side benefit of the FGC process is that it often initiates reconciliation and the healing of ruptured family relationships. Increasingly, this approach to case planning is adapted to other practice settings, such as juvenile probation, mental health, institutional placement of an older person, and education.

The FGC can be used with most families. Those most likely to benefit are ones in which family members (and others) can focus on the needs of the child, rather than their own issues, and will communicate honestly and strive for a consensus in decision making. Here are several guidelines for using family group conferencing regarding the well being of a child:

1. The FGC is to be used only when the parent(s) has agreed. All of those invited to attend the meeting first must be "nominated" by the parent. The parent is encouraged, however, by his or her social worker to invite all family members, relatives, and friends who are genuinely concerned about the situation, even if the parent does not like them. If the parent wants his or her attorney present, the attorney can be invited if the attorney agrees to allow a free-flowing discussion and takes a non-adversarial approach to the problem-solving effort. (In some states, the child protection agency is required to invite the parent's attorney to a family group conference.)

When making decisions about whom to invite to the conference, the FGC coordinator and the parent also must consider safety issues. A person who is extremely intimidating, violent, or under the influence of drugs or alcohol may need to be excluded.

2. A Family Group Conference can be used at any point, but it is usually tried in these situations: (a) when the agency and the parent have reached an impasse; (b) when the out-of-home placement of a child or the child's return home is under consideration by a child protection agency or court; and (c) when the parent's change effort is "stuck" and his or her family and friends need to help the parent get back on track and more effectively cope with current problems. (In some states, the use of an FGC can be court-ordered in an effort to arrive at a plan for a child in need of care.)

3. The FGC coordinator or facilitator of the meeting should possess a neutral attitude toward the parent and not have an ongoing or prior relationship with the parent or the family. Thus, the parent's current social worker, case manager, therapist, or service provider should not assume the role of coordinator.

4. For a family group conference to be successful, the coordinator or facilitator must carefully prepare the potential participants. During this preparation phase, the coordinator meets with each potential participant (i.e., someone nominated by the parent) to explain the purpose and process of the FGC, to answer questions, to encourage him or her to attend, and, if necessary, to arrange for transportation, child care, and so on. Typically, a coordinator will invest 30 to 40 hours in preparing for a single FGC meeting.

5. At the beginning of an FGC session, certain ground rules must be explained and displayed for all to see. For example:

- The coordinator will guide the process without imposing his or her views or ideas on the group.
- Keep the focus on the needs of the child and on making decisions and a plan that are in the child's best interests.
- Keep the focus on finding solutions. Focus on what can be done in the future, not on what happened in the past.
- Be respectful of each other. No name-calling, blaming, shaming, or threatening. No one will be allowed to intimidate another person or prevent another from speaking.
- It is important for everyone to voice his or her ideas and suggestions. It is OK to disagree, but do so in a respectful manner.
- Only one person will speak at a time.
- After this meeting, be sure to maintain confidentiality about what was discussed.

6. A typical FGC session will unfold as follows:

- The coordinator welcomes the participants and explains the purpose of the meeting. For example: "We are here to see how we can help Margaret and her children and make it possible for the family to stay together."
- Coordinator explains the ground rules for the meeting (see Guideline 5). At the beginning of the meeting, a ritual that is meaningful to the family may be used to set the tone for the discussion. This ritual might be, for example, a prayer, recalling the family's traditions, or recalling some special time in the family's history.
- All who are present introduce themselves and briefly explain their relationship with the parent(s) and children.
- Parent is asked and helped, if necessary, to describe his or her goals for the meeting and the hoped-for outcome.
- Coordinator guides a discussion of the parent's and the family's strengths.
- Coordinator guides presentations by selected child protection personnel, service providers, and family members. This serves to describe the current problem or troublesome situation, the needs of the child, and the possible legal ramifications or court action if the problem is not resolved. The professionals in attendance answer all questions asked by those in attendance. (Professionals may be asked to leave after their presentations.)
- Family and friends are asked to propose their ideas on how the child can be protected from further maltreatment and how the parent might be helped to make needed changes. In cases in which the child must be separated from the parent, the group decides where the child might live. (These discussions may take place with or without the coordinator being present.)
- The coordinator reviews the group's recommendations and decisions and a follow-up plan is formulated.
- Meeting is adjourned and perhaps followed by a celebration ritual and sharing of food.

7. The use of family group conferencing does not abrogate the responsibilities of the social worker, agency, or court in protecting the child. They can, if absolutely necessary, veto the plan. However, if the plan generated by the family conference will keep the child safe, it should be approved by the child welfare agency or court.

8. Following the meeting, the coordinator compiles notes on the meeting and puts the agreed-upon plan into written form and sends this report to all participants and the child protection agency.

Selected Bibliography

American Humane Association. *Family Group Decision Making: Technical Assistance Notebook.* Englewood, CO: American Humane Association, 1998.

Burford, Gale, and Joe Hudson, eds. *Family Group Conferencing.* New York: Aldine de Gruyter, 2000.

Connolly, Marie, and Margaret McKenzie. *Effective Participatory Practice: Family Group Conferencing in Child Protection.* New York: Aldine de Gruyter, 1999.

Pennell, Joan, and Gray Anderson, eds. *Widening the Circle: The Practice and Evaluation of Family Group Conferencing.* Washington, DC: National Association of Social Workers, 2005.

12.8   THE SMALL GROUP AS A RESOURCE

When planning an intervention, the small group should always be considered a potential helping resource. Small groups can be an invaluable resource to both individuals and families who are struggling with some problem or trying to learn how to cope with a difficult situation. Small group approaches are essential to work with clients who are defensive and manipulative, as is frequently the case with clients whose problems revolve around substance abuse, sexual offenses, and domestic abuse.

A group provides its members with acceptance and encouragement and with opportunities to acquire new skills, develop self-awareness, and help others. In many instances, a group experience is superior to one-on-one counseling. Many clients are more open to the suggestions and confrontations voiced by their peers than to those offered by a professional. For example, an adolescent is more likely to listen to another adolescent than to a 50-year-old social worker. Peers and group members are often willing to say things to each other that a social worker hesitates to say out of fear of offending a client or making a mistake. For example, a social worker might be reluctant to confront a client who seems to be lying but another group member may quickly voice this suspicion.

For the most part, the groups utilized in direct practice are *formed groups*, meaning that they are purposefully planned and created by a social work practitioner. By contrast, a *natural group* is one that develops spontaneously among friends, peers, and neighbors. There are occasions when a social worker will work with the naturally occurring groups in neighborhoods, schools, and institutional settings.

When a group meets for several sessions it will typically move through five **stages of group development**: (1) preaffiliation, (2) power and control, (3) intimacy, (4) differentiation, and (5) separation. During the first stage, *preaffiliation*, the members size each other up, consider what they might have in common, and decide whether they want to be a part of the group. Unless individuals feel comfortable in the group and see that it is somehow beneficial, they are likely to avoid meaningful involvement, even if they remain physically present. During this first stage, members tend to look to and depend on the designated leader for direction and structure.

During the *power and control stage*, members test each other and come to a decision of where they fit in the group. They may challenge each other for position, rank, and leadership. Some members may challenge the designated leader. At this time, some informal rules emerge to govern what is and what is not acceptable behavior within the group. As the members get to know each other, they gradually let down their defenses and the group enters the fourth stage, *intimacy*, during which the members recognize and come to value what they have in common.

Next, the group moves to the *stage of differentiation*, wherein differences are exhibited but accepted and respected. Members begin to learn more about each other's roles and responsibilities outside the group. As the life of the group approaches its ending, it enters the *separation stage* and each member must struggle with the loss of meaningful relationships.

For those who want to make a group experience available to their clients, these guidelines are suggested:

1. Before attempting to plan or design a group, be clear as to its purpose and why the group experience might benefit your clients. A group's purpose might be education, recreation, socialization, therapy or behavior change, mutual aid, and self-help. Answers to most questions about how best to structure and guide a group will relate directly back to the group's purpose or desired outcome. As a general rule, the more specialized the group's purpose, the better it serves the members. If all the members have similar concerns and similar reasons for being in the group, they are more likely to participate and share their thoughts and experiences.

2. Decide which clients are to be offered the group experience. Some social group workers hold definite beliefs about the mix of personalities they want in the group (e.g., having outgoing members to balance those who are reserved). Also, some group workers may want to eliminate from consideration those who tend to be resistant or uncooperative. However, in many practice settings, the worker does not have the luxury of using detailed selection criteria and must include in the group those who have a need for a group experience and have at least a minimal capacity to form relationships and tolerate differences. A voluntary member should be free to drop out if the group is not meeting his or her needs or expectations.

When screening or selecting potential members, the group worker must balance the needs of the individual with the needs and safety of other members. People exhibiting bizarre or truly dangerous behavior should be eliminated from membership unless the meetings occur within an institutional setting that can provide monitoring and safety. Individuals who are at high risk of suicide or actively using or selling illegal drugs may not be appropriate for inclusion.

When extending an invitation to join a group, be prepared to explain how the group will be of benefit, what will usually occur during the meetings, and the atmosphere you hope to create (e.g., informal, fun, learning, sharing). Also, offer information that might elevate interest and reduce fears about participating.

3. It is not possible to predict with accuracy how an individual will behave and function in a group. As a general rule, however, people will behave in a formed group much like they behave in other situations. For example, if an individual does not express feelings to family and friends, he or she will usually carry this same pattern into the group. Likewise, the person who controls and dominates others at home and at work will most likely try to dominate and control the group.

4. Decide an appropriate group size. Size depends on such factors as the age of the clients, concerns to be addressed by the group, and your professional experience as a leader or facilitator. You will want the group to be small enough so all members have a sense of belonging and a chance to actively participate but large enough to yield a variety of opinions and minimize pressure on those who are shy or fearful. For preadolescents, a group of only three or four is often workable. For adolescents, a group of six to eight is about right. For adults, a group of eight to ten is a comfortable size. You must also anticipate the inevitable problem of nonattendance and dropouts. The group must be large enough to continue functioning when some members miss a meeting and after a member or two decides to drop out.

5. Decide on the frequency of meetings and the length of each session. For adults, a meeting lasting 1½ to 2 hours is about right. Because children and adolescents have a shorter attention span, it is usually best to have shorter but more frequent sessions. The practice setting will also dictate the frequency of meetings. In an institutional setting, daily meetings are often possible and desirable. When members are drawn from the larger community and must travel long distances, it may not be feasible to meet more often than biweekly or monthly.

6. Decide when and where the group will meet. A meeting space should be quiet, private, comfortable, and large enough for people to move around and to accommodate a circle of chairs. The decision of when to meet must consider each member's work and family responsibilities, matters of personal convenience, travel required, and, of course, the availability of a meeting room.

7. Decide on the approximate number of times the group will meet. This is, of course, tied to purpose. An information sharing or training group might meet only once or twice, whereas a support or therapy group might meet weekly for several months or longer. Consider setting a limit (e.g., three, five, or ten meetings) with the understanding that at the end of that period the group will decide whether the meetings should continue. This can help keep members involved because they will know there is a planned time to terminate and it can prevent a group from continuing to meet even when there is no longer a need to do so.

8. Decide whether the group will be open or closed to additional members. This is sometimes a decision for the group to make. If the group is to decide, this decision needs to be made during the first or second meeting. Incorporating new members into an already functioning group has the advantage of maintaining group size if some members drop out. Also, new members may bring fresh perspectives. However, the frequent introduction of new members can interfere with the development of group cohesion and entering the intimacy stage.

9. Decide if the group is for voluntary clients, involuntary clients, or both. Obviously, there are advantages to limiting membership to persons who want to attend. Although individuals can be mandated by court order to attend a group, they cannot be made to interact in a meaningful and productive manner. However, the use of group approaches in correctional settings, chemical dependency, and domestic abuse treatment programs demonstrates that groups composed of involuntary clients are both feasible and effective (see Items 10.7 and 10.8).

The addition of involuntary or mandated members to a mostly voluntary group will usually work if the group has been functioning well for a time and the new involuntary member is cooperative to at least a minimal degree. On the other hand, it is usually problematic to bring a mandated and resistant member into a newly formed group or into one that is not functioning very well. Before adding such a member, it is best to wait until the group has reached the intimacy stage. The addition of new members, especially ones who are manipulative or domineering, should definitely be avoided during the power and control stage. In all groups, whenever members are resistant and manipulative, the group leader must be strong and highly skilled.

10. Be prepared to establish rules to govern the behavior of group members. Possible rules include the following:

- Members are expected to attend all meetings.
- Members are expected to maintain confidentiality.
- Members cannot smoke nor do drugs during the meeting.
- Members cannot remain at the meeting if they are under the influence of alcohol or drugs.
- Minor-aged members must have parents' written consent to participate.
- Members are to avoid romantic involvement with other members.
- Members who bring weapons, threaten violence, or engage in sexual harassment will be excluded.

11. As the group moves through the usual stages of development, it is important to monitor the functioning and behavior of each group member and, when necessary, use various techniques to deal with problems (see Items 8.4, 11.11, and 13.25). A fairly common problem in small groups (and in family counseling) is that a few members dominate the discussion. The *talking stick* technique, which is commonly used in Native American cultures, addresses domination. An object, the talking stick, is passed around the group from person to person. Whoever is holding it has permission to speak while all others are silent and give the speaker their undivided attention. It is passed around the group as many times as necessary to assure that everyone has the opportunity to speak, to clarify their message, and to be heard. In a session with a family, the talking stick might be an object that commands the family's respect (e.g., family photo, religious symbol).

12. Select activities (programs) for each meeting (e.g., introductions, ice breakers, refreshments, structured discussion, role-play, guest speaker). These activities should be consistent with the group's purpose and encourage the type of activity relevant to the group's stage of development (see Item 13.21).

13. Anticipate how you can handle the numerous practical problems associated with a meeting, such as the room is too hot, too cold, or too small; members arrive late; members bring uninvited guests; conflict between smokers and nonsmokers; deciding if there will be refreshments and, if so, who will bring them or pay for them; the leader must miss a meeting; and so on.

Selected Bibliography

Garvin, Charles, Maeda Galinsky, and Lorraine Gutierrez. *Handbook of Social Work with Groups*. New York: Guilford, 2004.

Gitterman, Alex, and Robert Salmon, eds. *Encyclopedia of Social Work with Groups*. New York: Routledge, 2009.

Jacobs, Ed, Robert Masson, and Riley Harvill. *Group Counseling: Strategies and Skills*, 6th ed. Belmont, CA: Brooks/Cole, 2009.

Toseland, Ronald W., and Robert Rivas. *Introduction to Group Work Practice*, 6th ed. Allyn & Bacon, 2009.

Zastrow, Charles. *Social Work with Groups*, 7th ed. Belmont, CA: Brooks/Cole, 2009.

SECTION B

TECHNIQUES AND GUIDELINES FOR INDIRECT PRACTICE

Social workers engaged in indirect service activities must give careful attention to the planning and contracting phase of the change process. As systems become more complex, it is increasingly difficult and time consuming to promote meaningful change in its ways of operating. When working with organizations and communities, one should also be aware that change in one system or one part of a system will reverberate not only through that system but through related systems, as well. Therefore, change efforts must be carefully planned and the responsibilities of each actor in the process should be clearly identified.

Planning Activities.   Community organization and community planning are forms of social work practice typically performed by social workers with advanced education. This book does not intend to address these more complex processes; rather, it provides some guidelines that are useful for the front-line social worker (i.e., the direct practice worker whose job sometimes involves indirect practice activities). Much of the front-line worker's planning activity related to organizations and communities involves the ability to assess various alternatives for remedying a problem, selecting the best alternative for achieving a positive outcome, and plotting the schedule of tasks and activities to make the change process as efficient and effective as possible.

Contracting Activities.   Once plans for organizational and community change have been developed, there must be explicit agreements among the participating parties about the responsibilities and timetable for carrying out the associated activities. In a community change effort, for example, once an assessment is made and a plan developed, individual or committee assignments for implementing the plan must be agreed upon. Typically, someone must prepare a position statement, someone must organize the people concerned with the issue to take action, someone must provide relevant information to the media, someone must lobby the decision makers, and so on. These actions must be orchestrated to be sure that they are done in a timely manner, as subsequent actions may depend on those tasks having already been completed.

12.9   ESTABLISHING AND CHANGING ORGANIZATIONS

Social agencies stake their claim to specific areas of service provision. They must clearly state their mission, the goals they intend to achieve, the services they will provide, and the policies and procedures they will follow. Only then can the public be accurately informed about the nature of the agency, can clients know what services to expect, can unplanned duplication and overlap of services among agencies be minimized, and can staff members plan and coordinate their work.

An effective social agency is dynamic; it must constantly adapt to community and societal changes, to new knowledge about the nature of personal and social problems, to changes in public attitudes, and to ever-changing fiscal and political realities. Thus, a social worker can expect to participate, to some degree and at some level, in efforts to modify agency goals, structure, and operations.

Public agencies are particularly reactive to any change in the state and federal laws relevant to their areas of service and to budget modifications. In response to such changes, the agency's own policies and procedures may need to undergo significant change within a short period of time.

Private agencies, too, must be capable of responding to a variety of forces. When a private agency is created, the bylaws spell out its mission and decision-making structure. Although the original bylaws may capture the intent of the founders, such agencies must change over time to keep pace with changing community needs and new concepts of service. Leadership for needed change by a private agency often falls first to the CEO and the staff, with the board and/or a broader membership group subsequently amending the bylaws or revising its policies to reflect the needed changes.

Although change is inevitable, an agency, like all social systems, will resist change; in fact, it may take considerable effort to make needed change. The following guidelines suggest what to consider when planning and initiating organizational change:

1. Begin by describing as precisely as possible the change that is needed and why. Then secure and study all documents that may pertain to the desired change. These may include, for example, federal and state laws and regulations, administrative and personnel manuals, union contracts, accreditation standards, agreements and contracts involving other agencies, and so on. The information drawn from these sources will determine, to some degree, what changes are possible, how the change process must proceed, and who must support or approve the change.

2. Assess the organization's readiness for change. Review its prior experience in accepting change. People are likely to resist change if prior change efforts have been misguided, ineffective, or frustrating. On the other hand, they will tend to accept change if they trust those promoting or leading the change effort, when they believe the proposed change is needed and feasible, and when the proposal has addressed their questions, concerns, and fears about changing.

3. Determine if the desire for change is shared across the various levels, departments, and units of the organization. Pay special attention to the views of those who will be affected most directly by the proposed change. A common error is to overlook or disregard the opinions of line workers and clerical staff—those who often know most about how the proposed change will affect day-to-day agency operations and agency clients.

4. Assess the degree to which the change is compatible with the agency's mission, traditions, and current goals. Determine the degree to which the change is desired and likely to be supported by top management and the board of directors.

5. Identify and assess the relative strength of the organizational subsystems and individuals who are likely to favor the change and those who will oppose it. Determine who stands to gain and who stands to be hurt by the proposed change. A strategy most likely to overcome resistance is one that either (a) increases the power of those within the agency that favor the change or (b) introduces innovative programs or brings new resources into the organization that will minimize the impact of the change on those who are resistant.

6. The agency, or a unit of the agency, will most likely adopt a proposed change if it can be shown that the change will result in an increase in scope, authority, autonomy, or funds and other resources. A change that decreases power and resources will be resisted. People will favor a change that makes their work easier or more successful; they will resist a change that makes their work more complex or demands more of their time.

7. The members of an organization will strongly resist a change that they perceive as a threat to their jobs, advancement, or opportunities within the organization. Also, they will be resistant whenever they suspect others are withholding information about the true intentions of the change.

8. An organization will be more open to a proposed change if it can be demonstrated that other similar organizations have successfully made this change.

9. A change is most likely to be accepted by the organization after its advantages have been demonstrated in a trial run or implemented within only a part of the organization. Thus, it is desirable that the first phase of a more far-reaching change effort begin by focusing on a specific program or activity of limited scope.

10. Whenever possible, changes should be integrated into current structures and procedures so as to minimize the disruption of existing relationships and patterns.

Selected Bibliography

Anderson, Donald L. *Organization Development: The Process of Leading Organizational Change.* Thousand Oaks, CA: Sage, 2010.

Kettner, Peter M., Robert M. Moroney, and Lawrence L. Martin. *Designing and Managing Programs: An Effectiveness-Based Approach,* 3rd ed. Thousand Oaks, CA: Sage, 2008.

12.10 THE PROCESS OF AGENCY PLANNING

To operate in an effective and efficient manner and to grow and develop as an organization, a social agency must formulate both short-range and long-range plans that guide its ongoing activity and decision making. All too often, agencies neglect long-term planning and then find that they must make hasty decisions and rapid changes in agency operations in response to a situation or crisis they did not anticipate and for which they were unprepared.

Ideally, an agency's planning process is proactive and forward looking. The plan should include a description of how it will utilize its resources (i.e., staff time, money, knowledge, skills, etc.), how it can capitalize on its strengths and opportunities, how it will correct its weaknesses, and how it can respond to certain unwanted but possible future events such as increased demand for service, loss of staff, or a reduction in funding.

A fruitful planning process is complex and time consuming. It can be especially difficult because all planning decisions rest on a set of predictions as to what will happen in future months and years. Unfortunately, it is difficult to predict accurately the ever-changing political, economic, and public opinion forces that may affect an agency's operation. Given these uncertainties, even the best of plans must be constantly reviewed and revised.

Broadly speaking, there are three types of planning processes: (1) problem-solving planning, (2) operational planning, and (3) strategic planning. They differ primarily in terms of the time period covered.

Problem-solving planning has a lifespan of 60 to 90 days. It focuses on some specific problem that is having an adverse effect on the agency's usual activity. The process involves (1) identifying and examining the problem, (2) selecting a set of corrective actions or measures, (3) planning the implementation of these measures, and (4) monitoring their effectiveness. If the agency is successful in its operational and strategic planning, the need for problem-solving planning will be minimized.

Operational planning refers to short-range planning covering a period of 3 to 12 months or perhaps one budget cycle. This planning process formulates objectives, details performance standards, and prepares an action plan to reach the stated objectives.

Strategic planning may cover a period of 3 to 10 years. Basically, the strategic planning process strives to develop a plan for achieving the agency's mission or long-term goals. This type of planning calls for the identification and analysis of broad social and economic trends, for speculation on what challenges and opportunities the agency will face in the next few years, and for forward-looking decisions about how best to use agency resources. Strategic planning is based on the belief that it is important to have a plan that considers all conditions and factors that may impact the agency, regardless of how uncertain the future must be. Because it is so speculative and based on so many uncertain variables, a strategic plan must be continually reviewed and revised.

Following these guidelines will enhance the planning process:

1. Make certain that adequate and accurate data are available to those engaged in the planning process. Such data should describe these factors:

- The agency's mission and goals
- Current and projected budgets and a history of the agency's fiscal condition
- Programs and services provided and the number of clients/consumers participating in each program or service area

- Characteristics of the persons served by the agency (e.g., age, income, ethnicity, religion)
- Agency staff (e.g., education, training, interests, skills)
- The agency's relationship with other local, state, or national agencies
- Requests and concerns voiced by staff/clients/consumers and other agencies and community groups
- Trends and projections (i.e., demand for services, capacity to raise funds, demographic changes in the community)
- Special problems faced by the agency

2. Keep the planning process as simple as possible so that all those who should participate can do so despite the day-to-day pressures of their other responsibilities. Do not demand more of their time than is absolutely necessary. Keep the number of meetings and the paperwork required to a minimum.

3. Make sure that all who might be affected by a decision or proposed change are invited to participate in the discussion and encouraged to voice their thoughts and concerns. Avoid top-down planning (i.e., decision making and planning by only the upper-level administrative personnel). Facilitate information flowing from both those who might be affected to the decision makers and from the decision makers to those who will operate and benefit from the changes.

4. Gather and organize ideas and promote creativity by performing a SWOPA analysis of the agency. The acronym **SWOPA** stands for Strengths, Weaknesses, Opportunities, Problems, and Action.

- *Strengths.*   Identify the services, programs, and activities currently provided at a level of quality that meets or exceeds professional standards.
- *Weaknesses.*   Identify the services, programs, and activities that fall below acceptable levels of quality or needed levels of quantity.
- *Opportunities.*   Identify the service or program activities that are promising for future development or expansion because of growing demand, available funding, staff interest, and so on.
- *Problems.*   Identify the areas of agency performance that are especially troublesome.
- *Actions.*   Identify activities or changes that would build on agency strengths, exploit opportunities, address areas of weakness, or better manage the problems faced by the agency.

5. Perform a *competition analysis*. This asks those participating in the planning process to examine the activities of other agencies, organizations, or professional groups to determine how they compete with the agency's current programs and services. For example, are other organizations developing services that would attract your agency's clients or staff or are other agencies making requests for the funds now utilized by your agency?

6. Perform a *stakeholder's analysis*. Stakeholders are those individuals, groups, or organizations that have an interest in the agency. Their beliefs, values, and possible reactions to changes in the agency must be given serious consideration. Examples of internal stakeholders are clients/consumers, agency staff, unions representing staff, members of the board of directors, and so on. Examples of external stakeholders include professional associations, politicians, other agencies, businesses and corporations, local newspapers, citizen groups, taxpayers, contributors, former clients, and the like.

7. Perform a *threat analysis*. A threat is some possible future circumstance or action by others that could harm the agency. Examples might include a lawsuit against the agency, an employee strike, loss of funding, loss of key staff, rapid change in community demographics, significant changes in the laws or regulations that affect the agency, damaging news stories, and so forth.

8. Make sure that the many facets of the planning process are coordinated and well integrated. For example, decisions concerning budget, staffing patterns, performance standards, and programs and services to be offered are all interrelated. In particular, financial planning must be incorporated into all other areas of planning. If the many components of the process are not properly coordinated and integrated, much time will be wasted, confusion will occur, and the planning process will flounder.

Selected Bibliography

Chen, Huey I. *Practical Program Evaluation: Assessing and Improving Planning, Implementation, and Effectiveness.* Thousand Oaks, CA: Sage, 2005.

Pawlak, Edward J., and Robert D. Vinter. *Design and Planning Programs for Nonprofit and Government Organizations.* San Francisco: John Wiley and Sons, 2004.

Sinofsky, Steven, and Marco Iansiti. *One Strategy: Organization, Planning, and Decision Making.* Hoboken, NJ: Wiley, 2010.

12.11 SELECTING CHANGE ISSUES FOR ADVOCACY

Social workers encounter many people who are experiencing a problem or social injustice caused by the policies, actions, or the inactions of a business, large corporation, or governmental agency. Not infrequently, the problem is one of discrimination based on social-economic class, race, ethnicity, gender, age, sexual orientation, or disabling conditions. When such a problem is affecting large numbers of people, perhaps even a whole neighborhood or community, it may be necessary to engage in political or social action in order to rectify the situation. The social worker can help the people impacted by these sorts of problems to clarify and express their concerns, to decide what kind of change is needed, and to mobilize and build coalitions to effect the desired change. Since the outcome of an advocacy action (e.g., a petition drive or demonstration) directed at a powerful organization or special interest group is always somewhat unpredictable and can have unwanted consequences, the issue to be tackled and the tactics to be used must be selected with great care. Si Kahn (1991, pp. 84–87), a well-known folk musician and social worker who has been successful in grassroots organizing, provides a helpful list of factors to consider when selecting an issue for social action:

- A good issue is winnable (i.e., it is reasonable to believe the desired change can occur).
- A good issue builds the organization or strengthens the group of concerned people.
- A good issue unites people.
- A good issue affects a lot of people.
- A good issue is strongly felt.
- A good issue is simple enough to be stated in one sentence.

Another important part of planning to address an issue is assessing the readiness of the community to change. These questions might prove helpful in examining the capacity of a community to engage in a change effort:

- Are efforts, programs, or policies that attempt to address this issue already in place?
- To what extent do community members know about these efforts and their effectiveness?
- How much do members of the community know about the extent of the problem and the consequences for the persons affected, as well as its impact on the community at large?
- Do elected officials and other influential members of the community support addressing this issue? If not, why?
- Is the prevailing attitude in the community toward this issue one of resignation or one of willingness to assume responsibility for addressing the matter?
- To what extent are people likely to commit time and other resources to bring about change in this situation?

As suggested by these questions, those people who select and define the issue to be addressed must grapple with the fundamental question of whether a particular change effort is feasible, realistic, and likely to succeed. The issue selected must be one that will motivate people and attract their involvement in the change process.

Once an issue has been selected and it has been determined that the community is ready to address it, the next critical step is to build a membership base. Typically, the effort to seek change is initiated by a few highly committed people, but unless the membership can build to a more substantial number, there is little hope for success. Politically, economically, and socially powerful people can best be influenced when the advocacy group's power comes, for example, from having members who might boycott a company or product, form a voting block, or conduct a public demonstration. In other words, the advocacy group must make the general public aware of the unwillingness of those in power to change. Of course, using these confrontational approaches may not be necessary if less polarizing tactics are successful, such as negotiating, collecting and analyzing data for a position paper, conducting a public education campaign, or using other techniques described in the following chapter of this book. However, knowing that an organization has the capacity to mobilize a large group of people for action will help to get the attention of powerful people and encourage them to consider solutions (perhaps requiring compromise from both sides) before a more conflictual situation develops. (For additional information on social change and advocacy, see Items 13.31, and 13.37.)

Selected Bibliography

Barlow, Andrew L., ed. *Collaborations for Social Justice: Professionals, Publics, and Policy Change.* Lanham: Rowen & Littlefield, 2007.

Kahn, Si. *Organizing: A Guide for Grassroots Leaders,* rev. ed. Washington, DC: NASW Press, 1991.

12.12 PROJECT PLANNING AND EVALUATION

Human services agencies are dynamic. They must constantly respond to changing needs and circumstances with new strategies (e.g., new services and methods) and special projects for accomplishing their organization's goals. The challenge is how to introduce such change with a minimum of disruption to the staff and the organization's day-to-day operations. This is possible only if those advocating for the innovation have carefully considered whether and why the proposed change is needed and how its introduction is to be scheduled.

STRATEGY SELECTION

Achieving a social agency's goals calls for the selection of the best possible strategies among the available alternatives. Those responsible for making these decisions should consider the following questions:

- Is this strategy consistent with the agency's overall mission and goals?
- Does the use of this strategy raise any legal or ethical concerns?
- Is this strategy likely to be successful in reducing or eliminating our problem or concern?
- Is this strategy an efficient use of agency or community resources?
- Are the actions called for by this strategy likely to have a lasting positive impact?
- Are there negative side effects that could result from using this strategy?

SCHEDULING

A variety of techniques have been developed to help schedule an activity such as the introduction of a new type of service into an agency. One scheduling tool called a **Gantt chart** provides a visual means of depicting the relationship between the activities required for a project and the timeframe

Activity	J F M A M J J A S O N D
1. Collect literature on parent-effectiveness training.	
2. Secure permission to initiate parent-effectiveness training group from supervisor.	
3. Interpret parent-effectiveness training in staff meeting.	
4. Request all workers in unit to nominate families for parent-effectiveness training.	
5. Send letters to nominated families, inviting them to participate and asking for preference on which night to meet.	
6. Set meeting times, reserve room, and notify families of first meeting.	
7. Make day-care plans for children of the participants.	
8. Prepare presentations and materials for parent-effectiveness training sessions.	
9. Hold 12 weekly meetings with participants.	
10. Assess the value of the sessions to the participants.	
11. Report results to supervisor and other staff members.	

FIGURE 12.4 **Sample Gantt Chart for Parent-Effectiveness Training**

for completing each. The activities are listed down the left column, and the periods of work on each activity, charted by month or week, are shown across the top of the page (see Figure 12.4). A Gantt chart is useful because it helps to identify the sequencing required for the entire project and helps to keep track of the completion dates for specific activities.

The Program Evaluation and Review Technique (**PERT chart**) is another useful scheduling tool. This chart is especially helpful for sorting out the proper sequencing of events and estimating the amount of time required to complete each activity or event. When developing a PERT chart, recognize that each *activity* will require staff time to complete. Thus, by adding up the days or hours devoted to the various activities, it is possible to estimate the cost in staff time to carry out the project. An *event* is an action taken by someone other than staff on a target date that affects the timeline of the project. By first identifying the dates on which various events are likely to be completed and then charting the activities that must occur to prepare for each event, it is possible to start with the intended completion date for the project and work backward to build the PERT chart. Figure 12.5 illustrates a section of a PERT chart developed for a client survey regarding the effectiveness of an agency's services.

TASK PLANNING

The final step in completing a special project is to identify and carry out the activities required for its implementation. This involves identifying the tasks to be completed, specifying the rationale for engaging in this activity, noting when it must be completed, who should be involved, and estimating the time required for completing the task.

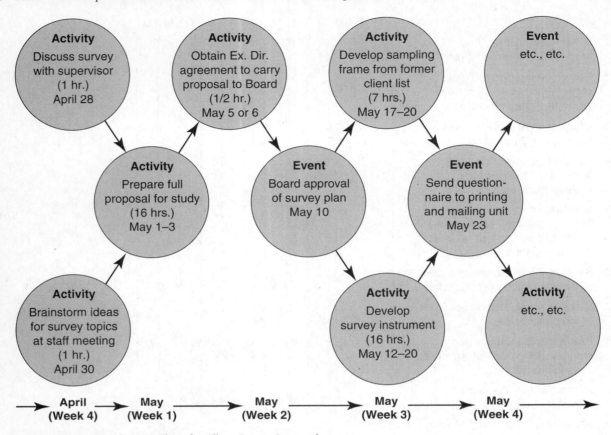

FIGURE 12.5 Sample PERT Chart for Client Survey Proposal

It is noteworthy that if you are seeking funding to support a project (see Item 13.36), you can provide evidence of careful planning (presented in Figures 12.4 and 12.5) to funding sources and demonstrate to them that you have a thoughtful and feasible plan for implementing the proposed project.

Selected Bibliography

Bender, Michael B. *A Manager's Guide to Project Management: Learn How to Apply Best Practices.* Upper Saddle River, NJ: FT Press, 2010.

Horine, Greg. *Absolute Beginner's Guide to Project Management.* Indianapolis, IN: Que, 2005.

Shore, Arnold S., and John M. Carfora. *A Guide to Proposal Development and Project Management: The Art of Funding Ideas.* Thousand Oaks, CA: Sage, 2011.

12.13   PLANNING A PRIMARY PREVENTION PROGRAM

Most social programs are initially created as a reaction to an existing problem and are designed to offer treatment or assistance to the people who experience this problem. Equally important are programs designed to prevent the problem from developing in the first place. Prevention efforts are desirable and logical, but the design of an effective prevention program is complex and difficult.

Although many view prevention as essentially different from intervention, it is useful to treat prevention as a type of intervention. **Primary prevention** consists of a set of actions intended to intervene and modify those conditions or situations that will, if not changed, lead to a problem. Thus, those engaged in planning a prevention effort must be able to identify the specific factors, conditions, and situations that cause or give rise to the problem and then engage in a set of actions and activities that will reduce or eliminate their impact.

Increasingly, primary prevention programs are built around ideas of risk and resiliency. In relation to children and youth, for example, considerable research identifies a high correlation between certain negative family, neighborhood, and community influences (risk factors) and the development of social problems such as delinquency, drug and alcohol abuse, school dropout, emotional disturbance, gang activity, and teen pregnancy. Among the corrosive influences that give rise to these problems are poverty, discrimination, lack of opportunity, family breakdown and dysfunction, feelings of low self-worth, easy access to drugs and alcohol, and poor schools. For reasons not well understood, some young people are more "resistant" to these influences than others. They have within their personalities, environment, and life experiences certain protective factors that shield them from the full force of negative influences. They are said to possess resiliency in that even when exposed to stress, trauma, and adversity, they do not develop serious problems.

The process of human development and adjustment includes many self-righting mechanisms that can compensate for trauma and life stressors. Some of these protective factors are found in the person's personality and behavior patterns (e.g., self-confidence, self-esteem, problem-solving skills), warm and supportive relationships within his or her family, the presence of caring people in the school or work environment, and/or supportive factors in one's ethnic, neighborhood, or community interactions. This is not meant to suggest that stages of human development do not exist or that what happens at one point in a person's development has no impact on what follows. Rather, it suggests that the developmental stages and the impact of significant events are more elastic than often assumed and it is possible for people to overcome serious problems that arise in their lives.

Efforts by social workers to prevent problems from occurring in the first place are helpful for both the resilient and not-so-resilient people. Thus social workers must be skilled at designing and implementing primary prevention programs. Following these general guidelines will help those planning to engage in primary prevention:

1. Enter the initial planning stage with caution and thoughtfulness; a poorly designed program is likely to fail. Early in the planning process, consult with those people who have experience in designing prevention programs and review the literature that reports efforts to address these target problems.

2. Clearly define and describe the problem or condition you are attempting to prevent. Without an operational definition of your target problem, you cannot design an effective program of prevention.

3. Identify the signs or indicators of the problem's existence and its current level of seriousness so that you can later measure the impact of your prevention effort. Without a way of measuring success, your program is not likely to attract funding and support for more than a brief demonstration period. Make sure that these indicators are understandable, measurable, and important to those who are paying for this prevention program. Consult the literature and people skilled at program evaluation (see Item 14.9) early in the planning process.

4. Recognize that any plan for prevention rests on the knowledge, beliefs, and assumptions made about when, why, and how this problem developed, as well as judgments about which individuals or groups are most likely to experience this problem. Thus, a critical step in planning is to formulate and articulate one's beliefs about the nature and causes of the problem to be prevented. This is a challenge because the social and behavioral sciences are seldom able to identify clear cause-and-effect relationships. Social problems are complex and a whole host of interrelated factors contribute to their development.

5. Once the factors that cause the problem have been identified, it is necessary to decide which contributing factors, if any, can be influenced and changed. Identify the specific risk and protective factors related to the problem you want to prevent. A *risk factor* is a condition, situation, or set of circumstances that increases the likelihood that a person will develop the problem. A *protective factor* is a condition or circumstance that reduces the chance that the problem will develop. The prevention program should be designed to weaken or reduce risk factors and, at the same time, strengthen or expand protective factors. As a general rule, a prevention program is most likely to be effective and efficient if it targets those at greatest risk of developing the problem.

6. Finally, determine how the necessary changes can best be accomplished. In many cases, important contributing causes (e.g., large-scale economic and societal forces) are beyond the reach of community-based prevention programs. A social worker may choose instead to advocate for change at the state or national levels. In other cases, the action plan would require intervention at the local level or at both the local and national levels.

Selected Bibliography

Cohen, Larry, Vivian Chavez, and Sana Chehimi, eds. *Prevention Is Primary: Strategies for Community Well-Being.* San Francisco: Jossey-Bass, 2007.

Gullotta, Thomas P., Gary M. Blau, and Jessica M. Ramos, eds. *Handbook of Child Behavioral Issues: Evidence-Based Approaches to Prevention and Treatment.* New York: Routledge/Taylor & Francis, 2008.

Intervention and Monitoring

The most visible phase in the change process is termed *intervention and monitoring*. Sometimes called the *action phase*, it is the time when the client, the social worker, and possibly others implement the plan that they believe will bring about the desired outcome. Each phase of the change process builds upon the prior ones. Thus, the success of the intervention depends on the validity of the conclusions reached during the prior phases, such as engaging with the client, data collection and assessment, and planning.

Because the intervention phase typically takes up most of the time and energy expended during a change process and because concrete actions by the social worker are part and parcel of an intervention, many intervention techniques have been developed for use in both direct and indirect practice. Often, the greatest challenge for the social worker, whether serving individuals, families, groups, organizations, or communities, is to select the most appropriate approach and techniques to facilitate change.

As the interventive activities unfold, the social worker must **monitor** what is happening and continuously examine the progress of the intervention. Depending on how it is proceeding, the social worker must decide if the intervention should be continued, modified, or possibly aborted, and a new plan negotiated. Monitoring differs from the evaluation phase, although both are discussed in Chapter 14, in that monitoring occurs while the intervention is happening, whereas evaluation takes place at the end of the change process, looking back to assess and measure overall progress.

A frequently overlooked element of monitoring is continuing to examine the client's situation for a period of time before completely terminating the professional relationship. Whenever change occurs, various systems are disrupted and there is often a tendency toward relapse or slipping back into a prior pattern. Thus, the social worker should determine if the observed change is more than a temporary accommodation to the interventive activities and ensure that the changes and improvements are firmly established and maintained as part of the ongoing functioning for the client and/or the relevant environment.

SECTION A

TECHNIQUES AND GUIDELINES FOR DIRECT PRACTICE

When working directly with individuals, families, and small groups, the social worker must adapt the intervention approach to the uniqueness of the situation and people involved and to support the clients as they strive to make needed changes. The worker, too, must constantly monitor the client's response to the change process and regularly assess progress toward the agreed-upon objectives.

Intervention Activities. As the social worker engages a client in a helping relationship and introduces the client to the process of change, he or she must select an appropriate practice framework to guide this process (see Chapter 6). In addition, the worker must choose a number of specific techniques and guidelines that are likely to facilitate and encourage the desired change. In Section A, an array of direct-service techniques and guidelines are presented. These are but a sampling. Social work literature, supervisors, colleagues, and workshops are sources of still others. None, however, is likely to be effective unless it is used by a caring and competent social worker.

Monitoring Activities. Monitoring involves keeping watch over the change process. To do this, the social worker must regularly interact in person or through other communication forms with the clients. The worker must be sensitive to how the change activities are affecting the client and also how other people or related social systems are being affected. If progress toward the agreed-upon objectives is lacking, the worker should suggest needed modifications in the intervention plan and possibly even cycle back to the beginning phases of the process to reexamine and clarify the issues being addressed and perhaps look for other solutions.

Whenever possible, the social worker should share the results of this monitoring with the clients. When clients are aware of the changes that are occurring, whether positive or negative, they are more likely to involve themselves in the change process and come up with useful modifications to the intervention plan. Most often, the monitoring results are fed back to the client in an informal manner. Increasingly, however, social workers are collecting empirical data about client change and feeding that information back to clients to assist them in understanding the effects of the services being provided. Some of the commonly used tools for organizing this data can be found in Chapter 14.

As explained in Chapter 7 and elsewhere in this book, the process of making change happen is often difficult and slow. When clients do not find a quick solution to their problems or when they slip back into an old and troubling pattern or habit, they may become discouraged and be tempted to give up. Change can be scary because it usually requires that clients do things differently, make difficult decisions, learn new skills, view their situation from a different angle, or place themselves in an unfamiliar social environment. When clients are hesitant about moving ahead, it can be helpful to remind them that when nothing changes, nothing changes. In other words, making a change requires doing something differently. Without that effort, nothing can possibly change.

13.1   PLANNING AN INTERVIEW

Just as there should be an overall intervention plan, there should be a plan for each contact or meeting with the client. One of the most common errors made by new workers is to go into a session without a clear purpose and plan. However, this plan must be tentative and flexible in order to respond to client concerns that could not be anticipated. The following questions can help the worker formulate such a plan:

1. What are the overall goals and objectives of the intervention with this client? How will my next session or contact relate to these goals and objectives?
2. What needs to be accomplished during the interview or meeting? What decisions need to be made during the session?
3. Should the next contact be a face-to-face or a telephone interview? Should it be a one-on-one, family, or group session? Who needs to be present?

4. Will other professionals and/or concerned individuals participate in this session (e.g., a family conference in a medical setting)? If so, what do they expect from the session?

5. How much time do I have to devote to the interview or meeting? How much time can the client and others devote to the session?

6. Where and when will the interview take place? What arrangements are necessary prior to the interview (e.g., scheduling a room, transportation, care for client's children)?

7. What techniques might be used during the session to complete important tasks and work toward intervention goals and objectives?

8. What factors related to the client's current emotional state (e.g., anger, fear, confusion, depression) must be considered in preparing for the session?

9. What factors related to the client's current physical functioning (e.g., mobility, pain, discomfort, hearing problems, effects of medication) need to be considered when preparing for the interview or meeting?

10. What factors related to the client's culture, values or religious beliefs, and social and family network need to be considered in preparing for the session?

11. What documentation of this contact is necessary for the agency record?

In every session, some time should be devoted to talking about client experiences that are positive and that help the client to feel good about himself or herself. This is important because all too often counseling or therapy sessions focus mostly on what is going wrong in the client's life. To counterbalance this attention to the negative, a social worker should create opportunities for clients to recognize and verbalize their successes and strengths.

Selected Bibliography

Murphy, Bianca, and Carolyn Dillon. *Interviewing in Action*, 3rd ed. Belmont, CA: Wadsworth, 2008.
O'Hare Thomas. *Essential Skills of Social Work Practice*. Chicago: Lyceum, 2008.

13.2   INFORMATION, ADVICE, AND PERSUASION

Change is difficult. Not infrequently, clients are ambivalent or fearful of taking the steps toward change. For example, a client may resist the idea of using a critically important service or program. In order to encourage action by the client, the worker may need to provide the client with information, possibly offer advice, and in some cases, persuade the client to move ahead.

As used here, the term *information* refers to providing a client with facts and observations so that he or she can make an informed decision or perform a task. The term *advice giving* refers to worker statements that recommend a certain decision or action. When using the skill of *persuasion*, the worker uses logical arguments to convince a client that a particular action is important and in his or her best interests.

When **providing information** to a client the social worker should keep these guidelines in mind:

1. Adapt your message to the client's educational background, intelligence, command of the language, and the like. Also, consider the client's state of mind. If, for example, the client is feeling anxious or overwhelmed, he or she may not comprehend or remember the information or instructions you provide. If the client is unable to grasp your message, seek his or her permission to also convey this information to family members or trusted friends so that they might help the client make use of the information.

2. Appreciate how easily a message can be misunderstood or forgotten. For example, the statement, "Fill out the form and take it to the person at the desk over there." could be confusing to someone who is not sure what the words "form," "it," "person," or "over there" are referring to. Always provide sufficient detail and description so there will be no mistake. Provide information or directions in a logical, step-by-step fashion. Complicated instructions (e.g., how to get to another agency), names, address, and phone numbers should be written out for the client.

3. Give the client time to think about what you are saying, and invite him or her to ask questions. Check to see that your message was understood. Say something like, "Now I want to make sure that I was clear in what I have been telling you. Would you please repeat to me what you heard me say?" Do not simply ask, "Do you understand?" All too often, people will answer that question in the affirmative, even when unsure or confused.

One of the common errors made by inexperienced social workers is to give advice when the client has not asked for it. This is an understandable error because often the worker knows how other individuals dealt with a certain problem and wants his or her client to benefit from those experiences. However, there are many pitfalls in **advice giving**, and the worker needs to be cautious. Follow these guidelines for advice giving:

1. Before offering advice to a client, reflect on how you feel when someone gives you advice. Often we feel annoyed or irritated, regardless of their good intentions. And very often, we do not follow their advice, even when we have requested it. When we do follow advice, it has usually been offered by someone we know well and trust completely.

Whether giving advice is appropriate depends largely on the purpose and nature of the worker–client interaction. If the purpose has to do with securing a needed service, making a referral, or case advocacy, advice giving may be important and necessary. When the worker is providing counseling or therapy, giving advice is only rarely appropriate.

2. Do not offer advice until you have determined that the client genuinely wants your opinions and suggestions. Test the client's receptivity by asking questions such as "Have you asked others for suggestions?" and "Would it help if I tell you what other people do in that situation?"

3. When you do give advice, present it in a way that says, in effect, "This is what I would do," or "This is what others have done." Explain the reasoning or logic behind the guidance you offer. Leave the responsibility for accepting or rejecting the advice with the client. And never give advice on a topic outside your area of training and expertise.

4. Consider the issue of legal liability if you advise a client and he or she later experiences a negative personal or financial consequence because of your recommendation. For example, beware of advising a client who asks questions such as, "Do you think I should get a divorce? Do you think I should quit my job and look for another? Do you think I should I cut back on my medicine?"

5. Be alert to the dangers of giving advice to a manipulative client, who may then hold you responsible if things do not turn out well (e.g., "I did what you said and it didn't work, so now it's your fault"). Also, be alert to the danger of encouraging dependency in a client who can and should take responsibility for decision making.

In some situations, it is necessary to use the skill of **persuasion** to encourage a fearful or hesitant client to take an important step. The worker should follow these guidelines:

- Present your suggested course of action through the use of personal stories that will engage and touch the client's feelings and emotions. When people do change their minds, it is usually in response to personal stories and observations, rather than in response to rational arguments or statistics.
- Use words, descriptions, and examples that the client can easily understand, given his or her background and life experiences.
- Present the suggested course of action after first identifying other options or positions that may appeal to the client. This demonstrates to the client that you understand the client's dilemma, hesitation, or ambivalence.

- Explain how the suggested action is compatible with the client's core values and goals and how not taking this particular action would be inconsistent with his or her personal goals and values.
- Describe the advantages of following the suggested action while also pointing out the negative consequences of not doing so.
- Describe how this course of action was helpful to others in similar circumstances.
- Offer an approach or plan that will allow the client to move ahead cautiously in small steps or phases so he or she can gradually try out or test the suggested course of action.
- Enlist the assistance of persons whom the client trusts and respects and ask them to encourage the client toward the suggested course of action.

Selected Bibliography

Cialdini, Rovert. *Influence: Science and Practice,* 5th ed. Boston: Allyn & Bacon, 2009.
Kotter, Jeffery. *A Brief Primer of Helping Skills.* Thousand Oaks, CA: Sage, 2007.
Shulman, Lawrence. *The Skills of Helping Individuals, Families, Groups, and Communities*, 6th ed. Belmont, CA: Brooks/Cole, 2009.

13.3   REINFORCEMENT AND RELATED BEHAVIORAL TECHNIQUES

The various behavioral techniques, drawn from learning theory, are some of the most powerful techniques available to the social worker when the purpose of an intervention is to help a client learn a new behavior or modify an existing one. They are used to either strengthen (increase) or weaken (decrease) a target behavior. The term **target behavior** refers to an operationally defined and observable behavior that is the focus of the intervention.

Reinforcement is any action that increases or strengthens a target behavior. There are two forms of reinforcement: positive and negative. **Positive reinforcement** involves adding, presenting, or giving something to the client (such as attention, objects of value, or privileges). A positive reinforcer is usually something that is desirable or pleasurable, but for some individuals, a painful event can become a positive reinforcer (e.g., self-mutilation, head banging). Thus, only by carefully observing its effects, can one determine for sure what is and is not a reinforcer for an individual. To do this, it is necessary to first establish a **baseline measurement** of the target behavior prior to the intervention or reinforcement.

There are two kinds of positive reinforcement: primary and secondary. **Primary reinforcers** are inherently rewarding and almost universally reinforcing. Examples include food, sex, and so on. **Secondary reinforcers** are learned, usually as a result of having been associated with primary reinforcers. Examples include money, toys, and privilege. Praise and attention are usually considered to be a form of secondary reinforcement but there is some evidence that they are universally reinforcing. As a general rule, what a person chooses to do when he or she does not have to do something else is a good indicator of what is reinforcing for that person (e.g., how a person spends extra time and money).

Both positive and negative reinforcements increase the frequency, intensity, or duration of a target behavior. **Negative reinforcement** involves subtracting or removing some condition that is aversive or unpleasant to the client, which then has the effect of increasing or strengthening the target behavior. Negative reinforcement is often confused with punishment, but they are not the same. Punishment weakens the target behavior, whereas negative reinforcement strengthens the behavior.

As a technique of behavior change, **punishment** involves the presentation of an unwanted or unpleasant stimulus (an event or action) that has the effect of suppressing a target behavior or reducing its strength. For ethical and legal reasons, the social worker must usually avoid the use of punishment. Most agencies and treatment programs prohibit the use of punishment for one or more of the following reasons:

- Often the results of punishment are short-term. When the threat of punishment ends, the target behavior may recur.
- A professional's use of punishment displays a poor model of behavior and might be imitated by the client.
- Punishment can become excessive when administered by a person who is angry or frustrated.
- Punishment may also suppress desirable behavior and make the client afraid to respond even in normal and functional ways.
- The use of physical punishment may make the worker vulnerable to a civil lawsuit or criminal charges (e.g., abuse, assault).

A behavior that is not reinforced tends to decrease in frequency, duration, or intensity. The term *extinction* describes the planned withdrawal of reinforcements so as to eliminate or weaken an unwanted behavior.

There are two basic **reinforcement schedules**: continuous and intermittent. *Continuous reinforcement* presents the client with a reinforcer each time the desired target behavior occurs. In *intermittent reinforcement*, the target behavior is only periodically rewarded. Continuous reinforcement is often used in the first stages of a program designed to teach a new behavior because it promotes faster learning than intermittent reinforcement. However, a behavior that has been continuously reinforced will often weaken or disappear when no longer reinforced. To make the newly learned behavior resistant to extinction, the initial continuous reinforcement should be replaced by intermittent reinforcement. A behavior that is maintained by *random reinforcement* (e.g., slot machine, bingo, fishing) or learned during a time of high emotion or personal crisis is highly resistant to change and difficult to extinguish.

A useful behavioral technique is to ignore an unwanted target behavior while at the same time, reinforcing an incompatible desired behavior. This is called **differential reinforcement**. When one behavior is described as incompatible with another, it means that a person cannot perform both behaviors concurrently. For example, a child cannot play basketball and watch TV at the same time.

The techniques of chaining, prompting, fading, and shaping are useful when the objective is to help a client learn a new behavior. These techniques are frequently used in training programs for people who are mentally handicapped, in speech therapy, and in certain aspects of physical rehabilitation. **Chaining** refers to a procedure that breaks down a complex behavior (e.g., dressing) into many separate steps and teaching only one step at a time. As a step is learned, it is "chained," or linked, to the ones already learned. The number of steps needed to teach a particular behavior will depend on the complexity of the behavior and the capacity of the client. There are two types of chaining: forward and backward. In *forward chaining*, the first step in a chain is taught first. For example, in teaching a man to put on his trousers, he would first be taught how to pick up and hold his pants. A second step might be to put his left leg into the pant leg. All subsequent steps are taught in the order of a usual or natural sequence as determined by having observed people perform the behavior (i.e., putting on pants).

In *backward chaining*, the last step in the chain is taught first. Thus, all the prior steps in the sequence would be done for the client except the one being taught. For example, when teaching a man to put on his pants, the first step to be taught would be to button the pants around his waist. The advantage of backward chaining is that the last step in the chain is always the one that is reinforced. Thus, the client is always reinforced at the very end of the behavior chain (e.g., when he has finished putting on his pants) and this prevents the client from getting stuck on a step before learning the total sequence. For some self-help skills, such as hand and face washing, backward chaining is not feasible.

The term **prompting** describes any form of assistance given by the trainer to help or guide the client in performing the target behavior. A prompt may be a verbal cue or instruction, a gesture or other nonverbal cue, or physically moving the client through the behavior. Prompting should be used only when necessary.

Fading is the process of gradually withdrawing prompts and decreasing the frequency of reinforcement as the client begins to learn the desired behavior. In the first steps of a training program, the trainer will use continuous reinforcement and frequent prompting to help establish the new behavior. Later, when the client regularly performs the behavior, the trainer will gradually fade out or decrease the frequency of reinforcement and prompting.

Shaping is a technique of building up a new behavior by reinforcing closer and closer approximations of the desired response. For example, a speech therapist teaching a child to say "cookie" may reward the child when he or she says "gowk." Perhaps later, the child is reinforced for saying "gook-koo" and still later, "gookie." Finally, after many weeks of reinforcing the child for closer and closer approximations of the desired sound, the child has learned to say "cookie."

Much of what we learn, especially social behavior, is learned by observing others and subsequently imitating that behavior. This learning process is termed **modeling**. Both functional and dysfunctional behaviors can be learned through modeling. A social worker can enhance a client's learning of functional behaviors by keeping several principles in mind:

- Individual A is most likely to imitate the behavior of individual B (the model) if he or she views B as having a valued status (e.g., power, prestige, attractiveness) and if he or she observes B being rewarded for the behavior.
- In addition, individual A must in some way identify with B and feel similar. If A views B as being significantly different (e.g., in age, education, social economic class), individual A may conclude there is no chance he or she could actually perform the behavior and/or that there is little chance that the behavior would be rewarded.
- Individual A is most likely to learn B's behavior if he or she has an opportunity to perform or practice the behavior soon after observing it and is then rewarded for the behavior.

Under ordinary conditions, licensed foster parents and child care staff working in hospitals, treatment centers, and group homes are prohibited from using any form of physical punishment. The procedure termed **time out** is an alternative to physical discipline. Consider this set of instructions given to a foster parent who is learning methods of nonviolent child care for use with a 7-year-old, male, foster child:

1. Find an area in your home that can be used for time out. If the child (Johnny) kicks, throws things, or has tantrums, be sure to choose an area that has no breakable or dangerous objects. You might use his bedroom or other quiet area that is well lighted and ventilated.

2. Identify the undesirable or unacceptable behaviors that will result in time out (i.e., clearly define the target behavior). For example, you may decide to use time out whenever Johnny hits you or another child.

3. Each time a target behavior occurs, use the time-out procedure immediately. Walk up to the child, explain what rule was broken, and tell him what must now happen—for example, "Johnny, whenever you hit your sister, you must go to time out." Accompany the child to the time-out area; do not look at or talk to him on the way. If he resists, carry him there as quickly as possible.

4. Leave him in the time-out area for a predetermined period of time. As a rule of thumb, use the formula of one minute per year of the child's age. At the end of the time-out period or when he is quiet and behaving well, go to the door and ask if he is ready to come out and behave correctly. For example, if he had thrown toys as "Johnny, are you ready to come out and put your toys away?" If he answers yes, have him come out and correct the earlier behavior. Reinforce the correct behavior with praise. For example, say, "I like the way you are picking up your toys."

If he does not answer yes or screams, cries, throws a tantrum, or displays other undesirable behavior, walk away from the door and wait until he is again quiet and behaving appropriately. Then go back and repeat the question.

5. At first, you may have to question him several times before he is ready to come out and correct the bad behavior. Do not be discouraged—just continue to follow these rules.

6. Arrange a special activity, privilege, or treat at the end of each day or half day that he did not have to be taken to the time-out and tell him that the reward is for his good behavior.

Selected Bibliography

Hersen, Michel, ed. *Encyclopedia of Behavior Modification and Cognitive Behavior Therapy* (three volumes). Thousand Oaks, CA: Sage Publications, 2005.

Martin, Gary, and Joseph Pear. *Behavior Modification*, 8th ed. Boston: Allyn & Bacon, 2007.

Sundel, Martin, and Sandra Sundel. *Behavior Change in the Human Services*, 5th ed. Thousand Oaks, CA: Sage, 2005.

13.4   BEHAVIORAL REHEARSAL

The technique of **behavioral rehearsal** is designed to teach a client how to handle a specific interpersonal exchange or a situation. Essentially, it is a form of role-playing that makes use of modeling and coaching as teaching tools. Like other forms of role-play, behavioral rehearsal provides the client with an opportunity to try out and practice new behaviors in a safe and accepting environment. The technique can be used, for example, to prepare a client for a job interview (e.g., the social worker takes the role of the employer and conducts a simulated job interview). Whether used during a one-to-one interview or during a group session, the steps are basically the same:

1. The client identifies the problem situation with which he or she wants help. The client is asked to demonstrate how he or she would usually behave in the situation.

2. The worker (and/or group members) makes suggestions on how the client might handle the situation more effectively.

3. The client is given an opportunity to provide additional information about the problem or concern and to ask the worker (or group members) to further explain or describe their suggestions.

4. A role-play is used to demonstrate for the client the behavioral changes being suggested. The worker (or group member) will usually take the role of the client.

5. After the role-play, the worker (or members) identifies the positive aspects of the performance and possibly offers additional suggestions. The role-play may be repeated to further illustrate the preferred way of behaving.

6. When the client understands how he or she ought to behave and is ready to do a role-play, he or she rehearses the behavior until satisfied with the performance. Homework outside the session can be used to further reinforce the new behavior.

A possible limitation of behavioral rehearsal is that the client may perform well in the presence of the social worker but may not be able to generalize this behavior to the real world. Sometimes the real situation poses problems that cannot be anticipated during a practice session.

Selected Bibliography

Rose, Sheldon. *Group Therapy: A Behavioral Approach*. Englewood Cliffs, NJ: Prentice Hall, 1977.

Spiegler, Michael, and David Guevremont. *Contemporary Behavior Therapy*, 4th ed. Belmont, CA: Wadsworth, 2003.

13.5   BEHAVIORAL CONTRACTING

Essentially, a **behavioral contract** is an agreement, usually written, that is designed to encourage a behavior change. It usually involves an exchange of rewards or positive reinforcements between two or more persons. There are two forms of behavioral contracting. In a **contingency contract**, one person (often a professional) arranges for a positive consequence to follow the performance of a target behavior by another person (such as a client). For example, a group home manager may agree to take a resident to a movie, if the resident cleans his room five days in a row. By contrast, a **reciprocal behavior contract** is an agreement between the members of a dyad (e.g., husband-wife), in which each agrees to reward the other for the performance of a desired behavior. For example, the husband agrees to take his wife to a movie of her choice if she will take the car to the repair shop, and she agrees to cook his favorite meal if he will clean the house.

Thus, we see that a behavioral contract might be negotiated between the social worker and the client or the worker may help two or more clients (e.g., a parent and adolescent) negotiate a contract. Any behavior can become the focus of a contract so long as it is observable and can be described clearly. When helping to formulate a reciprocal behavioral contract to be used by a couple or family, the following guidelines are important:

1. Assist all parties to select a change (or target behavior) that will provide some immediate reward or relief from their problems. Make sure that each person stands to receive a desired payoff for participating and completing the assigned tasks.
2. Select tasks or behaviors that everyone agrees are worthwhile and possible, given the current circumstances.
3. Allow for approximations. It should be possible to observe even a partial success and a person's genuine effort to complete the task.
4. Set up a simple plan for recording performance and the exchange of rewards.
5. Before the participants leave the negotiation session, ask each one to describe and explain the contract and the tasks he or she has agreed to carry out. Make sure there is no misunderstanding.

Variations of the contingency behavioral contracting, often called point systems or token economies, are frequently used in special educational settings and residential treatment facilities. Under such systems, a client earns points or tokens for performing desired behaviors (e.g., completing homework, cleaning one's room) and can then use the tokens to "purchase" privileges or valued objects such as snacks, movie tickets, and so on.

When using a contingency contract, the reinforcement (rewards) for compliance, along with any adverse consequences for noncompliance, should be clearly described and understood by all. Whenever noncompliance could have serious repercussions for a client, the contract should be in writing. In other situations, a verbal agreement may suffice.

Selected Bibliography

DeRisi, William, and George Butz. *Writing Behavioral Contracts*. Champaign, IL: Research Press, 1975.
Gambrill, Eileen. *Social Work Practice*, 2nd ed. New York: Oxford University Press, 2006.
Stuart, Richard. *Helping Couples Change: A Social Learning Approach to Marital Therapy*. New York: Guilford, 1980.

13.6   ROLE REVERSAL

When people begin to understand one another's point of view their relationship changes, usually for the better. When applying the technique known as **role reversal**, the social worker asks a client to temporarily adopt and act out the perspective or vantage point of another person in order to better understand that person. This technique also allows the individual to observe and hear his or her own attitudes and messages, as interpreted and dramatized by another. The technique is especially useful during marriage and family counseling when, for example, a husband and wife or a parent and child are in conflict and one or both have little awareness of how the other is thinking or feeling. The best time to use role reversal is when the communication between the two individuals has reached an impasse.

The worker might initiate the role-reversal by saying something like, "Joe and Susan, would you be willing to try something? I would like you to reverse roles to see how it feels being the other person in your relationship." The two people are then asked to switch chairs (if the clients do not change chairs, they often become confused as to which role they are playing). The worker might explain, "Joe, when in this chair, you are yourself. In that chair, you are Susan."

The social worker might get the role reversed discussion going by focusing attention on a particular line of repetitious or contentious dialogue, for example: "Joe, I want you to start playing Susan's part in this conflict and begin with the line, "Joe, you don't realize or care about how much work I have to do." And Susan, in the role of Joe, I want you to respond by saying how those words make you feel. As their discussion unfolds, the worker uses various interviewing techniques to encourage each to express the thoughts and feelings of the other, as they imagine it. Given the nature of this technique, the clients should be instructed to approach their effort at role reversal with a spirit of lightheartedness and humor so that they can, hopefully, laugh at themselves and their situation.

After a few minutes of role reversal, the worker asks each person to return to his or her own chair. The content of what was said during the reversal is then discussed so each will better understand the other's perspectives and feelings regarding the issue causing the conflict. The role reversal technique may be assigned as homework, asking, for example, the couple or family members to take time to experiment with role reversals prior to the next session.

Selected Bibliography

Brock, Gregory, and Charles Barnard. *Procedures in Marriage and Family Therapy*, 4th ed. Boston: Allyn & Bacon, 2009.

Sprafkin, Robert, N., Jane Gershaw, and Arnold Goldstein. *Social Skills for Mental Health*. Boston: Allyn & Bacon, 1993.

13.7   MANAGING SELF-TALK

The term **self-talk** refers to what we tell ourselves about ourselves and about our situation. What we say to ourselves reflects our unique interpretations of what we have experienced. Consider, for example, how you might feel about yourself if you really believed the following statements: "I will be alone and rejected by everyone unless I meet all of their expectations." "Worthwhile people always give a 110 percent effort to everything they do." "I cannot be happy until I have lost 50 pounds."

If a person habitually thinks about his or her life experiences in distorting and irrational ways, he or she generates inner turmoil and also creates problems in interpersonal relationships. Negative self-talk evokes emotional reactions, which can, in turn, draw us into self-damaging and self-limiting behaviors. Here are some common types of distortions:

> *All or nothing.* We evaluate experiences in the extremes of either all right or all wrong, all bad or all good; there is no middle ground (e.g., we conclude that a single mistake proves we are a complete failure).

Jumping to conclusions. We draw conclusions on the basis of little or no evidence (e.g., we conclude that something is undesirable or unworkable even before we have gathered information).

Selective attention. We pay attention only to those facts that support our preconceived ideas; we dismiss facts that point to different conclusions.

Catastrophizing. We anticipate the worst possible outcome; we always expect something bad to happen.

Magnification of failure. We exaggerate the meaning or importance of a setback or mistake (e.g., we may have ten successes and one failure, but we focus only on the one failure).

Minimization of success. We downplay a positive experience or success (e.g., we attribute our success to dumb luck).

Negative beliefs about self, others, and the world. We hold tightly to the belief that everything and everybody is bad, hopeless, and getting worse.

Personalization. We assume every problem is caused by our own inadequacy. We take responsibility for things over which we have little or no control.

External locus of control. We believe that whatever happens to us is caused by external factors beyond our influence.

By helping a client learn to think more critically, the social worker can help him or her control troublesome emotions and behave more effectively. This is, of course, much more difficult than it sounds. Patterns of thinking are habits; they are not easily changed and are themselves a barrier to change. A five-step approach can help a client modify distortions and control a tendency toward negative self-talk. Ask the client to do the following:

1. Identify what you are feeling and thinking right now.
2. Get in touch with your self-talk. Pay attention to extremes in your thinking as suggested by your use of words, such as *never, always, everybody, completely*, and so on.
3. Examine the facts and objective reality of your situation. Once the facts have been identified, relax, take a deep breath, and repeat them out loud three times.
4. Notice that, when you hold to the facts and avoid using inaccurate and extreme words, you begin to feel differently and more hopeful.
5. Keeping the facts of your problem situation in mind, what you can do about it?

This five-step method is illustrated below in the dialogue between a social worker and a college student who has just learned that he failed a math exam:

CLIENT: I cannot believe I am so stupid. I had a B average in math and I got an F on the last test. I might as well leave school and get a job as a dishwasher. I am a complete failure. I don't deserve to be in school.

WORKER: Wait a minute! You have said before that you wanted to learn how to stop putting yourself down. Let's try something. Start by telling me again what you are feeling and thinking right now.

CLIENT: Well, I just can't pass math tests. I'm stupid. I am embarrassed. I hate myself. I am never going to get through college. My parents are going to kill me. This is the worst possible thing that could have happened. My future is down the drain. Everything is just awful and ruined.

WORKER: Let's take a look at that kind of negative self-talk. Try to recognize what you are saying to yourself; notice your extreme language. Let's take a look at the way things are in reality. Is it true you cannot pass math tests?

CLIENT: Well, not really. I passed all of them before this one and I still have a B average in college.

WORKER: Are your parents really going to kill you?

CLIENT: Well, of course not, but they will be disappointed.

WORKER: Is failing a test really the worst possible thing that could happen to you?

CLIENT: Well, no, but it seems awful right now.

WORKER: Does failing this test really mean you have no future?

CLIENT: Well, I still have a future. I know what you are saying and I agree that I am over-reacting. But I don't know how to put a lid on those negative thoughts and feelings.

WORKER: Do this for me. Repeat the truth—the reality, the facts—of your situation, which is as follows: I flunked one math test. My parents will be unhappy. I have a B average in college. I can remain in college. My life is not over.

CLIENT: (repeats above)

WORKER: Now take a couple of deep breaths and relax. Now say that again, three times.

CLIENT: (client follows instruction)

WORKER: How do you feel when you change your self-talk?

CLIENT: Well, I guess it isn't as bad as I thought. I feel less upset than before.

WORKER: Our emotions react to what we tell ourselves. If your self-talk is distorted, your emotions are going to be more extreme and more negative than they need to be. You can use this technique yourself when your mind starts to race and your feelings start to get out of control. Certainly, your situation is not as bad as it seemed when you were telling yourself those awful things. But you still have to make plans on how to prepare for your next math test. Now let's talk about that.

Once a client is able to describe his or her pattern of maladaptive self-talk, the cognitive restructuring techniques of self-instruction, visualization, and journaling may prove helpful. **Self-instruction** (also termed *positive self-talk, covert speech,* and *countering*) refers to a set of statements that are repeated by the client on a regular basis, perhaps three times a day, and especially in times of distress. Often, they are said aloud in front of a mirror. These messages are to be factual and incompatible with the client's habitual negative self-talk. They are meant to counteract the dysfunctional pattern and foster self-acceptance and self-confidence. The use of this technique rests on the observation that when an individual actively argues against his or her own irrational thoughts, those thoughts are weakened.

This technique should not be confused with positive thinking that is blindly optimistic and may gloss over important realities and allow self-deception. Rather, self-instruction requires that the messages be truthful and realistic, given the client's abilities and situation. The messages should be as specific as possible and tied directly to the client's concerns. Self-instruction works, but it works slowly. Consistent practice for a year or more may be needed to make a significant and lasting change. Consider, for example, the woman who avoids taking a better job because her dysfunctional self-talk tells her: "If I make a mistake on the job, people will think I am stupid and will criticize me." This woman might be taught to repeat the following message: "Each time I make a mistake on the job, I have an opportunity to learn something very important. If someone criticizes me, he or she is either right or wrong. If the person is right, I have learned something. If he or she is wrong, I can ignore it."

In using the technique of **visualization**, the client is taught to prepare for a future worry-causing event by repeatedly imagining this event and mentally rehearsing the steps necessary to handle it successfully. It is important that the images are ones of activity, vividness, and detail. For many individuals, visualization reduces their fear of the event and builds confidence in their ability to do what they know they must do. For example, a client might prepare for a frightening job interview by visualizing being asked hard questions and giving clear and appropriate answers. This might need to be practiced dozens of times before the interview.

The technique of **journaling** asks the client to keep a daily log of significant thoughts and feelings. It is especially useful for clients who like to write. It helps them recognize recurring themes and patterns in the meaning they assign to their experiences. As a way of structuring this homework, the client might be instructed to respond in writing to specific questions, such as: What have I learned about myself today? What feelings and moods did I experience? What thoughts gave rise to these feelings? What were the two most significant events of the day? What thoughts and feelings did I have in relation to these events? What personal strengths did I observe in myself today? What troublesome thoughts do I need to work on and what is my plan for doing so? How will my plan build on my personal strengths?

Selected Bibliography

Berlin, Sharon. *Clinical Social Work Practice*. New York: Oxford University Press, 2001.
Corcoran, Jacqueline. *Cognitive Behavioral Methods: A Workbook for Social Workers*. Boston: Allyn & Bacon, 2006.
McMullin, Rian. *New Handbook of Cognitive Therapy Techniques*. New York: W. W. Norton, 2000.

13.8   BUILDING SELF-ESTEEM

Our need to see ourselves as worthwhile is a powerful motivating force. While food, water, and shelter are critical to our physical survival, our psychological and spiritual survival depends on whether we find value and worth in ourselves. We need to know that we are worth something, that we mean something to other people, that our existence makes a difference, and that we are a person worth knowing and caring about.

The term **self-esteem** refers to one's belief about his or her worth as a person. Individuals who do not value or respect themselves struggle with a multitude of self-imposed limitations. Often, they lack self-confidence, engage in self-defeating and destructive behaviors, and are vulnerable to exploitation and abuse by others. They may spend an inordinate amount of time dwelling upon the situations that cause them to feel devalued and rejected and those that make them feel worthwhile. By following these guidelines the social worker can help the client build self-esteem:

1. Help clients understand that feelings of personal worth (i.e., our level of self-esteem) are rooted in how we think about ourselves and how we compare ourselves to others. These self-evaluations are highly subjective, not always accurate, and not necessarily consistent with the judgments and evaluations of people who know us. Consequently, person "A" who is violent, narcissistic, and dishonest, may have high self-esteem, whereas person "B" who others view as a genuinely good and wonderful human being may have low self-esteem.

2. Self-esteem cannot be taught but it can be learned from one's experiences. Certain types of experiences can provide learning opportunities that cause the client to reconsider and reevaluate his or her beliefs about self. Seek to place or draw the clients into situations or environments that create some cognitive dissonance and compel the client to reconcile a seemly positive outcome or experience with their negative opinions and expectations of self. For example, if an individual participates in a support group, personal growth group, or faith community they will usually have the experience of being accepted and respected by others. When that occurs they may reexamine their beliefs about themselves and hopefully conclude that they are appreciated and worthwhile. In a similar vain, taking a job, changing occupations, returning to school, becoming a volunteer, or forming new friendships can set in motion such self-examination. Needless to say, persons with low self-esteem are often fearful of new experiences. They will need encouragement and help to understand that to get something you have never had, you must do something you have never done.

3. People with low self-esteem often have a habit of comparing themselves with the best in the field (e.g., with the best musician, the best student, the most attractive person). Given that mode of thinking they will always suffer by comparison, and this reinforces their beliefs that they are not as good or as worthwhile as other people. Help clients recognize this self-defeating pattern of thinking. Help them to see that another person may indeed be outstanding in a certain area but will not be outstanding in all areas because all people have strengths and limitations. Self-awareness and self-acceptance are the building blocks of self-esteem.

4. As a way of helping the clients to examine their beliefs and assumptions about themselves, encourage them to imagine specific conditions or circumstances that—if they existed—would elevate their feelings of self-worth. Then engage them in an examination of the values implicit in those conditions and whether these particular values are suitable criteria for measuring the worth of a person. For example, many people believe they would be happy and would feel good about themselves if only they were attractive, popular, rich, or famous. A critical look at those assumptions reveals that they are the shallow values of a society obsessed with physical appearance, possessions, and self-aggrandizement. There are numerous examples of individuals who have these things and still lack happiness, contentment, self-worth, and a sense of purpose in life. Other values such as generosity, compassion, honesty, and kindness are more authentic and lasting measures of personal worth. Help clients to understand that their own value is not dependent on what others may think is important.

5. Self-esteem grows from experiences of success and achievement. Thus, encourage clients to establish realistic and achievable objectives for themselves. Assist them in working toward those objectives and call to their attention their successes (see Item 12.4).

6. Encourage and assist clients to develop a sense of purpose and meaning and a healthy spirituality. Self-worth grows from knowing that you are living your life in accord with your ideals and moral and ethical standards. For this reason, when clients are facing difficult decisions they should be encouraged to do what they know is right so they can maintain a sense of personal integrity (see Item 15.17).

7. For some clients, low self-esteem is tied to one or more significant separations and loss experiences (e.g., separation from bio-family, loss of one's childhood through sexual abuse, loss of respect from valued others). Help these clients recognize and grieve for what they have lost (see Item 15.16).

Selected Bibliography

Kernis, Michael. *Self-Esteem: A Sourcebook on Current Perspectives.* New York: Psychology Press, 2006.
McKay, Matthew. *Self-Esteem Companion.* Oakland, CA: New Harbinger, 2005.
Mruk, Christopher. *Self-Esteem: Research, Theory, and Practice*, 3rd ed. New York: Springer, 2006.

13.9 CONFRONTATION AND CHALLENGE

A *challenge* or a *confrontation* refers to a gentle and respectful effort to help the client recognize that he or she is engaged in a self-deception, rationalization, or evasion that is a barrier to more effective functioning. This technique invites the client to take a careful look at a negative or self-defeating attitude or behavior such as the client's refusal to acknowledge an obvious problem. Or it may point out a discrepancy between the client's stated moral principles and how the client is actually behaving. Here is an example:

CLIENT: I should be more involved with Jason, my son. His mother, my ex-wife, says that Jason feels like I don't care about him. I feel bad about that but I just don't have the time. I have a new wife and my job is very demanding.

SOCIAL WORKER: What do you mean by the word "involved"?

CLIENT: Oh, you know, I should spend time with Jason—take him to a ballgame, that sort of stuff.

SOCIAL WORKER: I recall you saying this very same thing several times over the past few weeks. You say that you should be more involved with Jason, but it is obvious that you are not doing what you think you should be doing. I am aware that you want to make your new marriage work and that you are a responsible employee. But I have the feeling that deep down you have decided to abandon your role of father. What is your honest reaction to what I am saying to you?

There is always some risk in using a confrontation. Clients who are highly defensive will usually reject the message by further rationalizing or verbally attacking the worker. If used with a client who is depressed or has low self-esteem, the client may feel criticized and withdraw from the relationship. Several guidelines need to be considered in the use of this technique:

1. For a challenge to be effective, it must be used at a point when the client appears open and ready to hear and consider the message. Moreover, someone who is trusted and respected by the client must offer it. Once a challenge or confrontation is offered, it is the responsibility of the worker to help the client understand it accurately and consider the validity of the message.

2. Do not confront or challenge a client when you are feeling angry or exasperated with the client. Unless you have a genuine concern and empathy for the client, a confrontation will be little more than an expression of your own frustration with a difficult client.

3. Your message must be presented in a nonjudgmental manner. Use an I-statement format throughout the challenge (see Item 8.2). Couple the confrontational message with positive observations about the client. In other words, present the message within a context of recognizing and supporting the client's strengths.

4. Present the facts or observations on which your message is based and make sure the client understands the distinction between your facts and the inferences you have drawn from those facts. An observation can be stated directly: "I observed you hitting . . ." or "Last Friday you specifically told me that . . ." or "I have received four reports that describe your fights in school." An inference should be stated tentatively: "Because of what I have been told, I have concluded that . . ." or "Unless you can offer another explanation, I have to assume that. . . ."

Selected Bibliography

Cormier, Sherry, Paula Nurius, and Cynthia Osborn. *Interviewing and Change Strategies for Helpers*, 6th ed. Belmont, CA: Brooks/Cole, 2009.

Egan, Gerard. *The Skilled Helper*, 8th ed. Belmont, CA: Brooks/Cole, 2007.

Hepworth, Dean, Ronald Rooney, Glenda Dewberry Rooney, Kim Strom-Gottfried, and Jo Ann Larsen. *Direct Social Work Practice*, 7th ed. Belmont, CA: Brooks/Cole, 2006.

13.10   REFRAMING

The technique known as **reframing** (also called *relabeling*) is used to help a client modify the negative meaning he or she has assigned to a particular event, behavior, or life experience. Reframing recognizes the wisdom of the first-century philosopher Epictetus, who said, "It is not the things themselves which trouble us, but the opinions we have about these things." The following example illustrates a social worker's use of reframing:

FOSTER PARENT: I get so upset with Anna [foster child]. So often, she blows up and gets angry with me. But I haven't done anything to make her angry!

SOCIAL WORKER: I can understand how frustrating and disappointing that you must feel. As you know, Anna is an angry child because of the severe abuse she experienced long before she met you. But, in one way of looking at it, Anna is paying you a big compliment. When she expresses her anger in your presence she is demonstrating that she feels safe with you and trusts that you will not retaliate and hurt her as others have in the past. If she did not feel safe with you, she would be too afraid to express her anger.

Another example of reframing is illustrated in the following statement to a 35-year-old client who has experienced a lifetime of physical and emotional pain related to a disabling car accident and having been physically and sexually abused as a child.

SOCIAL WORKER: I have been thinking about your life experiences. Despite all you have been through, here you are at age 35 still alive and still struggling to do the best you can. In the school of life, you have received a very expensive and a good education— much better than what a Harvard or a Yale could provide. What I am saying is that because of your painful experiences you have learned things about people and about life that most people never learn, no matter how long they go to school. Your tuition has been paid in the form of personal pain and suffering but in return, you have acquired great wisdom.

An alternative to the social worker providing the new or a reframed perspective is to encourage the client to brainstorm several new and different interpretations. A client will usually agree that five people will most likely tell five somewhat different stories about the same experience. Using that agreement as a foundation, the worker can encourage the client to come up with additional stories (interpretations) about the life experience being discussed. After thinking up several alternative perceptions, the client will usually soften his or her original position and acknowledge that there may indeed be a different and more positive way to interpret the situation.

Still another use of reframing is to help a client redefine his or her troublesome behavior as a basically positive action or a motive taken to an extreme. In other words, a problem is viewed as a client strength spinning out of control. For example, consider the young mother who has injured her 3-year-old child as a result of harsh spanking as discipline. The discussion of her abusive behavior might be approached by first recognizing that the mother wants to teach the child proper behavior but in this situation her motive to be a good mother jumped off the track or went spinning out of control. When the worker redefines the client's problem as a good motive that has gone wild the client feels less defensive, less accused, and more hopeful. From the client's perspective it seems easier to try to tone down or get control of a personal strength than to get rid of a problem behavior. The words that a helper uses do make a difference.

Selected Bibliography

Berg, Insoo Kim. *Family Based Services*. New York: W. W. Norton, 1994.
Ronen, Tammie, and Arthur Freeman, eds. *Cognitive Behavior Therapy in Clinical Social Work Practice*. New York: Springer, 2006.
Schuyler, Dean. *Cognitive Therapy*. New York: W. W. Norton, 2003.

13.11   HELPING CLIENTS MAKE DIFFICULT DECISIONS

Decision making can be especially difficult for clients who face multiple problems and feel overwhelmed. All too often, they tend to either avoid making decisions or make decisions impulsively without adequately considering the ramifications of each option. To facilitate decision making by clients, the social worker can use some relatively simple ideas and tools.

1. Help clients to consider their usual approach to decision making. Encourage clients to think about significant decisions they have made previously and describe how they usually go about making decisions. Do they make decisions mostly on the basis of feelings or mostly on the basis of logic and reasoning? Do they tend to act impulsively? Do they consult with others or do they resist the advice offered by others? Do they often regret the decisions they have made? Do they avoid making a decision until forced to do so by circumstances or a deadline? Also, encourage the clients to think about personality factors that influence decisions. Examples might be a strong desire to please others, an intense fear of making a mistake, or a lack of self-confidence. Once the client has gained some awareness of the factors that influence his or her decisions, encourage the client to consider how he or she can capitalize on the strengths and avoid being pushed and pulled by negative factors.

2. Guide the client through a discussion that will help them to make a clear distinction between the problem to be solved and the options available for addressing that problem. In other words, help the client **distinguish the means from the end**. Consider, for example, the client who is struggling to figure out how to get money to buy a car because he or she needs to get to and from a new job. In this case, the client has confused means and ends. The client's problem is a lack of transportation, not the lack of a car. Owning a car is only one means of transportation; others might include public transportation, walking, bicycling, or paying for a ride with another employee.

Creating a simple listing of the various means of reaching a desired end may help the client keep these ideas separate. For example, consider a young, single mother who had approached a family services agency and requested the foster care placement for her child because she could not care for her child while holding a job. With some encouragement she was able distinguish between the problem and the means of solving the problem and to brainstorm four other possible solutions: licensed day care, paid baby sitter, informal exchange of baby sitting with friend, change jobs, and change hours of work. As can be seen in this example, once the client's presenting problem was redefined as the need for child care, rather than a need for placement, several new options emerged.

3. Another tool, the **decision-making matrix**, can help a client think through the pros and cons of various options and arrive at a decision. The matrix has three columns: (1) Alternative, (2) Cost, and (3) Benefit. In the *alternative* column, the client lists the options being considered. Then, to the right of each alternative, in the other columns, the client describes both the drawbacks (costs) and the advantages (benefits) associated with each option. After all the pros and cons have been outlined, the client selects the best option. Figure 13.1 is an example of a matrix completed by a social worker and a battered wife during an interview focusing on question of whether she should return to her husband or leave him and end her marriage.

4. A social worker familiar with the key issues and common client thoughts and feelings surrounding a particular type of decision can facilitate a client's decision making by constructing a **decision-making worksheet**. It serves to focus the client's attention on the important questions, factors, and possible consequences that need be considered. Figure 13.2 contains excerpts from a decision-making worksheet designed for use with pregnant teenagers who are considering whether to relinquish their babies for adoption. As can be seen from this sample, a worksheet is simply a format for raising questions and helping clients analyze their situation. Obviously, skilled interviewing could accomplish the same thing, but the worksheet can provide added structure and can also be used as homework between sessions.

Selected Bibliography

Lutheran Social Services. *Decision-Making Plans for the Baby*. Missoula, MT: Lutheran Social Services. Handout, no date.

McClam, Tricia, and Marianne Woodside. *Problem Solving in the Helping Professions*. Belmont, CA: Brooks/Cole, 1994.

Alternative	Cost	Benefit
1. Return to John	a. Abuse would probably continue b. Children are fearful c. Would have to face same hard decisions in future d. I could get seriously hurt or killed e. Medical expenses	a. Preserve family b. Hard decision is delayed until later c. Would have place to live and money d. John says he cares for me
2. Leave John and end the marriage	a. Fear of the unknown (I need to be with somebody) b. Trauma of divorce for me and kids c. Would have less money to live on d. Legal costs e. Custody battle over children	a. Abuse would end b. Decision would have been made and I could try to put my life together c. Children would be less nervous and upset d. I could find out if I can function on my own e. Opportunity for fresh start

FIGURE 13.1   Sample Decision-Making Matrix

Planning for My Baby

I. Questions about my relationship with my baby's father.
   A. Can I count on him for financial support?
   B. Can I count on him for emotional support?
   C. Has my relationship with him changed since I got pregnant?
   (and so on)

II. Questions about my relationship with my parents.
   A. What do my parents want me to do?
   B. Can I go against their wishes?
   C. If my mother helps take care of my baby, is it possible the baby will become "her baby"?
   (and so on)

III. Questions about my life after having the baby.
   A. If I keep the baby, how will this affect future dating, marriage, and children?
   B. If I give my baby up for adoption, how will this affect my future dating, marriage, and children?
   (and so on)

IV. A daydream exercise.
   A. If I could pick the ideal time for having a baby, when would it be? Where would I be? What would the baby's father be like?
   B. How does the above ideal situation compare with my real situation?
   (and so on)

V. Picturing myself.
   A. Draw a picture of yourself one year ago. Around your picture, indicate in words or pictures the things that were important to you then. What were your activities, how did you use your time? What were your goals and aspirations one year ago?
   B. Think about yourself now. Change the above picture of yourself one year ago to fit things today. Cross out those activities in which you are no longer involved. Have your goals and aspirations changed?
   C. Draw a picture of yourself one year from now. Again, around your picture, write in those things that you will be involved in one year from now. How will you spend your time? In one year, what will be your goals and aspirations?
   (and so on)

Source: Lutheran Social Services, mimeographed item (no date), pp. 1–2, 4–5. Used with permission.

FIGURE 13.2   Sample Decision-Making Worksheet

13.12   HELPING CLIENTS WITH HARMFUL HABITS

A *habit* is a learned and deeply ingrained behavior. Bad habits have been described as the barnacles we accumulate through life that keep us from doing what we would like to do and from being the kind of person we want to be. Because bad habits can adversely affect one's health, relationships, career, and financial situation, it is not uncommon for a social worker to become involved in helping clients find ways of dealing with their habits. Examples of bad habits are gambling, overeating, spending too many hours on the Internet, excessive TV watching, yelling at one's children, procrastinating, excessive shopping, knuckle cracking, nail biting, spitting, annoying table manners, and so on. For some individuals, activities such as shoplifting, viewing pornography, and promiscuity are habits.

The ancient philosophers were very aware of how good habits could help a person find happiness and success, while bad habits were a source of frustration, misery, and failure. Throughout much of history, good habits were termed *virtues*, while bad habits were called *vices*. Many of the spiritual practices and techniques taught by the major religions are intended to help people cultivate and develop good habits such as compassion, patience, self-awareness, and honesty. For example, if we respond to others with compassion and do that over and over again, we gradually become a person of compassion. In a sense, we become what we practice.

Some clients need help in developing new and positive habits. For example, basic social skills are essentially habits. Thus, some clients may need help in establishing the good habits of paying attention and listening to others, making eye contact, initiating a conversation, cooperating with others, and so on. Success in school and on the job is dependent upon possessing good habits such as time management, punctuality, self-discipline, following instructions, and treating others with respect. An effective parent, teacher, mentor, or job supervisor is someone who can encourage and guide others to develop good habits.

Habits are a natural part of living. In fact, we could not function at all if not for our capacity to develop habits and routines that allow us to perform many important tasks (e.g., keyboarding, playing a musical instrument, driving a car, reading) with little conscious thought and effort. Habits develop slowly over many months and years. Many are learned during childhood. The process by which habits are formed is fairly well explained by learning theory. A behavior that elicits some sort of reward or reinforcement (e.g., pleasure, release from stress, attention) is likely to be repeated. After many repetitions, the behavior is so ingrained that we are easily drawn to perform the behavior, often without even noticing what we are doing.

In some ways, a habit is like a non-chemical addiction. However, habits do not involve the physiological phenomena of tolerance, withdrawal, and craving associated with a chemical addiction to a chemical substance (see Item 15.11). Our intentions and will power can exert some control over a habit. By contrast, loss of control is a defining feature of an addiction or a compulsion. However, it is important to recognize that a habit can be the beginning stage of an addiction. For example, smoking is, at first, a habit but then gradually develops into an addiction as the body becomes accustomed to and starts to crave the nicotine. An addiction to pornography may start out as mostly a matter of curiosity or seeking stimulation, but over time develop into a compulsion.

Breaking a bad habit is no easy matter. Many of us start each New Year with a resolution to break one or more of our bad habits, but we seldom succeed. Philosopher George Santayana wrote: "Habit is stronger than reason." Even when we know that our bad habits are irrational we repeat them over and over again. Below are suggestions and techniques that a social worker might offer to a client who wants to break a bad habit or establish a good one.

1. Accept the reality that you cannot break a bad habit unless you acknowledge that it is a firmly established behavior and its elimination will require the application of special techniques. You cannot wish it away. Breaking a habit requires motivation, persistence, and a plan.

2. Analyze the habit. Write down your answers to the following questions: How long have I had this habit? What rewards or reinforcements (pleasure, relief of tension, stimulation, attention) do I get from this behavior? In what situation is it most likely to surface? What moods and feelings precede, accompany, and follow this behavior? If I get rid of this bad habit, what else will I be losing or giving up? If I give up the habit, what will I gain? Given what I have to gain and what I have to lose, do I really want to get rid of this bad habit?

It is best to work on only one habit at a time. For at least one week, make a detailed written record of where, when, and how often you engage in this habit. This frequency count will serve as a baseline from which you measure progress (see Items 14.5 and 14.6). In some instances, the act of carefully monitoring a habit will, by itself, decrease its frequency.

3. A study of the habit will usually identify the reinforcers or rewards that maintain its existence. It should also reveal the existence of *triggers* that precede or set up its occurrence. Triggers may take the form of certain environments, thoughts, moods, or little rituals that increase the likelihood that the habit will follow. For example, many who have a habit of excessive eating do so when feeling bored, worried, or lonely. Or perhaps, they start to think of food whenever they sit down to watch TV. Being alert to and avoiding such triggers can help control a habit.

4. Formulate and write out a plan for eliminating the bad habit. Carry the plan with you at all times and review it frequently. Keep the plan simple and make sure it fits with your other normal routines and responsibilities. For example, a simple plan to exercise at least 30 minutes, three times a week is more likely to be followed and successful than a complex one that requires exercising on Monday, Wednesday, and Friday from 4 to 5 p.m. by walking on Monday, biking on Wednesday, and weights on Friday. Obviously, the second example is too specific and rigid and easily disrupted by the ebb and flow of daily life.

5. List the disadvantages of having this bad habit. And, list the advantages of being free of this habit. The point of this analysis is to make you more conscious and aware of the fact that each time you feel the urge to engage in the habit you are about to choose between a set of disadvantages and a set of advantages. Review these lists frequently.

6. Create an environment that will strengthen your commitment to change and provide encouragement. For example, announce to your friends that you are embarking on a plan to eliminate a habit and ask them to call this habit to your attention whenever they observe it. Perhaps, give a friend a hundred dollars and explain that he or she is to return the money if you succeed in breaking the habit but he or she may keep it if you fail. Consider wearing a rubber band on your wrist and snapping it whenever you are about to engage in the habit. If, for example, your bad habit is spending too much time on the Internet, set a kitchen timer to remind you that your allotted time is up. If you snack too much, make an entry into you log as soon as you feel the desire to eat and keep a list of everything that you do eat.

7. One of the most effective methods of breaking a bad habit is to develop a replacement habit that is incompatible with the habit you want to eliminate. For example, if you snack while watching TV it may be because you usually eat meals in front of the TV and have been conditioned to associate food with TV. As a correction, cultivate the habit of eating only at a table and without TV.

When you set out to develop a desirable habit, begin with a written description of this behavior and then formulate a plan. Appreciate the power of making conscious and deliberate choices and frequent repetition. Maintain a record of your progress and find ways to reward yourself for success.

8. As people struggle with a habit, it is not uncommon for them to develop rationalizations as to why their bad habit is not so bad, why it cannot be changed, and why it is futile to even try. In order to make progress you will need to honestly confront and carefully examine this type of self-talk (see Item 13.7).

The first month or so of trying to either extinguish or establish a habit is especially difficult because you must rely heavily on choice and will power to bring about this change. After a couple of months of success, the new pattern will begin to feel more natural. After a year, it will be fairly firmly established. However, as you make progress guard against complacency because it is easy to slip back into old patterns.

Selected Bibliography

Clarborn, James. *The Habit Change Workbook*. Oakland, CA: New Harbinger, 2001.

Huebner, Dawn. *What to Do When Bad Habits Take Hold*. Washington, DC: Magination Press, 2009.

Ladouceur, Robert, and Sella Lachance. *Overcoming Pathological Gambling*. New York: Oxford University Press, 2006.

LeVert, Suzanne, and Gary McClain. *Breaking Bad Habits*. New York: Alpha Books, 1998.

Schaefer, Charles E., and Theresa DiGeronimo. *Good Kids/Bad Habits*. New York: Prince, 1993.

13.13   HELPING CLIENTS WITH FINANCIAL PROBLEMS

A job loss, large medical expenses, a divorce, and a variety of other factors can rather quickly plunge an otherwise fiscally responsible individual into a serious financial bind. Some individuals slip gradually into a serious problem because their income is inadequate or because they lack the self-discipline necessary to monitor their expenditures and control overspending. The power of advertising, peer-group influences, and feelings of low self-esteem draw many people into buying on credit and buying more than they need. Regardless of cause, individuals in financial difficulty face the daunting task of working their way out of a financial hole. The following information and suggestions may apply when working with clients immersed in a serious financial problem.

1. Every individual and family needs to construct a budget but more importantly, they need the discipline and motivation to adhere to that budget. A budget anticipates and plans to cover the costs for food, housing, utilities, insurance, transportation, debt related to credit cards and loans, health care, clothing, recreation, charitable contributions, communications, taxes, and so on. A budget should also include provisions for regular savings and possible emergencies. It can be as simple as a set of columns and entries in 3-ring notebook or software for a home computer. Whatever its form, the budget needs to be monitored on a daily or weekly basis for this will reveal problems that need to be addressed and items that can be trimmed.

A special budgeting challenge arises when the client cannot do arithmetic and deals only in cash. The method known as **envelope budgeting** can be taught to clients who need a very simple method for keeping track of their money. If the client can only count, he or she can usually use this approach. The first step in setting up an envelope budgeting system is for the client to identify the key categories of expenditure (e.g., food, rent). The next step is to determine how many dollars need to be spent on each category during a spending cycle, such as a two-week period. An envelope for each category is prepared and labeled. In the "food envelope," for example, the client places the cash allotted for food. All of the envelopes are kept together in a box or folder. As cash is removed from an envelope and spent, the client has an observable measure of cash flow and can view the balance that remains. The client is encouraged to resist the temptation to shift money from one category to another, but this may sometimes be necessary. As the client secures income, cash is again distributed across the envelopes for the new spending cycle.

2. Consider referring the client for **credit counseling**. A consumer credit-counseling program can help a client prepare a budget, develop self-discipline, and possibly avoid bankruptcy. However, do not confuse the credit-counseling services that are available for little or no cost from nonprofit agencies with those offered by for-profit businesses that do debt adjustment for a high fee and interest. There are unscrupulous and unethical businesses that prey on desperate people by promising a quick and easy method of getting out of debt. Thus, before referring a client to a credit counseling–type program, find out who sponsors the program, what fees are involved, and the program's reputation for honesty and effectiveness.

3. Help the client analyze his or her debt situation. To do so, make four columns on a piece of paper. In column 1, list all of the items that are billed on a regular basis (e.g., loan payment, credit card, utilities, rent, insurance). In column 2, list the expected payment due for each item in column 1. In column 3, list the amount that the client can actually afford to pay each month toward each item. In column 4, total the amount owed for all items. Next, have the client mark all of the column 1 items for which interest is charged; these should then become high-priority targets for payment. If the client must skip a payment or reduce the amount paid toward a bill, the payment should be on an item that does not involve interest or late payment charges. Also prioritize the interest-related items according to the amount still owed. The client should concentrate on paying off those items on which the least amount is owed, for this will eliminate all credit charges associated with that bill and free up money for other bills. Completely paying off a bill also helps the client see progress. Moreover, this record of progress in paying off debt can be used to argue for a payment extension from a business or lender because it demonstrates the client's ability and resolve to pay what is owed.

4. Paying some bills while deferring payment on others is sometimes necessary, but this will damage a credit rating and possibly have legal ramifications. If a client cannot pay a bill or must miss a payment, he or she should immediately contact the creditor or business and explain the problem. If the client demonstrates a genuine desire to pay, the creditor or business may be willing to temporarily adjust the bill or negotiate a less burdensome payment plan.

If a company concludes that an individual is ignoring a bill, it may eventually turn the matter over to a collection agency or seek legal action such as the garnishment of wages. A collection agency does not want to repossess property or do anything that will decrease the individual's ability to pay in the future. What it wants is payment. If the individual avoids the bill collectors and shows no effort to make payments, the collection agency will do whatever is legal to obtain the money owed or repossess the items not yet paid for. Those being pursued by a collection agency need to be aware that some collections personnel make statements and threats that are untrue and illegal. If a collections agent is saying things that seem unfair, unreasonable, or abusive, an attorney should be consulted.

5. When a client's bills exceed his or her income, he or she must find a way to trim spending, increase income, or both. Obtaining a loan or buying on credit is a short-term emergency fix but this makes the problem even worse in the long run. Credit cards are convenient but for many individuals they are the cause of serious money problems. No one should enter into a credit card contract without reading the fine print and understanding the amount of interest, service fees, and late charges. Paying a high rate of interest can set in motion a spiral of ever-growing debt. If the overuse of credit cards is a problem, the client will need to destroy the cards and close the account. If paying by cash is not practical and the use of credit cards is necessary, the client should strive to pay each credit card bill before incurring an interest payment or other fees.

When excessive spending is driven by emotional needs and a lack of self-discipline, it is important to help the client address this issue and modify these harmful habits (see Item 13.12). A self-help group like Debtors Anonymous may prove helpful to persons who are prone to impulsive and indiscriminate spending.

In some situations, the client may need to sell non-essential possessions and use the proceeds to pay off debt. The client might consider selling a car, unless it is essential for work-related transportation. A car loan creates a cycle of debt because by the time it is paid off, the car must often be replaced.

6. When less drastic methods fail to reduce the client's debt, *loan consolidation* might be considered. In this approach one takes out a new loan (a new legal contract) that is sufficient to pay off all other loans and overdue accounts. The single payment on this new loan is designed to be smaller than the combined total for the current loan payments. However, a consolidation loan stretches one's payments over a longer period of time. The client must still pay all that is owed before becoming debt free and that requires paying interest throughout the life of the new loan. Another disadvantage of consolidation is that the new payment may seem small in comparison to previous bills and it is easy to forget how much is actually owed, making it tempting to make unneeded purchases.

7. When a client is overwhelmed with debt and has no practical way of paying it off, the client may need to consult an attorney and consider seeking the legal protections offered by a court declaration of bankruptcy. For individuals and married couples, the Federal Bankruptcy

Act provides two types of **bankruptcy**: Chapter 7 (called a *straight bankruptcy* or *liquidation proceeding*) and Chapter 13 (called a *wage-earner plan*). A means test is used to assess the petitioner's ability to pay off his or her debts and determines which type can be used. As a general rule, if the individual earns more than the median income for his or her state, that individual must file for a Chapter 13 proceeding. People seeking bankruptcy protection must avail themselves of credit-counseling services.

A Chapter 13 bankruptcy proceeding requires payment of some or all debt. This proceeding allows the individual to keep personal possessions while he or she pays the debt under an installment plan monitored by a court-appointed trustee. The plan provides for the repaying of debts over a designated period, usually three to five years. If the judge approves this plan, creditors must stop all collection efforts and cease charging interest and late fees on most types of debts. Each payday, a fixed amount of the client's wages or other income is turned over to the court trustee who then pays the creditors.

In the case of a Chapter 7 bankruptcy proceeding, the bankruptcy judge notifies the creditors of their right to file claims for their losses and to question the individual filing for bankruptcy on the witness stand. The creditors are given the opportunity to object to the individual not having to pay what is owed. If there are no compelling objections, the bankruptcy judge grants a discharge in bankruptcy that relieves the individual from legal liability for all debts at the time of this bankruptcy. All the person's possessions, except those exempted by law, are then turned over to a trustee to be sold and the proceeds are distributed to the creditors who filed claims. The remaining dept is then legally erased. Certain debts such as child support, alimony, taxes, fines, and/or debts obtained under false pretenses cannot be discharged.

Bankruptcy has a number of negative consequences. Because it is a matter of public record it can never be hidden from those who take the time to find this information. Also, a bankruptcy remains on one's credit rating report for many years and affects one's ability to secure loans and other credits. If a client reaches a point of needing to consider bankruptcy, he or she should consult with an attorney and carefully weight the pros and cons of this legal procedure.

Selected Bibliography

Lawrence, Judy. *The Budget Kit*, 5th ed. New York: Kaplan, 2008.
Leonard, Robin. *Credit Repair*, 8th ed. Berkeley, CA: Nolo, 2007.
Stouffer, Tere. *The Everything Budgeting Book*, 2nd ed. Avon, MA: Adams Media, 2008.
Sutton, Garrett. *The ABC's of Getting Out of Debt*. New York: Warner Business Books, 2004.
Ventura, John. *The Bankruptcy Handbook*. New York: Kaplan Publishing, 2008.

13.14 HELPING CLIENTS IN CRISIS

Although the word *crisis* is widely used, it has a specific meaning within the field of mental health. Essentially, a **crisis** is a sudden but temporary breakdown in a person's capacity to cope and function, which is brought on by some overwhelming and threatening event. Situations that might precipitate a crisis include the sudden death of a loved one, a diagnosis of a life-threatening illness, loss of a job, a house fire, rape, witnessing a violent death, or some other traumatic event. For the individual, this experience is so unbearable that he or she reacts with anxiety, panic, despair, confusion, and disorganization.

By definition a crisis is *time limited*. Within a matter of about 4 to 6 weeks, the person will begin to reestablish a plateau of adjustment and functioning. However, that plateau may be either better or worse than the level of adjustment that existed prior to the onset of the crisis. Thus, a crisis is a time of both danger and opportunity. It is dangerous because if the crisis is not resolved constructively, it can set in motion a downward spiral that results in a lower level of functioning and chronic emotional problems. However, if the crisis is managed well it can turn out to be an opportunity to learn new coping skills, reevaluate one's perspectives on life, and actually elevate the person's overall social functioning. The outcome is dependent, in large part, on how others respond to the person during the crisis.

It is important to distinguish between a genuine personal crisis (i.e., a time-limited period of distress and readjustment) and a lifestyle in which there is one emergency after another, year after year, but no real change in how the person behaves, copes, or functions. For individuals immersed in this crisis-ridden mode, life is a roller-coaster ride and, for some individuals, the ever-present emergencies are energizing and almost addicting.

The concept of crisis overlaps, to a degree, with two mental disorders: Acute Stress Disorder and Posttraumatic Stress Disorder (PTSD). The essential feature of an **Acute Distress Disorder** is the appearance of certain symptoms within one month after exposure to a traumatic event. Symptoms include anxiety, "numbing" (or an absence of emotional responsiveness), reduced awareness of one's surroundings, a feeling that life is unreal, a feeling of being detached from one's body, an inability to concentrate, and an inability to remember important details about the traumatic event. If this condition goes untreated and/or if the person experiences additional traumatic events, the second condition, PTSD, may develop.

A **Posttraumatic Stress Disorder** is characterized by the occurrence of the above-mentioned symptoms plus flashbacks, recurring frightening dreams about the event, and reactions of distress when reminded of the event. PTSD may arise three or more months after exposure to an intensely emotional and/or life-threatening experience, such as rape, kidnapping, torture, an auto accident, combat, and witnessing the traumatic death of another person. If an individual is not making progress in working his or her way through the crisis period (a matter of weeks) and if symptoms of an Acute Stress Disorder or PTSD become evident, he or she should be referred for appropriate psychiatric treatment.

The following guidelines will be useful when dealing with a person in crisis:

1. Individuals who are in crisis are preoccupied with the precipitating event and their own fears and anxiety. They often feel a sense of failure because they are unable to cope and perform even the ordinary tasks of everyday life. They are unable to stay focused and to think clearly. Before the client can consider alternatives, make good decisions, or plan ways of addressing his or her challenging situation, he or she needs to feel safe and understood. He or she needs time to sort things out and comprehend what has happened. Thus, do not rush or push the client to take action before he or she is ready. A client in crisis should be advised to delay, if possible, making important decisions that will have a far reaching impact on his or her future (e.g., selling a house, moving to another city). Listen attentively and guide the discussion in ways that will help the client assess his or her situation realistically. Offer support that may range from simply acknowledging the existence of the upsetting experience to offering reassurance (e.g., "You did the right thing in leaving that violent situation and coming to our shelter").

2. Involve others in the helping process. People in crisis are usually most receptive to the assistance and support offered by persons they know and trust (e.g., family, friends, employer, minister, neighbors). Encourage the client to reach out to others, or, with his or her permission, contact these significant others and enlist their help on behalf of the client.

3. The person in crisis feels as if he or she is confronting a giant, insolvable problem. Thus, a social worker might use the technique of *partialization* to break this frightening situation into numerous components and smaller steps and decisions so that they seem more manageable to the client and can be addressed one at a time. As the client starts to take even very small steps, he or she will begin to regain confidence in his or her own capabilities.

A person in crisis may feel paralyzed and may be unable to take action or may act impulsively. Emotional reactions can make a situation feel worse than it is. Misunderstandings and misinterpretations can exacerbate the crisis and intensify emotional reactions. Thus, provide factual information, a realistic perspective and give honest feedback to correct misunderstandings. Help the client weigh the pros and cons of various options and anticipate the consequences of his or her decisions and actions. It may be necessary to provide very specific directions and instructions as to what the client needs to do in order to address a concern.

4. A hopeful attitude is an essential element in responding to a person in crisis. Convey confidence in the client's ability to deal with his or her challenges. If you communicate belief in the client's ability to cope, he or she will be less frightened and insecure. Help the individual recall times when he or she effectively dealt with such problems. Consider using a behavioral contract (see Item 13.5) as a means of providing the client with structure and a plan of action. This can help the client maintain a focus and mobilize inner resources.

5. When several individuals or a whole family is in crisis because they have experienced the same traumatic or distressing event, a group approach or a family-therapy approach may prove useful. In such a meeting, all are encouraged to talk about their experiences and feelings and offer to others their perspectives, support, and mutual aid.

Selected Bibliography

James, Richard. *Crisis Intervention Strategies*, 6th ed. Belmont, CA: Brooks/Cole, 2008.
Kanel, Kristi. *A Guide to Crisis Intervention*, 3rd ed. Belmont, CA: Brooks/Cole, 2007.
Roberts, Albert. *Crisis Intervention Handbook*, 3rd ed. New York: Oxford University Press, 2005.

13.15   HOMEWORK ASSIGNMENTS

The technique known as **homework** refers to various types of activities that the client is asked by the social worker to perform between sessions. Homework is often used when the objectives of the intervention involve teaching the client new skills that need to be practiced within the client's natural environment. For example, given a client whose problems revolve on low self-esteem and an inability to interact comfortably with others, a homework assignment might be for the client to strike up at least two conversations per day while riding on the bus to and from work.

The homework assignment must be given with clear and precise instructions. Often, these need to be written instructions and both the client and worker should have copies. The instructions that accompany homework might include, for example, one or more of the following types of statements:

> *Do statements* that begin with action words such as talk, read, write, observe, count, obtain, and give.

> *Quantity statements* such as "Observe three people who are doing . . ." and "Spend 30 minutes talking to . . . "

> *Recording statements* such as "Write down the number of times that you . . ." and "Mark on your chart . . ."

> *Bring statements* such as "Bring your list of . . . to our next session."

> *Contingency statements* such as "If you succeed, then reward yourself with . . ." and "Each time you get angry and curse others, you are to donate $2 to an organization that you dislike."

Obviously, the homework assignment must seem possible and make sense to the client. The use of this technique presumes that the client is willing to accept direction from the worker.

Selected Bibliography

Hecker, Lorna, and Sharon Deacon. *The Therapist Notebook II: Homework Handouts, and Activities for Use in Psychotherapy.* New York: Haworth, 2007.

Rosenthal, Howard. *Favorite Counseling and Therapy Homework Assignments*. Philadelphia: Brunner-Routledge, 2001.

Schultheis, Gary. *Brief Therapy Homework Plann*er. New York: Wiley, 1998.

13.16   THE FEELINGS LIST

Many of the clients known to social workers grew up in dysfunctional families (e.g., alcoholic, abusive) where they learned to deny and suppress their feelings. Often, they were punished for expressing emotion or for asking the "wrong" questions. Many were exposed to a childrearing pattern that invalidated or discounted the feelings they did express such as when a mother tells her angry child, "You're not really angry; you're just tired." As these individuals grow older, they carry with them a tendency to mistrust and misinterpret their emotions and feelings. Many cannot distinguish one from another and can speak of feelings in only broad words such as sad, upset, or OK.

Simplistic as it sounds, a written list of feeling words can help a client find a word to express his or her feelings. For example, as the client struggles to describe what he or she is feeling, the client is offered this list and asked to review it in search of the right word. Even a short list of 25 to 50 words can serve as a starting place and help the client identify feelings and distinguish one from another.

A feelings list can prove useful in work with individuals, families, and groups. If you believe such a list might help your clients, the authors suggest that you prepare one consisting of words that will be meaningful to individuals served by your agency. A client's age, life experience, culture, and educational level need to be considered when compiling this list. It should be a mix of both positive and negative feelings. Examples of positive feeling words might be, safe, relieved, freedom, valued, dependable, confident, hopeful, rescued, content, grateful, courageous, compassion, reassured, forgiven, reconciled, elation, excitement, responsible, and anticipation. Examples of negative feelings that might appear in the list are betrayed, bewildered, abandoned, hateful, desperate, heart broken, disgusted, disloyal, misunderstood, controlled, rejected, embarrassed, ashamed, guilty, manipulated, lost, vulnerable, and lonely.

It is often helpful to remind clients that feelings and emotions are a natural and normal part of living. Although some feelings are pleasant and some unpleasant, they are neither good nor bad. How one chooses to behave in response to feelings may be appropriate or inappropriate, but the feelings themselves are neither right nor wrong in a moral sense (see Item 8.6).

Selected Bibliography

Black, Claudia. *It Will Never Happen to Me*, 2nd ed. Center City, MN: Hazelden, 2002.

Mayer, Adele. *Incest: A Treatment Manual for Therapy with Victims, Spouses and Offenders*. Homes Beach, FL: Learning Publications, 1983.

Porter, Eugene. *Treating the Young Male Victim of Sexual Assault*. Syracuse, NY: Safer Society Press, 1986.

13.17   CLIENT ADVOCACY

When a social worker assumes the role of an advocate, he or she speaks for, argues and bargains for, and negotiates on behalf of another. In **client advocacy** (or case advocacy) the worker represents the interest of an individual. In **class advocacy** the worker represents the interests or a whole group of people (see Item 13.31). Client advocacy may be necessary when a specific client has been unable to obtain services to which he or she is entitled or has been subjected to unfair treatment by an agency and is unable to respond effectively to this situation without the worker's help. When a social worker is considering the need for advocacy on behalf of a particular client, he or she should remember these guidelines:

1. Make sure your client wants you to become his or her advocate. Do not engage in advocacy unless you have an explicit agreement with your client and he or she understands both the potential benefits and the possible disadvantages of this action. To the extent possible, involve your client in all decisions concerning the actions that you take.

2. Because client advocacy is a form of confrontation, there are some risks in using this tactic. For example, your advocacy can damage your relationship with the other agencies, service programs, or professionals. Such a damaged or strained relationship may create problems in the future when you need their cooperation and good will in order to serve clients. A decision to assume the role of client advocate should arise out of a genuine desire to be of service to your client and never from a desire to castigate or embarrass another agency or professional.

3. Before you decide to use this tactic be sure that you understand the facts of the matter. Do not base your decisions on hearsay or on a one-sided description of what has occurred. Realize that clients sometimes misunderstand, misinterpret, and even misrepresent events and explanations. Secure and review copies of all letters sent and received as well as other documents relevant to the issue. If an individual has been denied a service, seek information on the various eligibility criteria. For example, it is often possible to use the Internet to access a public agency's policy manual, eligibility criteria, and so on. A review of these criteria can clarify the client's concern or complaint and help determine if case advocacy is indeed appropriate.

4. Once you decide that the tactic of advocacy is required, arrange a meeting with the appropriate agency or program representative. Face-to-face meetings are almost always more effective than phone calls, emails, and letters. However, a letter outlining your client's situation and your own concern and questions may be helpful as preparation for a face-to-face meeting.

Respect an agency's chain of command. For example, do not ask to speak with a supervisor until you have spoken to the employee who was in contact with your client. Do not ask to speak with the administrator until you have spoken with the supervisor.

5. Before you speak with the agency representative, prepare an outline of what you intend to say and the questions you will ask. Begin your conversation with a courteous request for an explanation of why your client was denied service or treated in a certain way. Communicate your concerns in a factual and respectful manner, but in a tone that conveys your resolve. Keep a written record of the people you have talked to and their response.

6. If the agency or program in question wanted to provide the service requested by your client but could not because of a technicality or an unreasonable procedural requirement, request information on how the decision can be appealed. Ask if administrators, board members, or legislators should be informed of the difficulty faced by your client or consulted on how this matter can be addressed.

7. If further action is required, you will need to secure information on how to file a formal complaint or initiate an official appeal. In some cases, you will need legal advice before proceeding. As preparation for an appeal you will need detailed documentation of what happened and what was attempted, step by step, to resolve the matter. You will need names, dates, and copies of all relevant documents.

Selected Bibliography

Ezell, Mark. *Advocacy in the Human Services*. Belmont, CA: Brooks/Cole 2001.

Hoefer, Richard. *Advocacy Practice for Social Justice*. Chicago: Lyceum, 2006.

Katz, Marsha. *Don't Look for Logic: An Advocate's Manual for Negotiating the SSI and SSDI Programs*. Missoula, MT: University of Montana Rural Institute on Disabilities, 2005.

Schneider, Robert, and Lori Lester. *Social Work Advocacy*. Belmont, CA: Brooks/Cole 2001.

13.18   CLIENT EMPOWERMENT

Many of the clients seen by social workers in direct practice settings have been beaten down by oppression, poverty, abuse, and other harmful life experiences. They want their situation to improve but often feel powerless and helpless. Some have a pervasive sense of failure and feel rejected and ignored. In order to counter or modify these negative and self-limiting perceptions, social workers and social agencies need to emphasize empowerment. The word **empowerment** literally means to invest another with power or to authorize or permit another to exercise a certain power. As a social work strategy, empowerment is a way of working with clients that assists them and to acquire and exercise the competencies and power they need to improve their own functioning and to change the public policies and other attitudes that are adversely impacting their lives. Implicit in this approach is the belief that many personal difficulties are the result of social and economic structures that makes it impossible for people to utilize the strengths and competencies they do possess. To apply this approach, the social worker should adhere to these guidelines:

1. Social workers and agencies that want to embrace the empowerment strategy must realize what it asks of them. Fundamentally, they must be willing and able to share power and responsibility. It asks workers and agencies to recognize and implement the principle of client self-determination and to create true partnerships with their clients. The client is viewed as an expert on his or her life and situation. Thus, the worker must seek out and be willing to accept the suggestions and ideas proposed by clients. The social worker's role is primarily that of a teacher/trainer or consultant, not an authority, expert, nor a therapist. The worker looks for and seizes all opportunities to teach clients how to solve problems and access and utilize resources. The worker refrains from doing things for clients if they can be taught to do it for themselves.

2. Fundamental to empowerment is the conviction that each individual is an important resource to others and also a potential participant in social and political action. Through the process of cooperating, sharing responsibility, teaching, and learning they come to understand the social, economic, and political context of their current situation. By working together, people can bring about needed change in their neighborhood, community, and in their own lives. As they work toward change they learn the skills or communication, problem solving, leadership, critical thinking, persuasion, assertiveness, and negotiation. As they grow in confidence, they are motivated to take additional steps that can improve their lives. When they work with others they no longer feel alone and realize that others share their struggles and ideals.

3. The term *power* refers to an individual's or a group's capacity to influence the behavior of others, such as the decisions of a politician, government official, agency administrator, or an organization's board of directors. Assist clients in making an inventory of the types of power they already possess, such as knowledge gained from life experience, motivation, time, energy, knowledge of the community, understanding of a particular problem, sense of humor, willingness to take risks, right to vote, solidarity with others, and the like.

Help your clients to experience the exercise of personal power by allowing and encouraging them to make decisions, individually and as part of a group. Also, allow clients to experience the consequences of those choices, whether positive and negative. One does not learn to make good decisions unless given the opportunity to make decisions and observe their effects.

4. Encourage and assist your clients to arrange, host, and attend meetings and events that will help them to understand the people, organizations, and systems they want to influence and change. An example would be for clients to arrange a meeting with their local legislators. When clients meet face-to-face with politicians, program administrators, and other decision makers they often come away with a better understanding of what change is possible and a greater sense of hope that they can make a difference.

5. Once your clients understand that they are not helpless and do possess some power, assist them to use this power in a planned and disciplined manner to bring about some desired and feasible change. However, keep in mind that there are some pitfalls at this stage. When persons who have been oppressed finally realize that they have some power to influence others, they may not always use this power in an appropriate manner. Sometimes built-up anger and a sense of injustice cause people to make impulsive decisions and become aggressive or combative and that may alienate potential supporters or attract added opposition to their goals. While encouraging clients to use their power, also help them understand that making social change can be frustratingly slow and that various realities may limit how quickly others can respond to their requests. For example, an agency may not be able to make immediate or far-reaching changes in its policies or programs because of budget limitations, existing laws, and the needs of others that they serve.

6. As people examine how they have been held back in life by public attitudes, policies, and the powers that be, they are sometimes engulfed by resentment. Some may get stuck at this point and become prisoners of their anger. Help these clients express and understand their feelings, but then to let go of and move beyond this bitterness. Make frequent use of reframing (see Item 13.10) to help the client view his or her prior experiences of mistreatment or injustice from a different angle. For example, help him or her view the past as a painful but invaluable source of wisdom about what is really important in life and how and why people behave as they do. Help the client see that if one chooses to be taught rather than hurt, he or she will uncover many opportunities to grow as a person. Help the client recognize that even personal distress can be beneficial if it pushes one to carefully reexamine his or her situation and take action to change those things that are causing pain or discomfort.

7. In selecting the empowerment strategy you are assuming that the client (individual or group) already has or can learn the prerequisite competencies needed to effect changes and also that his or her current difficulties are caused primarily by social barriers and a lack of resources. If these are not valid assumptions for a given client, this approach, by itself, will not be effective or sufficient.

As an overall philosophy, empowerment is applicable in work with most clients and in most settings. However, what a social worker can actually do to empower others will vary depending upon the setting and the types of clients served. For example, an empowerment strategy is highly applicable in work with women who have been abused and with persons with physical disabilities. It would have much less applicability in direct practice with nursing home residents who are mentally confused. In work with inmates in a correctional facility, legal context and security concerns would not allow a professional to relinquish decision making to his or her clients.

Selected Bibliography

Eamon, Mary. *Empowering Vulnerable Populations: Cognitive Behavioral Interventions.* Chicago: Lyceum, 2008.

Lee, Judith. *The Empowerment Approach to Social Work Practice*, 2nd ed. New York: Columbia University Press, 2001.

Linhorst, Donald. *Empowering People with Severe Mental Illness.* New York: Oxford University Press, 2005.

Wise, Judith. *Empowerment Practice with Families in Distress.* New York: Columbia University Press, 2005.

13.19 RESOLVING CONFLICT THROUGH COUNSELING AND MEDIATION

Social workers are frequently involved in helping clients resolve or minimize conflicts. For example, conflicts might arise between spouses or partners, perhaps over divorce and child custody; between a parent and child; between landlords and tenants; and even between social workers. Interpersonal conflicts have many root causes such as differences in beliefs and values, inaccurate or incomplete information, or differences in how an event or experience is perceived and interpreted. A social worker can often help people to resolve some types of conflict by fostering better communication and mutual understanding. However, resolving a fundamental disagreement requires a more structured means of intervention known as *mediation*. And it must be recognized that not all conflicts can be resolved.

For some social workers, conflict resolution has become a practice specialty. Organizations such as the American Arbitration Association (AAA), the Association for Conflict Resolution (ACR), and the Institute for Advanced Dispute Resolution offer training programs and certifications to social workers and other professionals who have the knowledge and skill needed to resolve conflicts. In addition, the AAA and ARC, along with the American Bar Association (2005), have created a "model of conduct" for mediators that like the NASW *Code of Ethics* offer guidelines for professionals engaged in conflict resolution interventions.

COUNSELING STRATEGIES

Compared to many social work interventions that involve advocating on behalf of one's client, the conflict resolution approach typically involves taking a neutral position while helping the affected parties examine their situation, identify and clarify the factors that contributed to the conflict, and consider alternative solutions. An application of basic social work counseling and facilitation skills that help clients to explore issues, engage in effective communication, and identify common interests can resolve many conflicts. Some guidelines to keep in mind when counseling clients and others in relation to a conflict include:

- As part of planning and scheduling a meeting to address the conflict, urge the parties to consider these questions: Do I really want to resolve this conflict, or do I have another motive or agenda? Is what I have stated regarding this matter true, or have I exaggerated or provided only partial truth? What relevant information can I add to the discussion? What can I offer as a constructive step toward resolving this matter?
- When beginning the session, appeal to the parties to demonstrate mutual respect while discussing the issue, to reflect a willingness to listen to one another, and to make an honest effort to understand their different perceptions. Invite the parties to designate you as the person in the discussion who will enforce basic rules of fairness so that each can speak his or her mind without interruption.
- To the extent possible, encourage the parties to identify the source of the conflict. For example, is it possibly caused by a lack of information? Do both parties have the same facts and information? Are there differences in how the facts are interpreted? Is there agreement on the facts, but a difference of opinion on what would be the most reasonable and desirable outcome or action?
- Use basic helping skills (e.g., clarifying, paraphrasing, reframing, summarizing) to assist each party to express and explain his or her viewpoint. It may be useful, at times, to ask each party to repeat what he or she heard the other party say in order to help each clarify points and develop some level of empathy for the other person's perspectives.
- Once there appears to be sufficient understanding of the issues, use brainstorming to identify potential solutions to the conflict (see Item 13.30). During this process, look for opportunities to remind the parties of their shared interests and what they have already agreed upon (e.g., values, compromises, concern for a third party who is potentially affected by the outcome) and to build possible solutions that do not violate those areas of agreement.

MEDIATION

A more structured alternative to counseling is *facilitative mediation*, a method where a neutral third party, who has no authority or decision-making power in the situation, works with both sides to help them agree to terms for settling the dispute. As opposed to *arbitration*, where the participants are bound by the decisions of the third party, mediation does not impose a resolution but rather engages the disputing persons as active participants arriving at a mutually agreed-upon solution, which leads to a win–win situation. **Mediation**, then, is essentially a dialogue between parties who are in conflict over such things as values, power, status, or access to resources, in which a social worker or other third party facilitates a balanced and even-handed search for a solution.

Moore (2003, pp. 64–65) has developed a typology that distinguishes five forms of conflict often addressed by mediation:

- *Relationship conflicts* are caused by experiences such as strong emotions, poor communication, misperceptions, and negative or antagonistic behaviors. In addressing this type of conflict, interventions should include helping participants to control emotions, to promote expression and clarity feelings, and to encourage positive problem-solving approaches.
- *Data conflicts* are created by a lack of information or misinformation, competing views on what is relevant information, or different interpretations of data. Addressing these conflicts requires determining which data are important and accurate, how additional data might be collected, and resolving issues about the interpretation of the data.
- *Interest conflicts* are caused by competition over substantive interests or resources. Thus, helping parties to resolve these conflicts requires minimizing entrenched positions, looking for objective criteria for developing possible solutions, and developing trade-offs to arrive at a mutually agreeable solution.
- *Structural conflicts* are created by destructive patterns of behavior, imbalance of power or resources, and time or geographical constraints that hinder cooperation. Structural conflicts are often the most difficult conflicts to mediate because it requires the parties to modify behavioral patterns, establish a mutually agreeable decision-making process, and/or modify or disregard the influence of external pressures on the parties.
- *Value conflicts* develop when the parties come from very different family or cultural backgrounds, have different goals, or operate from different religious perspectives, worldviews, or ideologies. In working with the parties to such a conflict, the mediator might help them search for agreement on a broader or more important goal, agree to disagree on some issues, or seek a way to define the problem in some way other than a value conflict.

Because the mediator does not operate from a position of power or authority, his or her primary strengths must be the ability to quickly build a trusting relationship with both parties and to effectively use basic social work helping skills (see Chapter 8). Especially important is the ability of the social worker to guide the change process (see Chapter 7) in order to assure that the parties are indeed equal and active participants.

Selected Bibliography

American Arbitration Association, American Bar Association, and Association of Conflict Resolution. *Model Standards of Conduct for Mediators.* http://www.adr.org/si.asp?id=2095, 2005.

Barsky, Allan. *Conflict Resolution for the Helping Professions*, 2nd ed. Belmont, CA: Brooks/Cole, 2007.

Folger, Joseph, Marshall Poole, and Randall Stutman. *Working Through Conflict*, 6th ed. Boston: Allyn & Bacon, 2009.

Mayer, Bernard S. *The Dynamics of Conflict Resolution: A Practitioner's Guide*, 2nd ed. San Francisco: Jossey-Bass, 2007.

Moore, Christopher W. *The Mediation Process: Practical Strategies for Resolving Conflict*, 3rd ed. rev. San Francisco: Jossey-Bass, 2003.

13.20   INDIRECT DISCUSSION OF SELF IN SMALL GROUPS

This small group technique is designed to stimulate members to discuss their own concerns or problems without having to claim them as their own and to do so with a bit of emotional distance. It is often effective in drawing reluctant or quiet individuals into the discussion.

To begin the process, each participant is given three blank 3″ × 5″ cards. Each participant labels the cards A, B, and C. On each card the participant will complete or finish a stem sentence or respond to a specific question. The questions are labeled question A, question B, and question C. Before they write, the social worker tells them that the cards will be collected, shuffled, and redistributed randomly for discussion. The participants are warned against writing a response that might reveal their identity. The participants can be completely honest in answering these questions, since the identity of the person writing the card will be protected.

The social worker using this technique selects beforehand the three questions. The questions are, of course, ones that the worker wants the group to discuss and ponder because he or she knows or suspects these are important or troublesome issues. The following is a set of stem sentences used in a session with a group for parents who have abused their children.

On Card A: (complete the statement) "Before a hitting episode, I feel . . ."

On Card B: (complete the statement) "The thing I feel most after a hitting my child is . . ."

On Card C: (complete the statement) "One thing I could do to prevent a hitting episode is . . ."

The technique is also useful in training sessions. The next example is a set of stem sentences used in a training session for foster parents who are struggling to get along with the biological parents of children in foster care:

On Card A: (complete the statement) "In my contacts with biological parents, I find it most difficult to . . ."

On Card B: (complete the statement) "I know I shouldn't have this negative feeling toward biological parents, but I sometimes feel . . ."

On Card C: (complete the statement) "The thing that would help me to improve my interactions with biological parents is . . ."

After all of the participants have finished writing their responses, collect the cards in sequence: first, all of the A cards, then all Bs, and then the C cards. Shuffle each stack separately. Then randomly distribute the A cards, then the B cards, and then the Cs. This ensures that each participant will receive a card holding a response to each of the three questions. (At this point each participant holds three cards.)

The next step is to have groups of three or four members (if part of a larger group) study and discuss the cards they have been given. The social worker might ask each small group to summarize what the cards seem to be saying or to find the common themes. The foster parents, for example, might be asked to study all their cards and answer the following:

1. Identify the difficulties experienced in contacts with biological parents.

2. Identify the possible causes of these difficulties.

3. Identify methods of improving relationships with biological parents.

Typically, what they find on these cards are thoughts, observations, and feelings quite similar to their own. This can be enlightening and reassuring. After a small group has studied its cards, participants are encouraged to trade their cards with other small groups in order to obtain even more data.

The technique works best in groups larger than about 15, but it can be adapted for use in smaller groups and even with families. When used with a group smaller than ten, the social worker should also submit a set of cards. Sometimes, the worker can move things along or "prime the pump" by writing responses that are sure to provoke discussion.

Selected Bibliography

Gitterman, Alex, and Robert Salmon, eds. *Encyclopedia of Social Work with Groups*. New York: Routledge, 2009.

Zastrow, Charles. *Social Work with Groups*, 7th ed. Belmont, CA: Brooks/Cole, 2009.

13.21   PROGRAMMING IN GROUP WORK

Within social group work, the term **programming** refers to the purposeful use of nonverbal media, recreation, and other activities in order to move the group process in a desired direction and create opportunities for group members to learn new skills and behaviors and to experience positive relationships. A broad range of activities can be used in programming. For example: drama, dance, camping, puppet shows, story telling, care of animals, art, crafts, basketball, community service projects, and the like.

Consider, for example, how playing a game might affect people's behavior and attitudes. Games are fun and engaging. They often allow for creativity and fantasy. They teach the importance of obeying rules and maintaining boundaries. They often challenge the players to test themselves against others. Complex games and those involving teams may teach a variety of important skills such as self-control, problem-solving, communication, decision making, planning, cooperation, leadership, and how to handle feelings related to success, failure, and authority.

An individual's behavior during an activity can provide important assessment and diagnostic information. For example, the observation of a child's interaction during a game may yield insights into the child's behavior that could not be obtained from a battery of psychological tests.

The type of programming used will depend on the social worker's assessment of individual members, their needs and strengths, the group's purpose, and the level of group functioning. Guidelines include the following:

1. The selection of a particular activity is always tied to the question: What behaviors, attitudes, and skills do I want to encourage and teach? The activity should elicit and reinforce prosocial and functional behaviors by members and help the group achieve its purpose. The chosen activity should not encourage or reward troublesome behavior such as bulling, ridicule, teasing, and dishonesty.

2. When selecting an activity, carefully consider such factors as the members' ages, intellectual abilities, physical capacities, motor skills, endurance, attention span, need for control and protection, social skills, and so forth. Also, carefully consider the prerequisite skills or knowledge required by the activity. For example, does the activity require writing, reading, oral communication, cooperation, competition, initiative, memory, quick judgment, self-control, or the ability to follow detailed instructions? An activity should offer some challenge to the members but not generate excessive frustration.

3. A group activity should be attractive and interesting. For example, young adults are often attracted to activities such as car maintenance, cooking, dance instruction, and woodworking because such activities are age appropriate and combine the learning of useful skills with social interaction. Those who are physically fit might enjoy hiking, volleyball, or swimming. Older people might prefer more sedentary activities such as bingo, cards, and sewing; they might enjoy dancing but only if the music is familiar.

4. Carefully consider what the activity will require of the social worker. For example, does the activity require the worker to function as a teacher, leader, rule enforcer, advisor, planner, referee, timekeeper, or a provider of transportation or food? Also critical in this consideration is the group's size. Obviously a large and diverse group presents the worker with more challenges than will a smaller group that is easier to manage and supervise.

5. Consider how the rules of the activity will affect individual members. For example, does a game involve the selection or ranking of participants, the choosing of sides, or the elimination of a "loser" from further competition? Can the members cope with the limits imposed and whatever frustration the rules may create?

6. The appropriateness of a particular activity will depend on the group's stage of development. For example, in the get-acquainted or *preaffiliation stage*, you would select an activity that encourages communication and friendly interaction; you would avoid activities that involve competition or requires a member to assume a leadership role (see Item 12.8).

7. Consider how the activity fits with scheduling constraints and the physical environment. How much time is required? How much space? Is it safe? Is it noisy?

Selected Bibliography

Barlow, Constance, Judith Blythe, and Margaret Edmonds. *A Handbook of Interactive Exercises for Groups*. Boston: Allyn & Bacon, 1999.

Benson, Jarlath. *Working More Creatively with Groups*, 3rd ed. Clifton, NJ: Routledge, 2009.

Carrell, Susan. *Group Exercises for Adolescents: A Manual for Therapists*. Thousand Oaks, CA: Sage Publications, 2000.

Cheung, Monit. *Therapeutic Games and Guided Imagery*. Chicago: Lyceum, 2006.

Furman, Rich, Diana Rowan, and Kimberly Bender. *An Experiential Approach to Group Work*. Chicago: Lyceum, 2009.

Haslett, Diane. *Group Work Activities in Generalist Practice*. Belmont, CA: Wadsworth, 2005.

SECTION B

TECHNIQUES AND GUIDELINES FOR INDIRECT PRACTICE

Due to the complexity and multiple layers of decision making in organizations and communities, facilitating change in these large systems is usually a time-consuming and labor-intensive process. The social worker engaged in these change activities should recognize that complex social organizations were built by people and can be changed by people, but the process of changing them is often difficult. Typically, large system change efforts must be sustained over a long period of time, although occasionally intensive work on a project during a somewhat limited time period is effective. Successful outcomes depend on such factors as timing, knowledge of alternative programs that have succeeded, and involvement of key people in the organization or community.

Intervention Activities.   Like all social work practice, much of the activity by social workers to change human services organizations and communities is based on relationships. As compared to direct-service practice where the central relationship is with clients, these relationships are with administrators, board members, media representatives, elected officials, and others who are in a position to make or influence decisions. It is useful to remember that many of the actions of the social worker to interpret problems or promote changes in the functioning of the agencies or the community occur through informal conversations with decision makers.

Most actions to change organizations and communities are best described as maintenance or incremental change activities. Much of that work is geared toward facilitating teamwork, resolving disputes within an agency, generating ideas for new or innovative services, raising funds for programs, or developing grant applications. These interventions are central to improving the services to clients or future clients.

The more dramatic change activities are those that attempt to solve immediate and stressful problems. Those interventions include activities such as promoting changes in agency programs, organizing staff to address issues, chairing a committee or leading a problem-solving group, designing new programs, helping the media interpret social problems to the public, advocating for vulnerable groups, and lobbying key decision makers.

Monitoring Activities.   Similar to the direct services, the monitoring of indirect-service activities uses techniques that can be used either to inform actions while the change effort is in process (i.e., *formative evaluation*) or to sum up the results of an action after it is completed (i.e., *summative evaluation*). The tools for both monitoring and evaluating practice are combined in Chapter 14.

13.22   WORKING WITH A GOVERNING OR ADVISORY BOARD

With the exception of for-profit human services agencies, social agencies operate at the will of the people. Governing or advisory boards made up of community representatives play a critical role in establishing the policies and programs that these agencies provide. Boards also serve as the interface between the community and staff and thus their actions and decisions affect the resources (e.g., funds, volunteers) available to support the services provided by the agency. It is essential that the social worker understand the authority and responsibilities of the agency's board because, for example, if the policies and programs fail to adequately meet the needs of clients, the social worker must know how to effectively advocate for change with that board.

Particularly in a private agency, the composition of the **governing board** is important as they, in fact, govern the agency. The board should be representative of the community but also bring expertise or resources that are needed. Some agencies, but not all, select members with the expectation that they will be major fund-raisers or donors. However, the responsibilities are far greater than fund-raising. The clear communication to the public of the agency's mission and services, the assurance of responsible allocation of funds, and the ongoing evaluation of services (see Item 14.9) are essential for building public trust in the organization.

In nonprofit social agencies, the governing board is legally responsible for the total management of the organization. However, board members cannot and should not be present on a day-to-day basis to manage the operation of the agency. That is the job of the executive director or chief executive officer (CEO). A governing board shares its authority with the executive director, who then employs staff members to provide the services. In this arrangement, the lines of authority must be clearly drawn so there is no confusion that interferes with the provision of client services by the professional staff.

In sum, the governing board of an agency is responsible for policymaking to establish the agency's goals, methods of operating, and programs; planning to link the agency with the needs of the community; fund-raising to assure the resources needed to operate the organization are available; securing a competent executive director; providing facilities in which to deliver the programs; communicating with the public regarding the agency's successes; and conducting evaluations to assure accountability for the trust placed in them to govern the organization.

In a public agency, by contrast, the **advisory board** (also called an advisory council or advisory committee) has no legal authority or responsibility for the operation of the organization. It is established either because the public officials responsible for the operation of the organization desire citizen input and/or because public law requires an advisory body as a channel for citizen participation. As the name implies, it offers advice but cannot require compliance with that advice. Why, then, would an agency have an advisory board? Advisory boards typically exist for the following purposes:

1. To help identify the needs of the community and recommend new or revised programs
2. To evaluate agency programs and propose new procedures for conducting the agency's business

3. To assist in fund-raising, public education regarding the agency's work, and advocate for support of the agency

Typically, the members of both governing and advisory boards volunteer their time and talents to the agency. The motivations of board members may vary from a desire to help others, to a desire to use their special knowledge to benefit the community, to seeking personal recognition and social status. It is important to understand these motivations and use this resource in a manner that both serves the agency and satisfies the board members' need.

Selected Bibliography

Eadie, Douglas C. *Extraordinary Board Leadership: The Keys to High-Impact Governing*, 2nd ed. Sudbury, MA: Jones and Bartlett, 2009.

Tropman, John, and Thomas J. Harvey. *Nonprofit Governance: The Why, What, and How of Nonprofit Boardship.* Notre Dame, IN: Corby Books, 2009.

13.23   CONDUCTING EFFECTIVE STAFF MEETINGS

An important factor in the successful operation of a social agency is the quality of staff communication, making the staff meeting a critically important tool in agency management. Properly used, the staff meeting enhances communication and can prevent organizational problems caused by staff who act on inaccurate or incomplete information. Improperly used, staff meetings can be both costly for the agency and frustrating for the staff. A one-hour meeting involving a staff of eight, for example, is the equivalent of a day's salary for one person. The cost of the meeting should be justified by its benefits for achieving the agency's purpose, as compared to the staff providing service to clients during that time.

It is important to distinguish between a staff meeting and other types of meetings, such as case staffings and consultations and the meetings used for case assignments or by special committees and project teams. The distinction between staff meetings and team meetings can be made in terms of purpose (e.g., exchange of information regarding the agency versus practice techniques related to specific cases); content (e.g., discussion of policies, procedures, organizational maintenance, and professional practice issues versus a specific issue of practice activity regarding a case situation); formality (e.g., a formal decision-making structure); membership (e.g., inclusive of practitioners and support staff); and size (e.g., typically larger than a team meeting).

Staff meeting time should not be spent on routine or easily understood information that can be disseminated by other means, such as memos and email. Staff meeting time is best spent only on matters that require verbal clarification, feedback from staff, or a staff decision. Also, staff meetings should be held at the same time each week or month, have a set starting and ending time, and last not more than one hour. Attendance should be mandatory, and the leader should prepare and circulate an agenda in advance of the meeting and take responsibility to keep the discussion moving. However, staff meetings are not solely a management responsibility. All staff members should be expected to contribute agenda items, be prepared for discussion of those items, and assume responsibility for following through on items that require their attention. If an issue requires extensive discussion, a separate meeting should be scheduled. In many settings, the preparation of minutes is useful to disseminate information and properly record staff decisions in order to keep upper levels of administration informed of the activities of this unit.

Barretta-Herman's (1990, p. 145) analysis of staff meetings in human services organizations identifies three elements of successful meetings:

1. They should fulfill their objectives by jointly involving management and practitioners.
2. They should provide a forum for active discussion, creative problem solving, and participation of staff members.

3. The structure of the meeting should ensure that decisions made are followed through with action.

Selected Bibliography

Barretta-Herman, Angeline. "The Effective Social Service Staff Meeting." In *Business Communication: New Zealand Perspectives,* edited by Frank Slegio, 136–147. Auckland, New Zealand: Software Technology, 1990.

Brody, Ralph. *Effectively Managing Human Service Organizations,* 3rd ed. Thousand Oaks, CA: Sage, 2005.

Tropman, John E. *Making Meetings Work: Achieving High Quality Group Decisions*. Thousand Oaks, CA: Sage, 2003.

13.24 BUILDING TEAMWORK AND COOPERATION

Given the complexity of human services, often requiring the involvement of both multiagency and multidisciplinary workplaces, there is a need for social workers to have good teamwork skills. Providing services through teams and cooperative efforts not only draws together the resources of multiple agencies but also provides opportunities for the knowledge and skills of several disciplines to be brought into a service plan. Thus, if the client is to be served, the social worker must be prepared to work as a team member and to encourage teamwork and cooperation from others. Following these guidelines can encourage cooperation and teamwork:

1. In general, individuals and organizations cooperate with each other when it is of benefit to do so. Those benefits may be personal, professional, organizational, political, or financial. Cooperation is fostered by emphasizing what the parties have in common and how they and the client will benefit from working together.

2. Genuine teamwork and interagency cooperation does not occur by accident; they must be encouraged and nurtured. Statements of thanks, recognition, praise, and taking a personal interest in other team members help to reinforce cooperative behavior. Where appropriate, invite other members of the team to social gatherings as a way of building relationships and promoting goodwill. Do not engage in activities that might diminish respect for other professionals or agencies.

3. Teamwork and cooperation is built on a common purpose. That purpose is to serve the client and to accomplish what no one professional or single agency can achieve alone. Whenever necessary, help the team members or agency representatives revisit the question "What are we trying to achieve for our clients?"

4. Encourage the selection of a leader or chairperson who is nondefensive, supportive of others, and respected by the group. Strive to be proactive and willing to plan and prepare carefully for team meetings and assume a leadership role when appropriate.

5. Concern for client confidentiality is a reason commonly given for not working closely with other agencies and professionals. Sometimes this issue is more imagined than real. Clients can be asked to sign a release of information, thus removing this barrier. If professionals or agencies want to work together but are hesitant to do so because of confidentiality, they should ask their agency's legal counsel to recommend a workable procedure.

6. Be alert to the fact that many interagency conflicts center on questions of which agency has primary fiscal responsibility for providing a particular service. In other words, many disagreements boil down to the question of whose budget is to be used to pay the cost of services.

7. Understand your role and responsibility and those of the people with whom you are working. Make sure everyone knows what they can and cannot expect of each other. Several forms of documents might be used to define interagency expectations such as contracts, letters of agreement, protocol statements, and purchase of service agreements.

8. Remember that even under the best circumstances, teamwork can be challenging. This is especially true when the team is attempting to make difficult, value-laden decisions. Members should be willing to address directly and openly the conflicts or hidden agendas that disrupt team efforts. Conflict that arises from thoughtful differences of opinion is healthy. However, conflict that stems from bias or thoughtless loyalty to actions of the past is disruptive. Attempts to suppress or avoid conflicts or significant differences of opinion by denial, capitulation, or domination often make the problem even worse. When it is necessary to express a difference of opinion, use I-statements and other communication skills that convey your message in a clear, straightforward, and nonthreatening manner. Try to resolve interprofessional and interagency conflicts by focusing on shared values and goals and by using negotiating skills.

9. Realize that some of those with whom you must work may not be committed to teamwork. When this is evident, be firm but diplomatic in expressing the need for cooperation and for putting the good of the client before other considerations.

Selected Bibliography

Garner, Howard. *Helping Others through Teamwork: A Handbook for Professionals*, 2nd ed. Washington, DC: Child Welfare League of America, 2001.

Gold, Natalie, ed. *Teamwork: Multi-Disciplinary Perspectives*. New York: Macmillan, 2005.

Housley, William. *Interaction in Multidisciplinary Teams*. Burlington, VT: Ashgate, 2003.

13.25 LEADING SMALL-GROUP MEETINGS

Group decision making has become increasingly popular in the human services. Therefore, social workers spend considerable time participating in groups, agency staff meetings, interagency team meetings, and various agency and community committees. While group consideration of issues potentially leads to better decisions, group meetings without proper planning and direction can waste much valuable time and reduce the opportunity for making change. As the leader of a small group, the social worker is responsible for making the meeting as productive and efficient as possible. The following principles and guidelines should be followed by the worker when he or she is in a leadership position:

1. *Prepare for the meeting by engaging in the following activities:*
   - Clearly identify the purpose of the meeting.
   - Decide who should participate.
   - Identify objectives for the meeting and anticipate what the participants will and should expect. You may want to involve them in the planning.
   - Decide the best time and place for the meeting, and determine how participants will be notified of the purpose, agenda, starting time, and location of the meeting.
   - Decide how much time will be required for the meeting and construct a realistic agenda. Plan to address high-priority items first.
   - Decide what physical arrangements are necessary (e.g., room reservations, seating arrangements, audiovisual equipment, refreshments.).
   - Decide if a written report will be needed and, if so, who will prepare it and how it will be distributed.
   - Decide if a follow-up meeting will be needed.

2. *Get the discussion off to a good start.*

- Make sure that all members are introduced to each other. Use name tags if members do not already know each other.
- Explain the purpose of the discussion and its relevance to the participants.
- Distribute materials needed for the discussion (e.g., fact sheets, outlines, case examples).
- Create an atmosphere that helps the participants feel valued, appreciated, and responsible for contributing to the discussion.

3. *Give all members an opportunity to participate.*

- Explain in your opening remarks that the role of the group leader primarily will be that of coordinator to ensure that all members have an opportunity to be heard.
- Address your comments and questions to the group as a whole, unless specific information is needed from a particular person.
- Scan the group every minute or two. Look for indications that a member wants to speak. If this is seen and the member has been quiet, bring that person into the discussion by asking if he or she would like to add something to the discussion.
- If the group contains members who dominate the discussion, try to control them for the benefit of the group. A number of techniques can be used; begin with a more subtle approach and become directive only if necessary. Here are some possible ways to deal with such members:
  a. Seat the talkative members where they are more easily overlooked by other members.
  b. When a question is asked of the group, meet the eyes of those members who have spoken infrequently and avoid eye contact with the dominant talkers.
  c. When a frequent talker has made a point, cut in with something like: How do the rest of you feel about that idea?
  d. Propose a rule that each person can make but one statement per topic.
  e. In private, ask the excessive talkers to help in getting the quiet members to speak more often.
  f. Point out the problem and ask others to contribute more—for instance: "We have heard a lot from John and Mary, but what do the rest of you think about . . .?"

- If asked by a member to express a personal opinion about a controversial issue, try to bounce the question back to the group, unless members already have expressed their opinions. Say, "Well, let's see how others feel about this first." If you must express a personal opinion, do so in a manner that will not inhibit others from speaking on the topic.
- Avoid making a comment after each member has spoken. Doing so tends to create a "wheel" pattern of communication, with the leader becoming the hub of the wheel and thus the center of attention.
- React to what members say with acceptance and without judgment, showing only that a point is understood or that it needs clarification. If evaluation seems necessary, invite it from others with a question such as "Does that fit with your perception on the matter?"
- Use nonverbal communication to promote discussion. Nods and gestures can be used to encourage participation, especially from the quiet members.

4. *Promote cooperation and harmony in a small group.*

- Be alert to the possibility of counterproductive hidden agendas, and, if necessary, call them to the attention of the group. The group usually can solve a problem of conflicting purposes if it is brought into the open for discussion.
- Emphasize the importance of the mutual sharing of ideas and experiences and the need for clear communication.

- Use the word *we* often to stress the group's unity of purpose.
- Keep conflicts focused on facts and issues. Stop any personal attacks.
- Do not let the discussion become so serious that the members do not have some fun. Humor can reduce tension. Effective discussion is characterized by shifting between the serious and the playful.

5. *Use questioning techniques to maintain attention on a topic and encourage analytical thinking.*

- Use open-ended questions, such as "What do you see as the merits of . . .?"
- Questions should be understandable to all. Vague or obtuse questions frustrate the members.
- Questions should be asked in a natural and conversational tone of voice.
- Questions should usually be addressed to the group as a whole, rather than to a particular individual. This motivates everyone to think and respond.
- Questions occasionally should be asked of persons who are not giving their attention to the discussion. This usually stimulates the individual and the whole group to redirect its attention to the topic.
- Questions should be asked in a manner that indicates the leader's confidence in the person's ability to respond.
- Questions should be selected to maintain the focus on the topic under discussion. Avoid questions that would cause the group to leave its task and go off on a tangent.
- Ask for more detail and specification. Dig for the rationale and assumptions behind an opinion or a belief. Help those offering opinions to furnish evidence for the positions they take.
- See that the evidence offered for a position is tested and not accepted at face value.
- Assign one or two members of the group to challenge ideas and play devil's advocate so that differences are aired openly.

6. *Keep the discussion orderly, efficient, and productive.*

- Keep the participants focused on the meeting's goals and purpose. For example, occasionally ask, "Are we still on target for reaching our objectives?"
- Be alert to extended departures from the topic. If the group is drifting away from the topic, call this to everyone's attention. Ask if the digression means that there is disagreement on the goal or if it is an indication that the group is ready to move on to another topic.
- If there is much repetition in the discussion, ask if the group has exhausted the subject at hand. If so, help them get started on a new topic.
- Be the group's timekeeper. Keep the group informed of the time limits so high-priority topics will get the attention they deserve.
- Bring the discussion to a conclusion, which might include any of the following:
  a. A summary of progress made by the group
  b. Comments about planning and preparation for another meeting
  c. Assignments for follow-up and implementation
  d. Commendations when appropriate
  e. A request for an evaluation of the meeting in order to improve future meetings.

Selected Bibliography

Fujishin, Randy. *Creating Effective Groups: The Art of Small Group Communication*, 2nd ed. Lanham, MD: Rowman & Littlefield, 2007.

Kaner, Sam. *Facilitator's Guide to Participatory Decision Making*, 2nd ed. Hoboken, NJ: John Wiley, 2007.

Kemp, Jana M. *Moving Out of the Box: Tools for Team Decision Making*. Westport, CN: Praeger, 2008.

Larson, James R., Jr. *In Search of Synergy in Small Group Performance*. New York: Psychology Press, 2010.

Young, Kathryn Sue, (et. al.). *Group Discussion: A Practical Guide to Participation and Leadership,* 4th ed. Long Grove, IL: Waveland Press, 2007.

13.26   THE RISK TECHNIQUE

At times, committees (and especially staff committees) need to address fears and concerns related to some perceived risk or threat. For example, when new policies are adopted by a board, when new legislation is passed that affects a social program and/or the resources available, or when administrators establish a change in routine, it becomes important to identify and clarify the facts and issues in the situation and set aside rumors and fantasized outcomes. In these situations, the RISK technique can be useful.

To use this technique, the leader must take a nondefensive posture and communicate an interest in having the group members express their fears, issues, concerns, complaints, and anticipated problems. Using this approach, the leader encourages members of the group to express their views and to listen and understand one another's fears.

For example, assume that a change is proposed in an agency that would double the number of days that social workers are on 24-hour call. To address concerns about this proposal, the supervisor might elect to use the RISK technique by taking the following steps:

1. The leader schedules a meeting with all agency workers and presents a detailed description of the proposed change in the on-call section of the agency's personnel policy.

2. The leader explains that he or she will utilize the RISK technique to help workers identify their concerns about this proposed change.

3. The leader begins by asking workers to voice any and all fears, concerns, and worries they have in relation to the proposed change. These "risks" are written on newsprint for all to see, with the wording of the statement acceptable to the person raising the concern. Discussion of the items is not permitted at this time. (Note that up to this point, the RISK technique is similar to brainstorming, Item 13.30.)

4. The leader continues to encourage workers to voice additional concerns about the proposed change. It is important to allow adequate time for this session because the most disturbing and threatening concerns often will not surface until late in the session.

5. At this point, the initial session ends and the leader schedules a second meeting to occur in the next three to seven days. Meanwhile, all workers receive a written listing of the risk items identified during the meeting.

6. At the second meeting, the leader encourages workers to voice any additional risks they may have thought of since the initial meeting or to change the wording of any risk statements. The group is then asked to discuss and react to each risk item and decide if it is, indeed, a serious and substantive concern or issue. The risks considered to be minor or of little concern are dropped from the list. Those remaining are further discussed and clarified. The second meeting is then ended with the understanding that the identified risks are viewed as those of the group as a whole, and not the person who first identified any risk.

7. The leader places the group's identified risks (i.e., the final list from the second meeting) on an agenda for a meeting between the workers and administrators.

Selected Bibliography

Galanes, Gloria J., Katherine Adams, and John K. Brilhart. *Effective Group Discussion: Theory and Practice,* 12th ed. Boston: McGraw-Hill, 2007.

13.27 THE NOMINAL GROUP TECHNIQUE (NGT)

Committees that depend on a consensus approach sometimes get stuck in reaching a decision. One technique that helps bring issues into the open and moves the group toward consensus is the Nominal Group Technique (NGT). It is particularly suited for groups of six to nine people; if used with a larger group, the committee should be divided into smaller groups. Depending on the scope and complexity of the matter being addressed, it might take from as little as an hour and a half to a much longer period to complete the process.

There are four main elements in the NGT process:

1. The participants generate ideas in writing.
2. Each group member is provided opportunity to record an idea in a terse phrase on a flipchart.
3. Group discussion of each recorded idea is held for clarification and evaluation.
4. Individual voting on the most important ideas establishes priorities with the group's decision being mathematically derived through rank ordering or rating.

The following guidelines are suggested to help structure an NGT session:

1. The chair acts as facilitator and does not vote.
2. The issue is stated on a flipchart.
3. The pros and cons are freely discussed for 10 minutes.
4. Each person is asked to spend 5 to 15 minutes working silently, writing down ideas or solutions on a piece of paper.
5. Each idea or solution is listed on the chart and numbered. The chair then polls each member for a second idea or solution and repeats this process until the lists have been exhausted.
6. An additional 10 more minutes are allowed for clarification of the ideas or solutions presented—not for defense of the position.
7. All members vote on a secret ballot, ranking their top five choices 1, 2, 3, 4, 5. By adding the scores for each idea or solution, the lower scores will reflect the most favored positions.
8. Discuss the several items at the top of the list. Encourage critical thinking, invite disagreement, and seek careful analysis of the items.
9. If a clear consensus is not reached, revote and then discuss the items again. This can be repeated until a synthesis of ideas is developed or there is clear support for one idea.

The NGT process encourages active involvement by all participants as they consider and write down their ideas. Too often, in a group process, a few members carry the discussion and others do not actively and creatively think about the issues from their own perspectives. The interactive presentation of the issues allows all committee members an opportunity to express themselves and respond to the ideas from both the verbal and less-verbal members.

Selected Bibliography

Galanes, Gloria, Katherine Adams, and John K. Brilhart. *Effective Group Discussion: Theory and Practice*, 12th ed. Boston: McGraw-Hill, 2007.

Toseland, Ronald W., and Robert F. Rivas. *An Introduction to Group Work Practice*, 6th ed. Boston: Allyn & Bacon, 2009.

13.28 CHAIRING A FORMAL COMMITTEE

The committee is a particular type of small group for which the social worker might assume a leadership function. As chairperson of a committee, the social worker should make use of the guidelines for working with small groups (see Item 13.25). In addition, chairing a committee requires the use of a formal task-oriented approach to groups.

Essential knowledge for both the chairperson and committee members is familiarity with parliamentary procedures. For more than a century, *Robert's Rules of Order* has been the accepted set of procedures to be followed in formal committee proceedings. Table 13.1 provides a summary of these rules.

Above all else, a committee chair must believe in the worth and wisdom of group decision making. The decisions made by a small group, as compared to those made by a single individual, are more likely to be based on accurate and complete information and on a wider range of considerations; thus, the decisions are more likely to be the best ones possible. That is not to say that committees do not make bad decisions. They do. But a group is less likely to make a bad decision or a serious error in judgment than is an individual acting alone.

The leader must recognize the danger of *groupthink*, a situation of false agreement or false consensus that arises when a powerful committee member takes a strong stand on an issue and other members simply acquiesce rather than argue an opposing point of view. Soon after the meeting, the other members will usually complain and agree among themselves that the decision reached was a bad one. Needless to say, this conflict could have been avoided if the chair had made sure all points of view were expressed and debated and no one member or faction dominated the meeting.

People are usually willing to serve on a committee if they believe their time will be used efficiently and the committee's work will result in a real and positive change. On the other hand, many people have reasons for disliking and avoiding committee work, especially when:

- There is a lack of clear purpose (e.g., members are not sure why they are meeting or what they are to accomplish).
- There is a lack of leadership and direction by the chairperson (e.g., the chair does not keep the group moving and focused; real issues are not addressed or difficult decisions are avoided).
- The chair and/or members do not take the assignment seriously (i.e., lack of motivation or interest in the work of the committee).
- The committee's work is disregarded by top management (e.g., a committee is asked to study an issue and make a recommendation but the recommendation is ignored; sometimes the committee discovers that there was never an intention to follow the committee's recommendation).
- Committee discussion is controlled or dominated by one individual or subgroup.
- There is a lack of preparation for the meetings (e.g., no agenda, needed information is not made available).
- There is a lack of follow through (e.g., members or the chair promises to do something but fails to do so).
- The chair or members have a hidden agenda (e.g., some members have an ax to grind or will accept only one outcome, regardless of majority opinion).

One means of helping a committee avoid pitfalls that can lead to unproductive meetings is to engage the members in setting goals and operating procedures for the committee. However, it is useful for the chairperson or other members to periodically review and renegotiate the objectives and methods of operation so that all members can fully participate in the work. Dyer, et al. (2007) identify several steps that should be followed in building a productive committee:

1. *Give the work realistic priority.* It is important to give members a chance to discuss why they are serving on the committee, clarify the relative importance of this work in the context of their total responsibilities, and indicate the amount of time they are able to commit to this activity. Sharing these matters helps to establish the pace at which the committee can operate and allows the chair to identify persons who have the time and interest to carry major responsibilities.
2. *Share expectations.* Each person should be asked to identify his or her greatest concerns about working on this committee, how he or she sees it functioning, and what actions are necessary to ensure positive outcomes.

TABLE 13.1 Summary of Parliamentary Procedures

Guidelines/Description	Type of Action	Purpose of Action	Interrupts Debate?	Requires Second?	Debatable?	Amendable?	Vote Required?
• #1–12 in order of priority	PRIVILEGED MOTIONS						
	1. Fix time to adjourn	Establish plan to discontinue meeting	No	Yes	No	No	Majority
• #1–4 supersede all other actions	2. Recess	Temporary break in meeting	No	Yes	Yes	Yes	Majority
	3. Question of privilege	Challenge rights of assembly or a member to take an action	Yes	No	No	No	None
	4. Point of order	Clarify or challenge process	Yes	No	No	No	None
• #5–12 facilitate action on other motions	SUBSIDIARY MOTIONS						
	5. Table the motion	Delay action to a specified meeting	No	Yes	No	No	Majority
	6. Previous question	Close debate and vote immediately	No	Yes	No	No	2/3
	7. Limit debate	Set limits on future debate	No	Yes	Yes	Yes	2/3
	8. Postpone definitely	Temporarily delay action to a specified time	No	Yes	Yes	Yes	Majority
• Each may be made while motion below is on the floor	9. Refer to committee	Delay until committee can review matter and report back	No	Yes	Yes	Yes	Majority
	10. Amend the amendment	One amendment to primary amendment is permitted at a time	No	Yes	Yes	Yes	Majority
	11. Primary amendment	Propose change in main motion	No	Yes	Yes	Yes	Majority
	12. Postpone indefinitely	Remove motion from consideration	No	Yes	Yes	No	Majority

Process Starts Here

Category	Motion	Action	Interrupt debate?	Require second?	Debatable?	Can be amended?	Vote required (proportion)?
MAIN MOTION OR RESOLUTION — *Routes to opening main motion*	• New motion	Introduce action for first time	No	Yes	Yes	Yes	Majority
	• Reconsider prior action	Reconsider previous vote	Yes	Yes	Yes	No	Majority
	• Resume consideration	Take up motion previously tabled	No	Yes	Yes	No	Majority
INCIDENTAL MOTIONS — *No order of precedence; Arise from process of debate and may occur at any time; Yield only to privileged motions*	• Move to appeal	Challenge ruling of the chair	Yes	Yes	Yes	Yes	Majority
	• Move to suspend rules	Override existing procedures	No	No	Yes	No	2/3
	• Request point of order	Correct parliamentary process error	Yes	No	No	No	None
	• Withdraw motion	Remove motion from consideration	Yes	No	No	No	None
	• Division of question	Act on parts of motion or amendment	No	No	No	No	None
	• Division of assembly	After voice vote, request vote count	Yes	No	No	No	None
	• Request for information	Seek clarification	Yes	No	No	No	None

Note: Parliamentary procedure requires study and practice before it becomes useful. An action can only occur after a motion or resolution is introduced, as indicated in the left column by "Process Starts Here." One of the three routes to opening the main motion must be selected, and then the chair can track across the columns from left to right to determine the process to follow. Does it interrupt debate? (Yes/No) Does it require a second? (Yes/No) Is it debatable? (Yes/No) Can it be amended? (Yes/No) Is a vote required? (Yes/No) is a vote required, and if so, what proportion at the voters must support it if it is to be approved? For any subsequent motion, the same process applies. Note that moving vertically up the page, the "Privileged and "Subsidiary" motion are listed in order of priority from the top (#1) to the bottom of the first page (#12). The "Incidental" motions (listed below the main motion) may be made at any time during debate, but they do not override the privileged motions.

3. *Clarify goals.* The committee members should collectively discuss and write down a statement that represents the group's core mission. Subgoals can then be developed to reflect the intermediate or short-range objectives necessary to accomplish this mission. During subsequent committee work, each decision and action should be examined for its contribution to the mission or subgoals that have been established.

4. *Formulate operating guidelines.* The committee members should then establish procedures for their operation. Answers to the following questions will provide guidance for the chair and allow members to know how to proceed:

- How will we make decisions?
- What will be our basic method of working as a group?
- How do we make sure everyone gets a chance to discuss issues or raise concerns?
- How will we resolve differences?
- How will we ensure that we complete our work and meet deadlines?
- How will we change methods that are not producing results?

In addition, it should be recognized that the formality with which a committee operates often depends on its size, the existing relationships among the members, and the speed with which it needs to make decisions. The purpose of some committees is best served by an open dialogue that explores topics in depth before action is taken. For others, the work is more task-oriented. Subcommittees consider the issues and prepare reports of their deliberations on which the full committee will act.

Selected Bibliography

Cook, Rita. *The Complete Guide to Robert's Rules of Order Made Easy: Everything You Need to Know Explained Simply.* Ocala, FL: Atlantic Publications, 2008.

Dyer, William G, W. Gibb Dyer, and Jeffrey H. Dyer. *Team Building: Proven Strategies for Improving Team Performance,* 4th ed. San Francisco: Jossey-Bass, 2007.

13.29   PROBLEM SOLVING BY A LARGE GROUP

At times, it is necessary for a social worker to initiate problem-solving activity within a large group. The technique described here is intended to elicit ideas from all members and provide an opportunity for participation, even when as many as 30 or more people are involved.

The technique begins with the group leader explaining the purpose of the meeting—for example: "We need to come up with a method of collecting information from the agencies in town on trends in the number of homeless people applying for help." These steps should then be followed:

1. *Each individual is asked to think privately about the problem and possible solutions.* Members are asked to make written notes on their thoughts.

2. *Dyads are formed.* Each person in the dyad is instructed to interview his or her partner and to try to understand that person's perspective on the problem and proposed solutions. The dyads work for 10 minutes.

3. *Quartets are formed.* For 15 minutes, each group of four people discusses the problem and possible solutions. Each quartet records the key points of its deliberation on a large piece of paper, which is hung on the wall for all to see.

4. *Each individual studies the papers for 10 minutes.*

5. *The whole group reassembles and shares their analysis of the problem and proposed solutions.* This final step sets the stage for the prioritizing of proposed solutions to be explored in more depth.

Selected Bibliography

Brody, Ralph. *Effectively Managing Human Service Organizations,* 3rd ed. Thousand Oaks, CA: Sage, 2005.

Tropman, John E. *Making Meetings Work: Achieving High-Quality Group Decisions*, 2nd ed. Thousand Oaks, CA: Sage, 2003.

13.30 BRAINSTORMING

Problem solving includes the important step of identifying all possible alternatives or solutions. Too often, some potential solutions are overlooked because they do not fit preconceived notions or expectations. Being rigid and following old habits of thought can limit creativity during the problem-solving process. The technique of **brainstorming** is designed to overcome this limitation. It can be applied to any problem for which there may be a range of solutions. The objective of brainstorming is to free persons temporarily from self-criticism and from the criticism of others in order to generate imaginative solutions to a specific problem. However, it should not be used until the problem has been clearly defined. Brainstorming is most often used in work with groups or committees, but many workers adapt its principles for use in one-on-one counseling sessions.

A brainstorming session begins with the identification and listing of a wide variety of possible solutions. Many may be unrealistic, but it is only after all alternatives have been identified that the participants are permitted to evaluate the proposed solutions in search of those that are feasible. A social worker setting up a brainstorming session should give several instructions:

1. Encourage participants to develop a large number of solutions. The goal is to generate a quantity of solutions—quality will be determined later.
2. Encourage participants to be freewheeling in their thinking. Even wild ideas should be welcomed and accepted without judgment.
3. Recommend that participants combine and elaborate on the solutions that are offered.
4. Do not allow participants to criticize or evaluate one another's proposed solutions.

During the brainstorming session, a recorder writes down all the ideas as fast as they come up. Do this on a whiteboard or flipchart so the visual record stimulates additional ideas. The leader of the session should quickly stop any criticism of ideas, whether verbal or implied by tone of voice or nonverbal gesture. Also, the group leader needs to keep the participants focused on the problem under consideration.

Once all of the proposed solutions or ideas have been heard and recorded, the session moves to a second stage: the critical examination of each idea. De Bono (1992) suggests a useful technique for ensuring that six types of questioning and thinking are applied during the evaluation stage. Each of these six categories of thinking is called a "hat," and each hat has a color. Thus, for example, when the group is asked by the group leader to "put on your red hats," the group is being asked to evaluate the proposed solutions in terms of hunches, intuition, and gut feelings. If asked to put on the "black hat," the group is to view the solutions in a highly critical and skeptical manner.

The six thinking hats are as follows:

1. *White hat* (focus on objectivity and data): What information do we have? How reliable is this information? What additional information do we need?
2. *Red hat* (focus on hunches and intuition): What are our gut feelings about this proposed solution? Does it "feel" right? Let's trust our instincts!
3. *Black hat* (focus on caution and risk): What are the legal, policy, political, and funding problems we will encounter? This cannot be done and will not work because. . .

4. *Yellow hat* (focus on optimism): It needs to be done, so let's try! Who cares if it has never been done before? Let's try something different! It will work if we really want it to work!

5. *Green hat* (focus on creativity and other combinations of ideas): Are there still other ways of thinking about this? Can we combine the best parts of several different proposals?

6. *Blue hat* (focus on the big picture and holistic thinking): How does this idea fit with other things we know about this issue? Are we missing something important? Let's summarize the conclusions we have reached and the decisions we have made so far. Is our way of discussing and approaching this issue working for us? Are we making progress toward a decision or solution?

Be sure to provide sufficient time for a brainstorming session. Considering that many ideas might be generated in a single session and that time will be needed to evaluate each proposed solution, a brainstorming session could easily take more than an hour.

Selected Bibliography

Adair, John. *Decision Making and Problem Solving Strategies*, 2nd ed. Philadelphia, PA: Kogan Page, 2010.

De Bono, Edward. *Serious Creativity*. New York: HarperCollins, 1992.

13.31   CLASS ADVOCACY

The term **class advocacy** refers to actions on behalf of a whole group or class of people. This is in contrast to client advocacy (see Item 13.17), in which the advocacy is on behalf of a specific individual. Because class advocacy seeks change in law and public policy at either the local, state, or national level, it is essentially a political process aimed at influencing the decisions of elected officials and high-level administrators. It entails building coalitions with other groups and organizations that share concerns about a social issue. The social worker typically participates as a representative of an organization, rather than as an independent practitioner.

Since the goal is to bring about a change, opposition should be expected. Not everyone is comfortable with this type of advocacy. Further, each organization must examine the pros and cons of taking on an advocacy role and decide whether having its representatives perform this role fits with the purpose of the organization.

For those who choose to become engaged in class advocacy, following these guidelines may increase the chance of success:

1. Realize that advocacy intends to help bring about needed changes in laws, policies, and programs. Bringing about change is difficult—but not impossible.

2. You cannot do it alone. Individual social workers will need to join with others. A group has more power than an individual, and several organizations working together have more power than a single organization working alone. Working with other organizations will mean that your own organization will have to share some resources, make some compromises, and perhaps do some things differently. In the long run, however, you will accomplish more as part of a coalition than by working alone.

3. Many improvements are needed in our human services systems. Since you cannot do everything that needs to be done, you must decide which concern has the highest priority. If you, or your organization, take on several causes at one time, you may be spread too thin. It is better to make real gains in just one area than to make minimal gains or fail completely in several.

4. It is also important to choose a cause where success is possible. Be realistic! Do not waste your time and energy on a lost cause. A successful experience generates hope and a feeling that other successes are possible. If participants can see even small successes, they will be more willing to invest themselves in future advocacy efforts.

5. Successful advocacy is built on a foundation of careful analysis and planning. It is important to clearly define and carefully study the problem before you make a decision on what to do about it. Do not launch an effort to change something until you know exactly what has to be changed, why it needs to be changed, and what will be involved in bringing about the change.

6. Before you take action, carefully assess what achieving your goal will require in the way of time, energy, money, and other resources. Do you have the resources? If not, it is best to scale down your goals or wait until later when you are better organized and more capable of reaching your goal.

7. Try to understand those who oppose you. There is always resistance to change, and analysis of the situation should include understanding why there is resistance. The advocate needs to be able to put himself or herself in the opponent's shoes (i.e., have empathy). People always have reasons for opposing change. You may not agree with their reasons, but you must understand them if you are to figure out a way to successfully overcome that resistance.

8. Successful advocacy requires self-discipline. One of the most serious errors one can make in advocacy is to act impulsively. If that happens, the other organizations in the coalition may pull back or be reluctant to cooperate because they fear that your recklessness will cause damage to their organization or to the coalition. Also, if you act impulsively, those who oppose you can more easily discredit you.

9. Advocacy involves the use of *power*. Essentially, power is the ability to make others behave the way you want them to behave. Think of power as a resource that can be used or "spent" for a particular purpose. There are different kinds of power. It is important to study your own organization and its membership in order to discover the type of power that you possess.

Among the types of power social workers have is the power that comes from knowledge and expertise. For example, if you are advocating on behalf of children, you have detailed information about children and troubled families, and you know how the system works or does not work. Information, if carefully assembled and presented, can have a powerful impact on legislators, agency administrators, and the public.

Perhaps some members of your organization are highly respected in the community and have credibility that gives them a type of power. Individuals who are respected can have a significant influence on legislators and administrators. You need to encourage and help those individuals to advocate actively in behalf of the issue.

Do not forget that personal commitment, time, and energy are also types of power. Much can be accomplished just by sticking with a task and seeing it through to the end. Organizational solidarity is also a type of power. If legislators and decision makers can see that members are solidly behind their organization, they will pay attention to what the organization's leaders have to say.

Within your organization are members who are natural leaders. Others may be charismatic and articulate with the ability to excite people and get them to work together on a cause. Charisma is a rare quality, but it is definitely a type of power. Identify charismatic individuals in your organization and let them speak for your cause.

10. There are times when class advocacy must take the form of a lawsuit. Many changes and reforms would never have happened without lawsuits and court decisions. For example, many of the reforms in the areas of mental health and mental retardation have grown out of legal actions. An organization committed to advocacy will, at times, need to encourage and support lawsuits that have potential for bringing about a needed change.

11. Most people in the United States depend on television and newspapers for information. If one wants the public to understand and support a cause, it is important to learn to market the services offered. If there is someone associated with the organization who knows how to work in advertising and the use of media, make use of that person's talent. If not, approach an advertising agency or perhaps a school of journalism and ask if someone would be willing to help get your message on TV or in the newspapers.

Selected Bibliography

Ezell, Mark. *Advocacy in the Human Services.* Belmont, CA: Brooks/Cole, 2001.

Schneider, Robert L., and Lori Lester. *Social Work Advocacy: A New Framework for Action.* Belmont, CA: Brooks/Cole, 2001

Sen, Rinku. *Stir It Up: Lessons in Community Organizing and Advocacy.* San Francisco: Jossey-Bass, 2003.

13.32   TEACHING AND TRAINING

Social workers do a lot of teaching. They frequently teach skills related to parenting, interpersonal communication, stress management, job seeking, independent living, and so on. Their teaching may be directed to clients, volunteers, colleagues, or concerned citizens. It may occur within the context of a one-to-one relationship, a workshop, or a formal classroom situation. Several guidelines can help the social worker increase his or her effectiveness as a teacher:

1. The adage "It hasn't been taught until it has been learned" underscores the difference between teaching and learning. Teaching activities are planned and controlled by the teacher, but learning is not. Learning occurs within the learner and is tied to such factors as motivation, ability, and readiness. The teacher's job is to find a way of engaging and motivating the learner to examine and consider the materials to be taught.

2. That which we teach and learn falls into three broad categories: knowledge, beliefs and values, and skills. Of these three, knowledge is the easiest to teach because there is an agreed-upon language to explain facts, concepts, and theories. This is not so when we focus on values and attitudes. In fact, values and attitudes can be introduced and modeled by the teacher, but the learner must adopt or adapt them to his or her own belief system. Skills, too, are best learned through modeling and demonstration. They then can be performed and practiced in a real or simulated situation in order to master the behaviors or actions related to the skill.

3. It is said that the truly educated person is one who has learned how to learn. How we learn varies with such factors as our sensory preferences (hearing, seeing, kinesthetic, etc.), our need for or resistance to structure and direction, our desire for either competition or cooperation, our tendency to move from the specific (parts) to the general (whole) or vice versa, our tendency to either break apart or build concepts, our need to read and write in order to learn, our preferences for either solitary or group learning, and so forth. An important first step in teaching, then, is to plan for differences in how people learn. An effective teacher must be prepared to use several different methods when teaching a single topic.

4. When teaching, begin by identifying and teaching only essential terminology and concepts. The acquisition of specialized vocabulary is a fundamental step in the acquisition of new learning. However, too much information too soon can overload a learner. For example, before someone can learn to do the work of the social worker, he or she must first master the terminology and basic concepts related to the profession's values, roles, principles, and practice theories. The teacher, however, should carefully pace the introduction of new concepts in order to avoid having the learner shut-down because too much new material is given at one time.

5. Help people learn by helping them practice skills and techniques.

6. When planning a class or training session, begin with an analysis of learner characteristics (e.g., developmental stage, formal education, prior experience) and the identification of the knowledge, values, and skills they are expecting (and expected) to learn. Then select the methods that are most likely to engage the learners and push and pull them toward the learning objectives.

7. Review and consider using existing curricula and teaching materials, but realize that such materials nearly always need to be modified. Materials and methods that worked well with one group of learners may not work for others.

8. To the extent possible, use teaching techniques that actively engage both the learner's mind and body (e.g., role-plays, simulation exercises, debates, and discussions). Reduce to a minimum the time spent in formal presentations. Lectures are among the least effective methods. In order to teach, we must attend to the learner's thinking, feelings, and behavior.

9. When teaching a skill, utilize the model known as "watch one, do one, teach one." First, have the learners observe someone performing the skill activity, then have them do it, and, finally, have them teach it to someone else.

10. Place emphasis on helping the learner immediately use the information, knowledge, or skill being taught. In the human services the primary reason for learning is to do something with whatever has been learned. Thus, encourage the learner to ask "Why am I interested in this topic?" "What can I do with it?" "How can I apply it?" "How will it help me answer some other question or solve a problem?"

11. Critically evaluate your teaching. We can assess our effectiveness as teachers on four levels:

- *Level 1.* Simply ask the learners if they liked it. This is the most commonly used method of evaluating teaching. The problem is that one can enjoy a class or a workshop, but learn little. Moreover, learning is not always an enjoyable experience.
- *Level 2.* Determine if the learners actually learned something new. Did they leave the session with knowledge or skills that they did not have when they began? To assess training at this second level, some type of pre-session and postsession testing is necessary.
- *Level 3.* Assuming that new learning occurred, then ask if the new knowledge and skills were used after the session. To assess training at this level, we need a follow-up system for monitoring the learner's behavior subsequent to the training session.
- *Level 4.* Finally, determine whether the learners' application of the new knowledge and skills had a positive impact on their lives or work. Unless what is learned has a real and a positive impact, the session was of little value no matter how enjoyable or how much was learned.

Selected Bibliography

Basarab-Horwath, Janet A., and Tony Morrison. *Effective Staff Training in Social Care: From Theory to Practice.* New York: Routledge, 1999.

Patterson, Sandra L. *Ready, Set, Patient Safety!: Questions, Games, and Other Strategies to Prepare Your Staff.* Marblehead, MA: HCPro, 2005.

13.33   PREPARING A BUDGET

A budget is an important planning tool that lists an agency's anticipated income and its intended use during a designated period, usually one or two years. Typically, a budget will be revised several times during the period it is in use. A *preliminary budget* is often used to estimate expenses and serve as the basis for securing funding. That budget will be revised once various commitments have been made by the funding sources. An *operating budget*, when approved by a legislative body (in the case of a public agency) or by a board of directors (in the case of a private agency), becomes the authorization for the agency's executive director to spend the amounts listed for each budget category. However, in the course of the budget period, there may be a shortfall in one or more income categories, unanticipated costs in expenditure categories, or emergent reasons to shift funds from one category to another. Given the relative fluidity of demand for services, agencies must have the capacity to make changes in programming or staffing during budget periods.

When building a budget, many questions should be asked and answered:

- What agency goals and objectives are to be emphasized during the budget period?
- What types and how many employees are needed to carry out the agency's programs? What salaries and benefits are needed to attract and retain them? What forms of insurance is needed to protect the employees and the agency? What training will be required for staff and volunteers—and what is the cost of that training?
- How might changes in program activities affect budget items such as numbers of staff with various competencies, training expenses, travel, supplies and equipment, consultation, and so on?
- What central office space and outreach locations are needed? What is required to keep the space clean, well-maintained, and safe? What will be the cost of rent, utilities, insurance, security, and so forth?
- What is required to develop and maintain community support for the agency such as printing and publications, postage, marketing materials, audits, and the like?
- What are the sources of income (e.g., agency fund-raising efforts, United Way, government appropriations, fees for service, grants, contracts, bequests) and how reliable is each as a base of support?
- If the budget must be cut at some later time, what reductions could be made that will do the least damage to the agency's capacity to carry out its mission?

In a stable organization, the budget should be built on past experience with allowance for anticipated changes in income or expenditures or to accommodate new programming. Since most human services agencies are highly labor intensive, without the infusion of new resources the personnel aspects of the budget become the most critical to consider if any substantial change is anticipated. In addition, the constant tug between *efficiency* (cost per unit of service) and *effectiveness* (ability to achieve service objectives) should be addressed as part of the budgeting process.

Three types of budgeting are commonly found in human services agencies: (1) line-item budgeting, (2) incremental budgeting, and (3) program or functional budgeting. Each yields different information about the cost of doing business.

LINE-ITEM BUDGETING

This type of budget is the most commonly used in social agencies. It requires that the various income and spending categories be identified and that the amount of money anticipated in each category be stated. The accounting system of the agency is organized around these categories, making it possible to obtain a historical picture of the income and expenditures that will serve as the basis for projecting the future. Since a preliminary budget is a planning device, it must be prepared in advance of the year it will be in effect. In other words, next year's budget must be based on incomplete information about how well this year's budget estimated income and expenses. Thus, a preliminary line-item budget will reflect educated guesses about how each budget line will play out during the remainder of the current year and how it will change during the subsequent year.

Typically the *income items* included in a line-item budget would include: any carry-over funds (positive or negative) from the previous year, contract or grant funds, contributions/gifts/bequests, fees from services provided, and, if a nonprofit agency, membership dues. The *personnel expenses* are usually the largest part of the budget and include salaries; employee benefits, such as insurance and Social Security taxes; and fees for consultation and staff development. The *operating expenses* are related to renting or maintaining office space, office supplies and equipment, telephone service, information technology support, any tangible goods (e.g., food, clothing) provided to clients, and travel required by staff.

The line-item budget must then be backed up by an audit report verifying the last year's actual income and expenditures and listing the amounts of any other assets, endowment, or building fund reserves that are excluded from the operating budget.

INCREMENTAL BUDGETING

Based on estimates of increases or decreases in revenue, a series of budget projections might be built on the basis of the current line-item budget. That is, using a "what if?" approach, the expense items of a budget might be developed to reflect the impact of 2 and 5 percent income reductions, no change in revenue, or 2 and 5 percent revenue increases. An incremental budget is particularly helpful in reflecting the impact of inflation and identifying the service implications of increases and decreases in revenue. Such a budget is useful in assessing the cost of adjusting an organization's current program to provide new services. The availability of spreadsheet programs (see Item 9.3) simplifies the process of developing incremental budgets and thus examining the impact of various alternatives.

PROGRAM OR FUNCTIONAL BUDGETING

A final type of budget used by social agencies is the program or functional budget. Again, this is built from a line-item budget and adds the feature of attributing portions of the total cost in each income and expense category to the various components or functions of agency operation. This approach makes it possible to estimate income and expenditures related to any function of the agency, thus providing a picture of the cost-effectiveness of that function.

Preparing a program budget involves estimating the distribution of income (e.g., fees, contributions) and expense items (e.g., salaries, operating expenses) according to their contribution to each of the various agency programs (e.g., adoption, foster care, family counseling).

Selected Bibliography

Edwards, Richard L. and John A. Yankey, eds. *Effectively Managing Nonprofit Organizations.* Washington, DC: NASW Press, 2006.

Kettner, Peter M. *Achieving Excellence in the Management of Human Service Organizations.* Boston: Allyn & Bacon, 2002.

13.34 MARKETING HUMAN SERVICES

Most social workers are not accustomed to thinking about their agency's services as a product to be advertised, displayed, and sold. Doing so, however, helps workers better understand what actions are necessary to attract funding, clients, board members, volunteers, and paraprofessional staff members such as foster parents.

Five distinct aspects of a marketing strategy should be considered when preparing a marketing plan.

KNOW YOUR PRODUCT

Successful salespeople are enthusiastic about their product and they can explain its advantages in a way that attracts the potential customer's interest. The most essential first step in marketing, then, is for the agency personnel to truly believe in the worth of their services. At a minimum, they must be able to explain its merits in simple language and be prepared to back up their beliefs with data drawn from independent evaluations.

FOCUS ON STAKEHOLDERS

In order to understand what attracts your supporters and clients, make a careful analysis of your agency and its services. What are the most and least attractive features of the agency in the view of the general public? Who are the community members most interested in having the agency succeed? How committed to the agency are the professional and support services staff members? What are the characteristics of those who use this service? The answers to such questions help an agency better understand its potential supporters and consumers and helps target marketing efforts toward those groups most likely to respond.

Although you should attempt to keep the general public aware of your agency and its services, your marketing focus should be on the **stakeholders**, that is, clients and other people who share common interests and values related to the agency and its services. It is useful to determine which subgroups are most likely to be interested in a particular program and target your marketing to them. For human services agencies, there are typically several subgroups of stakeholders that a marketing strategy might address:

- *Agency family.* This includes the agency's board, members of various agency committees, and the staff.
- *Volunteers.* People who give their time to assist the agency in providing services have a special commitment and are especially interested in its activities.
- *Clients, former clients, and their families.* Those who have benefited from the agency's efforts can become valuable advocates for an agency.
- *Supporters.* Many agencies have a group of members or other interested supporters who provide various forms of assistance such as financial contributions, assistance with fundraising efforts, and speakers' bureau participants.
- *Community influencers.* Each community has a few people who help shape public opinion or make important decisions that affect human services (see Item 11.20). You should make an effort to keep them informed about the services of your agency.

PROJECT AN IMAGE

Develop a representative symbol or image (e.g., photo, drawing, emblem) of the organization that will both reflect what the agency does and help stakeholders feel positive about what is done there. Use this symbol throughout your marketing efforts. The response to the marketing approach will partly depend on people's first impressions which begin with this image. First impressions are exceedingly powerful, but can quickly evaporate if stakeholders do not have a rewarding experience when interacting with the agency.

PAYOFF FOR STAKEHOLDERS

The payoff in human services is what people gain by supporting or using the services. When contributors or volunteers give their money and time, they are not able to give those dollars or hours to some other worthy cause and thus need to know that their gifts are appreciated and will make a real difference in someone's life. Or perhaps they want to make sure their association with the agency will yield some personal benefit, such as interesting training, job-related experience, or a feeling of being useful. Clients, too, must be treated courteously and with respect by all staff members and receive high-quality services to justify expending their time, money, and emotional investment with this agency.

GETTING OUT THE MESSAGE

The final part of a marketing strategy is to be sure your message gets out to both stakeholders and the general public. Your goal is to keep people informed of the agency's services through speaking to various community civic, social, and religious groups, becoming the subject of stories in newspapers and on TV, and maintaining an appealing and informative website for the agency.

When **addressing community groups**, it is useful to recognize that satisfied customer is the best advertisement an agency can have. As a general rule, presentations by satisfied customers (e.g., long-time financial supporters, enthusiastic volunteers, clients pleased with agency services) are more persuasive than presentations by agency staff, although pairing these stakeholders with staff can increase the depth of understanding of the agency's services.

When working with the **radio, newspaper, and television media**, social workers should:

- *Be proactive.* Rather than hoping the media will come to you for information or a story, reach out to them. Work at creating opportunities to describe your agency and program in a positive way. Remember that human interest stories are especially appealing.

- *Have the authority to speak for the agency.* Make sure you are authorized to represent the agency and, if more than one person from the agency is authorized to deal with the media, make sure the efforts are coordinated. Also, be clear if at any time you are speaking for yourself rather than for the agency and avoid professional jargon.

- *Establish personal relationships with the media.* If the reporters and photographers know and trust you and are aware that you are willing to help them prepare a story, it can mean the difference between just getting your program covered and getting good coverage.

- *Be prepared.* Keep an up-to-date "press kit" in which you include agency information (e.g., a brochure, annual report); your business card; a description of the program, or if conducting a fund-raising effort (see Item 13.35), the campaign's goals; a fact sheet about the agency's clients and services; and a draft news release of the event or program activity you hope to have reported. If you are to be interviewed or be a guest on a talk show, be clear in advance about what you want to say and then rehearse. Have in mind some case examples, but be sure to disguise them in a way that will protect confidentiality.

- *Be available.* Make it easy for the media to contact you by providing your email address and your cell and office telephone numbers, as well as the contact information for someone else to call if you are not available.

- *Be fair.* If you release a story about an agency event, make sure that all media organizations get your news release or a phone call as close to the same time as you can manage.

- *Be understanding.* If your story is not used, there may be good reasons. It could have been dropped at the last minute for something considered more urgent news value. It is all right to ask your media contact if there was something wrong with the story—something that could be corrected in future stories.

- *Make corrections only when necessary.* Handle errors in stories carefully. Unless a serious error has been made, no comment is usually necessary. When a comment is in order, go to the reporter who made the error and handle the correction in private. Explain the error and indicate any damage that may have been caused. Control your emotions and focus only on the facts.

- *Say thanks.* Express your appreciation every time you submit material, whether it is used or not. At least once a year, thank your media professional's boss for the interest and investment in your program.

Finally, your marketing strategy should be backed by a high-quality **webpage.** Today, most people wanting to learn about an agency or program first visit that agency's webpage. Although social workers are rarely the webpage designers, their involvement in determining what should be included and how it should be presented is important. The following steps should help create a useful webpage.

- *Understand your stakeholders.* Be clear about who are the target users of the webpage, that is, your stakeholders. Each subgroup will have different needs and interests and thus the initial page stakeholders open should have something that capture's their interest and then provides tabs to help them locate the appropriate information in more detail.
- *Engage your stakeholders in building the webpage.* Include representative stakeholders on the design team and possibly lead a focus group or conduct a survey to learn their level of computer comfort, what they already know about the services, and what they would expect from a webpage. This process might typically identify the need to describe each program and service; how a potential client should apply; how someone could donate money or volunteer time; provide a list of major donors; present short case summaries of successful services; and include an "about us" tab where information about the board and staff, as well as including the most recent annual report.
- *Develop a prototype webpage.* Working with someone with the technical skills to develop the page, determine what should be included. In general, it is important that the page is easy to navigate, the language is simple, it contains pictures or videos of clients or services being delivered, and provides links to related topics.
- *Test the prototype webpage with stakeholders.* Once again return to your representative stakeholders, ask them to review and critique the page, and then revise and place the material on the web.

Selected Bibliography

Andreasen, Alan R., and Philip Kotler. *Strategic Marketing for Nonprofit Organizations,* 7th ed. Upper Saddle River, NJ: Pearson/Prentice Hall, 2008.

Dunham, Sarah. Brandraising: *How Nonprofits Raise Visibility and Money through Smart Communications.* San Francisco: Jossey-Bass, 2010.

Frost, Raymond, and Judy Strauss. *Building Effective Web Sites.* Upper Saddle River, NJ: Prentice Hall, 2001.

Sheehan, Robert M. Jr. *Mission Impact: Breakthrough Strategies for Nonprofits.* Hoboken, NJ: Wiley, 2010.

13.35 FUND-RAISING FOR A HUMAN SERVICES AGENCY

If a private, not-for-profit human services agency is to survive and develop its programs, it must have a secure and diversified funding base. In the final analysis, that depends on the willingness of people to contribute their money to the agency. A key to agency survival is **fund-raising**, or what some prefer to call *friend-raising*. This refers to the identification and nurturance of those supporters who genuinely believe in the value of the agency and can be counted on to make a contribution to the agency, year after year. The "care and feeding" of this important base of continuing support is one important target of an agency's marketing plan (see Item 13.34) that results in on-going fund-raising.

On occasion, a major fund-raising campaign is planned in which funds to start a new program or build a facility are solicited which requires a different approach to fundraising. Inexperienced agency personnel are seldom prepared for the demands and complexity of such a campaign. It takes time, energy, and know-how to successfully raise funds. Because many local health and human services agencies are affiliated with large federated campaigns such as the United Way or the American Cancer Society, a small, independent agency must compete with these experienced and sophisticated fund-raising agencies for the interest, goodwill, and money of potential contributors.

GUIDELINES FOR FUND-RAISING

Following these principles can assist social workers in a major fund-raising effort:

- Realize that even under the best of circumstances raising money for human services agencies is a difficult and time-consuming activity.
- It is critical to plan ahead. Allow plenty of time (i.e., several months), remembering that the most difficult time to raise funds is when you urgently need them. It is estimated that it will take a minimum of three months to plan and raise funds from individuals and local businesses (e.g., through canvassing and direct mail); three to six months to raise funds from local foundations, service clubs, and unions; and at least six to eight months to raise funds from a national foundation, United Way, or financial institution. Also, that investment of time and energy usually means that other responsibilities in the agency must be set aside in order to free time for fund-raising. Thus, it is important to assess the need and the chances of success before embarking on a fund-raising effort.
- Look for money at the local level first. Local people are the ones most likely to have a vested interest in seeing the program succeed.
- Fund-raising is a very personal activity. In reality, people usually give money to other people, not to an organization or cause. Build networks and get to know key people in the organizations you plan to solicit and have those individuals help you gain access to and establish credibility with others in that organization.
- It costs money to raise money. Make sure that the cost of fund-raising is built into the agency's budget.
- Get volunteers and the agency board of directors involved. They will have credibility in the community and their involvement increases their ownership of the program.
- It is important to research the priorities of potential funding sources and match their priorities with yours. Considerable helpful information is usually available on the website of the funding source.
- Fund-raising involves asking people for their money. If you do not ask, you will not get it. (Some suggestions on how to ask are given later.)
- Get expert advice if you are unsure of how to proceed in a fund-raising campaign. You can damage future efforts if you attempt to carry out a poorly developed plan.

ELEMENTS OF A FUND-RAISING CAMPAIGN

Hundreds of decisions and actions make up a successful fund-raising campaign. Here are some of the major steps to follow:

1. *Formulate a goal.* After a careful examination of agency needs, establish a realistic goal as to how much money is intended to be raised and set a realistic timeframe for reaching that goal.

2. *Consult those with expertise.* Draw together the people who have worked on previous campaigns and determine what has and has not worked. Consider hiring a professional fund-raiser if your own prior efforts have not been successful, if you are unsure how to proceed, or if you need to raise more than $100,000.

3. *Develop a plan.* Draw on the agency's prior experience and use an approach that has worked in the past. Be cautious about attempting an approach with which you have no experience. When constructing your budget, factor in the amount of staff time needed and the cost of postage, supplies, public information materials, and travel.

4. *Select a chairperson.* This person should be a respected and trusted individual with good name recognition in the community. Most important, the chairperson must be someone who has the energy and time required and is committed to achieving the campaign goal. Recruit the chairperson during the planning stage so he or she can help shape the overall strategy. This individual must be capable of recruiting other volunteers.

5. *Build an organizational structure.* A successful campaign requires an organizational structure that ensures rapid communication, coordination, and careful monitoring of campaign activities and volunteers. Because many of the contributions will come from those working on the campaign, the effort should embrace and involve many individuals, community groups, and organizations. Many campaigns use a pyramid structure made up of several team captains, each responsible for overseeing the work of several campaign workers. A campaign might also have several divisions or special units that seek contributions from certain segments of the community (e.g., labor unions, civic clubs, small businesses).

6. *Recruit and train the campaign workers.* Workers must be asked to help people seldom volunteer for fund-raising. The campaign chair, board members, and friends of the agency must actively recruit persons who have the contacts and influence necessary to secure contributions. Some of the individuals willing to help may not be comfortable asking for money, yet they can help with other important tasks such as preparing informational packets, doing office work, and arranging appointments.

7. *Prepare informational material.* Simply written brochures should explain the agency's program, what money is needed, and how it will be spent. This information may also need to be presented in the form of newspaper, television, and radio ads, as well as being added to the agency's webpage. Agency staff members who know the various programs the agency offers should play a key role in identifying appropriate content.

8. *Maintain proper records.* The campaign must maintain a complete and accurate record of persons contacted, contributions, and expenses. Any hint of dishonesty, fraud, or incomplete bookkeeping will seriously damage the agency's ability to raise funds in the future.

9. *Be generous with recognition.* All those who contributed and all those who worked on the campaign should receive recognition and thanks. This creates a sense of pride and goodwill and increases the chances that these people and groups will assist in future campaigns.

10. *Evaluate the campaign.* After the campaign is complete, the agency board, campaign chairperson, and other key leaders should carefully evaluate what worked, what did not work, and how future campaigns could be improved.

ASKING FOR MONEY

Many of us are hesitant to ask others for money, but that is what fund-raising is all about. Following these suggestions may help reduce this problem:

- Those who ask others for money must have already given their fair share. Those doing the asking must be able to say, "I have given $500; I am asking that you give at least $250."
- Small amounts of money can be raised by mail, email, and telephone campaigns. Big money is raised through face-to-face contact with the donor.
- It is critically important that the right person ask another for money and that the request be made in the right way, for the right reason, and at the right time. This is a further reminder that people do not give money to agencies or even causes; people give primarily because a specific person (e.g., someone they know and trust) has asked them to give.
- Ask for a specific amount of money and be sure to ask for enough (e.g., "We need $1,000 to send five children to camp").
- Assess the person's capability of giving before you ask. In other words, do some background research and determine what an individual or company is capable of giving. Ask for that amount.
- Be persistent. Keep asking until you get what you want or receive a firm "no."
- If an individual cannot make a cash donation, ask if an in-kind donation might be possible (e.g., time, used equipment, expertise).

Selected Bibliography

Fredricks, Laura. *The Ask: How to Ask for Support for Your Nonprofit Cause, Creative Project, or Business Venture*. San Francisco: Jossey-Bass, 2010.

Kihlstedt, Andrea. *Capital Campaigns: Strategies That Work,* 3rd ed. Sudsbury, MA: Jones and Bartlett Publishers, 2010.

Klein, Kim. *Reliable Fundraising in Unreliable Times: What Good Causes Need to Know to Survive and Thrive.* San Francisco, Jossey-Bass, 2010.

13.36 DEVELOPING GRANT APPLICATIONS

The resources available to a social agency are usually fully committed for operating existing programs and any incremental increases in funds obtained each year are often consumed by normal salary increases and inflation. The opportunity to demonstrate or test program innovations or conduct research on some aspect of the agency's program frequently cannot be done without the infusion of grant funds. A social worker who is knowledgeable about locating sources of grant funds, able to facilitate the work of a team to prepare grant applications, and skilled at preparing such applications, is a valuable asset to his or her agency.

Before grant writing team can begin the grant-writing process, three prerequisites must be met. First, the idea or program innovation to be demonstrated or studied must be clearly thought out. Second, the agency's administrators and governing body must be committed to the idea. Finally, an assessment of the competence and capacity of both the individuals and the agency to carry out the proposed activity must indicate that this work can be successfully completed. The grant development team should be prepared to invest considerable up-front time and effort into preparing a grant application, which frequently must be done in addition to ongoing work assignments. Yet, obtaining grant funding is often the only way to improve services.

SOURCES OF GRANT FUNDING

A variety of funding sources might be considered. Sometimes, a local or national business will underwrite a project that is of interest to them. A computer company, for example, might donate equipment to demonstrate the potential effectiveness of a computerized interagency referral network. Other times, a group of persons interested in a project might undertake a fund-raising effort to help support this activity. However, the primary sources for a project are grants from government agencies or private foundations.

Government Grants. The largest amount of money is available through agencies of the federal government, although states may also allocate such funds. Most government grants relate to areas that the sponsoring agency has defined to reflect its priorities. The public is notified of available funding through a *Request for Proposals* (RFP) or *Request for Applications* (RFA). Grant applications are reviewed by a panel of experts and awarded on a competitive basis. Some discretionary funds may also be available to allow for innovative program ideas that are not currently among the granting agency's established priorities, making it is helpful to discuss your ideas with persons in the regional and national offices of the government agencies who administer the funds in your area of interest (e.g., aging, child welfare, AIDS) before investing much time and energy in developing a proposal. These staff members can help you assess the fit between your proposal and the agency's interest and provide such information as the typical size of grants and the odds of success.

Two published sources of information are particularly useful regarding grant possibilities from the federal government. The *Catalog of Federal Domestic Assistance* contains a comprehensive listing and description of federal programs. Programs are cross-referenced by function (e.g., housing, health, welfare), by subject (e.g., drug abuse, economic development), and by the federal agency that administers the program. The description of each program includes information such as uses and restrictions on the funds, eligibility requirements, and the application and award process. A second source is the *Federal Register*. It is published every government working day and contains notices, rules and regulations, guidelines, and proposed rules and regulations for every federal grant-giving agency. Both the *Catalog of Federal Domestic Assistance* and the *Federal Register* are usually available through many libraries and on the Internet.

Private Foundations. A more likely source for the small grants an agency might request to support innovative program ideas is the private foundation. Most foundations develop specialized areas of interest, and some make resources available only for programs located in a specific geographic region. Perhaps the most helpful source is The *Foundation Directory*. Part 1 of that directory includes those foundations that give away more than $200,000 per year, and Part 2 contains those that give smaller amounts. The Foundation Center periodically publishes a series of specialized directories of grant sources that are focused on areas such as children, youth, and families; aging; the economically disadvantaged; health; and women and girls. Another directory, The *Directory of Corporate and Foundation Givers*, provides background information about potential funding sources in the private sector. Once again, many local libraries and universities will have copies of these publications. Once a foundation that appears to be a good match with your interest is identified, go to that foundation's website where considerable information on their selection criteria and process is listed.

GUIDELINES FOR DEVELOPING A PROPOSAL

The planning and preparation of a proposal is a labor-intensive process. Make sure you have the necessary time and motivation. A hastily written proposal, or the so-called all-purpose proposal, has little chance of success. Several guidelines are of critical importance:

1. *Do your homework.* Make a thorough study of the potential funding source (foundation or government agency) before deciding to submit a proposal. Pay special attention to the published funding priorities, history of prior awards, eligibility, geographical limitation, type and size of grants available, funding cycle, process for selection, and so on. Secure the name, address, and phone number for the contact person should you have questions.

2. *Make informal inquiries.* Save time for yourself and for the funding agency by informally inquiring about its possible interest in your ideas. However, assume that the recipient of your inquiry is busy, impatient, skeptical, not especially interested in your problems, and faced with many more requests than he or she can read thoroughly, let alone fund. Be very businesslike in your approach and be prepared to describe your proposal clearly and concisely in one or two pages or in five minutes on the phone. If you think you will be making an application, request an application packet and all relevant instructions.

3. *Write the proposal.* Study the instructions in the funding agency's guidelines and follow them to the letter, addressing every section or question. You should anticipate answering at least the following questions:

- What do you want to do, how much will it cost, and how long will it take?
- How does the proposed project relate to the funding agency's interests and priorities?
- Are you aware of other projects like the one you are proposing and how is yours similar or different? (You will need a good literature search.)
- How do you plan to carry out the project? Does the proposed staff have the necessary training and experience? Why are you particularly prepared to conduct this project, rather than someone else?
- Who stands to benefit from the proposed project? What impact will it have on your agency, clients, discipline, community, state, or nation? How will you measure, evaluate, and report the impact?
- If successful, how will you continue the work after the grant support has ended?

The written proposal must be very clear and well organized, with justification for the various expenditures described in detail. Often, the proposal cannot exceed a certain number of pages and has a firm closing date. Usually the closing date is a designated postmark, but sometimes the proposal must be in the hands of the granting agency either physically or electronically by that date. If a team is writing a proposal, designate one person who will have final authority to edit the materials into a coherent document.

4. *Be a good salesperson for your project.* Your written proposal and/or oral presentation should reflect knowledge, enthusiasm, and commitment. Focus your proposal on its alignment with the funder's goals and how you can contribute to clients or improve the provision of human services if you are funded. Coming across as helpless and needy (e.g., "We really, really need the money") will pretty much assure that you will not be funded. However, if those selecting proposals to be funded become convinced that the people associated with the program are capable and responsible, they may work especially hard on finding a way to fund the proposal. Obtaining letters of support from related agencies and key people in your community can help sell your proposal. Ask these people to address specific areas of the proposal (e.g., the need, the agency's history of sound management, the staff's ability to carry out the project, community support for the program).

5. *Be accountable.* If you receive the grant requested, be prepared to carry out the project according to your written plan and within the proposed budget. The acceptance of a grant carries with it the responsibility for managing the money properly, submitting regular progress reports, reporting project results, and giving appropriate credit to the funding source. Good stewardship of the grant funds is very important and is essential if future grant requests from that source are to be funded.

Proposal Contents.   Stress the quality of what you can do with grant support, as opposed to stressing why you have not done it before. Remember that your proposal is in competition for scarce grant resources and that it likely will be evaluated against the criteria set out in guidelines. In general, the following components will be expected:

1. *Cover page.* Include the project title, principal investigators, name of agency, dates for project activity, total budget request, and signatures of authorized agency personnel approving the application.

2. *Abstract.* Prepare a short statement of the objectives and procedures to be used, methods of evaluation, and plan for disseminating results.

3. *Statement of problem and objectives.* Indicate the rationale for this project and prepare a clear statement of the objectives in measurable terms.

4. *Methodology, procedures, and activities.* Describe the design and approach of the project, identify who will be served, and discuss the administrative structure for the project. Lay out a clear plan of action with phases and dates for activity detailed. The use of Gantt and PERT charts (see Item 12.12) can help make processes and timelines clear to reviewers.

5. *Evaluation methods.* Describe how the results or outcomes of the activity will be assessed. Your application will be strengthened if the evaluators are not directly associated with your agency or personally invested in the outcome of your demonstration or research project.

6. *Dissemination of results.* Indicate how the results of the project will be disseminated so that others can benefit from the knowledge gained from this activity.

7. *Personnel and facilities.* Describe the staff required to carry out the project, include short resumés of key personnel who will be assigned to this activity, and indicate how any new staff will be selected. Also, describe any special equipment required, and indicate how the agency will make space available to accommodate project activities.

8. *Budget Justification.* Provide a detailed budget of the anticipated costs of the project and an explanation or justification for those expenditures. Indicate what will be required from the funding source and what will be contributed by the agency or other sources. Many funding sources require that matching funds from local sources be identified as a requirement for funding. In some instances, a cash match is required, but in others, in-kind contributions (e.g., staff time or office space) are acceptable. A budget will usually include personnel costs (including fringe benefits), outside consultants or evaluators for the project, consumable materials (supplies, printing, postage, etc.), equipment, travel, and indirect costs. The latter relates to the real costs to an agency (space, heat, light, etc.) consumed by the project staff that cannot readily be documented. Some public agencies limit indirect cost to as little as 8 to 15 percent of the project expenses and some foundations do not allow charging for any indirect costs. Also, be prepared to describe what will happen to the project after the grant funding has ended.

Selected Bibliography

Bauer, David G. *The "How To" Grants Manual: Successful Grantseeking Techniques for Obtaining Public and Private Grants*, 6th ed. Westport, CT: Praeger Publishers, 2007.

Carlson, Mim, Tori O'Neal-McElrath, and the Alliance for Nonprofit Management. *Winning Grants: Step by Step,* 3rd ed. San Francisco: Jossey-Bass, 2008.

Catalog of Federal Domestic Assistance. Available online: https://www.cfda.gov.

Directory of Corporate and Foundation Givers. Washington, DC: Taft Group, most recent edition.

Federal Register. Available online: www.gpoaccess.gov/fr/index.html.

13.37 ORGANIZING NEIGHBORHOODS AND COMMUNITIES

Terms such as *social activist* and *progressive* have been branded as negative by right-wing political advocates. Yet, part of the mission of social work is to not only help individuals change to adapt to issues they experience but also help them change to environments in which they live to prevent these issues from occurring in the first place. Facilitating progressive change in the social structures in our neighborhoods and communities requires the social worker to become an **activist**, that is, have skill in organizing people to identify and address the sources or causes of the issues, and then to mount strategic change efforts to rectify the problems. Changing the status quo is sure to find opposition.

Some issues can be addressed only through very broad social change efforts best described as **movements**. These efforts require skills in national or statewide organization that attempt to change the public's basic thinking and understanding of the issues at stake. Some examples that have been of special concern to social workers include the Civil Rights Movement, the Women's Movement, the Community Mental Health Movement, and the Gay Rights Movement. Some social workers may be a part of local organizing efforts affiliated with a movement, but few would be in the role of orchestrating the movement's overall actions.

More typically, social workers are involved in neighborhood and community efforts to bring about social change locally. In the United States, relatively few social workers have jobs that focus primarily on neighborhoods or communities. Rather, U.S. social workers are largely concerned with individuals, families, groups, and sometimes organizations. However, when social workers provide services to a number of people experiencing similar issues, it becomes clear that something more than individual abilities or choices is at the root of the issue. For example: "Why are so many African American males in jails and prisons?" "What is behind the excessive violence against people who are gay or lesbian?" "Why is the suicide rate so high for older males?" "Why are so many of my clients unable to find stable employment?" "What are the reasons so many people use the hospital's emergency room as their primary health care provider?"

Two forms of organizing characterize social workers' efforts to affect community and neighborhood change. One form has been labeled **community organization**. This is largely interagency work or efforts to strengthen the service delivery system in the neighborhood or community at large. Due to social workers' unique focus among the professions to aid people in using the resources in their communities, social workers become keenly aware of the difficulties clients have in accessing services, as well as recognizing the gaps in services where there simply are not sufficient resources. This change effort, then, is largely interagency work. The skills required for this work include leading small-group meetings (see Item 13.25), sometimes chairing committees (see Item 13.28), helping groups of interested people problem-solve about the issue (see Item 13.29), and engaging in community advocacy (see Item 13.31).

At a more grassroots level, social workers help facilitate the efforts of people who experience an issue to come together to better understand the causes and plan strategies to remedy, or at least decrease, the impact of the issue. This form or organization is known as **neighborhood or community development** with the goal of increasing *social justice* for local people. Depending on the issue, this might involve energizing people living in a neighborhood (e.g., trailer park, ghetto, or barrio) or it might require engaging people from throughout a community concerned with specific social problem (e.g., various expressions of discrimination, restricted access to public resources, or experiencing poverty). This approach to social work practice leans heavily on the principle of *empowerment* (see Chapter 5) where the social worker facilitates the change-oriented activities of the people most affected by the issue.

Two goals are dominant in this neighborhood/community development work: (1) helping the individuals recognize and develop their own skills in leading change efforts and (2) helping to bring about change in the neighborhood or community to address the issue. This is essentially behind-the-scenes activity where one guides the neighborhood/community leadership only when needed or requested. With this mind-frame, the social worker largely depends on critical thinking, unobtrusive guidance of the change process, and the basic communication skills discussed in Chapter 8. Typically this type of social work practice begins with the formation of an ad hoc group that disbands when the issue is resolved, but at times resolution of the issue is more long-term and results in the formation of a formal organization that may have a continuing life of its own.

Selected Bibliography

Chetkovich, Carol and Frances Kunruther. *From the Ground Up: Grassroots Organizations Making Social Change.* Ithaca, NY: Cornell University Press, 2006.

DeFilippis, James, Robert Fisher, and Eric Shragge. *Contesting Community: The Limits and Potential of Local Organizing.* New Brunswick, NJ: Rutgers University Press, 2010.

Gamble, Dorothy N., and Marie Weil. *Community Practice Skills: Local to Global Perspectives.* New York: Columbia University Press, 2009.

Rothman, Jack, John L. Erlich, and John E. Tropman, eds. *Strategies of Community Intervention,* 7th ed. Peosta, IA: Eddie Bowers Publishers, 2008.

13.38   INFLUENCING LEGISLATORS AND OTHER DECISION MAKERS

Decisions that are made at the local, state, and national levels by elected representatives and other public officials have substantial impact on the human services. Because social workers are in a unique position to observe how public social policy helps or hinders the most vulnerable members of society, their perspective needs to be articulated lest client needs and concerns are overlooked. When social workers are not politically involved, the insights and experiences of the social work profession are not made available to the policy development process.

When planning an effort to influence a decision maker, the worker should keep several guidelines in mind. First, a social worker is more likely to influence a decision when he or she has an established relationship with the decision maker. Of course, when someone is new to a community or organization it will take time to build such relationships and, as new decision makers appear on the scene, it will also take time to cultivate a relationship with them. The worker should make a point to initiate such relationships before attempting to influence a particular decision if at all possible. Second, the decision maker is more likely to be influenced by the worker if he or she presents information that can be trusted. The social worker should make a careful analysis of the issue and the people making the decision (see Items 11.20 and 11.21), never distort the facts or give information that cannot be substantiated, and be thoroughly prepared to discuss the matter. Finally, the worker should be selective about the issues presented to decision makers. One's credibility with decision makers can be diminished if too many issues are addressed. When a social worker decides to attempt to influence a decision, it should be done in a carefully planned and assertive way. In short, when formulating an approach the worker should remember that decision makers are most likely to be persuaded by persons they perceive as well-informed, competent, engaging, and genuinely committed to the issue.

Because social workers do not usually have the power or status necessary to exert pressure on decision makers, they must often work through others who are in a better position to exercise influence. At other times, however, the worker should directly communicate with the decision maker through personal contact, in writing, or both.

VISITING WITH A POLICYMAKER

Many legislators and other key decision makers spend their time in a somewhat restricted environment; they speak primarily with staff members, lobbyists, and colleagues. Hence, they often welcome the opportunity to hear the positions of people who have firsthand knowledge of issues they must decide. This communication might occur by attending a legislator's open forum or town meeting or by talking individually with the decision maker. Sometimes, when a decision maker is difficult to schedule, effective communication on a subject can occur with his or her aide or advisor can be effective.

The following guidelines can help to make visits with decision makers (or their advisors) productive:

- *Use time efficiently.* The decision maker's time is valuable. If you are to get that person's full attention and have a favorable climate for communicating your information, you must be efficient. When planning an individual meeting, schedule an appointment in advance and ask that a specific amount of time be reserved for the meeting. Be on time, even though you may have to wait for the legislator to complete other responsibilities before meeting with you. Also, get to the point quickly. Have your presentation planned so that you can pack a lot of information into a short time period.
- *Be positive.* Begin on a friendly note. Find a reason to praise the decision maker for some action taken in relation to prior contacts (if appropriate) and thank him or her for being willing to take time to hear your position on this matter.
- *Express your conviction.* Let the legislator know that, as a social worker, you are in a unique position to recognize the implications of this decision. Leave no doubt in the legislator's mind that you believe in what you are proposing. Back up your view with facts and examples. If the information is at all detailed, prepare a handout that can be left with the decision maker and others who may be present.
- *Be specific.* Be very sure that the person knows what you want him or her to do. For example, do you simply want him or her to understand the situation better? Do you want him or her to propose an amendment to a piece of legislation? Do you want him or her to vote in a particular way?
- *Follow up in writing.* Send or leave a statement that reflects your position and provides the facts that you presented. The purpose of this document is to supply material that will be placed in the legislator's file on the topic and as a reminder of your position when it is time to take action. Be sure that your name, street address, email address, and telephone number are on the materials so you can be contacted to clarify points or provide information on related matters.

WRITING A POLICYMAKER

Although face-to-face contact is probably the most effective way to influence a legislator or other decision maker, many times that is not possible because of constraints of time, distance, resources, or the availability of the decision maker. Letters, fax messages, email, and telephone calls, when properly timed, can also be effective in influencing decisions. The addresses and telephone numbers of public officials will usually be listed periodically in newspapers or are readily available through an Internet search. Locating other officials may require more research.

Observe these guidelines when writing to a decision maker:

- *Be accurate.* Be sure that you use the correct spelling of the person's name, the proper title, and the accurate address. Be sure that the decision maker has correct information about you in case he or she wants to respond to your communication.
- *Be brief and to the point.* Limit your communication to one page. Focus only on one issue or piece of legislation in each communication. If you are interested in several matters, send separate correspondence so each can be filed with materials about those matters.
- *Clearly identify the issue or bill that concerns you.* Provide identifying details (e.g., the bill's number, name, and dates) so there can be no misunderstanding of what you are writing about.
- *Write simply and clearly.* Remember that those who will read your material are very busy and may receive many pieces of correspondence each day. Make it easy for them to understand the points you wish to make.
- *Begin in a positive manner.* Address the legislator in a respectful manner and use titles appropriate to the office. If possible, praise or compliment the legislator for some previous action or statement and, if possible, relate the preferred action on this matter to other positions he or she has supported.
- *Provide facts and figures that support your position.* Explain the impact of the decision and how many people will be affected. Short case examples are often effective in helping the reader understand how the issue affects individuals.
- *Clearly identify the action you desire.* Make sure the reader knows what you want to happen (e.g., vote for HR 254, oppose the filibuster of SB 1543).
- *Pay attention to timing.* Be sure to time communicating your opinion to just precede the debate on the topic. Typically, a legislator will make up his or her mind early in the hearing process and long before time for a final vote.
- *Follow up the action.* After the decision or vote is completed, write again, thanking the legislator for considering your viewpoint if he or she took the action you requested. If not, express regret about that action. Such follow-up reminds the person that you are truly concerned about the issue and will continue to observe his or her actions on this matter.

Selected Bibliography

Haynes, Karen, and James Mickelson. *Affecting Change: Social Workers in the Political Arena,* 6th ed. Boston: Allyn & Bacon, 2006.

Richan, Willard C. *Lobbying for Social Change*, 3rd ed. New York: Haworth Press, 2006.

Schwartz, Heather E. *Political Activism: How You Can Make a Difference.* Mankato, MN: Capstone Press, 2009.

CHAPTER 14

Evaluation and Termination

Every helping relationship must end. Counseling must be concluded and groups or committees must eventually be disbanded. The change process ends with the termination of service and a final evaluation of the intervention. **Termination** is that important final phase in helping clients, the time when the worker guides the concluding activities in a manner that is sensitive to issues surrounding the ending of a relationship.

If a meaningful relationship has been formed between client and worker (a key to successful helping), it is not surprising that this ending phase is often experienced with mixed emotions. One common reaction is that the client and worker are pleased that their work together has been concluded. Consequently, the client will no longer need to invest time, resources, and emotional energy in the change process and the worker can move on to new responsibilities. A competing emotion is the sense of loss. Clients sometimes feel anger, rejection, sadness, and anxiousness when the relationship ends. Thus, the worker must provide an opportunity for the client to express his or her feelings and concerns and the worker must lay the groundwork for a resumption of service in the future, should that be needed.

Occasionally, service will unexpectedly end at a time other than that originally planned or expected by the worker and client. For example, an abrupt termination may occur in these circumstances:

- The client, for personal or financial reasons, decides to stop participating.
- The worker accepts employment elsewhere.
- The helping process is blocked by a problem or conflict in the worker—client relationship necessitating transfer to another worker.
- The client requires specialized services that are best provided by another social worker, professional, or agency.

If the termination is prompted by the worker or agency, the worker should clearly explain what is happening and why. If the client simply stops participating, the worker should attempt to make a final contact to bring their relationship to an amicable closure.

Also, a final **evaluation** should occur at the conclusion of the change process. At this time, the degree of client change is measured and the social worker assesses the success of the intervention. The growing impact of various funding sources on the practice of social work today, coupled with an already important obligation for accountability to clients, agencies, and the community, makes it imperative that social workers are skilled at evaluating their practice. As compared to the ongoing monitoring that occurs throughout the helping process, the final evaluation occurs during or after termination.

Two forms of evaluation are of primary concern to the social worker. **Direct practice evaluation** is the assessment of the interventions and their impact on a specific client (e.g., an individual, family, or small group). This evaluation can serve two purposes. It can be *formative evaluation*, which is used to inform and guide the ongoing practice decisions related to the intervention and, as such, is a tool for monitoring and changing the planned intervention when necessary. Direct practice evaluation can also be a *summative evaluation*, in which one assesses the final outcome and identifies the factors that contributed to the relative success or failure of the intervention.

The second form, **program evaluation**, attempts to evaluate the effectiveness and efficiency of a program that serves many clients or perhaps even a whole community. Program evaluation, too, can be both formative and summative. It is formative if it is used for assessing a program and changing aspects of its functioning to better serve the agency's clients or community. It is summative when, for example, it is used to report the results of a demonstration program to a board of directors or a funding source.

The planning of an evaluation should begin at the point when the intervention's goals and approach are selected. Unless the desired outcomes are specified and measured in the early phases of the change process, the worker will not be able to adequately judge its effect. Additionally, the worker must specify the criteria by which to measure the variables (e.g., client behaviors, community knowledge) that are expected to change during the intervention. In research terms, the client's, agency's, or community's functioning is considered the *dependent variable* and the intervention used is the *independent variable*. In the evaluation of a counseling program, for example, improvement of client functioning (dependent variable) may be viewed as an indicator of the success of services provided (independent variable).

The perception reflected here is that social work practice is all about change—helping clients change, helping their environments change, and helping agencies or communities change. The philosophy behind the evaluation of social work practice, then, is that the change that occurs during a practice intervention can be measured based on the following logic:

- If a social problem or negative social condition does not exist, then there is no need for intervention.
- If a problem or negative situation exists for a client, then it exists in some quantity (e.g., frequency, intensity, or duration) and can, therefore, be described and measured.
- If it can be measured, then it is possible to measure or document the degree to which it changes over time.

In short, the outcomes of all social work practice can be evaluated. The challenge is, of course, to figure out how to measure the dependent variables and to determine the amount of change that occurred.

When deciding what approach to use to measure change in client functioning, the social worker should consider the following factors and questions:

- *Validity.* Does the measurement procedure actually measure what it is assumed or believed to measure?
- *Reliability.* Does the procedure yield similar results when the measurement is repeated under similar circumstances?
- *Ease of application.* Is the procedure sufficiently brief, easy to use, and understandable to the nonspecialist?
- *Sensitivity.* Is the measurement procedure able to detect relatively small levels of change and degrees of difference?
- *Nonreactivity.* Can the procedure detect differences without modifying or influencing the phenomena being measured?

When selecting standardized measurement tools, the social worker should review the manuals that accompany the instrument or published articles about the tool's development for descriptions of how they are to be used and their strengths, limitations, and psychometric properties.

If this information is not available, the social worker should make only tentative and cautious judgments based on the measurement.

The measurement techniques included in this chapter can be used for both monitoring practice (formative evaluation) and making a comprehensive or final assessment of the intervention activity (summative evaluation). Thus, these techniques could be placed in either Chapter 13 or Chapter 14 of this book. Due to the large number of intervention techniques reported in Chapter 13, the measurement techniques are located in this chapter to give them more visibility.

SECTION A

TECHNIQUES AND GUIDELINES FOR DIRECT PRACTICE

The social worker is ethically obliged to be accountable for the quality of services provided. The *NASW Code of Ethics* recognizes that "social workers should monitor and evaluate [their] . . . practice interventions" (Section 5.02.a). Also, it is important to engage clients in the review of the change process, encouraging them to judge the success and usefulness of the experience from their vantage point, and to express their thoughts on the worker's performance. From this information, the worker can more accurately assess his or her practice strengths and limitations and, where appropriate, seek consultation or training to enhance the quality of future practice.

Evaluation Activities.   There is a growing emphasis on the need for data-based or empirical evaluation of social work practice, suggesting that social work should become a profession of *scientific practitioners*. This development is not without controversy. Four primary themes are reflected in this debate:

1. It is argued that social work intervention is primarily an act of human caring and that the whole person cannot be broken down into discrete components and measured in any meaningful way. Proponents of direct practice evaluation, however, argue that people come to social workers for help with specific problems and conditions, and that change in the client's situation is what demonstrates that the intervention was effective.

2. Opponents of empirical evaluation contend that it is time-consuming to select or design measurement scales, collect and analyze data, and then interpret the results and all this takes valuable time away from therapeutic interactions with clients. Those on the other side of the debate contend that much of the data needed for evaluation will usually have already been gathered for purposes of assessment and monitoring. The only additional time required is that needed to organize these data in a way that allows systematic analysis. Once the worker develops the skill, it takes little additional time to evaluate an intervention. Moreover, because the evaluation process actively engages the client, it can help increase his or her motivation and involvement in the change process.

3. Persons who object to empirical practice evaluation suggest that only a relatively few social workers and agency administrators have the skills needed to implement this type of evaluation. In addition, the opponents of evaluation contend that because systematic data collection and evaluation is not yet a common activity or what clients usually expect, the clients will resist this practice. Proponents, however, contend that the profession cannot wait around for some future generation of social workers to be trained in the use of these evaluation techniques. Given the demands from managed care companies and the general public for evidence that social work interventions are effective, the profession must move quickly to adopt systematic evaluation as a regular component of practice. Further, it is usually the social workers, not the clients, who resist collecting these data. Most clients are accustomed to physicians measuring and recording changes in their body temperature, blood pressure, and weight—or even asking for a patient's judgment on a 1 to 10 scale regarding less quantifiable factors, such as how much pain is being experienced. For the clients there is little difference between being asked by a social worker to record the number of anger outbursts experienced in a week or completing a questionnaire that measures the level of marital conflict, and keeping a record of changes in one's temperature for a physician.

4. Some social scientists contend that it is not possible to arrive at clear cause-and-effect conclusions from the methodologies available for the evaluation of a social work intervention. These scientists suggest that there is too little control over extraneous variables, that the evaluation designs and procedures must be adapted to unique client situations (thus minimizing one's ability to generalize the results to other cases), that the range of designs is too limited to accommodate the breadth of social work practice, and that the conclusions are suspect because the social worker, as a practitioner-researcher, cannot remain sufficiently objective. Proponents counter that this form of evaluation is not intended to yield the same kind of information as traditional research, and they agree that the results should not be generalized to other clients. Rather, these methods are primarily intended to help assess one social worker's intervention with one client (or group of clients). Also, proponents call for caution in concluding that the measures alone provide sufficient evidence to prove that an intervention by itself *caused* a change in a client's attitudes, behaviors, or actions. Additional information would be needed to arrive at a genuine cause-and-effect conclusion. Even so, those supporting empirical evaluation conclude that it is valuable for what it can measure—for example, to substantiate that the client or situation did change, that the change occurred following introduction of a specific intervention, or that the client's condition improved and that the improvement was sustained over time.

These four basic criticisms of the empirical evaluation of social work practice should signal the worker to be cautious not to overestimate the power of the data to predict outcomes. These data should supplement, rather than replace, other indicators of practice success. The worker can feel most confident about client change when empirical data are consistent with his or her own practice observations, the client's self-reports and perceptions, and the views of collateral resources or observers, such as parents or other professionals. If at least three assessments are comparable (i.e., *triangulation*), the social worker can feel relatively confident about the results.

When collecting data to be used in the evaluation of a direct services intervention, the social worker should follow these guidelines:

1. *The informed consent of the client is more important than the data.* The client should be fully informed about how these data will be collected and used and should give his or her consent for participation in the evaluation process (see *NASW Code of Ethics,* 1999, Section 5.02.e). Clients may fear that the data collected could potentially be used against them, for example, by a court, school, or family member, and should have the right to refuse to supply this information. In addition to the obvious ethical matter of collecting and maintaining such information without client permission, it is also unlikely that much useful data will be obtained if the client is not a willing and active participant in the process.

2. *Practice requirements should take precedence over data collection.* It is sometimes tempting to structure and manipulate service delivery in a way that makes it easier to collect the data needed for evaluation. But compromising client services for the purpose of evaluation (e.g., delaying intervention to obtain baseline scores, continuing services beyond the client's needs to obtain additional data) is not in the best interest of the client and thus should be avoided.

3. *The questions to be answered through the practice evaluation should be viewed as fluid.* The traditional research process begins with identifying the research questions or hypotheses, selecting the methods for data collection, determining the sampling process for the population to provide data, and so on. There is little flexibility once the process is begun. By contrast, direct practice evaluation begins with developing a service plan for a client (individual, family, group) and only after that is the research question (or questions) generated, the measurement tools selected, and the evaluation design adopted. The range of questions one might attempt to answer could relate to change concerning:

- *The client.* A fundamental purpose of monitoring and evaluating practice is to determine if the client was, in fact, helped. For example: If change occurred, was the change in the intended or desired direction? If a family or a group showed positive change, did each member also experience positive change? Did the client accomplish the agreed-upon tasks? To what extent did the client achieve his or her goals? Was the change accomplished during the intervention sustained after termination?

- *The intervention.* We sometimes want to study the effectiveness of the interventions we use. We might ask questions such as these: What specific aspects of the intervention produced the change? If the client participated in several interventions or services, was one more effective that another? Was an intervention more effective when used alone or in combination with other interventions? With what types of clients or under what circumstances is a particular intervention effective or ineffective?

- *The worker.* We also may want to use practice evaluation as a means of answering questions about ourselves and the success of our service provision—for instance, to what extent do my clients achieve their goals for this service activity? Do I provide some services more successfully than others?

Also, unlike traditional research, the questions one attempts to answer may change as the practice situation unfolds. For example, a client's service plan may begin with the premise that a particular intervention approach will be the best means of serving a client but as the worker monitors the client's progress it may become apparent that a different approach should be tried. Thus, the questions asked of a direct service evaluation may need to be altered as the client and worker gain experience during the change process.

4. *The evaluation design should be viewed as changeable.* Once the questions to be answered by the evaluation have been framed, the worker can select the most appropriate ways to measure change in the dependent variables (i.e., the client's actions, emotions, behaviors) and establish the process by which measurements will be taken, organized, and analyzed. However, if the anticipated service plan for the client changes, it is both appropriate and necessary to revise the evaluation process, as well.

A critical feature of any evaluation is to identify and accurately measure the variables or factors (e.g., client's behavior, attitudes, skills, decisions, situation) that the intervention is intended to change. One form of measurement is to count and record such factual information (i.e., numerical data) as school attendance, acts of violent behavior, number of family arguments, and so on. A second form of measurement is to develop a tool specifically tailored to the issues or problems faced by the particular client (see Item 14.1), or an *individualized scale.* Finally, in some cases, scales may already exist that will accurately measure the client on the factors being considered (see Item 14.2). These *standardized scales* might be utilized both to initially assess the client and periodically measure changes in the client's condition.

With measurement data in hand, the social worker can then organize the information in a manner that will allow him or her to answer the practice evaluation questions and reach conclusions about the degree of success. Items 14.3 through 14.6 provide examples of tools one can use to conduct these tasks.

Termination Activities.   Although termination is recognized as a key element in planned change, it has been given surprisingly little attention in the social work literature. With the increased limits placed by managed care and other funding sources on the number of sessions a social worker can have with a client, this ending point increasingly is arbitrary and often premature. However, termination should be discussed at appropriate times throughout the helping process, and concluded in a manner that leaves the client with positive feelings and improved capacity to sustain gains made during the period of service. Item 14.7 provides some guidelines for the worker closing a case and terminating a professional relationship.

Social workers should remember, too, that the *NASW Code of Ethics* (1999, Section 1.16) states that termination should be planned with the needs of the client as the primary consideration. If termination is necessary before the change process is completed, there should be an appropriate referral to other helping sources.

Selected Bibliography

Corcoran, Jacqueline, and Joseph Walch. *Clinical Assessment and Diagnosis in Social Work Practice*. New York: Oxford University Press, 2006.

Dudley, James R. *Social Work Evaluation: Enhancing What We Do*. Chicago: Lyceum Books, 2009.

National Association of Social Workers. *NASW Code of Ethics*. Washington, DC: NASW, 1999.

Weinbach, Robert W. *Evaluating Social Work Services and Programs*. Boston: Allyn & Bacon, 2005.

14.1   MEASURING CHANGE WITH INDIVIDUALIZED RATING SCALES

As suggested earlier, there are numerous reasons why social workers need to measure various aspects of a client's condition or situation. For example, knowing about the duration, intensity, frequency, severity, and so on, of a client's problem is prerequisite to determining if an emergency exists, if the client or someone else is at risk, or if a referral should be made. Such measurements also allow the worker and the client to track the amount and the direction of change occurring during the helping process and to decide if the current service plan or approach should be modified. A comparison of the measurements taken at the beginning and end of a service period or an intervention (i.e., a before-and-after measurement) can determine if the desired change actually occurred. A close examination of evaluation data drawn from work with a number of clients can inform a social worker about his or her strengths and weakness as a helper and lead to a professional development plan to strengthen his or her competence. Such data, if drawn from a number of social workers, can help an agency design its overall staff development plan.

In short, accurate measurement can benefit clients, workers, and agencies alike. It must be acknowledged, however, that measurements of human behaviors, attitudes, feelings, and interactions are rarely completely accurate. Yet, with careful selection of appropriate indicators and a rigorous process of data collection, usually a good approximation of a factor being measured can be achieved.

One approach to measurement is to construct an **individualized rating scale** that is developed or adapted to fit the client's unique situation. This "homemade" scale is particularly useful if the client can be involved in the process of developing the scale. Often, clients become clearer about their situations and what it might take to bring about a desired change when they work on creating a scale to measure the change they want to make. In this process, vague thoughts and feelings are translated into concrete descriptions of what it is that they hope to change. Thus, the development of an individualized rating scale can become a valuable part of the helping process. Further, when scales reflect the respondent's own descriptions of the variables, the *face validity* of the scale is high and repeated measurements can be relatively accurate indicators of the client's experience. Finally, some factors that social workers help clients address defy standardized descriptors that can be universally interpreted for the purpose of measurement. For example, how does one standardize a person's feeling of grief, or a spouse's level of listening, or someone's motivation to change? With individualized scales, it is possible to "start where the client is" and construct measures of differing degrees of change from the perspective of that client.

Follow these steps when constructing an individualized rating scale:

1. *Help the client recognize the value in measuring behaviors, attitudes, and feelings.* Unless the client is invested in measuring his or her condition, the results are unlikely to be very helpful. This measurement, however, should be a familiar experience for most clients. Just as other professionals routinely utilize indices of a patient's physical health, social workers require indices of a client's social health or social functioning to perform most effectively. Many clients will welcome a close look at such indicators and find the results confirming of their own observations.

2. *Carefully identify what is to be measured.* Many times, the problem or concern being addressed cannot directly be measured. If measured indirectly, it is critical that the items selected for measurement are valid or logical indicators of the problem being addressed. For example, just as an elevated body temperature might be an indicator of infection, the number of arguments a couple has might be an indicator of marital discord. It is also important that each scale is designed to measure only one dimension of client functioning. If more than one dimension is involved, a separate scale for each dimension should be created. Further, if there are multiple indicators for a single dimension, the use of several indicators can help to confirm or raise caution about the results from any one indicator.

3. *Develop a scale in which the client's status on a continuum from negative to positive functioning can be designated.* When developing a scale, one task is to determine how many points on a continuum—that is, from most to least or best to worst—will be identified. There can be as few as two points (e.g., yes or no, more or less), although this allows for very little variability and should be avoided if possible. More informative scales typically range anywhere between 3 and 10 points. A general guideline is to have only as many points as the client can clearly distinguish—usually five to seven points. Whether to have an odd or even number of points depends somewhat on the item being scaled. For some items, it is appropriate to have a midpoint, but often that creates a situation in which the respondent simply takes a noncommittal middleground that provides little definitive information. An even-numbered scale, by contrast, forces the respondent to at least lean toward one direction or the other.

Once the number of points on the scale is determined, anchoring statements should be developed that describe each point. One method is to describe the most negative point on the scale (e.g., "I lost my temper at least once each day") and then define the most positive anchor point (e.g., "I did not lose my temper at all during the week"). With the two ends of the continuum identified, some or all of the points between them can be defined. Care should be taken that the client can identify differences in the increments between points. Another method for developing anchor points is to begin describing the client's functioning at the current time and making that description the midpoint. A description of what it would be like if things should get worse (a worst-case scenario) would become the negative end of the continuum and progressive levels to the midpoint on the negative side identified. Then the process is repeated on the positive side of the continuum.

When the anchor points use the client's own words (e.g., "I feel encouraged," "I am furious," "My thoughts are fuzzy," "I flew off the handle"), the scale is referred to as a *self-anchored scale* and the face validity of the scale is enhanced. At other times, it is helpful to use anchor points that have been utilized in other scales and are generally accepted as reflecting progressive scale values. When numerical categories are placed on a scale, be sure there are no gaps or overlaps in the numbers (i.e., *mutually exclusive categories*). It must be possible to place every potential number on the scale and impossible for any score to fall into more than one category. Some frequently used response categories include the following:

Frequency

- rarely > seldom > occasionally > frequently > almost always
- none > 1 or 2 times > 3–5 times > 6–7 times > more than 7 times
- never > rarely > sometimes > often > very often > always

Duration

- 0–20% of the time > 21–40% > 41–60% > 61–80% > 81–100% of the time
- never > some of the time > most of the time > almost always

Intensity

- strongly disagree > disagree > agree > strongly agree
- totally disagree > disagree slightly > neutral > agree slightly > totally agree
- not at all > slightly > moderately > very much > extremely

Amount

- substantial decrease > some decrease > no change > some increase > substantial increase

One last decision is whether to present the scales horizontally or vertically. Most people are accustomed to horizontal scales, as they are convenient to produce on a computer and are regularly used in survey instruments. Usually, the negative end of the continuum is placed on the left side of a page and the progressive steps (i.e., identified by the anchor points) flow from left to right. For some clients, however, a vertical scale communicates the more or less dimension more clearly. Children, for example, sometimes find a scale that looks like the portion of a glass that is filled is more understandable.

4. *Determine how the data will be collected.* Determining a process for completing the scales is the next step. Who should do the rating? The client? The worker? A teacher? A relative? When should the rating be made? The rating scale might be completed just before each counseling session, first thing each morning, Sunday evenings, and so forth. Where should the rating be done? At home? In the agency's waiting room? In the worker's office with the worker participating? There are any number of suitable places where the client can give thoughtful responses. Perhaps the most important general guideline is to attempt to achieve consistency regarding the conditions under which the ratings are made.

5. *Present the data in a form that allows them to be easily interpreted.* Just charting scores, possibly in different colors, on the scale itself is often sufficient visual evidence of change. However, if a series of measurements are taken to reflect change over time or to compare changes in two or more variables, it is useful to create simple line graphs to track the progression. Such organization of the data can provide a useful basis for discussion of change or lack of change with clients.

Selected Bibliography

Bloom, Martin, Joel Fischer, and John Orme. *Evaluating Practice: Guidelines for the Accountable Professional*, 6th ed. Boston: Allyn & Bacon, 2009.
Nurius, Paula S., and Walter W. Hudson. *Human Services: Practice, Evaluation, and Computers*. Pacific Grove, CA: Brooks/Cole, 1993.

14.2 ## MEASURING CHANGE WITH STANDARDIZED RATING SCALES

In many instances, the social worker can measure a client's social functioning by using one of the many standardized measuring instruments. **Standardized rating scales** are indices of behaviors, attitudes, feelings, and so on. They consist of a set of questions that measure a clearly defined construct such as, for example, depression, self-esteem, or satisfaction with one's marriage. These scales have been subjected to sufficient psychometric testing to confirm the instrument's accuracy when used with particular populations. As opposed to individualized rating scales that are designed for a specific individual client or client group (see Item 14.1), standardized indexes can be used to measure the experiences of many different clients. Typically, they are copyrighted and often they must be purchased.

Using standardized scales has three main benefits. First, because they have already been developed and tested, standardized scales are ready for immediate use and can be applied in a practice situation even before the client and worker have established the rapport necessary for an ongoing professional relationship. Thus, they can be used for diagnostic purposes where it is necessary to quickly assess the severity of a client's problem or condition. Second, periodic application of standardized assessment scales when working with a client can identify changes over time to inform practice decisions regarding the desirability of continuing or changing the intervention plan. These scales can also be used to help a social worker sum up the results or the outcome of the intervention with one client (i.e., comparing the client's score on the scale before the intervention begins and at the conclusion of service). In addition to the social worker's general ethical obligation to be accountable to clients and agencies for the quality of services provided, empirical analyses of practice outcomes as reflected by standardized measurement tools are increasingly requested by funding agencies.

Although standardized self-report scales vary in length, most contain between 15 and 30 one-sentence statements that a client is asked to rate on a 3- to 7-point scale. Therefore, these scales can be completed in a short period of time. One set of scales, known as the *WALMYR Assessment Scales*, illustrates a typical format used to measure constructs applicable to social work practice. For example, one of the WALMYR scales, the *Index of Self-Esteem (ISE)*, is designed to measure the extent of a client's problems with self-esteem. Here are 5 of the 25 items on that scale:

1. I feel that people would not like me if they knew me really well.

4. When I am with others I feel they are glad I am with them.

8. I feel that I need more self-confidence.

16. I feel very self-conscious when I am with strangers.

20. I feel I get pushed around more than others.

The client rates each item on a 7-point scale with (1) none of the time, (2) very rarely, (3) a little of the time, (4) some of the time, (5) a good part of the time, (6) most of the time, and (7) all of the time. To prevent respondents from slipping into a pattern of responses in which the words or content of each item is not carefully considered, some of the items are presented as a positive statement and others as negative. In these cases, the responses must be *reverse scored*. To illustrate, an answer of "most of the time" on Item 1 would be a negative statement about the client's self-esteem, while on Item 4, a response of "most of the time" would reflect a positive attitude. Clear instructions are provided with the scales to guide the worker in reverse scoring.

A well-established research methodology underpins the development of standardized instruments known as **psychometrics**. During their development, the scales are examined to assure that they not only represent the meaning of the construct being measured (**validity**) but that the scale would also yield approximately the same result each time it is administered (**reliability**). In the development phase, the scales are administered to a large number of respondents and the responses are statistically analyzed; then the results are compared to other indicators of that condition. The scale is then revised and adjusted until it meets the criteria for a valid measure.

The descriptions and user instructions provided with the scales help inform the social worker when he or she is in search of an appropriate measurement scale. For example, published data should always be available on the instrument's validity and reliability. Although there are no strict guidelines, generally when judging a scale's *validity* in the human services area, a correlation coefficient of +.60 or greater when compared to other indicators is acceptable. For *reliability*, an Alpha score of +.80 or greater is sufficient. Some scale descriptions will also specify the age and reading levels for which the measure is acceptable. Finally, the worker must decide if it is feasible to use the instrument in the particular practice situation. For example, the worker should determine if the measure has been normed with the cultural or age group that includes the client, is of appropriate length to use in the practice situation, is sensitive to the

---

- Corcoran, Kevin, and Joel Fischer. *Measures for Clinical Practice: A Sourcebook,* 4th ed. New York: Oxford University Press, 2009. (This two-volume handbook of measures was developed specifically for social work practice and describes more than 300 different standardized instruments for use with children, couples, and families and problematic adult characteristics. For each scale, a short description is provided, its psychometric properties presented, and sources for obtaining permission to use the scale (with or without a fee) included.)
- Hudson, Walter W. *WALMYR Assessment Scales Scoring Manual.* Available online: www.walmyr.com. WALMYR Publishing Co., P.O. Box 12217, Tallahassee, FL 32317–2217. E-mail: walmyr@walmyr.com. (This is a collection of nearly 30 short self-report scales, including personal adjustment measures, problems with spouse or partner, family relationship problems, and measures of organizational outcomes. The psychometric properties and a description of the construct being measured by each scale are also included with the set of scales.)
- Rush, A. John, et al., eds. *Handbook of Psychiatric Measures.* 2nd ed. Washington, DC: American Psychiatric Association, 2008. (This sourcebook contains 230 carefully selected measures of various psychiatric conditions. For each measure, the authors identify the goal of the measurement tool; describe what it measures; identify practical issues of test administration, availability, and cost of instruments; report the psychometric properties; and discuss its clinical utility.)
- Sajatovic, Martha, and Luis Ramirez. *Rating Scales in Mental Health,* 2nd ed. Cleveland: Lexi-Comp, Inc., 2003. (Primarily written for psychiatrists, this sourcebook provides information on more than 100 scales. Especially useful for social workers are scales measuring anxiety, depression, social/family functioning, client satisfaction, substance abuse, suicide risk, eating disorders, geriatric issues, and others.)

FIGURE 14.1 **Sources of Standardized Scales for Social Workers**

issues on which the practice is focused, and does not take an inordinate amount of money to secure or time to score.

Another feature of some scales is that cutting scores can be established. **Cutting scores** indicate the point on a scale where a client's score reflects a very serious problem or, at the other end of the continuum, does not indicate a problem that would typically require professional intervention. Many of the WALMYR scales, for example, measure the severity of problems with scores ranging from 0 (low severity or intensity) to 100 (extremely high level). A cutting score of 70 on these scales has been standardized to indicate the level of severity at which the client begins to be at high risk to self or others. Similarly, a score below 30 is an indication that intervention is probably not required.

Finally, to interpret the scores from a standardized scale, it must be recognized that the scale contains a certain amount of error and cannot precisely reflect the factor it measures. Known as the **standard error of measurement (SEM)**, SEM represents the amount of change that must occur in either direction that can be considered significant. For example, the WALMYR Index of Self-Esteem (mentioned earlier) has an SEM of 3.70, meaning that any change in a client's score of less than 3.70 on repeated tests could just be the inability of the test to measure self-esteem and should not be considered real change in the client.

Reports on standardized scales are scattered throughout the social work and psychology literature and are often difficult to locate. Several sources that contain collections of standardized rating scales are described in Figure 14.1.

Selected Bibliography

Abell, Neil. *Developing and Validating Rapid Assessment Instruments*. New York: Oxford University Press, 2009.

Bloom, Martin, Joel Fischer, and John G. Orme. *Evaluating Practice: Guidelines for the Accountable Professional*, 6th ed. Boston: Allyn & Bacon, 2009.

| 14.3 | THE SERVICE PLAN OUTCOME CHECKLIST (SPOC) |

The **Service Plan Outcome Checklist (SPOC)** is a tool for collecting summative data on client progress in achieving identified outcomes. Unlike most other monitoring tools, the SPOC can be developed and used with multiple clients (e.g., a group or a worker's caseload), as well as with an individual client.

A SPOC is relatively easy to construct and is in some ways an elaboration of a client problem checklist (see Item 11.12). The central feature of the SPOC is a menu of outcome goals the agency or worker typically helps the clients address. (Note that a SPOC need not focus just on outcomes. A SPOC could be adapted to focus on how much was learned, how well skills were developed, how satisfied the client was with the intervention, and so on. It would be important to also adapt the descriptors of the assessment ratings [see Figure 14.2] to be consistent with the change being assessed.) The SPOC is also useful for identifying the content that group members hope to address during group sessions, information that can help in planning the group experience, as well as in assessing what was achieved during the group sessions. Although the format of the SPOC is standardized, the list of outcomes included in the menu will be unique for each type of service offered. Such a list can be derived from interviews with clients, analysis of client records, a review of the agency's manual, and interviews with experienced workers. The menu of outcomes in Figure 14.2 was created for clients in a substance abuse group.

The first step in using the SPOC is to ask the client or clients during the initiation of service to review the list of desired outcomes (left-hand column of Figure 14.2) and to place a check (✓) by each goal he or she wants to achieve. This selection might be done independently by the client or with the assistance of the worker. Workers often find that discussion of these items yields helpful information and provides a way to focus an initial interview or adapt plans for a group's content or activities. To assist in prioritizing services, the two or three most important service outcomes for the client should also be identified (circled).

If used with a client over an extended period, the client's perception of achievement might be obtained at interim points in the change process to assess the progress of the intervention effort. At a minimum, all items on the menu of possible outcomes should be rated at the point of termination (shaded section of Figure 14.2). A by-product of this final evaluation is that clients find it helpful to revisit their initial selection of outcome goals, as well as the other outcomes addressed, and reflect on what was actually achieved. When applied to an individual client, examination of the client's view of the level of outcome achievement is an indicator of the success of the intervention relative to the various items the client believed were important.

When the SPOC is applied to a group of clients, it yields information that can help the worker identify both the importance of and level of achievement for the various menu categories. The menu in Figure 14.2 was developed in relation to the items the worker anticipated addressing when using group therapy in a substance abuse treatment program with adult outpatient clients.[*] Before the group sessions began, the worker constructed the items in the menu (left column) by scanning literature on the treatment of substance abuse and listing items that typically concern clients, interviewing staff members who offered the group in the past, and discussing a draft menu with potential group members. The group members were subsequently given a copy of the SPOC and asked to place a checkmark by every item they would like to address while in the group and then to circle the two or three items that would be their highest priority. In addition, a final item was an open-ended question allowing group members the opportunity to identify topics to address that may have been omitted from the menu. At the last group session, the worker returned the SPOCs to the group members and asked them to rate their achievement for each item on a five-point scale.

---

[*]Prior editions of this book contained outcome menus from a child and family services agency (4th edition), community mental health center (5th edition), hospice agency (6th edition), medical trauma center (7th edition), and a pain management group (8th edition).

Steven Christopher	Angela Silvernail	7/6/2010
Client/Family	Worker	Service Initiation Date

Instructions: Complete Steps 1–2 within two weeks of the initiation of service.

Step 1 In the far left column, select and (✓) check all outcomes for intervention. If a desired outcome does not appear on the menu below, add items in the space provided at the end of the questionnaire.

Step 2 Review the items checked in Step 1 and circle the two or three that you consider the most important or of highest priority.

When services are terminated and/or at an interim point in service activity, complete Step 3 (i.e., the shaded area).

Step 3 Rate each checked item from "no progress" to "fully achieved" by circling the number from 1 to 5 that best represents your judgment about progress made to date.

Place a checkmark (✓) by each desired outcome for this service. Then circle the two or three most important outcomes you want to achieve.

Circle Your Assessment at Time of Discharge

	No Progress		About Half Achieved		Fully Achieved
___ 1. Understand the disease concept as it relates to addiction	1	②	3	4	5
___ 2. Understand the myths of addiction	1	2	3	4	⑤
✓ 3. Understand the grief process	1	②	3	4	5
___ 4. Understand Post-Acute Withdrawal Syndrome (PAWS)	1	2	③	4	5
✓ 5. Become better at recognizing, setting, and maintaining healthy boundaries	1	2	3	④	5
✓ 6. Learn how to develop more trust in my personal relationships	1	2	③	4	5
✓ 7. Become more efficient in coping with stress without chemicals	1	2	3	4	⑤
✓ 8. Become more assertive when speaking to others about my addiction	1	2	3	④	5
___ 9. Learn how my defense mechanisms affect my addiction					
✓ 10. Learn to recognize my relapse warning signs	1	2	3	④	5
___ 11. Learn about the "science" of brain recovery from addiction	1	2	③	4	5
___ 12. Become better at giving and receiving support during my recovery	1	2	③	4	5
✓ 13. Understand if increased spirituality may aid my recovery	1	2	③	4	5
___ 14. Additional outcomes I would like to address:	1	2	③	4	5

How to get referral to different clinic

Advantages of group vs. individual therapy

Source: Adapted and modified from evaluation conducted by Angela Silvernail, Colorado State University.

FIGURE 14.2   Service Plan Outcome Checklist (SPOC): Adult Male Addictions Recovery Group

To determine the importance of each item to the group members, the social worker summarized the group members' responses as reflected in Columns 2 through 5 in Figure 14.3. The steps followed were as follows:

- In Column 2, the worker recorded the number of group members who had selected that item and computed a percentage of the total (i.e., 12 of the 12 clients, or 100.0 percent, selected Issue #6, I want to "Learn how to develop more trust in my personal relationships" as an issue they all wanted to address).

Column 1		Column 2		Column 3		Column 4	Column 5
Item #	Issue Selected	# and % Selected		# and % Priority		Importance Index	Mean Achievement
6	Learn how to develop more trust in my personal relationship	12	100.0	6	50.0	150.0	4.33
12	Become better at giving and receiving support during my recovery	10	83.3	4	33.3	116.6	3.67
8	Become more assertive when speaking to others about my addiction	6	50.0	6	50.0	100.0	2.00
7	Become more efficient in coping with stress without chemicals	10	83.3	2	16.7	100.0	2.33
5	Become better at recognizing, setting, and maintaining boundaries	8	66.7	1	8.3	75.0	3.55
10	Learn to recognize my relapse warning signs	4	33.3	3	25.0	58.3	4.22
4	Understand Post-Acute Withdrawal Syndrome (PAWS)	4	33.3	2	16.7	50.0	3.50
9	Learn how my defense mechanisms affect my addiction	4	33.3	0	0.0	33.3	3.82
13	Understand if increased spirituality may aid my recovery	1	8.3	1	8.3	16.7	3.00
3	Understand the grief process	2	16.7	0	0.0	16.7	1.75
2	Understand myths of addiction	1	8.3	0	0.0%	8.3	3.50
1	Understand disease concept as it relates to addiction	1	8.3	0	0.0	8.3	3.22
14a	Other: How to get referral to different clinic	Not Scored		Not Scored		Not Scored	Not Scored
14b	Other: Advantages of group vs. individual therapy	Not Scored		Not Scored		Not Scored	Not Scored
						Group Mean	3.24
		N = 12 clients				**Possible Range** = 1.00 to 5.00	

Source: Adapted and modified from evaluation conducted by Angela Silvernail, Colorado State University.

FIGURE 14.3 **Adult Male Addictions Recovery Group: Service Plan Outcome Checklist (SPOC) Summary**

- In Column 3, the worker followed the same procedure and arrived at the number and percentage for each item selected as one of the two or three priority issues to address by the group members.
- Given that both the expression of interest and the priority given an item are valid indicators about how important an item is for each member, an *Importance Index* (Column 4) was compiled by adding the two percentages from Columns 2 and 3. Note that this is an index number, not a percentage.
- At the time of termination, each group member rated his or her achievement on the five-point scale in the shaded section of the SPOC form (see Figure 14.2). The social worker then recorded each client's rating, computed a mean achievement score for each item, and entered that in Column 5.
- Finally, the worker used a spreadsheet program to sort the items, using Column 5 (in descending order) as the first sort. Doing so produced a list of the items in order of the Importance Index score, with the most important items at the top of the chart. The mean or average achievement score for the group members was the parallel to the importance score for each item.

Having completed these calculations, the worker could then interpret the group members' perceptions of success by visually comparing Columns 4 and 5. For example, in Figure 14.3, Item 6 had a 150.0 Importance Index and an above average achievement score (4.33 of a possible 5.00), suggesting the group believed they had been very successful in addressing this issue. However, Item 8 had a high importance index (100.0), but only a 2.00 mean achievement. According to these data, the group was not successful in helping members "Become more assertive when speaking to others about my addiction." This would suggest that the worker should seek additional knowledge or training about how to engage and encourage members to become more assertive in discussing their addictions. The "other" items contributed by two group members would suggest that these items should be added to the menu the next time this SPOC is used. Also, it should be noted that the "other" items were not scored and not included in the summary data since all members did not have the opportunity to rate them.

Two additional uses of the SPOC can strengthen social work practice. First, a social worker might administer the SPOC to all or a sample of his or her clients and compute the scores as in the group example mentioned earlier in order to identify areas where clients could benefit from the worker gaining additional knowledge and skill. Second, a supervisor on a unit of an agency might give a SPOC with a menu of the unit's services to a sample of clients in order to judge overall unit performance and to identify workers who are particularly strong in addressing specific outcomes so that the most competent workers could be assigned to clients with these specific needs.

Selected Bibliography

Horejsi, Charles. *Assessment and Case Planning in Child Protection and Foster Care Services*. Englewood, CO: American Humane Association, 1996.

14.4 TASK ACHIEVEMENT SCALING (TAS)

Task Achievement Scaling (TAS) was developed for use with the task-centered practice approach wherein work toward the client's goals and objectives is broken down into many small and separate tasks and then worked on sequentially. A **task** is an action by the client or worker that is necessary in order to reach a desired outcome. A task is usually something that can be accomplished in a matter of days or, at most, in a few weeks. For many clients, this process of breaking down the work toward an objective into many small steps or tasks makes the work more manageable and elevates their confidence that it can be achieved. Usually, not more than three or four tasks are worked on at a time. Each session with the client begins with a review of the progress on tasks selected for attention during the previous session and ends with identifying tasks to be undertaken before the next session. Because the TAS reports the percent of attempted tasks that were actually achieved, some tasks may be completed or judged to be no longer needed and dropped, some may be continued, and others added at each session.

TAS is especially applicable as a means of evaluation when the service is relatively brief and when activities are concrete. For purposes of illustrating the use of task achievement scaling, consider the situation of Millie and her two daughters. Millie, who has the beginnings of dementia, was recently hospitalized after a minor stroke. Her two daughters, who both live in another state, then needed to locate a safe assisted living facility and secure finances to support their mother's care. While examining their mother's finances, the daughters discovered that a "companion" that Millie had taken into her home to help meet some of her basic needs had drained Millie's bank account. Given that the daughters were unsure how to proceed, a hospital nurse had arranged for them to speak with a social worker. The immediate goal of the social worker was to help the daughters make appropriate plans for the mother's care before she was to be released from the hospital the next week.

Given that the two daughters felt overwhelmed by all that needed to be accomplished in such a short time, the worker utilized a task-centered approach to help them focus and structure their activity. The worker helped them identify three key tasks that needed to be completed. The tasks for the first day were to (1) select an appropriate facility, (2) establish a legal address for Millie's Social Security checks, and (3) obtain Power of Attorney and Medical Durable Power of Attorney in behalf of their mother.

In order to construct a method of evaluating their progress, the worker and daughters identified four incremental steps or levels of progress toward the completion of each key task. Each step was assigned a numerical value of 0 to 4 that represented five levels of achievement: no progress, minimally achieved, partially achieved, substantially achieved, and completely achieved. By combining the percentage of accomplishment for each of the three key tasks, an overall task achievement score could be readily computed each day when the daughters and worker met, and discussion would then focus on how to continue to make progress the next day.

Figure 14.4 represents the first day's task achievement scale completed by the daughters and worker. They achieved 50 percent of the task related to choosing an assisted living center when they visited a facility that day. They were also able to find the phone number where they could reach a Social Security representative, but by then the office was closed and the next step would need to wait another day (25 percent of this task was achieved). Third, the daughters were 75 percent successful in gathering the mother's legal documents, meeting with an attorney to establish Power of Attorney and Medical Durable Power of Attorney, getting the forms notarized that day (75 percent of the task achieved). The overall percent of achievement for Day #1 (a total change score of 6 steps compared to a possible change score of 12) was 50 percent. For Day #2, the three tasks were continued, but since the third was almost completed a new task was added for that day—collecting the necessary materials and applying for Medicaid.

A useful means of tracking a client's level of task achievement is to cast the weekly scores into a time-series chart as described in Item 14.6, where various single subject designs are introduced. Such graphing of the percent of task achievement from day to day or week to week can be useful in reinforcing positive task achievement, or a downward trend can signal a decline in client interest or motivation. Using the time-series format also makes it possible to graphically compare the percent of task completion with some other variable to answer a practice question such as "To what extent is the level of task achievement associated with the client's level of personal stress?"

Selected Bibliography

Coady, Nick, and Peter Lehmann, eds. *Theoretical Perspectives for Direct Social Work Practice: A Generalist-Eclectic Approach*, 2nd ed. New York: Springer, 2008.

Naleppa, Matthias J., and William J. Reid. *Gerontological Social Work: A Task-Centered Approach*. New York: Columbia University Press, 2003.

Overall Goal: *Secure Assisted Living for Millie*
Client: *Millie's Daughters*   Worker: *Judy Moore*
Date: *10/7/2010*   Week #1

	Task 1: Select an assisted living center for Millie	Task 2: Change Millie's Social Security Address	Task 3: Obtain Power of Attorney and Medical Power of Attorney
No Progress (0)	Did nothing for now	Didn't take time for this	Put off addressing this matter
Minimally Achieved (1)	Identified two assisted living centers to consider	Found telephone number for Social Security, but did not call (✓)	Searched Millie's possessions to determine if someone already had this Power of Attorney
Partially Achieved (2)	Visited one assisted living center, but made no decision (✓)	Called Social Security and got information, but did not take steps to change address	Looked for the two Power of Attorney forms on-line
Substantially Achieved (3)	Visited two assisted living centers but made no choice	Spoke to Social Security representative and copied on-line forms	Completed the power of Attorney and Power of Medical Attorney forms and had Millie sign them with notary present (✓)
Completely Achieved (4)	Visited two assisted living centers and selected one for Millie to enter	Completed Social Security address change process and confirmed change made	Delivered the two Power of Attorney forms to lawyer, hospital, and assisted living facility
Change Score	2	1	3
Possible Change	4	4	4
% of Possible Change Achieved	50%	25%	75%
Total Percent of Change for all Three Tasks: 50.0%			

Source: Adapted and modified from evaluation conducted by Judy Moore, Colorado State University.

FIGURE 14.4   Task Achievement Scale (TAS)

14.5   GOAL ATTAINMENT SCALING (GAS)

Goal Attainment Scaling (GAS) is a procedure that provides an estimate of the degree of movement toward goals that accrues from an intervention with an individual or family. The basic format for a GAS is the same for all clients, although adjustments must be made to accommodate the number of goals selected. It consists of several five-point scales (usually two to four or five) that are individualized for the specific client to represent a set of possible outcomes related to the agreed-upon goals. These scales could take the form of frequency counts, various levels of performance on individualized scales (see Item 14.1), scores on a standardized assessment instrument (see Item 14.2), or a combination of these. Here are the steps in constructing a GAS:

1. *Identify two to five goals, and develop a five-point scale for each.*   To establish a GAS, the worker and client begin by describing in a few words the client's condition or situation before the intervention was started in relation to each identified goal. Ideally, this description should be viewed as indicating the second-lowest point on a five-point scale where a score of 2 is assigned. The lowest point (assigned a score of 1) on the scale is then described, indicating what a step backward would represent. Next, the best outcome that could reasonably be expected should be described; a value of 5 is assigned. Then, two levels of improvement between the current situation and the best possible scenario can be identified and assigned scores of 3 and 4. The result should be a five-point ordinal scale for each goal where the worker and client have created explicit descriptions (anchor points) for each of the five levels.

The GAS in Figure 14.5 was created by a social worker in the child welfare unit (a county human services agency) who was helping Kyle, a 17-year-old boy, prepare for "aging-out" after spending most of his life in foster homes and residential treatment centers. Kyle feels he has damaged relationships with his family and is anxious to start fresh by living

Client: Kyle Gandy
Worker: Lindsay Ishman

(✓) = Beginning Level (✗) = Terminating Level	Goal 1: Increase Self-Esteem	Goal 2: Develop and use a personal support system	Goal 3: Manage conflict in life
Attainment Level	Weight: 45	Weight: 30	Weight: 25
(1) Most unfavorable outcome thought likely	Index of Self-Esteem Scale score = 70 or above	Makes no effort to identify people to offer support	Demonstrates no interest in managing conflictual situations ✓
(2) Less than expected success	Index of Self-Esteem Scale score = 57–69 ✓	Identifies up to 3 strategies for building his personal support system ✓	Is able to describe signs that conflict is likely to occur
(3) Expected success	Index of Self-Esteem Scale score = 44–56	Identifies his personal support system with 1 to 2 appropriate people to help with problems ✗	Can describe 1 way to manage conflict with his peers
(4) More than expected success	Index of Self-Esteem Scale score = 31–43 ✗	Describes his personal support system with 2 to 3 appropriate people to help with problems	Can describe 2 or more ways to manage conflict with his peers
(5) Best anticipated success	Index of Self-Esteem Scale score = 30 or lower	Demonstrates appropriate use of support system to address an issue	Describes a conflictual situation with peers and identifies how he managed the conflict ✗
Summary	Goal 1: Self-Esteem	Goal 2: Anger Outbursts	Goal 3: Discipline Referrals
Weight	45	30	25
Change Score	2	1	4
Weighted Change Score	90	30	100
Possible Weighted Change	135	90	100
Percentage Attainment	66.7%	33.3%	100.0%

Total Weighted Change (220) / Total Possible Weighted Change (325) = 71.5%

Source: Adapted and modified from evaluation conducted by Lindsay Ishman, Colorado State University.

FIGURE 14.5   Goal Attainment Scale (GAS) for Kyle Gandy, 9/27/2010 and 12/15/2010

independently. The social worker and Kyle identified three goals to address during the intervention period: (1) increase self-esteem; (2) develop and use a personal support system; and (3) learn to manage conflict. Kyle participated in a weekly money management/life skills development oriented group and met regularly with his social worker where supportive counseling and case management were provided. Early in the counseling sessions, Kyle and the social worker developed three 5-point scales to measure his success (or lack of success) in attaining each of the three goals. Five levels of change, ranging from "Most unfavorable" to "Most favorable," were identified for each goal.

2. *Assign a weight to each goal to indicate its importance in relation to the other goals.* Since most people are accustomed to working in sets of 100, clients usually understand dividing 100 points among the several goals to reflect the degree to which each is important. In Figure 14.5, the social worker and Kyle decided that increasing self-esteem would partially contribute to developing a personal support system and would also help him manage conflictual situations in his life. Therefore they gave Goal #1 the highest weight of 45, Goal #2 a weight of 30, and Goal #3 a 25 weighting. By assigning a weight to each goal, not only could the progress on each goal be identified, but an indicator of overall goal achievement (due to the fact that the goals were interrelated) also could be computed.

3. *Place a checkmark (✓) in the cell that best describes the client's condition for each goal at the point that intervention begins.* Usually this checkmark will appear in the "2" cell, the "Less than expected success" level, since at the start of the intervention the client is likely to be having difficulty at that degree of problem. Sometimes, however, the checkmark will appear in a different attainment level, for example, Goal #3 in Figure 14.5. The checkmarks, then, become the baseline or "before" measurement for the GAS.

4. *When the service or intervention is terminated, place an (X) in the cell that best describes the client's condition for each goal at that time.* This mark (✗) represents the "after" measurement, and the difference in measurement from the initial check mark (✓) reflects the change that occurred during the time of service. In some long-term cases, however, it may be useful to locate an interim attainment level for each goal as a means of monitoring the change process.

5. *Determine the weighted change score for each goal.* Computing the change score involves subtracting the beginning score (✓) from the ending score (✗) and multiplying by the weight assigned to that goal. In Goal #1 of Figure 14.5, for example, the client's level of self-esteem increased from the "2" attainment level to the "4" attainment level—a change of two levels. The change score is then multiplied by 45 (the established weight for Goal #1), and a weighted change score of 90 was recorded.

6. *Compute the percentage of possible change for each scale.* Determine the highest score a client might generate for each scale by identifying the change that would have occurred if the client had fully reached the goal (i.e., the "5" level) and record that score. Then divide the actual weighted change score by this possible change score. For Goal #1 in Figure 14.5, this would involve dividing 90 by 135, yielding a percentage change score of 66.7 for that goal.

7. *Compute an overall goal attainment score.* Perhaps the most valuable information derived from a GAS is the combined score from the several scales, which gives a comprehensive indication of the client's overall level of goal attainment. To derive that score, the possible weighted change scores for all the goals are summed and then divided into the sum of the actual weighted change scores. In Figure 14.5, the percentage of overall change is reflected at the bottom of the chart (i.e., total weighted change [220] divided by possible weighted change [325], which yields a percentage change of 71.5 percent). In sum, this intervention resulted in a generally favorable outcome, although Kyle would need to work more on developing a support system before he leaves the foster care system.

If goal attainment scaling is used widely in an agency, data can be gleaned from GAS charts that will also be useful in program evaluation. For example, data might be accumulated regarding the following:

- The types of goals chosen as targets for intervention, their frequency, and the percent of goal achievement on each

- The amount of progress made on particular goals by the clients served by a specific worker
- The relative success in goal achievement with particular groups of clients (e.g., age, ethnicity, gender)

Selected Bibliography

Bloom, Martin, Joel Fischer, and John G. Orme. *Evaluating Practice: Guidelines for the Accountable Professional*, 6th ed. Boston: Allyn & Bacon, 2009.

Kiresuk, Thomas J., Aaron Smith, and Joseph E. Cardillo. *Goal Attainment Scaling: Applications, Theory, and Measurement*. Hillsdale, NY: Erlbaum, 1994.

14.6   SINGLE-SUBJECT DESIGNS (SSDs)

The most well-known method for direct practice evaluation is single-subject research design—also known as single-system, single-case, $N = 1$, and time-series design. As compared to more traditional forms of research that accumulate data from multiple respondents, either before and after or with experimental and control groups, **single-subject designs (SSDs)** involve accumulating repeated measurements from a single subject (e.g., individual, couple, family, or group) over time.

Two fundamental assumptions underpin SSD. First, it is assumed that if left unattended, the client's condition or problem will stay about the same or worsen. Second, it is assumed that barring evidence to the contrary, one can cautiously conclude that if change occurs after the introduction of an intervention, the intervention is a dominant force in that change. Thus, by clearly specifying the client's behavior, attitude, or functioning *before* the intervention begins (i.e., a baseline measurement), any change that occurs during the period of intervention can be attributed to the intervention. Although it is not possible to conclude that the intervention *caused* an identified change it can be said that there is (or is not) an *association* between the client's change and the intervention.

There is no uniform format for a single-subject design. In fact, one of the strengths of this methodology is its flexibility. Because the SSD monitors what occurs in practice, the design must be adaptable to changing practice situations. Unlike traditional social science research, therefore, it is acceptable to modify the design during the change process if a decision is made, for example, to alter the intervention or to take advantage of a temporary secession of service such as a vacation period to obtain another baseline. The following steps reflect a process for conducting a single-subject evaluation:

1. *Select a case situation in which it will be possible to take several measurements over time.* Because data that reveal trends in a client's actions or feelings provide the basis of this design, repeated measurements must be taken. These measurements might occur before the intervention is begun, during the intervention, and even retrospectively after the intervention is completed. The frequency of measurement will depend on the case situation and could be daily, weekly, or even monthly. The characteristic way of organizing SSD data is a graph that depicts the independent variable (e.g., client's behavior, attitude) on the left axis (*y*-axis) and a timeline in days or weeks along the bottom (*x*-axis). Figure 14.6 depicts the typical format for graphing the basic components of a single-subject design.

2. *Select the target behaviors/attitudes/beliefs, and determine how each is to be measured.* During the assessment and planning phases of the change process, the factors, conditions, or patterns targeted for change will have been identified and, in order to monitor change, a valid and relevant numerical measure must be selected. This may be a frequency count (how often something happens) or a score on a standardized or individualized scale (see Items 14.1 and 14.2). The worker and client should establish a plan for taking the measurements under similar conditions (e.g., same location, just prior to counseling sessions) so that as far as possible, each time a

FIGURE 14.6   Components of Single-Subject Design (SSD) Graphing

measurement is made, the context when collecting data will be consistent. If measuring more than one client variable it might be useful to alternate the times scales are administered, for example, alternating scales every other session.

3. *Select a single-subject design, and designate the phases of the process on a chart.* (Note that a little practice with Microsoft Excel or a similar program makes charting these data relatively easy.) The different phases (e.g., baseline, intervention, and follow-up) of the process are identified across the top of the graph with dashed vertical lines separating each phase. *A* is always used to represent a *baseline period.* The letters *B, C, D,* and so forth (except for M and F-U) denote distinctly different interventions. If multiple interventions are used simultaneously, a slash is placed between the letters representing those interventions (e.g., *B/C*). If there is a modification in the frequency or intensity of an intervention (e.g., shorter sessions or increased medication), those modifications can be noted with a superscript designation (e.g., B^1 B^2). *M* designates a period in which a minimum level of service is maintained before a case is closed (the maintenance phase) and *F-U* denotes a follow-up measurement after service has been terminated. Either include a descriptor (e.g., *B* = family therapy, *C* = individual supportive counseling) or provide a key for each phase of the process somewhere on the chart.

The variations in SSD depend on the practice situation, the worker's creativity, and the questions the worker intends to answer. The most elementary SSD is the *B* design or a case study in which there are no baseline or follow-up data and the worker simply tracks what happens in regard to the independent variable(s) while the intervention is occurring. This approach allows the worker to record what is changing during the intervention phase in order to adjust the practice approach, if necessary, or to inform future practice decisions.

The most commonly used form of SSD, the *A B* design, allows the worker and client to examine any changes in a relevant client characteristic between a baseline period and the intervention phase. This type of study might also allow the worker to examine any change in the key client variable(s) associated with introducing a different intervention (an *A B C* design) or adding a second intervention, such as group therapy, to the individual counseling already in process (an *A B B/C* design) to assess the relative effectiveness of each approach or combination of approaches. In sum, these designs can be used to provide data to guide practice decisions (i.e., if an intervention isn't working, it can be replaced with another) or to adapt to changing practice activities to track the relative success at each phase of the process.

Figure 14.7 reflects a single-subject practice evaluation conducted in a community mental health setting. The client, Michael Douglas, was a 44-year-old divorced man living alone, but

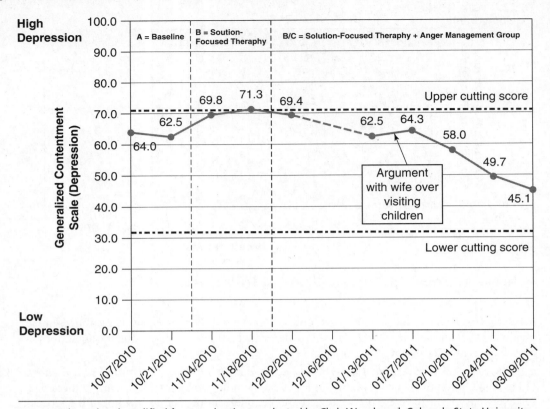

Source: Adapted and modified from evaluation conducted by Chris Woodward, Colorado State University.

FIGURE 14.7   Generalized Contentment [Depression] Scores (GCS) for Michael Douglas

having occasional contact with his three children. The divorce had been particularly contentious and Michael continued to be angry about his wife's decision to leave him and restrict his contact with his children. In addition, Michael was previously diagnosed with depression for which he was taking medication and had been referred to the social worker for counseling after he self-reported suicidal ideation. The worker and Michael developed a safety plan, but suicide seemed unlikely as Michael could not identify any serious plans about how he might commit that act and reported that he "couldn't abandon his kids, anyway." The worker's search of the evidence-based litera-ture for "best practices" intervention approaches in such situations, and with consultation from his supervisor, suggested that solution-focused therapy (see Chapter 6) would be a sound initial intervention approach.

When assessing this case situation, the social worker had Mr. Douglas complete the Generalized Contentment Scale (GCS) which measures a person's level of depression (Hudson, 1997). As indicated in Figure 14.7, he scored 64.0 during their first session and 62.5 the next ses-sion. Those two scores varied slightly but were well within the Standard Error of Measurement (SEM = 4.26) for that instrument (see Item 14.2) indicating that no substantial change had oc-curred. These scores were plotted on a single-subject design (SSD) chart as the baseline scores (A), suggesting that a stable pattern of relatively high depression was present.

Once the solution-focused therapy (Intervention B) began with Mr. Douglas, the social worker met with him every week and measured his level of depression every other week. Four sessions into intervention phase, the B phase on the SSD chart, the GCS scores indicated that Michael's level of depression was worsening. In fact, the depression scores of 69.8 and 71.3 were at the crisis cutting score indicating that Michael or others around him may be at risk. When dis-cussing this finding, the client and the social worker concluded that solution-focused therapy alone was not sufficiently helpful and it might be productive for Michael to also join an anger management group (Intervention C) that was beginning that week in the agency.

During the B/C phase, Michael's depression started to subside. He was far from well when his GCS score dropped to 45.1, but he was making progress. However, as too often happens, Michael experienced a crisis when his son threatened suicide and he decided to move to the community where the son was living and dropped out of contact with the social worker. When Mr. Douglas called to report this move, a referral was made to a community mental health center in the new community, but the social worker did not know if Michael followed up.

As in Michael's case, single-system designs can be used to test the impact of an intervention. By establishing the baseline (A) level for a client characteristic and then starting an intervention (B), the social worker reached the reasonable conclusion that solution-focused therapy was not sufficiently effective. By joining that with attending the anger management group (B/C) and finding a gradual decline in Michael's depression, there was evidence that the combination of approaches was starting to make a difference.

Another variation might have been to assess change in depression for all members associated with the anger management group. A group mean score from measurements taken periodically might be useful, but the chance that a group approach might be helpful for most members yet damaging to others would have to be considered. The scores for each member could be charted, as well as the mean score for the group, to compare both individual and group scores. In sum, once the rudiments of SSD are mastered, the opportunities for developing a wide variety of designs to inform one's practice are limited only by the worker's creativity.

4. *Collect and record baseline, intervention, maintenance, and/or follow-up data on each factor.* When scores are obtained on each variable, the score should be plotted on the client's graph. Because the chart reflects the sequence of related scores through time, a *line chart* as depicted in Figure 14.7 is the preferred format. The known data points should be connected with solid lines. If there are missing data at an interval when data regularly would have been collected (see 12/16 and 12/30 missing data points in Figure 14.7), the two known points should be connected by a dashed line, which represents the assumption that the missing data would have fallen along the line between the two known points.

Ideally, baseline measures should be repeatedly taken until a stable score on the variable is established. However, the realities of social work practice rarely permit many measurements. A minimum of three baseline measurements (before the intervention is begun) should be collected if at all possible, but as in Michael's case, when suicide was a possibility, one ethically could not withhold service while a baseline was established. These measurements might be made during the assessment and planning phases of the change process (*current baseline* data) or might possibly be based on information already on record (*retrospective baseline* data), such as records of prior services or previous scores on assessment instruments. It is also important to note on the *y*-axis if a high score represents a positive or negative outcome on each factor.

5. *Interpret the data and compare empirical evidence with other practice observations.* When data points have been entered on a chart, it is then possible to examine the data and make judgments about the success of the intervention. Several cautions should be considered when interpreting SSD data. First, if there is a sequence of interventions being evaluated, such as in the A B B/C design, there could be a *carryover* effect in which the change made in one phase affects the next. Withdrawing all interventions (i.e., returning to a second baseline) can help to reveal if there has been a cumulative influence from the series of interventions. The *order of presentation* of various intervention strategies can also affect the impact of a specific intervention. This problem can be addressed in subsequent practice situations by changing the order of introducing the various intervention strategies. If one strategy appears most effective regardless of order, a worker can feel more confident about using that strategy in similar practice situations. Finally, SSDs often suffer from *incomplete and inaccurate data.* The realities of practice are that clients miss sessions, data collection instruments are not fully completed, clients sometimes provide incorrect information, and so on. These problems do not weaken the rationale for conducting direct practice evaluation, but rather they argue for cautious interpretation of the results and reinforce the importance of *triangulation.*

Visual examination of the direction of change will often produce a clear picture of the client's situation. However, when data are erratic, it may be difficult to detect trends. When this happens, it is helpful to compute a *mean* or *median* score to identify the most typical responses. For each phase of the process, then, horizontal lines can be drawn to represent the central tendency. Other more sophisticated analyses of data can be conducted, in which *trend lines* or *celeration lines* project the future direction of client performance on the factor being measured. Moreover, if there are sufficient data, it is possible to determine if a change is *statistically significant*. Rubin and Babbie (2009), for example, describe procedures for determining if the intervention phase scores are more than two standard deviations from the baseline scores (i.e., statistically significant at the 0.05 level). Also, statistical tables have been developed that identify levels of significance based on the proportion and frequency of observations above and below a trend line before and after the intervention is begun. However, one should be cautious about using elaborate statistical manipulation, as it can imply more rigorous data collection than the SSD methodology permits. The effort devoted to determining statistical significance might be better spent on examining the *practical significance* of the information (i.e., the importance of the change).

Selected Bibliography

Bloom, Martin, Joel Fischer, and John G. Orme. *Evaluating Practice: Guidelines for the Accountable Professional*, 6th ed. Boston: Allyn & Bacon, 2009.

Hudson, Walter W. *WALMYR Assessment Scales Scoring Manual*. Tallahassee, FL: WALMYR Publishing, 1997.

Rubin, Allen, and Earl Babbie. *Essential Research Methods for Social Work*, 2nd ed. Belmont, CA: Brooks/Cole, 2009.

Weinbach, Robert W., and Richard M. Grinnell, Jr. *Statistics for Social Workers*, 8th ed. Boston: Allyn & Bacon, 2010.

14.7 TERMINATION OF SERVICE

Closing a case, or terminating services to a client, should be viewed as a planned component of the helping process. In many cases the service is time-limited and the social worker and client know from the start there will be a limited number of sessions or that services will cease on an identified date. In other cases, the worker and client must decide when termination is appropriate and the following factors should be considered:

- Have the intervention objectives been achieved?
- Is the problem or situation that brought the client to the agency sufficiently resolved so the client can now function at an acceptable level and not be at risk of harming self or others?
- Has the worker and/or agency made a reasonable investment of time, energy, and skill without sufficient results?
- Has the client and/or worker reached a point where one or both do not anticipate significant benefit from future contacts?
- Has the client become inappropriately dependent on the worker or agency?
- Would the client benefit by changing to another agency or professional?

In some situations, a transfer of the client to another worker within the agency is necessary. This, too, is a type of termination. An intraagency transfer is necessary when any of the following occurs:

- The worker will no longer be available to serve the client (e.g., worker moving to another job, a student internship is completed).
- The client will be better served by another agency staff member.
- A conflict between the worker and client cannot be resolved and is interfering with client progress.
- For some reason, the worker cannot develop necessary empathy and warmth for the client.
- There is a serious and insurmountable gap in mutual understanding and communication caused by difference in values, religious beliefs, language, or cultural background.

Ideally, termination is a mutual decision that occurs when the service objectives have been reached and both client and worker are happy about completing their work together. Many situations are far from ideal, however. All too often, the client decides to end the relationship before reaching the objectives, and sometimes circumstances dictate that the worker decides unilaterally to terminate. Examples of the latter include the following:

- The client is considered to be a physical danger to the worker or continually harasses the worker.
- The client files a lawsuit or an official complaint against the worker.
- The client violates, without good cause, a financial agreement regarding the payment of fees for service.

In the case of an intraagency transfer or a termination by the worker, the client should be notified in writing, and, if possible, during a face-to-face meeting. The reasons and circumstances surrounding the transfer or termination should be clearly documented in the case record. The social worker has an obligation to make a termination or transfer as positive an experience as possible. Several guidelines can aid in this process:

1. The worker should do everything possible to keep termination from being abrupt or unexpected. Termination should be discussed during the planning and contracting phase of the helping process and the client should be reminded from the beginning that intervention is goal-oriented and time-limited. The client will be gradually prepared for termination if the intervention includes, as it should, an ongoing monitoring of progress.

2. In a case where an adult client wants to terminate but the social worker thinks he or she should continue, the worker should explain to the client the possible consequences of terminating. If the client still wishes to terminate, his or her decision should be respected. Usually, a child or adolescent client does not have the authority to decide the termination of services; in cases involving a minor, the minor's parent or guardian must make the decision.

3. Special attention should be given to any termination prompted by an administrative decision to cut back on services provided, restrict case transfers within the agency, or modify a client contract due to either a change in the worker's status with the agency, or the end of financial reimbursement from a third-party payer (e.g., an insurance company, Medicaid). When necessary, the worker is obliged to advocate on behalf of the client. Additional care must be observed if services were being provided under court order to be sure that all terms of the order have been met. When making decisions about termination, the worker should be guided by Section 1.16 of the *NASW Code of Ethics* (1999).

4. The social worker should anticipate how the termination might affect other people in the client's family and social network. In situations where a termination may place the client or others at risk of harm, it may be appropriate to notify others of the termination. This notification must, of course, be done in ways consistent with the law and ethics concerning confidentiality.

5. In some cases, termination can be difficult because of a social worker's own psychological needs. A worker may want to be needed and appreciated so strongly that he or she maintains regular contact with a client even when there is no professional reason for doing so. If the need to be needed by one's clients is a recurring problem, the worker and/or his or her supervisor must address it (see Item 16.3).

6. As termination approaches, it is desirable to gradually decrease the frequency of contact. If the client is quite dependent on the worker, this weaning process should be accompanied by efforts to connect the client with natural helpers and informal resources within his or her neighborhood or social network.

7. The feelings of loss and anger that often accompany the ending of any important relationship should be broached by the worker, even if not mentioned by the client. The scheduling of a follow-up interview or telephone contact (i.e., a booster session) several weeks after official termination may be reassuring to the client who fears separation. Also, the client should be informed that he or she can return to the agency if the need arises.

8. The ending of a meaningful professional relationship should utilize some type of ritual to mark this transition. Fortune (2009) notes that such markers include culturally appropriate goodbyes such as hugging and shaking hands and, in the case of terminations within a support group or treatment group, they might involve the exchange of token gifts, potluck meals, and celebrations at which the participants recall highlights in the group's experience. Such ending rituals are especially important in work with children.

Selected Bibliography

Fortune, Anne E. "Terminating with Clients." In *Social Workers' Desk Reference,* 2nd ed. edited by Albert R. Roberts, 627–631. New York: Oxford University Press, 2009.

National Association of Social Workers. *NASW Code of Ethics.* Washington, DC: NASW, 1999.

Walsh, Joseph. *Endings in Clinical Practice,* 2nd ed. Chicago: Lyceum, 2007.

SECTION B

TECHNIQUES AND GUIDELINES FOR INDIRECT PRACTICE

Many of the guidelines for termination and evaluation identified in the introduction to Section A of this chapter also apply to indirect practice. However, a few modifications should be made.

Termination Activities. Organization and community change do not come easily. Although the effort to prevent problems can lead to dramatic savings in both human and financial costs, efforts to make agencies run more smoothly or to help communities address problems are not usually included in a social worker's job description. In order to engage in large system change, social workers typically invest or contribute their personal time or squeeze indirect service work into an already packed schedule. Usually, it is a team of staff members or a special committee from the community that works on bringing about the desired change. The conclusion of a successful organization or community change effort is therefore a time for celebration, or if unsuccessful, a time for critique and recognition of the significance of making the effort. Pizza in a conference room, dinner out together, a gathering at someone's home, or some other symbolic recognition can be important concluding activities that terminate the process.

Evaluation Activities. A number of techniques are available for evaluating indirect practice. Some are used in conjunction with the evaluation of an agency's workers, and other techniques offer guidelines for a comprehensive program evaluation.

14.8 WORKER PERFORMANCE EVALUATION

Worker performance appraisal involves systematically assessing how well agency staff members are performing their jobs. The appraisal of its employees is a fundamental part of the agency's obligation to be accountable to its clients, its community, and those who provide financial support. This *accountability evaluation* is the most common form of worker assessment and typically occurs on a regular basis and is viewed as a quality control mechanism for the agency. Often, salary increases, promotions, the extension of employment contracts, or other rewards are at stake in these evaluations of job performance.

A somewhat different type of evaluation, one separate from regular accountability evaluations, is used to formulate a plan for the worker's further professional growth. For example, an *empowerment evaluation* (Fetterman and Wandersman, 2005) involves considerable self-assessment and reflection by the worker. In this evaluation, rewards (e.g., salary) are not at stake. During this process the worker is assisted in candidly evaluating his or her strengths and limitations. The steps of this process require the worker to take stock of himself or herself, set performance goals, develop strategies to reach those goals, and document progress over time.

Matheson, Van Dyk, and Millar (1995, p. 1) suggest that, if properly conducted, the following positive outcomes can accrue from worker performance evaluations:

- Increase the person's motivation to perform effectively.
- Increase the self-esteem of the person being evaluated.
- Allow new insights for the person(s) doing the appraisal.
- Promote more clarification and better definition of the job of the person being evaluated.
- Facilitate valuable communication among the individuals taking part.
- Promote a better understanding among participants, of themselves, and of the kind of staff development activities that are of value.
- Clarify organizational goals and facilitate their acceptance.
- Allow the organization to engage in human resource planning and to develop training programs.

Certainly, the outcome of a performance evaluation may have either positive or negative consequences for the worker. To minimize the negative factors, an evaluation should be factual and objective to the degree possible. However, even a well-designed procedure requires judgment by the supervisor or agency human resources personnel. Consequently, there will be times when there is disagreement on the conclusions.

In general, an evaluation can be considered relevant when the following criteria are met:

- It focuses on areas of performance or competency that are related to the worker's job and the agency's mission and goals.
- The evaluation criteria and standards, as well as the agency's preferred practices and outcomes, are clearly stated in writing and are made known at the beginning of the time period to be evaluated.
- The work of the person being evaluated is compared to written performance standards and criteria that are realistic for the work assigned.
- The worker has been given ongoing feedback regarding his or her performance prior to the formal evaluation.
- The evaluator can cite and describe examples of performance that form the basis of the ratings.
- The evaluation process identifies and records differences in level of performance among workers.
- The evaluation takes into consideration the nature and complexity of the assignments given to the worker.

Horejsi and Garthwait (2002) caution supervisors about the pitfalls that exist whenever one person attempts to evaluate or rate another's performance:

- The *halo effect*. A supervisee is rated the same in all standards based on the observed performance in a few areas.
- The *attraction of the average*. Every supervisee is evaluated about the same or about average, regardless of real differences in their performances.
- The *leniency bias*. All supervisees are evaluated as outstanding or are assigned inflated ratings so as to minimize arguments or conflict or to avoid hurting their feelings.
- The *strictness bias*. All supervisees are evaluated and rated on the low side because the supervisor has unrealistically high expectations or holds the belief that low ratings will motivate them toward even higher levels of performance.

To avoid these pitfalls, the following three elements should be addressed when conducting a performance evaluation:

1. *People.* The evaluator must be competent. That person must know what constitutes good practice and be able to develop a trusting relationship with the worker. That trust must center on the desire to help the worker develop his or her potential as a social worker. The evaluator must be able to identify both worker competencies and deficiencies in performance and be able to articulate them in a way that builds on worker strengths in order to correct deficiencies. The evaluator must understand that new workers will usually have unevenness in their performances.

2. *Criteria.* The criteria on which the performance evaluation will be based must be made clear *before* the worker enters the time period to be covered by the evaluation. The lack of clear criteria can cause confusion and hard feelings and possibly a lawsuit. A typical direct-service worker's performance appraisal would focus on areas such as these:

- Capacity to establish and maintain appropriate relationships with clients (e.g., attitudes, values, and ethics as manifested in behavior toward clients; self-awareness and self-discipline; ability to manage especially difficult relationships)
- Knowledge and skills in the helping process (e.g., engagement of clients, data collection and assessment, planning and intervention, interviewing and communication skills, documentation of work, and recordkeeping)
- Knowledge of and adherence to agency policies, procedures, and objectives
- Use of supervision and learning opportunities
- Management of workload and job stress
- Intraagency relations (e.g., communication and teamwork with other staff members)
- Interagency relations (e.g., creation and maintenance of working relationships with other agencies, programs, and resources)
- Productivity (e.g., numbers of clients served, new programs started, fees generated)

3. *Process.* The examination of performance must focus on worker behavior, not on explanations or rationalizations for the behavior. The written aspect of the evaluation may take the form of a narrative statement, rating scales, or a combination. Once prepared, these written materials should be reviewed, discussed, revised, if necessary, and signed by both the worker and evaluator, with notation regarding any disagreements, and then placed in the worker's permanent personnel file. The documentation of disagreements could help the worker defend against arbitrary personnel actions. From discussion of the evaluation materials, the worker and supervisor can establish goals, adjust assignments, and plan activities that will strengthen the worker's performance prior to the next evaluation.

Selected Bibliography

Fetterman, David M., and Abraham Wandersman, eds. *Empowerment Evaluation Principles in Practice.* New York: Guilford Press, 2005.

Edwards, Richard L., and John A. Yankey, eds. *Effectively Managing Nonprofit Organizations.* Washington, DC: NASW Press, 2006.

Horejsi, Charles, and Cynthia Garthwait. *The Social Work Practicum*, 2nd ed. Boston: Allyn & Bacon, 2002.

Matheson, Wayne, Cornelius Van Dyk, and Kenneth Millar. *Performance Evaluation in the Human Services.* New York: Haworth, 1995.

14.9   PROGRAM EVALUATION

Because an agency program (e.g., a parent training program) is a planned sequence of activities designed to achieve desired individual and social change, its success in achieving that change is partially determined by its ability to respond to changing needs, concerns, and circumstances. **Program evaluation,** then, is the systematic examination of a program to determine the degree to which and the means by which it is achieving its goals and objectives. Unless programs are regularly evaluated, they can rapidly become out of touch with client needs and lose the support of the community. Furthermore, sound program evaluation and the correction of any identified deficiencies are essential if the program is to be supported by funding agencies or if services are to be reimbursed by managed care companies.

The following guidelines should be followed when considering a program evaluation:

1. *Identify the users of the evaluation data and report.* (e.g., administrators, practitioners, program planners, legislators, fund-raisers). What do they really want and need from this evaluation? What type of information can they understand and use? Is it reasonable to believe that evaluation results will affect the continuation, modification, or termination of the program? It is not a good use of time to begin a program evaluation effort unless the results can make a real difference in terms of the program's operation and the services provided.

2. *Decide if an evaluation is feasible.* Do you have the necessary time, money, and skill available? Do you have access to experts in program evaluation for consultation? Are the data you need readily available? Are key staff members committed to the idea of evaluation? Is the program stable enough to undergo scrutiny? Has the program been in operation long enough to make an evaluation worthwhile?

3. *State the goals and objectives of the program.* Are there clear statements of the program goals and objectives? You cannot evaluate a program until you know precisely what it is trying to accomplish.

4. *Describe the program's activities that are to be evaluated.* The activities must be logically connected to program goals and objectives and must focus on factors or forces over which it has control. Clearly describe the program's units of intervention or services. For example, to describe when an intervention activity is happening, you might ask: When does it begin and end? Does the worker decide when an intervention has occurred or does the client or someone else? Can you distinguish an intervention from other client-staff interactions? Can you decide when a service has been used? (For example, if a client attended only two of five scheduled sessions of a parenting class, has he or she received parent training?)

5. *Select measurable indicators of change.* Once you are clear as to the specific attitudes, behaviors, or conditions your program is trying to change and you are clear as to the interventions used to bring about those changes, you need to select indicators of change that can be detected and measured. Make sure these indicators are ones that can be reasonably attributed to your program's intervention. Also, decide if it is reasonable to believe that the desired effects of the intervention will occur within the time frame you are using. If you cannot wait to measure long-term benefits, you must choose indicators that reflect more immediate changes.

6. *Select appropriate and feasible data collection and measurement tools and/or instruments.* Developing a valid and reliable instrument is a complex, time-consuming, and expensive process, so try to use available instruments. Look online for evaluations done on similar programs and use or adapt instruments that others have found useful.

7. *Plan how you will collect, tabulate, and analyze the data.* Do not collect more data than you can manage and use. Make sure the data you want are actually available. For example, if you plan to gather data from case files, are you sure all of them include the information you need? If your data are stored in the computer system, can you get them out? Can the information you seek be obtained without a release from the client? If your evaluation design involves contacting former service consumers, will you be able to locate them?

8. *Interpret the results of your evaluation.* The final product of your effort is to report the results. Caution should be used in making this interpretation because factors other than the nature of the intervention may account for a program's success or failure. For example, low staff morale may produce poor outcomes despite a well-conceived program.

A useful tool for guiding program evaluation is known as the **logic model**. The essence of this model is to create a structure appropriate for the evaluation to be conducted and to ensure a rigorous and logical assessment of each aspect of a program. According to the logic model, the following items should be considered in conducting a program evaluation:

1. *Priorities established for the program.* The fundamental criteria for evaluating a program are first expressed in the "broad strokes" of the agency's mission, vision statement, specification of whom to serve and how to serve them, mandates from the public, and so on. Thus, the first step in program evaluation is to review these priorities as expressed when the program was created and then to update them to reflect any changes in emphasis that have occurred.

2. *Inputs into the program.* Inputs are the resources the agency invests in the program—for instance, staff, volunteers, money, equipment, information technology, and other elements necessary to carry out the day-to-day program activities. How much of each resource is needed? How much is being used? What does each cost?

3. *Outputs from the program.* Outputs are a program's activities—for example, the manner in which the various programs are delivered, the successful engagement of the people/clients who are served, and the more tangible products that are produced. An evaluation must carefully identify the desired outputs in order to develop appropriate measures of a program's format and method of functioning. Some human services programs can be evaluated in terms of the individual/family/group sessions conducted, others in terms of the training provided to volunteers, and yet others in the amount of consultation given or the number of research studies conducted. Outputs, too, might be reflected in the number of clients served, groups facilitated, or participants in community education meetings.

4. *Outcomes, impacts, and results.* The impact or effect of an agency's activities might take several forms—for instance, people gaining awareness or knowledge of a social issue, client success in addressing personal problems, or workers developing skills to better serve their clients.

In sum, the logic model provides a tool for carefully specifying the factors that should be considered when engaging in program evaluation. Particularly good illustrations of this model can be found online at many cooperative extension programs throughout the United States (e.g., www.uwex.edu/ces/pdande).

Selected Bibliography

Fretchling, Joy A. *Logic Modeling Methods in Program Evaluation*. San Francisco: Jossey-Bass, 2007.

Grinnell, Richard M., Jr., Peter A Gabor, and Yvonne A. Unrau. *Program Evaluation for Social Workers: Foundations of Evidence-Based Programs*, 5th ed. New York: Oxford University Press, 2010.

Martin, Lawrence L., and Peter M. Kettner. *Measuring the Performance of Human Services Programs*, 2nd ed. Los Angeles: Sage, 2010.

Smith, Michael J. *Handbook of Program Evaluation for Social Work and Health Professionals*. New York: Oxford University Press, 2010.

14.10   THE CLIENT SATISFACTION QUESTIONNAIRE (CSQ)

The **Client Satisfaction Questionnaire (CSQ)** is a method for soliciting client opinions about the services provided by a human services agency. It asks clients to rate important aspects of the helping process, such as the atmosphere of the agency, the success of the intervention, the competence of the staff, and so on. Typically, a questionnaire is administered at the point of termination or shortly thereafter, although some agencies administer a CSQ after three to five interviews and periodically thereafter if the client receives services for a longer period.

Figure 14.8 is an example of a typical CSQ. Although CSQs vary in length, they should be easy for a client to complete; therefore, they should not request too much detailed information. If more information is desired, administration of the CSQ might be coupled with an in-depth interview

Evaluating Your Experience at ABC Agency

Thank you for taking a few minutes to evaluate the services you have received at our agency. Your answers to this brief questionnaire will help us improve our services. Feel free to offer additional comments in the space provided or on the back of this page.

Instructions: For each question below, check (✓) your answer.

A. How do you feel about the way you were treated by the receptionist?
—— (1) dissatisfied
—— (3) no feelings either way
—— (5) satisfied
Comments:

B. How do you feel about the length of time you had to wait before our agency provided you with service?
—— (1) unhappy or dissatisfied
—— (3) no feelings either way
—— (5) pleased or satisfied
Comments:

C. Did you accomplish what you expected to achieve when you came to this agency?
—— (5) yes, completely
—— (4) mostly accomplished
—— (3) some accomplishment
—— (2) no real progress
—— (1) worse off than before
Comments:

D. Did you feel your situation/problem(s) changed when you became involved with this agency?
—— (1) things became much worse
—— (2) things somewhat worse
—— (3) no change
—— (4) things somewhat better
—— (5) things became much better
Comments:

E. Which of the following statements comes closest to your feelings about the impact of this agency's services on your situation or problem?
—— (1) made things much worse
—— (2) made things somewhat worse
—— (3) no change
—— (4) made things somewhat better
—— (5) made things much better
Comments:

F. How competent do you feel the social worker was to deal with your situation or problem?
—— (5) very competent
—— (4) moderately competent
—— (2) somewhat incompetent
—— (1) very incompetent
Comments:

G. If a friend needed services from an agency like ours, would you recommend our agency?
—— (1) never
—— (2) probably not
—— (4) probably yes
—— (5) definitely yes
Comments:

H. Overall, how do you feel about your experience with our agency?
—— (1) very dissatisfied
—— (2) dissatisfied
—— (4) satisfied
—— (5) very satisfied
Comments:

It is helpful to know something about the person completing this questionnaire.
—— Male
—— Female
—— Client
—— Parent of agency client
—— Spouse of agency client
Client's age:
—— under 21
—— 21–50
—— 51–65
—— over 65

FIGURE 14.8   Sample Client Satisfaction Questionnaire

(by phone or in a face-to-face setting) or perhaps a focus group of clients on specific variables related to one's satisfaction or dissatisfaction.

A limitation of the CSQ format is that it records only the client's perceptions of what happened as a result of the intervention. Certainly, reality may differ from that perception or the perception may change over time. Also, there is a tendency for satisfied clients to return a greater portion of the questionnaires (particularly if a mailed questionnaire) than those who are dissatisfied—skewing the data toward positive responses.

The process for implementing a CSQ is as follows:

1. *Decide what population of clients to sample.*   The sample could be representative of agency clientele in general, of clients who have received a particular type of service, or of clients who make up a particular demographic group (e.g., clients over age 60). Unless all members of the target group are to be included in the study, basic knowledge of sampling methods is required in order to draw a representative sample. Criteria for CSQ distribution should be determined by the evaluator and relate to the purpose of the evaluation, statistical requirements, and administrative convenience.

2. *Design the questionnaire.*   Keep it as simple and brief as possible and avoid professional jargon. The agency may want to gather certain client and demographic information in order to determine if satisfaction with or complaints about services are related to factors such as the client's ethnicity, age, socioeconomic status, and the like. However, asking for such information tends to weaken assurances of anonymity.

3. *Administer the questionnaire.*   This step can often be carried out by clerical staff, volunteers, or social service aides; however, those administering the questionnaire must be trained in its use in order to increase reliability. The assurance of confidentiality to respondents is very important. A mailed CSQ can provide the client with anonymity but does presume that the client can read. If the target population consists of former clients, the questionnaire can be mailed, emailed, or administered by phone. If it includes clients who are still in regular contact with the agency, the questionnaire can usually be administered by a receptionist. The greatest amount of work in administering the questionnaire will probably be in following up on those clients who fail to return the questionnaire; these clients will have to be called individually or sent a letter to obtain a reasonable return rate. If the responses are to be anonymous, there will be problems in follow-up; therefore, a guarantee of confidentiality without the added assurance of anonymity may be preferable. Statistical techniques can determine whether there are significant differences between those who return the questionnaire immediately and those who require urging.

4. *Tabulate and analyze the questionnaire data.*   Manual tabulation may be possible for short questionnaires. Computer processing is desirable for long questionnaires and when a large number must be tabulated.

Selected Bibliography

Clow, Kenneth E., and Robert E. Stevens. *Concise Encyclopedia of Professional Services Marketing.* New York: Routledge, 2009.
Sue, Valerie, and Lois A. Ritter. *Conducting Online Surveys.* Thousand Oaks, CA: Sage, 2007.

14.11   AGENCY EVALUATION

Social agencies are expected to demonstrate that they are efficient and effective in the provision of services. Agency boards, legislative bodies, and other funding sources regularly demand that agencies review their functioning and report the results of that evaluation. Individual workers, too, are often interested in performance indicators that might stimulate organizational changes necessary to improve the quality of services provided. Thus, it is useful for social workers to be familiar with some of the indicators typically used in agency performance reviews.

Evaluation must be preceded by a clear statement of goals. Often, the first task in agency evaluation is for the governing board or other policymakers to explicate the current goals and objectives for the organization. It is only with this information that appropriate performance indicators can be selected and methods of data collection identified.

An agency's evaluation should address the degree to which its programs respond to community need, the quality of services offered, the satisfaction of clients, efficiency in use of resources, and so on. Here are some of the areas that should be considered in specifying an agency's goals:

- *Responsiveness.* Does the agency and its programs respond to public and community needs and identified concerns?
- *Relevance.* Do sponsors, constituents, and consumers find the agency's programs appropriate to the needs they seek to address and do they consider them supportive of community values?
- *Availability.* Are the amount and type of services provided sufficient to meet the needs of the community?
- *Accessibility.* Are the location, cost, and times services offered appropriate for the clientele of the agency? Are there other potential constituent groups who do not receive services due to accessibility issues?
- *Quality.* Do the services meet expected standards of quality as judged by client satisfaction and expert opinion?
- *Awareness.* Is the general population, as well as other human services providers, sufficiently aware of the services offered to assure that persons who need the services know how to obtain them?
- *Productivity.* Does the program efficiently use its resources to accomplish the agency's goals?

With clarity about the questions to be answered when collecting data, it is then possible to select a set of *performance indicators* that will help to measure the agency's level of success and, when appropriate, lead to improvements. Selecting appropriate indicators and finding accurate data regarding them is a complex task. The following sampling of indicators illustrates a few essential areas to include in measures of agency success:

- *Personnel-related factors.* Rate of turnover, absenteeism, staff vacancies, number of hours contributed by volunteers, frequency of in-service training, and so forth
- *The intake process.* Data on the number and sources of referrals, number of telephone contacts, number of people on the waiting list, average length of time between first contact and initiation of service, and so on
- *Service-related factors.* Number of new cases opened each month, average length of service per case, number of clients served, number and type of cases referred elsewhere, number of former clients returning for service, average cost per client, client satisfaction with services, and so on
- *Staff productivity.* Size and type of caseload per worker, number of counseling sessions provided each day, number of hours spent per case, amount of inter- and intraagency contacts per month, number of miles of work-related travel each week, and the like
- *Cost of providing services.* Average cost of staff time per case, number of clients paying a fee for service, average travel cost per case, average time spent in case recording, estimated value of volunteer hours per week, and so on

These data, once collected, must be carefully analyzed. Data collected over time will allow for the examination of trends within the agency and adjustments to improve the efficiency and effectiveness of the agency. Also, the data can be compared to data from similar agencies, making it possible to gain a relative picture of the agency's functioning.

Selected Bibliography

Harrison, Michael I. *Diagnosing Organizations: Methods, Models, and Processes*, 3rd ed. Thousand Oaks, CA: Sage, 2005.

Knapp, Stephen A., and Gary R. Anderson. *Agency-Based Program Evaluation: Lessons from Practice.* Thousand Oaks, CA: Sage, 2010.

Posavac, Emil J., and Raymond G. Carey. *Program Evaluation: Methods and Case Studies.* Upper Saddle River, NJ: R. G. Carey and Associates, 2007.

Specialized Techniques and Guidelines for Social Work Practice

The techniques and guidelines described in prior sections of this book could be used by almost all social workers, regardless of their practice setting. In addition to these generic tools of the social worker's trade, specialized knowledge and skills are required for some social work practice activities. Part V concludes the book with two chapters on these specialized aspects of social work.

Some client groups require special sensitivity by the social worker. For example, unique insight and understanding is required to help a client deal with the devastating impact of poverty, to provide services to a woman who has been battered, or to intervene when a client is at risk of committing suicide. Clients of different sexual orientations and those of different age groups call for special sensitivity, too. Working with a child or adolescent requires knowledge of developmental factors and communication skills that connect with young people. And at the other end of the age spectrum, older people have unique needs that must be recognized. Specialized knowledge and skills are also required when clients have a physical disability, brain injury, intellectual disability, chemical dependence, mental illness, eating disorder, or is an immigrant. Chapter 15 identifies guidelines for working with these clients.

Another set of specialized guidelines can help the social worker and have a satisfying and productive career. Chapter 16 presents guidelines that will assist the worker in obtaining employment, preparing for licensing and certification exams, dealing with job-related stress, testifying in court, avoiding malpractice suits, and addressing issues of sexual misconduct. Finally, to support the social worker in carrying out his or her professional obligations, this chapter also provides guidance on how to provide and utilize supervision, consume and contribute to social work knowledge, improve the social work image, and assume a leadership role within the human services.

Guidelines for Working with Vulnerable Client Groups

Social workers practice within a wide variety of settings, and consequently, they encounter a wide variety of clients with many different types of concerns, problems, and requests. Even though the clients served by a particular program may have presenting problems that are quite similar, each client will react to his or her situation and to the social worker in a unique way. Thus, social workers must always adapt their approaches and techniques to the special needs, characteristics, and circumstances of the clients they serve.

The items selected for this chapter illustrate how a social worker might adapt his or her approach to the client by providing information on several different client groups and offering guidelines for addressing their special needs, characteristics, and challenges. By comparing the approaches recommended for these diverse client groups, the reader will come to a deeper appreciation of why direct-service practitioners, as well as those who design and administer programs, must always consider the uniqueness of the clients they serve. In addition, the reader will understand more clearly why an approach that works well for one group may not be appropriate for another.

15.1   THE CLIENT WHO IS EXPERIENCING POVERTY

Many of the individuals and families encountered in social work practice are struggling with financial problems. Many live in poverty. Poverty is fundamentally an issue of social and economic justice. No matter what the cause—whether individual factors or large-scale economic forces—no person should have to live in poverty in the relatively wealthy U.S. society. No one should have to go without food, housing, and medical care. No one should have to live in conditions that are dehumanizing, unsafe, and unhealthy. Social workers, regardless of their practice settings and job titles, have a responsibility to collaborate with others in order to advance social and economic policies and programs that will prevent or reduce the incidence of poverty and assist those facing economic hardship.

Poverty has devastating effects on individuals, families, and communities. It is a contributing factor to personal and social problems, such as the breakup of families, violence, crime, substance abuse, suicide, and disease. Children experiencing poverty are also especially vulnerable to the effects of poor nutrition, disease, family insecurity, and social instability.

The causes of poverty are complex and will vary, depending on whether one is examining poverty in a developed or a developing country. The ultimate causes of widespread and persistent poverty are to be found in a society's economic system and in its political and economic decisions regarding what it will produce, how it is produced, and for whom. Regrettably, when it comes to matters of social and economic justice, there are no completely fair economic systems. None of the systems—whether free market economies, planned economies, or mixed economies—are able to deliver all that their theory promise.

A war or an economic recession or depression can quickly push large numbers of people into poverty. Regional and localized pockets of poverty can result from natural disasters such as floods and earthquakes and from a shrinking or loss of major industry such as steel, textiles, or lumber. The more immediate or situational causes of poverty among the individuals and families encountered in social work practice are usually job layoffs, inability to secure a job that pays a living wage, and an illness or injury that precludes employment.

Even in good economic times, some groups are at high risk of being poor, including those lacking in education and marketable job skills and also those with an intellectual limitation, mental illness, addiction, or debilitating health problem. Individuals and families can quickly slide into poverty after loss to the family's breadwinner because of death or imprisonment, a house fire, a serious health problem, and the like. People on a fixed income, such as the elderly, are at risk when faced with a high rate of inflation and rapid increases in the cost of food, housing, utilities, and health care. Racism, sexism, and other forms or discrimination also restrict the economic opportunities available to various segments of a population.

In the United States, many of those who are poor are the so-called working poor—those who may be working two or three part-time jobs but still not earning an adequate income or receiving benefits such as health insurance. Many of those living in poverty are single mothers and their children. Families headed by very young mothers are at very high risk of being poor. Mothers who are raising their children after a divorce are often unable to make ends meet because many fathers do not or cannot pay adequate child support. Women with limited education face special challenges since many of the jobs available to them (e.g., waitress, maid) pay low wages, do not provide health insurance, and often the time of their work is at night or on weekends when child care is especially expensive and transportation is harder to arrange.

Direct-service social workers responding to individuals and families who are poor will find this additional information and guidance useful:

1. When designing or selecting an approach to working with clients who are poor, recognize that once an individual becomes poor, he or she encounters a multitude of forces and barriers that keep him or her in poverty. For example, in order to get a job, an individual must have appropriate clothing, transportation, recent job experiences, a telephone, email, and a permanent address—things that many poor people do not have. A parent who wants to work may discover that the cost of child care will consume much of the pay received from a minimum-wage job. Working one's way out of poverty requires not only the motivation and the capacity but also the opportunity to do so. It is a slow process that requires planning and methodically executing a multitude of small steps. Changing one's life circumstances is difficult for anyone, but doing so when poor is especially difficult, given the demoralizing and exhausting effects of poverty (see Item 13.13).

2. Social workers must possess a working knowledge of the various government programs and private agencies that provide financial assistance. The most effective programs are those designed to address an array of personal and family needs and concerns in addition to financial problems. Providing access to education and technical training is one of the most cost-effective approaches to addressing poverty among people who are healthy and of working age. However, education and job training programs are usually not, by themselves, sufficient. Accessing and utilizing education and training opportunities can be difficult for those who are overwhelmed by other personal problems and family responsibilities and by persons who suffer the psychological effects of domestic violence, child abuse and neglect, death of a loved one, and other traumatic life events. Thus, counseling, child care, transportation, and other supportive services are essential components of successful adult education, job training, and employment programs.

Securing a job and financial independence is a feasible goal for many who are poor. However, for some individuals of working age, this is not a realistic goal because their capacity for gainful employment is severely limited by serious and chronic conditions such as mental illness, mental retardation, brain injury, and substance abuse.

3. Be alert to the fact that existing welfare policies, rules, and eligibility criteria can be obstacles to people who desperately need government assistance and services. Client or *case advocacy* by the social worker is often needed to help individuals secure welfare assistance. *Class advocacy* is necessary to make these systems more responsive to the needs of the people they serve (see Items 13.17 and 13.31).

4. A client's views and beliefs about being poor are of importance because they can influence his or her response to current circumstances. Among those who are poor there are a variety of beliefs, attitudes, and feelings about being poor. For example, an individual who has always been poor may view living in poverty differently than an individual who for many years had an adequate income before becoming poor. Moreover, a person who lives in a community made up of mostly poor people will view their situation differently than the poor person who lives in a community where few others are poor. Some who are in poverty, as officially measured by government standards or other objective criteria, may not define themselves as being poor. To better understand the client's responses to the current situation, consider the following questions:

- What personal and family characteristics, situational factors, and economic forces are contributing to the client's economic problems?
- Did the client grow up in a community where most others were poor? If yes, what meaning did he or she assign to being poor?
- Are the client's family and relatives also poor or is he or she economically different from family and relatives?
- Has the client been abandoned or rejected by family, relatives, and friends who are better off economically? If yes, did a problem such as mental illness, substance abuse, or criminal activity contribute to this ostracism?
- Who are the client's sources of social support and everyday assistance? Are these persons also poor?
- What strengths or resiliency factors have the client relied on to cope with the challenges of living in poverty?

5. Living in poverty is extraordinarily stressful because so many aspects of a poor person's life are worrisome, unpredictable, and exhausting. This commonly gives rise to anxiety, fear, and frustration. Consequently, some who are poor are quick to anger and resentful toward anyone who might somehow make their life even more difficult. Still others feel hopeless and respond to their circumstances and to service providers with passivity and emotional dependency.

Because the dominant American culture values work, money, material possessions, and independence, persons who are poor are prone to developing feelings of inferiority and shame. They may feel inadequate, rejected, and shunned. They may feel guilty about being poor, especially if they are the parents of young children and see that their children are being harmed by their life circumstances. Some cope with these painful feelings by withdrawing from ordinary social relationships. Some express their embarrassment and resentment by criticizing and tearing down the work and performance of other people, including those working in programs that address the problems faced by the poor.

Some of the people who live on the streets or in shelters for the homeless are especially challenging clients. Their economic situation may be complicated by substance abuse, mental illness, inadequate nutrition, and disabling and untreated health problems. Some of these individuals are so immersed in a lifestyle of day-to-day survival that they approach all relationships in a calculating and manipulative manner. Some are belligerent and aggressive. A client's frustration, sense of hopelessness, and unpredictable lifestyle can be barriers to his or her effective utilization of professionals and human service programs that expect their clients to be cooperative, adhere to schedules, and follow through on plans.

6. Strive to reduce the social distance and power differential between yourself and the client. Do this by looking for opportunities to talk with clients about the very ordinary aspects of life, such as their interests, hobbies, and special times in their lives. Invite your clients to share their music, art, and other creative skills. When possible utilize in-home interviews and when appropriate to the practice setting, share meals with clients (see Items 10.6 and 10.10). Above all, recognize their humanness, their uniqueness, worth, and dignity.

7. Identify and arrange opportunities for clients to share their knowledge and skills for dealing with poverty. For example, many who are poor have learned to be frugal and thrifty in shopping and stretching their limited resources. Many have located and learned to use community resources that have been overlooked by others. Many are very creative in working out arrangements that permit several individuals or families to share what little they have and to help each other cope. Still others have arrived at profound insights into the human condition and developed a truly inspiring spirituality. These are all important strengths that need to be recognized and, if the client is willing, shared with others who struggle with many of the same issues.

8. In keeping with the empowerment strategy, offer clients opportunities to shape the programs they utilize by serving on agency boards, advisory groups, or by testifying at a legislative hearing. Many clients have a need to express appreciation and reciprocate in some way for the help they receive. If this is important to a client, arrange opportunities for him or her to make an in-kind contribution to the relevant program or agency. For example, a client might want to do volunteer work at a homeless shelter or somehow assist other clients. Unfortunately, issues of facility insurance and concerns over legal liability may be barriers to arranging reciprocity (see Items 13.17, 13.18, 13.31, and 13.38).

9. Living in poverty often leads to a life of desperation. Frustration can push a person into making decisions that others judge to be unwise and imprudent. For example, a mother with very little money may splurge and buy her child a pair of expensive shoes. Fear and worry over a lack of money may draw a person into activities that are illegal and that violate his or her conscience. For example, in an effort to secure money, a desperate individual may sell drugs, steal, or engage in prostitution. As a professional, you will probably feel disappointed and irritated because such choices by your client make things even worse. While you cannot condone illegal behavior, try to see the world through your client's eyes and understand why clients make these choices. Do not allow yourself to become judgmental or moralistic for that would only create a barrier to further work with the client.

10. Many professionals (e.g., social workers, physicians, nurses, psychologists) admit to feeling somewhat uncomfortable when working directly with persons who live in truly desperate economic circumstances. This discomfort stems, in part, from the obvious fact that the client has so little and that, by comparison, the professional has so much. In addition, the professional realizes that he or she does, in fact, have the ability (i.e., the money) to alleviate this client's immediate financial distress, at least for a few hours or a few days. It is this awareness that tugs on the professional's conscience and sense of fundamental justice. In working with clients who have other types of problems, the professional knows that he or she does not have the ability to bring about such an immediate change. In working with the economically poor, the professional must struggle with the question: If I have the ability, do I have the responsibility?

Selected Bibliography

Albert, Raymond, and Louise Skolnik. *Social Welfare Programs.* Belmont, CA: Brooks/Cole, 2006.

Midgley, James, and Amy Conley, eds. *Social Work and Social Development.* New York: Oxford University Press, 2010.

Minuchin, Patricia, Jorge Colapinto, and Salvador Minuchin. *Working with Families of the Poor*, 2nd ed. New York: Guilford, 2007.

Payne, Ruby, Philip De Vol, and Terie Smith. *Bridges Out of Poverty: Strategies for Professionals and Communities*. Highland TX: aha! Process Inc., 2006.

15.2　THE CLIENT WHO IS A CHILD

Children are not miniature adults. Thus, many techniques that are effective with adult clients may not work with children. When their clients are children, social workers must add some new skills to their repertoire, such as the use of play. The sections that follow provide guidelines for a range of tasks involved in working with a child under the age of 12.

PLANNING THE INTERVIEW

1. Be clear about why you are meeting with the child and what it is that you hope to accomplish. Plan several alternative methods to accomplish your goal. Anticipate what could go wrong (e.g., child will not talk, child cries, child will not leave parent) and consider how you might handle such awkward situations.

Conduct the interview in a room that is familiar and comfortable to the child. If that is not possible, consider an open space such as a park or playground. Be cognizant that only limited confidentiality can be provided to a child. Parents will usually have access to records kept on their child.

2. Consider using some form of play to put the child at ease and facilitate communication. Prior to the interview, assemble play materials that may be helpful. For young children, provide art materials (e.g., finger paints, clay, building blocks) as well as objects that can be used to portray family members and situations (e.g., dolls, hand puppets, doll house, toy animals). For older children, consider simple board games, toy telephones, puzzles, and electronic games.

INTRODUCING YOURSELF AND GETTING STARTED

3. Place yourself at the child's level physically; sit or squat so you do not tower over the child. When introducing yourself, inform the child how you want to be addressed and give a simple description of your role (e.g., "My name is Ron Hoffman. Please call me Ron. My job is to help children who have problems at home."). Be prepared to offer a simple and truthful explanation as to why you need to speak with the child. It may be necessary to assure the child that he or she is not in trouble and that the interview is not a punishment.

If the child is at least 6 or 7 years of age, ask what he or she has been told about the purpose of the interview. This may reveal what the child is expecting. You might ask if someone (e.g., a parent) has told the child what to say or do during the interview.

4. You might begin with some friendly conversation and showing an interest in what the child is wearing or carrying or asking about the child's school or favorite activities or TV shows. If the child is frightened, attempt to normalize the situation by saying something like, "When I was your age, I was afraid to talk to new people." If the child appears reluctant to talk for fear of retaliation by others, you may need to describe what you can do to keep him or her safe. But do not make promises you cannot keep.

If the child refuses to talk or interact, try engaging him or her in a parallel activity and then gradually initiate conversation about the activity. For example, if the child does not talk but begins to play with a doll, pick up another doll and engage in similar play. This will often lead to some interaction and opportunity for verbal exchanges.

Young children who are frightened and withdrawn will sometimes relax and let down their guard in response to a bit of clowning around. However this clowning must be done in a way so the child knows for sure that you are trying to be silly. For example, if you put on a clown nose, the child will understand your intentions. Another technique is to do something rather unexpected, such as, "Brian, while we are talking, we may get thirsty. Should we go get some juice now or should we wait until later?"

GATHERING INFORMATION FROM CHILDREN

5. Because young children have limited verbal ability, much of the information you gather will come from observing the child's nonverbal behavior during play and social interactions. However, in order to draw valid inferences about a child's personality or behavioral patterns, you must observe the child in several different situations. Do not base a conclusion or assessment on a single observation.

6. Children act out their concerns in play and often project their concerns and feelings into the stories they make up and into their play, drawings, and art. Thus, consider using these activities to set up imaginary or pretend situations that are relevant to the topics you wish to explore. For example, present the child with a set of dolls and ask the child to make up a story about what makes the dolls happy or afraid. Or, you might ask the child to draw a picture of a family or children at school and then tell a story about the people in the picture. If the child is hesitant, you may need to initiate the storytelling about the dolls or pictures, but once the child is attentive, ask the child to continue the story.

While it is true that young children incorporate their thoughts, feelings, and experiences into their play, stories, and drawings, they will also incorporate themes drawn from TV programs, books, and incidents described by their friends. Thus, you must be cautious about interpreting what you observe because it may be difficult to pinpoint the source of the themes that appear in a child's play or stories. It is important to remember that themes of violence are quite common in the play of normal children. Thus, violence-related talk and play, especially by boys, is not by itself an indicator that a child has experienced or observed violence.

7. Children between the ages of about 3 and 6 are usually eager to please adults. They are also suggestible, especially if asked leading questions. Children of this age may modify what they have to say in order to make it fit with what they believe the adult wants to hear. Children who sense disapproval from adults will often cease talking.

Young children are easily distracted and move quickly from one topic or activity to another. Consequently, they may express only once what they think or feel about a particular concern. Asking a child to remain focused on a topic is seldom successful. If pressured to stay focused on a painful or sensitive topic, the child may become noncommittal or silent.

8. Most children older than about 6 years are able to answer simple and age appropriate questions. However, they may need assistance to fully describe a situation or event. For example, you may need to ask: What happened next? Then what did you do? Where were you when this happened? Who was with you? As a general rule, avoid asking "why" questions because children find it difficult to describe the reasons behind their behavior.

9. Special techniques like story completions, doll play, and drawings may still be necessary and useful when interviewing children between about 7 and 9, but many children who are older than this will usually give a thoughtful response to a clear but uncomplicated question. By age 9 or 10, children pay attention to the meaning and implications of words and can often detect phony or insincere messages. They will become suspicious when they observe incongruence between a person's words and actions.

Many children of this age group find it easier to talk about personal matters if they can do so while engaged in some non-demanding activity such as a simple card game or a board game like checkers that does not require much concentration. Talking back and forth on a toy telephone works and puppet-to-puppet interaction can facilitate meaningful communication. Sentence completions may prove useful with older children (e.g., "When at home, I am afraid of . . . ").

10. The game of "Hot or Cold" may prove useful to an effort to explore a particular topic. For example, if the child is reluctant to describe a concern, you might say something like the following:

> "Jimmy, I am going to make some guesses about what is bothering you. If my guesses are getting closer to what is troubling you, tell me that I am getting warmer. If my guesses are wrong, tell me that I am getting colder."

HOW CHILDREN THINK

11. Children between the ages of about 3 to 6 are concrete, and egocentric in their thinking. For example, they believe an event or activity that makes them happy will have the same effect on all people. Their thinking is characterized by an all-or-nothing pattern; the child is unable to understand mixed feelings or ambivalence. The child may describe a person as mean and then just minutes later describe the same person as nice or fun. Such thinking in extremes and absolutes leads them to categorize both themselves and others as, for example, good or bad, smart or dumb, and so on. Children of this age typically describe themselves and others in terms of external characteristics (e.g., age, hair color, grade in school); they seldom mention personality traits except in global terms such as "She is happy" or "He is a bad person."

12. At about age 6, the child's thinking starts to become more objective and logical. Gradually, the child acquires the ability to imagine being in another person's situation and understand that different people have different feelings and experiences. However, even a 7-year-old may still believe that he or she is the total cause for how others, especially parents, feel and behave. It is not until about age 9 or 10 that children understand that they do not cause the behaviors and emotions they observe in others.

13. By around age 10, children can view themselves as an individual with a mixture of characteristics and abilities (e.g., skilled at some things but not in others, sometimes good and sometimes bad). At this age, the child realizes that it is possible to have conflicting thoughts and feelings and opposing emotions simultaneously (e.g., to be angry at someone you love). The child can now anticipate how others will probably behave in a particular situation or react to certain information. Thus, the child can now manipulate words and information in order to influence how others will respond.

ASSESSING THE TRUTHFULNESS OF A CHILD'S STATEMENTS

14. A social worker responsible for investigating reports of abuse and neglect or conducting child custody evaluations will often need to form an opinion about whether a child is telling the truth. As a general rule, the younger the child, the less able and the less likely he or she is to fabricate a falsehood. However children, like adults, may misunderstand and misinterpret their experiences and they may lie to get what they want or escape punishment.

15. Sometimes, a parent or another adult will pressure a child to lie to a social worker in order to avoid the disclosure of some problem or criminal activity or perhaps as a way of hurting another person, such as an ex-spouse. If an adult has coached a child on what to tell a social worker, the child will often use adult-like language, use few gestures and few facial expressions, and speak without displaying genuine and appropriate emotions. Moreover, the child will be either inconsistent regarding the major elements of the story or, on the other hand, extremely consistent on certain points but unable to describe supporting or connecting details.

16. Assessing the truth of a child's statement is a special challenge in the case of alleged child sexual abuse. As a general rule, sexually abused children are reluctant to report the abuse and do not want to talk about it. When children do self-report sexual abuse, they seldom lie about such matters. Deliberate false reports (i.e., actual lying by the child) are rare among children below about age 12 and infrequent among teenagers. Nonetheless, the possibilities that the child is lying, misinterpreting a situation, or has named and accused the wrong person must always be kept in mind. The probability of a deception and false report increases whenever the child is the focus of a custody or visitation dispute. In these situations, one parent may instruct the child to accuse the other parent of some wrongdoing. Indicators of a possible deception by a child and/or his or her parent include the following:

- Disclosing of and talking about the incident seems too easy for the child (i.e., child is not afraid or reluctant to tell others what happened).
- The child does not show expected or authentic emotion when describing what happened (e.g., does not cry or display distress, embarrassment, fear, anger).
- The child uses adult-like words to describe sexual activity (as if coached or rehearsed by an adult).
- The child describes the sexual activity using only visual images and not information drawn from the other senses (i.e., smell, taste, touch, sound).
- The child does not seem to be afraid of the alleged offender (e.g., the child does not seem hesitant to meet with the alleged offender when that possibility is mentioned).
- The child is not hesitant to talk about the sexual abuse in the presence of a non-offending parent. (Most children try to shield this parent from the details and thus the pain of what happened.)
- The child talks about having been sexually abused but does not display any of the other behavioral signs and symptoms associated with child sexual abuse (see Item 11.14).
- When a parent is encouraging the child to report the sexual abuse, the parent does not display the expected emotions. For example, the parent does not seem genuinely shocked, sad, depressed, anxious, worried, alarmed, or fearful. The parent may express anger at the alleged offender and seek revenge yet not display genuine alarm or distress over what has supposedly happened to the child.

17. Children from about age 4 to 6 will frequently exaggerate or boast when describing their abilities and experiences; however, when asked, "Is that pretend or real?" or "Is that really, really true?" they will usually acknowledge the difference between a truth and a make-believe story. They may tell a simple lie in order to avoid punishment but they do not have the cognitive abilities necessary to fabricate an untrue and complex story having several interrelated elements, actions, or actors. In trying to describe something that happened, they will usually recall key actors or central events but not the connecting details, such as what happened before and after the event and how one thing led up to another. They can remember special times and rituals such as a mealtime or a birthday party but they do not accurately remember things that are unconnected to their routines and familiar activities.

18. Preschool age children do not grasp the concept of time and can seldom accurately describe when something happened. They do not use clocks or calendars to measure time. Children in the first and second grades will still use events such as nap time, lunch time, Christmas, start of school, and other events as markers of time. Reference to such markers can help to establish timeframes.

19. Children between about 7 and 11 place a high value on fairness and honesty. They are quick to notice cheating or rule-breaking in a game. They may, however, embellish the truth in order to tell an exciting story. At this stage, they possess the cognitive ability necessary to deliberately mislead others by selectively withholding information and using other simple deceptions. Children in the age range of about 9 to 11 are usually eager to please adults and tend to say what they believe adults want to hear. They have good memories of central actors and events and can usually recall relevant specifics with a little probing by an interviewer.

ADDITIONAL SUGGESTIONS

20. Children will behave differently in different situations and when with various people. Thus, you get only a sample of the child's behavior during an interview. The farther removed the child is from his or her usual social and family context, the more cautious you must be in drawing conclusions about the child's behavior. For example, the child who is anxious or withdrawn during an office interview may be responding to an unfamiliar environment. Multiple interviews with the child and in-home interviews are important to securing an accurate assessment of a child's functioning.

21. Because young children are responsive to nonverbal communication, it may be helpful to make deliberate use of facial expressions and gestures. Light physical touch may be appropriate but do not hug or caress a child for this makes many children uncomfortable. In addition, this could be misinterpreted as inappropriate sexual contact. Touch can be especially confusing and even threatening to a child who has been physically or sexually abused.

22. Answer a child's question honestly and directly (e.g., "I believe you will be in foster care until the school term ends"). Do not use euphemisms and avoid elaborate or complicated explanations. When giving information to a child, present it as simply as possible and in small doses.

23. When behavior-control rules are necessary during an interview, explain the rules, along with any consequences for breaking them (e.g., "You are not permitted to hit me; if you hit me, I will put away the toys.").

24. During an interview, give the child as much choice as possible. But be sure to offer choices that you can accept. This point is illustrated in the following statements:

Misleading: "Well, Ellen, what would you like to do? We can do whatever you like."

Better: "Ellen, today you can use either the finger paints or the crayons. Which one do you want to use?"

25. Be cautious about offering gifts or treats to a child. Although they are an extension of normal adult–child interaction and may be helpful in building a relationship, children and parents can easily misinterpret them. Make sure that your gift to a child is not viewed as competition with the child's parents.

26. Children are protective of their parents. They will usually defend their parents, even abusive parents. Be objective and non-judgmental when talking about the parents' behavior (e.g., "Your dad does have a problem with alcohol. When he is drinking he says and does bad things. That is why your parents are getting a divorce."). Avoid statements that the child could construe as a criticism of his or her parents.

CHILDREN IN OUT-OF-HOME PLACEMENTS

27. Many of the children known professionally to social workers are in an out-of-home placement (i.e., foster family care, group homes, institutional care). Many of these children were exposed to severe abuse or neglect. Regardless of the reason for the placement, a separation from parents and family is usually a disruptive and emotionally traumatic experience for children. The children may be confused about why they are in placement. Children often blame themselves for the family problems that led up to the placement and view their separation from family as a punishment for some real or imagined wrongdoing. Once apart from family, many children worry intensely about the well-being of their parents and any siblings still at home. Assume that the child has many questions about his or her current situation and future. Make it as easy as possible for the child to ask questions, and be as factual and honest as possible in answering.

28. Do everything possible to maintain frequent contacts and visitation between the child in placement and his or her parents, siblings, and other relatives. If a child has little or no contact with family, he or she will usually create an imaginary story or a fantasy that explains the situation. In the long run, visitation is helpful to the child, even if the visits are upsetting. If, for example, the child's mother is addicted to drugs and acting irresponsibly, it is important for the child to see this behavior and recognize that the parent is in no shape to provide care. It is better for the child to struggle with an unpleasant reality than to live within a pleasant but untrue fantasy.

29. Relationship losses, especially a series of losses, have long-lasting, negative effects on a child. It is critically important to minimize the number of separations and placements experienced by a child. If a child must be separated from someone to whom he or she is emotionally attached, the move should be as gradual as possible, thus giving the child an opportunity to prepare and adjust. A ritual such as a going-away party helps the child make this transition by symbolically ending one relationship and beginning another. Without such a ritual, the child might feel as if he or she was given away or rejected. A transition ritual gives the child permission to let go of one relationship and embrace a new one. After the physical separation, it is important that the child be able to return to his or her former home for occasional visits.

30. Because foster children experience so much change and uncertainty, the child's social worker must be prepared to become a predictable figure in the child's life. The foster child is especially sensitive to any hint of rejection. Contacts with the child should be regular and predictable. If you must miss an appointment, explain this directly to the child.

31. Children often feel shame and embarrassment about being in foster care, and consequently they may fabricate a story to explain their situation. When a teacher or school classmates discover this fabrication, the child may acquire a reputation as being a spinner of tall tales or a liar. Thus, it is important to help these children develop a truthful and understandable explanation of why they are in an out-of-home placement so they can more comfortably describe their living situation to teachers, friends, and others.

32. When speaking with a child's foster parents, adoptive parents, or group care staff, be truthful about the child's behavior, situation, and history. Efforts to conceal the child's life experience in an attempt to somehow protect the child or because you fear others will not understand or accept the child almost always backfire.

Selected Bibliography

Poole, Debra, and Michael Lamb. *Investigative Interviews of Children*. Washington, DC: American Psychological Association, 1998.

Rose, Steven R., and Marian Fatout. *Social Work Practice with Children and Adolescents*. Boston: Allyn & Bacon, 2003.

Sommers-Flanagan, John, and Rita Sommers-Flanagan. *Tough Kids, Cool Counseling*, 2nd ed. Alexandria, VA: American Counseling Association, 2006.

Timberlake, Elizabeth, and Marika Cutler. *Developmental Play Therapy in Clinical Social Work*. Boston: Allyn & Bacon, 2001.

Wilson, Claire, and Martine Powell, eds. *A Guide to Interviewing Children*. New York: Brunner-Routledge, 2001.

15.3   THE CLIENT WHO IS AN ADOLESCENT

The developmental period known as adolescence—between about ages 12 and 18—is a time of rapid physical and psychological change and awakening sexual desire. It is often a time of conflict and tension between adolescents and their parents regarding issues of authority and control. Parents typically worry that their adolescent children will become involved with drugs, have irresponsible sexual experiences, or be injured by recklessness.

The problems most likely to bring adolescents to the attention of a social worker include family conflict, alcohol and drug use, running away, behavior problems in school, violence, delinquency, pregnancy, threat of suicide, and the need for foster care or residential treatment. The following background information and guidelines are useful when working with adolescents:

1. Adolescents are typically idealistic, painfully self-conscious, struggling with authority issues, fiercely attached to peers, preoccupied with their appearance and sexuality, seeking popularity and conformity within their peer group, and desperately trying to develop an identity apart from their family. Adolescents want and need positive adult role models and mentors who can prepare them for adulthood but they will often resist the influence of their own parents. They need opportunities to learn skills—whether athletic, academic, musical, or vocational—that provide a sense of accomplishment and competence.

2. Many of the adolescents encountered in social work practice are involuntary or mandated clients who are sent to a social worker or a social agency by parents, school officials, a juvenile court judge, or a probation officer. This is, of course, a very uncomfortable and awkward situation for the adolescent because of the authority struggles common to this developmental period. The adolescent may respond with silence, non-cooperation, rudeness, or abusive language. In such a situation, a social worker's patience and self-control can be severely tested. In addition, the worker's own unresolved parent-child and authority issues may surface and intrude in the professional relationship.

Despite the challenges they present, adolescents are usually resilient and have a great capacity to grow and change. Effective social work intervention during this developmental period can prevent serious problems and have lifelong, positive effects. Because they are usually lively and inquisitive, work with adolescents can be stimulating, fun, and truly rewarding.

3. Adolescents need an environment that is predictable and provides structure, boundaries, and limits. In many practice settings, such as group homes and treatment centers, social workers have the responsibility for creating this environment and deciding what rules are necessary. Adolescents will typically test whatever rules put in place by adults. Thus, before you create a new rule, make sure it is really necessary, can be enforced, and worth fighting over. Once you have decided that a particular rule is necessary, inform the adolescent of the rule and the consequences for violating it. When enforcing rules, it is critically important to be fair and consistent. Behavioral contracting works fairly well with adolescents (see Item 13.5).

4. Because the peer group is so important during adolescence, group approaches (e.g., group discussion, psychodrama, and group counseling) can be especially useful. Most adolescents are more accepting of a group-related intervention than to one-to-one interviews. Adolescents in need of out-of-home placement usually do better in a group home setting rather than in foster family care.

5. Because of adolescents' high energy level, a meeting or interview should be planned around movement and physical activity. If possible, avoid office interviews; rather, try talking with an adolescent while walking, shooting baskets, working out in a gym, or riding in a car. Movement seems to make it easier for adolescents to interact, talk, and express feelings.

6. Adolescents are sensitive to any hint of artificiality in others, even though they themselves may pretend to be someone they are not. Thus, it is important for the social worker to be real and genuine. Do not try to speak or act like an adolescent. It is nearly impossible to keep up with the latest adolescent fads, music, and slang. Imitating adolescent talk is likely to make you appear phony.

7. Most adolescents are focused on the here and now. They tend to be somewhat impulsive in their decision making and may not anticipate the consequences of their choices. This, of course, can lead to bad choices that are potentially harmful to themselves and others. When counseling an adolescent who is struggling to make a decision, gently encourage him or her to examine their options in light of their goals and hopes for the future. When their thinking is clearly unrealistic, it is usually best to tell them so, along with the reasoning behind your conclusion.

8. Adolescents have an intense need to be heard. They want others to pay attention and take them seriously. Listen carefully and be alert to the underlying meaning in what they are saying. Encourage them to share their perspectives and experiences. Ask about their hopes, dreams, values, significant life experiences, the times when they learned something important, and what adults do not understand about their life, interests, and challenges.

9. When an adolescent is sullen and refuses to speak, the technique of "passing a note" might break the impasse. The social worker simply stops talking, pulls out a pencil and paper and, in silence and in a deliberate manner, writes a note to the client. In the worker's own words, this note should say the following:

- There are times when people do not want to talk. That is ok.
- Being asked personal questions can be irritating.
- Sometimes being quiet just feels better.
- I apologize if I have said something that was offensive.
- If you would like to do so, please write back.

When finished writing, the worker announces: "I have written you a note. Here it is." Most likely the client expects the message to be some kind of criticism. Receiving a personalized note, especially one that is positive and displays empathy may cause enough of a surprise that it alters the client's mood and prompts an interaction with the worker.

10. Because of estrangement and conflict between the divorced parents, and high rates of single motherhood, many children and adolescents do not have a meaningful relationship with their biological fathers. In the United States, for example, about 40 percent of boys are "father-less" in the sense that they are being raised apart from their biological fathers and have little or no contact with their fathers. The absence of an interested and caring father has negative effects that are especially noticeable among boys. These effects include poor school performance, school dropout, delinquency, drug use, violence, and gang membership. One of the most reliable predictors of whether a boy will succeed or fail in high school is whether he has in his life a responsible and positive adult male model and mentor. Both girls and boys need healthy adult role models. Ideally, the parent will be this positive model but when that is not the case, modeling and mentoring by other adults (e.g., concerned relatives, family friends, big brothers, big sisters) is critically important.

11. Some adolescents are drawn into gang activity. They join gangs for a variety of reasons, but often because the gang meets their needs for a sense of identity and belonging, self-esteem and pride, recognition, and camaraderie. For many adolescents, the tribal nature of a gang serves as a substitute family. In some instances, they join a gang because membership offers protection from other gangs.

Youth gangs or street gangs have existed in major U.S. cities since the nineteenth century. In the past, their illegal activity was mostly theft. At present, many youth gangs have adult leaders, have grown more violent, and are involved in very serious criminal activity such as drug dealing, extortion, and murder.

Selected Bibliography

Geldard, Kathryn, and David Geldard. *Counseling Adolescents*, 3rd ed. Thousand Oaks, CA: Sage, 2009.
Gullotta, Thomas, and Gerald Adams, eds. *Handbook of Adolescent Behavioral Problems*. New York: Springer, 2005.
Malekoff, Andrew. *Group Work with Adolescents*. New York: Guilford, 2004.
Mckenzie, Fred. *Theory and Practice with Adolescents*. Chicago: Lyceum, 2008.
Taffel, Ron. *Breaking Through to Teens*. New York: Guilford, 2005.

15.4   THE CLIENT WHO IS A PARENT OR GRANDPARENT

Parenting is a difficult and demanding undertaking, one that is a mix of joy and worry. Even when the parent is skillful and conscientious the outcome is uncertain. Many influences besides the parent's actions will shape a child's behavior, values, and choices. Many of the factors important to child development such as the child's temperament, genetic makeup, physiology, and socio-cultural environment are beyond a parent's influence. Even with good parenting and a supportive environment, a child will grow into an individual who has some self-doubt, some anxieties, some feelings of inadequacy and will, on occasion, make bad judgments or cause harm to self and others. Such is the human condition.

Many social work clients are parents, and many of the organizations that employ social workers provide services that focus on the role of parent and problems in the parent–child relationship. A significant number of grandparents also provide full-time care for their grandchildren when the child's parents are incapacitated, called for military duty, or otherwise absent or unavailable. Below are some factors that social workers should keep in mind as they work directly with parents or grandparents or work on behalf of them when administering or designing programs that impact children and families.

1. A social worker must be always cognizant of a **parent's legal rights and responsibilities**. According to the American Bar Association (2004, p. 62), "Parents have a right to direct the care, control, and upbringing of their [minor-aged] children. . . . This gives them the power to make various decisions on behalf of the child including where to live, what school to attend, what religion to follow, and what medical treatment to obtain. Only in life threatening or extreme situations will the court step in to override the parents' decisions."

Parents have a right to control, discipline, and punish their child but they may not injure the child, for that would constitute abuse. They have the right to control and manage the earnings and property of their minor-aged child and to receive proper legal notice of any action instituted on behalf of or against the child. Parents have the right to consent to marriage and military service by their minor-aged child and the right to consent to medical procedures and surgery needed by the child. It must be noted, however, that specific statutes may sometimes allow a mature minor to obtain certain forms of health care (e.g., mental health counseling, birth control, treatment for venereal disease, abortion) even without parental permission.

Parents also have certain legal responsibilities. These include the responsibility to provide the child with maintenance (e.g., food, shelter, clothing), provide the child with basic health care, supervise and protect the child from harm, and to provide the child with a basic education. A failure to meet these responsibilities may constitute child neglect (see Item 11.14).

2. Research has identified a number of parenting behaviors that contribute to the development of healthy and wholesome children. These include listening to the child so as to understand his or her thoughts, feelings, and motives; sensitivity to and respect for the child; providing comfort, affection, and nurturance; providing encouragement and using praise to reward the child's effort and accomplishments; providing structure with clear and reasonable rules and expectations; using consistent and reasonable consequences for misbehavior; spending time playing, reading to, and working with the child; engaging in activities that promote attachment and bonding between parent and child; and anticipating problems and being proactive to minimize their effect.

3. As parents we tend to raise our children the way we were raised. This tendency is an asset if we were lucky to have had experienced a loving and caring relationship with our parents. On the other hand, the tendency to imitate our parents can be a source of serious problems if our parent role models were troubled or dysfunctional. Many parents have been jolted when they heard themselves saying things to their children that they hated hearing from their own parents. An individual may enter parenthood resolving never to repeat the mistakes of his or her parents but later discover (or worse, be unaware) that he or she is visiting those same patterns on the next generation. This is most likely to happen when the parents are stressed and frustrated. Needless to say, not all parents repeat the mistakes or the dysfunctions of their own parents, but breaking this cycle takes self-awareness, conscious efforts, and often parent training and counseling.

4. The parent–child relationship is always two-sided; the child's behavior affects the parent and the parent's behavior affects the child. In fact, the parent–child relationship is an interaction of two unique personalities. An approach to discipline and guidance that works well with one child may not work with another. A parent may do an adequate job with a child at a certain stage of development but have problems when the child moves into another stage. For example, most parents are severely tested when their child enters adolescence. A parent may do well with a normal child but become distraught and overwhelmed when caring for a child who has special needs or unusual behavioral problems.

Some special challenges and conflicts can arise if the parent and child are very different in terms of their temperaments, intellectual abilities, or interests. For example, a gregarious and outgoing parent may feel inept and frustrated if his or her child is by temperament shy and introverted. An athletic father may secretly resent a son who shows no interest in sports.

5. When parents do not have easy access to persons experienced in the ways of parenting, they can easily feel alone, unsure, and overwhelmed. Stress and social isolation are contributing factors to the problems of child abuse and neglect. A parent who has little contact with other parents and children may form unrealistic expectations of his or her own child. Social workers should look for opportunities to promote friendships and to build social support networks among parents so that the parents gain knowledge and perspectives on how to be a parent.

Parents must have the emotional and psychological maturity to give of themselves and manage their emotions of anger and frustration. Parents who are fearful, frustrated, or self-absorbed will have difficulty being attentive and responsive to their children and are likely to act impulsively and make bad parenting decisions. Those with serious personal problems (e.g., addiction, mental illness, domestic violence) and those who grew up in families who experienced such problems will, almost always, face some special challenges in the parenting role. The young and immature parent and the parent with cognitive delays will find the demands of parenting especially difficult. Parents who are busy, overwhelmed, or disorganized may overlook a child's need for adequate sleep, good nutrition, and a predictable daily routine, the lack of which causes behavioral problems, irritability, and poor school performance. In order to help a parent become more effective in the parent role, the parent's other personal concerns and problems must be addressed.

Parents cannot give what they do not have. For example, if a mother does not feel physically safe, it will be difficult for her to help her child feel safe and secure. If a father does not possess a sense of personal worth, it will be difficult for him to help his child develop healthy self-esteem.

6. Most parents struggle in their efforts to create and enforce rules. To be effective in the area of discipline, the parent must, first of all, have a truly caring, trusting, and loving relationship with his or her child. Within the context of that positive relationship, the parent must be able to distinguish between behavior that arises from the child's immaturity and inexperience and behavior that is truly defiant and a deliberate violation of known and reasonable rules. Boundaries and protections should be the response to immature behavior. To truly defiant behavior, the parent needs to respond firmly with nonviolent but real and realistic consequences.

7. Some of the grandparents who are raising their grandchildren are ambivalent about assuming this responsibility. On one hand, they want to provide this care out of their love for the children but, on the other hand, caring for grandchildren may strain their finances and disrupt a hoped-for retirement. Some find this responsibility burdensome because it often comes at a time when they are experiencing health problems and lack the energy needed to look after a young child or teen. It is important for agencies to develop programs that will address the concerns of these grandparents.

8. Most parents can benefit from parent training, parent support groups, and counseling focused on the parent–child relationship. The most effective programs zero in on concerns that are of high priority to the parent. They strive to reach out to parents during difficult times, such as after the arrival of a first child or when the child enters the teen years. Successful programs also recognize the unique challenges faced by certain groups of parents. For example, a foster parent, an adoptive parent, and the parent of a disabled child will usually have a unique set of concerns and questions about being a parent. Being a single parent is inherently stressful simply because all of the responsibilities fall to one person. Because of societal attitudes and prejudices, parents in same-sex relationships and those in interracial marriages sometimes face special challenges, too.

Successful parenting programs build on the parents' strengths. They operate on the assumptions that most parents do the best they can but often have difficulties because the parent lacks important knowledge and skills or is overwhelmed by other personal, family, or economic problems. Rather than focusing solely on the parent role, the successful programs also give attention to the situational and contextual factors that are adversely impacting on the parent. Effective parent training programs collaborate with other agencies and connect parents to other needed resources (e.g., health care, financial assistance, housing, counseling, job training).

As a general rule, fathers are less involved than mothers in the care of children and less likely to avail themselves of opportunities to learn parenting skills. Thus, the professionals and agencies must actively reach out to fathers and design programs that connect with the ways men think and feel. Whenever possible, parenting classes for men should be taught by a man.

Most parent training programs presume that the parent can read and write and will make use of written materials, workbook assignments, and the like. Unfortunately, there are many parents who are not literate. Special efforts should be made to identify those parents so that alternative modes of teaching can be utilized.

Ironically, the parents most likely to utilize parent training and other parenting resources are parents who are already doing an adequate job. The parents who are most in need of these services seldom seek them out. In order to attract those parents, programs must be welcoming and have a vigorous outreach component.

9. Most agencies deliver parent training within the context of a small group because that environment provides the participants with opportunities to learn from each other and receive assurance that they are not alone in having worries, frustrations, self-doubts, and questions. A fairly typical parent education group meets once a week for about eight weeks. A session should last about one and one-half hours. The optimal size is between 8 and 16 parents. The group can be larger if the teaching format is mostly didactic but smaller if it utilizes techniques of role-play and discussion. It is usually preferable to have both members of the parenting couple participate (e.g., both mother and father). Parents are expected to attend all sessions. Members should not be added after the group is formed and underway. Ideally, groups for parents will have two leaders or trainers, a male and a female. It is best to have separate groups for the parents of adolescents since their concerns are significantly different from the parents of younger children.

When feasible, each potential participant should be interviewed before being admitted to the group in order to determine if what the group has to offer is appropriate for the parent. The parents who have been referred to the group by a child protection agency or mandated to attend by court order should be carefully assessed because they are often angry and resistant and sometimes disruptive to the group process. However, a skilled facilitator can usually successfully integrate them into the group (see Item 12.8).

For parents who will not or cannot attend a group, the use of home visitation and a parent-to-parent approach is a helpful alternative. In a home visitation program, a parent trainer or a "resource mom" meets the parent in the parent's own home. This highly individualized approach is tutorial in nature and their discussions focuses on the parent's child and unique concerns and circumstances.

10. Social workers must sometimes evaluate a parent's capacity to provide his or her child with safe and appropriate care. For example, a social worker employed by a child protection agency might be asked to prepare a report and recommendation to the court concerning whether a mother who had neglected her child is now able to resume the care of her child who is in foster care. When conducting such evaluations the social worker must remember that there is no one, always right, way of raising a child and that every parent makes some mistakes. Children do not need perfect parents but they need and deserve parents who can provide at least a minimally acceptable level of care.

In order to assess a parent's capacity and performance in the parent role, it is essential to observe the parent interacting with his or her child in several different situations and contexts. It is important to gather information on parent-related values, attitudes, and knowledge, as well as how the parent has come to terms with his or her own parents and possible troublesome experiences. And of course, it is important to determine if the parent's capacity is diminished by problems of addiction, mental illness, and the like.

Within the context of a non-threatening interview, a social worker can initiate a discussion about parenting by asking a number of simple questions, such as: Tell me about your child, Mary? In what ways is Mary like other kids her age? In what way is she different from other children? Does Mary have a personality and temperament similar to yours or different from yours? In what ways are Mary's experiences as a child similar to or different from what you experienced as a child? What have you liked most about being a parent? Is being a parent fun for you? What is most difficult about being a parent? Has being a parent gotten more or less demanding as your child has grown older? How would you rate the parenting abilities of your own parents? Many people say they want to be a better parent than their own parent; have you ever had that thought? If you could start over, is there anything you would do differently as a parent? Have you ever made a big mistake in how you dealt with your child? What is it like for Mary to have you as a parent?

A social worker must guard against the possibility of favoring the child to the detriment of the parent. Since a child is more vulnerable than an adult, it is natural to be attentive to the child and possibly value the child over the parent, especially when the parent has been irresponsible or damaging to the child. This very human inclination can, however, give rise to an unfair and biased assessment and treatment of the parent.

Selected Bibliography

American Bar Association. *Family Legal Guide*, 3rd ed. New York: Random House, 2004.

Bigner, Jerry. *Parent-Child Relations: An Introduction to Parenting*, 7th ed. Columbus, OH: Pearson/Merrill, 2006.

Bornstein, Marc, ed. *Handbook of Parenting*, 2nd ed. (in five volumes). Mahwah, NJ: Lawrence Erlbaum, 2003.

Briesmeister, James, and Charles Schaefer, eds. *Handbook of Parent Training*, 3rd ed. Hoboken, NJ: Wiley, 2007.

Hilarski, Carolyn. "Best Practices in Parenting Techniques." In *Social Worker's Desk Reference*, 2nd ed. Edited by Albert Roberts. New York: Oxford University Press, 2008.

Istar, Arlene. *The Complete Lesbian and Gay Parenting Guide*. New York: Berkeley Books, 2004.

15.5   THE CLIENT WHO IS AN OLDER PERSON

In most developed countries, a growing percentage of the population is in the older age range. Given this trend, social workers and human services programs must give increased attention to the concerns of persons in their seventies, eighties, and nineties. The background information and guidelines presented below will assist the social worker serving these clients.

1. As people grow older, they experience numerous losses (e.g., the death of loved ones and friends, loss of health and mobility). They often feel less independent and more vulnerable. They begin to worry about their ability to care of themselves and possibly becoming a burden to their children or other family members. In response to these fears, they may hold rigidly to whatever independence they still possess. They may resist any offer of help or service that they view as limiting their freedom and choice. Thus, when working with older clients allow them to make choices and retain control over their lives, to the greatest extent possible.

2. Most older persons will prefer a friendly and outgoing social worker, but some will react negatively to a professional who seems too casual and informal or appears to take the relationship for granted. When addressing older clients, use the title Mr., Mrs., or Miss until you have their permission to use a first name. Some older persons may be bothered or offended by what they judge to be immodest clothing, unusual hairstyles, or strange jewelry worn by a professional or other service provider.

3. For both physical and psychological reasons, older clients often prefer to meet with a professional in their homes rather than in an office setting. When in a client's home or room, a good way to break the ice and start a conversation is to show an interest in family pictures, homemade items, or decorations. Begin building a professional relationship by focusing first on the client's most obvious and concrete concerns and needs such as transportation, medical care, and social activity. Only after a positive professional relationship has been formed is the older client likely to feel comfortable discussing more personal concerns such as family conflicts, money problems, grief, feelings of isolation, and so on.

4. Many older clients are concerned about the cost of services and their ability to pay. Some find using public programs and "taking charity" to be humiliating and embarrassing. Some will simply reject a service rather than reveal their inability to pay.

5. Most older people experience some degree of diminished vision, hearing, energy, and mobility. The pace of an interview may need to be slower with an older person and a client's lack of stamina may limit the length of the interview. It is important to speak clearly and repeat your message if necessary. Nonverbal communication is important as a means of helping the client with an auditory deficit to grasp your message.

6. As people grow older, many will think more about death and dying and their spirituality. Many will not fear death but most will fear the disease, disability, dependency, and suffering that so often precedes death. Many will value more deeply their relationships with children and grandchildren. Contacts with family and long time friends take on added importance. Some may want to reach out to others in order to patch up conflicts or make amends for harm they have caused.

As an individual approaches death, it is important for him or her and for family members to express the thoughts and feelings that might heal past hurts and conflicts. Professionals who work with the dying identify these special words as: "Please forgive me," "I forgive you," "Thank you," and "I love you." To the extent possible, a social worker should facilitate intergenerational family communication and reconciliation.

7. Allow and encourage the older client to reminisce. Thinking and talking about the past is a normal activity—it is not a sign of deteriorating mental abilities. Listen carefully to the reminiscence for they may reveal much about the client's values, feelings, and concerns. A few open-ended questions will often encourage an older client to speak about meaningful life experiences. For example: What was the world like when you grew up? What was the most significant event of your childhood? How did you meet your spouse? What was the happiest time of your life? What do you consider to be your greatest accomplishment? What was your greatest disappointment or regret in life? What are you most thankful for? What has your life taught you about what is really important and worthwhile? What do you most want the younger generations to know about life? What were your biggest surprises in life?

8. Given that racism, discrimination, and prejudice can inflict so much pain on people, strive to be especially sensitive when interacting with older people who are members of racial or ethnic minorities. As a general rule, they will be more suspicious and distrustful of agencies and more sensitive to anything that might appear demeaning and disrespectful. The values common to a particular ethnic group can make life more or less difficult for the aging person. For example, in certain ethnic groups (e.g., Chinese American, Native American), older people occupy a position of respect and influence within families. On the other hand, the importance of hard work and productivity within an ethnic group (e.g., Slavic American) may make the nonworking elderly person feel useless and unworthy.

9. Be alert to indicators of elder abuse and neglect (especially self-neglect), such as unusual bruises, cuts, and burns; untreated injuries that are explained in a vague or defensive manner;

improper clothing for the weather; wandering outside at odd hours; mail and newspapers that have not been picked up; person has sufficient financial means but has many unpaid bills or is facing a utility shut off or an eviction; highly unusual or strange behavior; unpleasant odors associated with poor hygiene or unsanitary housekeeping; inability to recognize familiar people, disoriented as to time or place; and the person is dependent on a caregiver who is overwhelmed, chemically dependent, or mentally ill.

10. Those who work with older persons should be alert to indicators or **symptoms of dementia**, a term that refers to an irreversible loss of mental abilities such as memory, judgment, and the ability for self-care. Dementia is different from depression or delirium in that it comes on insidiously over months and years. The four major types of dementia are Alzheimer's disease, Lewy Body Dementia, Frontotemporal Dementia, and Vascular Dementia. In the United States, Alzheimer's disease accounts for about 65 percent of all dementia cases.

In the beginning stages of a dementia, a person's family and caretakers notice that the individual is gradually becoming more and more forgetful and confused. He or she may, for example, forget frequently called phone numbers, lose the ability to balance a checkbook or pay a bill, engage in repetitive activities and statements, become disoriented as to time and place, withdraw from normal activities, and exhibit personality changes. When such symptoms are apparent, a medical evaluation is called for.

When a dementia like Alzheimer's has progressed further, it is very apparent that something is terribly wrong because the individual now needs full-time supervision. In later stages, the individual cannot read, add or subtract, or recognize family members. They may lose their ability to speak, wander about, become combative, and engage in other inappropriate behaviors.

Needless to say, family members experience a gut-wrenching sadness as they watch the deterioration of a loved one. A medical social worker can often provide guidance to the family on caring for and planning for a family member with a dementia and also connect the family to resources such as specialized nursing home care, legal advice, and relevant family support groups.

11. Older people and their families will typically face a number of legal issues and decisions. These include preparing a will, estate planning, advance directives related to end-of-life choices, legal guardianship, power of attorney, long-term care insurance, and the like. When such matters are encountered the social worker should refer the client and family to competent legal counsel.

Selected Bibliography

Berkman, Barbara, ed. *Handbook of Social Work in Health and Aging.* New York: Oxford University Press, 2006.

Lymbery, Mark. *Social Work with Older People.* Thousand Oaks, CA: Sage, 2006.

McInnis–Dittrich, Kathleen. *Social Work with Older Adults*, 3rd ed. Boston: Allyn & Bacon, 2009.

15.6   THE CLIENT WHO IS A BATTERED WOMAN

As used here, the term *battered woman* refers to an adult who has been physically, sexually, and/or emotionally abused by a spouse or intimate partner. This type of abuse is all too common and results in many serious injuries and deaths. In the United States, a woman is more likely to be assaulted, injured, raped, or killed by a her male partner than by a stranger or any other type of assailant. The vast majority of the abusers are men and the abuse occurs most often within a heterosexual relationship. However, it may also occur within gay and lesbian relationships. (For ease of discussion, the authors will refer to the offender or abuser as male and the victim as female.)

The abuse can take several forms, but all are intended to control the woman—for example:

- *Physical injury or threats of injury*   (e.g., choking, punching, beating, forced sex, threatening to hurt her or the children)

- *Emotional abuse*   (e.g., humiliation, making her the object of demeaning jokes, blaming, undermining her confidence, saying she is crazy, insisting that she deserves to be punished, denying her opportunity to make decisions)
- *Isolation*   (e.g., controlling and limiting who she talks to and where she goes, oppressively monitoring her activities)
- *Economic manipulation*   (e.g., controlling her access to money, giving her only an allowance, preventing her from having a job, threatening to take all possessions and leave her with nothing)
- *Intimidation*   (e.g., displaying weapons, abusing pets, destroying her property, threatening to commit suicide if she does not do what he wants)
- *Using the children*   (e.g., threatening to take the children, threatening to report the woman for child abuse)

Typically, there is a cycle of abuse with three major phases: (1) tension building, (2) the explosion, and (3) the honeymoon. In some cases, the cycle may be short, such as a matter of days; in other cases, it may take several months to cycle through these phases:

- *Phase 1—Tension building.*   Tensions between the two people begin to rise. Some outbursts may occur but these are minimized and rationalized away often by both parties. The woman tries to protect herself and maintain some control over the situation by being compliant and not showing anger.
- *Phase 2—Explosion.*   The abuser finally explodes. Anger is expressed in extreme verbal abuse, physical violence, and/or rape.
- *Phase 3—Repairing the damage (Honeymoon).*   The abuser expresses sorrow for what he has done. To keep her from leaving he becomes very attentive, loving, and thoughtful. Since this loving behavior does not fit with his abusive behavior, the woman is confused and may doubt her own perceptions and sanity. She may want to believe that the episode of abuse was atypical and out of character. She may conclude that she is the one responsible for the abuse and think: "If only I would have done things right, he would not have gotten angry." This period of good behavior by the abuser eventually runs its course and the cycle begins once again.

The men who abuse women typically have several of the following characteristics:

- Extreme and irrational jealousy and possessiveness toward the woman, often coupled with an unjustifiable belief that she is interested in other men.
- Desire to control the woman and isolate her from friends and family by saying such things as "All we need is each other—no one else."
- Quick to anger and an explosive temper.
- Moods and behavior fluctuate from being kind and gentle to being violent and oppressive.
- Denies or rationalizes his outbursts and abusive behavior; blames others, especially the woman, for whatever goes wrong in his life.
- History of being abused as a child or a witness to family violence.
- A history of legal violations related to violence.

There are a number of reasons why battered women are reluctant to leave an abusive relationship or will return to it after only a brief separation:

- Fear of retribution and even more serious violence.
- Lack of money and a suitable place to live.
- Fear of losing children, home, and economic security.
- Self-doubt, low self-esteem, shame, or a distrust of others.
- Fear of not being believed or blamed for causing the abuse.
- Religious beliefs that emphasize maintaining a marriage.
- Desire to preserve the family for benefit of the children.
- Wanting to believe that the abuse will stop or a tendency to deny or minimize the seriousness of the abuse.
- Tendency to equate love with dependency.

An abusive situation should be considered especially dangerous if there is a pattern of frequent and/or severe violence, the abuser and/or the abused woman use drugs or alcohol, the woman or her children have been threatened with death, the abuser has easy access to deadly weapons, either the abuser or victim has a psychiatric impairment, the abuser has a history of criminal activity, the abuse has taken the form of forced sexual acts, the abuser has threatened suicide, the abuser has tortured or killed animals as a display of his willingness to take extreme action, and the woman has made suicide threats or attempts.

Social workers and programs offering services to battered women must strive toward the following goals:

- Make sure that the woman and her children are safe and protected.
- Help the woman understand the nature and cycle of abuse and that she has options that can keep her and her children safe.
- Help her make decisions, formulate plans, and obtain the services she will need in order to be safe.
- Help her and her children heal from the psychological effects of abuse and reestablish a sense of personal boundaries.

Those working directly with abused women should keep the following guidelines in mind:

1. Give immediate attention to the issue of her safety and her basic needs such as the need for food, housing, medical care, transportation, child care, legal counsel, and so on. Do not immediately assume that the battered woman is in a heterosexual relationship; refer to the abuser as "partner" until you learn the gender of the offender.

2. Focus on the woman's strengths, such as the decisions and behaviors that have kept her alive or that protected her children; help her to identify and name her survival skills as a way of counteracting her feelings of self-doubt and helplessness.

3. If she decides to remain with or return to the abuser, assist the woman in developing an escape plan (safety plan) that she can immediately implement if she is again threatened. The plan should include packing and then hiding from the abuser a bag that contains money, clothing, personal items, and copies of legal documents that she (and her children) would need to live apart from the abuser.

4. Anticipate that the woman's emotions will fluctuate widely and that she will experience great ambivalence about ending the relationship. Discourage her from speaking with the abuser when she is feeling especially insecure and confused. At such times she is especially vulnerable to his manipulation and is likely to return to him without considering the danger.

5. Do not assume that the abused woman has some underlying psychological need or problem that caused her to enter or remain in an abusive relationship. However, as a response to ongoing abuse, the woman may indeed develop problems such as alcohol or drug abuse, depression, anxiety, and posttraumatic stress disorder.

6. Understand that the woman may have to leave and return to the abuser several times before she is finally convinced that the abuse will not end unless the abuser is motivated to make use of a program of therapy and training. Couples counseling (i.e., both partners attend same session) is not an appropriate mode of intervention because the abused woman will likely be afraid to speak honestly in the presence of the abuser and the abuser will typically accuse her of exaggeration or lying.

7. After leaving an abusive relationship and even with counseling, it may take from two to four years before the battered woman recovers emotionally and becomes significantly less fearful, anxious, and depressed. The same can be said for the children who have experienced the terror of seeing their mother beaten and threatened.

Selected Bibliography

Barnett, Ola, Cindy Miller-Perrin, and Robin Perrin. *Family Violence Across the Lifespan*, 2nd ed. Thousand Oaks, CA: Sage, 2005.

Roberts, Albert, ed. *Battered Women and Their Families*, 3rd ed. New York: Springer, 2007.

Walker, Lenore. *The Battered Woman Syndrome*, 3rd ed. New York: Springer, 2009.

Wexler, David. *Stop Domestic Violence: Innovative Skills, Techniques, Options*. New York: Norton, 2006.

15.7 THE CLIENT WHO IS AT RISK OF SUICIDE

Given the high rate of suicide among teenagers, young adults, and older adults, the social worker will encounter clients who are at risk of taking their own lives. The **warning signs of suicide** include intense depression, preoccupation with death and pain, giving away prized possessions, unexplained changes in behavior, sudden increase in the use of drugs and alcohol, and impulsive or reckless behavior. Clinical data indicate that most suicide victims have consulted a physician within six months of their suicide.

Although not all people who end their lives are clinically depressed, studies reveal that depression is often present. The **symptoms of depression** include pervasive sadness, feelings of hopelessness, lack of interest in activities once enjoyed, inability to concentrate, thoughts of suicide, unexplained aches and pains, fatigue and restlessness, changes in appetite, withdrawal from others, early waking from sleep or erratic sleep patterns, irritability, and unexplained crying. Whereas depression in adults usually results in a retardation of activity, depression in children and youth is often expressed in agitation.

Legally and ethically, the social worker must make every reasonable effort to prevent a client's suicide. This includes providing or trying to provide counseling, staying with the person during times of high risk, and, if necessary, calling the police. State laws dictate when police can detain a suicidal person and when involuntary hospitalization is permitted. However, it must be noted that it may not be possible to prevent the suicide of a person who is firmly committed to taking his or her own life. If the person really wants to die, he or she will probably find the opportunity and the means.

The following guidelines will help the social worker in assessing a client's suicide potential and responding to the client who is at risk of suicide:

1. Take every message about suicide seriously. It is always significant that the person is talking about harm to self rather than expressing unhappiness and frustration in other ways. It is a myth that people who talk about suicide will not kill themselves. Unfortunately, their message may be veiled and, in some cases, it is not until after the death that its meaning becomes clear. In 10 to 20 percent of suicides, there are no noticeable warnings prior to the death.

2. Listen for subtle and indirect statements of suicidal intent, such as "I won't be around much longer," "There is nothing worth living for anymore," and "I just can't stand the pain any longer." Be especially concerned about such statements if the person has very recently experienced the loss of an important relationship, a loss of status, an episode of family violence, or is in the throes of dealing with chronic pain, a life-threatening illness, or a serious physical limitation.

3. If you believe that a client is at risk of suicide, always consult with other professionals on how best to proceed. Do not allow yourself to be "hooked" by the suicidal client into a promise of complete confidentiality. Ordinary rules of confidentiality must be broken in order to prevent a death.

4. The person thinking about suicide is experiencing intense **ambivalence**—the desire to live and, at the same time, the desire to escape pain, even if by death. At a fundamental level the person does not want to die but does want to escape his or her pain. Reach out to and support that part of the person holding on to life.

Most suicidal people have "tunnel vision"—they can think only about their pain and help-lessness. It is important to help them identify and consider alternative methods for dealing with the situation. How has the individual managed stressful situations in the past? Will any of these methods work in the present situation?

5. Do not be afraid to ask if the individual is thinking about suicide. Speaking openly will not increase the likelihood of suicide. Direct questioning tells the suicidal person that you are concerned and not afraid to talk straight. Examples of questions include the following: Are you thinking of killing yourself? Can you tell me why suicide seems like the answer? Who else knows that you are thinking about suicide? What has happened recently that caused you to think more and more about suicide? Why do you believe your situation will not improve or change? How might your situation be different two or six months from now? Have you attempted suicide in the past? If you thought about suicide in the past, what caused you to change your mind?

6. Determine whether the person has worked out a specific suicide plan. Ask questions such as: Do you have a plan for killing yourself? How do you plan to get the gun you intend to use? Where do you plan to kill yourself? What time of day do you plan to kill yourself? The more detailed and specific the person's plan the higher the risk of suicide. Many suicidal people have thought about a suicide plan but most have not thought about an alternative plan or a "plan B." Thus, if you can interfere with a key element of their plan, you can often thwart their suicide.

7. The person who has chosen a method of suicide and has access to it is at high risk. The more lethal the chosen method, the higher the risk and the more likely a suicide attempt will result in death. Highly lethal methods include shooting, jumping, hanging, drowning, carbon monoxide poisoning, car crash, or taking high doses of barbiturates, sleeping pills, or aspirin. Less lethal methods include wrist cutting, gas stove, or tranquilizers and nonprescription drugs (excluding aspirin and Tylenol).

8. Many who commit suicide feel alone, ignored, or cut off from people. The risk of suicide increases when a person is widowed, divorced, or separated. Encourage significant others to come to the support of the suicidal person.

9. Help the person see that suicide is a permanent solution to a temporary problem. Identify other possible solutions to dealing with the pain the individual is experiencing. If necessary, ask him or her to agree not to commit suicide for a specific period (e.g., two weeks) or to promise not to commit suicide before talking to you one more time. Urge the person to call the toll free suicide prevention lifeline at: 1-800-273-TALK. Urge the person to immediately enter counseling. If a referral for counseling is made, you or someone else should possibly accompany the client to the initial interview. Follow-up is necessary to ensure that the client is making use of the service.

10. In extreme situations and when nothing else seems to be working, attempt to engage the person in a discussion of what will happen when he or she is found dead. Sometimes this will jar the person into thinking more clearly about the real consequences of a suicide. For example, you might ask the following questions: Who is likely to find your body? Who should be notified of your death? Should the people to be notified be approached or talked to in a certain way? What question might they ask? Can we make a list of all the people who should be notified of your death so they can attend your funeral? What kind of a funeral service do you want? Would you want a burial or cremation? What do you want your obituary to say? Who do you want to have your favorite possessions?

11. When dealing with persons who are actively suicidal, it is important to remember that they may have no hesitation about also killing you or someone else in the process of taking their own life. For example, a suicidal person with a gun may shoot you if you attempt to take away the gun.

Selected Bibliography

Bonger, Brice; *The Suicidal Patient*, 2nd ed. Washington, DC: American Psychological Association, 2002.

Quinett, Paul. *Suicide: The Forever Decision*. New York: Crossroad, 2004.

Schneidman, Edwin. *Comprehending Suicide*. Washington, DC: American Psychological Association, 2001.

15.8   THE CLIENT WITH AN INTELLECTUAL DISABILITY

Three features that define an **intellectual disability**: (1) an IQ below 70, (2) significant limitations in adaptive behaviors such as communication, self-care, memory, problem solving, social interaction, and academic skills, and (3) these impairments or limitations existed prior to age 18. The four levels of severity are *mild* (IQ between about 50 and 70), *moderate* (IQ between about 35 and 55), *severe* (IQ between about 20 and 40), and *profound* (IQ below 20). There are dozens of causes such as inborn errors in metabolism, chromosomal aberrations, head trauma, malnutrition, infections, and the ingestion of toxic chemicals.

The terms *intellectual disability* and *mental retardation* are synonymous. Because of the stigma attached to the word "retardation," parents and professionals have sought an alternative terminology. Gradually, the term *intellectual disability* is gaining acceptance. However, the term *mental retardation* is still used by many health-care professionals because it has been utilized for many years in the *Diagnostic and Statistical Manual of Mental Disorders*.

Roughly 3 percent of the population has an intellectual disability. Of those, about 80 percent have a mild level of impairment and about 10 percent are in the moderate range. Those with a mild and moderate level of disability can usually achieve at least an upper grade school level of education and as adults hold unskilled or semi-skilled jobs. Many will marry and have children. Persons with a severe level of impairment can learn simple counting and some written word recognition. They require much assistance and close supervision. The 1 to 2 percent with a profound impairment will usually have serious neurological disorders and other complex medical problems. Most need round-the-clock nursing care.

People with an intellectual disability tend to be friendly, trusting, and naïve. Consequently, they are vulnerable to manipulation, exploitation, and abuse. Because they often experience frustration and social rejection, they are at risk of developing emotional problems and patterns of unusual and inappropriate behavior.

The term *developmental disability* is a legal and programmatic category. Although definitions vary slightly from state to state, a **developmental disability** is often defined as a severe disability caused by a physical or mental impairment that limits a person's development, appears before the age 18 (or 22), is likely to be lifelong, and affects the person's functioning in self-care, learning, self-direction, language, independent living, mobility, and/or economic self-sufficiency. The developmental disabilities include mental retardation, cerebral palsy, autism, severe dyslexia, and epilepsy. Of these, mental retardation (intellectual disability) is the one most frequently diagnosed. All persons with intellectual disability have a developmental disability, but not all persons with a developmental disability have subnormal intellectual ability. Early diagnosis and medical and educational intervention are of critical importance to minimize the effects of these conditions (see Items 11.13 and 11.17).

The following guidelines and information will aid the social worker serving an adult client with a significant intellectual disability:

1. Throughout history and in most societies, individuals with this disability have been subjected to ridicule and rejection. Their parents were made to feel somehow different and defective and often suffered from feelings of guilt, shame, and embarrassment. In recent years, this state of affairs has improved but remnants of those negative attitudes remain. Social workers and other professionals must examine their own attitudes and rid themselves of any prejudices and stereotypes.

Most of all, they need to recognize that a person with intellectual limitations has the same basic human needs (physical, emotional, social, sexual, and spiritual) as everyone else.

2. Certain medical disorders and behavioral patterns are associated with some types of mental retardation. Among them are neurological problems and limitations in the areas of vision, hearing, coordination, mobility, and physical strength. A familiarity with such medical conditions is of critical importance in assessment and case planning and when working as part of a team with other disciplines, such as medicine, psychology, physical therapy, occupational therapy, speech therapy, special education, and vocational rehabilitation.

3. Many with an intellectual disability will have limited verbal ability and at best, only rudimentary skill in the areas of reading and writing. Consequently, the verbal counseling and helping skills commonly used by social workers will have limited applicability with this client. Alternative skills and techniques are needed. These include behavioral techniques, modeling and demonstration, special teaching methodologies, nonverbal group work, and the creative arts.

Because the client's attention span may be short, the length of a meeting with a client needs to be adjusted accordingly. And because the client's memory may be limited, each contact should be planned as a discrete event rather than assuming it will be a continuation of previous conversations. Your communications and vocabulary must be adjusted to the client's level of comprehension. They need to be clear-cut and simple, but never patronizing.

4. When formulating an intervention or a helping strategy, focus on and build upon the client's abilities—on what he or she can do rather than on limitations. To the extent possible, the client should participate in making decisions that will affect his or her life circumstances. However, such participation may be quite limited if the client is severely disabled. Because the client's situation is typically influenced, supervised, or controlled by others (e.g., family, legal guardian, group home manager), the social worker must engage and involve those individuals in the formulation of a service plan. The practice roles of client advocate, case manager, and broker are especially important in work with this client group (see Items 12.3 and 13.17). The skills of teamwork are essential in planning and providing services to persons with disabilities.

5. In your interactions with your client, avoid doing anything that might reinforce or reward inappropriate social behaviors or mannerisms. For example, hugging is not a conventional greeting among adults who do not know each other well. Thus, the social worker should teach and model the use of a handshake rather than allowing one's self to be inappropriately hugged by the client.

6. In order to maximize appropriate learning and socialization by persons with an intellectual disability and also reduce the chances that they will be stigmatized, the principles of normalization and social integration should guide the design and delivery of social services and the formulation of case plans or habilitation plans. **Integration** exists when persons with a disability participate, to the greatest extent possible, in the ordinary and usual activities of family, community, and society. **Normalization** is a philosophy of service planning and delivery that emphasizes the utilization of helping approaches and services that are culturally normative. The phrase *culturally normative* refers to that which is typical, ordinary, or conventional within the community. An example may illustrate the notion of what is culturally normative. Where does a man get a haircut? The answer is a barbershop. Thus, a man with a disability should also obtain his haircut at a barbershop. It would be a violation of the normalization principle for a case manager to arrange for a barber to visit a group home in order to give haircuts to all the residents.

The term *normalization* should not be misunderstood as "being normal" but instead as an effort to decrease separation and deviance (i.e., socially created differences). Moreover, the principle of normalization does not dictate that a person with a disability be placed in situations that would generate unusual frustration or impossible competition just because those situations are typical for the average person. However, normalization does call for the removal of unnecessary overprotection and recognizes that learning and living involves some degree of risk-taking and possible failure.

7. It is in relation to clients with severe disabilities that a social worker is likely to encounter the legal procedures known as guardianship and conservatorship. In a **guardianship** arrangement, a court finds a person to be legally incompetent because of young age or mental or physical incapacity and therefore invests another person (the guardian) with the power to manage the incapacitated person's money and property and to make certain other decisions such as those related to health care. In a **conservatorship**, the court appoints another (the conservator) for the more limited purpose of managing the legally incompetent person's estate. Neither of these legal procedures should be confused with **power of attorney**, which does not involve a court finding of legal incompetence, but simply involves the use of a notarized document in which one legally competent person voluntarily gives to another the legal power to take certain actions such as selling a property, depositing or withdrawing funds from a bank, or paying bills.

Selected Bibliography

Belrne-Smith, Mary, James Patton, and Shannon Kim. *Mental Retardation: An Introduction to Intellectual Disabilities.* Upper Saddle River, NJ: Merrill, 2006.

Parette, Howard, George Peterson-Karlan, and Ravic Ringlaben, eds. *Research-Based Practices in Developmental Disabilities.* Austin, TX: Pro-Ed, 2007.

Schalock, Robert, et al. *Intellectual Disability: Definition, Classification, and Systems of Support,* 11th ed. Washington, DC: American Association of Intellectual and Developmental Disabilities, 2010.

15.9   THE CLIENT WITH BRAIN INJURY

Advances in emergency medical treatment can now save the lives of many people who have a stroke or a traumatic head injury. Consequently, a growing number of individuals in society have survived a life-threatening event but then struggle with the aftereffects of brain injury.

The consequences of an injury to the brain depend on what parts of the brain are damaged and the extent of that damage. For example, the effects of stroke (cerebral vascular accident, or CVA) can be quite circumscribed because a blocked blood vessel will cause damage to just one area of the brain. For this reason, once the location of stroke-caused damage is known, the aftereffects can be predicted with some accuracy. By contrast, the consequences of a traumatic brain injury, such as one acquired in an auto accident can be rather unpredictable because there is usually a tearing and shearing of tissue in several different parts of the brain.

Individuals with significant brain injury, especially if caused by trauma, will often develop a pattern of rigid thinking. They tend to hold tightly to their ideas and beliefs because they have difficulty interpreting subtle differences among ideas and nuances in meaning and are frustrated by complexity and ambiguity. They are inclined to view an issue or position as either entirely right or entirely wrong. They have difficulty accepting a middle ground and find it hard to examine and consider both the advantages and disadvantages of a proposal. This black-or-white type of thinking can make it difficult for them to make good decisions and may cause others to perceive them as rigid, abrasive, opinionated, and narrow-minded.

Stroke.   Typically, the most visible sign of a stroke (CVA) is a paralysis on one side of the body. Damage to the left side of the brain results in right-sided paralysis and problems with speech and language (termed *aphasia*). In addition, the person tends to be slow, hesitant, and disorganized when faced with an unfamiliar situation.

Stroke-caused damage to the right brain results in left-side paralysis and causes difficulties in perception. The person tends to be impulsive, have poor judgment, and overlook his or her limitations. This individual can often describe tasks that are to be performed but is not able to do them. He or she has trouble both expressing emotions and accurately perceiving the emotional signals of others.

Many who have suffered a stroke have what is termed one-sided neglect, meaning that they may have lost sections of their visual field or have lost sensory signals to parts of their bodies. For example, a man with a paralyzed arm may be unaware that his arm is dangling near a hot stove. Another illustrative example is the woman who sees her own leg and becomes upset because she thinks someone is lying in bed beside her. Persons with such perceptual problems are easily confused while traveling or moving about.

Other problems commonly associated with a stroke include (1) the person becomes careless and neglectful of personal grooming and appearance; (2) loss of memory retention span (i.e., a decrease in the number of things that can be retained and attended to at one time); (3) decreased capacity for short-term memory, which makes new learning difficult; (4) difficulty in generalization (i.e., applying what was learned in one situation to another); (5) emotional liability (i.e., erratic emotions such as laughing or crying for no apparent reason); (6) sensory deprivation (i.e., loss in the ability to taste, hear, see, perceive touch); and (7) fatigue.

Traumatic Brain Injury.   Trauma to the brain may result in paralysis or other physical symptoms such as seizures and a decrease in strength and coordination. However, it is quite common for the person with this type of brain injury to appear physically normal but have a number of significant cognitive, behavioral, and emotional problems. Difficulties in memory, judgment, attention, perception, and impulse control can cause major problems in social interaction and job performance.

For the social work practitioner who may encounter a client who has had a stroke or a traumatic brain injury, several guidelines are important:

1. Be alert to the possibility of brain injury effects whenever a client's presenting problems involve personality changes, impulsiveness, poor memory, and poor judgment. Inquire if there is a history of a concussion, coma, stroke, skull fracture, or other injuries to the head caused by, for example, car accidents, sports injuries, or violence. If there is reason to suspect the existence of a brain injury, consult with a rehabilitation specialist, neurologist, or neuropsychologist and determine if a referral for an in-depth evaluation is indicated. A medical doctor who specializes in physical rehabilitation and in treating the aftereffects of stroke and head injury is called a *physiatrist*. This medical specialty is known as *physiatry,* not to be confused with psychiatry.

2. Individuals with brain injury may fabricate an explanation or make up stories to hide their problems of poor memory and learning difficulties. They may hold tightly to a false belief because the belief helps them make sense out of the unorganized bits of information they possess and the confusion they experience. The family may be distressed and frustrated when the person with brain injury insists on the truthfulness of an obviously false assertion.

3. Rehabilitation programs can be successful in teaching patients how to compensate for some of the deficits caused by brain injury. They are most beneficial when started as soon as possible after the brain damage has occurred.

4. The family of a person who has a brain injury will need information, guidance, and support in learning to cope with the many stressful changes they face. Their loved one may now seem like a very different person. The personality changes associated with brain injury will put a severe strain on a marriage and on relationships with children. The family or spouse should be encouraged to review relevant legal documents, contracts, wills, financial agreements, and the like and to develop legal protections against impulsive decisions and poor judgments by the brain-injured family member. Organizations such as the National Head Injury Foundation and the American Stroke Association provide information as well as support to the survivors of head injury and stroke and their families.

5. State departments of vocational rehabilitation may have special employment programs for persons with cognitive deficits caused by head injury. Such services may include job coaching and extended or supported employment programs. Cognitive deficits that preclude competitive employment may qualify a person for Social Security Disability Income benefits (see Item 15.10).

Selected Bibliography

Applegate, Jeffery, and Janet Shapiro. *Neurobiology for Clinical Social Work.* New York: Norton, 2005

Berg, Richard, Michael Franzen, and Danny Wedding. *Screening for Brain Impairment*, 2nd ed. New York: Springer, 1994.

Dell, Arthur, and Paul Power. *Brain Injury and the Family*, 2nd ed. Houston, TX: HDI Publishers, 2000.

Senelick, Richard, Peter Rossi, and Karla Dougherty. *Living with Stroke: A Guide for Families.* Chicago: Contemporary Books, 2000.

15.10   THE CLIENT WITH A SERIOUS PHYSICAL DISABILITY

Many people live with physical impairments of one sort or another. An *impairment* is a long-term or permanent bodily or sensory limitation caused by disease, injury, or advanced age. If this limitation significantly hampers a person's capacity to perform his or her major social roles and the ordinary activities of living (e.g., self-care, employment), it is termed a **disability**. Whether a particular impairment is a disability depends on its severity, on whether assistive technology can help compensate for the limitation, and on the physical and social barriers that exist within the person's environment. A set of stairs is an example of a physical barrier for a person using a wheelchair. An example of a social barrier for that same person would be a prejudice that keeps him or her from being hired for a job for which he or she is qualified and for which the ability to walk is not a requirement. Eliminating physical and social barriers and using adaptive technology and equipment can go a long way in keeping an impairment from turning into a disabling condition.

The following information and guidelines will prove helpful when working with persons who have a physically disability:

1. People are more than their bodies; they are also mind and spirit. That fact is easily overlooked in a society obsessed with physical appearances, sex appeal, and celebrity based on physical beauty. Despite malfunctioning nerves and muscles and despite often painful and tiring daily routines of self-care, those with a serious disability hold demanding and responsible jobs, are active in the community, and engage in the creative and expressive arts. Those who have faced squarely their own limitations often acquire a deep human understanding, true compassion, and an authentic spirituality. By contrast, many who are "normal" remain rather superficial and in denial of their own limitations and imperfections.

2. Social workers must also be able to see beyond a client's disability and focus mostly on the client's abilities. In work with this client group, the strengths perspective, maximizing client self-determination, empowerment, and advocacy are especially important.

Persons with a serious physical disability are at risk of being avoided and marginalized. Thus, the social worker should strive to normalize as much of the client's life as possible and prevent social isolation. Help and encourage the client to meet people, build friendships, pursue interests, explore new opportunities, and participate in community activities. Securing or retaining employment will be priority for many clients. However, employment may not be a possibility for persons with fragile and complex medical conditions.

3. In recent decades, federal laws such as the 1973 Rehabilitation Act, the 1975 Education for All Handicapped Children Act, and the 1990 **Americans with Disabilities Act** (ADA) have greatly benefited persons with disabling conditions. Schools, primary and higher education, are required to provide educational services to and make reasonable accommodations for students with a disability. The ADA, which has been described as the "emancipation proclamation for the disabled," provides a national mandate and the legal mechanisms to remove barriers for and eliminate discrimination against persons with disabilities, especially in the areas of employment, access to public services and public transportation, access to goods and services offered by businesses, and access to telecommunications. The ADA is a solid basis for social work advocacy with and in behalf of persons with disabilities.

4. A social worker must be familiar with the programs and services relevant to a client with a disability. The two most significant federal programs are worker's compensation, which provides financial assistance to persons recovering from a work-related injury, and programs under the Social Security Act, including Supplemental Security Income (SSI) and Social Security Disability Insurance (SSDI). In most communities, there will be state programs (e.g., Vocational Rehabilitation) and numerous service organizations and private agencies that focus on specific disabling conditions (e.g., cerebral palsy, arthritis, multiple sclerosis, spinal cord injury, blindness). Support and informational groups are invaluable resources to persons with a disability and their families.

5. Encourage and assist the client to secure the medical evaluations and treatments, rehabilitative services, training, and assistive technology that can maximize his or her independence and functioning. Such services and equipment are expensive and may be difficult to access, depending on where the client lives. Thus, a social worker must build bridges with and cultivate working relationships with programs and service organizations that might be able to provide financial assistance, transportation, and other services. The worker must be prepared to engage in case advocacy when the client is not receiving needed and available services and perhaps even pursue a special fund-raising effort in order to help cover some of the incurred costs. It is important to note that how a fundraiser or a benefit is set up can affect the individual's eligibility for certain government programs.

6. Occupational therapists, physical therapists, and other rehabilitation specialists can provide guidance on the selection of the assistive technology that will be helpful to a particular client. Be alert to the fact that this technology needs to be maintained and adjusted on a regular basis. For example, if a brace or a wheel chair is not properly fitted to a person's body, it can cause discomfort and exacerbate medical problems. A child's growth, weight gain, or changes in a person's medical condition are just a few of the factors that should prompt adjustments in such equipment.

7. A home or workplace assessment by an occupational therapist can identify physical barriers and offer specific recommendations for remodeling that can make a bathroom, kitchen, or bedroom more useable to a person with conditions that limit mobility and self-care. In the absence of recommendations by an experienced professional, a well-intentioned but uninformed remodeling project by family or friend can be a wasted effort. For example, it is not uncommon for friends to build a wheel chair ramp that is too steep and therefore unsafe.

8. Because an individual with a very serious disability may be dependent upon direct care provided by family or a paid caregiver, these care personnel should be involved in formulating a service plan for the client. Care giving is demanding and at times exhausting. Thus, it is important to insure that the caregivers have adequate social and emotional social support and sufficient rest and respite.

Selected Bibliography

May, Gary, and Martha Raske. *Ending Disability Discrimination: Strategies for Social Workers*. Boston: Allyn & Bacon, 2005.

Mackelprang, Romel, and Richard Salsgiver. *Disability*, 2nd ed. Chicago: Lyceum, 2009.

Oliver, Michael, and Bob Sapey. *Social Work with Disabled People*, 3rd ed. New York: Palgrave Macmillan, 2006.

Rothman, Juliet. *Social Work Practice Across Disability*. Boston: Allyn & Bacon, 2003.

15.11 THE CLIENT WHO IS CHEMICALLY DEPENDENT

Many of the individuals and families receiving services from social agencies and social workers are affected, directly or indirectly, by alcohol and drug-related problems. The use and abuse of various substances or chemicals is a contributing factor in many other problems, such as marital discord, marital discord, parent–child conflict, spouse abuse, child maltreatment, poor job performance, financial difficulties, and health problems. Substance abuse also contributes to the spread of AIDS by way of intravenous injections and by indiscriminate sexual behavior related to the disinhibiting effects of drugs and alcohol. The use of alcohol and drugs by a pregnant woman can damage the fetus and result in various birth defects and neurological and developmental problems.

Individuals who have an alcohol or drug problem are often difficult and challenging clients because of the pathological denial, rationalization, and self-delusion that are part of a dependency or addiction. They typically reject offers of professional help and will see an addictions counselor only after being court ordered or coerced into treatment by family or friends. The social worker's response to these clients must be based on an understanding of how alcohol and drugs affect the mind and body and on the realization that it is seldom possible for an individual to overcome an addiction without great and persistent effort and specialized treatment.

Many of the abused chemicals alter the body's neurochemistry and physiology resulting in the development of *tolerance* (i.e., an ever-increasing amount of the chemical is required to bring on the desired mood-altering effect) and symptoms of *withdrawal* (i.e., the individual becomes anxious, panicky, or physically ill when unable to take in the chemical). An individual may engage in reckless and extreme behaviors (e.g., stealing, violence, deceit) in order to escape distressing withdrawal symptoms.

Treatment and prevention specialists often distinguish between abuse and dependency. *Chemical abuse or substance abuse* refers to a recurrent but non-compulsive use that has negative consequences for the individual, but perhaps in only one area of functioning (e.g., occasional missed work, an arrest for drunk driving). By contrast, *chemical dependency* refers to a pattern of frequent and possibly compulsive use that is often accompanied by the existence of tolerance and symptoms of withdrawal and has a negative impact on several areas of functioning (e.g., family, job, health, finances).

Patterns of dependency and addiction are rooted in a learning process. Each time a mood-altering substance provides the user with a desired effect (e.g., relaxation, self-confidence, euphoria) usage is thereby rewarded or reinforced, thus increasing the likelihood that the substance will be used again. Individuals who suffer from a mood disorder (e.g., depression, bipolar disorder, anxiety) are particularly vulnerable to developing a dependency. Individuals with low self-esteem, feelings of powerlessness, loneliness, and other types of emotional pain are also drawn to the mood-changing and numbing effects of certain chemicals.

An individual with an alcohol or drug problem will typically exhibit several of the following behaviors and patterns:

- Continues to use the chemical or substance even though it causes personal, family, health, and work-related problems.
- Displays an increased tolerance to the chemical.
- Experiences withdrawal symptoms and often uses the chemical to relieve those uncomfortable experiences.
- Uses more of the chemical, uses it more often, and uses it over longer periods than intended and as a result is often late for or misses work-related appointments and family events.
- Abandons previously important activities and relationships in favor or drinking and/or drug use.
- Voices a desire to cut back on use but is unsuccessful in efforts to control use.
- Neglects appearance, grooming, and hygiene.

- Experiences a decrease in physical and intellectual capacities, such as physical stamina and ability to concentrate and think logically.
- Participates in reckless and/or illegal activities in order to obtain the chemical.

It is important to note that the information presented here is of a basic and general nature. The reader should consult the DSM for more precise criteria used in diagnosis and in identifying the existence of tolerance and withdrawal (see Item 11.16).

Generally speaking, the chemicals or substances most sought after are those with a rapid onset of effects. Onset of effect is related to chemical properties, dose, method of intake, and the user's personality characteristics. The psychosocial setting of its use can also influence a person's response to a chemical.

There are local and regional differences in the popularity of various substances and the preferred methods of intake. There are continual changes in the street lingo applied to illegal substances and new chemical combinations appear frequently. Presented below are brief descriptions of the legal and illegal chemicals that are most often abused and involved in dependency problems.

Nicotine.   The nicotine found in tobacco is highly addictive. Because this stimulant is widely used and a contributing cause in cancer and heart and lung disease, nicotine may possibly cause more illness and death than all of the illegal street drugs combined. Tobacco is usually smoked but is also chewed or placed next to the gums in the form of "snuff." The cessation of smoking brings on a physical withdrawal syndrome and a craving. These uncomfortable effects can be alleviated almost immediately by returning to the nicotine. This makes quitting exceedingly difficult.

Alcohol.   If one considers the number of individuals and families affected, the number of injuries and deaths caused by drunken driving, and the number of health problems either caused or exacerbated by drinking, the abuse of alcohol (a legal drug) is the number one drug problem in the United States. Because alcohol depresses the central nervous system (CNS), it can be very dangerous when used along with other drugs or medications that also depress the CNS.

The American Medical Association, the National Council on Alcoholism, and the American Society of Addiction Medicine all view alcohol dependence as a chronic disease that is often progressive and fatal. Genetic, psychosocial, and cultural factors influence the development and manifestations of this disease. There is no cure for this disease; at best, it can be controlled through complete abstinence from alcohol. Treatment experts generally agree that once addicted, the individual can never again become only a casual user of alcohol (i.e., a social drinker). If the alcohol-dependent person tries to drink in moderation, he or she will soon resume a pattern of uncontrolled problem drinking. There is some research to support the *harm reduction model* of treatment, but the vast majority of experts endorse complete abstinence as the only sure way to maintain control over this addiction.

In its early stage, alcohol dependence is difficult to recognize because the symptoms are subtle and the person's drinking pattern may be indistinguishable from those who on occasion drink too much. It has been noted that the individual who will eventually develop a dependency can typically consume an unusual amount of alcohol without showing the effects; this phenomenon may be genetic in origin. The person who is becoming dependent will drink more than others and alcohol plays a part in most of his or her activities. Yet, during this early stage, the consumption of alcohol may not significantly interfere with job or family functioning.

In the middle stage, the alcohol-dependent person becomes physically addicted. When his or her blood-alcohol level is lowered, he or she will experience withdrawal symptoms, including anxiety, agitation, tremors, and sweating as well as fluctuations in blood pressure and blood sugar levels. Increasingly, the individual will have trouble remembering what occurred while drinking, a phenomenon called a *blackout*. He or she will drink more and for longer periods. Family and job functioning will be adversely affected. Family and friends may ask the individual to please cut back. The individual may quit drinking for a few weeks at a time but will eventually start again. Experiencing these short periods of abstinence will convince the person that it is possible to quit whenever he or she really wants to and, therefore, drinking is not a problem. Concerned family members may reach out for professional help, but typically, the alcohol-dependent person will deny that there is a problem.

In the late stage, the seriousness of the problem is apparent to everyone but the alcoholic, for paradoxically, the more serious the addiction becomes, the less he or she will be aware of what is happening. By this point in the addiction process, the individual may have lost his or her family and job and may have alcohol-related health problems. However, the denial and self-delusion will continue, and possibly only a major personal or health crisis will temporarily shake him or her into reality.

The progression of alcohol dependency may be somewhat different for different individuals. Adolescents who engage in heavy drinking may develop a dependency after only 6 or 18 months of drinking. Others may drink for 15 or 20 years before the onset of dependency.

A client's answers to the four so-called CAGE questions will help to identify an alcohol problem:

- Have you ever felt you ought to *Cut down* on your drinking?
- Have people *Annoyed* you by criticizing your drinking?
- Have you ever felt bad or *Guilty* about your drinking?
- Have you ever had a drink first thing in the morning (*Eye opener*) to steady your nerves or get rid of a hangover?

If one or more answers are positive, the social worker should further explore the possible existence of an abuse or dependency problem.

Amphetamines.   All of the amphetamines are CNS stimulants. Some like Dexedrine and Benzedrine are prescription medications used in the treatment of narcolepsy, brain dysfunction, and obesity. Other forms (i.e., the methamphetamines) are illegally manufactured and widely abused because of their strength and low cost. Among the chemicals used in making methamphetamine in a "meth lab" are various cold and allergy medicines that contain pseudoephedrine, acetone, ether, sulfuric acid, rubbing alcohol, brake cleaner, rock salt, farm fertilizer, iodine, red phosphorus from matches or road flares, and lithium. Several of these chemicals are extremely toxic and flammable, especially when heated. Illness can result from exposure to the chemicals. Meth labs have been found in basements, bathrooms, kitchens, garages, and hotel rooms.

Small batches of a methamphetamine can be made in a pop bottle by mixing crushed cold medication tablets containing pseudephedine with certain other chemicals. This method does not use a flame to heat the chemical mix but it leaves a toxic waste and can explode.

Among the forms of methamphetamine are methamphetamine sulfate (i.e., "crank"), methamphetamine hydrochloride (i.e., "crystal meth"), and dextrometh-amphetamine (i.e., "ice"). These highly addictive chemicals produce feelings of self-confidence and an intense and long-lasting euphoria. Depending on their form, they may be snorted, swallowed, smoked, or injected.

The abuse of these stimulants is indicated by hyperactivity, nervousness and anxiety, dilated pupils, irritability, and going for long periods without sleep or food. Some users experience a dry mouth, sweating, headache, blurred vision, dizziness, and sleeplessness. High doses can cause rapid or irregular heartbeat, tremors, loss of coordination, and physical collapse. Long-time use can lead to malnutrition, skin disorders, ulcers, weight loss, kidney damage, dental problems, depression, and speech and thought disturbances. A methamphetamine injection causes a sudden increase in blood pressure that can precipitate a stroke or heart failure.

Heavy use can result in a psychosis involving hallucinations (seeing, hearing, and feeling things that do not exist), delusions (having irrational thoughts or beliefs), and paranoia. In such a state, the person may exhibit bizarre and violent behavior. Methamphetamine use is often a contributing factor in child abuse and neglect, domestic abuse, and other forms of violence. Withdrawal (often referred to as crashing) is very uncomfortable and characterized by fatigue, nightmares, insomnia, depression, and a wildly fluctuating appetite.

Cocaine.   Cocaine is a CNS stimulant derived from the coca plant native to the mountain regions of South America. It is smuggled into a country as a fine, white, crystalline powder (cocaine hydrochloride) and then diluted, or "cut," to increase its bulk and stretch the supply for selling.

A common method of intake is intranasal or snorting the diluted powder. When snorted, the euphoric effects begin within a few minutes, peak within 15 to 20 minutes, and disappear within about 45 minutes. During this brief period, the user often feels confident, energetic, talkative, and omnipotent.

Chemical procedures can be used to separate or free the pure cocaine from the other usual additives in powdered cocaine. The process of freebasing involves adding ammonia and ethyl ether to powdered cocaine and burning it to free up the "base" cocaine, a dangerous process. This yields "freebase" that can be smoked is a more direct and rapid way to transmit the chemical to the brain. Since freebase cocaine is water soluble, it can also be injected. Because injection produces an immediate and intense euphoria, intravenous use is highly addictive.

Smokeable crack or "rock cocaine" is made by mixing powered cocaine with baking soda and water and then burning off the liquid to form tiny "rocks." It came to be called crack for the crackling sound of the cooking process. Smoking crack cocaine produces a short but very intense high. It is highly addictive.

Regular users of cocaine often report feelings of restlessness, irritability, anxiety, and sleeplessness. Cocaine causes physical and mental damage similar to that caused by the amphetamines. High doses over a long period may precipitate a psychosis with hallucinations of touch, sight, taste, or smell. Because cocaine stimulates the body and its nervous system, it is not uncommon to experience a physical "crash" and a mental depression following a period of use. These depressions and mood swings can be debilitating and last from a few hours to several weeks. The uncomfortable psychological and physiological effects of withdrawal are a source of worry for many cocaine abusers.

Marijuana.   Marijuana is the common name for a tobacco-like, dried leafy substance derived from the cannabis sativa plant. The main psychoactive ingredient in marijuana is THC (delta-9-tetrahydrocannabinol). The amount of THC in the marijuana determines its strength and effects on the user. Concentrating the resin found in the plant's leaves and flowers makes *hashish*, which contains more THC. Marijuana and hash are usually smoked but sometimes taken orally.

Research and the experiences of drug-treatment programs identify several potentially adverse effects. Some individuals become psychologically dependent, and heavy users may develop *amotivational syndrome*, such that they lose interest in life's major activities and feel increasingly passive and sluggish. Marijuana users do not experience the physiological withdrawal syndrome, but it is not uncommon for them to report a degree of psychological withdrawal that includes intense cravings.

An individual high on marijuana or hashish will have dilated pupils and feel euphoric and may speak rapidly and loud. Some individuals experience sensory distortions. The drug can impair short-term memory, alter sense of time, and reduce the ability to perform tasks that require concentration and quick reactions such as in driving a car or operating machinery.

Because marijuana is not physically addictive and because it can provide relief from the discomforts of chemotherapy and chronic pain, there has been some public support for decriminalizing its use.

PCP.   Phencyclidine (PCP) was developed as an anesthetic but later taken off the market for human use because it sometimes caused hallucinations. It continues to have use in veterinary medicine. PCP is easily manufactured and available in several forms (i.e., white crystal-like powder, tablet, or capsule). It can be swallowed, smoked, sniffed, or injected. PCP powder, sometimes referred to as angel dust or "dust," may be sprinkled on marijuana and smoked.

The sought-after effect of PCP is euphoria. For some users, small amounts act as a stimulant. For many, it changes how they perceive their own bodies and objects and movements and time are slowed. The effects of PCP are unpredictable, and for this reason many "experimenters" abandon its use. Others, unfortunately, become dependent.

Negative effects of PCP include increased heart rate and blood pressure, flushing, sweating, dizziness, and numbness. Users may show signs of paranoia, fear, and anxiety. Frequent use negatively effects memory, perception, concentration, and judgment. The effects of large doses include drowsiness, convulsions, coma, and sometimes death. Its use can produce violent or bizarre behavior. When under the drug's influence, some become aggressive; others withdraw and have difficulty communicating. A PCP-induced psychosis may last for days or weeks.

Hallucinogens. The hallucinogens or psychedelics are chemicals that affect a person's perceptions, sensations, thinking, self-awareness, and emotions. This category includes LSD, mescaline, and psilocybin. *LSD* is manufactured from lysergic acid found in a fungus that grows on grains. LSD is sold on the street in tablets, capsules, or occasionally in liquid form. It is usually taken by mouth. *Mescaline* comes from the peyote cactus and, although it is not as strong as LSD, its effects are similar. Mescaline is usually smoked or swallowed in the form of capsules or tablets. *Psilocybin* comes from certain mushrooms. It is sold in tablet or capsule form or the mushrooms themselves may be eaten.

The effects of psychedelics are unpredictable and depend on dosage as well as the user's personality, mood, expectations, and surroundings. Several different emotions may be felt at once or swing rapidly from one to another. Sensations become mixed and seem to "cross over," giving the user the feeling of hearing colors and seeing sounds. A person feels a change in one's sense of self and time. For some, these strange sensations are frightening and cause a "bad trip" that may last a few minutes or several hours and involve confusion, suspiciousness, anxiety, feelings of helplessness, and loss of control. Physical effects include dilated pupils, higher body temperature, increased heart rate and blood pressure, and often sweating, irregular breathing, and tremors. Some users sit in a stupor, whereas others become agitated.

In recent years, a manufactured hallucinogenic known as MDMA, or "Ecstasy," has become popular in the United States and Europe. It is usually taken by capsule or tablet. Its use brings on mild distortions of perceptions, has a calming effect, and, for many, creates a feeling of empathy with others. It does not cause the visual illusions often associated with the psychedelics. Physical dependency is not a major problem, but psychological dependence develops in many users. Growing evidence indicates that frequent and heavy use of MDMA causes damage to the brain.

The use of hallucinogens can unmask underlying mental or emotional problems. Some users experience flashbacks (i.e., intense and intrusive memories and emotions that can occur days and even weeks after having taken the drug). Heavy users sometimes suffer impaired memory, loss of attention span, confusion, and difficulty with abstract thinking.

Sedative Hypnotics. Sedative hypnotics are prescription drugs often referred to as sleeping pills, sedatives, and tranquilizers. Two major categories are the barbiturates and the benzodiazepines, which include Xanex, Valium, Librium, Ambien, and Ativan. These pharmaceutical drugs are only available by a physician's prescription but sometimes the prescription forms are altered or forged by addicts. These pills are sometimes stolen and sold on the street.

Sedative hypnotics depress the CNS, have a calming effect, and promote sleep. If an individual takes a higher than prescribed dosage, he or she may appear drunk (e.g., staggering, slurred speech, sleepiness) but will not smell of alcohol. When taken with alcohol (also a depressant), these drugs can cause unconsciousness and death.

The sedative-hypnotic drugs can result in both physical and psychological dependence. When regular users stop, they may develop withdrawal symptoms, ranging from restlessness, insomnia, and anxiety to convulsions and death. Barbiturate overdose is a factor in many drug-related deaths such as suicides and accidental poisonings.

Inhalants. These chemicals produce semi-toxic vapors that are inhaled in a practice sometimes called "huffing." The inhalants are grouped into four classes: (1) volatile solvents (e.g., certain glues, gasoline, paint thinner, nail polish remover, lighter fluid); (2) aerosols (e.g., spray paints); (3) anesthetics (e.g., ether, chloroform, nitrous oxide); and (4) amyl and butyl nitrates. Nearly all of the inhalants depress the body's functions. At low doses, users may feel slightly stimulated and some, like butyl nitrite, produce a "rush" or high lasting for a few seconds or a couple of minutes. Young people are likely to abuse inhalants, in part because they are readily available and inexpensive.

Possible negative effects include nausea, sneezing, coughing, nosebleeds, fatigue, bad breath, lack of coordination, and a loss of appetite. Solvents and aerosols decrease the heart and breathing rates and affect judgment. Deep breathing of the vapors may result in a loss of self-control, violent behavior, and unconsciousness. Inhalants can cause death from suffocation by displacing oxygen in the lungs and by depressing the CNS to a point that breathing stops. Moderate to long-term use can damage the brain, liver, kidneys, blood, and bone marrow.

Opiates.   The chemicals known as opiates or narcotics are used medically to relieve pain. They are potentially addictive and habit forming. Some opiates (opium, morphine, heroin, and codeine) are derived from the Asian poppy plant. Others, such as meperidine (Demerol), are manufactured. Heroin is the opiate for most often abused in the United States.

Opiates are ingested, snorted, smoked, or injected intravenously. After causing an initial rush, they relax the user. Indicators of opiate abuse include needle scars on the arms and the backs of hands, drowsiness, frequent scratching, red and watering eyes, sniffles, and a loss of appetite overall but an attraction to sugar and candies. In contrast to the effects of most other abused drugs that dilate the eye's pupils, the opiates constrict the pupils. When an opiate-dependent person stops taking the drug, withdrawal symptoms begin within 4 to 6 hours. These symptoms include anxiety, diarrhea, abdominal cramps, chills, sweating, nausea, and runny nose and eyes. The intensity of the symptoms depends on how much was taken, how often, and for how long. Withdrawal symptoms for most opiates are stronger approximately 24 to 72 hours after they begin but subside within 7 to 10 days.

Most of the physical dangers associated with opiate abuse result from overdoses, the use of non-sterile needles, contamination of the drug by other chemicals, or combining the drug with other substances. Long-time opiate users may develop infections of the heart, skin abscesses, and congested lungs.

Pain Medications.   Dependency on prescription pain medications is a growing problem. These addictive compounds include Darvon, Darocette, Percodan, Percocette, Demerol, Vicodin, Hydrocodone, and OxyCotin. Many individuals get caught up in dependency and illegal use after first taking one of these drugs as a doctor prescribed medical treatment for pain. Once dependent, the individual goes through withdrawal symptoms that are similar to those associated with the opiates. Being addicted to a pain medication may give rise to reckless and criminal behavior, as the individual desperately attempts to secure the drug.

GUIDELINES FOR DEALING WITH A CHEMICALLY DEPENDENT CLIENT

Throughout their professional relationships and interventions with a chemically dependent client and his or her family, social workers should carefully consider the following guidelines:

1. Because the abuse of and dependence on alcohol and other drugs is so pervasive in society, the social worker should be alert to the possible existence of this problem even when neither the client nor the client's family has mentioned it. In all individual and family assessments, some questions should be asked about the client's use of alcohol and drugs. However, it must be recognized that chemically dependent persons are seldom willing or able to accurately describe their use of chemicals and are often adamant in denying any connection between their personal problems and the use of drugs and alcohol. In many cases, the social worker's application of *motivational interviewing* will increase a client's willingness to acknowledge and address a dependency or addictions (see Items 8.5 and 11.4).

2. Never underestimate the psychological power of alcohol and drugs. A dependency or addiction is a pathological relationship with a mood-altering substance. The dynamics of this relationship resemble those of a neurotic love affair, but in this case, the love object is a chemical. It can turn a kind and honest person into a self-centered individual who may lie, cheat, and even injure loved ones in order to continue using a chemical.

3. When, in the course of your professional activity and/or when within your agency setting, you encounter an intoxicated individual you must be alert to the potentially life-threatening danger of delirium tremens or a drug overdose and also to the issue of public safety. A consideration of legal and ethical duties would suggest that a professional must make a reasonable effort to prevent a foreseeable injury, death, or tragic occurrence. For example, if you know that this intoxicated person intends to drive a car, you have a duty attempt to prevent it and, if necessary, to notify law enforcement in order to prevent an auto accident.

4. If your client is intoxicated when he or she arrives for a scheduled interview or meeting, explain in a polite but firm manner that you need accurate information and his or her full attention to do your work so you must reschedule the session for a time when he or she is sober. The client may argue and become angry but remain calm and hold firm to your decision.

5. Do not allow yourself to become part of an enabling system. For example, do not lend the client money and do not write letters or make phone calls that provide excuses or "cover" for his or her irresponsible behavior. Do not shield or protect him or her from the real-life consequences of substance abuse.

6. Learn about the behavioral pattern of *codependency* that develops as a result of living for many years with someone who is chemically dependent. Those who are codependent typically protect and provide excuses for the irresponsible behavior of the person who is using and abusing chemicals. They tend to assume responsibility for the behavior of others (e.g., the alcoholic) while neglecting their own needs. They are often hostile because of how they have been treated by someone they love, controlling because their own situation is so out of control, manipulative because manipulation is the only way to get things done, and indirect and vague in their communication because they live in a family system or a relationship that cannot tolerate truthfulness.

7. Because a person who is chemically dependent is seldom able to stop using without the help of a treatment program, a referral for treatment likely will be necessary. However, before attempting a referral, it is best to consult with a treatment specialist on how best to approach the client and how you might handle his or her denial and resistance to the idea of securing treatment.

The available options for securing treatment will need to be examined and planned within the client's health insurance program or perhaps an applicable tax-supported program. In some cases, inpatient medical care will be needed to manage physiological withdrawal (detoxification). After undergoing medically supervised detoxification, if needed, the individual will enter a treatment program that will take one of several forms (e.g., inpatient, outpatient, day treatment). Ongoing weekly or twice-weekly outpatient counseling sessions (both individual and group) may continue for six months to one year or longer.

Most recovering addicts will likely be involved in a *12-step program* (e.g., Alcoholics Anonymous, Cocaine Anonymous, Narcotics Anonymous), which provides encouragement and teaches methods of day-to-day coping. These self-help programs emphasize the development of spirituality and help the individual develop a lifestyle free of alcohol and drugs.

8. The assistance and support of the client's family and friends will probably be needed in making a referral to a treatment program. Thus, it may be necessary to reach out to these individuals and engage them in the assessment, planning, and helping process. However, be alert to the possibility that they too may have a substance abuse problem and/or may be contributing to your client's problem through enabling and codependency behaviors.

9. Learn about 12-step recovery programs by attending open meetings. Members are usually eager to consult with professionals who want to learn about the recovery process and effective ways of dealing with the many challenges presented by clients who are chemically dependent.

Encourage family members to make use of Al-Anon and Alateen groups, along with other resources such as COA (Children of Alcoholics), ACOA or ACA (Adult Children of Alcoholics), and programs that address the problem of codependency.

10. Once the individual stops using chemicals, special attention must be given to planning for relapse prevention. This involves helping the individual develop a plan for coping with those times and situations when he or she will be at highest risk of resuming the use of alcohol and drugs. Once an individual has been addicted to one type of chemical, he or she is vulnerable to becoming addicted to another. Help the recovering addict be vigilant with regard to use of both prescription and over-the-counter medications. Recovering addicts should inform their physicians of their prior problems with the abuse of chemicals.

Selected Bibliography

Doweiko, Harold. *Concepts of Chemical Dependency*, 7th ed. Belmont, CA: Brooks/Cole, 2009.

Hart, Carl, Charles Ksir, and Oakley Ray. *Drugs, Society, and Human Behavior,* 13th ed. Boston: McGraw Hill, 2009.

McNeece, C. Aaron, and Diana DiNitto. *Chemical Dependency*, 3rd ed. Boston: Allyn & Bacon, 2005.

Perkinson, Robert, and Arthur Jongsma. *The Addiction Treatment Planner*, 4th ed. Hoboken, NJ: Wiley, 2009.

van Wormer, Katherine, and Diane Davis. *Addiction Treatment: A Strengths Perspective*, 2nd ed. Belmont, CA: Brooks/Cole, 2008.

15.12 THE CLIENT WITH SERIOUS MENTAL ILLNESS

There are three major categories of serious mental illness: schizophrenia, bipolar disorder, and major depression. All three are caused primarily by biochemical abnormalities within the brain. Each may be episodic and vary in intensity and the degree to which it impairs a person's functioning. Some of those who experience these illnesses may become psychotic and lose touch with reality.

Schizophrenia is a baffling and debilitating illness. About 1 percent of the population is afflicted with this disturbance. The usual age of onset is between 15 and 25 years, when the frontal lobes of the brain are rapidly maturing. Many experts believe that a stressful environment, infections, and other physiological conditions may trigger the onset of this illness in those predisposed by heredity. Genetics plays a role in this disease. An individual with schizophrenia will exhibit several of these symptoms:

- *Delusions*   (e.g., holds to false beliefs that have no factual basis)
- *Hallucinations*   (hearing voices is the most common hallucination; visual hallucination [seeing nonexistent things] is relatively rare but is more likely if the individual is also abusing drugs; olfactory and tactile hallucinations are less common, but possible)
- *Disordered thinking*   (e.g., loose or illogical connections among thoughts; reaches conclusions unrelated to facts or logic; makes up words or uses sounds or rhythms that are meaningless to others, shifts rapidly from one topic to another)
- *Blunted or inappropriate affect*   (e.g., narrow range of emotional reactions; emotions or feelings do not fit the situation; speaks in monotone)
- *Extreme withdrawal*   (e.g., withdrawal from ordinary life and social interactions; deterioration in work or school performance; apathy in regard to appearance and self-care)

About one-fourth of those who have a schizophrenic episode will recover and never have another episode. Some have occasional relapses. Between 20 to 30 percent develop symptoms that persist throughout life.

The other two types of serious mental illness—major depression and bipolar disorder—are known as *mood disorders or affective disorders*. Individuals with a **major depression** experience persistent feelings of sadness and melancholy. They often become tearful, irritable, or hostile for no apparent reason. Other symptoms common to depression include the following:

- Intense feelings of worthlessness, hopelessness, or guilt
- Anxiety and rumination over problems and situation
- Diminished ability to think, concentrate, or make decisions
- Loss of interest in friends, family, and usual activities
- Recurrent thoughts of death and suicide
- Poor appetite and weight loss or increased appetite and weight gain
- Change in sleep pattern (sleeping too little or too much)
- Excessive fatigue; loss of energy, decreased sexual drive
- Change in activity level (either increased or decreased)

About 1 percent of the population suffers from **bipolar disorder**, which is characterized by swings between periods of depression and mania. Mania, state of hyperactivity, is often characterized by these qualities:

- Exaggerated, intense, or irritable moods
- Decreased need for sleep
- Inflated self-confidence and grandiose ideas
- Increased energy and activity; unusually high levels of involvement in work, pleasurable activities, and sex
- Unrealistic optimism, poor judgment, impulsive decision making
- Rapid and pressured speech and racing thoughts
- Distractibility

Most often, the depressive phase follows the manic phase. Sometimes, the two phases are separated by periods of near normal functioning. These episodes may come and go and last from several days to several months. Without treatment, there is usually an increase in the frequency of the episodes and the severity of the symptoms.

Some individuals experience the bipolar disorder with only the depressive or only manic symptoms, rather than both. These are termed *bipolar disorder, depressive type* and *bipolar disorder, manic type*. Often, a person's mental health history will predict how the bipolar disorder will manifest itself in the future. For example, a person who historically experiences depression in the autumn may continue to experience more severe symptoms during these months of the year. There is evidence that this disorder has a basis in heredity.

When working with a client who has a serious mental illness, the social worker should follow these guidelines:

1. These illnesses, especially the mood disorders, can usually be treated effectively with proper medications. An individual with a serious mental illness should be under the care of a physician, preferably a psychiatrist, who can monitor the effects of medications. For most individuals, some combination of medication, psychotherapy is the preferred treatment (see Item 15.13).

2. Because depression gives rise to feelings of hopelessness, the risk of suicide must always be considered. Of those with schizophrenia, about one in four attempts suicide and about one in ten dies of suicide. Thoughts of suicide or self-mutilation by someone with schizophrenia place him or her at high risk (see Item 15.7).

3. Delusions are a common symptom in schizophrenia. A *delusion* is a set of ideas and beliefs that remain fixed, even in the face of clear evidence to the contrary. The individual holds to these delusional beliefs because they help to make some sense out of his or her mental or perceptual confusion. Be very cautious about how you respond to a person's delusions. Listen carefully and try to understand the assumptions on which the delusion is built, but do not criticize, challenge, or confront the delusional thoughts for that will probably destroy the relationship you have with the individual. Also, confronting a delusion increases the risk that you will become part of the delusional system of thought and possibly defined as an enemy or part of a plot or conspiracy.

4. A small percentage of persons who become psychotic will experience command hallucinations—voices that tell these individuals to hurt themselves or hurt others (e.g., a voice telling them to jump off a bridge or kill the mayor). These command hallucinations, although rare, are very dangerous. If this symptom cannot be controlled by medication, the individual should be hospitalized.

5. The individual with persistent and serious mental illness is usually in need of services that will assist him or her with the everyday tasks of living. Such services include case management, counseling, case advocacy, budgeting, and assistance in securing income, a job, housing, transportation, medical care, and the like. The *clubhouse model*—which provides peer support, acceptance, meaningful work, social activity, and other services—is especially helpful and important to persons with a persistent mental illness.

When appropriate, encourage the client to authorize the release of confidential medical and therapy-related information to trusted family members or close friends so they will understand the client's condition and treatment and be in a better position to help him or her utilize needed services.

6. An individual's mental illness has a profound and painful impact on his or her family and close friends. The social worker should address the concerns of the family by doing the following:

- Provide practical information about the mental illness and its usual treatment. Ask about their possible fear of physical assault and worry over irresponsible financial decisions by the individual who is mentally ill.
- Encourage family members to join a self-help or support group such as the National Alliance for the Mentally Ill.
- Help the parents and siblings recognize their rights to a life apart from the anguish and worry they feel toward the family member who is mentally ill.
- Assist family members to secure services such as case management and respite care to relieve them of the daily responsibility of care giving and provide opportunities for rest and renewal.
- Encourage the family to secure legal guidance on how to address the questions and concerns they may have related to, for example, involuntary hospitalization, their loved one's finances, legal obligations, unpredictable behavior, and the refusal of medical treatment.
- Help family members grieve the loss of their loved one who, because of mental illness, may now seem like a stranger.
- Remain accessible to the families, especially during family crises that can be precipitated by relapses.

7. The treatment and management of a mental illness can be further complicated by the presence of another serious problem such as substance abuse, a personality disorder, brain injury, or a developmental disability. The term **dual diagnosis** is applied to such a situation. A **personality disorder** is a deeply ingrained, inflexible, lifelong, and maladaptive pattern of emotional responses and behaviors that are often harmful or distressful to others. Individuals with a personality disorder seldom see anything unusual about their own behavior and typically blame others for whatever difficulties they encounter in life. Because they do not feel an inner pain or anxiety, they do not usually voluntarily seek treatment. There are several types of personality disorders. They are not brain disorders and appear to develop in response to family and social influences.

Selected Bibliography

Gray, Susan, and Marilyn Zide. *Psychopathology: A Competency-Based Treatment Model for Social Workers*, 2nd ed. Belmont, CA: Brooks/Cole, 2008.

Lefley, Harriet. *Family Psychoeducation for Serious Mental Illness*. New York: Oxford University Press, 2009.

Linhorst, Donald. *Empowering People with Severe Mental Illness*. New York: Oxford University Press, 2005.

15.13   THE CLIENT ON PSYCHOTROPIC MEDICATION

A social worker will encounter many clients who take or are in need of medications that can control psychiatric symptoms. These medications fall into several major groups: drugs for depression, anxiety, bipolar disorder, psychotic disorders, and drugs for insomnia. Each medicine has a chemical name, a generic name, and sometimes a brand name. Each drug varies in effectiveness, adverse effects, in formulation, daily dosage, and cost. The selection of a medication for a particular patient is based on the patient's medical history, physical exam, laboratory tests, potential drug interactions with other chemicals such as other prescribed medications, alcohol and street drugs, and, of course, the disorder being treated. In especially complex cases, the doctor may consult with a clinical pharmacist.

A psychotropic medication can exacerbate other medical conditions such as hypertension, liver disease, epilepsy, and glaucoma. Among the side effects associated with certain psychotropic medications are dry mouth; weight gain; drowsiness; oversensitivity to the sun; menstrual cycle disturbance; muscles spasms of the eye, face, neck, and back; blurred vision; shuffling gait; and tremors. Children and the elderly are particularly prone to experience side effects. Because a child's brain is still developing and because an adolescent is going through biological changes, doctors must be knowledgeable and cautious when prescribing these drugs for young persons. The effects and risks of psychotropic medications in children are not well understood. Medications that are effective in adults may not work the same way in children and may produce different and unexpected reactions.

Despite the possibility of side effects, symptom control is critically important to persons suffering from a major mental illness. In general, a physician will reduce side effects by prescribing the lowest dosage that produces the desired effects, discontinuing a problematic medication and trying another, avoiding the simultaneous use of two medications that have a similar effect, and, whenever possible, treating only one symptom at a time.

Some prescription medications can cause psychiatric symptoms, but the causal link is often difficult to establish. During medical treatment and a course of drug therapy, psychiatric symptoms could also be due to an underlying illness, a previously unrecognized psychopathology, or a psychosocial factor. In some instances, withdrawal from a prescription medication can cause symptoms such as anxiety, psychosis, delirium agitation, or depression.

When an individual is hospitalized and/or is experiencing disabling symptoms, he or she may be started on a quick-acting medication or given a fairly large dose. Most will not need to take the same dosage after leaving the hospital or after the symptoms subside, and a physician may reduce the dosage or switch to a medication that is slower acting but has other advantages. A physician will usually reduce the dosage to the minimum effective level. This reduction is best done gradually—a process that may take several weeks or months. Even when on a maintenance dose, some patients find that their symptoms worsen from time to time. This may be due to stress, biochemical changes, or other factors.

Some patients are frightened when a doctor suggests that they take less medication because the patient fears a return of symptoms. On the other hand, some patients are reluctant to take medications because they fear side effects or because it is perceived as a loss of control or a blow to their self-esteem.

When working with a client who is taking psychotropic medications, keep several guidelines in mind:

1. The decision to prescribe a medication is a complex and technical medical judgment to be made only by a physician, preferably a psychiatrist. A social worker must never give medication-related instructions unless directed to do so by the physician.

2. Encourage your client to maintain regular contact with a medical professional so that the effects of the drug can be monitored. If you observe what appears to be an unusual or unexpected side effect, but your client is unwilling to see a physician, get the name and dosage of the medication and consult with a physician about what might be the best course of action.

3. Alert your client to the dangers of using alcohol or street drugs while taking a medication and the dangers of modifying the prescribed dosage and exchanging medications with others. If your client takes more than one medication, an adverse drug interaction could occur. This happens when the two drugs mixed together have an effect very different from when each is taken alone. Side effects can also occur when the client mixes a psychotropic medication with nonprescription drugs such as a cold medicine. Some foods (e.g., aged cheese) may cause adverse reactions when eaten by a person on certain medications.

4. As in the case of other forms of medical treatment, an adult has a right to refuse psychotropic medications. Exceptions are when a court has declared that the individual is legally incompetent to make that decision and/or when his or her behavior constitutes an imminent threat to self or others. Because the decision to reject a needed medication can have tragic results when symptoms recur, you should do everything possible to inform the patient of the possible consequences. In the final analysis, however, the decision of a legally competent adult must be respected.

Selected Bibliography

Bentley, Kia, and Joseph Walsh. *The Social Worker and Psychotropic Medication*, 3rd ed. Belmont, CA: Brooks/Cole, 2006.

Dziegielewski, Sophia. *Social Work Practice and Psychopharmacology,* 2nd ed. New York: Springer, 2009.

Preston, John, John O'Neal, and Mary Talaga. *Handbook of Clinical Psychopharmacology for Therapists*, 5th ed. Oakland, CA: New Harbinger, 2010.

15.14 THE CLIENT WHO IS GAY, LESBIAN, BISEXUAL, OR TRANSGENDER

In all practice settings, social workers will encounter clients who are lesbian, gay, bisexual, or transgender (LGBT). We humans are classified and labeled by our parents and society as either a male or a female, on the basis of anatomy and genitalia. However, our sexuality, sexual orientation, and sexual identity are not always so clear-cut. In reality, human sexuality exists as a range of orientations and identities.

The term **sexual orientation** refers to a person's enduring romantic and sexual attractions. Most people are heterosexual or "straight." Probably 6 to 10 percent of the population is homosexual and perhaps 30 percent are bisexual, meaning that they experience some sexual attraction to both males and females. It is difficult to determine with precision the number of people who are homosexual or bisexual because such statistics rely on self-report and some individuals may not want to reveal their sexual orientation. (For additional information on the concepts of sex and gender, see the *Feminist Perspective* presented in Chapter 6).

The developmental processes that give rise to homosexuality and bisexuality are not well understood; the same can be said about heterosexuality. Sexual orientation exists as a continuum: from very straight to the very gay. Researchers are not able to fully explain why some individuals are sexually attracted to the opposite sex, some to their own sex, and some to both sexes. However, there is growing evidence that sexual orientation is rooted in early stage, in-uterus biological processes. For most individuals, sexual orientation is firmly established by adolescence. Thus, it is inaccurate to speak of either homosexuality or heterosexuality as a choice or a preference. It is helpful to view homosexuality as something like left-handiness; it is a departure from the majority but an otherwise normal condition. Research indicates that growing up with homosexual parents has no impact on a child's sexual orientation.

The poorly understood phenomenon of **transgender** is usually described as a matter of gender identity, rather than sexual orientation. Gender is more subtle and complex than sexual attraction and orientation. It has to do with one's sense of being a male or a female and with the feelings, attitudes, and perceptions related to femininity and masculinity. One's gender is formed by a complex interplay of genetics, physiology, brain function, hormones, and culture. At a fundamental level, persons who are transgender do not feel comfortable or at ease with their physical or "assigned sex." For example, a transgender male may feel that he would be more real and authentic if he had a female body. Transgender individuals may feel awkward or uncomfortable wearing the clothing typically worn by their physical sex, they may prefer to take part in activities traditionally associated with the other sex and, in rare instances, they may seek out sex reassignment surgery in order to have a body more like the other sex. Transgender people may be heterosexual, homosexual, or bisexual.

About one in every 2,000 babies is born with ambiguous and abnormally developed genitalia, and or a mix of both male and female genitalia. In such cases, it is not possible to determine the baby's sex (male or female) with certainty by examining the child's genitals. The occurrence of this **intersex** condition requires a difficult decision by parents and their doctor. Should surgery be performed to "make" the baby a male or a female? (Constructing female genitalia is usually an easier surgery than is the construction of male genitalia). In the past, a sexual assignment surgery was performed shortly after birth but increasingly doctors delay this surgery until later in childhood when it appears as if the child clearly leans toward one sex or the other. Needless to say, a child growing up with intersex condition is at risk of developing social and psychological confusion and problems.

Within the United States and in most countries around the world, people who are LGBT are often maligned. The term **homophobia** refers to an irrational fear and hatred of homosexuality and sexual diversity. It can lead to discrimination in employment, housing, health care, social services, and other areas. Sometimes homophobia foments violence directed against persons who are known to be or suspected of being LGBT.

A fear of rejection, discrimination, and violence, as well as a desire to protect their families from embarrassment and worry, causes some who are LGBT to hide or deny their sexual orientation or gender identity. The inability to acknowledge and be at peace with something so basic as one's sexuality can be a source of emotional turmoil. Increasingly, gay and lesbian persons are emerging from the closet, identifying themselves publicly and demanding equal rights, justice, and societal acceptance.

The following guidelines will be useful in working with clients who are LGBT:

1. Carefully examine your own attitudes and moral standards for signs of possible bias, prejudice, and discrimination toward people who are LGBT. Consider, for example:

- Your beliefs on whether differences in sexual orientation and gender identity are pathological conditions or a normal variation of human sexuality
- Your level of comfort in hearing of affection and sexual activity within a same sex relationship
- Your beliefs and attitudes regarding same sex marriage and the parenting of children by persons who are gay, lesbian, bisexual, or transgender

2. Do not be afraid to acknowledge your lack of understanding and to face up to your own prejudices. Also, realize that an ignorance of variations in sexual orientation and gender identifications may exist among those in the helping professions, among clients who are straight, and even among some who are themselves lesbian, gay, bisexual, and transgender. Work hard to learn about the concerns of persons who are LGBT. Get to know leaders and professionals within the LGBT community and seek their consultation when unsure about how best to work with clients who are LGBT.

Leaders of LGBT-related organizations and advocacy groups should be consulted regarding the design and delivery of health and social services. Such consultations will help to make these services more accessible and acceptable to persons who are LGBT. And, of course, the professional staff working in health and human services programs must be alert to how their practices and approaches fit with or accommodate differences of sexual orientation and sexual identity.

3. It is fairly common for persons who are homosexual, bisexual, or transgender to go through many years of confusion and uncertainty before finally recognizing and accepting their true sexual orientation or gender identity. For example, they may suppress their sexual attractions. They may become sexually active with the opposite sex and even enter into a marriage in order to reassure themselves and demonstrate to family that they are "normal" and heterosexual. Such confusion and turmoil is especially difficult for the adolescent and may lead some to consider suicide.

4. Because many who are LGBT have been hurt by prejudice and discrimination, they may be cautious when seeking professional services and entering into a helping relationship. Some may speak openly about their sexual orientation or gender identity; others will not. When LGBT individuals seek health care, social services, or counseling, their sexual orientation or sexual identity, per se, will seldom be the presenting problem. Thus, as a general rule, it is not necessary for social workers or other professionals to ask about or discuss a client's sexuality unless it is clearly related to the client's presenting concern or request. In those practice settings where the professional may need to know about the client's sexuality and sexual activity (e.g., public health, counseling), a social worker might approach this topic by saying something like: "In order for us to provide an individualized and appropriate service, I ask all my clients about their sexual orientation. Would you be comfortable discussing this matter?"

In all practice settings, a social worker should strive to create a welcoming and non-threatening atmosphere that makes it as easy as possible for a client to speak about deeply personal matters. Clients who are LGBT may hide their sexuality until they are sure the social worker is free of demonstrable prejudices. If a social worker is LGBT he or she may elect to self-disclose in order to lessen the client's fear. Or, a social worker might use some personal stories to reveal that he or she understands the insidious effect of stereotypes and prejudice and thereby demonstrate to the client a capacity for acceptance and understanding.

5. When working with a same-sex couple, expect that their relationship problems will be similar to those of heterosexual couples. For example, their conflicts will most likely revolve around matters such as money management, unfaithfulness, domestic abuse, substance abuse, balancing home and work responsibilities, child care, and an unsatisfactory sexual relationship. However, their relationship may be unclear and uncertain if it lacks the legal status and protections that come with a marriage. In the absence of a legally recognized marriage, ordinary concerns like securing health insurance for one's partner, arranging survivor benefits, inheritance, child custody, hospital visitation, and adoption can be complex and troublesome. Thus, it is important to help these couples find the legal guidance they may need to address such matters and construct special legal arrangements. Laws providing for same-sex marriages or civil unions prevent or resolve many of these legal concerns and dilemmas.

6. If your client is considering the decision to come out, help him or her weigh the pros and cons of this option. On the surface, coming out may seem to be personally liberating and politically courageous, but a person choosing this action may pay a high price. Unfortunately, ignorance, prejudice, and discrimination still exist and this is more of a problem in some communities and occupations than in other. An individual should not ignore the possible negative ramifications of coming out, which may include alienation from family or even the loss of housing or a job.

7. As a group, gay men have been especially hard hit by *Acquired Immune Deficiency Syndrome (AIDS)*, a deadly disease caused by a virus known as *Human Immunodeficiency Virus (HIV)*. Many gay men have suffered the loss of friends or lovers to the disease, and others live in fear of contracting the disease. The symptoms of AIDS typically do not develop until several years after being infected. The virus is spread primarily by having vaginal, anal, or oral sex with an infected person (whether male or female) and by sharing needles for injecting drugs with someone who is infected. The virus can be passed from an infected mother to her baby during pregnancy or childbirth and in rare instances through breastfeeding. Promiscuity, whether heterosexual or homosexual, increases the risk of contracting the infection. The use of condoms, other safe sex techniques, and HIV testing can reduce the spread of this disease.

Selected Bibliography

Bieschke, Kathleen, Ruperto Perez, and Kurt DeBord. *Handbook of Counseling and Psychotherapy with Lesbian, Gay, Bisexual, and Transgender Clients*, 2nd ed. Washington, DC: American Psychological Association, 2007.

Mallon, Gerald, ed. *Social Work Practice with Lesbian, Gay, Bisexual, and Transgender People*, 2nd ed. New York: Haworth, 2008.

Morrow, Deana, and Lori Messinger, eds. *Sexual Orientation and Gender Expression in Social Work Practice*. New York: Columbia University, 2006.

Omoto, Allen, and Howard Kurtzman. *Sexual Orientation and Mental Health*. Washington, DC: American Psychological Association, 2006.

15.15   THE CLIENT WITH AN EATING DISORDER

Increasingly, social workers are serving clients with eating disorders. The term *eating disorder* is an umbrella term that describes any of several problems linked to a person's relationship to food. The three most prevalent and serious eating disorders are anorexia nervosa, bulimia nervosa, and obesity. At one extreme is the person who self-starves; at the other extreme is the person who eats to excess.

There are many other examples of actual or potentially harmful behaviors related to food and nutrition. For example, it is not uncommon for male athletes to intentionally overeat to gain weight (e.g., offensive linesmen in football) or lose weight (e.g., wrestlers seeking to reach certain weight divisions). Nor is it uncommon for older people to experience food-related problems when, for example, their food intake is insufficient because they are lonely and "cooking for one" seems like too much trouble or when the food of a nursing home lacks a preferred taste. Fad diets and misguided fasting can disturb body chemistry and give rise to health problems.

Anorexia Nervosa.   The condition known as *anorexia nervosa* is characterized by intentionally maintaining a body weight substantially below normal (i.e., 15 to 25 percent below normal). This disorder is most commonly found in middle- and upper-class female adolescents, with symptoms typically beginning between ages 12 and 18. The exact causes of anorexia are not known, but it is often associated with high stress, pressure from one's cultural group, presence of an eating disorder among other members of the person's family, as well as the person's biological predisposition.

Some psychological *indicators of anorexia* are a distorted perception of one's own body size, weight, and shape; an intense fear of gaining weight; and high self-expectations or perfectionism. Some physical symptoms are excessively low weight, the absence of or irregularity in the menstrual cycle, dry skin, loss of hair, refusal to eat normal amounts of food, anxiety about eating, and episodes of spontaneous or induced vomiting.

The recommended interventions are first to assist the person to take steps to restore physical health and regain a normal weight and then to implement the necessary psychological interventions to prevent the recurrence of this condition. When a person is literally starving, his or her physical condition must be addressed before the social and psychological factors. Treatment may involve a period of hospitalization and possibly the use of various medications.

When intervening with the anorexic (and also the bulimic) person, it is important to be very direct about the person's behaviors and the consequences of those behaviors, as well as to gain the person's trust as a foundation for helping him or her reestablish a sense of self-worth. Specific psychosocial interventions may include individual and family therapy, ongoing supportive treatment of the individual, cognitive therapy, behavior modification techniques, and participation in self-help groups. Recovery from anorexia nervosa requires actions on many fronts, including a team of professionals, family, and other significant people in the client's lives. Eating a sufficient amount of nutritious food is difficult for the anorexic to accomplish without considerable encouragement and reinforcement from others. It is thought that about one-half of the diagnosed and treated anorexics recover within two to five years. Yet, about 18 percent never recover and, for them, the possibility of death from suicide or health problems resulting from the person's depleted physical condition is quite high.

Bulimia Nervosa. This condition is characterized by a morbid fear of becoming fat. With this disorder, a person usually stays within 10 percent of normal body weight but experiences a lack of control over eating behaviors. As opposed to the person with anorexia who avoids food when under stress, the bulimic deals with stress by turning toward food. Periodically (i.e., three times or more a month), the person with this disorder experiences a severe craving for food and he or she binges, followed by induced vomiting, use of laxatives, severe dieting, excessive exercise, or fasting as a means of preventing weight gain. This bulimic cycle can be understood as the fear of becoming overweight leading to self-starvation, with a periodic eating frenzy followed by guilt and efforts to void the weight produced by the food, thus reinforcing the fear of becoming fat—and the cycle continues.

The causes of bulimia are not known. Symptoms usually begin in adolescence or early adulthood. The typical bulimic is thought to be a successful white woman in her mid- to late-twenties. Because of this stereotype, bulimia is considered a "woman's disease" and men tend to deny or hide the fact that they experience this disorder. Estimates of the number of young women experiencing bulimia are as high as 15 to 20 percent; however, young men, too, experience bulimia at the rate of about 5 to 10 percent. The binge-and-purge cycle can have disastrous effects, causing fatigue, seizures, and muscle cramps as well as having long-term damaging effects on the person's esophagus, teeth, and bone density.

It is often difficult to determine if a client might be experiencing bulimia because there are no obvious physical symptoms such as the weight loss or emaciation that occur in cases of anorexia. However, some clues are periodic consumption of large amounts of food, usually eaten alone or secretly; preoccupation with food or one's weight; excessive exercise or fasting; trips to the bathroom following meals; diminished sexual interest (sometimes); and depression or self-loathing.

As compared to persons who are anorexic, bulimics are more likely to seek and accept treatment, but their strong need for perfection leads to frustration when there are no immediate cures. Some interventions focus on helping them become more accepting of failure and imperfections in life, improving nutrition, and the use of medication to deal with depression, if it exists. Cognitive-behavioral therapy is often used to assist the client in interrupting the binging, establishing normal eating patterns, and modifying distorted view of foods and body image. The client is helped to reveal the problem to family and other significant people and to seek their help in maintaining a balanced diet. Finally, group approaches have been successful in helping bulimics disclose and discuss their problem, reduce their guilt, learn to self-monitor their eating behaviors, gain nutrition information, examine alternatives to the binge-and-purge cycle (e.g., relaxation techniques), and address cultural pressures they experience regarding body weight.

Overeating and Obesity. Overeating and excessive weight gain is a problem for many people. They are aware that they eat too much but are drawn into a pattern of overeating by the pleasure of eating, how foods are engineered by the food industry, their social surroundings, and by advertising. Weight gain occurs when an individual takes in more energy (as measured in calories) than he or she expends in activity. About 3,500 excess or unburned calories result in a gain of one pound.

Weight gain over a long period leads to the condition known as **obesity**. The term *moderate obesity* applies to a person who is 20 to 100 percent above recommended weight for his or her age, gender, and height, whereas a person experiencing *morbid obesity* would exceed the 100 percent level. Obesity is an epidemic in the United States and a growing problem in other developed countries. Those who are excessively overweight are at higher risk of developing numerous health problems such as high blood pressure, heart disease, stroke, diabetes, joint problems, and complications of pregnancy.

A variety of biological, psychological, and social factors are associated with excessive weight gain and obesity. Psychological factors include overeating as a compensation for boredom, unhappiness, depression, and painful life events. Research points to some connections between being overweight and one's genetic makeup. The eating patterns common to one's family and culture also contribute to weight gain and to the social acceptance of being overweight. Many processed and refined food products and store-bought snack or pleasure foods are loaded with sugar, fat, and salt and deliberately designed or blended to promote craving and make them difficult to resist. People with low incomes are susceptible to weight gain because they often purchase inexpensive processed foods that are high in calories.

Achieving weight loss requires a significant decrease in daily calorie intake (e.g., to 1,200 or 1,500 calories) and an increase in physical activity. While many individuals can achieve a weight loss by adhering to a prescribed diet, once they end their structured diet most will regain the weight in a few years. Changes in eating habits and lifestyle are essential to maintaining a weight loss.

A social worker's interventions will typically include helping the client learn to self-monitor food intake, create a social environment (e.g., family and friends) that has a positive influence on eating patterns, participate in an appropriate exercise program, connect to support groups wherein feelings of isolation and embarrassment are diminished, and provide the client with individual and group therapeutic services as warranted.

Social workers are sometimes in a position to assist with nutrition education and to offer guidance on identifying foods that can achieve a balanced diet at a reasonable cost. Most clients will benefit from learning to apply behavior self-modification techniques designed to change eating habits and reward their commitment to a weight loss plan. Individual counseling or therapy may be helpful for those clients who are exceedingly self-conscious and embarrassed by their appearance. Group counseling and support groups are helpful to adults willing to speak about their problems. Group approaches can be especially useful in work with overweight children. Purely medical or drug interventions have not proven successful in most cases of obesity. The *bariatric surgeries* designed to reduce food intake carry some risks and are usually recommended only for persons who are morbidly obese and suffering from serious health problems caused by the obesity.

Selected Bibliography

Kessler, David. *The End of Overeating*. New York: Rodale, 2009.

Lask, Bryan, and Rachel Bryant-Waugh, eds. *Eating Disorders in Childhood and Adolescence.* New York: Taylor and Francis, 2007.

Natenshon, Abigail. *Doing What Works: An Integrative System for Treating Eating Disorders*. Washington, DC: NASW Press, 2009.

Yager, Joel, and Pauline Powers, eds. *Clinical Manual of Eating Disorders*. Arlington, VA: American Psychiatric Association, 2007.

15.16   THE CLIENT EXPERIENCING GRIEF OR LOSS

The experience of grief is as old as humanity itself. **Grief** is the intense emotional suffering brought on by the loss of or separation from someone or something deeply loved. A sudden and unexpected death is one of the most common precipitators of intense grief. However, other types of loss can also precipitate grief reactions; for example: a divorce, loosing a job, a planned or spontaneous abortion, placing one's child in foster care, the termination or relinquishment of one's parental rights, loss of physical mobility, loss of a house to bankruptcy, and the destruction of possessions in a house fire or natural disaster.

A grief reaction to the death of a loved one, and the mourning of this loss, typically moves through four phases:

1. *Numbness.*   The person is shocked, dazed, confused, and overwhelmed. Physical symptoms might include nausea, tightness in the chest and throat, shortness of breath, disturbed sleep, loss of appetite, and headaches. This phase lasts from several days to several weeks.

2. *Yearning.*   The grieving person is preoccupied and withdrawn and may seem to wander about as if in search of the deceased person; he or she may even report seeing and being with the deceased individual. Intense crying and feelings of anger, guilt, anxiety, and frustration are common.

3. *Despair and disorganization.*   As the reality of the loss settles in, the person experiences feelings of helplessness, despair, depression, and fatigue.

4. *Recovery and reorganization.*   Over a period of many months or even years, the person gradually resumes his or her usual routines at home and at work and feels less depressed, sleeps better, and has more energy.

The term **acute grief** describes the reaction that occurs at the time of the loss, such as a parent's immediate reaction to his or her child being killed in an auto accident. It is a response to a sudden and unexpected loss. Another pattern, **anticipatory grief**, is set in motion by the realization that a serious loss will occur in the near future. The diagnosis of a terminal illness may prompt this type of grieving. The term **anniversary reaction** describes a recurrence of grief precipitated by remembering a prior loss, such as the sadness that occurs each year during the month when one's child or spouse died.

When a client is in the throes of grief, a social worker should keep several guidelines in mind:

1. The intensity of a person's grief is affected by the nature of his or her relationship to the person or object that has been lost, prior experiences with loss, cultural and ethnic background, gender, age, circumstances surrounding the death or loss, access to social supports, the person's usual coping patterns, and so on.

2. In order to grieve successfully, an individual must work through certain tasks or phases such as accepting the reality that the person or object is gone forever; confronting, experiencing, and coming to terms with the emotions and conflicts associated with the loss; constructing a life without the loved person or object; reinvesting emotional energy in other relationships and activities; and honoring the memory of the lost person or object. These tasks are, of course, overlapping and the grieving individual will revisit each one many times before achieving a satisfactory adjustment.

3. The initial and most intense feelings of grief will slowly diminish in six months to a year, but some level of grieving may continue for three to five years (or even longer). Time is the great healer. With time and the support of family and friends, most people are able deal with their loss without the professional assistance.

Not infrequently, significant personal growth occurs as a person deals successfully with grief. An individual may, for example, uncover previously unknown strengths, grow in self-confidence and competence, discover new areas of interest, and form new and rewarding relationships. People can and do learn valuable lessons about life and living from their misfortunes. It has been said that experience is the best teacher. Although experience is an effective teacher, experience is not a good teacher. A good teacher would never give the test before providing the lesson.

4. Support groups can be helpful to many who are struggling with a loss. These groups can offer advice about day-to-day tasks such as handling finances or taking on new household tasks and provide emotional support and a safe place where the grieving person can talk about the loss and learn that their emotions and feelings are a normal part of the grieving process. Many who are grieving find comfort and strength in their religious beliefs and rituals and in a faith community.

5. Sometimes the normal grieving and healing process stalls and the grieving person develops dysfunctional behavior or sinks into depression. In these situations, clinical interventions are appropriate. This usually begins with *supportive counseling* which would consist of active listening, encouraging the client to talk about their feelings, providing information about the grieving process, helping the person to think through and complete important tasks of living (e.g., handling legal matters, filing insurance claims), and guiding and encouraging the client to resume their roles and responsibilities such as managing the home, returning to job, budgeting, paying bills, and so on.

As the client makes some progress in accepting the loss and resuming usual activities, the social worker might then help him or her to remember positive experiences from before the loss occurred. For example, if the client is grieving the loss of her husband, the worker might help her to recall and appreciate their good times together by viewing and talking about photo albums or by visiting places that were special to her husband. Some clients use art, stories, poems, and music as a means of getting in touch with their feelings and honoring the person they have lost. *Guided mourning* is a cognitive-behavioral approach in which the grieving client is encouraged to recall the details of the loss experience and to find appropriate ways to say good-bye through ritual and journaling.

6. When very intense and complicated grief reactions are giving rise to serious psychological problems or affecting a person's marriage or family, some form of individual, couple, or family therapy and/or medical intervention is needed. Some individuals suppress or hide their grief or deny the pain of a loss. If they do not work through the normal grieving process, their mental health may be adversely affected years after the loss. In such situations an approach termed *regrief therapy* may be used to activate or restart the grieving process and help the individual to relive, confront, and resolve the loss experience.

Selected Bibliography

Hooyman, Nancy, and Betty Kramer. *Living Through Loss: Interventions Across the Life Span.* New York: Columbia University, 2008.

Pomeroy, Elizabeth. *The Grief Assessment and Intervention Workbook.* Belmont, CA: Brooks/Cole, 2009

Walsh-Burke, Katherine. *Grief and Loss.* Boston: Allyn & Bacon, 2006.

Worden, J. William. *Grief Counseling and Grief Therapy*, 4th ed. New York: Springer, 2008.

15.17   THE CLIENT WITH CONCERNS RELATED TO SPIRITUALITY AND RELIGION

Various surveys suggest that about 90 percent of the adults in the United States believe in a God and for a majority of these, religion is important to how they live their lives. Many of those who are not drawn to organized religion and many of those who do not believe in a God strive to nurture their spirituality. Thus, if a social worker serves a cross-section of the population, religion and or spirituality will be of some significance to most of his or her clients. Yet, many social workers feel poorly prepared to discuss these matters with clients.

Social workers, psychologists, and other professional helpers are often taught to avoid or sidestep discussions of religion with their clients. Folk wisdom also warns against discussing religion (and politics) with friends because these discussions so often turn into arguments that strain the relationship. So, how should a social worker respond to clients concerns that are intertwined with their religion, spirituality, and faith? On the one hand, spirituality and religion will be of importance to many clients and possibly a valuable resource to the helping process. On the other hand, an attempt to explore these aspects of a client's life carries some risk of alienating the client or perhaps giving the appearance of proselytizing. Handling this practice dilemma requires sensitivity and knowledge.

Most people in the world would not, and probably could not, speak of their spirituality as separate from their religion. However, making such a distinction is fairly common in the United States and it is a useful one because some individuals appear to have an active spiritual life but engage in few religious practices. And some individuals participate in religious activities without seeming to possess a deep spirituality.

Spirituality is especially difficult to define because it is deeply personal and unique to each individual. Even if two people practice the same religion, their spirituality will differ. The word *spirituality* has its origin in images of the invisible wind, or the "breath of God." For many, **spirituality** is their connection to a higher power or ineffable presence, which many name God. It involves awareness or a mindfulness of the mystery, beauty, and awesomeness inherent in human life and the universe. Spirituality has been variously described as an inward journey, a holy longing, a yearning for meaning, one's enduring values, the essence of one's character, the way one lives his or her life, how a person channels his or her inner unrest and desires, one's lived experience with the mystery of life, and that which puts life in our life. The idea of mystery is a common theme in people's attempt to describe their spirituality. In this context, mystery refers to a dimension or a level of experience and awareness that the person knows to be real but is beyond description and understanding.

Spirituality is the ultimate source of all religion. A **religion** is a set of beliefs, traditions, stories, rituals, and practices that support and sustain spiritual growth and offer some answers to the persistent questions of life, such as: Who am I? What is the purpose of my life? How should I live my life? Is the universe a friendly place? Why does evil exist? Why does goodness exist? What happens when we die? How am I to pray or communicate with my God?

We are drawn to spirituality and religion because, deep within, we have a sense that we are somehow adrift, incomplete, and lack wholeness. We seek an anchor or a foundation as we encounter and cope with life's challenges. For many people, religion and or spirituality provide a sense of meaning, direction, hope, and a moral compass. A religion can help people live creatively and peacefully with troublesome realities such as mortality, pain, grief, despair, and outrage at the injustice and cruelty of life. For others, however, their experiences with religion and their spiritual struggles are a source of inner turmoil, family conflicts, shame, and guilt. At its best, a religion can transform people's lives for the better. At its worst, a religion can impede human progress and give rise to a narrow-mindedness and intolerance.

Below we offer background information and guidelines for the beginning-level practitioner who has clients for whom spirituality and/or religion is related to their concerns:

1. Examine your own experiences with and attitudes toward religion and spirituality. Be alert to any presumptions or prejudices that may limit your ability to serve clients who have beliefs different from your own. An effective social worker has the capacity to accept and respect persons with strong religious beliefs and also those with none at all. Addressing issues and concerns related to a client's religion and spirituality requires of the social worker a high degree of self-understanding and self-discipline (see Item 16.3).

2. Approach these concerns much as you would approach matters related to a client's culture (see Item 8.10). A person's religion is, in fact, like a culture in that it is a lens through which the client will view, understand, and interpret life's experiences. A client's religion or spirituality can influence what the client defines to be a problem, its cause, and its solution. It includes a person's definitions of right and wrong, as well as their moral standards that are often rooted in a religious or spiritual orientation. A religion, like a culture, will seem reasonable and common sense to the person immersed in that religion.

3. It is important for social workers and human services programs to build working relationships with a variety of local clergy, leaders of faith communities, and trained spiritual directors so that these individuals can be consulted on how best to approach especially complex issues related to clients' religion or spirituality. When a client's concern is primarily within the realm of religion, faith, and spiritually, and therefore outside the domain of professional social work, the social worker should refer that client to the appropriate religious or spiritual counselor or clergy person.

4. If the client wishes to discuss spiritual and religious matters that are related to his or her concerns, the social worker must demonstrate a readiness to do so and be at ease with the topic. If that openness is not apparent, clients may withhold important information because they fear that their beliefs will be misunderstood or dismissed as irrelevant. The social worker must display an accepting and nonjudgmental attitude but this can be a challenge if the client's beliefs seem highly unusual or harmful. The worker must not redefine a client's spiritual or religious concerns and struggles as merely a psychological issue or problem.

5. During the data-gathering and assessment phase, the social worker should do at least a cursory exploration of the client's spiritual and religious beliefs and practices in order to determine whether the client's presenting concern is tied to his or her spirituality and/or religion and to identify possible client strengths and helping resources. Simple and straightforward inquiries will usually work—for example: What do I need to know about your values and beliefs to better understand what is really important to you? How do you find encouragement and strength during difficult times? Is religion and spirituality a part of your life? Are you a member of a church, synagogue, mosque, temple, or a faith community? The nature of the client's responses to such exploratory questions will dictate if a more in-depth assessment is necessary and appropriate.

In some situations it may be necessary to probe more deeply. For example, a practitioner in direct practice (e.g., counseling, case management) might ask specific questions about the client's spirituality and/or religious beliefs and background when the client is experiencing troublesome thoughts and feelings, such as guilt, regret, grief, despair, and meaninglessness and when the client is struggling with a moral dilemma. Client statements such as the following illustrate these situations: "I feel like a failure as a parent because none of my children go to church." "I have hurt so many people; I need to make amends for the harm I have caused." "My life is empty and meaningless." "I wish I had some type of faith, but I don't know how to develop one." "The people in my 12-step program talk about their Higher Power, but I'm not sure I even have one." "So often, I pray that my illness will be cured, but my medical condition is getting worse." "As I approach my death, I wonder if there is an afterlife." "My daughter is under the influence of evil spirits." "I want to forgive my father for what he did, but I am consumed by bitterness and festering with anger."

The social worker in indirect practice (e.g., community organization, administration, program management) must understand the religious beliefs, traditions, and practices common to an agency, neighborhood, or a community. This knowledge is needed in order to develop programs and policies that are respectful and relevant to the people who are to benefit from an agency's programs.

6. The numinous mystery or power that is named God (or another sacred name) cannot be described in words and is, by definition, beyond the grasp of the human mind. Nevertheless, people use words and concepts and form images as they think about and speak of God. Even those who do not believe in a God will possess some notion that describes the God they have rejected as fiction. People's images and ideas about God vary widely.

When a client is troubled about his or her relationship to God, it may be prove helpful to encourage him or her to critically examine his or her image of God and consider how and when these images were formed. This can be important because it is through this image that he or she relates to God and depending on how God is conceived, it can cause him or her to feel loved or rejected, secure or fearful, accepting or intolerant. For example, some individuals may imagine God in very personal terms and perhaps as somewhat like a nearby and caring parent. Others may conceive of God as an impersonal and remote power or energy. Descriptions may range from God as father, mother, or brother to abstractions like "pure being," "ultimate concern," and "the something more." In general, people's various images and notions of God will tend to emphasize either immanence or transcendence. *Immanence* refers to God as within and around us whereas *transcendence* views God as beyond and outside the world as we know it.

7. It is often during a personal crisis or a time of painful self-examination, that people realize that they are in need to cultivate a deeper spirituality and find a better way of living their life. When working with a client who is seeking a more meaningful spiritual life, it may be helpful to discuss the difference between a spiritual search and a spiritual journey. A person on a search is always looking for something more satisfying and always exploring new possibilities. By contrast, a person on a spiritual journey has chosen a particular path and strives to follows that path. A search is often necessary and important but a constant search gives rise to restlessness and dissatisfaction. Spiritual growth can begin only after one commits to a path. In every person's search, there comes a time when, despite unanswered questions and doubts, he or she must step off the diving board and say, in effect: "This is my choice, this is how I choose to live my life." The philosopher Kierkegaard called this choice the "leap of faith." The path chosen must fit the individual's authentic self at the deepest level. Regardless of the path taken, the person must set aside regular time for quiet reflection, solitude, prayer, or meditation. All of the great spiritual traditions and the world religions agree on that point.

The metaphor of a spiritual journey is not meant to suggest that spiritual growth is lineal. Rather, it is circular or a spiral in that the core struggles and life's questions must be revisited and confronted again and again. Spiritual growth involves going deeper within one's self and being truthful and honest with what one finds there. Many will resist this self-examination because they fear what they will learn about themselves. Indeed, the self-understanding that comes from prayer and meditation can be a source of discomfort. Still others are ambivalent about pursuing spiritual growth because they fear that a deeper and authentic spirituality will demand changes in their lifestyle and priorities that they are not prepared to make. In many ways, spiritual growth is a process of changing one's perspectives, of seeing things in a different way, and letting go of the desire for control, power, possessions, and prestige. The fear of letting go is the greatest barrier to spiritual growth.

8. At a fundamental level, both spirituality and religion have to do with our choices and distinguishing the important from the unimportant, the lasting from the fleeting, and the ends from the means. Choices have consequences and different choices have different consequences. The importance of our choices is captured in a Native American parable.

> A grandfather sought to teach his grandson an important lesson about how to live his life. The grandfather told his eager young listener that every person has two wolves inside and the two wolves are engaged in an on going fight for dominance. One is the wolf of generosity, honesty compassion, contentment, and justice. The other is the wolf of selfishness, deceitfulness, hatred, and greed. "Which one will win?" asked the grandson? The grandfather replied, "Whichever wolf we feed."

This story teaches us that even the small choices that we make every day will have consequences and a cumulative effect that will orient our life in one direction or another. If, for example, we "feed" our tendency to be self-centered, we gradually become a selfish person. If, on the other hand, we "feed" our desire to be honest and kind, that is the sort of person we will become. Our spirituality is displayed in our choices and in how we live our out life.

Striving for intellectual honesty and for moral integrity are prerequisites to developing an authentic spirituality. The individual must be true to his or her conscience and adhere to what he or she believes to be true and right. To depart from one's core beliefs and to violate one's moral code precludes achieving a sense of contentment and wholeness and will often result in a loss of self-respect and feelings of guilt, shame, and remorse.

Spiritual growth is a life-long process and never a quick fix for personal problems. Neither is it a solitary activity. Rather, it is mostly communal in the sense that one's deepest questions can only be honestly examined when in dialogue with others. Self-scrutiny requires the support and guidance of others and especially from persons who are experienced in living a spiritual life for they can help the beginner avoid discouragement, self-absorption, self-deception, and spiritual arrogance. Religious institutions are centers of spiritually and exist to cultivate spiritual living. While composed of and led by persons who are very human and flawed, religious organizations are the primary means of passing on spiritual wisdom and are an invaluable resource.

Spiritual growth involves cultivating a sense of gratitude and thankfulness for whatever life offers us. Ironically, it is often the people who face great challenges or suffering who develop this sense of gratitude for gratitude involves understanding ourselves and accepting our limits. Contrary to the assumptions of our can-do culture and the teachings of some self-help gurus, not everything is possible if we only think positive and work hard. We have real limitations such as those set by age, intelligence, temperament, physical abilities, and the like. We need to be honest with ourselves, recognize both our strengths and our weaknesses, and then strive to be all that we can be within the circumstances and conditions that are beyond our control.

9. Much like those who belong to an ethnic or cultural minority group, many who are religious and spiritual must struggle to live in two worlds and negotiate, socially and economically, within an environment they often perceive as foreign, unsympathetic, and sometimes hostile to their way of life. When people feel that their cherished values, beliefs, and practices are being threatened, they may strike out at the perceived threat. Or they may refuse to participate in the social, school, and community activities they view as threatening. Parents, especially, will take action to protect their children from societal influences they perceive as destructive to their children's spiritual well-being.

Appreciate the dilemmas faced by deeply religious and/or spiritually oriented individuals as they try to live, work, and raise a family within a social environment that often undermines their cherished beliefs and values. The dominant values of U.S. society are materialism, consumerism, competition, and individualism. By contrast, authentic religion and spirituality emphasize a very different set of values and virtues, such as honesty, truthfulness, justice, humility, modesty, compassion, reconciliation, forgiveness, and service to others.

10. The usual challenges of direct social work practice are compounded when the client's presenting problem involves a clash between his or her conscience or personal moral code and a civil code. Consider, for example, that for one person a particular action is immoral but legal (e.g., war, abortion, blood transfusion) whereas, for another individual, an illegal action is morally right (e.g., refusing to pay taxes that support a war, abusive punishment in child-rearing). Helping a client think through and resolve such conflicts between one's moral principles and the law of the land may call for consultation with religious or spiritual leaders who have an in-depth understanding of the client's moral reasoning and in some cases, the advice of an attorney.

11. A social worker faces a challenging situation when a client's religious and/or spiritual beliefs and practices are unhealthy and harmful to the client or to others. In such cases, the social worker can at least try to help the client examine the observable effects and consequences of these beliefs and practices. It must be recognized, however, that people hold tightly to their core beliefs and values and are not easily swayed by what others may view as reason and logic.

A healthy religion or spirituality recognizes that humans are complex with many interrelated dimensions (i.e., physical, spiritual, psychological, emotional, intellectual, sexual, social). All human dimensions are valued, not just the spiritual. There is an emphasis on being fully human on the qualities of wholeness, integration, and connectedness.

By contrast, an unhealthy spirituality or religion is unbalanced, fragmented, or one-sided. It can cause harm to one's body, mental health, social relationships, and community. It can fracture families and friendships and sow the seeds of intolerance, violence, or oppression. When attempting to decide whether a particular spirituality or a religion is healthy or unhealthy, consider these questions: Does it make for joy or fear, hope or helplessness, self-worth or shame, openness or rigidity, freedom or constraint, intellectual honesty or self-deception? Does it encourage, lift up and support the person or does it drag the person down? Is the person helped or haunted by his or her beliefs?

12. When a client is an active member of a faith community (e.g., a church, synagogue, mosque), that community may be a potential resource and support to the helping process. Depending on the client's concern or need, the possible use of this resource might be explored. However, it is important to understand that some individuals will describe themselves as belonging to a certain religion or faith community when, in fact, they have only a tenuous connection to it. Thus, a client's self-identification with a particular religion or faith tradition does not necessarily signify that he or she will have access to the informal social support network or other resources usually associated with active membership (see Item 12.6).

The social worker should never assume that he or she knows about a client' beliefs and practices when all he or she really knows is that the client identifies with a particular religion. Within most religions, there are subgroups or branches that differ in a variety of ways. For example, within Christianity there are numerous denominations and within each of these there is usually further divisions along a conservative–progressive continuum. Not infrequently, a religion's traditions and practices are intertwined with a particular nationality, culture, or ethnic group.

13. A social worker must be prepared to respond to questions a client may ask about the worker's religion or spirituality. A client may have several motives for asking such questions. As a general rule, people are most at ease with those who have beliefs, values, and life experiences similar to their own. Thus, a client may want to know if the social worker is capable of understanding certain spiritual and religious beliefs and practices and perhaps, whether the worker is accepting or disapproving. Some clients may ask about the worker's religion simply because they are curious about how the worker has approached the questions of life's meaning. Still other clients may be trying to manipulate the worker into taking their side in some interpersonal or family conflict. How a social worker responds to such questions will depend on why the client is asking and how various answers might affect the professional relationship and their ongoing work together. (See Item 8.4 for guidance on responding to personal questions.)

Selected Bibliography

Becvar, Dorothy, ed. *The Family, Spirituality, and Social Work.* Binghamton, New York: Haworth, 1998.
Canda, Edward, and Elizabeth Smith, eds. *Transpersonal Perspectives on Spirituality in Social Work.* New York: Haworth, 2001.
Derezotes, David. *Spiritually-Oriented Social Work Practice.* Boston: Allyn & Bacon, 2006.
Pargament, Kenneth. *Spiritually Integrated Psychotherapy.* Washington, DC: American Psychological Association, 2007.
Van Hook, Mary, Beryl Hugen, and Marian Aguilar. *Spirituality within Religious Traditions in Social Work.* Belmont, CA: Brooks/Cole, 2002.

15.18 THE CLIENT WHO IS IMPACTED BY THE CRIMINAL JUSTICE SYSTEM

In every practice setting, social workers will meet people who have had their lives changed and disrupted by crime. Some are the victims of crime, some have committed crimes, and some have a child, spouse, parent, or friend serving a sentence in a correctional program. Increasingly, social workers are employed in probation and parole, juvenile courts, pre-release centers, halfway houses, diversion programs, and prisons. In these settings they learn first hand about the complexity and problems within the criminal justice system.

The United States has a serious crime problem and an extremely high rate of incarceration. With about 5 percent of the world's population, the United States has nearly 25 percent of the world's prisoners. At times, one of every one hundred adults is in jail or prison while many others are on probation and parole. Of those who are incarcerated, most are males and most are economically disadvantaged. Most of the incarcerated have low levels or education and few job skills. About one-half of those entering a prison are between the ages of 18 and 27. Many are non-violent drug offenders. A disproportionate number of those in prison are members of a racial or ethnic minority. Many, but certainly not all, grew up in fractured or dysfunctional families.

The Victim.   Many of the clients known to social workers have been harmed (physically, emotionally, and economically) by a crime such as assault, rape, homicide, robbery, fraud, drunken driving, identity theft, and extortion. Whole neighborhoods and communities are impacted by crime. For example, those living in a high crime neighborhood are often afraid to leave their homes to visit friends, do their shopping, and attend school. Local businesses may be challenged to continue operating when their expenses are increased by robberies and extortion. The victims of crime have a very personal interest in the operation of the criminal justice system and in the actions and decisions of those who work within this system. The victims of crime typically want increased police protection, stricter laws, stern courts, and they want offenders convicted and imprisoned so they cannot harm others.

When working with a client who has been injured or traumatized by a crime, the social worker should be aware that most states have some type of a victim compensation program. If an individual meets the eligibility requirements, such a program may provide assistance in paying for medical expenses, mental health counseling, loss of income, and funeral or burial expenses. Individuals who have been traumatized by crime will usually benefit from counseling, therapy, and self-help or support groups.

Increasingly, communities are developing programs of *restorative justice* that focus attention on the personal harm caused by crime rather than only on the laws that have broken. Such programs are designed to give the victim an opportunity to speak with the offender and voice how they have been harmed. The program gives the offender an opportunity to learn about the consequences of his or her crime, take responsibility, provide restitution, and offer an apology. Programs of restorative justice promote healing by both the victim and the offender. They are a supplement to ordinary court activity and punishments but not a substitute.

The Offender.   Crimes are committed by many different types of people and for a wide variety of motives. A significant number of crimes are related, directly or indirectly, to the use of drugs and alcohol and to the distribution of illegal drugs. Some crimes are very deliberate and calculated acts. Others are thoughtless and impulsive. Some people who commit a crime, even minor crime, experience intense feelings of guilt and remorse. On the other extreme are those who seem devoid of guilt and only regret that they got caught. Some who have committed even terrible crimes appear to be fundamentally good, truthful, and compassionate people. Others consistently display a tendency toward dishonesty, violence, and even cruelty.

Social workers employed in non-correctional settings and also private practitioners will occasionally have a client who is arrested and drawn into the criminal justice system. When a worker's client (e.g., an individual who has been receiving counseling from the worker) is arrested, the worker should do what is possible to make sure that the client secures competent legal representation. If the accused is held in jail, a visit and discussion by the social worker may assist him or her to better cope with the situation and make good decisions about how to proceed.

Those who are poor are at a distinct disadvantage within the judicial and criminal justice systems. Because they cannot afford a private defense attorney, they are dependent on an overburdened public defender. If offered the opportunity to be released on bail, they may not be able to raise the money needed for bail and consequently, they may spend months in jail awaiting their trial.

Classification.   All who enter the correctional system are subjected to some type of assessment and classification. For example, on one extreme are *situational offenders*, those for whom the criminal act was unexpected and out of character. On the other extreme are the *habitual offenders* or career criminals who have a decades-long history of criminal behavior. A career criminal may view time in jail as simply the "cost of doing business." The situational offender is probably a good candidate for rehabilitation; the habitual offender is probably not.

Those who administer the correctional system have little choice but to use classifications and categories in order to manage programs and prisoners. However, when a person is placed in and treated as a category or a class, individualization is sacrificed. Correctional programs seldom have capacity or resources to adequately address such problems as inadequate education, lack of job skills, lack of reading ability and language skills, substance abuse, learning disabilities, mental disorders, and so on.

Probation and Parole. If an individual is placed on *probation or parole* he or she must maintain regular contact with a probation or parole officer and adhere to a set of rules and conditions such as: keeping the officer informed of living arrangement and employment status; at the discretion of the officer, submit to drug testing, a body search, and/or home search; avoid contact with known felons; stay away from places that sell alcohol or display pornography; secure and utilize treatment for an addiction or mental health problem; avoid contact with the victim of the crime; and adhere to a curfew. A violation of these rules may result in the imposition of an additional sentence or a return to prison.

Prison Environments. The physical and social surroundings of a prison will vary greatly depending upon whether it is a minimum-security facility or a maximum-security prison. When an individual enters a *maximum-security prison* he or she encounters a frightening and disorienting environment. These prisons are designed to hold persons for whom violence, intimidation, and manipulation are a way of life. Within such an institution one finds a status hierarchy, a code of conduct, and an economic system that governs the distribution of goods, services, and opportunities. Like all people, inmates want to be respected and taken seriously, but in this degrading environment being feared by others is a substitute for genuine respect. A new inmate may want to just serve out the sentence and be left alone. But that seldom works. New inmates are typically tested and challenged and they usually need to join a group for self-protection. Inmate groups typically divide along racial and ethnic lines, or by gang affiliation.

By contrast, a minimum-security correctional facility will typically have a very different atmosphere. The inmates usually feel safer and have more privacy, freedom, and choice within the prison. They also have more access to visits by friends and family.

The Impact of Imprisonment. Most people sent to a correctional facility are eventually released after serving a sentence. They then return to their community and to their family, if they have one. Ideally, their time of incarceration is a time of positive change and rehabilitation, a time of making the best of a very difficult situation, and a time to prepare for life that follows prison. For that to occur, two elements must be present. First, the facility must offer a wide variety of educational, training, and therapeutic programs. Second, the inmate must have the motivation and the capacity to make use of those programs.

All too often, time spent in a prison is a negative and damaging experience that reinforces and solidifies criminal thinking and activity. It causes many to feel embittered and angry. Many inmates come to believe that they have been treated unfairly when they hear of others who committed the same crime but received a lesser sentence.

The time spent in prison will often weaken the inmate's already fragile ties to family. When finally released and returned to the community, the ex-cons are usually poorly prepared for the job market and are frequently feared and avoided by ordinary citizens. Having a criminal record makes it difficult to find a decent job, obtain housing, and to enter into a positive and helpful social network.

Of critical importance are rehabilitation programs that help inmates examine and understand their behavioral patterns and habitual ways of thinking (see the following paragraph); identify their personal goals; and construct a framework of moral and ethical principles to be used in making choices and decisions. For many inmates, reducing the chances of recidivism means making significant changes in their lifestyle and social network. Once released, they need to create and maintain a set of healthy and pro-social friendships that provide guidance, encouragement, and support.

For some prison inmates, faith-based programs are attractive and beneficial. Such programs can offer the individual a new set of values, a new way of understanding his or her life, and a sense of purpose, hope, and identity. When the individual is released, these programs can provide valuable social support and encouragement, help in finding a job and housing, and counseling.

Criminal Thinking.   It is important to recognize that many who are repeat offenders and career criminals have a way of thinking that is significantly different from that of situational offenders and the typical law-abiding citizens. The existence of this pattern often explains why they persist in criminal activity. Basically, *criminal thinking* is a set of erroneous beliefs and distorted values. Unless this pattern can be changed, the chances for rehabilitation are quite limited. Below are the key components of criminal thinking:

- Playing down or dismissing the seriousness of their crimes and blaming others or circumstances for their bad choices and behavior.
- A lack of empathy and compassion for their victims. They experience little or no remorse or guilt for the harm they inflict on others.
- A belief that their victims got what they deserve because the victims are naïve, stupid, weak, and of no value.
- A persistent belief that they are above the law and can violate laws because the laws are stupid and unfair and because they have a right to take a share of the good things in life, if necessary, by fraud or force.
- Frequent use of lies, deception, manipulation, and intimidation to get what they want. They have no hesitation to use, abuse, and discard people when it serves their purposes.
- Their manipulations often take the form of charming and endearing themselves to others by appearing to be helpful and generous so as to win trust and secure the emotional leverage they need in order to exert influence and control.
- A strong desire to exert power and control over others. When not in control, they feel nervous, weak, and frustrated. Interpersonal conflicts are resolved by threats and shouting rather than by respectful discussions and compromise.
- Impulsivity in decision making and taking action without anticipating or appreciating the likely consequences. Decisions are made in response to current circumstances and opportunities rather than on the basis of fundamental moral and ethical principles. In many cases, this mode of decision-making style reflects a real lack of reasoning and critical-thinking skills.
- They have trouble sticking with a plan and following through on the commitments and promises they have voiced. They are easily influenced and swayed by the current or immediate situation.
- A belief—often based on experience—that they can get away with their crimes and are too smart to get caught. Over time they may become overconfident and feel invulnerable. When their self-confidence begins to weaken, drugs and alcohol are often used to pump up their courage or cover their fears.

For additional information on distorted thinking patterns and persons who are manipulative and dangerous, see Items 10.8, 10.9, and 13.7.

The Offender's Family and Children.   When an individual is convicted of a crime and sent to a correctional program or prison, his or her family usually experiences emotional turmoil and economic hardships. Feelings of frustration, grief, loss, shame, embarrassment, anger, guilt, self-blame, and regret are common. Some family members may be angry with the offender for getting in trouble while others feel guilt because they could not keep the offender out of trouble, or perhaps because they did not protect him or her from getting caught. Many family members worry about the offender's safety and mental health, especially if he or she has been sent to a maximum-security prison.

Separation by imprisonment places great strain on a marriage or partner relationship. The spouse or partner left behind may seek professional help in deciding whether to pursue a divorce and end the relationship. They may need help with practical problems such as finding a less-expensive place to live, securing health care because the person in prison has now lost the heath insurance utilized by the family, adjusting the family budget, arranging child care, finding a job, and so on.

Children react in various ways to the incarceration of a parent. For most, it will be a troubling, confusing, and upsetting experience. For some, however, such as those who have been mistreated by the parent, the parent's removal from the home may allow them to feel safer than ever before. A variety of factors will determine how a child is affected. These variables include: the child's relationship and closeness to the incarcerated parent, age at time of separation, temperament and personality, prior separations, length of separation, strength of family, reactions by the other parent and family members, nature of parent's crime, reactions to crime by community, and so on. These children often experience humiliation, teasing from other children, social isolation, difficulties in school, and various other problems such as mood swings, developmental delays and regressions, depression, outbursts of anger, and violence. Studies suggest that the children of imprisoned parents are at increased risk of poor school performance, school dropout, drug abuse, early pregnancy, and gang involvement. A social worker in contact with these children should help them express their pain and concerns and provide or secure for them appropriate counseling. Mentoring programs and Big Brother/Big Sister programs are important for these children.

Visiting an Inmate. When a social worker is providing services to the family of an inmate, the worker needs to give attention to issues related to visitation. As a general rule, visits by family and friends help the inmate cope with the loneliness and stress of confinement because it gives them something to look forward to. Regular contact with family helps retain some semblance of family bonds and social support. Encouragement from family is an added incentive for the inmate to make use of rehabilitation programs and prepare for a life after prison. Visiting can reassure the family that the person they care for is doing as well as can be expected under the circumstances. Visiting helps the family work through their mixed-up thoughts and feelings about what has happened. Visits may be helpful to the family as they face important decisions such as those related to personal finance, housing, and care of the children. Visits also help the family visualize and anticipate the challenges that lie ahead when the inmate is released.

The effect on children visiting their parents in prison has not been well researched. Needless-to-say, the physical structure of the prison and the security procedures can be frightening to a child. It is disturbing to see one's parent in that environment. However, many child-welfare specialists suggest that visiting by a child is usually beneficial because the visits help the child recognize, understand, and gradually accept the realities of the situation. It is better for a child to struggle with and adjust to a painful reality (e.g., Daddy is in prison because he hurt someone) than to live with a fantasy, a lie, or deception (e.g., Daddy is a soldier and in a foreign country).

Visitation by children is especially important when it is the mother who is incarcerated. Frequent visits with the mother can reassure the child that he or she has not been abandoned and is not responsible for the mother leaving home. Seeing his or her children reassures the inmate that the children are okay and can be an additional incentive to make good use of available training and rehabilitation programs as preparation for an eventual release.

If the child's caretaker is unsure about whether a child should visit the parent in prison, he or she should request guidance from prison personnel (e.g., prison psychologist, prison social worker) and/or specialist in child development.

A child visitor, like all visitors, must be on the prison's list of approved visitors. The parent or foster parent who will be taking the child to the prison should visit the inmate one or two times before taking the child there so that the caretaker knows what is involved and can prepare the child.

All who wish to visit an inmate, whether the visitor is a family member, friend, or a social worker, must submit the required application to visit. Only those on the list of approved visitors can enter the facility. Persons with a criminal record may not be given permission to visit. Most institutions allow visiting only on certain days and times. The rules that govern visitation can be obtained by mail. Most jails and prisons have a website describing these rules and procedures. Visitors should know the rules before they arrive at the facility. The visitation rules in a maximum-security facility are very strict. For example:

- Only those listed on a pre-approved visitor's list are allowed to visit. The falsification of an application to visit will result in the suspension of the visiting privilege.
- Visitors must clear a metal detector (shoes with a steel shank, jewelry, and bras containing wire will set off the alarms and may need to be removed before a visit).
- Visitors are subject to the search of their person, belongings, and vehicle.
- Visitors are prohibited from bringing food items, cameras, cell phones, and other electronic equipment to the visiting area.
- Visitors and inmates must remain seated during the visit.
- Visitors are not permitted access to inmate restrooms.
- Visitors caught with illegal contraband will have their visiting privileges suspended and may be referred for possible criminal prosecution.
- Visitors who use inappropriate, foul, or abusive language will be removed from the visiting area.
- Sexually provocative behavior and sexual contact between inmates and visitors such as petting, fondling, prolonged kissing, and bodily contact are prohibited.
- Visitors must be fully clothed, buttons and zippers must remain fastened, female visitors must wear a bra and undergarments.
- Children who are visiting are not allowed to use restrooms without supervision by the visiting parent or another approved adult.

It is important for all visitors to understand that prison officials view visiting as a privilege and not a right. Moreover, they are usually ambivalent about visitation. On the positive side, visitation improves inmate morale and creates a better prison environment. On the negative side, visitation programs are difficult to manage and visitors are the main source of contraband (e.g., drugs, weapons) entering a prison. Visits can be disappointing and highly emotional. Sometimes a visitor does not show up as the inmate had expected. Sometimes an inmate refuses to meet with the visitor. Sometimes a family argument erupts. Sometimes an inmate will ridicule or humiliate other visitors in the room. Sometimes a last-minute security concern cancels a scheduled visit.

Prison officials are concerned that some of inmates will seek out and cultivate a manipulative relationship with naïve and gullible pen pals, prison ministry personnel, and volunteers who "just want to help." Some inmates convince sympathetic visitors to bring them drugs and money. Some visitors, knowingly or unknowingly, assist inmates to continue operating their criminal enterprises.

Those who intend to visit an inmate should prepare themselves mentally and emotionally before they go. For example, seeing a family member or loved one in shackles and behind glass, bars, and wires can be upsetting. Crying or emotional outbursts by family members make the inmates feel worse than they already do.

Basically there are two types of visits. In a *non-contact visit* the visitor and inmate are separated by glass or wire mesh. In a *contact visit* the visitor and inmate share the same space and are allowed to offer a brief hug and touch.

The space available for visiting varies widely among prisons. However, a visitor should anticipate a lack of privacy and limited space and few activities for small children.

Issues Related to Social Work Records and Confidentiality. If a social worker's client (or a former client) is convicted of a crime, an officer of the court (e.g., a probation officer) may contact the social worker and request information that the officer wants in order to prepare a pre-sentence investigation report. In addition, the defense attorney may request information from the social worker that might help secure a more lenient sentence for the defendant. How is the social worker to respond?

In such situations, the ordinary *rules of client confidentiality* still apply (see Item 10.5). Client data should not be released unless the client has authorized it by signing a proper release of information or a formal court order requires the release of specified information. A judge's routine request for a pre-sentence investigation does not, by itself, authorize a social worker to release client information to the officer of the court.

The same principles on the handling of client records and information will apply if, at a later date, correctional program staff invites a social worker to participate in a case conference aimed at formulating a rehabilitation or treatment plan for a former social work client now in a correctional program.

Selected Bibliography

Alder, Freda, Gerhard Mueller, and William Laufer. *Criminal Justice*, 5th ed. New York: McGraw Hill, 2009.

Coggins, Kim, and J. Eli Fresquez. *Working with Clients in Correctional Settings*. Peosta, IA: eddie owers, 2007.

Council on Crime and Justice. *Children of Incarcerated Parents*. Minneapolis: Council on Crime and Justice. January 2006.

Sharp, Boyd. *Changing Criminal Thinking: A Treatment Program*, 2nd ed. Alexandria, VA: American Correctional Association 2005.

Walsh, Anthony. *Correctional Assessment, Casework, and Counseling*. Alexandria, VA: American Correctional Association, 2006.

Wright, Lois, and Cynthia Seymour. *Working with Children and Families Separated by Incarceration: A Handbook for Child Welfare Agencies*. Washington, DC: Child Welfare League of America, 2000.

15.19   THE CLIENT WHO IS AFFECTED BY WAR

Since 1941, when the United States entered World War II, this country has been at war over 45 percent of that time. When a nation is at war nearly every person and every social institution is affected in some way. At the macro level, U.S. culture has been impacted, for example, by the increased taxes and the allocation of resources to support the war instead of other human needs such as poverty and health care, or by the eroding international status of the United States in the eyes of many throughout the world. At the micro level, it is estimated that during those 70 plus years, nearly 390,000 U.S. military personnel (Army, Navy, Marine, Air Force, Coast Guard) have been killed in combat and more than three times that number have suffered significant physical and mental injuries. Needless to say, the families and friends of those who are killed or injured are also impacted. These countless individuals experience many years or a whole lifetime of pain, grief, and distress (Clancy and Sheafor, 2010, p. 203). All of these people—the dead, the injured and their families, and U.S. society as a whole—are casualties of war.

Social workers, both those in the military and those employed in virtually every type of human services agency, have a role to perform in serving the casualties of war. To effectively address these issues, social workers must understand the stress war places on military personnel and the sacrifices made by family, friends, and other loved ones who remain at home.

STRESS ON INDIVIDUALS AND FAMILIES ASSOCIATED WITH MILITARY SERVICE

In a war, military personnel are called upon to commit acts that challenge conventional notion of morality. If committed by civilian and in other circumstances, these acts would be considered both criminal and immoral. The social worker should understand that those who have experienced the horrors of combat are usually reluctant to talk about it, except possibly with other combat veterans. They may be justifiably proud for having served their country but deep within may not be proud of actions they had taken in order to perform that service (see Killology.com). They sometimes carry vivid and disturbing memories of what they have seen, heard, smelled, tasted, and felt, as well as guilt about what they did and what they failed to do. In the extraordinarily stressful and chaotic environment of combat, military personnel discover many things about themselves. For example, they may have discovered that they could perform under extreme pressure and were surprisingly loyal and devoted to their comrades. On the other hand, they may have discovered that they could be immobilized by fear and were capable of extreme brutality and perhaps other behaviors that they view as shameful. Not infrequently they feel some degree of guilt, regret, and remorse over what they think they should have done, but did not or could not do. Such feelings are especially intense if they feel somehow responsible for the death or injury of a comrade.

It is not uncommon for families and friends to report that the returning veteran has changed and is not the same person who left them for military duty. The veteran of combat may seem distant, detached, and preoccupied or perhaps he or she drinks too much and appears depressed, angry, or reckless. Those coming home from war need the understanding and support of family and friends. However, as supportive as family and friends may want to be, they seldom fully appreciate what the veteran actually experienced and are often unsure of what they should or should not be doing in order to make things better. Both the veteran and his or her family may feel frustrated and confused. They may worry and wonder if they will ever again have a normal life.

SERVICES PROVIDED BY SOCIAL WORKERS

Most social workers, regardless of practice setting, will have some veterans and/or their family members as clients. However, the social workers who are part of the military or employed by the Department of Veterans Affairs (VA) will regularly provide services to this population. The social work skills of referral, case management, counseling, crisis intervention, advocacy, the creation and facilitation of support groups, program development, and community organization are especially relevant to serving this client population.

Evidence-based practice research and guidelines developed by the military and the VA are indispensible resources to the social worker (e.g., Iraq War Clinician Guide, 2004). The following programs and guidelines should be kept in mind by these social workers.

Prevention. Increasingly, efforts are being made to help soldiers and their families anticipate adjustments they will need to make when the person returns from war. For example, the veteran returning home on leave or being discharged should be helped by a social worker to give careful thought to how he or she will handle questions from family members and curious friends about war experiences. If such recall is harmful, he or she should be encouraged to simply announce, "I don't want to talk about the war. So please do not ask me any questions." Family members should be prepared to avoid such questions and to ask others not to discuss these matters unless the subject is introduced by the veteran. However, unless the veteran can find a safe place to talk about these matters (e.g., a support group, individual therapy) he or she will remain at risk for emotional problems.

Preparing family members for the absence of military personnel during a duty tour is another important professional intervention. If a mother or father is to be away from the family for an extended period of time, plans must be made and assistance provided for assuming family roles for parenting and child care, home maintenance, management of the family's finances, and so on. When the serviceperson returns, these roles again must be renegotiated. Failure to attend to these matters is one reason military families experience a high and growing divorce rate. The deployed person's spouse or partner should be encouraged to maintain supportive contact with other service families and perhaps to participate in a formal support group.

Advancing technology is allowing deployed personnel to stay in closer contact with loved ones back home which can help to decrease the number of devastating Dear John/Jane letters announcing the unexpected end of a relationship. Nevertheless, social workers have a role to play in addressing both the maintenance and dissolution of relationships strained by military duty.

Disrupted Families. It is evident that military families experience numerous changes and disruptions while the soldier is away on duty. In addition to dealing with their own issues of coping with separation, family members will worry about the military person's safety, especially if he or she is stationed in a combat zone. However, they can gain some comfort and reassurance through friendships with other families facing similar concerns, an experience a social worker might arrange and facilitate. The family, including older children, should be encouraged to join and participate in support groups so that they have an opportunity to feel understood and supported and know they are not alone in their worries.

When facing deployment, it is critically important for the parents to spend time with their children to explain what is happening and assure the children that they are loved, even though the parent must leave for military duty. Young children, in particular, may sense the parents' anxiety and become anxious themselves or perhaps misinterpret why the deployed parent has gone away and thus feel abandoned. The child's other parent or caretaker should be helped to explain, as well as possible at the child's level of understanding, what has happened and that the parent's departure is not a sign that the child is not loved.

These families are not only missing the person's parenting and other contributions to family life, but usually experience high levels of stress during the deployment. One indicator of this stress is found in a study indicating that child maltreatment was three times greater among Army wives during the husbands' deployment than when not deployed (Savitsky, Illingworth, and DuLaney, 2009). Reduction in income can be another stressor. For families of Reservists or members of the National Guard who had successfully established nonmilitary careers, the income reduction can be substantial and the family's lifestyle severely impacted. Funds simply may not be available, for example, to cover mortgages or car payments to which the family is legally obligated.

Death. Sadly, military personnel are killed in battle or duty-related accidents. Others may die of disease or suicide. Spouses, partners, children, parents, and other loved ones will feel this painful loss for years and possibly for the rest of their lives. Depending on their practice setting, social workers may have a significant role in helping these individuals deal with their immediate crisis and grief reactions, their eventual adjustments, and possible related mental health problems (see Items 13.14 and 15.16).

In addition, suicide is a significant cause of death for military personnel, especially those who have been in combat and those with multiple deployments. It has been estimated that veterans are twice as likely to commit suicide as non-veterans. The method of suicide is frequently by gunshot as these weapons often have been an intimate part of the person's existence while in the military. In addition to the suicide risk factors described in Item 15.7, there are some warning signs that are unique to military veterans: increased frequency of cleaning or handling a weapon, staying up at night to "watch over" the house and a preoccupation with home security measures, frequent visits to military cemeteries, wearing a uniform or part of the uniform in civilian life, contacting old military friends to say good-bye, speaking frequently about the honor of military service, obsession with news coverage of the war, and becoming overprotective of children.

Physical Injury. The tactics and armor used in modern warfare result in fewer combat deaths than in previous wars. Concurrently, there has been a dramatic increase in number of individuals who have survived combat but are left with a severe disability. Social workers in VA hospital settings will be part of the team working with the veterans during long, painful, and frustrating periods of rehabilitation. Adjusting to disfigurement, amputations, use of prosthetics, and changes in self-image are always serious challenges. The veteran's loved ones will struggle in their acceptance and adjustment to these same concerns (see Item 15.10).

Increasingly, it is recognized that many veterans experience Traumatic Brain Injury (TBI) (see Item 15.9). Depending on the location of the injury in the brain, the veteran may develop a pattern of rigid black-or-white thinking, experience seizures, memory difficulty, and other cognitive

functioning problems. Rehabilitation programs can be helpful for persons exper
the social worker should be prepared to link that person to such programs.

Psychological Injury.   There is no such thing as getting used to combat—the
intense the exposure the more serious its impact. Some veterans will say somet
I was in combat and it didn't affect me." Often associated with that belief is t
strong. I could handle it. I could tough it out. I'm not a whiner." In reality, no or
the effects of combat. It is not a question of whether, but rather when the effect
stress and trauma will surface. For some veterans, the effects are delayed and do
years later.

The social worker should be alert for the cluster of symptoms that signal
Stress Disorder (PTSD), that is, intrusion, avoidance, and hyperactivity. The form
PTSD include sleep disturbance, intrusive thoughts, flashbacks, nightmares, nigh
reaction, survivor guilt, emotional numbness, wanting to be alone, eruptions of r
ing isolated, inability to concentrate, anxiety, depression, and sexual dysfunction.
with these distressing symptoms many with PTSD will medicate themselves
drugs. The seriousness of PTSD and its symptoms will vary from person to pers
a loved one with PTSD is extraordinarily stressful.

Flashbacks are one of the many delayed reactions to combat stress. They a
ening experience. If you are working with a veteran who is in the midst of a fl
wait for the flashback to be over. Given time, they will come out of it but afterw
angry, scared, and embarrassed that it happened. It might be helpful to encourag
view PTSD and a symptom like a flashback as something like an infected cut th
and periodically breaks open. This infection needs to be cleaned out before it ca
Talking about the trauma is the necessary, but painful, cleaning process.

Sleep disturbance and nightmares are other common symptoms of PTSD.
will try to avoid sleeping in order to escape recurring nightmares. Some will stay
can sleep only in daylight because their experiences of combat in the dark of nigh
ly terrifying. A long-term lack of sleep has a devastating effect on one's physi
health and exacerbates other PTSD symptoms.

If the PTSD is not recognized and treated it can have long-term negative e
son's life and functioning (see Item 13.14). An individual with PTSD is at increa
stance abuse, committing domestic violence, and suicide. Treatment of PTSD u
the application of cognitive and behavior modification therapies, psychotropi
arousal reduction and anxiety management stress reduction techniques, or exp
In exposure therapy, a specially trained social worker or other therapist encoura
clients to repeatedly talk about their traumatic experiences and confront the ver
feelings that are trying to avoid. The goal of this therapy is to gradually gain contr
ing thoughts and learn that they need not be afraid of those memories. Support gr
of veterans are another effective means of helping veterans come to terms with th
and make a successful transition back into civilian life.

Other conditions with a strong emotional component to which social wor
alert when serving military veterans are chronic pain, sexual trauma, and sl
Further, the government's "Don't Ask, Don't Tell" policy created an added laye
strain on gay and lesbian members of the military who either had to be secretive a
ual orientation or be discharged from the service of their country.

Military to Civilian Transition.   In order to understand some of the adjustme
combat veterans after their discharge from the military it is helpful to think of thi
a loss experience. Even those who voluntarily leave the military may feel ambiva
be glad to be out of harms' way and happy to rejoin their families, but recognize th
giving up a sense of identity, purpose, structure, and comradeship found in the
such factors as giving up one's weapon that has been a constant companion and so
tion is no small matter.

addition, an individual with military experience typically has developed a strong work
l the qualities of self-discipline and goal-directedness. Consequently, they become valued
es in civilian jobs. However, the transition from the military to the civilian employment
an be difficult. For example, the military attitude and job skills may not translate easily
vilian context. Whereas the military is highly regimented and one's work assignments are
of following the orders issued by a superior, in civilian life work assignments are often
and even open to negotiation. Social workers may be able to help veterans anticipate,
ze, and adjust to these different expectations in the work environment.

t present, the United States has an all-volunteer military. By contrast, a military draft
individuals into World War II, the Korean War, and the Vietnam War. Today's military per-
have deliberately chosen to serve their country and many entered the military with an eye
ing it a career, a training ground for civilian jobs, or a route to support for attaining higher
ion. Thus, if an injury forces them out of the military it has also disrupted their career
identity, and sense of belonging. For the veteran's spouse and children, leaving the military
losing the mutual support and sense of community that exists among military families.
ocial and emotional losses add to the crisis and adjustment problems related to a veteran's
al or psychological injury.

Too often the emotional scars from military service make it difficult for many veterans to
on well in the private life. For example, it is estimated that one-third of the adult homeless
ation in the United States are veterans of wars dating back to World War II and the domes-
lence rate in military families is high.

ral.   Veterans often need access to many different services. The VA offers a vast array of
es, including over 50 hospitals and 900 local points of contact. Services in rural areas are
e, although advances in technology are starting to reduce this problem.

Eligibility for veteran-related service is very complex to determine and depends on such
rs as the time and place of one's military assignments, the risks involved in that assignment,
whether the veteran was in the regular military, the National Guard, or the Reserves. Because
rent programs use somewhat different eligibility criteria, it is often a difficult and lengthy
ess for a veteran to identify and enroll in needed services. The social worker should help the
an find needed information and negotiate this complex sometimes frustrating system. One
l entry point for these services is a VA benefits telephone number (1-800-827-1000).
ther first step is to contact a state Office of Veterans Affairs or one of the many local veter-
services organizations (e.g., American Legion, Veterans of Foreign Wars, Vet Center).

Military families, too, should be encouraged to make use of services and programs that will
specially knowledgeable and sensitive to their concerns. These would include, for example,
r military base's Family Assistance Center, Deployment Support Groups, Family Advocacy
gram, Military Medical Clinic, Military Mental Health Services, and Military Chaplains.

lected Bibliography

ncy, Joanne E. and Bradford W. Sheafor, "Social Work with U.S. Casualties of the Middle East Wars" in
    Bradford W. Sheafor, Armando T. Morales, and Malcolm E. Scott, *Social Work: A Profession of
    Many Faces*, 12th ed., Boston: Allyn & Bacon, 2010, pp. 203–217.
q *War Clinician Guide,* 2nd ed. National Center for Post-Traumatic Stress Disorder. http://www.ptsd.va.
    gov/professional/manuals/manual-pdf/iwcg/iraq_clinician_guide_v2.pdf (June 2004)
ngman, Phillip. *Best Care Anywhere: Why VA Health Care Is Better Than Yours*, 2nd ed. Sausalito, CA:
    PoliPoint Press, 2010.
ason, Patience. *Recovering from the War: A Guide for All Veterans, Family Members, Friends and
    Therapists.* High Springs, FL: Patience Press, 1990.
vitsky, Laura, Maria Illingworth, and Megan DuLaney. 2009. "Civilian Social Work: Serving the Military
    and Veteran Populations." *Social Work* 54(4): 327–339, 2009.
healin, Julia M., Lorie T. DeCarvalho, and Edward M. Vega. *Clinician's Guide to Treating Stress after War:
    Education and Coping Interventions for Veterans.* Hoboken, NJ: John Wiley and Sons, 2008.

15.20 THE CLIENT WHO IS AN IMMIGRANT OR REFUGEE

A significant number of the people in need of health and human services have the designation of being an immigrant or refugee; thus, a social worker must acquire at least a basic knowledge of the problems they face and how their special status might affect access and eligibility for human services.

The United States has been described as a country of immigrants and refugees. Nearly all U.S. citizens have a family genealogy that leads back to another nation and culture. Many people reading this book have parents, grandparents, or great-grandparents who were born in another country. Throughout its history, the United States has been a sought-after destination for persons migrating from countries that have fewer freedoms and opportunities. The United States has been a safe haven for those who sought escape from political and religious oppression and from other forms of injustice. This theme is captured by an inscription on the Statue of Liberty:

> *Give me your tired, your poor,*
> *Your huddled masses yearning to breathe free,*
> *The wretched refuse of your teeming shore.*
> *Send these, the homeless, tempest-tossed, to me:*
> *I lift my lamp beside the golden door.*

Those welcoming words and the country's rich immigrant history belie the challenges actually experienced by many who enter the United States as immigrants or refugees. Whether from Europe, Africa, Asia, or parts of the Western Hemisphere, these individuals commonly experience personal, social, and economic problems because of the inherent difficulty of adapting to a new culture; many lack language facility and/or job skills relevant to the American economy. Many live in complete or near poverty. In addition, some encounter hostility because segments of society perceive newcomers as a threat and disruption to the status quo, an added competition for jobs and housing, and an additional tax burden. Social workers often feel caught between a grudging public that wants to deny services to the new arrivals and the immigrants and refugees themselves who often face extraordinary problems and clearly need the help of educational, health, and social programs.

THE IMMIGRANT/REFUGEE POPULATION

Based on data from the "Current Population Survey" by the U.S. Census Bureau, foreign-born population in the United States had reached a total of 37.3 million persons by 2008. Included in this population were approximately 15 million naturalized citizens; 11.1 million currently legal permanent residents; and 11.2 million unauthorized migrants—some entering clandestinely or with fraudulent documents and others overstaying their visas. Among the foreign-born population were 11.6 million from Mexico, 8.4 million from other Latin American countries, 10 million from Asian countries, 4.7 million from Europe, 10.0 million from Asia, and 2.6 million from other areas. There were an additional 2.5 million refugees, and 1.2 million temporary legal residents—including students and temporary workers (Pew Hispanic Center, 2005).

The term *immigrant* refers to any person who voluntarily leaves one country in order to permanently settle in another country. However, as part of an effort to limit the allocation of resources to immigrants, various laws and regulations contain additional distinctions and definitions. Some immigrants, for example, have been declared *legal permanent residents* as a means of recognizing those who have legally entered the country through the existing structure. Congress has established quotas for the maximum number of immigrants from each country, facilitating the entry of those who have certain job skills or close ties to family members already living in the United States. Legal permanent residents can, after a period of time and a demonstration that they possess knowledge of U.S. law and culture, become naturalized citizens. The average family income of legal permanent residents is comparable to native families and the 18–24-year-old youth are slightly more likely than resident youth to attend college (Pew Hispanic Center, 2005). This part of the immigrant population, then, is unlikely to make more of a demand on human services than other U.S. residents.

Some persons receive permission to temporarily enter the United States to attend school or perform certain needed jobs. When the visas of these *temporary legal residents* (also known as nonimmigrants) expire, they must return to their homelands. Generally speaking, this segment of the immigrant population has only limited income and few benefits. Social workers may meet persons from this group in hospitals and clinics, mental health centers, schools, and in child welfare agencies (Garrett and Herman, 2006).

People who have entered the country illegally, i.e., without meeting the immigration requirements, fare rather badly in the United States. These *unauthorized immigrants* tend to be young, have limited education, live in crowded housing, and yet have high employment rates in farming, cleaning, construction, and food preparation jobs. These families have low income ($27,400 per year), 39.9 percent of the children live in poverty, and 53 percent have no health coverage (Pew Hispanic Center, 2005). Although taxes are withheld from their paychecks and they pay sales taxes, these unauthorized immigrants must live under the radar of government scrutiny, are not eligible for Temporary Assistance for Needy Families (TANF) and most other government programs, have few legal rights, and risk deportation at any time. For social workers, this population is difficult to serve. Many of the usual health and welfare resources are not accessible due to the client's legal status. Moreover, unauthorized immigrants are often reluctant to ask for services due to the risk of deportation if their status is discovered.

The Personal Responsibility and Work Opportunity and Reconciliation Act of 1996, referred to as PRWORA and commonly known as welfare reform, ". . . institutionalized the concept of immigrant exceptionalism" (Zimmerman and Tumlin, 1999, p. 5), thereby denying most public benefits to nondocumented immigrants. Specifically, that federal law bars most immigrants from receiving food stamps and Supplemental Security Income (SSI) and also blocks use of "federal means-tested benefits" for five years from their date of arrival in the United States, including TANF, Medicaid, and the Child Health Insurance Program (CHIP).

In addition, PRWORA gives states the option to deny immigrants who arrived in the United States prior to August 22, 1996, from receiving TANF, Medicaid, and services under the Social Security Block Grant. It also allows individual states the right to bar immigrants who arrived in the United States after August 22, 1996, from TANF and Medicaid, following the mandatory five-year ban. This federal legislation, in effect, denies unauthorized immigrants access to all federal public benefits, and grants to the states the legal right to discriminate through restrictive eligibility criteria for federal, state, and locally funded social services. For example, access is denied by requiring verification of immigrants' legal status prior to the provision of social services.

Refugees enter the United States under a different set of circumstances. They have been victims of oppressive conditions in their home countries and have fled persecution, usually without time to gain legal immigration status or to plan for the disposition and transfer of their property and financial resources. Often families are not able to escape together and may temporarily relocate in one or more countries before finally arriving at their final destination. Refugee status provides a temporary legal means of entering the United States and can be a first step toward becoming a legal immigrant. Social work practice with refugee populations requires that practitioners explore client problems from two interrelated dimensions: (1) issues originating from the individual's perceptions and interpretations that are a result of culture, values, or "ethnic reality" influences and (2) the after-effects of the individual's migration journey and reception by the host country.

Because of federal legislation such as the Refugee Act of 1980, most refugees are eligible for public health and human services programs including cash and medical assistance, social services, and preventive health services. A social worker should be alert to the possibility that other organizations and social agencies working with an individual who is a refugee may not understand his or her cultural background and special immigration status and might have policies and procedures that unwittingly deny their services to refugees (see Item 8.9). In such a situation, interagency negotiation or perhaps client advocacy or class advocacy may be necessary (see Items 13.17 and 13.31). When working with refugees, social workers need to be especially sensitive to the interplay of such factors as the client's ethnicity, religion, nationality, legal and immigration status, age, gender, family context and characteristics, education, economic situation, and acceptance in the community (Puig, 2001).

GUIDELINES FOR ASSISTING IMMIGRANTS AND REFUGEES

Depending on the social worker's job responsibility and agency context, a worker may have a role in assisting individuals and families in planning a migration or escaping as a refugee to a different country; the social worker might also assist those who have entered the country in successfully resetting and adapting to life in the United States.

Migration.   When clients are preparing to migrate, social workers should help them to focus on several concerns. For example, clients should be helped to address the probable economic and social impact on the family members who leave, as well as on those staying behind. Will there be a loss of income? Can they cope with the emotional pain of a separation and loneliness? Can they successfully adjust to a strange culture and new environment? Can they negotiate a language barrier? Is it safe to make this journey? How can they stay in communication with family and friends? Might this migration require detainment in a refugee camp? Does the migration require waiting for an official decision by the foreign government? If so, how long will the wait be, and what financial and other resources will be needed during the wait for an official decision? What if the person is refused entry?

Resettlement.   Social workers should help clients adjust to the new environment and learn how to secure employment, housing, health care, social relationships, and so on. In addition, social workers should help clients examine such issues as their *acculturation* (i.e., changes in beliefs toward those of the host society), *assimilation* (i.e., the degree of adoption of the values, norms, and behaviors that dominate the society), and *adaptation* (i.e., the ability to adjust one's way of life to fit into the new country). More specifically, workers should help clients consider and address possible discrepancies between their expectations and reality, the degree of stress encountered throughout the migration experience, and the effects on friends and loved ones left behind. Some other factors that social workers should help clients consider as possible impediments to or supports for successful adjustment to the new culture include the following:

- Language and the individual's degree of bilingualism
- Differences in expected housing or living arrangements between the cultures
- Variations in work patterns and expectations by employers
- The degree of commonality between values and social norms of the old and new cultures and societies
- The availability of cultural mediators or teachers for new arrivals
- Corrective feedback (positive and negative) needed to assist adaptation
- Tension between adapting to a new environment while holding on to important elements of the original culture
- The degree of similarity or dissimilarity in physical appearance with the dominant population groups in the culture

Guiding the Path to Naturalization.   Both legal permanent residents and refugees may require the assistance of the social worker in attaining naturalization. Typically the social worker helps by informing the person(s) of the naturalization process and helping to make connections to resources that help to accomplish the various steps of the process. The requirements for *naturalization* (the process of awarding U.S. citizenship to a person after birth) include the following. The individual must:

- Be at least 18 years of age
- Have resided continuously in the United States for at least five years (three years for the spouse of a U.S. citizen)
- Have demonstrated good moral character as determined by the absence of conviction of any criminal offenses
- Be able to read, write, and speak English well enough to understand commonly used English words and phrases, and
- Demonstrate the ability to pass a citizenship exam in U.S. government and history

Selected Bibliography

Balgopal, Pallassana, ed. *Social Work Practice with Immigrants and Refugees.* New York: Columbia University Press, 2000.

Garrett, Kendra J., and W. Randolph Herman. "Foreign-Born Students in Baccalaureate Social Work Programs: Meeting the Challenges." *The Journal of Baccalaureate Social Work* 12 (Fall 2006): 24–38.

Pew Hispanic Center. "Unauthorized Migrants: Numbers and Characteristics." www.pewhispanic.org/files/reports/46.pdf. June 14, 2005.

Puig, Maria. "Organizations and Community Intervention Skills with Hispanic Americans." In Rowena Fong and Sharlene Furuto, eds. *Culturally Competent Practice: Skills, Interventions, and Evaluations*, pp. 269–284. Boston, MA: Allyn & Bacon, 2001.

U. S. Bureau of Census. *Characteristics of the Foreign-Born Population by Nativity and U.S. Citizenship Status*: 2008. http://www.census.gov/population/www/socdemo/foreign/cps2008.html#cit

Zimmerman, Wendy, and Tumlin, Karen C. *Patchwork Policies: State Assistance for Immigrants under Welfare Reform.* Washington, DC: Urban Institute, 1999.

15.21 THE CLIENT OR COMMUNITY EXPERIENCING AN EMERGENCY OR DISASTER

Various natural disasters and catastrophic events have the potential to disrupt whole communities and inflict death, injury, trauma, and financial hardship on large numbers of people. Examples include earthquakes, floods, hurricanes, tornadoes, forest fires, airline crashes, terrorist attacks, spills of toxic chemicals, and war-related invasions and bombings.

The defining characteristics of a **disaster** are that it affects many people simultaneously and that its scale requires a highly organized and disciplined emergency response by a range of governmental and private organizations. The roles and activities of social workers at the site of a disaster must fit within an organized rescue and emergency response—one characterized by a military type of decision making and coordinating structure. The leaders of emergency response organizations will have certain objectives and priorities and these will determine what types human services are most needed and when, where, and to whom they will be provided. In an emergency or disaster situation, the highest priorities are the following:

- Rescue or evacuate people in danger, to treat the injured, and to prevent an outbreak of contagious diseases through inoculations, proper care of the dead, and provision of sanitation facilities.
- Address the immediate physical needs of the survivors by providing shelter, water, food, blankets, and the like.
- Maintain public order to prevent panic, looting, and riots. (This requires police or military units.)

Once these priorities have been addressed, the emergency response organization will attempt to deal with the psychological, social, and spiritual needs of the survivors by dispatching mental health, social services, and pastoral personnel.

INDIVIDUAL AND FAMILY RESPONSES

How an individual responds to a disaster is related, in part, to the nature of the disaster and whether he or she had time to prepare for what was coming. For example, people who have lost their house to a flood, hurricane, or a forest fire will usually have had a day or two of advance warnings and some opportunity to plan, save some possessions, and share their fears with family and friends. By contrast, an earthquake, terrorist bombing, or a plane crash is a complete surprise and more disorienting. Those exposed to a disaster or catastrophic event will experience some or all of the following:

- Overwhelming feelings of shock, fear, horror, and grief
- Preoccupation with death brought on by remembering the sights and sounds of persons with severe injuries, and people dying, and corpses
- Preoccupation with what they have lost, such as a loved one, a house, important papers, and other possessions
- Worry that they may never be able to reestablish a normal life or manage financially
- Feeling that they survived at the expense of those who died (i.e., survivor guilt)
- Feelings of helplessness and a loss of trust, self-confidence, and control

Responses to a disaster often unfold in three stages: impact, recoil, and post-trauma. During the first stage, *acute impact*, people are just absorbing the reality of what has happened. During this initial phase, which usually lasts for an hour or two, people respond in a variety of ways, particularly when some are still in danger. While a few manage to remain surprisingly calm, make rational decisions, and care for themselves and others, most are in a state of emotional shock and disorientation. They experience intense fear and anxiety and have physical symptoms such as sweating, trembling, and stomach upset. These individuals are, however, able to communicate and follow instructions given by emergency personnel. Of all who are caught up in the disaster, a small percentage will be hysterical or paralyzed by their fear, unable to make rational choices, and behave in ways that are dangerous to themselves and others.

During the second phase, *the recoil phase*, survivors realize more clearly what they have been through. Typically, this phase begins some hours after the disaster has hit. At this point, many of the survivors are in a state of emotional exhaustion and many will break down and weep. Most have an intense need to talk about their experience. Attention must be given to meeting the immediate needs for food, clean water, shelter, and sleeping arrangements. Many will need help securing items for grooming and personal care, arranging access to communication networks so that they can contact worried relatives and friends, and also replacing lost eyeglasses, prescription medications, and so on. Mental health counseling and crisis intervention work should begin in this phase (see Item 13.14).

The third phase of adjustment to a disaster or catastrophic event is termed the *post-trauma phase*. The major adjustments that individuals and families must make are basically those of dealing with and grieving for their losses, rebuilding their lives, and reestablishing ordinary and predictable patterns of living. This phase may last for months, years, or the rest of a person's life, depending in part on the adequacy of the crisis intervention services (see Item 15.16).

COMMUNITY RESPONSES

According to Webster (1995), whole communities that have experienced a disaster typically move through four rather predicable phases: heroism, honeymoon, disillusionment, and reconstruction. The *heroism phase* begins soon after the disaster has hit when the people of the community bond together, provide mutual support, and display cooperative behavior. Former divisions of social and economic class, race, and ethnicity are set aside. During this phase, people often experience a positive sense of community and belonging. They take great pride in how they have been helpful to each other and in how well they are working together.

During a second phase, *the honeymoon*, the community feels hopeful and confident that it can and will recover and perhaps become even stronger than before. Prior conflicts, tensions, political disputes, and power struggles within the community are temporarily forgotten.

The honeymoon gradually gives way to a sense of disappointment, known as the *disillusionment phase*. At this point, the people of the community recognize the enormity and complexity of rebuilding. Typically, the available emergency relief programs are time limited and provide less than what people need or expected. Program limitations and the associated eligibility rules and regulations may elicit anger and a sense of unfairness. It is during this phase that former community conflicts and divisions resurface and people begin to fragment into competing groups. Rumors and misinformation are special problems during this phase. Thus, community meetings and disseminating accurate information are critically important.

Eventually, the community moves beyond its disillusionment and enters the long and difficult phase of *reconstruction*. Some communities are successful in rebuilding after a disaster, whereas others never fully recover. Among the variables that affect a community's capacity for and level of recovery are the extent of the destruction, the economic base, the community's prior level of cohesion, the availability of needed resources, and leadership.

GUIDELINES FOR A DISASTER RESPONSE

The following guidelines will help social workers to respond to the human needs and problems created by a disaster or catastrophic event:

1. Representatives of human services agencies and social work organizations, such as the National Association of Social Workers (NASW), should be involved in local and statewide disaster-planning activities. Long before a disaster occurs each agency should have formulated a plan as to how it can and will respond and how it will coordinate its work with the local emergency response organization and with disaster relief organizations such as the American Red Cross. In order to provide the appropriate services at the time of a disaster, social workers and agencies must understand how emergency and disaster relief organizations will respond and function. Social workers who expect to work at the site of a disaster must first secure the proper authorization from those directing and coordinating the emergency response.

2. In the first hours and perhaps days following a disaster, the collection of accurate information is of critical importance to the conduct of rescue operations and other emergency responses. It is important to identify who is still missing and who has been killed or injured. Also, it is important to document where each survivor is now located (e.g., whether the person was taken to a shelter, transferred to a hospital). Obtaining accurate and complete information will reduce the level of confusion, facilitate communication between the survivors and their worried relatives and friends, and allow for the reunification of families.

3. Certain individuals will require special attention, even if they have escaped physical injury. These include, for example, young children, the elderly, those with a physical or mental illness or disability, and those without access to family or a social support network. Because children are especially vulnerable to turmoil and social disruption, they should not be separated from their families at times of crisis. If at all possible, families should be evacuated as units and housed together in emergency shelters.

4. Information and referral services are especially important in the months that follow a disaster. Thus, social workers in contact with survivors should be familiar with the state and federal disaster assistance programs that may provide direct money grants, low-cost loans, temporary housing, and other resources. Regularly scheduled informational meetings will help people keep abreast of the actions or anticipated actions of government agencies and emergency relief organizations.

5. If a hundred people die in a disaster, thousands of survivors must cope with the loss of a loved one in addition to the loss of property and possessions, the possible loss of their jobs, and a fundamental disruption to their usual way of life. Many who live through a disaster will experience adjustment problems and psychological symptoms for many months and even years after the event. Some will develop Posttraumatic Stress Disorder (see Item 13.14). Increased levels of financial problems, depression and anxiety, suicide and homicide, domestic violence, problem drinking and drug use, psychosomatic illness, poor job performance, and the like can be anticipated, as well. Thus, mental health and social services agencies should formulate plans to address an increased need for their services and engage in case finding and active outreach to those who may need them.

6. When possible and feasible, the survivors of a destructive disaster such as an earthquake or hurricane should be directly involved in the cleanup and rebuilding effort. This not only provides them with needed jobs and income but also helps them to regain a sense of control and self-confidence.

7. Be alert to the possibility that a professional or emergency worker may develop a condition known as *vicarious trauma*. After repeated exposures to people who have been traumatized, social workers and other helpers may themselves develop symptoms of trauma, such as intrusive thoughts and images, sleeplessness, bystander guilt, and feelings of vulnerability, helplessness, self-doubt, and rage. Workers who previously suffered severe emotional trauma and those who are inexperienced in disaster-related work are especially vulnerable to developing these symptoms. Ongoing self-care, including the opportunity to talk about one's experiences and feelings and receive reassurance and support from other professionals, is of critical importance in helping social workers cope with the stress of disaster-related work.

Selected Bibliography

Halpern, James, and Mary Tramontin. *Disaster Mental Health*. Belmont, CA: Brooks/Cole, 2007.

Ritchie, Elspeth, Patricia Watson, and Matthew Friedman, eds. *Interventions Following Mass Violence and Disasters*. New York: Guilford, 2006.

Rosenfeld, Lawrence, Joanne Caye, Ofra Ayalon, and Mooli Lahad. *When Their World Falls Apart: Helping Families and Children Manage the Effects of Disasters*. Washington, DC: NASW, 2004.

Webster, Stephen. "Disasters and Disaster Aid." In *Encyclopedia of Social Work*, 19th ed., edited by Richard L. Edwards, 761–771. Washington, DC: NASW, 1995.

Techniques for Sustaining Social Work Practice

Social work is a demanding profession but also a rewarding one. However, the rewards are mostly intrinsic. By selecting social work as a career, one is virtually assured of never attaining wealth or prestige. Social work is about caring, sharing, and social responsibility; these are not the values rewarded by our economic system that emphasizes competition and individualism.

From its beginnings, the social work profession has demonstrated special concern for those who are powerless, stigmatized, and devalued—the people who most others tend to avoid or ignore. Because social workers encounter so many people who are desperate and in need and see firsthand the inadequacy of available professional, agency, and societal resources, they frequently experience the anguish of knowing that no matter how hard they work, many people will not receive the services and attention they need and deserve. This is a frustration with which social workers must learn to live.

Because many clients are economically poor, few are in a position to pay directly for services. For this reason, most social workers are employed by governmental or nonprofit agencies. Most workers are employed in resource-poor organizations—ones with few perks and with limited opportunities for additional education and training.

This chapter provides social workers with guidance for developing their skills, coping with frustrations, and dealing with some ordinary but complex work-related tasks. It offers background information on finding a social work job, taking competence tests, dealing with job-related stress, making use of and contributing to professional literature and making presentations, and serving in leadership roles. In addition, the chapter provides guidance on testifying in court, avoiding malpractice suits, addressing sexual misconduct, and developing mentoring relationships.

16.1   GETTING A SOCIAL WORK JOB

Once a social worker has completed his or her professional education, the next task is to secure employment. That usually takes time and effort, as human services agencies are necessarily careful in their selection of staff to serve their clientele. (To examine this process from the viewpoint of the agency, see Item 10.12.)

The first step in finding employment is to identify the job openings. In most communities, several sources of information might be examined. Agencies will typically advertise their positions; thus, job seekers should read the classified advertisements in the local newspaper, visit agency websites, and watch for openings on bulletin boards. In addition, informal networks among professionals are an excellent source of information. Attending local NASW meetings is a good way to tap into the professional network in most communities.

Once an open position is located, the application materials must be prepared. It typically has two parts: a cover letter and a professional resumé, although sometimes an application form must also be completed either online or as hard copy. The **cover letter** should focus on the particular job being applied for and stress the applicant's qualifications for that position. It should be approximately one page in length and must be carefully written with no spelling, punctuation, or grammatical errors. The letter should indicate that it and the resumé represent an application for the position, describe why the applicant is interested in that job, and discuss qualifications for the position. The cover letter is not the place to discuss salary expectations or reasons for leaving past jobs. Indicate that a list of references will be provided on request (unless the job announcement asks that references be supplied as part of the application). Be sure to obtain permission in advance from anyone named as a reference. The letter should be upbeat about the position for which one is applying.

The **professional resumé** is more generic than a cover letter and might be used when applying for several positions. It is an organized summary of one's professional qualifications and skills. Its purpose is to present the applicant's background in a manner that will convince the employer to invite him or her for an interview. There is no prescribed format or style for a resumé. Rather, use a creative approach to attract the attention of members of a screening committee who may be selecting a few finalists from a large number of applications; however, avoid being cute or clever. Often, photocopy shops provide layout consultation, have high-quality printers available, and can recommend distinctive paper, making it relatively inexpensive to prepare an attractive resumé. In addition, many colleges or universities have offices that provide workshops and consultation to students in preparing job applications.

At a minimum, a resumé should include the following information; other items may be added at one's discretion:

- *Personal data.* Include your name, street address, email address, and phone number. If you have a cell phone where you can be easily reached, be sure to include that number to facilitate scheduling an interview.
- *Education.* Give the name of your degree(s), your major, the colleges or universities you attended, and graduation dates. List all schools you have attended (listing in reverse order) and possibly add grade-point average, honors, special projects, or any special skills or training that might be relevant to a social work job (e.g., computer, foreign language).
- *Experience.* List employment in reverse order (i.e., beginning with your current or most recent job), giving the job title, name of organization, dates of employment, and job duties. It is also helpful to list any volunteer experience that might have contributed to your social work competencies.
- *Activities and interests.* Identify your professional interests as well as those that extend beyond social work. Note membership in professional organizations, your participation in various clubs or organizations and any offices held, and any hobbies or special interests.
- *References.* A statement such as "References Available on Request" is usually best to place on a resumé. If a job announcement calls for references, they should be listed in the cover letter. This flexibility allows you to list the most appropriate references for each position. In general, the persons selected as references should be able to comment on your skills and might include a faculty member, a field instructor, and/or job supervisors or persons who supervised volunteer experiences. In many instances an agency will prefer to contact the references by telephone, so be sure to provide telephone numbers.
- *Other information.* It may be desirable to add other information such as publications, travel experiences, and unique experiences that may enhance your competence as a social worker.

If the application is successful, the applicant will be invited to an interview. Typically, the interview process will involve appearing before a panel of interviewers, although there will usually be some one-to-one discussions, as well. Many review panels will present the applicant with hypothetical situations or case vignettes and ask how he or she would handle the situation.

The interviewing procedures used by government agencies are usually highly structured and many will require a written exam (see Item 16.2) in addition to oral interviews.

Preparation is essential. First, research the agency thoroughly. Know the services it offers, its target clientele, and something about its structure and goals. This information might be obtained by stopping by the agency in advance to pick up informational materials, by visiting the agency's website, or by discussing the agency with other social workers in the community. Second, dress professionally and be as relaxed as possible during the interview process. Third, be prepared for questions about your personal and professional interests, as well as your preparation for the specific job duties.

Here are some examples of questions that are commonly asked in an interview:

- What are your qualifications for this job?
- What are your strengths? Your weaknesses?
- Why do you want this job?
- What are your career goals?
- Why should we hire you?
- As a social worker employed by this agency, how would you handle the following situation? (For example: A client tells you he or she plans to take his or her own life. How would you respond?)

Also be prepared with questions you would like to ask about the agency and the job. An interview is a two-way street—both the applicant and the agency are deciding if there is a good match between one's skills and interests and the requirements of the job.

If offered the position, be sure to know what will be expected of you on the job, and negotiate the salary or other benefits at this time with the employer. Before accepting a new position, (1) you should obtain a letter of appointment that states the starting salary, duties, and other pertinent information; and (2) you should review the agency's personnel manual to be sure that you understand the working conditions and benefits.

Selected Bibliography

Doelling, Carol. *Career Development: A Handbook for Job Hunting and Career Planning*, 2nd ed. Washington, DC: NASW, 2005.

George, Laura, *Excuse Me, Your Job Is Waiting: Attract the Work You Want*. Charlottesville, VA: Hampton Road Publications, 2007.

Sidell, Nancy, and Denice Smiley. *Professional Communication Skills in Social Work*. Boston: Allyn & Bacon, 2008.

16.2   PREPARING FOR SOCIAL WORK COMPETENCY EXAMS

Test taking does not end when one secures a BSW or MSW degree. At some time in his or her career, most social workers will need to complete a competency examination. Passing an exam is often a part of applying for a job and/or a step in obtaining a sought-after credential, such as securing a state license to practice social work or becoming a private (independent) practitioner. Although occasionally oral exams are used as part of the job application process, all state licensing exams are made up of multiple-choice questions on a paper-and-pencil or computerized test.

Examinations developed at the agency or state levels typically focus on the knowledge and skills relevant to the performance of a specific job. For example, if a state agency test is part of an application process for securing a job as a child protection worker, the exam questions will focus on such matters as relevant state laws, testifying in court, signs of abuse and neglect, understanding child development, and methods of working with abusive and neglecting parents. By contrast, the licensing exams are constructed for nationwide use, such as those developed by the Association of

Social Work Boards (ASWB), and focus more broadly on the range of activities typically per-formed by social workers regardless of setting. The ASWB tests are available for several groups of social work practitioners: the social work associate, the new BSW, the new MSW, as well as the experienced advanced generalist and clinical MSWs.

Although data are not available on the pass rates for state or agency developed tests, the 2009 pass rates for persons taking ASWB's national licensing tests for the first-time were: Associate level, 69.3 percent; Bachelors level, 79.3 percent; Masters level, 74.5 percent; Advanced Generalist, 57.0 percent; and Clinical, 74.6 percent (*Association News*, 2010a). Because the failure to pass a test can prevent a person from qualifying for employment, the courts have ruled that the test questions must be representative of the work required for the jobs and professional level being tested. In order to write relevant test questions and construct a fair test, a formal research effort is periodically conducted that identifies the frequency and impor-tance of tasks performed by social workers. This task analysis provides a "blueprint" for each exam and determines the percentage of the exam questions that will focus on a specific topic or content area. Beginning in 2011, the percentages of questions for each examination level in each content area are listed below (Association News, 2010b).

Bachelor's Examination

- Human Development, Diversity, and Behavior in the Environment, 27%
- Assessment, 28%
- Direct and Indirect Practice, 26%
- Professional Relationships, Values, and Ethics, 19%

Master's Examination

- Human Development, Diversity, and Behavior, 28%
- Assessment and Intervention Planning, 24%
- Direct and Indirect Practice, 21%
- Professional Relationships, Values, and Ethics, 27%

Advanced Generalist Examination

- Human Development, Diversity, and Behavior, 18%
- Micro Assessment and Planning, 22%
- Micro Practice and Social Work Relationships, 18%
- Macro Practice, 18%
- Professional Values and Ethics, 25%

Clinical Examination

- Human Development, Diversity, and Behavior, 31%
- Assessment, Diagnosis, and Treatment Planning, 26%
- Psychotherapy, Clinical Interventions, and Case Management, 25%
- Professional Values and Ethics, 18%

When preparing for an exam, the social worker should allocate his or her study time and effort somewhat in the proportion to the number of questions expected in each content area. For example, given the above percentages, one could anticipate that on a 150-question BSW exam, there will be 40 or 41 questions ($0.27 \times 150 = 40.5$) focusing on understanding of biological, psychological, and societal factors related to human development, diversity, and people's behavior in the environment (i.e., concepts related to individuals, families, groups, organizations, and communities).

Test questions fall into three categories: recall, application, and problem solving. If ques-tions were all at the recall level (e.g., "Which of the following is the *most accurate* definition of domestic violence?" or "Who was author of the eight stages of human development?"), taking the test immediately after completing one's degree might be best. However, application-level questions (e.g., "If a school social worker suspects a child has been abused, his or her *first* action should be:" or "Which of the following would be the *most effective* technique when preparing to present at a case conference?"), experience would strengthen one's ability to pick the correct answer. For problem-solving questions (e.g., "Which of the following criterion *best* differentiates between persons with low income from those who live in poverty?" or "Select from the following cultural competencies the one that is *most immediately* applicable when working with an immigrant family that is experiencing . . ."), practice experience and critical thinking will be valuable assets in selecting the correct answer.

When answering questions, it is instructive to understand the language and concepts used in developing the questions. When questions are composed, the item writer begins by identifying the content area (see earlier paragraph) the question is intended to address. Next, a *stem* or the stimulus for the answers (i.e., the opening statement) is prepared. It is important to read and think about the stem very carefully when answering the question as it provides the focus for selecting an answer. Look for such words as *most, first, best,* etc., that emphasize what the question is aimed at and this will clue you to address frequency, sequence, priority, and so on in selecting the correct answer. The correct answer is known as the *key*. When the question is pretested, the key should be most frequently selected and also chosen by those who score well on the overall test, otherwise the question is not used as a test question. Finally, the item writer prepares (usually) three *distractors*. Distractors are answers that may seem plausible if the test-taker is guessing or not truly knowledgeable about the topic, and are clearly not as good an answer as the key. When taking an exam, it is best to read the stem and answer A together, then read the stem again and answer B, and so on through the answers. By that time you should be fully familiar with the stem and its intent and should be able to rule out answers that are clearly not the best answer. Typically that will leave only one or two answers in consideration. This is the time to apply critical-thinking skills (see Chapter 7) to work out which answer you will select as your final choice.

There are two schools of thought regarding when one should ideally take such exams. One position is that a person should sit for these exams as soon as possible after completing a social work degree program—while the content of that education is still fresh and the person is accustomed to taking exams. This is especially true when preparing for the bachelors and masters exams as these tests have a greater proportion of recall and application items. The alternative view suggests waiting until the social worker has more experience. With a year or two of practice experience one learns a great deal about how various concepts play-out in work with people and agencies. Thus, the more experienced worker is better able to apply critical thinking when answering the test questions.

The *NASW News* usually carries advertisements for schools of social work, NASW chapters, or entrepreneurial companies that offer written materials, workshops, flash cards, and other tools for licensing exam preparation. Like most marketed items, it is difficult to judge the merits of these offerings and sometimes they are quite expensive. A useful and not too costly preparation source can be found at http://www.aswb.org/SWLE/SWLE.asp, the website for the ASWB. At this site study materials and practice exams are available, providing the reasons the key is correct and the distractors are not the *best* answers for the questions. ASWB also maintains a list of recommended books (usually textbooks) that one might review in preparation for each level of licensing exam.

Selected Bibliography

Association of Social Work Boards, website, http://www.aswb.org.
_____. "Consistency, and a Growing Population." *Association News* 20 (April 2010a), http://www.aswb.org/pdfs/April10Newsletter/PassRates.pdf
_____. "Change in the Works." *Association News* 20 (April 2010b), http://www.aswb.org/pdfs/April10Newsletter/NewBlueprints.pdf
DeAngelis, Donna. "Social Work Licensing Examinations in the United States and Canada: Development and Administration." In Albert R. Roberts (ed.). *Social Workers' Desk Reference,* 2nd ed. New York: Oxford University Press, 2009.

16.3   DEVELOPING SELF-AWARENESS

Professional social workers emphasize the need to develop self-insight in order to use themselves effectively in serving others. The **self-awareness** one develops refers to an accurate perception of one's own beliefs, values, attitudes, and habits and how they might influence decisions and behavior in social work practice. Efforts to develop self-awareness should focus on identifying both strengths and limitations. Many of the strengths that are of importance in social work practice are discussed in other parts of this book. Chapter 3, for example, describes the qualities of courage, compassion, hopefulness, empathy, genuineness, warmth, creativity, imagination, flexibility, energy, good judgment, knowledge, and so on (also see Chapters 2 and 8). The worker can increase his or her self-awareness through activities such as the following:

- Keep a daily journal or log that helps you sort out and think about experiences and get in touch with feelings.
- Ask for constructive criticism. Seek feedback and evaluations from trusted and experienced colleagues familiar with your performance, responsibilities, and agency setting.
- Obtain and then study audio or video recordings of your interviews, group sessions, and other work-related meetings. (Note: Secure permission of others before making such a recording; clients should sign a written authorization.)
- Use role-play. Practice and evaluate your performance in simulated sessions that focus on or act out situations that are especially difficult.

In this section, the focus is mostly on factors that can interfere with effective practice. This is not to suggest that strengths are of less importance but rather to counter the human inclination to deny or ignore personal limitations.

Many individuals are drawn to the helping professions because they believe the problems they have faced in life give them a special understanding or sensitivity to the problems of others. Indeed, life's problems can be a powerful teacher and provide a degree of empathy that others may not have. However, this will be the case only after one has honestly examined those experiences and successfully worked through the residual painful memories and feelings associated with them.

When a social worker becomes aware of some factor that interferes with client service, he or she must be willing to correct the problem or, if change is not possible, to seek a practice setting where this factor will not have a negative impact on clients. Below are some of the factors that can interfere with the formation of a positive professional helping relationship and client service:

1. *Personal issues.* To a considerable degree, our core beliefs and attitudes toward people and toward life in general have been shaped by childhood and family experiences. Most people carry a certain amount of emotional baggage into their adult lives, including unresolved parent–child conflicts, prejudice, aftereffects of traumatic events, and so on. Sometimes this baggage is carried to the workplace, where it has a negative impact on clients and work performances—for example:

- Preoccupation with personal problems, resulting in an inability to give one's full attention to the client
- Inability to control one's reactions or exercise self-discipline when in an emotionally charged situation or when under the ordinary pressures associated with social work practice
- Inability to demonstrate warmth, empathy, and genuine caring for clients served by the agency
- Inability to work cooperatively with persons in positions of authority (e.g., judges, physicians, administrators, supervisors)
- Difficulty separating personal experience (e.g., having been a victim of child abuse, growing up with alcoholic parents) from the concerns and problems presented by clients

- Defensiveness that prevents a critical examination of one's job performance
- Avoiding certain clients or especially difficult tasks
- Personalization of client anger and frustrations (i.e., inability to maintain an appropriate level of objectivity)
- Imposing one's values, political beliefs, religious beliefs, or lifestyle on clients
- Inability to respect the religious beliefs and cultural values of a client
- Alcohol or drug abuse
- Misuse or abuse of one's authority or position (see Item 10.10)
- Extreme level of shyness or nonassertiveness resulting in an inability to express opinions and engage in the give-and-take of client work, peer supervision, and team work

2. *Appearance, clothing, and grooming.* To a large extent, people form their impressions of others—especially the powerful first impression—on the basis of appearance. Thus, the social worker must pay attention to his or her clothing and grooming because it matters to clients and will affect how they respond to the worker and their utilization of agency services. Of course, what is offensive to one client may be acceptable to another, and what is appropriate dress in one agency setting may be inappropriate in another. The staff in a particular setting must make decisions on what is appropriate. Many agencies and most hospitals establish dress codes as a way of providing guidance to staff. When examining your appearance and its possible impact on clients, remember these guidelines:

- Some choices of clothing, hairstyle, perfume, makeup, body decoration, or jewelry may offend or distract clients served by the agency.
- Deficiencies in grooming and personal hygiene may offend clients.
- Uncovered infections, skin irritations, and similar conditions may distract the client or cause him or her worry and anxiety.

3. *Behaviors that devalue others.* Social work values dictate that every client should be treated with dignity and respect. The social worker must avoid behaviors that are disrespectful, including the following:

- Using words, phrases, or gestures that are in bad taste or known to offend clients and staff (e.g., cursing, sexual overtones)
- Telling sexist or ethnic jokes
- Discriminating or showing prejudice against particular client groups
- Making sarcastic, insulting, cruel, or disrespectful comments about clients

4. *Distracting personal habits.* Most people have some undesirable mannerisms and habits that their friends and families have learned to accept. However, the social worker must be willing to modify habits that may annoy clients, such as:

- Fidgeting, pencil tapping, knuckle cracking, nail biting
- Pulling or twisting hair
- Chewing gum or tobacco and smoking
- Scowling, frowning, or other facial gestures that seem to express scorn
- Excessive nervous laughter, frequent clearing of throat, or other distracting mannerisms

5. *Difficulties in cognitive functioning.* A social worker must absorb information quickly and apply complex principles. A capacity for abstract thinking is essential. The following examples illustrate insufficient cognitive functioning:

- Cognitive deficits that interfere with attention, memory, and judgment
- Inability to explain the reasons behind one's judgments, conclusions, and decisions
- Difficulty processing new information, drawing logical inferences, and solving problems
- Lack of reading speed and comprehension needed to understand records and reports, agency policy, and professional books and journals

6. *Difficulties in verbal communication.* The social worker's verbal communication must be understandable to clients and other professional persons. Problems such as these could hamper work with clients:

- Mumbling, speaking inaudibly, loud or penetrating voice tones, halting or hesitant speech, rapid speech
- Frequent use of slang not understood by or offensive to clients
- Errors of grammar or awkward sentence construction that confuse clients
- Inability to adjust vocabulary to client's age or educational level
- Uncorrected vision or hearing problems

7. *Problems in written communication.* Because so much of the social worker's service to a client involves the exchange of information with other professionals, the worker must be able to communicate in writing. If letters, reports, emails, and agency records are carelessly written and difficult to understand, those attempting to read them will be frustrated and conclude either that the worker does not care enough to communicate clearly or is incompetent. The worker's reputation and effectiveness is seriously damaged if the client or other professional persons form such negative impressions. Serious writing problems that merit correction include the following:

- Inability to prepare letters, reports, and records that are understandable to clients, agency staff, and other professionals (see Chapter 9)
- Not recognizing and correcting errors of spelling, grammar, and syntax
- Difficulty selecting words that adequately express thought
- Inability to write at a speed sufficient to manage required paperwork

8. *Poor work habits.* Poor work habits may have a direct or indirect impact on the clients served by an agency. Here are some examples:

- Being late for client appointments, team meetings, case conferences, and other scheduled events
- Missing deadlines for the completion of written reports that are important to clients or agencies and professionals serving the client
- Incomplete or sloppy recordkeeping and documentation
- Lack of preparation for meetings with clients and other professionals
- Not following through on assignments or tasks
- Distracting other staff members or keeping them from their work
- Unwillingness to seek and utilize direction from the supervisor
- Blaming clients or others for one's own ineffectiveness; unwillingness to acknowledge mistakes or limitations of knowledge and skill
- Unwillingness to follow established agency policies and procedures
- Behaviors occurring outside work hours that draw negative attention and thereby lessen client and public respect for the social agency and/or the worker

In order to grow in self-awareness, we need to examine our beliefs, assumptions, and behavioral patterns. We must remember, however, that our most significant advancements in self-awareness do not come from self-scrutiny but rather are "gifts" from others, such as comments made by our clients, the constructive criticism offered by a supervisor, professional peers, and others who care about us and our performance as social workers.

Selected Bibliography

Corey, Marianne, and Gerald Corey. *Becoming a Helper*, 5th ed. Belmont, CA: Brooks/Cole, 2007.

Thompson, Neil. *People Skills*, 3rd ed. New York: Palgrave Macmillan, 2009.

16.4 AVOIDING COMPASSION FATIGUE AND STRESS MANAGEMENT

Job-related stress can have three sources. First, there is the stress that is simply a part of a particular job. Everyone placed in a high-stress job will feel stressed—it comes with the territory. Second, there is stress caused by a lack of skills necessary to do the job. For example, a particular job may not be stressful for most people, but will be for the individual who does not have the requisite knowledge and skill. Third, some individuals create their own stress because they have unrealistic expectations or take on an excessive number of responsibilities.

Every social worker responds to the demands of the profession and his or her job in a unique manner; some thrive while others grow weary. There are two especially maladaptive reactions to job stress: burnout and compassion fatigue. The term **compassion fatigue** (also known as secondary trauma and vicarious trauma) describes a set of reactions that may develop when a professional is helping persons who have just experienced some extremely traumatic event, such as an earthquake, train wreck, or terrorist bombing. The *symptoms* that arise in the helper include recurring images of the suffering and injured people, guilt over not being able to help certain victims, self-doubt, a dread of returning to work, anxiety, anger, difficulty sleeping, depression, and hypervigliance. The onset of those symptoms is relatively rapid and clearly connected with a particular event or experience. Efforts to treat this condition involve the opportunity to discuss in detail the distressing or frightening events with others who also experienced it, education about the phenomena of compassion fatigue, emotional support and reassurance, and individual counseling (see Item 15.21).

The term **burnout** refers to a state of physical, mental, and emotional exhaustion caused by an inability to adequately cope with the demands and stress of a job. A professional experiencing burnout often feels emotionally disconnected and numb, has lost interest in his or her job, dislikes going to work, is irritable and cynical, and treats clients in a routine and insensitive manner. Burnout develops gradually, often over a period of years. An affected professional may feel that something is not right about his or her job performance and attitude toward clients but usually does not recognize or acknowledge the problem. Counseling and perhaps a job change may be necessary to reverse burnout. Burnout is not inevitable; it can be prevented if the professional is committed to self-care and to developing a strategy for stress management. The following guidelines suggest ways to handle job-related stress:

1. The key to preventing negative stress reactions is to find your proper niche in the world of work. There must be a good fit or match between you as a person and the demands of your job. As a social worker, you must feel positive about your chosen profession and feel that you are effective in what you do. Before stress reactions were studied as a problematic human condition, an unknown author wisely stated, "In order that people may be happy in their work, these three things are needed: they must be fit for it, they must not do too much of it, and they must have a sense of success in it."

2. Examine the fit between your work and your values. Are you spending your time and energy on activities you consider important? For example, if you value relationships with family and friends, are you making choices that enable you to be with them? On the other hand, if you find that your job is more important and exciting than your family life, then that too must be faced with honesty. As a general rule, people find time for what they really want to do and for that which they truly value. Part of stress management is to become clear about what you value.

3. Make an honest attempt to recognize stress in your life. Listen to those who care about you for clues that you are under more stress than you realized (e.g., "You're so crabby when you get home," "You're not as much fun as you used to be," "You never go anywhere anymore," and "You look so tired"). Possible signs of dangerous levels of stress include frequent colds and sore throats, skin eruptions, persistent soreness in muscles and joints, frequent low-level headaches, inability to relax or sleep, fatigue, sluggishness that lingers from day to day, frequent stomach upset, weight loss, diarrhea or constipation, nervousness, depression, irritability, unexplained drop in job performance, and a loss of interest in what had been interesting hobbies and exciting activities.

4. Regular exercise, proper nutrition, and adequate sleep help to reduce stress and build natural defenses against the harmful effects of stress. Take several simple and brief physical exercise breaks during the workday (e.g., take a walk at lunch time, do some isometric exercises, or climb a few flights of stairs). Reduce or eliminate the use of alcohol, nicotine, caffeine, and other drugs. Obtain regular medical checkups. If you are having personal or family problems, seek help from trusted friends or professionals.

5. A major source of stress is the feeling that your work and responsibilities are excessive and beyond your control. In such a situation, you must start making some changes or the problem will get worse. Learning to manage your time is of critical importance. Time management is, in effect, stress management. When we use our time wisely we accomplish more and are more effective, and that contributes to a feeling of satisfaction and achievement (see Item 9.5). Consult with experienced peers who seem to effectively manage their workload and enjoy what they do. What are they doing that you might try? Like a long-distance runner, set a pace in your work activity that you can maintain without wearing down. Arrange work activity so you will accomplish at least one really important thing each day, for this can produce a surprising amount of job satisfaction. It is usually more satisfying to have done a few things well rather than to have done many things poorly.

6. Recognize that perfection is not required in most work-related tasks. Avoid placing unrealistically high expectations on yourself and on others. Also, avoid dwelling on the negatives and on what is lacking in your work. Take time to recognize and enjoy the positives in both your personal and professional lives. Help yourself recover from setbacks by recalling your prior accomplishments and maintaining a realistic perspective on your disappointments.

7. Build a support group of friends or colleagues with whom you are able to share your frustrations. Find enjoyable ways to spend time together—eat out, see a movie, take a walk, or travel together. Also, develop hobbies and outside interests that lead you into activities that are different from what you do at work. Doing something that is new and different is like a mini-vacation.

8. Apply to yourself the techniques you use with clients. For example, when faced with a stressful interpersonal task, use behavioral rehearsal to reduce anxiety and build confidence (see Item 13.4). As a technique for handling your fears, try exaggerating them out of proportion. For example, if you fear being embarrassed, visualize yourself blushing to the point of turning beet red, sweating profusely, and shaking so hard your watch vibrates off your wrist. Exaggerating your fears to the point of being ludicrous may help you laugh at yourself and put your fear into perspective.

9. Apply problem-solving and organizational change techniques to the stressors common to most work settings: including poor working conditions, unreasonable deadlines, heavy workloads, interruptions, and problems with co-workers and supervisors. Serious problems require careful analysis and intervention. They will not go away without intervention. Do something about them!

10. Visitors to the United States observe that the lifestyle is characterized by a fast pace, competition, materialism, and a coolness or emotional distance in human interactions. These characteristics contribute to the stress we experience, but we are not often aware of their influence. Look for ways to simplify your life and slow its pace. For example, simplify your wardrobe and your meals so you have fewer decisions to make about what to wear and what and where to eat. Give up nonessential possessions and activities that demand your attention and consume your time but provide little in the way of joy and relaxation. Replace unpleasant things in your life with meaningful and positive relationships with family and friends.

Selected Bibliography

Figley, Charles R., ed. *Treating Compassion Fatigue*. New York: Brunner/Routledge, 2002.

Keen, Samantha. *Recovering Vitality: Overcoming Chronic Fatigue, Burnout, and Stress*. Tuscon, AZ: Wheatmark, 2008.

Meisinger, Sarah E. *Stories of Pain, Trauma, and Survival: A Social Worker's Experiences and Insights from the Field*. Washington, DC: NASW Press, 2009.

Rothschild, Babette, and Marjorie L. Rand. *Help for the Helper*. New York: W.W. Norton, 2006.

16.5   DEALING WITH SEXUAL MISCONDUCT

The structure of professional relationships is inherently unequal, making clients vulnerable to exploitation. Clients enter these relationships in order to receive assistance from a competent professional and they trust the workers to treat their needs and interests as primary. In turn, it is expected that the professional will be responsible to avoid any misuse of this trust and will not exploit the client in any form (i.e., financial, sexual, or in any other way of personal gain). In addition, professional responsibility requires that any social worker in a position of power must avoid manipulating that situation for personal advantage. For example, a supervisor should not manipulate a supervisee, an administrator should not take advantage of workers, and a teacher or a field instructor should not exploit a student.

The National Association of Social Workers (1999) *Code of Ethics* provides guidance in several areas in which there is a potential conflict of interest for a social worker. There is recognition that the potential for sexual exploitation in the human services is high and professions take strong positions when sexual misconduct occurs. Section 1.09 of the *Code of Ethics* is explicit in prohibiting sexual contact with clients or former clients, the relatives of clients, as well as providing services to persons with whom the social worker has previously had a sexual relationship. In addition, Section 2.07 of NASW's *Code of Ethics* clearly prohibits sexually exploiting colleagues in a vulnerable position in the workplace (i.e., supervisees, students, trainees, or others for whom there may be a conflict of interest).

One form of sexual misconduct is **sexual harassment**, which federal law defines as any unwelcome sexual advance, request for sexual favors, or other verbal or physical conduct of a sexual nature made under these conditions:

- Submission to such conduct is explicitly or implicitly made a term or condition of an individual's employment or participation in an education program or activity.
- Submission to or rejection of such conduct by an individual is used as the basis for academic or employment decisions affecting that individual.
- Such conduct has the purpose or effect of substantially interfering with an individual's academic or work performance or creating an intimidating, hostile, or offensive working or educational environment. (Equal Employment Opportunity Commission, 1980)

Note that sexual harassment may comprise either heterosexual or homosexual advances.

Two strategies are available for dealing with sexual harassment: organizational and individual. At the *organizational level*, it is important to create agency policy that clearly prohibits sexual harassment and identifies procedures for making a complaint. That policy should be published in the agency's personnel manual, and the agency director should periodically post or circulate the statement. Regular training, too, helps to sensitize all staff to the problem and can prevent harassment.

At the *individual level*, if you feel that you are being harassed, you should first speak directly to the harasser, insisting that he or she stop the offensive behaviors. If you are not able to directly confront the harasser, an effective strategy is to send a letter that specifies the nature of the harassing incidents and when they occurred, how you were affected, and how the conduct should change in the future. If the harassment persists, it is advisable to keep a diary of events and a list of any witnesses, as well as consulting with other workers, informing your supervisor, and seeking resolution using agency procedures. (Note: Some employers require an official complaint within 30 or 60 days of an incident.) If the situation is not resolved within the agency, consultation with a lawyer is suggested. Options include contacting your state human rights commission or the U.S. Equal Employment Opportunity Commission—making an official complaint within 180 days of the incident. If you file a complaint, be prepared for possible negative reactions from the harasser and others in the organization.

Selected Bibliography

Celenza, Andrea. *Sexual Boundary Violations: Therapeutic Supervisory, and Academic Contexts*. Lanham, MD: J. Aronson, 2007.

Equal Employment Opportunity Commission. "Guidelines on Discrimination Because of Sex, Title VII, Section 703." *Federal Register* 45 (11 April 1980): 2505.

National Association of Social Workers. *Code of Ethics*. Washington, DC: NASW, 1999.

16.6 AVOIDING MALPRACTICE SUITS

Many social workers underestimate their legal vulnerability. In fact, a growing number are being sued for malpractice or professional negligence. Broadly speaking, a worker may be held liable if he or she has done something or neglected to do something that resulted in causing harm or injury to a client.

In this type of lawsuit, the person who files the lawsuit and alleges malpractice or negligence is termed the *plaintiff*. The person who is being accused of malpractice or negligence is termed the *defendant*. In order to win the lawsuit, the plaintiff must prove four points:

1. The defendant (e.g., the social worker) was obligated to provide the plaintiff with a particular standard of care or professional conduct.

2. The worker was derelict because he or she breached that obligation (or duty) by some act or omission that had a foreseeable consequence.

3. The client suffered some injury or harm (physical, financial, emotional, etc.).

4. The worker's conduct was a direct or proximate cause of the injury or harm.

Whether a breach of duty has occurred is determined by measuring the allegedly harmful act or omission against published standards of practice, agency policy, and the performance of social workers in similar settings. The plaintiff's (e.g., client's) injury must be one that would not have occurred had it not been for the social worker's action or negligence. Despite this traditional proximate cause requirement, juries are increasingly finding liability without fault (i.e., finding providers of services negligent even when they are not the proximate cause of the injury).

The professional duties that, if breached, place social workers and social agencies at greatest risk of legal liability include the following:

- Duty to avoid sexual misconduct
- Duty to warn others when a client discloses intent to harm them
- Duty to prevent a client's suicide
- Duty to properly diagnose and treat a client
- Duty to ensure continuity of service to a client under the care of a worker or agency
- Duty to maintain and protect confidentiality

- Duty to maintain accurate professional records and a proper and legal accounting of payments and reimbursements

In addition to allegations of misconduct based on the preceding duties, other allegations may give rise to a lawsuit:

- Failing to report or properly investigate suspected abuse or neglect
- Placing or contributing to the placement of a client into a facility or foster home in which he or she is subsequently abused or neglected (i.e., failing to properly select or supervise the placement)
- Inappropriately placing a child or adult into foster care, an institution, a hospital, or jail
- Inappropriately or prematurely releasing a client from foster care, a hospital, an institution, or another protective setting
- Failing to supervise a child or a person with a mental or physical disability while he or she is participating in an agency program
- Failing to supervise the work of others, including the work of volunteers and students
- Providing or arranging the transportation that involves a client in a vehicular accident causing bodily injury
- Practicing social work while impaired by use of drugs or alcohol or failure to report a colleague known to be impaired and a danger to clients
- Failing to inform a client of eligibility rules or regulations, resulting in avoidable financial costs or hardship to the client
- Failing to consult with or refer a client to a specialist
- Failing to recognize an obvious medical problem and not referring the client to a physician
- Practicing medicine without a license (e.g., suggesting changes in the client's use of medications)
- Misrepresenting one's professional training and qualifications
- Using a radical or untested approach, technique, or procedure
- Providing inaccurate information or advice to a client
- Providing birth control information or abortion counseling to a minor without consent of the parent
- Acting in a prejudicial manner in the selection of an adoptive home or in the licensing of a foster home, day-care facility, or the like
- Failing to be available to a client when needed (e.g., failing to provide professional coverage during the worker's vacation)
- Inappropriately or prematurely terminating a treatment relationship
- Causing alienation between parent and child or husband and wife

Of course, there is a very big difference between being accused of some wrongdoing and being found negligent by a jury. But even if the suit is eventually dropped or dismissed for a lack of evidence, the social worker and/or the agency will have incurred legal expenses during their defense and will have experienced the emotional turmoil of being accused and sued. Most malpractice lawsuits do not go to trial but are settled out of court.

Most lawsuits name as defendants both the social worker and the employing agency because the agency is assumed to be indirectly responsible for the harm caused by an employee. A social worker employed by an agency can be found personally liable, although this is not likely if the worker was acting within his or her job description, was following agency policy, and did nothing of a criminal nature.

In some cases, a social worker is held liable for harm caused by a person under his or her supervision (e.g., another social worker, volunteer, or student). Also, a worker might be held liable if he or she somehow contributed to the harm caused by another professional. An example of this is when a worker refers a client to an incompetent professional or when a worker provides a social assessment report to a psychiatrist who then makes a poor decision based in part on that report.

If named in a malpractice suit, the social worker should immediately contact an attorney (the worker's agency may provide legal representation) and also notify his or her supervisor, agency administrator, and insurance company. The social worker should not speak with anyone about the allegations before securing legal counsel. The worker must never alter case records or other documents related to the case. Such alterations are easily detected and may constitute a crime. An attempt to alter a client record after being named in a lawsuit will be viewed as an effort to destroy evidence and cover up a wrongdoing.

Legal experts note that the key to avoiding a malpractice suit is adherence to reasonable, ordinary, and prudent practices. In order to defend one's self against allegations, the worker must show that his or her actions were fair, in good faith, and consistent with how other professionals would behave under similar circumstances. One of the best defenses is to be able to show that the client gave his or her informed consent to the professional's intervention. This underscores the need to document client involvement in problem identification, assessment, and case planning and the value of written service agreements (see Item 12.5).

By following a number of additional guidelines, the social worker can avoid a malpractice suit or at least minimize its damage:

1. Always adhere to the NASW *Code of Ethics* and the NASW *Standards of Professional Practice* relevant to your area of practice and guidance from the NASW Legal Defense Fund (www.socialworkers.org/ldf). Also, adhere to your agency's policies and procedures, as well as state and federal laws affecting your agency's program and services.

2. Do not enter into dual relationships. A **dual relationship** is one in which a second set of obligations or expectations is introduced into the social worker–client relationship. Examples include dating a client, renting an apartment to or from a client, loaning money to or borrowing money from a client, hiring a client to perform some service (e.g., repair worker's car), selling some item or product to a client, and so on. Dual relationships must also be avoided in supervisor-worker and faculty-student interaction.

3. Do not become sexually or romantically involved with a client. Sexual misconduct toward a client is one of the most common allegations giving rise to malpractice suits in social work. Any sexual involvement with a client is a clear violation of the NASW *Code of Ethics*, a violation of state professional licensing statutes, and, in some states, a violation of criminal law. Avoid situations that could be misinterpreted as sexually inappropriate or give rise to false allegations of sexual misconduct. For example, male workers should be very cautious about visiting a female client in her home. A third party (potential witness) should be within earshot whenever a male worker interviews a female adult or a child.

4. Before providing services to a child or adolescent, be certain that your program or agency has secured the proper authorization from the parent or guardian and that it is lawful for you to provide these services to the minor in question. As a general rule, the parent has the legal right to control and consent to the medical care and other professional services provided to his or her minor-aged child. However, the laws of most states allow for some exceptions to this principle. For example, minors may be allowed to consent to their own medical care in regard to pregnancy, sexually transmitted disease, mental illness, and substance abuse. When in doubt, consult with your agency's attorney.

5. Know your level of skill and conduct your practice within those limitations. Secure the training and supervision needed to perform job-related tasks responsibly. Become aware of the types of clients or situations that touch your "hot button" personal issues and lessen your ability to be objective. Obtain supervision and/or consultation when you are having unusual difficulties with a client. Consult with your peers, supervisor, and/or attorney when faced with difficult ethical or legal issues.

Be especially vigilant when dealing with situations that present high legal risk. Examples include clients who may attempt suicide, clients who are violent and a threat to others, clients who have a history of filing lawsuits, clients who are very manipulative, and clients who quickly find fault or perceive bad intentions in the behavior of others. Be very cautious about giving advice that will impact the client's health or finances (e.g., advising a client to get a divorce, suggesting how a client should invest money, telling a client that his or her physical symptom is of no significance).

6. Base your practice on a professionally recognized and accepted approach or model. Keep your client fully informed of decisions, plans, and any risks associated with the intervention. Be careful not to give your client false hope about what you will be able to do. Convey a realistic picture of what you and your agency's services can accomplish. Maintain records that document your actions and decisions and any events or circumstances that have a significant impact on the client.

7. Inform clients of any circumstances that may affect confidentiality. Confidentiality must be broken in order to report suspected abuse or neglect, to warn others of your client's intention to harm them, and to alert others of your client's intention to commit suicide.

8. Reach out to the client who has been angered by your actions and attempt to rebuild the relationship and address his or her complaint. Many malpractice suits could have been prevented if only the worker or agency had followed up on client complaints. If you work for a fee-charging agency, make sure that financial arrangements are handled in a completely businesslike manner so as to minimize the possibility of misunderstanding regarding cost and the collection of insurance payments.

9. If served a *subpoena* to release client records, consult immediately with an attorney and your agency supervisor. It is important to understand that you must respond to the subpoena, but one possible response by your attorney is to claim confidentiality and to contest the request to release the records. Contesting the request will result in a court hearing and a decision by the judge on whether your claim is valid or if you must indeed turn over the records (see Items 9.4 and 10.5).

10. Adhere to agency policy whenever a client presents you with a gift. As a general rule, food and inexpensive gifts valued at not more than a few dollars can be accepted as a matter of common courtesy and etiquette, but a more expensive gift should not be accepted before consulting with your supervisor. Do not transport a client in your private car unless this is in keeping with agency procedures and allowed under your auto insurance policy.

11. Never agree to an interview with an attorney or other investigator before first consulting with your own attorney. (It is a common practice for attorneys to attempt to secure statements or information before you are even aware that you are the target of a lawsuit.)

12. The social worker should secure malpractice insurance. It can be purchased through the National Association of Social Workers by NASW members and from some insurance companies. Before accepting a job with an agency, check into the agency's policy regarding providing legal defense for employees who are named in a lawsuit.

Selected Bibliography

Guttmann, David. *Ethics in Social Work*. Binghamton, NY: Haworth Press, 2006.

Houston-Vega, Mary Kay, Elane Nuehring, and Elizabeth Daguio. *Prudent Practice: A Guide for Managing Malpractice Risks*. Washington, DC: NASW Press, 1996.

Reamer, Frederic G. *Social Work Malpractice and Liability: Strategies for Prevention*, 2nd ed. New York: Columbia University Press, 2003.

Reamer, Frederic. "Risk Management in Social Work." In *Social Workers' Desk Reference*, 2nd ed. Albert Roberts, ed. New York: Oxford University Press, 2008.

16.7   TESTIFYING IN COURT

Social workers employed in protective services, probation, and parole settings testify frequently in court. Sooner or later most social workers are called on to provide testimony. Following guidelines such as these can help the worker perform effectively on the witness stand:

1. Prepare for the court appearance. Consult with the attorney who will call you as a witness and learn of the questions he or she will ask, as well as the questions you are likely to be asked by the opposing attorney who will do a cross-examination.

Inform the attorney representing the side for which you are testifying of any uncertainty, inconsistency, or gaps in information that will surface or become apparent in your testimony. He or she should know of these concerns before you are called to testify.

2. A social worker's testimony will probably fall into one of three categories: personal observations, reading from a client's case file, and expert testimony.

If you are testifying as to your personal observations you should be prepared to do so orally with few, if any, references to notes. If your observations occurred over a long period of time, you should prepare a chronology or list of events to refresh your memory and keep your recollections organized. The opposing counsel and judge will probably look at this list, but it will not usually be introduced as evidence unless it differs from your oral testimony. Memorize the facts, but avoid sounding as though you are giving a recitation.

If portions of a client's case record or other documents such as letters have been admitted into evidence, you may be asked to read aloud the words you wrote. Prepare by being thoroughly familiar with the content and organization of the record. You should be able to explain why you wrote these particular words into the document and also the method for producing, transcribing, and storing a case file or document in your office.

In some situations a social worker may be qualified in court to offer *expert testimony*. An individual who the judge has designated as an expert witness is permitted to offer opinions as to the meaning of certain facts and observations. All other witnesses must confine their testimony to facts and observations. Opposing attorneys will often argue over whether a particular person should be qualified as an expert witness. If an attorney plans to qualify you as an expert, be prepared to explain: (1) your professional qualifications (e.g., degrees, license, certifications, experience, special training, publications), (2) the knowledge base and method used in forming an opinion, and (3) your mode of practice and how it is similar to or different from that of other social workers or professionals in your field of practice or area of expertise.

3. Tell the truth. Remember that you will be under oath. Any exaggeration or departure from facts will probably be uncovered and your credibility as a witness will suffer.

4. Appearance and demeanor are critical in a court. You should be properly dressed and well-groomed to reflect the solemnity of the courtroom. When seated in the witness chair, you should be attentive and courteous.

5. Listen carefully to the questions you are asked. If you do not understand a question, ask that it be rephrased or explained. If you do not know the answer, say so. Never speculate or guess. Answer only the question that is asked. Answer questions in a confident manner. Avoid phrases such as "I feel" or "I guess so" because they weaken the impact of your testimony. Speak clearly and avoid using slang and jargon. Much of the professional jargon used by social workers is incomprehensible to judges, attorneys, and juries.

6. If an objection is made during the course of your testimony, stop speaking immediately. If the judge overrules the objection, you will be told to answer the question. If the objection is sustained, you will not be permitted to answer and a new question will be asked.

7. When being cross-examined by the opposing attorney, keep in mind that he or she is not your friend. Even a polite, respectful, and friendly cross-examiner is looking for ways to trip you up and to discredit your testimony. Do not volunteer information that is not requested. Do not explain why you know something unless you are asked. And finally, remember that the attorney offering your testimony has a chance to follow up and ask additional questions after the other attorney's cross-examination. This may help clear up any problems in your testimony.

8. When being cross-examined, do not lose your temper at questions you consider impertinent or offensive. Exercise self-control. If you maintain your composure, you will be less likely to become confused and inconsistent. If the questioning is truly improper, your attorney will object. Pause before answering a provocative question to allow the objection to be made, but not so long that you appear hesitant or unsure. Judges are familiar with the histrionics of some trial attorneys and are rarely impressed by them.

9. Do not get caught in the "yes-or-no" trap. If, on cross-examination, the opposing attorney asks a question and ends it with, "Answer yes or no," don't feel obliged to do so if you believe such an answer will be misleading. Instead, begin your answer with something like, "Well, that needs explaining." The attorney may again push you to answer yes or no and the judge may require you to give a yes or no answer, but the judge and jury will understand your position and look forward to your explanation when your attorney clarifies the situation on redirect examination.

10. Many times, cross-examiners ask compound questions. When responding to a compound question, divide it into sections and then answer each part. Do not agree with a partially untrue statement, because the opposing attorney may cut you off and not allow you to complete your response, thus giving an erroneous impression of your actions or beliefs.

11. A witness is sometimes asked a question regarding his or her sympathy for one side or the other in the case. If asked, admit your beliefs or sympathies honestly. It is absurd to deny an obvious sympathy, and an honest admission will not discredit a witness.

Selected Bibliography

Bernstein, Barton, and Thomas Hartsell. *The Portable Guide to Testifying in Court for Mental Health Professionals.* Hoboken, NJ: John Wiley and Sons, 2005.

Madden, Robert. *Essential Law for Social Workers.* New York: Columbia University Press, 2003.

Springer, David W, and Albert R. Roberts, eds. *Handbook of Forensic Mental Health with Victims and Offenders: Assessment, Treatment, and Research.* New York: Springer, 2007.

Vogelsang, Janet. *The Witness Stand: A Guide for Clinical Social Workers in the Courtroom.* Binghamton, NY: Haworth, 2001.

16.8   PROVIDING AND RECEIVING SUPERVISION

Throughout most of its history, the social work profession has considered supervision critical to the preparation of new practitioners as well as a means of quality control in the delivery of services. Unlike those professions in which the private practice or independent practitioner model of service delivery has been dominant, social work extends supervision well beyond the worker's period of training. As a primarily agency-based profession, social work depends upon a layer of the agency's administrative structure (i.e., supervisors) to continue training new workers and provide ongoing professional guidance. Thus social workers must learn how to use the supervisory process to enhance their own professional development.

The supervisor plays dual roles. The first, **administrative supervision**, involves monitoring the work of supervisees to assure that it meets agency standards. Thus, supervisors are part of an agency's middle-management team and play an important role in agency policy, program, and personnel decisions. The second role is called **supportive supervision**. In this capacity, the supervisor is concerned with workers' job satisfaction, morale, and development of job-related knowledge, values, and skills. New social workers often move rather quickly into roles supervising other staff and volunteers because the basic helping skills they acquire in social work education translate into the skills needed by supervisors.

There are two sides in the supervisory process: the provider and the user, or the supervisor and the supervisee. As students and new workers, social workers will need to know how to make good use of supervision. Later in their careers, they must be adept at giving supervision in order to assist others in their professional development.

Both supervisors and supervisees should recognize that supervision must be carefully planned and the process adapted to the individual supervisor/supervisee situation. Here are the most typical ways in which supervision is given and received:

- *Individual supervision.* These one-on-one meetings between the supervisor and super- visee are the most prevalent form of interaction. Every supervisee needs and deserves regularly scheduled private time with his or her supervisor during which the worker's performance can be candidly examined with sufficient emotional safety to address practice successes and failures.
- *Group supervision.* Holding regularly scheduled meetings between a supervisor and a small group of supervisees provides a time-efficient opportunity for new workers or volun- teers to process events, share information and perceptions, and help each other gain knowl- edge and skill in service provision and meeting agency expectations.
- *Ad hoc supervision.* These brief and unscheduled meetings respond to questions and is- sues as they arise during daily practice activities. These impromptu meetings are particu- larly useful for preventing problems and capturing so-called teachable moments.
- *Formal case presentations* At regularly scheduled meetings, one or more supervisees present in-depth descriptions of their work on specific cases and projects. The supervisor and other participants then offer advice and guidance on how the presenter's client services could be improved.

GUIDELINES FOR USING SUPERVISION

Remembering guidelines such as the following can help the social worker make appropriate and effective use of supervision:

1. Realize that your supervisor will expect you to do these things:
   - Follow agency policies, procedures, and specific instructions.
   - Demonstrate an eagerness to learn the details of your job, to become more efficient and effective, and to accept constructive criticism and suggestions on how you could improve the quality of your work.
   - Take initiative and assume responsibility for work that needs to be done.
   - Consult with your supervisor when you are unsure about how to proceed or when a course of action is raising unforeseen issues or encountering unexpected problems.
   - Immediately inform your supervisor when you become aware of an ethical, legal, or procedural violation that could give rise to a formal complaint or in some way harm the agency or its clients.
   - Work cooperatively with and be respectful of colleagues and engage in behaviors that improve staff morale.
   - Maintain accurate and up-to-date records of your work with clients.

2. Expect your supervisors to do the following:
   - Evaluate your performance on a regular basis and offer specific suggestions on how it can be improved.
   - Provide needed on-the-job training.
   - Provide encouragement and support when your work is particularly difficult and frustrating.
   - Keep you informed of changes in agency policies or procedures.
   - Give you a clear warning when your performance falls below standards.

3. Establish a regularly scheduled time to meet with your supervisor. This should be at least once a week. Having adequate time to discuss work and job-related concerns is of critical importance.

4. Seek your supervisor's assistance in formulating an individualized professional development plan that will build on your strengths and address limitations in your performance. Such a plan should be in writing. It should identify specific tasks and objectives to be accomplished over the next 6 and 12 months, and list specific learning activities (reading, study, conferences, workshops, etc.) to help accomplish the objectives.

5. Recognize that there are some intangibles that your supervisor will look for and would come into play if he or she is making a recommendation for a promotion or move to another position. For example, a supervisor is likely to be especially attentive to the quality and quantity of your work, your understanding of the agency and the work to be done, your ability to formulate a feasible plan and carry it out, your leadership skills and the ability to win the respect of others, your time-management skills, your capacity to learn and adapt to change, your initiative and willingness to assume responsibility, and your emotional stability and dependability.

GUIDELINES FOR SOCIAL WORK STUDENTS

Horejsi and Garthwait (2002, pp. 12–13) explain that the social work student has the following special set of responsibilities to his or her practicum agency:

- Meet with the practicum instructor (field instructor) on a regular basis (at least weekly).
- Prepare for all meetings with the practicum instructor and inform him or her of the topics that need to be discussed during the upcoming meeting.
- Be present at the agency on days and at times agreed upon by the student and practicum instructor. If unable to attend, notify the agency supervisor prior to or at the start of the workday.
- Behave in a professional manner, taking responsibility as an adult learner to understand and carry out assigned duties, meet all deadlines, and seek direction when needed.
- Carry out agency-related assignments, tasks, and responsibilities in a manner consistent with agency policy and procedures and prepare all records and reports in accord with the prescribed format.
- Identify learning needs and, if required, prepare an agreement that identifies learning outcomes and learning activities.
- Complete all practicum monitoring and evaluation forms and reports required by the agency and school (e.g., time sheets).
- Discuss with the practicum instructor and/or the school's practicum coordinator any areas of significant disagreement, dissatisfaction, or confusion related to the practicum experience.

GUIDELINES FOR PROVIDING SUPERVISION

Assuming the role of supervising other workers or volunteers is a substantial step in a social worker's career. This is a serious and important responsibility because the supervisees count on the supervisor to guide their own development and because the clients being served by these supervisees trust that the services they receive will be properly monitored and that their interests will be protected. The following guidelines should assist the new supervisor in carrying out his or her responsibilities:

1. Social workers who assume the role of supervisor have special ethical obligations. According to the National Association of Social Workers (1999) *Code of Ethics*, social workers who provide supervision:

- Should have the necessary knowledge and skill to supervise appropriately and should do so only within their areas of knowledge and competence.
- Are responsible for setting clear, appropriate, and culturally sensitive boundaries.

- Should not engage in any dual or multiple relationships with supervisee and in which there is a risk of exploitation or potential harm to the supervisee.
- Should evaluate the supervisee's performance in a manner that is fair and respectful. (NASW, 3.01 a–d)

2. Reward good performance. Because supervisors in human services agencies can seldom offer monetary rewards, they must be creative in utilizing other types of rewards such as recognition, offering desirable or stimulating work assignments, and special privileges.

3. Hold supervisees accountable for their performance. When it is necessary to correct or discipline a supervisee, do so immediately after the infraction is discovered and in private. Disciplinary actions must be fair, decisive, very clear, and based on facts. Such actions must communicate to the supervisee exactly what is expected in the future and the consequences if performance is not improved. A failure to hold a supervisee accountable for his or her performance can frustrate and demoralize other agency staff and create personnel problems that consume an inordinate amount of a supervisor's time and energy.

4. Remember that example is the best teacher. The supervisor must constantly model the values, attitudes, and behavior he or she expects of supervisees.

5. Make sure that work assignments are clear and appropriate to the supervisee's level of knowledge, skill, and experience. The supervisee should be helped to learn job-related skills and obtain the training he or she needs to perform at a high level. Adjust the frequency and intensity of the supervisory process to the supervisees' level of competency and experience and to their job responsibilities.

6. If dismissal of the employee is a possibility, the supervisor must understand and strictly adhere to the relevant procedures outlined in the agency's personnel manual. Such procedures should reflect state and federal law on employee–employer relations. These procedures typically require that the employee be given written warnings of possible termination, a written description of his or her unacceptable performance, and a reasonable opportunity to improve his or her performance prior to termination. When attempting to terminate the employment of an individual, the supervisor must operate on the assumption that the individual may file a lawsuit and that the dismissal will have to be explained and justified in court. Some behaviors by the employee are so serious that they should result in an immediate move to terminate employment. These include:

- Clear and serious violations of the NASW *Code of Ethics* (e.g., sexual relations with a client, verbal abuse of a client, or sexual harassment of staff)
- Theft of agency money, equipment, or property
- Concealing, consuming, or selling drugs on agency premises
- Reckless or threatening actions that place clients or staff at risk of harm

[text obscured] a supervisor or agency personnel that
[text obscured] e clients and maintain the integrity and

[text obscured] from clients in exchange for preferential

Practicum, 2nd ed. Boston: Allyn & Bacon,

[text obscured]s. Washington, DC: NASW, 1999.

[text obscured]lo. *Strategic Supervision: A Brief Guide for* [text obscured]ks, CA: Sage, 2010.

16.9   BUILDING AND MAINTAINING MENTORING RELATIONSHIPS

In a **mentoring relationship** an experienced professional and/or seasoned agency employee guides a less-experienced colleague in learning the unwritten rules of the organization and how to successfully navigate the practice setting, demonstrates how to deal with common frustrations and disappointments associated with social work practice, and teaches what one should do to grow and develop as a professional. The experienced colleague is termed the *mentor*; the less-experienced one is often termed the *protégé* or *mentee*.

Elements of mentoring exist within a supervisor–supervisee relationship (see Item 16.8). However, in a true mentoring relationship, the mentor is not the protégé's administrative supervisor and does not assign work to him or her, oversee his or her daily work activities, or conduct the agency's formal evaluation of the protégé's job performance. A mentoring relationship is characterized by friendship and mutual trust, rather than by the structure of authority or chain of command.

BENEFITS OF MENTORING TO THE PROTÉGÉ

From the vantage point of the protégé, having a positive mentoring relationship can provide these five benefits:

1. *Support and understanding.* Beginning a new job or assuming a new set of responsibilities can be a time of uncertainty and self-doubt. During such a time, a wise and seasoned employee or professional can be of considerable help to a new or less-experienced employee. A mentor's support, empathy, advice, and encouragement can boost the confidence of a protégé and calm his or her fears and anxieties.

2. *Orientation to and assimilation into the agency.* A mentor can help a protégé learn about the practice setting or agency as an environment of professional activity. The mentor can orient the protégé to the organization's culture and traditions as well as help with understanding "office politics" and avoiding political pitfalls. A new employee who is mentored tends to learn the job faster, is more easily socialized into the organization, and is more likely to succeed.

3. *Access to important "insider" information.* A mentor is a valuable source of insider information that the protégé could not easily obtain through other means. Examples include information related to the key events that have shaped the organization, informal policies and procedures that do not appear in written manuals, patterns and personality traits of other colleagues, ongoing interpersonal conflicts within the organization, and the like. The protégé must honor the expectation of confidentiality and trust inherent in the sharing of this information and be prudent and discreet in using it.

4. *Career guidance.* Mentors can help protégés plan their careers, set goals, and develop the skills they need for career and professional advancement. Mentors can also help protégés connect to professional organizations, select professional learning experiences, and participate in community groups.

5. *Role modeling.* An intangible benefit of the mentoring relationship is that the mentor becomes an important role model for the protégé. Much of the protégé's learning and development will occur as a result of observing and imitating his or her mentor.

BENEFITS OF MENTORING FOR THE MENTOR

Mentoring is a two-way interaction, and the mentor should derive at least the following benefits from the mentoring relationship:

1. *Professional stimulation.* Social work practice is far from repetitious. Nonetheless, a certain amount of routine develops in agency practice, and it is easy for workers to fall into the pattern of approaching practice on a "business as usual" basis. The fresh perspectives and insights brought by the protégé can challenge the mentor to examine his or her practice through a different lens and thus stimulate his or her own professional growth.

2. *Updated knowledge.* The protégé can help the mentor learn about and stay abreast of new developments in the field. Likewise, the protégé can motivate the mentor to reexamine old assumptions and update any outdated knowledge and skills.

3. *Agency information.* The mentor can often obtain information from the protégé about personnel, problems, and issues in the organization that other employees might be reluctant to share with a senior staff member.

4. *Professional contribution.* Helping others make the most of their potential is the primary reason most social workers enter this profession. As the protégé grows in competence and effectiveness, the mentor will have the satisfaction of contributing to the growth and development of a colleague. What's more, the mentor may become more valued and respected by others in the organization based on the success achieved by the protégé.

MATCHING THE PROTÉGÉ AND THE MENTOR

Within most organizations, mentors voluntarily take on the mentoring role because they care about or are interested in the professional development of particular individuals. However, in some organizations, mentoring is encouraged by policy, and the organization sets up formal mentoring assignments that match new employees with more experienced ones. It is not uncommon for an organization to create mentoring relationships in order to assist women and minority employees, who may face unique challenges in performing some organizational roles where role models are too often in short supply.

When there are cross-gender mentoring matches, some potential problems must be considered. For example, the assignment of a male mentor to a female protégé may reinforce stereotypical roles of male power and female dependence. Others in the organization may perceive a cross-gender mentoring relationship as a romantic involvement. Mentors, protégés, and the organization as a whole must be aware of these possible complications and make sure that mentoring facilitates, rather than impedes, professional development and advancement.

GUIDELINES FOR MENTORING RELATIONSHIPS

A social worker who is seeking a mentor or is responsible for matching a mentor and mentee should keep the following guidelines in mind:

- Pick or assign a mentor with great care. Seek a mentor who has a reputation for competence and effectiveness within the agency or practice setting. The mentor must possess the knowledge and skills the protégé hopes to learn.
- The mentor–mentee relationship must be comfortable and safe, take place in an environment of open discussion and mutual trust, and maintain an atmosphere in which the protégé can freely accept advice and constructive criticism.
- The mentor and protégé must commit sufficient time and energy to the relationship. Some mentor–mentee relationships work best with regularly scheduled meetings; others work well on an on-call basis. Expectations about how the interactions will occur should be clearly established at the start of the relationship.

Social workers who are interested in mentoring or providing guidance to a protégé should keep the following points in mind:

- Pick a protégé with great care. A protégé should be someone whom you genuinely care about and someone you want to see advance within the agency and the profession.
- Above all else, be willing and able to separate your own goals and values from those of your protégé. He or she is a unique individual, and you must recognize and honor individual differences. Do not enter a mentoring relationship expecting to create a clone of yourself.

- Listen carefully to your protégé's questions and concerns. Do not assume that he or she has exactly the same concerns that you had at a particular stage in your professional development. The younger generation of professionals grew up in a different time, received a somewhat different type of professional education, and may have a set of personal and family concerns quite different from your own.

Selected Bibliography

Wilson, Pamela P., Deborah Valentine, and Angela Pereira. "Perceptions of New Social Work Faculty about Mentoring Experiences." *Journal of Social Work Education*, 38 (Spring–Summer 2002): 317–333.

16.10 CONSUMING AND CONTRIBUTING TO PROFESSIONAL KNOWLEDGE

The professional social worker makes a career-long commitment to engage in *evidence-based practice*. When consuming the available knowledge, the worker must carefully select and adapt that knowledge to the unique client and practice situation. Thus, social work needs a strong body of literature as a resource for practitioners, and practitioners need the ability to sort through and draw from that literature. At the same time, the social worker has an obligation to contribute his or her knowledge to other social workers through both writing and presenting his or her insights to professional colleagues.

CONSUMING THE LITERATURE

The social worker's ability to understand and apply information from the literature to inform practice decisions is critical to successfully serving clients. The worker is obligated to locate the most relevant literature and carefully examine that material for the facts and ideas that may be most useful in work with his or her clients. Doing so may be difficult for many social workers because of their heavy and time-consuming caseloads, leaving little time for reading and study. Moreover, up-to-date libraries are inaccessible to many social workers.

Fortunately, an increasing amount of helpful information is available online, and articles can readily be obtained and downloaded from one's own computer. Once relevant articles and reports have been identified, the social worker must decide if the information is reliable and trustworthy enough to use as a basis for practice decisions. An online abstract of a research report or journal article may not contain enough information on which to base a conclusive decision, but a summary will usually be sufficient to inform a decision on whether the complete article or report should be secured.

When reviewing published research, it is important to identify the basic design of the study. Although some studies combine quantitative and qualitative designs, most can be characterized as using just one of these. **Quantitative research** typically involves collecting a large amount of data from a representative sample of respondents. Statistical analysis may then be used to summarize and reduce those data to understandable generalizations and to identify relationships among the data. **Qualitative research**, by contrast, has the capacity to produce a more in-depth understanding of the thoughts, values, and experiences of a smaller number of respondents. Qualitative research is most appropriate when the basic characteristics of the phenomenon being studied are unclear or poorly defined.

A reader of qualitative research literature should be aware of these research characteristics:

1. Data collection is a highly interactive process. The qualitative researcher involves the respondents in interviews, focus groups, and other interactive processes, in which the respondent is given stimulus materials. Through the use of questions and other efforts at clarification, understanding of the phenomenon is deepened.

2. The researcher delays making an in-depth literature review until the data are collected in an effort to prevent researcher bias from affecting the data. Typically, the researcher will connect the findings to the literature only after the data have been collected.

3. Because the researcher interacts with respondents and can be biased in how he or she asks questions or interprets the information gathered, the researcher is expected to acknowledge his or her perspective on the matter under study. In doing so, he or she gives consumers of the research clues to researcher bias that may have entered the process.

4. Sample size is not a significant consideration in qualitative research. Although the respondents should be representative of the population that is interested in the topic, the goal is to secure more in-depth information from a small number of respondents rather than more general information from a large number. Often, 5 to 10 respondents are seen as a sufficient sample size in a qualitative study.

5. Methods used in qualitative research include (a) gathering information directly from respondents through interviews and focus groups, (b) case study analysis to evolve themes and patterns from case observations, and (c) ethnographic research, in which the researcher becomes immersed in the respondent's physical, social, cultural, and work environment to gain in-depth understanding of that person's perspectives and experiences.

6. The information collected is recorded as fully as possible, which is sometimes called the *thick documentation method*. It is then necessary to identify and code the themes and subthemes that appear in order to sort, organize, and reorganize the data and thus better understand the phenomenon being studied. Several computer software programs are available to facilitate this manipulation of data.

7. A central concept that guides the interpretation and analysis of qualitative data is *triangulation*, or applying multiple data-gathering methods, multiple observers or investigators, and/or multiple perspectives to the same data set. If those results are in agreement, there can be greater confidence in the validity of the information.

When consuming qualitative research, the social worker should be especially concerned about how researcher bias may affect the conclusions drawn. As noted earlier, because the researcher usually interacts with the respondents, it is relatively easy for him or her to slant the data and/or the interpretation of what they mean.

Quantitative research is the more customary form of knowledge development and testing in Western society. It is patterned after the scientific method used in the physical sciences. If studying the success of an intervention approach, for example, the researcher might engage in the following:

1. Review the literature and determine the current state of knowledge about that approach.
2. Formulate a hypothesis about the impact of the intervention.
3. Identify, define, and isolate the various factors and elements that must be examined in order to test the hypothesis.
4. Select a statistically valid sample from the population being studied.
5. Utilize control groups to hold constant the influence of extraneous factors.
6. Apply the intervention to the experimental group.
7. Collect and apply appropriate statistical analysis to the data.
8. Draw conclusions.

While this scientific process works well under laboratory conditions where many variables can be controlled, it is much more difficult (and sometimes inappropriate) in working with people. For example, can one ethically encourage or even require a person to remain in an abusive family in order to be part of a control group during the study of a domestic violence intervention? It is possible, however, to examine natural experimental and control groups (e.g., clients who did and did not receive a particular intervention) and then arrive at some conclusions about the merits of the intervention.

Much of the strength of quantitative social science comes from the statistical analysis of the data. **Statistics** are the numerical representations of the characteristics of individual cases—in social work, the characteristics of the people the researcher has chosen to study. The group of cases selected for study may be either a *sample* (i.e., part of a population) or the *population* itself (i.e., the complete group of cases to which the researcher may want to generalize the results). The consumer of this research must have confidence that the sample is indeed representative of the population in order to consider the findings valid.

The consumer must also be confident that statistical analysis was rigorous and appropriate. *Statistical analysis* involves assembling, analyzing, summarizing, and interpreting numerical data in order to inform thinking. Three general questions should guide the social worker in considering the validity of the statistical analysis conducted in a quantitative study:

1. *What was the purpose of the statistical procedure?* Some statistics simply help to reduce data to numerical indicators. These **descriptive statistics** include frequency distributions, percentages, measures of central tendency (i.e., reflections of the most typical response, such as mean, median, or mode), and measures of variability (i.e., descriptions of the spread or disbursement of the data, such as the range or standard deviation of responses).

A more complex set of statistical tools, **inferential statistics**, allow the researcher to draw conclusions from a sample regarding the differences in that sample from the population. One set of inferential statistics, *measures of difference,* project the likelihood that the differences occurred because of the intervention or other factors being studied, rather than simply by chance. For example, in the social sciences, the typical criterion for accepting a finding as significant is $p < 0.05$, meaning the probability is less than 5 in 100 that the outcome would occur by chance.

A second group of inferential statistics known as *measures of association* identify the correlation between two or more variables. In social research, it is seldom possible to establish a clear cause-and-effect relationship, but it is possible to identify patterns of interaction among variables. If the relationship between two variables is completely random, or a zero (0.00) correlation, the variables are considered unrelated. However, if one variable increases when the other increases (i.e., a positive correlation), the correlation coefficient will be somewhere between $+0.01$ and $+1.00$. Similarly, in a negative correlation, where one variable increases as the other decreases, the scores might vary from -0.01 to -1.00. When interpreting measures of association, a correlation coefficient (either $+$ or $-$) of less than 0.30 is considered a weak relationship, one from 0.30 to 0.70 is moderate, and one above 0.70 is strong. Other statistical tests reflect the relationships among more than two variables. These *multivariate statistical procedures* include multiple regression analysis, analysis of variance (ANOVA), cluster analysis, and factor analysis.

2. *Was the statistical test appropriate for the level of measurement?* The application of many statistical tests depends on the level of the data being analyzed. The three levels are nominal, ordinal, and interval or ratio. **Nominal data**, the most basic level, is a construction of mutually exclusive categories. Gender, ethnicity, and various yes or no questions (e.g., parent or nonparent) are examples. One category is not considered to have more or less value than another. The next level, **ordinal data,** represent information that can be ranked from low to high, but for which it would not be reasonable to assume that there is equal value between each category. For example, many scales used in the social work literature are three- or five-point ratings of a factor (e.g., frequently, occasionally, seldom) but there is no assumption of equal intervals between ratings—only indication of more or less, or higher or lower. For example, a rating scale may be used to indicate that Client A has higher self-esteem than Client B, but in measuring a variable like self-esteem, one is not able to say that Client A has three times more self-esteem than Client B. Similarly, a score on an IQ test is an example of ordinal data. **Interval or ratio data**, the most precise level of measurement assume the categories are divided into equal units and thus permit more precise measures. Examples would be age, population density per square mile, and the number of school children who have been immunized. As the consumer of a research report or article, it is important to be sure that the statistical procedures selected were appropriate for the level of data collected in the study. Otherwise, the statistic may misrepresent the outcome.

3. *Was the type of sample correct for the statistical test used?* The type of sample (in combination with the level of measurement) determines which statistical procedures can be appropriately used. The most powerful (i.e., more rigorous in a mathematical sense) statistical tests are **parametric tests**, which require independent or random samples and interval- or ratio-level data for at least one variable. For a sample to meet the sampling criteria for parametric tests the different cases being compared must have been independently assigned to groups or randomly selected and there must be reason to assume that the population from which the sample was drawn has a normal distribution. **Nonparametric statistics**, in contrast, are less powerful predictors but allow work with data that are nominal and ordinal. Also, since they compare the outcomes observed in the study with expected outcomes for those respondents, they do not assume a normal distribution. Nonparametric statistics fit almost all research situations and are frequently used in social work research.

Like the ability to communicate in a foreign language, one's facility with statistics quickly diminishes if he or she does not work with these procedures on a regular basis. Thus, making judgments regarding the correct application and interpretation of statistical data is often perplexing for the social worker who works with these procedures infrequently. To help such a worker, Figure 16.1 provides a "crib sheet" for use in examining quantitative research–based literature. It identifies several commonly used statistical procedures by the symbol commonly used in the literature and gives a brief description of its purpose.

ANOVA	*Analysis of Variance.* This test examines the variation in the means of two or more independent or predictor variables to determine the likelihood that the results could have occurred by chance. This parametric test requires that the dependent variable is measured by interval-level data, while the predictor variable or variables may be nominal or ordinal. The ANOVA is similar to the *t*-test (see below) but can also be applied when three or more groups of data are being compared. By consulting an *F* table, the probability (e.g., $p < 0.05$) of a distribution occurring by chance can be estimated.
d	*Effect Size Index.* Effect size indices have three important applications in research. First, they indicate the strength of the relationship between the independent and dependent variables. This is particularly important in describing results of a complex research study because statistical significance only indicates a relationship between two variables. Second, they are used as a summary statistic when many articles are combined as in a meta-analysis. Last, they are part of the process of computing statistical power prior to performing a study—in most cases determining how large a sample is needed to reject a false null hypothesis. When interpreting the value of *d,* a general rule of thumb for the social sciences is that 0.2 represents a small effect on the dependent variable, 0.5 suggests a medium effect, and 0.8 or greater indicates a large effect. A similar result can be obtained using the *r* value from a Pearson Product-Moment Correlation (see below), although the interpretation must be adjusted in that 0.1 suggests a small effect, 0.3 indicates a medium effect, and 0.5 or larger reflects a large effect of the independent variable on the dependent variable.
DF	*Degrees of Freedom.* *DF* indicates the number of ceils in a set of data that are free to vary. This freedom to vary is an important factor in estimating the probability of an outcome occurring by chance. *DF* is computed by multiplying the number of rows minus one in a table by the number of columns minus one. Thus a 2×3 table would have 2 *DF*, whereas a 3×4 table would have 6 *DF*. *DF* is a necessary number when the researcher interprets the probability tables for the different statistical tests.
f	*Frequency.* An *f* will usually be reported in a table and simply reflects the number of responses in each category or interval.
F-ratio	*F.* Usually based on an ANOVA or a multiple regression analysis, this parametric test of significance is a measure of variability that requires interval or ratio data. It tests for difference between the standard deviations of two variables or samples. The *F*-ratio compares estimates of variance *between* the samples with variance *within* the samples. If the between-group variance is higher than the within-group variance, increasing the likelihood that the variance did not occur by chance, the *F*-ratio will be larger. The *F* value has little meaning until it is applied to a table that identifies the probability of that distribution occurring by chance.

(Continued)

FIGURE 16.1   Statistical Notations Frequently Used in Social Work Literature

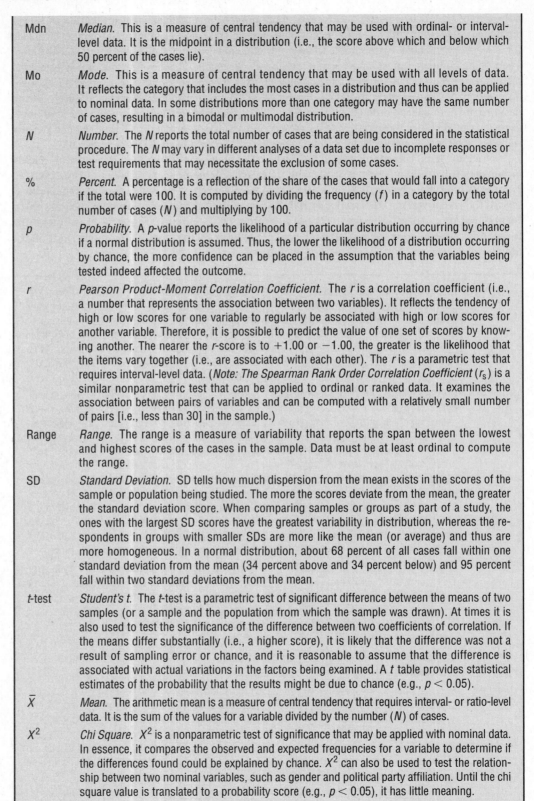

Mdn   *Median.* This is a measure of central tendency that may be used with ordinal- or interval-level data. It is the midpoint in a distribution (i.e., the score above which and below which 50 percent of the cases lie).

Mo   *Mode.* This is a measure of central tendency that may be used with all levels of data. It reflects the category that includes the most cases in a distribution and thus can be applied to nominal data. In some distributions more than one category may have the same number of cases, resulting in a bimodal or multimodal distribution.

N   *Number.* The *N* reports the total number of cases that are being considered in the statistical procedure. The *N* may vary in different analyses of a data set due to incomplete responses or test requirements that may necessitate the exclusion of some cases.

%   *Percent.* A percentage is a reflection of the share of the cases that would fall into a category if the total were 100. It is computed by dividing the frequency (*f*) in a category by the total number of cases (*N*) and multiplying by 100.

p   *Probability.* A *p*-value reports the likelihood of a particular distribution occurring by chance if a normal distribution is assumed. Thus, the lower the likelihood of a distribution occurring by chance, the more confidence can be placed in the assumption that the variables being tested indeed affected the outcome.

r   *Pearson Product-Moment Correlation Coefficient.* The *r* is a correlation coefficient (i.e., a number that represents the association between two variables). It reflects the tendency of high or low scores for one variable to regularly be associated with high or low scores for another variable. Therefore, it is possible to predict the value of one set of scores by knowing another. The nearer the *r*-score is to +1.00 or −1.00, the greater is the likelihood that the items vary together (i.e., are associated with each other). The *r* is a parametric test that requires interval-level data. (*Note: The Spearman Rank Order Correlation Coefficient* (r_s) *is a similar nonparametric test that can be applied to ordinal or ranked data. It examines the association between pairs of variables and can be computed with a relatively small number of pairs [i.e., less than 30] in the sample.*)

Range   *Range.* The range is a measure of variability that reports the span between the lowest and highest scores of the cases in the sample. Data must be at least ordinal to compute the range.

SD   *Standard Deviation.* SD tells how much dispersion from the mean exists in the scores of the sample or population being studied. The more the scores deviate from the mean, the greater the standard deviation score. When comparing samples or groups as part of a study, the ones with the largest SD scores have the greatest variability in distribution, whereas the respondents in groups with smaller SDs are more like the mean (or average) and thus are more homogeneous. In a normal distribution, about 68 percent of all cases fall within one standard deviation from the mean (34 percent above and 34 percent below) and 95 percent fall within two standard deviations from the mean.

t-test   *Student's t.* The *t*-test is a parametric test of significant difference between the means of two samples (or a sample and the population from which the sample was drawn). At times it is also used to test the significance of the difference between two coefficients of correlation. If the means differ substantially (i.e., a higher score), it is likely that the difference was not a result of sampling error or chance, and it is reasonable to assume that the difference is associated with actual variations in the factors being examined. A *t* table provides statistical estimates of the probability that the results might be due to chance (e.g., $p < 0.05$).

$\bar{X}$ *Mean.* The arithmetic mean is a measure of central tendency that requires interval- or ratio-level data. It is the sum of the values for a variable divided by the number (*N*) of cases.

X^2 *Chi Square.* X^2 is a nonparametric test of significance that may be applied with nominal data. In essence, it compares the observed and expected frequencies for a variable to determine if the differences found could be explained by chance. X^2 can also be used to test the relationship between two nominal variables, such as gender and political party affiliation. Until the chi square value is translated to a probability score (e.g., $p < 0.05$), it has little meaning.

FIGURE 16.1   **Continued**

CONTRIBUTING TO THE PROFESSION'S KNOWLEDGE

Social workers are not just consumers of professional literature; they are also obligated by the NASW *Code of Ethics* to build the knowledge base and make it available to other social workers (NASW, 1999). This knowledge usually is made available through conference presentations or preparing written materials to be made available through either online or published journal articles. Determining the best way to transmit one's knowledge to professional colleagues depends somewhat on the nature of information to be communicated, the interaction one wants with an audience, and the number of professionals one wants to reach. Figure 16.2 compares these forms of knowledge transmission.

Making Oral Presentations.   It is important for social workers to develop skill in public speaking not only for conference presentations but also for addressing community groups and legislators in public education efforts. One's preparation for speaking can vary considerably. At one extreme is an "off-the-cuff" presentation and at the other extreme is reading from a prepared paper. Neither is usually very effective. The former is likely to be difficult to follow and the latter can easily lull the audience to sleep. Somewhere between the two extremes is the recipe for an effective oral presentation.

The presenter must carefully plan the speech so that the intended message is accurately received by the audience. A presenter should always remember that the listening audience does not have the opportunity to reread something that is not understood. Thus, clarity is of critical importance and some repetition of key points is appropriate. The following guidelines may help to plan a successful speech.

Presenter/Author Viewpoint	Conference Presentation	Journal Article
Ability to shape how audience consumes the information	Presenter has complete control. Audience can leave the room, but otherwise must accept the presenter's structure. Presenter must anticipate audience ability to consume information.	Reader has complete control. Reader can skim, change order of material, or turn to another article. Author must capture and hold the reader's interest in the topic.
Relationship with person receiving the information	Presenter is face-to-face with the audience and can adjust presentation based on verbal and non-verbal audience reaction.	Author has no personal interaction with the reader and must anticipate the reader's beginning knowledge of the subject matter and interest in depth on the topic.
Delivering numerical or detailed information	Power-point and overhead transparencies can help audience navigate the organization of the presentation and examine any detailed information. Hard-copy handouts allow the audience to take home the information for further study.	Reader can change the order of the presentation to fit his or her learning style. All information must be contained in the article narrative and associated figures that the reader can examine at will.
Size of audience	Audience size is limited to the capacity of the room where the presentation is made. Typically this is a small number.	Subscriptions to social work journals range from a few hundred to 160,000 for *Social Work*. It is not possible to know how many articles are actually read.
Process for selection	A conference announcement invites an abstract and a committee screens and selects presenters. The full presentation is usually not developed until the paper has been selected. The conference is usually within 4 to 6 months after selection.	The full paper developed and submitted to an appropriate journal for consideration. Committee and editor select articles to be published. Acceptance rate varies by journal, but the typical range is 15 to 20 percent of submissions published. Once selected, an article may take 1 to 2 years before it is published.

FIGURE 16.2   Comparison of Methods for Sharing Professional Knowledge

Step 1   Know the content and be familiar with the audience.   When presenting at a conference, remember that the audience will usually have several choices of presentations to attend and any one time. A title in the program that both reflects your topic and yet shows a little pizzazz helps to attract an audience. When a conference participant selects your session, the expectation is that you will know your subject matter thoroughly and have important information to transmit in an interesting way.

Step 2   Select and adapt the content to your audience.   For example, a presentation on your adaptations of a specific practice approach would be quite different if presenting to a group of social work practitioners, as opposed to presenting to agency administrators. It is helpful to visualize a person you know who might be like people you anticipate will be in the audience and prepare as if you are speaking to that person.

Step 3   Carefully organize the flow of information.   In broad terms, the speech should include three major components: a preview of the topic, the main body of the speech, and a summary pointing out the conclusions reached about the topic. Be prepared with visual aids and handouts to help the audience follow the flow of the presentation and hand out hard copy of detailed information to minimize the need for note-taking. Organize the materials so that sufficient background information has been presented to support the audience understanding the conclusions or summary you make at the end of the presentation.

Step 4   Select creative ways to make the presentation interesting.   Your enthusiasm for the topic and confidence in your conclusions will go a long way in keeping the audience interested. In addition, using case examples can help the audience understand how they can apply that information. Such case examples must, of course, be altered to protect client confidentiality. Presenting two sides of an issue with a point/counterpoint format might assist an audience in considering a topic from different perspectives.

Step 5   Prepare your notes to help maintain the planned organization of the presentation.   Notes may be prepared as a script of what you have to say with key words highlighted or in a set of note cards. In either case, these notes should be viewed as reminders of what you want to say and when you want to say it. Never read aloud from these notes. The pages of a script and your note cards should be numbered in case they get out of order.

Step 6   Be as relaxed and comfortable as possible when presenting.   Careful preparation is a prerequisite to building confidence in making a speech. To reduce anxiety further, go to the room where you are presenting 15 to 20 minutes ahead of the session to be sure any audio-visual equipment is working and the room is arranged in an appropriate way for your presentation (e.g., chairs in a circle, a table where you can place your notes). Also, it is helpful to mingle with the audience before the session begins. Introducing oneself to audience members who arrive early, asking what they hope to get from the session, and simply cultivating a few familiar and responsive faces in the audience can increase the comfort level of the presenter considerably.

Step 7   Be aware of your mannerisms while speaking.   Words and phrases such as "you know" and "uh" are annoying and distracting, as are physical mannerisms such as elaborate hand movements or excessive pacing while presenting. Practice delivering the speech in front of a mirror to get a sense of the time required (although the time it takes to deliver a speech is often underestimated). Also, be sure to dress appropriately for the nature of the meeting, as attire that is out of place can be distracting to the audience.

Step 8   Leave time for discussion.   Conference schedules rarely leave a speaker with all the time he or she would want to fully develop a topic, and the tendency is to fill every minute with what you want to present. However, an advantage of a conference setting over written materials (e.g., a journal article) is the opportunity for interaction with the audience. Give them a chance to ask for clarification, to identify areas that they want discussed in more detail, and the opportunity to express their own opinions about the topic. In that way it can become a learning experience for both the audience and the presenter.

Preparing a Journal Article or Other Written Work.   When preparing written material, it is important to remember that whether it is accessed online or through the hard copy of a journal, the reader ultimately decides if the material will be read at all and, if so, how it will be approached. The first screen many readers will use is the title, asking themselves, "Does this appear interesting enough to spend my time reading this material?" Some readers will begin with the first paragraph and read each word as the author has presented the material. Some will first skim the whole article and return to read more carefully the parts that interest them. Others may read the introduction and conclusion and, if their interest is not captured, move on to other materials. The author, then, must write to help the reader determine if he or she will read the article.

The following steps should be followed when preparing written materials:

Step 1 **Have a clear and important message.**   Although some articles are built on original ideas and data, most update and expand existing information, synthesize or combine available knowledge in a unique way, or simply express something already known in a form that makes it more understandable. Since article manuscripts are limited in length (usually 15–20 double-spaced pages), the scope of the article cannot be too broad nor the content too complex. A good test of scope is to see if the key ideas can be stated in a single paragraph. If it is not possible to be this succinct, the topic is probably too broad and may need to be broken into subparts and presented in more than one article.

Step 2 **Select an appropriate journal.**   A large number of journals address matters of interest to social workers. Some publish articles on a wide range of topics, but most specialize. NASW's *Author's Guide to Social Work Journals* (2010) contains information about publishing requirements for over 200 different journals. Each has its own focus and will attract a specific readership.

Before beginning to write, examine several issues of the journal(s) most appropriate for your content and make an assessment of the probable readership, type of articles published, and typical format of the articles (e.g., research-based, theory development, case applications). Each issue of a journal will usually include a statement of its publishing requirements and provide information on preferred topics, length, style, and procedures for submitting articles. Social work journals typically use the APA style (*Publication Manual of the American Psychological Association*, 2010) and usually identify a maximum length. Remember, too, that it is considered unethical to submit the same article to more than one journal at a time.

Step 3 **Picture the audience.**   It is often helpful to imagine that you are writing to some specific individual. Select someone who would be likely to read the article, and write to that person. Use language that communicates your ideas clearly to him or her, and use concepts familiar to that person.

Step 4 **Prepare an abstract.**   Most journals require a 75- to 100-word abstract to accompany the article. Although it is often easier to write an abstract after the article is completed, preparing a first draft before writing the article can help focus attention on the most important points. The abstract should be clear, concise, and factual, as it may ultimately appear in databases where potential readers are searching for specific information.

Step 5 **Develop an outline.**   The readers' ability to comprehend the information in the article will be influenced by how well it is organized. Think through the logical connections between elements to be included. Preparing an outline will help you ensure that smooth and understandable transitions are provided to link the various parts of the article in a coherent fashion.

Step 6 **Write the introduction.**   The opening two or three paragraphs should tell the reader what the article is about, explain why it is important, and suggest which social workers might be especially interested in this material. Tying the subject to a current issue or including a short case example related to the topic may help the reader recognize the benefit in reading the entire article. For many writers, getting started is the most difficult part of writing. Do not let frustration over the introduction block the process. Some writers find it helpful to write a rough introduction with the intent of completely rewriting it later.

Step 7   **Set the context or background.**   It is important to let the reader know where this material fits in social work (e.g., practice theory, practice techniques, social welfare policy issues). The reader also needs to know the theoretical context in which this material is placed. A literature review or even clarification of its relationship to a particular concept, school of thought, or model of practice helps provide this background information. However, this contextual material cannot be extensive and must be focused clearly on the topic of the article.

Step 8   **Prepare the body of the article.**   Concisely report the facts and observations that are the heart of the article. It is helpful to supplement narrative material with alternative means of presenting the information (e.g., charts, figures, tables, and lists). If case examples are used, be sure that they are presented in a way that helps the reader generalize from that example to other situations.

Make frequent use of headings and subheadings so the reader can easily follow the flow of ideas and information. Articles are most readable when they contain short paragraphs with clearly focused content.

Write simply and clearly and avoid social work jargon. Omit gender-specific language and any terms that might reflect bias or stereotyping based on race, ethnicity, gender, age, handicapping conditions, or sexual orientation.

Step 9   **Prepare a summary and/or conclusion.**   End the article with a short statement that pulls together the key points and presents conclusions that can be drawn from this material. If relevant, point out additional research that is needed to further develop the subject.

Step 10   **Collect and format references.**   Using the format appropriate for the selected journal, list the references that support the ideas and information presented. Endnotes or some type of reference list are most often used.

Step 11   **Rewrite, rewrite, rewrite.**   Expect to revise and rewrite a number of times before determining that the article is completed. Polishing the structure, content, and language time and time again is an essential part of good written communication. It sometimes helps to read the manuscript aloud, thinking about how it might sound to someone else and checking for any errors that might have been overlooked.

Step 12   **Let it cool.**   Avoid sending an article to a journal as soon as it comes out of your printer. A few days or a week away from the material provides a fresh perspective and may yield alternative ideas for presenting the material or strengthening the way ideas are expressed. It may be helpful to use this time to get colleagues to review the work and offer comments. Remember, however, that it is your article, and you must own the final result. Do not feel obligated to incorporate all suggested changes. Also, do not allow this cooling period to become an excuse for procrastination. You may never be completely satisfied with your writing, but you must stop refining it at some point.

Step 13   **Dealing with acceptance or rejection.**   Typically, the editor of a journal will send out your manuscript to three or four reviewers. It often takes six or more months for the reviews to be completed and the editor to determine if the article is to be included in an upcoming issue of the journal. Online journals usually have a shorter timeline. Reviewers conclude their work with a recommendation to (a) reject, (b) accept if revised in specific ways, or (c) accept for publication without major changes. Some journals will, on request, provide the reviewers' comments if the article is rejected. If that occurs, seriously consider those comments and either revise and resubmit the article, send it to another journal, or drop your plan to publish.

Step 14 Finalize the manuscript. If the article is accepted, you will work with professional editors who will offer suggestions for strengthening the presentation. You will have the opportunity to be sure that their editing does not distort or misrepresent the content. In addition, when an article is accepted, the author will be required to assign the legal rights to this material to the publisher. It will then be necessary for the publisher to approve any subsequent reprinting or extensive quoting of the article in other books or articles, including your own.

Selected Bibliography

American Psychological Association. *Publication Manual of the American Psychological Association,* 6th ed. Washington, DC: APA, 2010.

Atkinson, John M. *Lend Me Your Ears: All You Need to Know About Making Speeches and Presentations.* New York: Oxford University Press, 2005.

Glicken, Morley. *A Guide to Writing for Human Service Professionals.* Lanham, MD: Rowman and Littlefield, 2007.

National Association of Social Workers. *Author's Guide to Social Work Journals*, 5th ed. Washington, DC: NASW Press, 2010.

Szuchman, Lenore T., and Barbara Thomlison. *Writing with Style: APA Style for Social Work.* Belmont, CA: Brooks/Cole, 2004.

16.11   IMPROVING THE SOCIAL WORK IMAGE

The typical citizen has little understanding of what social workers actually do and the impressions they have are often erroneous. On TV and in the movies, the social worker is often portrayed as either a judgmental and mindless busybody or someone who breaks up families by removing children for no good reason. All too often, the only newspaper or magazine articles that mention social workers are ones describing how the acts or omissions of an agency or a social worker contributed to a client's harm or distress. Additional image problems are created when the media uses the term *social worker* in a generic manner and applies it to all human services workers.

If they are to make their maximum contributions to improving the society, social workers must create a more positive image. Such changes will not result from wishful thinking; they must be made to happen. The image will change in a positive direction when it becomes evident to the public that social workers are truly experts in what they do and are able to get results that nonsocial workers are unable to match. The financial rewards and the status associated with certain other professions (e.g., medicine, engineering) came about not through exhortation but rather because their members completed long and difficult training, acquired a definite expertise, and promoted legislation providing clients with legal protections concerning the outcome of their decisions and actions.

In order to promote a greater public understanding, social workers should adhere to certain guidelines:

1. Assume a personal responsibility for improving the profession's image. Three actions are essential. First, provide the highest quality service possible. Second, behave in a highly professional and completely responsible manner when dealing with clients and the public. Third, remind those observing your performance that you are a social worker.

2. Use the title of *social worker*. If you must also use words such as counselor or psychotherapist to clarify your role, describe yourself as, for example: "I am a social worker—I provide psychotherapy to troubled youth," "I am a social worker specializing in the planning and development of services for persons with AIDS," "I am a social worker who administers a family support program," "I am a social worker who teaches at a university," and so on.

3. When being interviewed for a news story, make sure the reporter understands that you are a social worker, that you have a degree in social work, and perhaps describe the special training that has prepared you for the work you do. Always operate on the assumption that reporters and the public at large have little or no idea that social work is a distinct profession. Otherwise, you will probably be termed a sociologist, welfare worker, counselor, or agency employee.

4. Speak of your work with respect. If you truly value what you do, others are more likely to adopt a positive attitude toward both you and your work. Avoid any action or association that would detract from the profession or damage your credibility and trustworthiness.

5. Work with other social workers and professional associations (e.g., the local NASW chapter) to plan and implement a media and public relations campaign aimed at educating the public about social work and social workers in your community. March is designated as "Social Work Month," but a strong local campaign should be conducted throughout the year.

6. Whenever a news story uses the term *social work* or *social worker* in an erroneous manner, send the newspaper, magazine, or radio or TV station a letter that explains the error. Also send a packet of informational materials that describes the nature of the profession and social work activities.

Selected Bibliography

Payne, Malcolm. *What is Professional Social Work?* Chicago: Lyceum Books, 2007.

Whitaker, Tracy. *Who Wants to Be a Social Worker? Career Influences and Timing.* Washington, DC: National Association of Social Workers (NASW Center for Workforce Studies), 2008. http://workforce.socialworkers.org/studies/BeaSocialWorker.pdf

Whitaker, Tracy. *The Results Are In: What Social Workers Say About Social Work.* Washington, DC: NASW Press, 2009.

16.12 BECOMING A LEADER

Social workers encounter many situations of social and economic injustice that cry out for attention and change. These injustices may occur in their own agencies where modifications in policies, programs, and practices are needed in order to make the agencies more effective, in their communities, or in the larger society. In order to change these situations, the social worker must be willing to step forward and assume the role and responsibilities of leadership. Desirable change does not happen by accident. Rather, it is set in motion by people who assert themselves, articulate their beliefs, and take on the hard work of leading.

Most efforts to define **leadership** speak of it as a process of using authority and interpersonal influence to guide people through a certain course of action and toward a particular goal. An effective leader draws upon his or her own sense of mission to create a climate and foster the attitudes that move a group or organization toward a desired end. The exercise of leadership always occurs within a context of competing and conflicting forces. A good leader can shape and guide those complex forces so as to move people toward the desired goal.

Leadership should not be equated with administration or organizational management. Leadership is the process of bringing about some significant change by inspiring people to let go of what is familiar and to embrace a new vision or mission. By contrast, the process of management seeks to bring about order and consistency within an organization through the use of various administrative tools and procedures, such as planning, budgeting, and coordinating staff. Not all who occupy administrative positions are effective leaders.

Although certain traits and characteristics—such as intelligence, dependability, verbal ability, adaptability, physical height, and attractiveness appear to be associated with leadership, no one set of traits predicts who will become a leader. Research does not support the belief that some people are "born leaders." In order to become an effective leader, one must build on his or her strengths and learn and practice the skills of leadership, just as he or she would develop any other set of skills. An aspiring leader must consciously cultivate the development of those qualities as well as the thought processes, attitudes, and interpersonal skills associated with leadership.

Drawing upon ideas presented in Horejsi and Garthwait (2002), these guidelines are offered for those who want to become effective leaders:

1. *Have a clear vision about what you want to accomplish.* Leaders must go beyond what was and what is and articulate a vision of what could be. It is the leader's vision that provides a critically important sense of purpose and direction and infuses the effort with the confidence not only to make difficult decisions but also to act on those decisions. However, leadership is about much more than having ideas about changing a situation. In fact, effective leaders are seldom the most creative and innovative thinkers. People who are attracted primarily to ideas and theory seldom make good leaders because they often move too quickly, become impatient with the slowness of change, and get frustrated with the hesitations and limitations of those they seek to lead.

2. *Articulate your vision for your followers.* This vision must be one that can be translated into clear language and achievable objectives and programs that are feasible within the existing political, economic, and cultural environment.

3. *Lead by example.* A leader cannot ask others to do what he or she is unwilling to do. Followers are inspired and motivated by the resolve, courage, hard work, and sacrifices of an effective leader. Leaders must exhibit the behaviors and attitudes they want to see in their followers.

4. *Cultivate a group of followers.* In order to attract and retain followers, leaders must respect and demonstrate genuine concern for the wishes, values, and abilities of those they want to lead. Leaders must be willing and able to curtail some of their own hopes in order to avoid moving too quickly or too far ahead of their followers.

5. *Maintain clear and continuing communication with your followers.* This communication must keep followers focused on the desired goal while also attending to the concerns, fears, and ambivalence they may have about investing their time, energy, and money in working toward this goal.

6. *Be prepared to make difficult decisions.* The social, political, economic, and organizational environments are constantly changing and leaders must be willing to take calculated risks, cope with uncertainty, and manage situations that are inherently unpredictable. Nothing destroys the capacity to lead more quickly than indecisiveness and unwillingness to take action when action is clearly necessary. It is often said that "It is better for a leader to occasionally make a bad decision than to be perceived as someone who cannot make a difficult decision."

7. *Develop and maintain a positive personal and professional reputation.* The capacity to lead is often tied to having a favorable reputation within one's organization or community, to possessing special knowledge of and prior experience with the issue that has drawn people together, and to having a well-developed network of personal and professional contacts.

8. *Develop the art of building consensus and coalitions.* Leaders create networks among individuals and organizations and facilitate their cooperation and collaboration. They reward others for their cooperation and share credit, even with those with whom they disagree. Leaders must also be willing to compromise when doing so is a necessary step toward reaching a sought-after goal.

9. *Work to identify and understand the various motivations of followers.* Leaders should anticipate possible disagreements among followers and take steps to prevent or resolve these conflicts before they distract from achieving the goal and splinter the followers into competing factions. At the same time, leaders must be willing to remove from the collective effort those individuals or groups that are creating unnecessary conflict or setting up roadblocks to achieving essential goals.

10. *Use your influence in a thoughtful and deliberate manner.* The type of power and influence available to a leader will vary, depending on the type of group or organization he or she is leading. If the leader occupies a position of leadership within a formal organization (e.g., executive director, high-level administrator, or elected official), he or she will possess the power of authority and legitimacy associated with that position. This leader may also possess the power to reward or punish the actions of others and can initially increase their level or cooperation or decrease their level of resistance to a proposed change. Such a leader must be cautious to avoid forcing actions that lead to artificial or tacit agreement that unravels when the policy or program is implemented. In most situations, a social worker providing leadership may possess only the influence that comes from being a person who commands respect and attracts a following because of his or her personal charisma, attractiveness to others, and knowledge or expertise.

11. *Develop a high level of self-awareness.* Leaders must understand their own strengths and limitations and constantly examine their own motives and behaviors. Many potential leaders destroy their capacity to lead by letting their need for public recognition and self-importance affect their decisions.

The following are some qualities and characteristics that are also important to effective leadership:

- The capacity to critically evaluate various ideas and proposals, including one's own decisions, plans, and actions
- The capacity to speak and write clearly so as to articulate a vision and purpose in ways people can understand
- Perseverance even in the face of disappointment and criticism
- The ability to delegate responsibility and to teach or empower others to perform as well as they can
- Willingness to take personal responsibility for one's decisions and actions
- Openness to new ideas and acceptance of persons with various abilities and diverse backgrounds
- The ability to create a sense of camaraderie and feeling of community among one's followers
- The ability to make effective use of available time and get things done

Selected Bibliography

Burghardt, Steve, and Willie Tolliver. *Stories of Transformative Leadership in the Human Services: Why the Glass Is Always Full.* Los Angeles: Sage, 2010.

Gardella, Lorrie Greenhouse, and Karen S. Haynes. *A Dream and a Plan: A Woman's Path to Leadership in Human Services.* Washington, DC: NASW Press, 2004.

Horejsi, Charles, and Cynthia Garthwait. *The Social Work Practicum*, 2nd ed. Boston: Allyn & Bacon, 2002.

APPENDIX A

Acronyms Commonly Used in Social Work

ACSW   *Academy of Certified Social Workers*. NASW's MSW-level certificate that identifies social workers qualified to practice at an advanced level.

APA   *American Psychiatric Association*, also *American Psychological Association*. Both APAs are professional membership organizations for their respective disciplines. Many social work journals use the APA (American Psychological Association) guidelines for article preparation.

ASWB   *Association of Social Work Boards*. The organization of boards from most states, and several Canadian provinces, responsible for the legal regulation of social work. ASWB provides board training and offers licensing/registration examinations.

BSW   *Bachelor of Social Work*. The social work degree offered at the undergraduate level includes the BSW, Bachelor of Science (BA), Bachelor of Arts (BA), or other titles, but the social workers refer to the CSWE-accredited degree as the BSW and graduates of these programs as BSW social workers.

CASW   *Canadian Association of Social Workers*. CASW is a federation of nine provincial and one territorial social work organizations that provides a leadership role in strengthening and advancing the social work profession in Canada. It publishes the journal, *Canadian Social Work*, position papers on social issues, and the Canadian social work Code of Ethics.

CSWE   *Council on Social Work Education*. The national organization responsible for the development of social work education and the accreditation of BSW and MSW social work education programs.

DHHS   *U.S. Department of Health and Human Services*. Department of the U.S. government that funds and delivers many of the federal programs designed to meet basic human needs that employ social workers.

DSW   *Doctorate in Social Work*. The degree may be a Ph.D. (Doctor of Philosophy). Doctoral-level programs in social work are not accredited by the profession and usually are not considered preparation for professional practice. Rather, most are directed at preparation for social work teaching and research and thus some social work educators have their doctorate in related disciplines.

EBP   *Evidence-Based Practice*. A term calling for social workers to draw on the strongest documented information to guide assessment of client situations, selection of intervention approaches (i.e., "best practices"), and/or the evaluation of one's own practice activities.

EPAS   *Educational Policy and Accreditation Standards*. CSWE-generated standards that set standards for quality and content in BSW and MSW social work education.

HIPAA   *Health Insurance Portability and Accountability Act*. HIPAA is the law that spells out federal requirements for the protecting of private information regarding health care.

IFSW   *International Federation of Social Workers*. Primary membership organization reflecting social work's values and policy positions on worldwide issues.

LBSW   *Licensed Baccalaureate Social Worker*. Designation varies from state to state, but this (or a similar) label is used to identify social workers the state deems qualified to practice with educational credentials at the bachelor's level (usually graduation from a CSWE-accredited program) and passing a licensing examination at that level.

LCSW   *Licensed Clinical Social Worker*. Designation used in most states to designate those social workers who have been licensed for advanced clinical social work practice. Typically this credential requires completing a CSWE-accredited master's program, passing a clinical practice examination, and two or more years of clinical practice supervised by an experienced social worker.

LMSW (also LSW)   *Licensed Master Social Worker*. Designation used in many states to designate those social workers who have been licensed for master's-level social work practice, but not necessarily in advanced clinical practice. A CSWE-accredited master's degree and a satisfactory exam score on a master's level test are typically required.

MSW   *Master of Social Work*. The MSW is considered the "terminal practice degree" in the field of social work. Sometimes universities use a different degree designation, for example, Master of Arts (MA),

Master of Social Service Administration (MSSA), but the common term in social work to indicate graduation from a CSWE-accredited master's level program is MSW.

NASW   *National Association of Social Workers.* NASW is the primary membership organization of social workers in the United States that serves to advance the profession and represent its viewpoint to the public. NASW maintains the social work *Code of Ethics,* generates positions on key social policies, advocates for the election of public officials with views compatible with these policies, publishes the journal, *Social Work,* and a number of books (NASW Press), offers several professional credentials in social work specialties, and houses the Center for (social work) Workforce Studies.

OASDHI   *Old Age Survivors, Disability, and Health Insurance.* Often known simply as Social Security, OASDHI is the federal social insurance program that provides monthly benefits to qualified retirees, their dependents, their survivors, and, in some cases, disabled workers.

RSW   *Registered Social Worker.* Most Canadian provinces and some states use this designation in a similar fashion to certification or licensing. This title may relate to any practice level, depending on the state or province.

SSI   *Supplemental Security Income.* SSI is a federal program designed to help aged, blind, and disabled people, who have little or no income. It provides cash to meet basic needs for food, clothing, and shelter.

TANF   *Temporary Assistance to Needy Families.* TANF provides cash assistance and other resources (e.g., assistance with employment, housing, child care, domestic violence, and other factors that affect family stability) to low-income families with children while they strive to become self-sufficient.

Note: This annotated list includes only a small sample of the acronyms most basic in social workers' communication. *The Social Work Dictionary* (Robert L. Barker [2003], Washington, DC: NASW Press) lists approximately 1,000 acronyms found in the social work literature.

APPENDIX B

Retired Techniques and Guidelines from Previous Editions

To avoid expanding the length and cost of this book as new editions are prepared, a number of items have been eliminated to make room for new materials. To access information eliminated or substantially modified from previous editions, readers may (1) look up the last edition in which it was included as listed below in parenthesis (e.g., 7th) or (2) obtain a copy online through the School of Social Work at Colorado State University (http://www.ssw.cahs.colostate.edu/faculty_staff/sheafor/). Permission to cite this information is not required, although the source should be identified.

Chapter 6 Practice Frameworks for Social Work

- The Family Preservation Model (7th)
- The Clubhouse Model (7th)
- The General Systems Perspective (8th)

Chapter 9 Basic Skills for Agency Practice

- Using a Dictating Machine (3rd)
- Letter Writing (8th)
- Process Recording (6th)
- Problem Oriented Recording and the SOAP Method (7th)
- Controlling Workload (7th)
- Planning for a Temporary Absence or Departure (7th)

Chapter 10 Intake and Engagement

- The Hard-to-Reach Client (8th)

Chapter 11 Data Collection and Assessment

- The ABC Model and Behavior Matrix (8th)
- The Stuart Clinical Aids (1st)
- Childhood Level of Living Scale (1st)
- Scale for the Selection of Foster Parents (1st)
- Multi-Problem Screening Inventory (3rd)
- Child Well-Being Scale (3rd)
- Family Life Cycle (4th)
- Homemade Data Gathering Tools (4th)
- Dual Perspective (6th)
- Life History Grid (6th)
- Multi-Worker Assessment Interviews (6th)
- Life Cycle Matrix (7th)
- The 4Ps, 4Rs, and 4Ms (7th)
- Assessing the Agency's Need for Computers (1st)
- Force Field Analysis (7th)
- Focus Groups (8th)

Chapter 12 Planning and Contracting

- Using Checklists in Goal Selection (8th)
- Decision Trees (4th)
- Developing Protocol Statements (5th)
- Establishing Formal Interagency Collaboration (7th)

Chapter 13 Intervention and Monitoring

- Paradoxical Assignments (1st)
- Priorities Weighting Grid (4th)
- Family Sculpting (5th)
- Distinguishing Means from Ends (4th)
- The Life Book (6th)
- Crisis Cards (6th)
- The Empty Chair (7th)
- Animal Assisted Intervention (8th)
- Developing Professional Cooperation (1st)

Chapter 14 Evaluation and Termination

- Goal Checklist (4th)
- Rapid Assessment Instruments (4th)
- Differential Impact Scoring (4th)
- Client Self-Rating Scale (6th)
- Peer Review (6th)

Chapter 16 Techniques for Sustaining Social Work Practice

- Learning from an Oral Presentation (1st)
- Learning from a Book or Article (1st)
- Building a Professional Library (3rd)
- Building Support Networks (3rd)
- Using Humor in Social Work (6th)
- Coping with a Bureaucracy (8th)
- Dealing with Managed Care (8th)

APPENDIX C

Useful Web Resources for Social Workers

PROFESSIONAL ORGANIZATIONS

www.aswb.org

Association of Social Work Boards (licensing requirements in all states and Canada, schedule of licensing exams)

www.casw-acts.ca

Canadian Association of Social Workers (CASW programs, Canadian Code of Ethics)

www.cswe.org

Council on Social work Education (CSWE programs, lists of accredited BSW and MSW programs, publications)

www.ifsw.org

International Federation of Social Workers (IFSW position papers, international Code of Ethics)

www.naswdc.org

National Association of Social Workers (NASW activities, Code of Ethics, publications)

EVIDENCE-BASED PRACTICE

http://www.socialworkpolicy.org/research/evidence-based-practice-2.html#EVP

Supported by NASW's Social Work Policy Institute, this site maintains a comprehensive list of evidence-based practice registries and databases. This site also provides links to a number of other online resources useful to social workers.

http://scholar.google.com

Inserting search terms into Google Scholar such as "evidence-based probation" or "evidence-based PTSD" yields a number of articles using evidence-based research.

http://guideline.gov

The National Guideline Clearinghouse is a comprehensive database of evidence-based clinical practice guidelines and related documents maintained by the U.S. Department of Health and Human Services. Search terms such as "mental health and aging" results in the identification of a large number of carefully researched articles on health and mental health-related topics.

http://www.nrepp.samhsa.gov

The National Registry of Evidence-Based Programs and Practices is a service of the U.S. government's Substance and Mental Health Services Administration (SAMHSA). The search menu helps to narrow searches by problem area, age, gender, race/ethnicity, study design, and other factors.

SEARCH ENGINES FOR SOCIAL WORK-RELATED TOPICS

http://www.nyu.edu/socialwork/ip

"Information for Practice" is a comprehensive site reporting current news and scholarship from the United States and around the world. The search engine maintained by the New York University School of Social Work provides links to information on a broad range of social work and social welfare topics.

http://cosw.sc.edu/swan

Maintained by the University of South Carolina School of Social Work, the "Social Work Access Network" provides links to social work education programs, upcoming conferences, social work-related organizations, and social work publications. It also maintains a social work chat room.

http://www.fedstats.gov

"Fedstats" is a centralized U.S. Government site providing state and national statistics generated by most government agencies. A search, for example, for "Rural Poverty" yields the latest data on that topic.

www.financeprojectinfo.org

The "Finance Project" offers a series of clearinghouses linking to policies and programs to strengthen services to children, families, and communities. Topics include promising practices, finding federal funding, youth programs and policies, and sustainability planning.

http://catalog.loc.gov

The U.S. Library of Congress maintains the search capacity to identify over 12 million books by title, author, keywords, or subject.

AUTHOR INDEX

SUBJECT INDEX